Degas: His Life, Times, and Work

Degas

His Life, Times, and Work

Roy McMullen

Houghton Mifflin Company / Boston   1984

Library of Congress Cataloging in Publication Data

McMullen, Roy.
Degas: his life, times, and work.

Bibliography: p.
Includes index.
1. Degas, Edgar, 1834–1917.   2. Painters — France —
Biography.   I. Title.
ND553.D298M38   1984   709'.2'4 [B]   84–677
ISBN 0-395-27603-9

Printed in the United States of America

A 10 9 8 7 6 5 4 3 2 1

Contents

Preface

EGAS has been provoking wonder and bafflement for well over a century. During the early years of Impressionism, his companions in the studios and cafés on the lower slopes of Montmartre, and also his hosts and fellow guests in the town houses he frequented, were fascinated and often irritated by his mixture of contradictory traits. Eventually, as he advanced into celebrity and then into his cantankerous, witty, and misanthropic old age, he alerted a small legion of Boswellian collectors of *mots* and anecdotes. Since his death, in 1917, and especially since World War II, he has been an exciting focus for art historians: his works have been catalogued, his subject matter analyzed, his acquaintances and sitters identified, his notebooks (brilliantly edited by Theodore Reff) published, and more of his correspondence unearthed. Yet he has not ceased to be regarded as a formidable enigma. Looking through some articles by American and British critics, one finds John Canaday, for instance, deploring the "set of maddeningly frustrating puzzles as to just exactly what kind of man Degas was"[1] and Benedict Nicolson referring to "the great mystery artist of the age."[2] Vivien Raynor has summed up the situation by remarking, "He said he wanted to be 'illustrious and unknown,' and that continues to be his fate."[3]

The present biography was written in the hope of doing something about this paradoxical accumulation of information that allegedly does not provide knowledge. We cannot, of course, discover exactly what kind of man anybody was, or is. Even so, it seems to me that we can now legitimately try again to understand Degas — by pulling together the many facts that have become available, by placing him in his social class and historical context, by staying as close as possible to primary sources, and by taking a fresh look at his much discussed attitude toward women. Such an effort is worthwhile in ways that go beyond the usual concerns of art scholarship, for the object of our inquisitiveness (which he would have loathed) was not only one of the finest painters of the nineteenth century but also, in spite of his idiosyncrasies, a peculiarly representative man, an exemplar of a kind of society that emerged after Waterloo and almost disappeared after Sarajevo. To get to know him better is to gain additional insight into both the creative process and our sociocultural history.

Although my debts are listed in detail in the notes and bibliography, I want to call attention here to what I have learned from Hélène Adhémar, Jean Adhémar, Jean Sutherland Boggs, Norma Broude, Lillian Browse, Pierre Cabanne, Françoise Cachin, Marcel Guérin, Eugenia Parry Janis, Paul-André Lemoisne, Sophie Monneret, Ronald Pickvance, Phoebe Pool, the already mentioned Professor Reff, and John Rewald. For help in obtaining access to material in Paris I am grateful to Andrée Lhéritier, chief librarian of the catalogue and bibliography rooms in the Bibliothèque Nationale. And I owe special thanks to Roland Gelatt for having suggested the project.

— R.M.
Paris, 1984

Degas: His Life, Times, and Work

1. Class Profile

HILAIRE-GERMAIN-EDGAR DEGAS, who from the first appears to have been simply Edgar to his family, was born in Paris around eight-thirty in the evening of July 19, 1834, at 8 Rue Saint-Georges, one of the partly new streets near the magnificently new church of Notre-Dame-de-Lorette and at about the point where the central plain of the Right Bank begins to rise perceptibly toward the windmills, vineyards, bistros, and artists' studios on the Butte of Montmartre. Jean-Auguste-Dominique Ingres — Monsieur Ingres, even to his detractors — was fifty-four years old, Eugène Delacroix was thirty-six, Honoré de Balzac thirty-five, Victor Hugo thirty-two, and Hector Berlioz thirty-one. In the working-class Beaubourg quarter, King Louis-Philippe's soldiers had just restored order after a series of riots; at the Opéra, balletomanes had just begun to thrill to the rivalry between the ethereal Marie Taglioni and the pagan Fanny Elssler. A railway line to suburban Saint-Germain-en-Laye was under consideration.

The baby's father and mother must have seemed, to the other inhabitants of the Rue Saint-Georges, an interestingly exotic and romantic couple. The father, Auguste Degas, was a twenty-six-year-old banker, half French and half Italian, who had spent most of his life closer to Mount Vesuvius than to the celebrated Butte in Paris; the mother, Célestine Degas, née Musson, was a nineteen-year-old American, a Creole from Louisiana, but of purely French descent and with a European education. Neither of the young parents, however, was nearly as important as the two grandfathers, René-Hilaire Degas and Germain Musson, in the creation of the dense network of clan and class outlooks that would determine the future painter's educational program, condition his attitude toward society, and influence, in a number of subtle ways, his artistic activity. And to understand why this was so, to see how the ideological web was spun, one must go back in time to the end of the eighteenth century and out in space to sites as distant from the Rue Saint-Georges as Verdun, Egypt, Naples, Santo Domingo, New Orleans, and Mexico.

In the first week of September 1792 an army of seventy-five thousand Prussians, Austrians, and Hessians, under the command of the Duke of Brunswick, was encamped near Verdun. The troops were lighthearted: they had just captured the town and its huge fortress after encountering only token resistance, and they were now loafing, amusing themselves, and fraternizing with the local population while awaiting orders to continue what promised to be a military promenade to the banks of the Seine. In Paris the tocsin was being sounded, and hundreds of prisoners, supposed traitors, were being slaughtered by mobs under the influence of patriotism and alcohol. At Verdun, however, many of the townspeople were disposed to regard the invading soldiers as liberators come to restore the sacred authority of Louis XVI and save France from the abominations of the Revolution. A group of young women, later referred to by Royalist martyrologists as the Seven Virgins of Verdun, formed an impromptu welcoming committee, went out to the camp, and distributed sugared almonds to the Prussian officers.

Then, on September 20, the French won a miraculous victory at Valmy. The Prussians, Austrians, and Hessians were soon in full retreat toward the Rhine, leaving Verdun and its collaborationists to the mercy of the Paris government. The Seven Virgins, after a spectacular trial, were convicted of treason; five were sent to the guillotine, and the two others, each of whom had the excuse of being only seventeen years old, were let off with six hours of exhibition on a scaffold and twenty years in prison.

A general witch hunt followed, during which the history of France suddenly impinged on the destiny of the future Edgar of the Rue Saint-Georges. One of the guillotined young women, perhaps the one listed in the trial records as Hélène Vatrin, had been engaged to marry a twenty-three-year-old Parisian, René-Hilaire Degas, who was present at the executions in the Place de la Concorde. He was immediately tagged as a potential saboteur of the Revolution. Possibly he had already been placed under surveillance by the agents of the Committee of Public Safety, for in spite of his youth he was a professional speculator on the grain market, at a time when shortages were provoking food riots in Paris, and he also seems to have been a money changer, at a time when the falling value of the Revolutionary currency, the assignat, was frightening the government and comforting its many foreign and domestic enemies.

There are slightly varying accounts of what happened next, because the whole story was told and retold, and probably embroidered on a bit, by four Degas generations. According to a version that may have come down from one of Edgar's aunts, René-Hilaire was again in the grim Place de la Concorde when Marie Antoinette was executed, on October 16, 1793, and he was moved to express his pity for the former queen and his disapproval of the obscene behavior of the crowd. When the spectacle was over a sympathizing stranger came up to him and said, "You've just time to escape. Your remarks were overheard by a spy for the Committee."[1] According to an apparently unexpurgated version relayed by the grown-up Edgar, who may have had the details firsthand from his grandfather, the latter was going about his business one day in the Palais-Royal, where the Bourse aux Grains was then located, when a friend glided past his back and whispered, "Get the fuck out of here. [*Fous le camp.*] They are at your house."[2] However the alert may have been given, the young grain gambler, on a hired horse and evidently with a sizable bundle of assignats, was soon galloping off in the direction of southwestern France — a detail that suggests he had protectors in the moderate Girondin party, which was strong in that part of the country. After riding two horses nearly to death, we are told, he reached the port of Bordeaux. From there he sailed to Marseilles, and from there, installed in the middle of a cargo of pumice stone (an odd piece of precision in Edgar's variant of the family epic), he reached Damietta and Cairo.

After five years of obscure Levantine activity, he resurfaced by joining the army with which Bonaparte had invaded Egypt. Somehow he extricated himself from the debacle that ended the Egyptian adventure, and in January 1799 he showed up in the forces under General Jean Etienne Championnet that chased the Bourbon monarch, Ferdinand IV, from Naples. When Championnet and the bulk of the French troops withdrew, René-Hilaire remained in the city, apparently working at first as a small-time money changer and lender but finally, with some help from a Swiss brother-in-law, becoming a full-fledged banker and real estate operator. He survived the savage rioting and the equally savage executions that marked the collapse of the French puppet Neapolitan state and the temporary return of the Bourbons. In 1804 he married a lively young Italian woman from Leghorn, Aurora Freppa, and with her began to produce a family that eventually comprised ten children, seven of whom would reach maturity and play important roles in Edgar's early life, both as sitters for portraits and as protective, affectionate relatives. First came Rosa (Rose or Rosine to the Paris branch of the family), then Agostino (Auguste, the painter's father), Enrico (Henri), Odoardo (Eduard), Achille (whose name required merely a French pronunciation), Laura (Laure or Laurette), and Stefanina (Fanny).

When the Bourbons were chased out again, in 1806, and Napoleon's brother Joseph was proclaimed king of Naples, René-Hilaire Degas achieved a position comparable with that of an assistant finance minister, and, using unorthodox methods developed in Paris in the first years of the Revolution, helped to refund the Neapolitan public debt. In 1808 he became the *agent de change du roi,* the king's personal banker, when Joachim Murat, Napoleon's brother-in-law, took over the throne from Joseph. In this post he remained loyal to the French imperial cause until — indeed, somewhat after — the last minute. His final official act in the disastrous summer of 1815, the summer of Waterloo, was to hire a fishing craft and, using his wife and older children to lend the semblance of an ordinary boating party, deliver a supply of gold to Murat, who had already abdicated but had paused on the island of Ischia in his flight toward France. Edgar's aunt Rosa, who was ten at the time, liked to tell how the weeping former king, with perhaps a premonition that he would shortly face a firing squad, kissed the children good-by and stood forlornly on the shore shouting "Au revoir! Au revoir!" as they prepared to sail back across the Bay of Naples.[3]

The second Bourbon restoration might have put an end to René-Hilaire's Neapolitan exploits. In fact, it accelerated his irresistible rise. The new government saw no reason to rid its territories of a financier who was competent and reasonably supple and who, though he insisted on keeping his French nationality, was almost Italian, well known to local citizens as Ilario. Nor did he lack opportunities for employing his talents. Naples, with a population of close to four hundred thousand, was about twice as large as any other Italian city, and it was on the verge of industrial progress, in spite of the endemic poverty of its lower classes. In 1818 the municipality would launch the first steamboat on the Mediterranean; in 1826 it would begin to remodel its great port; and in 1839 it would build, between the city and the royal resort of Portici, the first railway in Italy. Moreover, in the years immediately after the upheavals of the Napoleonic era there were excellent opportunities, if one had the right connections, for investing in confiscated real estate. The fortune that emerged from all this is impossible to estimate but was obviously enough to make it unthinkable that a grandson, even if he were a painter, would ever become a bohemian.

Ultimately the former grain speculator and money changer had a hundred-room palazzo in the center of Naples, an imposing villa at San

Rocco di Capodimonte in the hills north of the city, and substantial holdings in four nearby Neapolitan localities. His three younger sons were his associates in his Naples bank, and the eldest, Auguste, was established in the branch at Paris. Each of the three daughters was supplied with a dowry of twenty thousand ducats and with what her father considered, sometimes after very lengthy negotiations, an acceptable suitor. The results, whatever they may have cost the young women in heartache, were undeniably brilliant in terms of social advancement. Rosa was eventually married to Don Giuseppe Morbilli, Duca di Sant'Angelo a Frosolone; Laura to Baron Gennaro Bellelli, who, after some political vicissitudes, became a senator of the Kingdom of Italy; and Stefanina to Gioacchino Primicile Carafa, Marchese di Cicerale e Duca di Montejasi.

In comparison with René-Hilaire's picaresque early career and final patriarchal glory, Edgar's other grandfather, Germain Musson, must have cut but a small figure in the Rue Saint-Georges. The known facts about him, however, reveal that he too was an adventurer and a self-made nabob, though his start was better than dabbling in cereals and assignats at the Palais-Royal. He was born in 1787 at Port-au-Prince, the capital of what was then the French possession of Saint-Domingue. His family was part of the territory's population of some thirty thousand whites, mostly French or Creole, who lived by exporting the sugar, cotton, coffee, cocoa, and indigo produced by half a million slaves shipped in from Africa. During his infancy life must have been sweet, from the white minority's point of view, for Saint-Domingue on the eve of the French Revolution was wildly prosperous: it accounted for two thirds of France's foreign investments, and in a particularly good year its trade called for the services of more than seven hundred seagoing vessels. But the ideas of liberty and fraternity that were being disseminated from Paris began to filter down to the black slaves, and a series of rebellions, led notably by Toussaint-Louverture and Henri Christophe, followed. In 1804 the colony, under its old Indian name of Haiti and with its economy badly dislocated, was declared independent, and it was perhaps around this date that the adolescent Germain made up his mind to leave the island for good. In 1810, after travels that may have taken him to Mexico, he settled in New Orleans, clearly with some capital, and married Marie Désirée Rillieux, the sixteen-year-old daughter of a prominent member of the local French community. The evidence indicates that it was a marriage of love, not just the family alliance common to the period.

New Orleans, with its tropical summers, its black slaves, and its rich mixture of French, Spanish, Creole, and African cultures, must have often reminded him agreeably of Saint-Domingue. But there were economic attractions as well. He bought some land at the corner of Canal Street and Royal Street, on the border between the eighteenth-century town nucleus, the Vieux Carré, and the bustling new business suburb that was called the Faubourg Sainte Marie. He was well established by 1812, when the first steamboat came down the Mississippi, and was soon participating in the boom that within a generation would quadruple the population of the city and transform the sleepy old Spanish colonial harbor into the fourth busiest port in the world (until rail lines altered the situation). His principal activity was exporting cotton, in his own ships, to the textile mills of Massachusetts. Probably his captains, like many of their colleagues, used as ballast on the return voyages the blocks of ice that were being harvested from New England ponds and for which there was a growing demand in the aristocratic homes of the Vieux Carré. When he had capital to spare, he invested it in Mexican silver mining, apparently somewhere in the vicinity of Perote, a picturesque village and eighteenth-century fortress in the Sierra Madre Oriental, northwest of Veracruz. By 1819, though only thirty-two, he was the head of what was beginning to look like an empire. But the sudden death of Marie Désirée in that year left him, for a long period, with no wish for further achievement. He abruptly ceased directing his various enterprises, gathered up his five motherless children — Eugénie, Michel, Henri, Eugène, and the four-year-old Célestine — and left New Orleans for Paris.

About a dozen years later he was still in the French capital, stylishly lodged in a town house at 4 Rue Pigalle, at a point where the street, after coming down the hill from Montmartre, paused to form with the Rue de la Tour-des-Dames a small triangle of trees and quiet gardens. His oldest child, Eugénie, had just been married to a French nobleman, the Duc de Rochefort. The oldest boy, Michel, had finished school and decided to return to Louisiana to become, with the aid of part of his father's fortune, a planter and exporter of cotton. The other two boys, Henri and Eugène, were about to emerge from their French lycée and were thinking of remaining in Europe. Only Célestine was left to be provided for, and propinquity was soon taking a hand in the problem, for by this time Auguste Degas had arrived from Naples and had rented an apartment just around the corner from the Rue Pigalle in the Rue de la Tour-des-Dames, on the other side of the small triangle of greenery. By looking down from his upstairs window Auguste could see Célestine when she came out to sit in her garden on a sunny afternoon; by glancing upward Célestine could see Auguste. They were married on July 12, 1832, in the nearby church of Notre-Dame-de-Lorette.

Germain Musson is referred to on the marriage certificate as "formerly a merchant."[4] Shortly after the wedding, however, having done his duty as a Frenchman to his children and to the memory of his wife, he went back to New Orleans and resumed, with the same energy, tenacity, and imagination he had displayed in the expansive years before the death of Marie Désirée, the role of an American entrepreneur. He had heard of the granite quarry at Quincy, Massachusetts, which had attracted national attention because its stone was used in the construction of the Bunker Hill Monument, so he instructed his ship captains to take on granite as ballast after unloading their cotton at Boston. When he had accumulated enough of this substitute for New England ice, he used it to erect an immense, severely functional building on his property at the corner of Canal and Royal streets. (The astonished residents of the Vieux Carré, who had been brought up on Creole cottage styles, delicate iron grillwork, and wooden Greek Revival façades, referred to the new structure as "Musson's fort.")[5] He returned to France for the birth of Edgar, stayed for a while at 8 Rue Saint-Georges, and commissioned Catherine Longchamp, a fashionable Swiss pastelist, to do a double portrait of Célestine and her sister Eugénie, which he took back with him to New Orleans. After that he seldom had time for trips to Europe, but he kept in touch, partly through Henri, with the Degas family on the Seine, and around the beginning of 1853 he came over for a visit, during which he posed, looking affluent and a bit truculent, for one of Edgar's earliest surviving portraits. He was soon back in the New World, however. On May 10, 1853, while inspecting his Mexican silver mines, he was killed when his coach turned over on a rough mountain road near Perote.

Two father figures as memorable as René-Hilaire Degas and Germain Musson should have been enough to satisfy any desire for distinguished ancestors. But they were not, and the fact is worth looking into, since it has caused both orthographical and critical confusion in Degas studies. During the early 1840s certain members of both the Naples and the Paris branches of the family, stimulated perhaps by the Neapolitan palazzo and the ducal marriages, began to sign themselves "de Gas," thus implying that they were entitled to the French nobiliary particle, the preposition that indicates that a name is derived from land holdings. The practice caught on firmly during the next twenty years. Edgar himself used the two-word form at school, in his letters of the 1860s, and as an artist until some time after 1870. He later explained his adoption of plain "Degas" by saying that he wanted to work and that aristocrats did not work. In the late 1860s a relative in the Paris branch, not satisfied with a mere prepositional implication, hired a genealogist to make things explicit, and the resulting document turned out to be what was wanted. The noble "de Gas" or "de Gast" family, it stated, was of very great antiquity and, though settled in western France by the eighteenth century, was originally from southern Languedoc and Bagnols-sur-Cèze, a town in the Rhone valley not far from Avignon. The name was purportedly "de Bagnols" until about the end of the fifteenth century. The coat of arms included, among other medieval devices, an eagle, a lion in gules with a double, partly intertwined tail, and a silver porcupine like the one on the escutcheon of the Orléans line of the French royal family.[6]

On such evidence (occasionally sharpened so as to place the family's more recent history in Brittany) art historians have repeatedly affirmed that Edgar Degas was of noble origins and have assumed that the spelling "de Gas" should be used in references to his relatives. On the same basis critics have sometimes felt authorized to detect signs of an aristocratic temperament in his work. All this has passed unchallenged, perhaps because it has not seemed worth fussing over, or because the use of "de Gas" for the relatives can be defended (and hence will be adopted in this book, with some exceptions) simply on the grounds that people have a right to spell their names as they wish. But the ancestry and the social condition of an important artist should not be dismissed as minor considerations, so a challenge is in order.

One can begin by noting that Edgar's remark about aristocrats and work may have been just one of his conversational pirouettes, designed to satisfy a questioner, since he was perfectly aware that his father, paternal grandfather, and three Neapolitan uncles all worked, or had worked, for a living. As for the claim to the nobiliary particle, one can observe that it was advanced at a very late date in the family's history, since the form "Degas" occurs in Naples on the birth certificates of Rosa, Auguste, Enrico, Odoardo, Achille, Laura, and Stefanina; in Paris on the marriage certificate of Auguste and Célestine; on Edgar's own birth certificate; and in letters written during the 1820s and 1830s by René-Hilaire and his wife, Aurora. One can continue by wondering why the family left its alleged fief in southern France, what had happened to its collaterals, why the genealogist did not come up with at least a minor title for Auguste, and so on. But such objections are unnecessary, for the whole edifice of genealogical charts, Languedoc lords, royal porcupines, and splendid prepositions collapses after one takes a single look at a parish register in Orléans for the year 1770, which records the birth of René-Hilaire and lists his father as "Pierre Degast, *boulanger.*"[7] (The bread business, incidentally, must have been what eventually steered the son into the Paris grain market.) Plainly, those descendants of Pierre the baker who in the 1840s began to call themselves "de Gas" were indulging in the foolish little parvenu trickery that was

laughed at during the reign of Louis-Philippe, and for a long while afterward, as "spontaneous ennoblement."

Their trickery was not, of course, particularly heinous, and they were
certainly not alone in practicing it. (By the end of the century, according
to a probably conservative estimate, more than half the nobiliary particles
in France were bogus.) Nevertheless, their foolishness is compounded when
one realizes that in their solid, respectable reality as members of the Parisian
grande bourgeoisie and of its Neapolitan equivalent, the urban *galantuomini,*
they belonged to a class that was far more important, and more stirring to
the historical imagination, than the decimated, mostly functionless, priest-
ridden French aristocracy of the period. An authentic *grand bourgeois,* as the
mature, anti-upstart Edgar, shortly after 1870, would tacitly announce in
his henceforth one-word signature, did not need a spurious particle.

Then as now, "bourgeois" was often used more as an epithet than as a
descriptive term, and there was disagreement about the exact nature, attri-
butes, and merits of the socioeconomic stratum in question. Hugo, who as
a poet and the son of an army officer could consider himself an objective
outsider, complacently observed that the French bourgeoisie was "simply
the contented part of the population."[8] Balzac, who had spontaneously
ennobled himself by tucking an unauthorized particle into his name, felt
that money was the determining factor after all, and tried to clinch the
matter by arguing that "an impoverished duke is still a duke, whereas an
impoverished bourgeois is a contradiction in terms."[9] The *Journal des Débats,* a thoroughly bourgeois (even mildly liberal) Paris daily, whose massively bourgeois founder, Louis-François Bertin, had sat for a celebrated,
aggressively bourgeois portrait by Ingres, thought that the whole discussion
was on the wrong track. "The bourgeoisie," the paper explained in an
editorial in 1847, "is not a class. It is a position. You can acquire this
position; you can lose it. Work, thrift, and capacity enable you to acquire
it. Vice, dissipation, and laziness cause you to lose it."[10] Karl Marx, a year
later in his *Communist Manifesto,* moralized in a different vein.[11] While
granting that the bourgeoisie had "rescued a considerable part of the population from the idiocy of rural life," he maintained that it had also "left
no other nexus between man and man except naked self-interest" and had
drowned all the old-fashioned sentiments "in the icy water of egotistical
calculation." In sum, such mid-nineteenth-century comments usually tell
us more about their authors than about the bourgeoisie, and often serve
mainly to suggest the fascination exercised by a class that had emerged as,
among many other things, the obvious winner of the French Revolution.

With the help of modern studies of the period it is possible to assess,
more clearly than before, the substance and psychology of the social cate-

gory to which the Degas family belonged. Statistical data have revealed, for instance, that the French bourgeoisie of around the middle of the century was much smaller than had been supposed, given the power it wielded and the talk it provoked. Seventy-five per cent of the total French population of about thirty-six million had not yet been rescued, as Marx put it, from rural life; and Paris, with something over a million inhabitants, was the only real metropolis in the country. Moreover, being rescued did not by any means transform one into a bourgeois. The figures for charity funerals between 1820 and 1860 indicate that more than 70 per cent of the citizens of Paris lived from day to day and died without enough francs to bury themselves. If we take the employing of servants as a criterion of the status we are looking for, only about 15 per cent of Parisian families were bourgeois.[12] But even that percentage should probably be halved, since some families with servants were aristocratic and hundreds of the so-called servants were young women and boy apprentices employed by shopkeepers and artisans dressed in workers' smocks. All in all, what can be called the indubitably upper middle class — the one in which the men always went to work wearing the regulation dark bourgeois frock coat and stovepipe hat — seems not to have been larger, in comparison with the mass of urbanized Frenchmen, than the white ruling minority in Saint-Domingue had once been in comparison with the mass of blacks. Naturally, the analogy should not be pressed too far. One can argue, however, that thousands of Frenchmen, especially in Paris, were mired in a squalid misery that was worse than what the average slave had experienced in the former pearl of the Antilles.

The numerical situation dictated a standard operating procedure for the upper classes: they let rioting and disorganized workers wrest political and economic gains for the bourgeoisie from reactionary governments, and then left the workers in the lurch. When the workers rejected the arrangement and continued to riot, the bourgeoisie and the aristocracy put them down with the army, which was composed largely of peasants who, in defiance of leftist theory, did not hesitate to shoot urban proletarians. The sequence, partly invented during the decade after the fall of the Bastille, was employed in the July Revolution in 1830, which brought Louis-Philippe to the throne, and again in the Revolution of 1848, which drove him into exile. It would reappear, with modifications and with unprecedented butchery, during the Paris Commune of 1871. The result was a semblance of stability, purchased at the cost of lasting bitterness. The most ordinary political decisions looked like momentous choices for society; class distinctions became pseudobiological ones; and even the more level-headed members of the bourgeoisie experienced a chronic feeling of insecurity that erupted periodically into a return of the Great Fear — the panic that had swept through the conservative part of France during the revolutionary summer of 1789. However well disposed a *grand bourgeois* might be toward workingmen as individuals, he tended to regard them in the aggregate as a separate race, innately inferior in intelligence, sensibility, and morals; and in times of stress he thought of them as a Redskin majority menacing the civilized Paleskins.

In the Degas family the latent Great Fear manifested itself as a repugnance for any kind of Jacobinism, perhaps because of the martyred Seven Virgins of Verdun and René-Hilaire's narrow escape from the Committee of Public Safety and possibly also because of Germain Musson's experiences during the insurrections at Port-au-Prince. René-Hilaire's revulsion was particularly strong and at the same time poignant, for during his walks about town when he visited Paris he always halted at the Place de la Concorde and refused to go past the spot where his fiancée had been guillotined. But the feeling was strong in him on other occasions, too, and in other places. In 1835, for example, when the Corsican republican Giuseppe Fieschi attempted unsuccessfully to assassinate Louis-Philippe with a twenty-five-gun "infernal machine," the patriarch in Naples immediately wrote to his wife, who was in the French capital at the time, deploring "this abominable catastrophe, which has plunged me into the saddest sort of reflections and into the consideration that such plots must inevitably lead to new revolutions, of which I know only too well the horror."[13] In fact, it is likely that the horror he referred to never really left him, in spite of his successful and mostly happy life, and that a vision of a terrible, sickening day in Paris in 1793 still haunted him when, in 1858 at the age of eighty-eight, surrounded by children and grandchildren, he died in his villa at San Rocco di Capodimonte. His last recorded words were an anguished refrain: "Ah, how much blood there was! How much blood . . ."[14]

But a sense of insecurity was not, of course, the sole response of the French mid-nineteenth-century bourgeoisie to the outside world, nor was it the only element in the class-conditioning of Edgar. And here some frequently forgotten sociological distinctions need to be remembered. René-Hilaire Degas and his immediate descendants did not belong, as did Germain Musson during part of his career, to the tough, sometimes vulgar, vigorously creative bourgeoisie Marx described in the *Manifesto* as "constantly revolutionizing the instruments of production, and thereby the relations of production, and with them all the relations of society." They did not, at least not directly, build Franco-Italian versions of the "dark Satanic mills" that had troubled William Blake, nor send tons of raw material scudding across the ocean from the far corners of the world; and they did not grind the faces of the poor. They were content, except during spells of yearning for the nobiliary particle, with belonging to a category that can be conveniently called the Louis-Philippe *grande bourgeoisie,* not because it existed only from 1830 to 1848, but because it reached its full and most characteristic flowering during that period, and because during the Second Empire and Third Republic it gradually yielded its importance in national affairs, first to big businessmen and eventually also to managers, technicians, and professional politicians. Typical members of the category were far from constituting a radically new social phenomenon: they were lawyers, magistrates, bankers great and small, prosperous doctors, publishers like the Monsieur Bertin of the Ingres portrait, speculators at the recently erected Paris Bourse, and rentiers who lived without professional status on their investments in land or commerce. In other words, they were pretty much a continuation and enlargement of the old Third Estate, which had snatched the French Revolution from the sans-culottes who had started it.

They were unlucky in having as their caricaturist an artist with the talent of Honoré Daumier, and so it is only fair to note that they were not always the heartless, cretinous monsters portrayed in his lithographs. Admittedly, they were usually no more interested in political reform than they were in becoming innovators in industrial production; in France until the fall of the July Monarchy they accepted a parody of democracy in which an income qualification limited the voting list for the entire country to about two hundred thousand. On the premise, however, that no change in the existing social structure was involved, they or their foreign counterparts might ardently favor a nationalist or quasi-liberal cause: Edgar's aunt Rosa let her twenty-year-old son, Gustavo, leave their house to die heroically in the abortive Neapolitan Revolution of 1848, which had links with the movement for the unification of Italy, and Aunt Laura's husband, Baron Bellelli, spent years in exile because of his participation in the same uprising. Again on the premise that no change in the existing social structure would ensue, the most representative members of the class were often charitable toward the underprivileged, kind toward children and animals, chivalrous toward women, and forgiving toward sinners. But their most attractive trait, and it was attractive enough to compensate for many unattractive ones, was their willingness to use their wealth to enrich their minds, sharpen their wits, and refine their sensibilities — to live somewhat in the manner of the enlightened section of the French eighteenth-century aristocracy. The result was often old-fashioned and even reactionary, but it was usually of a quality that the more up-to-date people in the society of the period, who were beginning to be swamped by the early aesthetic consequences of the Industrial Revolution, should have envied.

In Paris the Louis-Philippe *grands bourgeois* rented family loges at the Opéra, listened to the symphonic orchestra of the new Société des Concerts du Conservatoire, and organized chamber music evenings at home; they liked such contemporary composers as Rossini and Meyerbeer, but also Gluck, Weber, and especially Cimarosa (whom Stendhal considered greater than Mozart). They made Taglioni the most worshiped of all ballerinas. Under their patronage the French theater acquired more vitality than it had displayed at any time since Beaumarchais. They cultivated the arts of dress, cooking, and conversation by dining regularly with one another. Among the painters they admired and collected were Poussin, the eighteenth-century French portraitists, David, the early Corot, and both the early and the later Ingres. Surviving auction lists of the contents of their private libraries reveal that they read the Latin, and occasionally the Greek, classics in the original; the standard French authors, both literary and philosophical, from Montaigne up through Voltaire and the Encyclopedists; a good many essays on morals and duties but relatively few religious works (only the women, who were often educated in convent schools, seem to have regarded Christianity as more than merely a basis for ethical behavior); a lot of history and travel books; French translations of Tasso, Cervantes, Shakespeare, Richardson, Fielding, and Scott; and a sprinkling of recent French writers that included Madame de Staël, Chateaubriand, and Lamartine.[15] In general, to borrow a term coined for some of the architecture of the late eighteenth century and the early nineteenth, their taste in all the arts tended toward the Romantic Classical. They mixed, in a manner appropriate to a postimperial and postrevolutionary generation, Silver Age nostalgia with a fondness for order.

Their favorite part of Paris, and therefore the urban image of their social and cultural aspirations, was the Ninth Arrondissement, a then somewhat outlying sector that stretched from the Boulevard des Italiens northward to the Boulevard de Clichy, and from the Rue d'Amsterdam eastward to the Rue du Faubourg Poissonnière. Much of this area, including 8 Rue Saint-Georges, has long since been transformed into office buildings, but enough of the old has been preserved so that one can imagine, with the help of contemporary descriptions, how things looked in the time of Louis-Philippe. Here and there in the vicinity of Edgar's birthplace were some eighteenth-century town houses and sizable vestiges of their gardens. In the 1820s, however, a group of financiers and real estate promoters had subjected the lots in and around the Rues Saint-Georges, Saint-Lazare, de la Tour-des-Dames, Notre-Dame-de-Lorette, and de La Rochefoucauld to an intensive development in the Romantic Classical manner, and the outcome was such a profusion of neo-Greek and neo-Roman façades (in those days the differences between the two were not very clear) that the whole quarter was nicknamed "the new Athens." Dominating everything was the church of Notre-Dame-de-Lorette, a five-aisled, richly decorated version of an Early Christian basilica — for the most part an imitation of Santa Maria Maggiore in Rome — with an unusually tall temple portico. Further down on the scale of handsomeness were five-story apartment houses that brought together, in a strangely evident symbiosis, yet with clear lines of separation, some extensive samplings of contemporary society, for the ground levels were shops and workrooms, the three main floors were residences for the well-to-do, and the attics were congested barracks for servants, seam-stresses, and the miscellaneous poor. In a special division of modishness were expensively charming pavilions of the sort Balzac described in 1834, with what seems like unwarranted irritation, in *Le Père Goriot:*

> Rastignac reached the Rue Saint-Lazare and one of those lightweight houses, with slender columns and paltry porticos, that constitute what is considered "pretty" in Paris — a real banker's house, full of costly studied refinements, stucco-work, and stair landings with marble mosaics.[16]

It is pleasant to think, it the absence of more substantial evidence, that Auguste and Célestine Degas's first place, which was not far away, was like the pavilion Rastignac visited, and in fact there is what appears to be an inlaid marble floor beneath Célestine's feet in the portrait commissioned by Germain Musson in 1835. But since the couple were soon at another address, it is probable that they rented one of the new flats and that Edgar was born on a *piano nobile* above a greengrocer or a shoemaker.

An impressive number of artistic enterprises, providers of pleasure, and creative people helped to give the arrondissement its recognizable aura, compounded of fresh franc notes, sophisticated sensuality, and aesthetic confidence. In the Rue Laffitte, on the axis of the nave of Notre-Dame-de-Lorette, picture dealers were beginning what would become an internation-ally known concentration of commercial galleries, eventually familiar ter-ritory for Edgar. The Opéra, which would also become familiar to him, was installed nearby, in the Rue Le Peletier (the present house was not ready until 1875), in a sprawling Romantic Classical pile topped by the colossal statues of eight muses — the missing one being, according to detractors, the muse of architecture. In convenient proximity were the smart cafés and restaurants on the Boulevard des Italiens. A few blocks away stood the Conservatoire de Musique, which offered an acoustically perfect little concert hall, deliciously decorated in the neo-Pompeian style. The eighteenth-century Théâtre Chantereine was a three-minute walk from 8 Rue Saint-Georges.

All was not, of course, on a lofty level: the Rue Notre-Dame-de-

Lorette, for example, in back of the new church, was notoriously the beat of the peculiarly ambiguous sort of demimondaine, neither frail sister nor strumpet nor successful kept woman, who was popularly referred to as a *lorette* ("a decent word," Balzac explained in *Un Homme d'affaires,* "for designating the status of a prostitute with a status difficult to designate").[17] But there was plenty of distinction to be encountered. When Auguste arrived from Naples he had as close neighbors in the block-long Rue de la Tour-des-Dames, besides Célestine on the other side of the greenery, the much admired painters Horace Vernet, Ary Scheffer, and Paul Delaroche, plus two even more admired theatrical stars, Mademoiselle Mars and François-Joseph Talma. (René-Hilaire, in Paris to check on the education of his son, took him to the Comédie-Française to see the famous pair perform, and wrote to Aurora that it was essential that the young man get to know them.)[18] Dumas *père* was in the Rue Saint-Lazare. When Auguste and Célestine moved into the Rue Saint-Georges, they had another celebrated painter, Théodore Chassériau, as a neighbor. Number 22 would be occupied by the composer Esprit Auber, who was especially in view during the July Monarchy because one of his operas, *La Muette de Portici,* had been the signal for a riot in Brussels that had turned into a rebellion. Soon Fromental Halévy, whose masterpiece, *La Juive,* was to become one of the operatic war-horses of the century, resided in the Rue de La Rochefoucauld, Delacroix in a vast, cluttered studio in the Rue Notre-Dame-de-Lorette, and Chopin and George Sand behind a Romantic Classical façade in the half-hidden Square d'Orléans. Clearly, a reference to "the new Athens" was more than an architectural pleasantry.

As has been suggested, Auguste Degas continued to be mobile, in the manner of many a less prosperous immigrant, for a good while after his arrival. By 1838 he was around the corner from 8 Rue Saint-Georges at 21 Rue de la Victoire, where he remained only until 1840. During the next twelve years he lived, at various times, near the Place Vendôme, near the top of Montparnasse, and in the Latin Quarter, before settling near the Place de la Concorde. Edgar thus became acquainted with large sections of both the Right Bank and the Left, and he developed into an inveterate, wide-ranging Parisian stroller and rubberneck. But he remained attached to his native part of town, ready to return to it when he acquired the freedom of full manhood. Between the Boulevard des Italiens and the Boulevard de Clichy he was to find most of the most characteristic subject matter of his art. On the approaches to Montmartre he would establish his several studios, evolve from Romantic Classicism into a personal style, negotiate artistic alliances, and sit in cafés, talking endlessly about painting. And there he would finally spend nearly sixty of his eighty-three years, often in the role of a stubbornly surviving *grand bourgeois* of the reign of Louis-Philippe. If cityscapes and what they contain — ballerinas, for instance, and laundresses, prostitutes, bassoonists, and bathrooms — were not so perishable, we might today refer to the Ninth Arrondissement of Paris as Degas country, much as we refer to the landscape around Aix-en-Provence as Cézanne country and to the county of Dorset as Hardy country.

2. An Unsentimental Education

T HE YOUNG EDGAR," we are told, "was very much loved and very much coddled."[1] Unfortunately for psychohistory, this important piece of information rates only as family hearsay, since it comes, long after the events it refers to, from Jeanne Fevre, an occasionally unreliable niece of the painter's. But it can be accepted as a significant probability, partly because of some scraps of supporting facts and partly because in the Louis-Philippe *grande bourgeoisie* a baby who was at once a firstborn, a first son, and a first grandson in the direct male line was automatically a treasure, an infant prince. There is a current of dynastic excitement, in addition to warm humanity, in a letter written by René-Hilaire Degas in Naples, on May 28, 1835, to Aurora, who had just arrived in Paris:

> By now you will have had the pleasure of hugging and kissing Célestine and the little monkey Edgar. Please tell me all about them. What is the funny little man up to? Has he got some teeth? He's a year old. Can he walk a little? Is he strong and healthy? Details, please. You'll give me pleasure.[2]

Although such testimony of affection is lacking for the rest of the early years, there is the evidence, for what it is worth, of two portraits, the first painted when the boy was perhaps four and the other when he was about seven or eight. In both pictures the eyes already have, or can be imagined to have, a hint of the mixture of ironic intelligence and veiled morosity later visible in many of the self-portraits. In both, however, the carefully combed hair, the white, shoulder-wide collar, and an air of timidity suggesting that the sitter was on the verge of tears are compatible with a notion that the child was much loved and much coddled.

The occasionally unreliable niece also says that he "really worshiped" his mother;[3] and again some pictorial evidence, for what it is worth, can be noted. In the double pastel portrait of 1835 Célestine is a fashionable vision of languid roundness and melting dark eyes in a swirl of skirts and immense bouffant sleeves; in a sharp miniature, probably painted for her marriage in 1832, she is more dramatic and at the same time more girlish, with hair parted in the middle and swept up on the back of her head Spanish style, a Cupid's bow mouth, a revealing décolletage, and a rose in her belt. On the whole, then, though she was a little too Romantic for a sophisticated Parisian taste and too much the Creole belle, she was certainly a mother whom a sensitive boy might easily have adored, so the niece's report cannot be rejected out of hand. It is considerably qualified, however, by the adult Edgar's omission of any reference to his mother in his letters and by his mentioning only two memories of her in his published conversation, neither of which suggests anything at all like a worshipful attitude.

The first, more detailed, and more distant of these memories can be linked to the Great Fear. It was of a visit he paid with his mother, when he was about five years old, to Madame Elisabeth Le Bas, a pleasant, elderly woman who was also, although he could scarcely have appreciated this at the time, something of a historical revenant, for she was the daughter of the revolutionary carpenter Maurice Duplay, who had sheltered Robespierre, and the widow of Joseph Le Bas, the radical member of the National Convention who in 1794, on the memorable Ninth of Thermidor that preceded the execution of the leading Jacobins, had escaped the guillotine by shooting himself. The visit, surprising in view of the Degas family's politics, came about because Madame Le Bas's son Philippe, a learned and, one may suppose, reasonably conservative man, had been the tutor of the uncles in Naples. (At Augsburg he had also been the tutor — and the fact indicates the level at which René-Hilaire functioned — of Louis-Napoleon Bonaparte, the future Napoleon III.) The floor of the Le Bas apartment, in the Rue de Tournon, near the Palais du Luxembourg, was covered with red tiles that had just been waxed (the painter's eye was already at work), and Célestine was holding Edgar by the hand. Suddenly she noticed that the walls of the entrance hall were decorated with portraits of Robespierre, Saint-Just, Couthon, and other guillotined extremists. He remembered her brutal exclamation: "What! You're still preserving the heads of those monsters?" And the quick rebuke of the still staunchly loyal old woman: "Célestine, shut your mouth. They were saints."[4]

The other memory was much simpler, but equally vivid and probably more significant, more representative. He was older than at the time of the Madame Le Bas incident, though from external evidence he could not have been more than about twelve. It was the noon hour, the family was having lunch, and his mother was drumming nervously, vigorously, on the table with her fingers. At intervals she interrupted the tattoo to say, impatiently, "Auguste, Auguste." The boy would remember that his father remained silent throughout the meal, and then dashed for the door, struggled into a coat, and disappeared, still silent, down the stairs.[5]

The episode was recalled as domestic farce, almost as a vaudeville skit, and it was undoubtedly recounted as such, for Edgar developed into a deadpan humorist and an accomplished mimic. But the farce is rather thin, and its having stuck in his mind for decades, to the exclusion of possibly happier domestic scenes, is hard to dismiss as accidental. Behind Célestine's drumming and Auguste's silent flight there seems to have been something worse than an ordinary, absurd quarrel between man and wife, something like the accumulated exasperation and routine resignation of a marriage that had gone sour — too sour to be hidden from an observant son. And that this was actually the situation becomes more probable when one looks at some of the consequences, for Célestine in particular but also for Auguste and Edgar, of what had begun as a meeting of eyes above the greenery next to the Rue de la Tour-des-Dames.

She was seventeen, it should be remembered, when she was married, and nineteen in 1834, when Edgar was born. During the next three years at 8 Rue Saint-Georges she had two more sons, each of whom died almost immediately after being born. Soon she, Auguste, and Edgar were at 21 Rue de la Victoire (where her brother Eugène, her brother-in-law the Duc de Rochefort, and her sister, Eugénie, also had apartments), and there in 1838 she gave birth to Achille, Edgar's first surviving brother. A little more than a year later, while the family was living at 241 Rue Saint-Honoré, near the Place Vendôme, she lost another child; and at this point her mother-in-law, Aurora, who knew from personal experience what it was like to have babies and to lose them, wrote to her from Naples:

> Come and spend a few months in the bosom of a family that loves you and that will do everything to provide you with some distractions. . . . I'll be expecting you, accompanied by your sons.[6]

The invitation pleased Auguste, and Célestine, who by this time was pregnant again, showed up in Naples in 1840, presumably with the two-year-old Achille and the six-year-old Edgar in tow. While in the city she gave birth to a daughter, Thérèse. But she was provided with the promised distractions, and it was perhaps during this period that she began a flirtation with one of Auguste's younger brothers, Edgar's uncle Achille, which turned, according to gossip from the Neapolitan branch of the family, into a serious love affair. Back in Paris the next spring, she wrote to her young Italian sisters-in-law, Laura and Stefanina, a letter in which the excitement of the recent visit was still bubbling:

> What did you do this winter? Did you have a good time? Were there lots of balls? Write to me a little more often, you silent beauties. . . . And tell me about your winter conquests, you lovely damsels. With complete frankness, above all.[7]

In the same letter, however, she could not refrain from revealing her own chronic boredom and her disillusionment with marriage:

> What can I tell you about myself that will be amusing? I am spending my life, my youth, seated in front of the fire. I have not gone to a single ball, not even to the least little soirée. Auguste is more and more disgusted with society, and he flatly refuses to listen to my pleading.

In 1842, in the Parisian suburb of Passy, she gave birth to a second daughter, Marguerite; and in 1845, at 24 Rue de l'Ouest (today part of the Rue d'Assas), to a third son, René. Two years later, at the age of thirty-two, she died, evidently worn out by childbearing, perhaps fatigued by an almost nomadic existence, quite certainly unhappy, and probably still dreaming of winter nights of dancing and flirting. Edgar was then thirteen years old.

In this tragedy of the bourgeois woman as adolescent sex object, immature wife, and doomed baby-producing machine, Auguste can be theoretically cast in the role of the villain; and in fact he seems to have had his share of such faults as inattentiveness and self-centeredness. Giuseppe Morbilli, Rosa's husband, referred to him in a letter of 1835 as "a perfect model of apathy and egotism."[8] René-Hilaire was always uneasy about his eldest son's common sense and afraid that the Paris bank would become involved in Germain Musson's risky New Orleans ventures, and for a while Achille, Célestine's reputed sweetheart, was stationed in France to keep an eye on the business.

But there is a case for the defense. Auguste was being an average nineteenth-century husband when he failed to imagine that his wife might be in desperate need of a respite from her round of pregnancies, and he was simply, if rather selfishly, being true to his own nature when he refused to take her to dances. For he was definitely not the dancing type; he was not cut out for the role of husband to a Creole belle — nor, one feels, for that of a banker. In an early miniature, perhaps a pendant to the small portrait of Célestine, he is a slightly out-of-date mixture of British Regency buck and Chateaubriand, with a white neck scarf, rippling Romantic cloak, a curl plastered to a temple, regular features and sensual mouth, and an air of listening. In Edgar's best-known portraits of him, painted more than thirty years later, he is still listening, this time to music. He played the piano and the organ almost professionally, composed fantasias, and taught his daughters, as they grew up, to sing Gluck to him. He cultivated the friendship of several of the most important art lovers of the period, and his own collection of eighteenth-century pastels included works by Maurice Quentin de La Tour and Jean-Baptiste Perronneau. A friend of the family once summed him up as "very gentle, very distinguished, unusually kind, and witty,"[9] which may be a bit partial but is not incompatible with his son's memory of him slipping silently down the stairs while Célestine drummed on the table.

Since there is no record of Edgar's early education, presumably the boy was tutored at home by his mother or by one of the maternal uncles from New Orleans, Henri and Eugène, who had remained in France. During visits to Naples, at his grandfather's palazzo on the Calata Trinità Maggiore and also at his aunt Rosa's house in the Via Toledo, where he had three little cousins near his own age to play with, he may have picked up the fluent, impeccable Italian (spiced with Neapolitan slang for special effects) he commanded as an adult. In Naples, too, observing and hearing the volatile, voluble, gesticulating natives of the city, he may have acquired some of the ingredients of his later conversational style — the bantering effrontery, for instance, and the gestures that turned into mimicry. Back in Paris, he must have occasionally had his values as a small *grand bourgeois* straightened by a visit to his father's bank, which was usually near the family apartment and at times in the same building. One can guess what this sanctum was like by reading a description, by the art critic Georges Rivière, of similarly private loan enterprises around the middle of the nineteenth century:

> No luxury at all. The offices were installed, more often than not, on poorly lit mezzanine floors. A personnel solemn, silent, not very numerous. The director himself received the visitors, for a banker was the confidant and counselor of his clients.[10]

There were other, more cheerful sanctums, however. In the family salon the child learned not only to enjoy but to need music and painting; and in the family library he developed, among more usual bookish cravings, an avid, lifelong appetite for *The Thousand and One Nights*.

Without venturing very deeply into psychological speculation, one can imagine that the death of Célestine provoked complex feelings of sadness, guilt, liberation, and reorientation in her thirteen-year-old son. Had he, as reported, really worshiped her? Or had he, as his two memories of her imply, distanced her with an early version of that morose, ironic look of his? He may have had one attitude at one stage, of course, and another attitude later on, and finally both at once, thus fixing in his mind the common, conflicting, allegedly creative infantile fantasies of the good-mother figure and the bad-mother figure — and also fixing a private prototype for the nineteenth-century middle-class man's common conception of women as idealized inferiors. In any event, she was now, with her décolletages, her levity, her nagging, and her pathos, forever what she had been; and he was henceforth, for the duration of his adolescence and well beyond, immersed in a clan dominated by somber masculine redingotes and male celibacy. Auguste, although he was only forty at the time of his wife's death, seems never to have even considered remarrying. Germain Musson had long been a confirmed widower, and René-Hilaire Degas had recently become one, Aurora having died in 1841, shortly after Célestine's last, flirtatious visit to Naples. Two of Edgar's Neapolitan uncles, Enrico and Achille, were bachelors and would remain such all their lives. The third, Odoardo, was a bachelor until 1862, when he was fifty-one and the authoritarian René-Hilaire was dead. In Paris this unusual concentration of wifelessness was rounded out by the presence of Uncle Eugène, Célestine's brother, who was yet another lifelong bachelor. When they were all together the effect must have been like that of a meeting of top-hatted monks in a refectory.

The shift away from crinolines and coddling and toward a male orientation may actually have begun, however, more than a year before the death of Célestine, for on October 5, 1845, Edgar was enrolled as a resident student in the Lycée Louis-le-Grand, which of course was exclusively for boys. (Lycées for girls were created only in 1880, and coeducational lycées much later.) By 1847 he was already getting used to the seven-year ritual, in some ways more inflexible than a tribal initiation ceremony, through which the sons of the Louis-Philippe *grande bourgeoisie* had to pass on their way from prepuberty to adulthood. Whatever his initial, inherited dispositions may have been, they were now being subjected to a carefully calculated effort to transform them into acceptance of an élitist cultural code, into attachment to his social and economic category, and into anxiety about living up to paternal expectations.

The Lycée Louis-le-Grand was located, as it still is, in the Rue Saint-Jacques, across the street from the Sorbonne, but it was then quite dismally different from the reconstructed, relatively humane secondary school of today. In the 1840s the principal buildings, huddling around a huge, windy courtyard and harboring a score of shops on the street side, were still mostly seventeenth-century ones, and they were in a state of damp, gloomy, picturesque dilapidation that was regularly and ineffectually denounced by government inspectors. There were dramatic occasions when a suddenly sagging beam menaced an entire class, and when a fragment of a decaying cornice fell into the courtyard with an echoing thump. Discipline was rigorously military: the students were dressed in tightly buttoned uniforms and short stovepipe hats, were organized into companies under sergeants, and were marched to all their classes and to the dark, fetid dining hall, where they ate unappetizing food on bare, marble-topped tables. They took foot baths every two weeks and full baths every three months. Violators of the rules were punished by severe beatings (the records reveal that sometimes the headmaster had to restrain sadistic teachers) or by solitary confinement in the jail, a row of thirteen cells directly under the roof, with barred windows, grated doors for permitting close surveillance, and no heat. Adolescence was regarded as a malady that could be cured by shock treatment; masturbators were constantly warned that they risked becoming idiots. Winter was a particularly difficult season for the roughly five hundred boys (about half the total enrollment) who, like Edgar, lived in the school. One of his near contemporaries, in a lugubrious remembrance of things past, wrote of frozen wash basins, convulsive shivering, stiff joints, chapped skin, chronic chilblains, and — in the crowded, overheated study rooms equipped with stoves — an unforgettable dunghill smell compounded of January mud, unwashed bodies, and stale food.[11]

But in spite of the slumlike plant and the medieval living conditions, Louis-le-Grand was beyond question the most prestigious lycée in the country. It was founded in 1562 by the Jesuits as the Collège de Clermont, and down through the centuries its importance to succeeding governments was reflected in names that read like a series of French historical trumpet calls. In 1682, under the Sun King, it became the Collège Louis-le-Grand; in 1793, at the height of the Revolution, the Institut des Boursiers Egalité; in 1798, under the Directory, the Prytanée Française; in 1803, under Bonaparte as First Consul, the Collège de Paris; in 1805, under Napoleon as emperor, the Lycée Imperial; in 1814, before the return from Elba, for the first time the Lycée Louis-le-Grand; in 1815, after Waterloo, the Collège Royal; and then, under Louis-Philippe, once again the Lycée Louis-le-Grand. Its list of illustrious former students included Molière, Voltaire, Robespierre, Desmoulins, Delacroix, Géricault, Hugo, and Baudelaire. (The last named, however, was expelled in 1839 for having defiantly swallowed a classroom note he had been summoned to deliver to the headmaster.) An official report, written shortly before Edgar's entry, described the students as belonging "to the most enlightened and most influential classes of society,"[12] which in practice meant that most of the boys were either solidly bourgeois or the sons of nobles, generals, and ministers. A poor boy, unless he happened to win one of the limited number of scholarships, had no chance, for though the school was run by the state, the cost of board and room for a year was more than seven hundred francs. (The average teacher's annual salary was five hundred francs.)

The curriculum had about as much relevance to the emerging world of the Industrial Revolution as a seven-year course in *The Tale of Genji* would have had (which is not to say that it had no relevance at all), and it had perhaps even less to do with the social and political realities of the period. Although the fighting during and immediately after the Revolution of 1848 raged into the Rue Saint-Jacques, the boys were kept safely locked in and uncontaminated, and the sole effect of the short-lived Second Republic was to change briefly, against the wishes of the faculty, the name of the school to the Lycée Descartes. Afterward, as before, there was some desultory teaching of history and geography, and a lot of recitation of set pieces from the works of French seventeenth-century writers. But the emphasis remained heavily on Latin, Greek, and rhetoric; and the grand objective of this emphasis was the composition of a classical discourse with a proper beginning, middle, and peroration, a correct subordination of parts to the whole, and a suitably elevated diction. In typical assignments the student was told to imagine that he was a noble historical personage in a situation that called for convincing arguments: the Roman emperor Maximian, for example, obliged to persuade his joint emperor, Diocletian, not to give up the empire; or King Francis I, after his defeat in the Battle of Pavia, forced to complain about his captivity in a letter to the victorious Charles V.[13]

Edgar dodged falling cornices successfully, endured the stink and the discipline, and took to the curriculum with enthusiasm. Later, he would astonish his painter friends with his ability to recite long passages from Corneille, Racine, Molière, La Fontaine, La Rochefoucauld, and Pascal; and he would continue to read, for pleasure and in the original, the Latin and Greek classics — in particular the works of Livy, Pliny, Herodotus, and Theocritus. He would also, as he grew older, return frequently, zestfully, to the merciless memoirs of Saint-Simon. The Louis-le-Grand archives reveal, however, that he was just a slightly above-average student. In his second year at the school he won a prize for handwriting; in his third year, a second prize for Latin themes; and in his fourth year, a prize for generally satisfactory achievement. Otherwise he had to be content with being a winner of routine and not always very high honorable mentions.[14]

Music was an important extra subject at the school. There were frequent concerts for the students and their families, and even some regular singing classes, in which Edgar participated to the extent of once winning a ninth honorable mention. Music was also the cause of one of the few rebellions in the generally placid history of the institution, and the affair is worth recalling as an indication of the cultural atmosphere of the place. The innocent instigator was Gustave-Hippolyte Roger, a tenor with an elegant, graceful silhouette, a charming voice, and a flair for theatrical business. He had made his début at the Opéra-Comique in 1838, at the age of twenty-two, and gone on to star, in the same house, in an unbroken series of successes by such popular tune-makers as Ambroise Thomas, Fromental Halévy, and Esprit Auber; by 1848 he had achieved the distinction of being, with the great diva Pauline Viardot-García, one of the two best-loved singers in France — and a lion in the Rue Saint-Jacques, for he was a Louis-le-Grand graduate. Then Meyerbeer, the most talked-about composer in Europe, decided to exploit the situation. With his usual knack for publicity, he let it be known that his next opera for Paris, to be entitled *Le Prophète* and to be staged, of course, in the big house in the Rue Le Peletier, would be a spectacular reconstitution of the orgiastic Anabaptist rising of the sixteenth century, and that the crushingly difficult role of John of Leyden would be sung by Roger. In the world of opera fanatics, which had many resemblances to a world of blood-sports fans, the news was electrifying. Could Roger bring it off? Meyerbeer fed the excitement by letting it be known that there would be a role for Viardot, a powder-magazine explosion, and a ballet with the dancers on roller skates — a recent invention. (He had, Dumas *fils* remarked, "the German wit to set a success simmering six months in advance on the stoves of the newspapers.")

The tension in the Rue Saint-Jacques finally became unbearable, and on the opening night, April 16, 1849, a sizable mass of the students, who had somehow managed to procure tickets, broke out of their quarters, crossed the Seine, and made for the Rue Le Peletier. There they were not disappointed, for their hero Roger was reportedly a sensational John of Leyden, and the roller-skate ballet well worth whatever punishment they received for playing truant.

Drawing was another important extra, nonliterary subject at the Lycée Louis-le-Grand; and here again Edgar, though he had certainly begun to draw and probably to paint at home at an early age, received no better than slightly above average marks from his teachers. His sketches obtained a third honorable mention in 1848, a second in 1849, a fourth in 1850, a third in 1851, a first in 1852, and no prizes at all. But — to judge by his later enthusiasms — he evidently enjoyed working from the engravings of Italian Renaissance masterpieces and from the plaster casts of ancient sculptures provided by the school in lieu of live subjects, and he profited from contact with an outside professional, Léon Cogniet, who came once a week to give assignments, examine the students' work, and function as the traditional head of an atelier. Cogniet belonged to the large group of conventional, frequently uninspired French painters who would one day be dismissed as *pompiers,* as firemen. (The derisive term arose, according to a suspiciously folkish theory, from the resemblance between the metal headgear of Parisian firemen and the helmets of the ancient Greeks and Romans who populated academic pictures.) He had dallied with the Delacroix kind of Romanticism back in the 1820s and then gradually lost his nerve and allowed his natural ponderousness to assert itself. This had not prevented him, however, from becoming a chevalier of the Legion of Honor, nor from garnering a number of lucrative commissions for the decoration of public buildings, nor from suddenly achieving wide popularity in 1845 with a fine piece of light and shade, *Tintoretto Painting His Dead Daughter,* in which old Romanticism vied with new Realism and with a convincing intuition of the imperative, at times inhuman nature of an authentic artistic vocation. He was a competent draftsman, an immensely influential preceptor whose pupils would win medals in the official Salon for the next fifty years, and the possessor, according to Baudelaire, of an unusually "unquiet" intelligence.[15] An earnest, aspiring teen-ager of the 1840s might understandably have regarded such a painter as an inspiration, and that Edgar did so, for a while at least, is suggested by some evidence in his surviving notebooks of a projected personal version of *Tintoretto Painting His Dead Daughter.*

The type of career, at once respectably aesthetic and respectably bourgeois, favored by Cogniet's influence was also favored by the presence at Louis-le-Grand of schoolmates who constituted an old-boy network in the making and an effective peer group, full of models with which an attentive, anxious, introverted adolescent could identify. Among the boys whom Edgar knew particularly well were Léon Bonnat, future portraitist of statesmen, director of the Ecole des Beaux-Arts, and eminent *pompier;* Henri Meilhac, future author of sophisticated Parisian theatrical successes; Louis Bréguet, a scion of the powerful Bréguet dynasty of instrument-makers, engineers, and physicists; Henri Rouart, future artillery officer, industrialist, painter, and owner of a fabulous collection of pictures; Rouart's brother, Alexis, future factory manager and also a collector; and Paul Valpinçon, future landscape painter, horse breeder, and Norman country gentleman. Occupying a special niche of affection was a bright Jewish youngster,

Ludovic Halévy, who would become a dramatist and novelist, a member of the Académie Française, and, in collaboration with Meilhac, a brilliant librettist. In the small, ingrown society of the Louis-Philippe *grande bourgeoisie* each of these comrades was potentially a center of new acquaintances and a source of reinforcing ties.

Auguste Degas contributed, although certainly not intentionally, to the small forces that were gradually determining his son's choice of career. During much of this period he was living at 37 Rue Madame, across the Jardin du Luxembourg from the Rue Saint-Jacques, and on Sunday mornings he would walk over to Louis-le-Grand and pick up Edgar for one of the authorized family outings. Love of art was the usual motivation for the expeditions. There were many visits to the Louvre, probably with much lingering in the rooms devoted to the Italian fifteenth-century painters who were among the elder Degas's favorites. Between the long wings of the museum, in what is now the open Place du Carrousel but was then a tangle of old buildings, there was an art market where one could buy, according to Edgar's recollection, possibly embellished by time, "drawings by Boucher and Watteau for a few sous."[16] Across the river near the Bourse, in the Rue des Jeûneurs, one could buy academy figures — large studies from the nude done as exercises — by Prud'hon. And it was perhaps during these Sunday rambles that the boy encountered, without daring to risk an approach, two of the great men of the time. One, in the Rue Mazarine not far from the Ecole des Beaux-Arts, was Delacroix, whom Degas would remember in the style of a film shot:

> He had his collar turned up and a scarf around his neck. He was walking fast, fast. I can see him stepping off the sidewalk, crossing the street at a rapid gait, and stepping up onto the other sidewalk, still going fast. Whenever, which is often, I go past that spot . . . I again see Delacroix in a great hurry.[17]

The other, on a Seine quay opposite the Louvre, was the anarchist philosopher Pierre-Joseph Proudhon, bugaboo of the bourgeoisie, who would be remembered, in the manner of a Degas portrait, as "a large frock coat, a crease in the back, a head like Socrates', and those glasses behind which he looked at you."[18]

Sometimes the Sunday outings were calls on the connoisseurs with whom Auguste was friendly; as usual Edgar's memories included the addresses, as if a litany of Paris street names could in itself conjure up the past. Near the Rue Madame in the Rue du Cherche-Midi, after threading his way through a town house, a coach house, and a stable, all stripped nearly bare of furnishings to make room for piled-up art, he could find the rich, passably eccentric Dr. Louis La Caze, who loved oil paint as some men loved absinthe, and whose collection of more than eight hundred pictures included Rembrandt's *Bathsheba,* Hals's *Gypsy Girl,* Ribera's *Boy with a Clubfoot,* Terborch's *Reading Lesson,* eight Watteaus, nine Fragonards, thirteen Chardins, and works by Rubens, Velázquez, the Le Nains, Philippe de Champaigne, Boucher, and Greuze. (La Caze had an excellent eye and a public spirit, as well as money: he had spotted Watteau's *Gilles,* for example, in a secondhand shop, and in 1869 he turned his collection into the most splendid donation in the history of the Louvre.) Also near the Degas family apartment, in a modest house, could be found the aging François Marcille, who devoted himself especially to Prud'hon, Nanteuil, Chardin, and Fragonard, and whom Edgar would recall with particular affection:

> The old fellow lived at the corner of the Rue Monsieur-le-Prince. . . . At the back of the courtyard you went up some steps, and the door opened directly onto the floor. A bedroom with canvases stacked pell-mell, an iron bed, and, well, a chamber pot under it. He wore a caped cloak and an old hat: in those days everyone had an old hat. La Caze, ah La Caze, he too had an old hat. . . . I can see the gaffer Marcille coming back from the Rue des Jeûneurs with a pair of Prud'hon's academy figures. He is holding one in each hand, with his arms spread out, like this, to keep the sheets from rubbing together. [Here the memory became mimicry.] [19]

Still another collector on Auguste's visiting list, and an especially friendly one, was Edouard Valpinçon, father of Edgar's schoolmate Paul, who maintained (in addition to a place in Normandy) a large town house, garden, and stable in the Rue Taitbout, just inside the southern frontier of the Ninth Arrondissement. In these comfortable surroundings Edgar was encouraged to admire, leisurely, discriminatingly, idolatrously, a selection of Ingres's drawings and the same master's oil *Bather* — the one with turbaned head, long back, and cushioned buttocks that is now in the Louvre and is often referred to as the *Baigneuse de Valpinçon.*

On the whole, these Sunday visits can scarcely be said to have fostered a progressive attitude toward painting. There was a notable emphasis on drawing, at that time the most backward-looking element in the art, and a notable absence of the great Romantics and of such younger anti-Classicists as the landscapists in the Forest of Fontainebleau, who were beginning to be known as the Barbizon school because of their favorite village, and the Realists, who were beginning to attract attention because of the loud voice, and the immense talent, of Courbet. Ingres, the principal contemporary represented in the collections, was a veteran nearing seventy, although still vigorous, and a notorious reactionary, although a genius. He had painted the *Valpinçon Bather* in 1808, when Neoclassicism had not yet spent itself.

In short, what Edgar saw was largely an illustration, for all its high quality, of the widespread bourgeois conviction that great art was by definition the art of the past. And yet, in the taste of men like La Caze and Marcille for eighteenth-century works — and of Auguste, too, with his pastels by Perronneau and La Tour — there was something that the boy may have seen, however obscurely, as a small sign of change. The Oedipal, or skipped-generation, law of art history, according to which sons reject the styles of their fathers and return to those of their grandparents, had begun to operate. Watteau, Boucher, Fragonard, and their followers, who had been denounced by the champions of Neoclassicism as frivolous and unmanly, were beginning to regain favor; and this shift in appreciation would become one of the preludes to a creative shift, away from bitumen and solemnity and toward a light palette and hedonism.

In the meantime, young manhood, if of a rather docile, timid sort, was approaching, and eventually there were evenings of authorized liberty that could be spent in the public dance halls with which mid-nineteenth-century Paris teemed. One of the best known of such places, at 251 Rue Saint-Honoré, was the Bal Valentino, where there were masked balls in which dandies, students, painters, grocers, seamstresses, and *lorettes* mingled in an atmosphere of intoxicating mystery, like that of a Venetian carnival. The establishment was also a monument of social history, for it was there that an inspired dancer, confronted by an acquaintance's shiny new boots, had startled the assembly by shouting, *"Ah! il a des bottes, Bastien!"* The shout, picked up by the other dancers and chanted to the two-four beat of a polka, and then repeated mindlessly on every kind of occasion, became the most popular of the many nonsensical catch phrases of the Second Empire. And it was while walking past number 251, when he was nearly eighty and the dance hall long since demolished, that Edgar indulged in his only recorded sentimental memory of his school years:

> This was once the Bal Valentino. One night I lifted the mask of a young woman. I had been to the ball. I had taken her there. I was very young then, and dressed as Pierrot. I was young.[20]

The night was probably in 1852, during his last term at Louis-le-Grand, for around that date his father moved the family from the Left Bank to an apartment house at 4 Rue de Mondovi, which was three blocks from the Bal Valentino.

3. Bonjour, Monsieur Ingres

ON MARCH 23, 1853, after successfully completing his studies at the Lycée Louis-le-Grand, the recent Pierrot conformed to paternal expectations by obtaining his *baccalauréat,* the degree that gave access to the university or to a comparable institution of higher learning. He thus became, to an extent hard to imagine in the egalitarian climate of twentieth-century education, a member of a minority of a minority, an exception even among the *grands bourgeois,* for in an average year of the early 1850s only about four thousand young Frenchmen, and no young women at all, managed to pass the comprehensive, unpredictably difficult *baccalauréat* examination.[1] Below them were the lycée students who had failed or had dropped out, and further down were the millions who were never given a chance to fail or to drop out. Recent analyses of primary school attendance, military recruits' records, and bridegrooms' signatures or marks indicate that at the start of the Second Empire approximately 40 per cent of French adults were unable to read or write and that another 40 per cent were fumbling through their lives in what today would be called semiliteracy.[2]

The choice of a career now became a matter of disagreement between father and son, with the former pulling toward the law and the latter, though at first, it seems, not very resolutely, toward art. (Auguste Degas was not, of course, the only nineteenth-century French parent to have such trouble in guiding a gifted child: Balzac, Courbet, Manet, and Cézanne also balked at entering the legal profession.) According to Jeanne Fevre, the niece already cited, whose account is worth mentioning if only because it tells us of family anecdotes, the situation reached a breaking point when her uncle Edgar, after a short period at law school, politely but stubbornly refused to continue and at the same time announced his determination to become a painter:

> Between [him] and his father, whom he loved and profoundly respected, there was the classic scene. Monsieur Degas threatened to cut off his son's allowance . . . but this had no effect. With great sadness and equally great nobility, Edgar left the paternal hearth and went to live in a garret. Concerning this part of his life, during which he must have suffered a great deal, both emotionally and physically, the great painter never wished to speak. He merely supplied, very much later, an important detail by saying, "It was in that attic that I caught cold in my eyes."[3]

At first Auguste believed, still according to the niece, that the harsh reality of life in a garret without money would rapidly bring about an abandonment of what he considered "the dangerous chimera of an artistic career." But finally, as time went by without any indication of such an abandonment, his initial firmness gave way to respect for his son's courage and to fatherly concern:

> He had not forgotten the scene in which Edgar, so deferential, so gentle, so good, so timid, had said, in a burst of desperate audacity, "I want to be a painter!" The banker made some inquiries about his son's situation, and through a friend he learned of an existence that was rigorous and noble. The future artist was not frequenting any pleasure spots. He was displaying a horror of bohemianism, and he was beginning to win the admiration of his professors.

A reconciliation followed, we are told, with Auguste granting his son full permission to become a painter, and then, "in a beautiful movement of tenderness, the father and the son fell into each other's arms."

How did the Romantic rebel, without his usual allowance, find the francs for rent, food, and painting materials? How did he pay the fees of his admiring professors? His niece's failure to answer such questions adds to the doubts one has about her touching story when one compares it with the well-documented account of Edgar's activities during these decisive first years of his career. On April 7, 1853, two weeks after receiving his *baccalauréat,* he applied for and obtained permission to make copies of works in the Louvre. (Although Courbet and his Realist disciples were already trumpeting their conviction that only the here and now should be depicted, reproducing museum masterpieces was still, as it would be for another half-century, the principal method of self-instruction for student artists and a method of research, of what may be called consultation, for older ones.) Two days later he also registered as a copyist at the Cabinet des Estampes, the print department of the Bibliothèque Nationale (the Bibliothèque Impériale under Napoleon III). On this occasion he listed his profession as "painter" and, to strengthen his chance of gaining entry, added the information that he was a pupil of the painter Félix-Joseph Barrias. The professional title was in a way justified, for by this time, since he was no longer quartered at Louis-le-Grand, he had been provided by his father with a room of his own, large enough to be described as a studio, on the fourth floor at 4 Rue de Mondovi. It was toward the back of the building, with windows that admitted the full light of the sky, looked out over the roof of the eighteenth-century Hôtel de La Vrillière, and offered a view of the nearby Place de la Concorde and the linden and chestnut trees in the Jardin des Tuileries.

On November 12, 1853, he registered at the Faculté de Droit, the ancient and grandly bourgeois law school next to the Panthéon; he did not, however, attend classes regularly enough to leave much of a trace, and at the end of his first term he did not renew his registration. In the meantime his father, acting on the advice of Ingres as transmitted by Edouard Valpinçon, had replaced Barrias with another painting professor, Louis Lamothe, who was presumably more competent and was at any rate certainly more Ingresque. Edgar did some intensive work in Lamothe's atelier, with sessions of copying at the Louvre and the Cabinet des Estampes, and then, on April 6, 1855, registered at the Ecole des Beaux-Arts.

All this scarcely implies a rejection of a paternal ultimatum and a decision to leave home and live bravely in a garret. Although a conflict of ambitions is evident, any estrangement that resulted must have been mild and brief, for one gets a clear impression of a generally obedient son, of a father who was far from being the supposedly typical nineteenth-century tyrant, and of an attempt, which was soon recognized on both sides as a mistake, to compromise by having the son undertake art studies and law studies at the same time. And the impression is strengthened when one notes some of Edgar's later remarks about his education. Questioned about the Faculté de Droit, he agreed that it was a boring institution, and added, "I spent my time drawing copies of all the Italian Primitives in the Louvre, and I finally told my father that that couldn't go on."[4] Asked about his parent's reaction, he said, "My father heaved a few sighs."[5] It is true that he once attributed his chronic trouble with his right eye "to the dampness of a room up under the roof, in which [I] had slept for a long period."[6] But that can be taken as a reference to the fourth-floor room at home in the Rue de Mondovi, which he did occupy "for a long period," and not to a lonely attic elsewhere.

Such details help to point up differences between Degas and some of the major figures with whom he became associated in the Impressionist movement. At the age of twenty-one Claude Monet, the son of a grocer and ship chandler, was in violent revolt against paternal guidance and was being punished (though he seems to have enjoyed the experience) by having to serve as a rifleman in the army in Algeria. Auguste Renoir, the son of a tailor, while still an adolescent was already a veteran artisan, capable of earning his living as a decorator of fans, porcelain plates, and cloth panels for French missionaries to hang in churches. At twenty-two Camille Pissarro — quadruply an outsider as a Creole, a Jew, an artist, and a socialist with anarchist leanings — ran away from a job in his father's general store in the Danish West Indies and made a valiant effort to set himself up as a painter in Caracas. Edouard Manet, although the son of the chief of personnel at the Ministry of Justice and in many respects a believer in the values of the Establishment, was at the age of sixteen independent enough to sail for Rio de Janeiro as an apprentice pilot on the transport vessel *Le Havre et Guadeloupe*. Superficially, the two members of the group whose backgrounds most resembled that of Degas were Alfred Sisley, whose father was a wealthy English trader and broker living mostly abroad, and Paul Cézanne, whose father, like Auguste Degas, was a prosperous banker. But Sisley scarcely counts in the present context, for he remained essentially an amateur painter until after the Franco-Prussian War of 1870, which ruined his family's business; and Cézanne, intimidated by a pitiless, despotic, philistine parent, took more than two years to escape from the Faculté de Droit in his native Aix-en-Provence. In sum, by comparison with the allies, all innovators, whom he would acquire in the mid-1860s, the Edgar of the mid-1850s was a papa's boy, both in the sense of having a relatively fond, indulgent father and in that of being a relatively tame youth who was not moving very rapidly toward emotional independence and full ego identity. He was a male counterpart of Berthe Morisot and Mary Cassatt, the two talented, wealthy, sheltered girls who were to join the innovators.

Neither of the young professors (each was only thirty-one in 1853) whom Auguste engaged was of a kind to encourage the growth of a strong artistic personality, although both, to judge by the results they achieved, seem to have been good at instilling academic fundamentals. Barrias, with whom Edgar studied for at most only a few months, was one of Cogniet's many pupils and the creator of pictorial costume pieces with titles like *Dante at Ravenna* and *Cincinnatus Welcoming the Deputies at the Senate*. During a long, prolific, and undistinguished career he was a stalwart of the official Salon, a decorator of part of the new Opéra that was under construction during the Second Empire, and an illustrator of the works of Virgil, Horace, Corneille, and Racine. Lamothe, who taught Edgar off and on for

about four years, was a pupil of Ingres and of the church decorator Hippolyte Flandrin (also an Ingres pupil), and a careful, incisive, dedicated draftsman; appropriately, one of his few paintings to attract critical attention was
titled *The Invention of Drawing.* He had come up from his native Lyons to
Paris with the intention of entering the Ecole Polytechnique, had struggled
through a period of poverty on a diet of fried potatoes, and had turned to
art after his scientific studies were interrupted by a nearly fatal attack of
typhoid fever. Since 1848 he had been showing his work at the Salon, with
enough success to become an occasional portraitist and to obtain a commission, around 1855, for paintings and stained glass windows in the iron-
roofed Gothic Revival basilica of Sainte-Clotilde (on the Left Bank, a long
way, in several senses, from the Romantic Classical Ninth Arrondissement).
His circumstances were still such, however, that what was referred to as his
atelier was just a room in his Montparnasse apartment, at 10 Rue du
Regard; and until his death, at the age of forty-seven, he would remain, in
the words of one of his former students, "a poor man fated for misfortune"
and an artist "who was prevented by his timid nature and by his general
misery from revealing his capacity as he should have."[7]

From the notebooks Edgar began to compile around 1853 and from
the known views of his teachers it is clear that, not unexpectedly, his
principal aim during his early studies was to learn to do well what had been
done well before — often long, long before. He spent many hours over
Jean Cousin's treatise on drawing, which had first appeared in 1571 and
had gone through twenty-four editions in succeeding centuries. He read
André Félibien des Avaux's imaginary conversations on the lives and works
of outstanding painters, which had become a school handbook during the
reign of Louis XIV. At Lamothe's apartment studio he worked to perfect
the skills he had begun to acquire at Louis-le-Grand, and he became familiar, through a thoroughly indoctrinated disciple, with the pithy, conservative, sometimes majestically absurd sayings of Ingres:

> Drawing is the probity of art.
> Pursue the lines of relief, like a fly running on a sheet of paper.
> The secret of beauty is to be found in truth.
> The ancients saw all, understood all, felt all, depicted all.
> I know the muscles, they are my friends, but I've forgotten their names.
> Raphael was a god, an inimitable being, absolute, incorruptible.
> Poussin was the most perfect of men.
> When passing Rubens, put on horse blinders.[8]

At Lamothe's studio also the pupil probably had his first chance to draw
from a live, naked model instead of from the plaster nudes, often pitted

and speckled by age, to which beginners were usually restricted. Rapidly, he acquired a liking for just looking, or doing a quick sketch, and then working without the model, and he later tried to explain the advantages of this procedure, which was sinful in the eyes of orthodox Impressionists, by pointing out, "It's a transformation in which your imagination collaborates with your memory. . . . Your recollections and your fantasy are liberated from the tyranny of nature."[9] He may have got some of these ideas, via student talk, from Horace Lecoq de Boisbaudrant, a teacher at the Ecole Impériale et Spécial de Dessin, the government drawing school, who in the 1850s was a warm advocate of the memory system.

The life classes at the Ecole des Beaux-Arts and in the private ateliers in Paris were usually held in the morning, and the result, on the days reserved by the museum for copyists, was that by one o'clock in the afternoon the Grande Galerie and the other painting and sculpture rooms at the Louvre were jammed with easels, stepladders, canvases, stools, and chattering painters. You had to get there early to find a good spot, and you had to keep an eye on your paint box, for many of the copyists were hard up and light-fingered. Edgar often must have been among the first, since he had to walk only a few blocks down the Rue de Rivoli from the Rue de Mondovi. But sometimes he continued on over to the Left Bank and to the now defunct Musée du Luxembourg, which was a purgatory for the Louvre (and also the world's first museum of contemporary art). Here he found the works of living, or very recently living, artists, who as a rule had to wait until at least ten years after their death to have a chance for immortality in the Grande Galerie. Sometimes, too, he continued down the Rue de Rivoli and up the Rue de Richelieu to the Bibliothèque Nationale and its Cabinet des Estampes. Here he could explore — in the dusty stillness of a seventeenth-century gallery once occupied by Cardinal Mazarin's hoard of statues and curios, and in the presence of a Romantic, black-cloaked curator, Achille Devéria, who was a clever if minor lithographer — not only a unique collection of original prints, but also, in the form of engraved reproductions, an immense imaginary museum of paintings.

During these years, largely under Ingres's influence as filtered through Lamothe's timidity and as modified by Auguste's taste for the so-called Italian Primitives, the student copied a wide variety of styles and periods: the Early Renaissance as represented by Mantegna and Perugino; the High Renaissance of Leonardo and Raphael, often by way of prints in the Cabinet des Estampes; the Mannerism of portraitists like Bronzino; the Neoclassicism and post-Neoclassicism of artists like David, Flandrin, and Ingres himself; and ancient Greek Classicism as represented notably by plaster casts of parts of the Parthenon frieze. The variety is such as to leave a modern viewer both impressed and bemused. Although pencil drawings of details predominate, one frequently marvels at an accomplished piece of draftsmanship and detects, with the help of hindsight, a hint of a significant selectiveness — an interest in isolated figures and movement, for instance, or a response to the cool, courtly detachment of Bronzino. Still, many of the copies are schoolboy exercises of a kind done by hundreds of future *pompiers* during the Second Empire, and that fact, combined with the observable pressure of Lamothe's Ingresque conservatism, raises a question. What kept Edgar from becoming a *pompier?* What saved him from the twin dangers of academicism and eclecticism?

In fact, he was not saved right away; he would need help. One can see, however, that in the period from 1853 to 1856 a process of salvation through excess was under way. Edgar, unlike many of his fellow copyists, was not just an apprentice chef learning to cook by dutifully nibbling traditional dishes. He was a gourmand for the past, and he was developing through experience into a gourmet. Ultimately, unlike the basically ignorant *pompiers,* who would fabricate insipid imitations of the treasures in the Grande Galerie, and also unlike the many modernists, including some of the Impressionists, who would reject museum art entirely, he would know the history of European painting intimately enough to avoid both academic historicism and a total break with the past, and so be able to use the past for his own artistic purposes. (But his gourmandise would continue, and late in life he was still adding to the hundreds of copies he had executed throughout his career.)

Toward the end of 1854 or early in the following year the play of influences focused in an incident he often recounted, with his habitual distancing humor and also with an unashamed delight in having met a legendary figure and having touched a link in the long chain of heroes that constituted, for him, the history of art. The general background was the preparation for the forthcoming Paris world's fair, the Exposition Universelle of 1855, which was to include two big retrospective one-man shows honoring Ingres and Delacroix, in addition to a mammoth survey of world art during the first half of the nineteenth century and a celebration of the industrial progress being fostered by Napoleon III. The incident began with a visit Degas made to the Valpinçons' house in the Rue Taitbout, probably with the intention of studying the Ingres *Bather,* for he made a copy of it that can be dated, on the basis of his notebooks, to about this time. In the course of the conversation, as recounted by Degas, the elder Valpinçon revealed that he had been pushed into an awkward position by the projected fair:

I saw your god yesterday. Yes, Monsieur Ingres was here. He came to ask me to lend my *Bather* for that barracks where his works are to be exhibited. He seemed very offended when he left, for I explained that I was not disposed to let my picture run such a risk. The building is really much too inflammable.

The usually well-behaved Edgar exploded into a tirade about "disgusting selfishness" and "an affront like that to a man like Monsieur Ingres," and finally the collector, "much shaken," agreed to reverse his decision. So the next day the two of them appeared at Ingres's studio, on the Quai Voltaire, in a handsome Louis XVI building with balconies overlooking the Seine and the Pont du Carrousel. The god himself, a massive, dewlapped, hierophantic figure with spaniel's eyes, answered the bell. Valpinçon begged pardon for his refusal, announced his change of mind, and gave his young companion the proper credit.

When the arrangements for delivering the picture were completed, Ingres rose to accompany his departing visitors, bowed ceremoniously (he had been educated under the ancien régime), and then, seized apparently by dizziness (he was seventy-four), suddenly tottered and fell "full length, with a great walloping sound, to the floor." Edgar helped to set the heavy body partly upright and, reassured by signs of consciousness, ran to summon Madame Ingres, who was at the family apartment in the neighboring Rue de Lille. When he came back with her, everything seemed all right, so he returned to his room in the Rue de Mondovi to begin nursing an indelible, if slightly disrespectful, recollection. More than half a century later, in the decade of Fauvism and Cubism, he was able to say "I once held Ingres in my arms." The adventure, however, was not quite over, for he saw the great man again, when he negotiated the recovery of the *Valpinçon Bather* after the exhibition, and on this occasion he let it be known that he too was a painter. "Draw lines, young man," Ingres said, "lots of lines, either from memory or from nature." (According to another version of the story, also by Degas, the advice was "never from nature, always from memory and the engravings of the masters."[10] The difference is considerable. But when Ingres spoke of nature he often meant correctly harmonious, or beautiful, nature, and by that he meant what one could learn to discern by studying Raphael and the Greeks.)

The Exposition Universelle of 1855 must have been both an exciting and a dismaying event for a painter who at twenty-one was still facing the problem of finding a personal style and subject matter — of finding out who he was. What Edouard Valpinçon had called an inflammable barracks was in fact the not inappropriately named Palais des Beaux-Arts, up to date in its use of glass and cast iron, which covered a vast tract of the fairgrounds between the Avenue des Champs-Elysées and the scaffolding of the uncompleted Pont de l'Alma. Crowded into the building were the works of more than two thousand exhibitors, who, though half of them were French, represented the current or recently current state of the fine arts in twenty-nine nations. A large square hall was occupied by forty-three of Ingres's major paintings and a selection of his cartoons for stained glass windows; here, to a viewer eager to simplify tendencies, was the realm of the linear, of the Raphaelesque, and of ancient history and mythology. Another hall was devoted to forty-three of Delacroix's major works; here was the realm of color, of baroque energy, and of Shakespeare, Byron, the Middle Ages, and North Africa. Landscapists, led by the luminous yet solidly traditional Corot, were grouped in a special section of the long central gallery. Alexandre-Gabriel Decamps, the leader of the Romantic *orientalistes,* who had made the Middle East a fashionable land of lovely houris, cruel pashas, and dramatic scenery, was favored with a retrospective show; and so was Horace Vernet, Auguste Degas's old neighbor in the Rue de la Tour-des-Dames, who specialized in battle scenes and horses and advocated a stylistic *juste milieu.* Courbet, vexed by the jury's refusal to hang two of his favorite pictures, had erected a small barracks of his own near the Seine and had defiantly installed in it forty-four of his more provocative works. Here was the realm of a rugged, mostly rural Realism and of juicy slabs of pigment; here also was the temple of the self-portrait, for the painter had depicted his own bulky, darkly attractive person with a frequency and a complacency that would provoke even a friendly commentator into referring to him as "the peasant Narcissus."

In spite of the optimism that pervaded the great exhibition, a thoughtful and sufficiently prescient viewer might have had some misgivings. After visiting the Palais de l'Industrie, where twenty thousand exhibitors had amassed the latest evidence of an accelerating rate of scientific, technological, economic, and social change, he might have wondered, in the galleries of the Palais des Beaux-Arts, how long sensitive artists would continue to be satisfied with a system of pictorial space that had been invented in the fifteenth century. After noticing that nearly everything and everybody in human experience was being painted, from Homer, the angels, and the ancient Romans down to Hamlet, the Forest of Fontainebleau, and the cows of Normandy, he might have observed that the glaring exception was what surrounded the fairgrounds: the buzzing life of a mid-nineteenth-century city. After looking at acres of pompous, numbing canvases by academic nonentities, he might have remarked that it was these very painters who were carrying off most of the two hundred—odd medals and the two hundred honorable mentions being awarded by the official judges of the show. The viewer's conclusion might have been that a telltale rigidity was setting in and that what he was actually seeing, for all the genius of men like Ingres, Delacroix, Corot, and Courbet, was a prelude to the end of an era — the end, in a sense, of the Renaissance. But if such a viewer existed, he did not commit himself in print. One French critic, Paul de Saint-Victor, did perceive that history painting, which in academic theory ranked as the noblest category of art and which traditionally included subjects drawn from mythology and Christian iconography as well as from classical heroic history, was in trouble, and he commented on the malaise in his review of the Exposition Universelle:

> The gods are departing from modern painting, the gods and the heroes. . . . The great typical figures of Christian art, Christ, the Virgin, the Holy Family, seem to be exhausted by four centuries of picturesque combinations. Greek mythology, which was resurrected by the Renaissance, is at the end of its new span of life.[11]

It did not, however, occur to him that the gods and the heroes might not have been alone in their fatigue and their loss of cultural relevance, and that the crisis in subject matter might be the forerunner of a series of crises involving long-accepted notions of color, brushwork, drawing, and composition.

Nor did it occur to Edgar, at least not in 1855. For the moment, though he visited Courbet's barracks and admired Delacroix's retrospective, he was concentrating, according to the evidence of the copying in his notebooks, on Ingres's hall. He had the satisfaction of seeing the *Valpinçon Bather* well hung, at eye level next to the huge, recent *Apotheosis of Napoleon I,* and being generally well received by the critics. (It had not been shown in public since 1808.) The finicky Goncourt brothers thought that "Rembrandt himself would have envied the amber tint of that pale torso." Delacroix, it is true, dissented totally: after walking through his rival's hall he went home and told his diary that the collected works were "highly ridiculous, the complete expression of an incomplete mind."[12] But Edgar was not privy to this heresy, and anyway Delacroix was being uncharacteristically unfair, for to less prejudiced viewers the show was a revelation of an Ingres who was more complex, and much more ingratiating, than the conservative stereotype he liked to project. If his admiration for Raphael and the High Renaissance was visible, so was the influence of Mannerism and of the fifteenth-century Italian Primitives. If he had an appalling predilection for a mixture of the frigid and the saccharine, he also had a lusty delight in female flesh, and even in his most embarrassingly uninspired moments he remained the master of a quasi-abstract arabesque, which made him arguably one of the most modern artists in the Palais des Beaux-Arts (and which would one day fascinate Picasso). His worshiper in the Rue de Mondovi had more than one paradox to digest.

Looking at pictures, however, was not the only aesthetic, or simply amusing, activity offered by Paris in the early summer of 1855 to a cultivated, inquiring bourgeois of twenty-one who was well supplied with pocket money. Although the Crimean War was killing thousands of French soldiers each month (more by disease and by logistical stupidities than by Russian gunnery), the Second Empire was already launched into a whirl of public entertainments, both popular and highbrow, that would give the reign an enduring reputation for insouciance and frivolity — and would incidentally nourish the Degas repertoire for decades. At the Bal Valentino and competing establishments the polka went on and on. The café-concert, or *caf'conç'*, a recently revived eighteenth-century invention that combined drink, song, and spectacle, was flourishing. At the Opéra there were the regular ballet nights and also Verdi's latest work, *Les Vêpres siciliennes,* which had been commissioned especially for the Exposition Universelle and was having a good run, in spite of the composer's rather tactless choice of a libretto that told of the slaughter, by local patriots, of the French occupants of thirteenth-century Sicily. (Saint-Saëns, a notorious xenophobe, acidly advised Verdi to follow up with another opera for French audiences on the subject of Waterloo.) Many Parisian theaters, inspired by the internationalism the world's fair had helped to make fashionable, were staging exotic attractions. At the Porte Saint-Martin, for example, there were Spanish dancers, and at the Hippodrome a troupe of supposedly Mexican midgets, who were billed as Les Aztèques Lilliputiens. At the Théâtre Italien (also known as the Salle Ventadour because of the name of the street it was on), catering to French intellectuals who understood Italian and to the large number of Italian political exiles then in the city, there was the touring Royal Sardinian Company, which had the renowned tragedienne Adelaide Ristori as its leading lady. During the 1855 season and the following one she became the idol of the Parisian public, adored both for her classical grand style and for her passionate outbursts of naturalism. She was compared favorably with Mademoiselle Rachel, the reigning star at the Comédie-Française, with the singer Pauline Viardot-García, and even with Viardot's dead sister, the great Maria Malibran. After one of her performances Dumas *père* rushed up onto the stage and covered her hands and then the panels of her robe with kisses. Musset called her an ancient Greek statue that had learned to speak. One of the few people to resist the waves of enthusiasm was Sainte-Beuve, who after seeing her reported that he had been "merely contented, and not transported."

That a banker's son might be shipped off to the Crimea to face bullets, mud, cholera, and scurvy was an extremely remote possibility, for during most of the Second Empire the conscription system was a lottery rigged in favor of the middle and upper classes: if you drew a bad number, your father paid the government to hire a replacement. (An irate father could use the system to punish a disobedient son, but Auguste was not the irate type.) So Edgar was free, when he was not working at his art, to start developing into the man-about-town he would be throughout his active life — an opera enthusiast, a first-nighter at the theater, a friend of musicians, a familiar of ballerinas' greenrooms, and a café-concert habitué. He also found time to have a fervent, if across-the-footlights, love affair, for in 1855 he saw Ristori in an Italian translation of Schiller's *Maria Stuart* and succumbed immediately. He sketched her and then, partly in Italian, talked to himself about her in his notebook:

> . . . a robe of velvet and black satin, a coiffure with curly dark blond hair. Such delicate, such beautiful hands. The goddesslike queen herself! [13]

The following spring she returned to the Théâtre Italien in an Italian version of a recent French tragedy, Ernest Legouvé's *Médée*. This time she wore an ample, blue, strikingly Grecian robe — designed by another of Auguste's Rue de la Tour-des-Dames neighbors, Ary Scheffer — and she managed, by some miracle of invisible corporal adroitness (which she mentions in her memoirs as having been a constant worry), to keep its large folds flowing back from her shoulders in a marvelously antique, sculptural fashion. Edgar was again enchanted:

> Tuesday evening, April 15, I saw Madame Ristori in *Médée*. I saw, walking and speaking, the most adorable of Grecian-vase figures. Ah, the divine artiste. . . . When she runs she often has the movement of the Nike of the Parthenon. [14]

Ristori might have corrected his Classical allusions, for his "Nike," which he had once copied from an engraving or a plaster cast, was the Parthenon east-pediment figure (in the British Museum since 1816) now identified as Iris or perhaps Hebe, and anyway the actress was actually imitating, as she explained later, the poses of the ancient statues in the Niobe group at Florence. But she could not have asked for a more generally attuned, more Romantically Classical, appreciator of her art.

His multiple activities as a Parisian student and man-about-town were interrupted in the summer of 1855 by a long holiday in southern France, his first extended trip outside the capital since his childhood, and also his first important taste of being his own person, free from immediate paternal pressure. During part of July and August he was in Lamothe's home town, Lyons, well equipped by the careful professor, who may have suggested the journey, with a list of people to call on. Before returning to Paris in the fall he went on from Lyons, following the recently opened Paris-Marseilles rail line and branching off in horse-drawn conveyances, to Avignon, Tarascon, Arles, Nîmes, Montpellier, and Sète — a collection of sunlit, dirty, mistral-tormented, lovely old places that was then beginning, thanks partly to the published travel notes of pioneer visitors like Stendhal and Prosper Mérimée, to qualify as tourist country.

In the local museums he worked hard at his copying, often under the influence of the Neoclassical tendencies of his teachers: at Avignon, in the tranquil Louis XV town house that had been transformed into the Musée Calvet, he took the time to do an oil version of David's disconcerting, heroic-sentimental, sexually ambiguous *Death of Bara.* Profiting from the fine weather, he sometimes remained outdoors to sketch his impressions of urban sites and monuments: at Lyons, the weathered streets and quays, the seventeenth-century abbey in which the museum was installed, and the Gothic façade, mutilated by vandals and inept restorers, of the Cathedral of Saint-Jean; at Arles ("a hole," Stendhal had written in 1837, "to which the traveler goes only for its admirable antiquities"), the great medieval cloister of Saint-Trophime, the crumbling ramparts, and the ruins of the Roman theater; at Nîmes, the famous vestiges of Roman glory; and at Avignon, those of the Middle Ages. ("Time," Stendhal had noted, "has given these stones . . . a uniform color of dry leaves that augments their beauty.")[15] In the Rhone valley and on the Mediterranean coast at Sète he even drew a few panoramic, Romantic landscapes, which was a display of maturity and independence in the light of the scorn for natural scenery that was part of the figure-painting tradition in which he was being trained. ("Study Phidias, Raphael, and Beethoven," Ingres had once advised a painter of fields and streams, "and you will be the best landscapist in the world.")[16] The maturity remained, however, only relative: on September 18, at Sète, after climbing to the top of the massive Fort Richelieu for a good view of the sea, the young traveler informed his friend the notebook, in a confidentially small hand and without forgetting the bogus nobiliary particle, "I wrote EdG on the last step of the stairway to the terrace."[17]

On his return to Paris he began attending classes at the Ecole des Beaux-Arts, for which he had merely enrolled before the start of the summer vacation. Judging by an allusion of Auguste's and by Lamothe's known associates, his professor was Hippolyte Flandrin. (Lamothe himself did not teach at the school.) If the supposition is correct, the instruction was conservative without being aggressively so, for Flandrin was a tender, pious, melancholic man who had little of Ingres's kind of self-confidence, and who was distracted from his teaching duties by a commission for covering with biblical scenes a large part of the nave and choir of the church of Saint-Germain-des-Prés. But the teacher's name is mostly beside the point, since the evidence plainly shows that Edgar was not at all impressed by the Ecole, nor the Ecole by him. He performed indifferently in some competitive examinations during his first semester, and after that seems to have rapidly come to the conclusion that he was too advanced for the courses he was being offered and that he would be better off on the outside, learning by copying the old masters or with the help of instructors of his own choice.

Among the latter, in addition to the still available Lamothe, was Nicolas Soutzo, an expatriate Greek prince who was a painter and engraver, a collector of prints by Daumier and Claude Lorrain, an insider at the imperial fine arts directorate, and a member of Auguste's circle of connoisseurs. One of Edgar's increasingly ethical-aesthetical notebook entries reads:

> Today, January 18, 1856, I had a grand talk with Monsieur Soutzo. What courage there is in his studies! . . . There is indeed courage in making a frontal attack on nature in its large planes and lines, and cowardice in an attack by facets and details. It's a war.[18]

This declaration, and his concentration on drawing natural scenery when he was in southern France, suggest that at this stage he was thinking seriously about becoming a landscapist. Although he abandoned the idea, there are other hints that he entertained it for a while. Early in 1856 he copied a Soutzo landscape. With the prince's help, he initiated himself into the craft of engraving by etching a Greek landscape, from an illustration for the *Odyssey*. One bright day when the Paris winter was over, he looked out his Rue de Mondovi room toward the Jardin des Tuileries with a sensibility that suddenly owed nothing to Phidias and Raphael, and he immediately told his notebook:

> The top of the tree in front of my window stands out against a springtime blue, and the lower part against a procession of great white clouds, full and strong. It is lit from in front by the sun. Around noon the shoots are like gold.[19]

Clearly, if the Ingres cult and the French figure-painting tradition had been a little less influential, he might easily have become an enthusiastic landscapist, one with both the "courage" to tackle the structure of nature and the "cowardice" to occasionally enjoy painting the facets.

The single human figure, however, is already dominant in the few original works he produced between his departure from the Faculté de Droit, in the spring of 1854, and his final disillusionment with the Ecole des Beaux-Arts, in the early summer of 1856. A particularly fetching example is a drawing of 1854 in which his twelve-year-old sister, Marguerite, dollish and defenseless beneath the fragile canopy of her first-communion veil, peers out at the approaching problems of womanhood. Other examples are some informal drawings, executed probably in 1854 and 1855, in which his brother René, about ten years old, is represented as a little animal, dozing, convalescing from an apparently mild illness, and even painting. In an oil portrait of about the same date René appears as a wild-eyed schoolboy, with a brown smock and red necktie, who has been forced to pose, cap in hand, alongside a table laden with a symbolically thick book and an inkpot. Brother Achille is the subject of an oil done about the middle of 1856, when he was eighteen; he is wearing the black uniform, trimmed in gold, of a student naval officer and is leaning nonchalantly, wearily, in an attitude common in the daguerreotypes of the period, against the back of a chair that is the only recognizable object in a shallow red space.

Often the drawings, lightly traced on white paper with a hard, carefully sharpened pencil that could produce a silver-point effect, evoke Ingres's pencil portraits, though there are touches of realism and softness in which the master himself would not have indulged. The two paintings are closer to the Florentine Mannerists, specifically to Pontormo and Bronzino. But what is apt to strike a viewer is not so much the visible influences as the level of competence, which is astonishingly high for a twenty-one-year-old with a less than excellent record as an art student. Evidently there was something in his talent that called for more independence than could be found in the school world of conformism, prizes, and honorable mentions — a world that was an image of the medal-awarding official Salon, which was itself an image of the competitive, alienating world of Second Empire capitalism. And he seems to have been quite aware of the problem, for he discusses it, under a sketch of a young man seated at a table and supporting his head with his right arm, in a notebook entry from the spring of 1856:

> It seems to me that today if you want to produce art seriously and make for yourself a little corner of originality, or at least keep for yourself a thoroughly guiltless personality, you must immerse yourself in solitude. There is too much tittle-tattle. It's as if pictures were being painted by stock exchange players, by the agents of people avid for profits. Apparently you are supposed to need the mind and the ideas of your neighbor in order to do anything at all, much as a businessman needs the capital of other people in order to earn a sou. All these transactions put your mind on edge and falsify your judgment.[20]

Twenty years later, at the time of the first Impressionist group shows, the problem would return in a peculiarly acute form.

Auguste does not appear in this first gallery of family portraits, nor does Edgar's sister Thérèse, who was sixteen in 1856. Perhaps they simply refused to be pestered into posing, or perhaps the artist felt too much awe for his father and too little sympathy with Thérèse (with whom he did not always get along when he was older). In any event, they could not have been much missed as sitters, for Edgar was obviously more than willing to be his own subject when no one else at 4 Rue de Mondovi was available. In several self-portraits done during these years he can be seen examining himself attentively in the mirror, watching over his technique, playing roles, and in general trying to discover and depict an adult, unique self. At one moment he is merely a puzzled, pouting boy in shirt sleeves with a palette in his hand, at another a Napoleon III version of Filippino Lippi, at still another an evocation of the young Ingres's self-portrait of 1804, which was at the Exposition Universelle on the same wall as the *Valpinçon Bather*. The series crystallizes, around the end of 1854 or the beginning of 1855, in the self-portrait with a charcoal stick, which is formal and finished enough to imply that it was intended as a definitive portrait of the real Edgar Degas at the age of twenty-one. Of course, it is at once a good deal less and a good deal more than that. Like all self-portraits, it is an example of the uncertainty principle at work in art: it pictures a self seeing a self seeing a self, an "I" attempting the hazardous operation of organizing a "me." Naïvely, it integrates the heroic history of art into the Degas "me" by means of a classic painter's pose and of references to the Ingres self-portrait, in which the older artist holds a piece of chalk, and to Bronzino's icily elegant *Portrait of a Sculptor,* which Edgar had copied at the Louvre. Almost the entire canvas is covered by shades of a rich brown, associated in the nineteenth century with museums and old masters, and the light is diffused, mild, academic. The drawing is unhesitating, except in the right hand, which seems to have had trouble being both executant and model. A thin beard and mustache betray a long adolescence. The *grande bourgeoisie* is integrated into the "me" via the white collar, black cravat, and fitted frock coat (not ultrafashionable, for by 1855 men's clothes were becoming looser). In the stiff posture, the troubled gaze of the brown eyes, and the fishlike expression of the mouth one can detect, with the usual risk of subjectivity, symptoms of chronic anxiety and also of a weary, youthful, Romantic disdainfulness — of what Baudelaire called "spleen":

> *Je suis comme le roi d'un pays pluvieux,*
> *Riche, mais impuissant, jeune et pourtant très-vieux,*

Self-Portrait, 1854–1855

Qui, de ses précepteurs méprisant les courbettes,
S'ennuie avec ses chiens comme avec d'autres bêtes.[21]

(I am like the king of a rainy country, rich but impotent, young and yet very old, who, despising the kowtowing of his tutors, is bored with his hounds, as with other creatures.)

Compared with Baudelaire, Edgar was a little angel of proper social adjustment and cultural conformism. But that he was beginning to feel a certain contempt for his orthodox, place-seeking tutors is implied by his reflections on the need for solitude and by his decision to drop out of the Ecole des Beaux-Arts. And that he was becoming aware of certain personality problems in himself, spleen included, is suggested by several entries in his notebook of the spring of 1856. "The people you love the most," he remarked, "are those you could hate the most."[22] Further on, in a partly unintelligible passage, he exhorted his "me" to pull itself together: "Let us try . . . more calmly . . . vanquish the . . . real artist."[23] On a neighboring page he was more philosophical, more sententious, but equally anguished: "The heart is an instrument that rusts if it is not used. Without a heart, can one be an artist?"[24] It was a question that would worry him throughout his career.

4. From Naples to Tuscany

DURING THE EARLY YEARS of the Second Empire, displaying an interest in Italy might have suggested, in certain Left Bank cafés and some Right Bank salons, that you were aesthetically behind the times. Paris had long since outstripped provincial Rome as an intellectual and artistic capital. Vanguard sensibilities were expected to respond more to Wagner, Shakespeare, and the Gothic than to Rossini, Virgil, and the High Renaissance. A number of French artists, on the lookout for a usable, modernizable past, were turning, if sometimes only in the Grande Galerie of the Louvre, toward the Holland of Rembrandt and Hals, the England of Constable, and the Spain of Zurbarán, Velázquez, and Goya. Romanticism, though waning, was still enough alive to be controversial, landscape painting was flourishing, Realism was gaining adherents, and all three of these trends were largely foreign to central Mediterranean traditions. For the first time in generations there were several prominent members of the school of Paris, among them Delacroix and Courbet, who had never traveled beyond the Alps, though they had taken the trouble to visit such places as Andalusia, Amsterdam, the casbah of Algiers, and Piccadilly Circus.

The old magnetism of the land of Raphael continued, however, to work on less advanced imaginations. Although the decline of Neoclassicism had altered itineraries, something like the eighteenth-century Grand Tour was still favored by well-to-do French fathers as the final stage in the education of their sons. And in spite of Italy's not having produced a painter of international stature since the triumphs of the Tiepolo family in the mid-1700s, there were still many French believers in the idea, widespread in Northern Europe since the founding of the first academies of art, that a thorough steeping in the monuments, pictorial wonders, and pellucid light of the peninsula was indispensable for the ripening of a serious visual talent. Ingres, who had spent twenty-three years of his career in Rome and Florence (with a short period in the Naples of Joachim Murat and René-Hilaire Degas), still exemplified the centuries-old Mediterranean conviction that the human figure was the painter's proper subject, and made known his admiration for Roman composition and Tuscan drawing, along with his contempt for the northern manner of Rubens. An Italianate bias was strong in the curriculum of the Ecole des Beaux-Arts and in the criteria of Paris Salon juries, and it was not unknown even among the landscapists who were planting their easels in the Forest of Fontainebleau, for no French artist, however much he might like Dutch naturalism, could quite overcome a nostalgia for Claude Lorrain's Virgilian, pastoral Roman Campagna, the last vestige of the myth of the Golden Age.

Moreover, the appeal of a sojourn beyond the Alps was renewed annually, as it had been since the reign of Louis XIV, by the Prix de Rome, which remained the most desired of all the prizes awarded by the prize-addicted French fine arts system. Each winter the band of winners in the nerve-racking competition — a composer from the Conservatoire de Musique and an architect, a sculptor, an engraver, and two painters from the Ecole des Beaux-Arts — left their disappointed schoolmates in Paris and went to Rome to become pensioners in the local Académie de France, a sort of postgraduate school installed in the sixteenth-century Villa Medici. There they were allowed to spend three and sometimes five years perfecting themselves in their chosen disciplines, with Greek, Roman, and High Renaissance masterpieces for inspiration, with the neighboring gardens of the Pincio for relaxation, with a panoramic view of the Eternal City for historical perspective, with all their expenses paid by the French government, and with no obligation except to send to the Paris authorities annually some samples, called *envois de Rome,* of progress. (The *Valpinçon Bather* had been one of Ingres's *envois* for 1808.) When the period of study ended, the laureates returned to France to find themselves, if they had not sent back some disturbingly original *envois,* well placed to pick up official musical, architectural, and decorative commissions, exhibit in the official Salon, obtain academic sinecures, execute portraits of *grands bourgeois,* and eventually acquire the rosette of the Legion of Honor.

In short, Italy was not a neutral, innocent place, not just a splendid museum combined with a beaker full of the warm south. It was a symbol of commitment to traditional Classicism and one of the devices, along with the Ecole des Beaux-Arts and the Paris Salon, by means of which the French Establishment co-opted unwary youthful talent. It was even, in the worst of circumstances, a device that transformed potential creativity into *pompiérisme,* for although in fairness one should grant that the Prix de Rome occasionally helped to reveal a great French composer — Bizet, for example, in 1857 — the extraordinary fact remains that during the entire nineteenth century not a single winner of the award for painting, with the very early exception of Ingres, went on to become an artist regarded today as major. The academy in the Villa Medici (aided, of course, by the rest of the system) seems to have inhibited any impulses toward originality.

At twenty-two Edgar Degas was not exactly unwary; he was even, according to the evidence of his notebooks, excessively alert to the danger of an invasion of what he called his "solitude." He was already, however, partly committed to Mediterranean Classicism and more than half co-opted by the Establishment, and hence ripe for Italy. A period of study there was an almost inevitable part of a sequence that had begun with a Neapolitan fortune and continued with a bank in the Romantic Classical Ninth Arrondissement, seven years of Latin, Greek, and Cogniet (Prix de Rome, 1817) at Louis-le-Grand, and then Barrias (Prix de Rome, 1844), Lamothe (a "Roman" without the prize), Ingres (Prix de Rome, 1801), Flandrin (Prix de Rome, 1832), and the Ecole des Beaux-Arts. Although the student had not been good at competitive examinations, and had dropped out of the running for what was referred to as *la récompense suprême* by leaving the Ecole, he was in many respects a typical pensioner of the Villa Medici, and at the moment his family's finances were such as to make feasible a self-awarded Prix de Rome. (Second Empire capitalism was particularly dynamic in the years immediately after the Exposition Universelle, and bankers were notoriously prosperous. "Business," Dumas *fils* remarked in the midst of the boom, "is really very simple: it's other people's money.")[1] So on July 15, 1856, notebook in hand, the nonlaureate sailed southward from Marseilles.

He went first to Naples, where he soon settled into a familiar routine, though instead of going down the arcaded, Romantic Classical Rue de Rivoli to the Louvre he now emerged from the eighteenth-century Late Baroque doorway of his grandfather's palazzo, at 53 Calata Trinità Maggiore, and crossed the Piazza del Gesù Nuovo on his way to the Museo Nazionale (then a royal Bourbon institution, for the city was still the capital of the Kingdom of the Two Sicilies). "Let me get it well into my head," he wrote in his notebook, "that I know nothing at all. That's the only way to advance."[2] In the museum he sketched the ancient statues and copied, among other things, Titian's portrait of Pope Paul III and several of the mural paintings that had been removed from the ruins of Pompeii, Herculaneum, and Stabiae; he also took note of "the most beautiful Claude Lorrain one can see. The sky is like silver, and the shadows speak to you."[3] Some time during the summer he went down the coast to Sorrento, celebrated for its sumptuous sunsets and for being the legendary aerie of the sirens of the *Odyssey;* the excursion yielded some sketches of people and scenery, and a memo, for a picture that was never painted, that "the women wear their hair braided into crowns around bandeaux."[4] Back in Naples, he did an oil of one of his cousins, the seven-year-old Giovanna Bellelli, and a now lost drawing of his grandfather that has survived in the form of a slightly later etching: at eighty-six, with spectacles perched partway down his nose and a large cap jammed onto his head, René-Hilaire looks like a retired seaman dozing over his newspaper.

By mid-September the portraitist was at the country house at San Rocco di Capodimonte, reading Dante and perhaps dreaming of the lovely Claude Lorrain he had seen at the museum, for during his stay, in one of the top-floor rooms, he painted what is usually called *Italian Landscape Seen from a Dormer Window* and is more precisely a view of Capodimonte, with the local fortress in the background. Although this bizarre little work is far from being a masterpiece, it qualifies easily, with its blend of the past, the present, the artificial, and the real, as an early symptom of what hostile nineteenth-century critics of the mature Degas regarded as perversity. The depicted scenery mixes the antique, idealized Campagna of Claude with a directly experienced time and place. The distant vista, the absence of a middleground, and the high vantage point recall the imaginary bird's-eye perspectives of the Renaissance and anticipate the realistic cityscapes executed by the Impressionists from upper-story windows. More than half of the painting is occupied, for no immediately clear reason, by the bare interior around the dormer, with the result that the small landscape itself suggests at first glance a picture hanging on a wall, or a theatrical backdrop glimpsed through a Punch and Judy proscenium. A pronounced slant in the horizon and the windowsill, combined with the randomly cropped composition, implies the presence of a casual spectator, who can be thought of as a photographer with a tilted camera. And the whole amalgam of contingent reality and artful illusionism is rounded out by a notebook hint that allows us to imagine the invisible photographer as a philosophical person who has been reading Dante, because one of the pencil studies for the painting bears as its caption a quotation from the *Purgatorio* (XIV, lines 148–151):

> *Chiamavi 'l cielo e 'intorno vi si gira,*
> *mostrandovi le sue bellezze etterne,*
> *e l'occhio vostro pur a terra mira.*[5]

(The heavens call you and wheel around you, showing you their eternal beauties, and yet your eye is still directed toward the earth.)

Scenery was not the only material available for study by an eye that was becoming more painterly and by a mind that was becoming more questioning. On the basis of the portrait of Giovanna Bellelli one can assume that her mother, Edgar's aunt Laura, was at the palazzo or at San Rocco di Capodimonte, along with her younger daughter, the five-year-old Giulia, and that thus no fewer than sixteen of René-Hilaire's descendants were present. There was the still fairly young Marchesa Montejasi-Cicerale — Aunt Stefanina, or simply Fanny — with her baby daughter (and presumably her aristocratic husband). There were the three bachelor uncles, Enrico, Odoardo, and Achille, who come through rather dimly from the 1850s, as if robbed of color by too many years in the shadow of their father. There was the severe (according to a contemporary photograph) Duchessa Morbilli — Aunt Rosa — with six surviving children, who included the grown-up Alfredo, Edmondo, and Adelchi, former Via Toledo playmates of their cousin from Paris. Rosa had lost her husband, Don Giuseppe, in 1842, and had managed to raise and properly educate her large family only with the help of a house and money from her father. Edgar revealed in his letters that he was fond of them all. But he clearly had a special affection, which was warmly returned, for Laura, perhaps because she was the right age to be a substitute for the dead Célestine, or simply because she was beautiful, intelligent, and manifestly unhappy. And it was possibly during this Neapolitan summer of 1856 that he began to think of her as the central figure in an ambitious picture, eventually entitled *The Bellelli Family,* that would grow in his imagination, as he gained insight into his subject, from an ordinary portrait into a summing up of a spoiled life.

His interest is understandable. In 1856, at forty-two, Laura was a reminder of a Bronzino, with dark eyes, black hair, smooth olive ivory skin, a fine-boned face, a stylish silhouette, long, tapering hands, and a look of proudly controlled despair. In her late girlhood she had fallen deeply, romantically in love with a young man whose credentials had been rejected by the socially ambitious René-Hilaire (and whose letters she kept until her death, at the age of eighty-three); and after that she had endured years of half-comic, humiliating attempts by the entire family to keep her from becoming an old maid. Although suitors, attracted by her beauty and by her dowry of twenty thousand ducats, had been plentiful, they had one after the other been found unsuitable. On a particularly distressing occasion an Englishman who had failed to measure up to the requirements laid down in the palazzo had lost his temper and denounced the whole proceedings as "more like a business negotiation than an affair of the heart."[6]

Her father had tormented her about the failures, her brother Odoardo had insisted that their mother do something, and her brother-in-law Giuseppe Morbilli had produced a list of theoretically eligible but very elderly candidates. At last, at the dangerously advanced age of twenty-eight, she had been married to Baron Bellelli, a thirty-year-old Neapolitan lawyer and politician whose family may have already had some French connections, for the title dated back only to the time of Murat. Then Bellelli had been driven into exile, and finally condemned to death in absentia, because of his role in the local Revolution of 1848 and his activities as a follower of Cavour who wanted to expel the Bourbons and create a greater Italy by uniting the Kingdom of the Two Sicilies with Piedmont. He and Laura had taken refuge in Marseilles, then Paris, and then London, and in 1852 had settled with their two little girls in Florence, where there was a sizable colony of Neapolitans.

During these years the marriage had deteriorated into a state of tension that can be felt in two family letters, both dating from the end of the 1850s but referring to what had plainly been going on for a good while. Laura's brother Achille, writing to Edgar shortly after the latter had completed his Italian tour, remarked in passing:

> The domestic life of the family in Florence is a source of unhappiness for us. As I predicted, one of them is very much at fault and our sister a little, too. [There is] incompatibility of personality and background and as a result a lack of affection and leniency that enlarges like a magnifying glass the individuals' natural faults.[7]

The "I predicted" indicates that the clan had had misgivings about the baron from the first, and had perhaps accepted him only as Laura's last chance. Still, he had his own desperation to present to the meddlers in the palazzo. Writing to his brother-in-law Odoardo in 1860, he said, "You can have no idea of what it is like to live with a family for several long years in furnished rooms."[8] In 1856 he may have been relieved by having his wife and daughters, who were not under the Bourbon ban, visit Naples and leave him alone in Florence for a few weeks.

In 1856, however, *The Bellelli Family* was just a project, if it was that, and Edgar was in Italy for other reasons than relatives. So on October 7, after some three months with them, he departed by sea for Civitavecchia, the principal port serving Rome. Soon he was at the Villa Medici, which he found more open and more stimulating than anything he had hoped for, and he immediately threw himself into what in his old age he would look back on as "the most extraordinary period of my life."[9] The director of the Académie de France at the time was Jean-Victor Schnetz (Père Schnetz to the pensioners), a veteran academic painter who had studied with David, had begun to exhibit at the Paris Salon during the First Empire, and had helped to decorate, among other public edifices, the church of Notre-Dame-de-Lorette, but who in spite of his successful bourgeois career had never lost his relish for the bohemianism and the eccentric Romanticism of the earlier part of the century. He enjoyed painting the dirtier, more picturesque aspects of Rome, and also Roman bandits, whom he had been known to shelter in the Villa Medici on the pretext, which had a certain legal validity, that a foreign art school, like a religious institution, was protected by the ancient right of asylum. (Some of the inefficient servants around the place were suspected of being former bandits who had decided to stay.) He had installed gaming tables in the elegant, historic salons where Cardinal Alessandro de' Medici had once entertained prelates and royalty. And his practice with nonlaureates, perhaps partly because he himself had not won the Prix de Rome, was as lacking in formality as the rest of his behavior: almost any reasonably qualified French artist — including the recent arrival from Naples — who happened to be in town was allowed to frequent the academy, profit from the presence of models, and listen to the music that was being composed and performed.

On the whole the students were extremely serious, hard-working young men — and several were no longer very young, for it was not uncommon to win the Prix de Rome on a third or fourth attempt. Among those with whom Edgar became friendly during the winter of 1856–1857 were Emile Lévy, a history painter who had begun to exhibit at the Paris Salon in 1848; Camille Clère, a Cogniet pupil who had also made his Salon début in 1848; Elie Delaunay, a Flandrin pupil and already a familiar face; and the sculptor Henri Chapu, who was called Monsieur l'abbé because of his beardless chin, timid air, and bookish habits. Seriousness, however, did not rule out collegiate high spirits, fraternalism, and talkativeness, and both Chapu and Degas took part in an art-discussion group whose motto was *Semper ardentes* and whose members, inspired by the incessant shouting of Roman street vendors, called themselves the Cald'arròsti, the Roast Chestnuts. Their regular meeting place, in the Via Condotti down the hill from the Villa Medici, was the famous, century-old Caffè Greco, where the coffee was supposedly almost as good as in Venice, pipe-smoking was permitted (exceptionally for a Roman café at the time), and the atmosphere was charged with memories of such former clients and talkers as Goethe, Byron, Shelley, Leopardi, Stendhal, and Berlioz.

The copyist was still tireless, and he was now working with what was for him some wonderfully fresh material: Leonardo's *Saint Jerome* and Canova's *Perseus* at the Vatican, the mosaic, attributed to Giotto, in the porch

of Saint Peter's, the engravings in the stock of the Villa Medici, Domeni-
chino's fresco in the chapel of Sant' Andrea, and Greek and Roman sculptures in the Vatican, the Capitoline Museum, and the Villa Albani. He
found time to see Adelaide Ristori again in a Roman production of the
Medée that had delighted him in Paris. Outdoors he sketched the Forum,
the Borghese Gardens, and the traditional race of riderless horses; at the
Villa Medici he painted traditional nudes and equally standard pictures of
women in brightly patterned Italian peasant costumes. But his imagination
was occupied with potential Salon works based on religious, mythological,
literary, and ancient historical sources. He devoted many studies, for example, some of them almost final versions, to a projected *Saint John the
Baptist and the Angel.* Another possibility that interested him, more briefly,
was the myth, which he may have read in Herodotus at Louis-le-Grand, of
how the dutiful sons Cleobis and Biton hauled their priestess mother's
sacred chariot to the temple of Hera, where the goddess rewarded them
with the best gift she could bestow on mortals — eternal sleep. Still other
contemplated subjects were some familiar incidents in Dante's *Commedia,*
which had been a constant companion since his departure from France, and
the story, which was in Herodotus and had been retold by Théophile
Gautier, of how King Candaules, proud of his beautiful wife, secretly
exposed her nakedness to another man's view and how she discovered the
shameful arrangements and had her husband murdered.

In all this there is not much evidence of a single direction, and there
are signs of a compulsion to work for work's sake, or to hide an absence of
accomplishment under interminable preparations. His morale went down
periodically, and then rose more as a result of self-encouragement than of
any external change. On one of his notebook pages he wrote, "Ah, how
doubt and uncertainty tire me!"[10] Four pages later there is a partly erased
scribble, dated March 5, 1857: "My head feels much more calm. I want to
try to keep busy all the time."[11] In a self-portrait painted during these
months he looks, with the help of a little round hat, like a worried young
Italian who might be thinking of entering a religious order or one of the
Roman seminaries. But in spite of his wavering courage and his procrastination, and of the co-opting process evident in his Salon projects, he was
capable at this time of brief advances toward his ultimately characteristic
responses to pigments, space, moments, movements, and psychological
nuances. In the self-portrait there is a new assurance in the brushwork, and
a substitution, in the foulard he is wearing, of a patch of orange for the
museum brown he had favored in the Rue de Mondovi. The notebook
contains a suggestion, typical of the mature Degas and accompanied by a
rapid drawing, that "it would be interesting to range theatrical spectators

in tiers on a stairway." [12] A sketched panorama of Rome carries an exact record, worthy of Constable, of the time of execution: "February 6, 5:45." [13] A pencil study of King Candaules' wife freezes the action at the instant when, undressed for the night and with one knee already on her couch, she turns her head and glimpses out of the corner of her eye the peeper as he slips from the room. A note above the drawing stresses the need for precise expressiveness in the finished painting: "The whole body should be simple and tranquil, the eye alone burning with sexual modesty and the idea of revenge."

Toward the end of July 1857 he was at Terracina, on the coast southeast of Rome, sketching the Romanesque reading stand in the cathedral. He went on, still sketching, to nearby Fondi and Formia (then called Mola di Gaeta). On the first of August he was back in Naples, where he resumed his copying of Pompeian murals. During the following weeks he also did drawings of his uncle Odoardo and of Alfredo and Adelchi Morbilli, probably a watercolor of Aunt Rosa (the date and identification are uncertain), and finally, in the villa at San Rocco di Capodimonte, an Ingresque oil portrait of his grandfather, looking fragile with age but tough-minded, and possibly amused by Edgar's insistence on the pose of Pope Paul III — reversed, apparently by an engraved reproduction — in the Titian portrait at the Naples museum. (The fragility should not distract attention from the tough-mindedness, for René-Hilaire seems to have remained in firm command of his affairs and the family right up to the end and even beyond: his last will, written six weeks before his death, substituted for the usual legalistic *desidero,* "I desire," a thumping repetition of *ordino,* "I order.") [14]

The copying of masterpieces and the planning for a Salon picture were under way again in Rome by mid-October, and the Roman winter of 1857–1858 was even more entertaining and convivial than the previous one. The nineteen-year-old Georges Bizet, a curly-headed, spectacled prodigy from the Ninth Arrondissement, enlivened the musical evenings at the Villa Medici and also the comradeship, in spite of his low opinion of the pensioners who quarreled about the respective merits of Delacroix and Ingres. ("The painters," he reported to his mother, "are still divided into two camps: the colorists and the draftsmen. Unfortunately, the colorists are as ignorant as the draftsmen concerning color, and the draftsmen as ignorant as the colorists concerning drawing.") [15] Léon Bonnat, one of Edgar's schoolmates at Louis-le-Grand, was another new arrival, equipped by his home town, Bayonne, with a substitute for the Prix de Rome. Although he was already a cautious painter, he soon became one of the more heated of the Cald'arròsti at the Caffè Greco. In the French colony that revolved around the Villa Medici, thanks to Schnetz's hospitality, there was Edmond

René-Hilaire Degas, 1857

About, a witty young novelist and polemical essayist who had studied at the recently created French archaeology school at Athens, and who gave the papal city a touch of Parisian sinfulness by living with a notorious demimondaine, Alice Ozy. An important older member of the colony was Joseph-Gabriel Tourny, a painter and engraver who had won the grand prize ten years earlier, had returned to Rome with his wife to make copies of Renaissance pictures for the collection of the Paris historian and statesman Adolphe Thiers, and had begun to keep open house for several of the student artists who were working at the academy. On July 15, 1858, during a prolonged absence from Italy, Tourny wrote a fatherly letter to Degas that reveals something of the latter's not always agreeable personality during the preceding months, along with his talent for inspiring affection:

> You know, my dear boy, how much we like you and, in spite of all the happiness at our return [to France], how the memory of our old Romans sticks with us. We think constantly of the Degas who grumbles and of the Edgar who growls, and we are indeed going to miss that grumbling and growling during the coming winter.[16]

In a postscript Madame Tourny continues in the same vein: "At Rome we quite often complained about a little bear, but now we often happen to regret his absence."

An even more important member of the colony was Gustave Moreau, who had not yet begun to paint the morbid, elaborately ornate visions of Orpheus and Salome that would make him a cult figure for the literary Decadents and Symbolists of the 1880s but who had already acquired the qualities that would make him a great professor in the Ecole des Beaux-Arts of the 1890s, capable of forming artists as different from himself as Matisse, Rouault, and Marquet. Looking back half a century later at the Villa Medici of 1857, Bonnat recalled that "we were all crazy about Moreau."[17] Part of the secret of this popularity lay in a knack for unobtrusively sharing an erudition few of the pensioners could equal, part in tolerance of other men's opinions and styles, and part in an exemplary humility, for at thirty-one Moreau, who had failed once in the Prix de Rome competition and had refused to try again, was still a hard-working learner: in one of his letters from Italy he wrote of copying in museums from the opening to the closing hours, and added that "at my age the profession of schoolboy is not easy."[18]

Edgar found such a combination of sensitivity and industry immediately attractive, and he soon entered into a relationship that was to some extent that of a dazzled disciple with a sympathetic master and to a considerable extent warmly personal, filial, and even physical — a matter of complementary appearances and manners. Moreau had a massive body, a philosopher's domed brow, a biblical beard, and a prophet's stare, and, though only eight years older than Degas, addressed him as "enfant." The younger man, a fuzzy-chinned stripling, responded by playing the assigned dependent role almost excessively. In correspondence with Moreau from a slightly later time, he wrote of how at Rome "I would rub myself like a bear against your shoulder to signify in no uncertain way that I was understanding you."[19] (Madame Tourny was evidently not the only one to think of him in ursine terms.)

The god Ingres was not forgotten. On a notebook page[20] his last name was jotted down whimsically in Greek capital letters, as if inscribed on a stone monument, and was preceded by the opening line, also in Greek, of the *Iliad:* "Goddess, sing the wrath of Achilles, son of Peleus." But there was a shift of interest, partly under the influence of the older friends in Rome, away from the dry manner of Lamothe toward more expressiveness and more color. Etching alongside Tourny, Edgar learned, for all his grumbling and growling, to understand and to imitate Rembrandt; drawing and painting beside Moreau in the Roman environs and at the Villa Medici, sometimes with the same model, he learned to appreciate more fully Delacroix and the Venetian masters. Was he beginning to be tempted by what had tempted Chassériau? By the idea, that is, of a painting style that would reconcile line with color, Neoclassicism with Romanticism, and Ingres with Delacroix? Certainly Chassériau must have often entered that winter's conversation, for he had been alive and young only two years earlier, Alice Ozy had been his mistress before taking up with About, and Moreau had been, and still was, one of his most enthusiastic defenders. There is no firm evidence, however, that Degas at this time was ready for anything as ambitious, and as dangerous, as Chassériau's kind of compromise; he was simply expanding his taste and, in the meantime, continuing with his own eclecticism.

He sketched some portraits of friends, painted an academic *Dante and Virgil* with Tourny posing as Dante, and enjoyed himself as usual with landscape and the vivid sense it gave him of an exact, passing (but arrested by art) moment of the world's and his own existence. On the road to the Villa d'Este he did a shaded drawing of the sun setting over the distant town, and noted, "Very curious effect, in that there were two large beams of light projected across the sky, very visibly but very lightly. Night fell within ten minutes at the most. Tivoli, 5:10 P.M., November 10, 1857."[21]

When he was not sketching, painting, or talking, he was apt to be reading — Homer, Herodotus, and Dante, and probably the poetry of Gautier and Leconte de Lisle, who were among Moreau's favorites. He must also have listened occasionally to his friend's performances as a singer, for in February Bizet qualified his contempt for draftsmen and colorists by reporting to his mother that "Moreau, a painter, has a charming voice and we are making a bit of music."[22] Presumably the music was not always classical, since Edgar copied into his notebook some verses, entitled *Drunkenness,* by the popular songwriter and operetta composer Gustave Nadaud:

> *Tout est doré, tout est vermeil,*
> *Le passé n'est plus qu'un nuage,*
> *Le présent dans mon verre nage*
> *Et l'avenir, c'est le sommeil . . .*[23]

(All is gilded, all is vermeil, the past is no longer anything but a cloud, the present swims in my glass, and the future is sleep . . .)

At the beginning of summer Tourny returned to France for his long stay, and Moreau departed for Orvieto, Siena, and eventually Florence. A letter from Naples brought the news that Aunt Laura was also scheduled to arrive in Florence shortly, with Giovanna and Giulia, to rejoin Baron Bellelli. So Degas decided that the occasion was good for carrying out a long-contemplated project — taking a leisurely sightseeing trip from Rome to the Tuscan capital in a hired *vettura,* one of the light carriages, or flies, that were at the time very popular with foreign tourists, in spite of the drivers' reputation for rascality. First he crated and sent to Paris, as his own version of the *envois de Rome* of the Villa Medici pensioners, a selection of his recent works that included the *Dante and Virgil.* An accompanying note to his father explained how he could keep the fresh oil paintings from turning yellow. Then, on July 24, 1858, at the end of the afternoon, so as to avoid the heat, he was rolling up the Via Flaminia toward the Ponte Molle, the northern Roman suburbs, and the road to Viterbo. His watch was in a handy pocket and his notebook open for a record of the journey and his reactions, written in a rapid, abrupt prose that frequently suggests the jerking and jolting of his *vettura:*

> I leave Rome, 6:45 P.M., arrive on a hilltop after the Ponte Molle — superb plain, the Italy of dreams! Yellow plain, cut wheat, mountains gray with the night that is falling at their base. Vaporous mountains, really azure — vapor half [illegible word] in the different planes of the mountains. Seven-thirty. All is grayish yellow. A very tiring night. I make out volcanic terrain, stony with clumps of trees — and here we are going past the foot of Sutri. Caves. [The village of] Capranica. Up, down. I'm astonished when I enter Viterbo. You would think you were in Avignon.[24]

After catching a few hours of sleep he spent the rest of the day looking at the monuments of Viterbo, in particular the medieval church of Santa Maria della Verità.

At ten o'clock in the evening he was on the road again, with the architecture and painting of Orvieto as his next objective:

> Moonlight. I make out the landscape and mountains. Superb terrain. Montefiascone. Mountains. Day is breaking, with fog covering the plain. We are going down into the Orvieto valley. The cathedral appears above the fog. We are climbing the ramp.[25]

Although he was a well-prepared traveler who could recognize, and had frequently copied from reproductions in the Paris Cabinet des Estampes, what he was looking for, his judgments were not ready-made. If the Gothic façade of the cathedral and its sculpture were admittedly "sublime," the much restored mosaics were "too fresh" and at least one of them was "frightfully decadent." And anyway the façade was not, for him, the real treasure of the place: "I enter and I run to Luca Signorelli."[26] Before the brutal vigor and the movement of the frescoes he was plunged into a confused reverie of "subjects from Dante, ingenious, throbbing arabesques, a sort of madness,"[27] which lasted until he returned to his hotel, "stumbling from lack of sleep."[28] He woke up at noon, went out to do some sketching of scenery, changed his mind, and then encountered a mood-shattering vexation: "I go to the cathedral, I begin to draw a seraph. Someone is playing *La Traviata* on the organ as loudly as possible. What a mockery! I go for a walk on the ramparts."[29] By the end of the promenade he felt better; he enjoyed a good sunset and decided, in spite of an invasion of fleas in his bedroom, to spend one more day at Orvieto.

On July 29 at five-thirty in the morning, after another moonlit night on the road, he reached Città della Pieve, where he found little in the way of art except, behind the cathedral altar, Perugino's sweet *Virgin and Child with Saints Peter, Paul, Gervasius, and Protasius,* which reminded him of a Perugino he had copied at the Lyons museum in the summer of 1855. He was beginning to miss the Cald'arrosti and his other friends at the Villa Medici, to the point of becoming bored with the theatrical Umbrian landscape. "When traveling alone," he noted, "you need to cross regions that have human life or are very full of works of art."[30] The time passed slowly at the hotel, with nothing to do but write a letter, watch the usual small-town street spectacle, recall idly that Città della Pieve was Perugino's birthplace, and wait for transportation: "Always some priests walking around. All the women look like Peruginos! Is that an illusion? At last, ten o'clock in the evening. Departure for Perugia."[31]

Now he was traveling with five other passengers in a small coach, which was just as well, for the night was heavy with approaching thunderstorms. Shortly after three in the morning a yoke of oxen replaced the horses for a long uphill pull, and then the walls of pious, mystical Perugia came into view. Although it was scarcely daylight, the town was already putting on a fine medieval show: two files of pilgrims were marching past the fifteenth-century Palazzo del Capitano, singing as they went. He allowed himself merely a nap at his inn: "At eight-thirty I am on the run."[32] By the end of the day, despite occasional rain and generally poor light, he had added to his memories the Gothic-Renaissance-Baroque and still unfinished cathedral ("restored in the most ignoble fashion I've ever seen"), the Gothic-Baroque church of San Domenico ("disfigured and yet superb"), the mid-fifteenth-century Collegio del Cambio ("delicious harmony"), the Romanesque-Gothic-Renaissance church of San Pietro ("the sky is very black; you can no longer see in the interior"), and paintings by Signorelli ("superb color"), Fra Angelico ("adorable"), Perugino ("I knew the compositions, but what beautiful color"), and Raphael ("indeed divine").

The next morning at seven o'clock he set off on foot from Perugia for Assisi, twenty-four kilometers away. By ten-thirty, with his face sunburned and his head aching so much that for a moment he feared he had caught some kind of brain fever, he was at Santa Maria degli Angeli, the church, recently rebuilt, at the base of the Assisi hill five kilometers from the town. High Mass was under way for a crowd of pilgrims, and the vox humana stop of the organ was excellent. He sat down to listen and, after leaving, recorded the experience:

> It played during the elevation of the Host. I felt myself really very affected. I am not religious, at least not in the practicing sense. But I had a moment of emotion. The music, which was very beautiful, must have been what touched me, more perhaps than the sight of the pilgrims, who were fervently beating their breasts.[33]

The "moment of emotion" returned when, having had the courage to climb the hill, he entered the light-flooded Upper Church of San Francesco and stood before the fresco cycle *The Life of Saint Francis,* then attributed (as it still is by some authorities) to Giotto:

> Everything breathes prayer. Everything is lovely, the details, the whole. I would rather not draw than do a rough sketch without having examined anything. My memories will be worth much more. There is expression and an astonishing drama in Giotto. He was a genius.[34]

His meditations were interrupted by a group of Italian peasants who began to gallop ecstatically around the altar, singing and shouting the names of their patron saints, and who accelerated this unusual kind of devotional activity until they were like a band of whirling dervishes. "How well," he reflected, "that explains the Crusades."[35] But he was tired of talking only to his notebook, so he approached a robed Franciscan whom he had overheard speaking French, and who introduced himself as Brother Pascal. The conversation continued on a terrace near the church and then for a long while in a cell at the monastery of Sant' Apollinare, where the friar revealed that he had once enjoyed the company of fashionable Parisians, that he now pitied such people, and that on the morrow, a Sunday, he was to take another step in his withdrawal from a worldly life, by becoming a subdeacon. Edgar was impressed enough to decide, though he had left his luggage in Perugia, to spend the night in Assisi and attend the ordination. What had started with a sunburn and a vox humana stop was turning into a troubling spiritual incident.

The ceremony in the monastery chapel the following morning was even more affecting than he had anticipated: "Tears came to my eyes. How many thoughts passed through my mind!" He sketched a choir boy holding a bishop's miter, and gravely hypothesized: "If I were fifty years old, alone, without children or unmarried, I would perhaps settle down here in the monastery."[36] After listening to the last swell of the organ and the final benediction, he returned to the basilica of San Francesco to do some copying and eventually found himself in the cryptlike Lower Church, looking at the frescoes by, or attributed to, Cimabue, Simone Martini, Maso, and the Lorenzetti brothers. Here the sentiments that had been building up during his visit to Assisi produced a sudden spell of weeping and a note he labeled "almost a prayer":

> Ah, these people had a feeling for life, for life. They never rejected it. . . .
> If I am not a religious painter, at least let me feel as they felt.[37]

In the afternoon he talked again with the friar, now Father Pascal, and then together they called on an English couple who had become part of the local French-speaking colony; the husband, it turned out, had studied painting with Paul Delaroche, another of Auguste's former neighbors in the Rue de la Tour-des-Dames. Edgar was by now thinking of changing his travel schedule — and also of not changing it:

> What a state of uncertainty I am in. I must leave Assisi in order to put my baggage at Perugia on the stagecoach for Florence. And I want to come back to Assisi. Yet I am afraid of returning. I am afraid of falling again into daydreams . . .[38]

Common sense won out; in the evening he went back down the hill to Santa Maria degli Angeli and found a carriage to take him to Perugia.

By five-thirty Monday morning his bags were on the coach leaving for Florence. Then a pair of Villa Medici comrades appeared, and his firmness of resolve melted:

> In front of the hotel I catch sight of Clère and Delaunay. I fall on their necks. Hot discussion with coachmen, the most grasping people on earth.

At last, at last. We'll leave Wednesday morning, the three of us, for Arezzo, and tomorrow I'll go to Assisi. I'm capering with joy. I am going to see Father Pascal again. Assisi, which I found so seductive I wanted to run away from it . . . and where I could perhaps be so much at home someday.[39]

On Tuesday he was again being reasonable. He took a painter's pleasure in the ride up the hill from Santa Maria degli Angeli, with its views of plains, mountains, and melancholy cypresses; and he ended his visit with a note that substituted a vision of bourgeois domesticity for his earlier thoughts of retirement to the Assisi monastery:

I'm glad to have again seen the English gentleman and his wife. There was happiness in their home. Perhaps I may find a good little wife, a simple, calm woman who understands my foolish ideas and with whom I can have a modest life of work. Isn't that a beautiful dream? I am going to re-enter the agitation of Paris. Who knows what will happen?[40]

After a moment he added: "But I will always be an honest man."

At this point he was running out of blank pages. "I hope," he told himself, "that my memory will make up for the little I have written, which is not even a résumé of what I have thought." He found space for brief remarks about some unidentifiable pictures in a private gallery at Perugia, about the panoramic Tiber valley view, a tourist attraction for centuries, from the loggia of the local church of San Pietro ("distant thunderstorm, the mountain of Assisi in blackness"), and about the frescoes by Pintoricchio ("more refined than Perugino") in the church of Santa Maria Maggiore at nearby Spello.

Then he temporarily halted his note-taking, and probably he did so with a feeling of relief, for he had gone through several nights and days of what were surely tiring physical and psychological adventures, accompanied by a seriocomic tour de force of self-analytical writing. He had been bumping over moonlit roads, gorging on masterpieces, burning under a July sun, weeping in Assisi, withdrawing into monasticism, capering in Perugia, contemplating matrimony, and dreaming of Paris, all in dizzying succession. And at the same time he had been whipping out his little memorandum book to scribble that he was at that precise moment in the process of weeping, capering, dreaming, or whatever. What had begun as simply a recording of impressions of the Italian landscape and Italian art had finally turned into a strenuous attempt, equivocal in its blend of objectivity and artifice, to play simultaneously the observed and the observer and thus to surprise the Degas "me" in the act of revealing its true — though obviously still very unsteady — focus.

5. Florence

ON AUGUST 4 the three Cald'arròsti from the Villa Medici reached Florence, presumably late in the afternoon because of their scheduled stopover at Arezzo, where they can be imagined lingering in the choir of San Francesco to look at Piero della Francesca's frescoes the *Legend of the Holy Cross.* (Degas does not, however, mention the cycle, and in 1858 Piero's timeless geometry and pale colors had almost none of the impact they would have on post-Cubist viewers.) Laura and her daughters had been detained in Naples by what was feared to be René-Hilaire's last illness. But the reputedly difficult baron was cordial, and the visiting nephew was invited to stay in the Bellelli furnished rooms and await his aunt's arrival.

In spite of his affection for his grandfather, his wish to see Laura again, and his probable eagerness to begin work on what seems to have been shaping up into a definite project to do a portrait of her with Giovanna and Giulia, he could not have been extremely unhappy about the situation. The Bellelli apartment was within comfortable walking distance of the Uffizi, the Palazzo Pitti, and other famous places where there were pictures to be copied; and Siena and Pisa were within easy reach by carriage for the son of a banker. Moreau was in town, along with Clère, Delaunay, and a number of other young French artists, some of whom Degas had already met in Paris or Rome. Tourny was expected.

Meanwhile, there was Florence itself. In the summer of 1858 the streets were apt to fill suddenly with soldiers, for Italy was on the verge of a new stage in its struggle for unification, and in a few months an army under Napoleon III would be moving across Lombardy to defeat the Austrian occupants at Magenta and Solferino. Leopold II, destined to be the last reigning Grand Duke of Tuscany, was becoming less and less liberal, in the hope of saving his dynasty. But the political situation did not keep the city from being, in the words of its long-time resident Elizabeth Barrett Browning, "cheap, tranquil, cheerful, and beautiful." At the Caffè Doney, in the Piazza Santa Trinità near the river, the ice cream was delicious, the confectionery varied, and the price of a buttered roll with tea or coffee about half what was charged in many Italian establishments. Wealthy tourists and a large Anglo-American colony provided touches of international sophistication, and also clients for an omnipresent firm of art photographers, the Alinari Brothers. The transparent atmosphere sometimes seemed slightly amber, perhaps because of reflections from the Arno, and then Brunelleschi's great dome, the fortresslike palaces, and the darting Florentines, when seen from the hill behind the Pitti, flattened into a magically unreal, freshly varnished oil painting.

The copyist was soon hard at work, with his usual wide-ranging eye but with a particular interest in Pontormo, Bronzino, and some fifteenth-century Italians: Gozzoli, Uccello, Ghirlandaio, Leonardo, and Filippino Lippi. The still unfinished *Saint John the Baptist and the Angel,* on which he had labored for a long while in Rome, was abandoned; instead, he planned a *David and Goliath.* In the new notebook he was using he devoted two pages to a sixteenth-century account, discovered in the anecdotal Seigneur de Brantôme's *Vies des dames illustres,* of Mary Stuart's sad departure from France in 1561. His opening paragraph hints at a sentimental history painting that might appeal to the jury of the Paris Salon:

> Without thinking of anything else, she leaned both her arms on the poop of the galley next to the tiller and began to shed huge tears while continually rolling her beautiful eyes toward the port and the land she had left, and while repeating over and over again, for nearly five hours and until night began to fall, the same doleful words: "Adieu, France."[1]

Twelve more pages were occupied by a detailed summary of Sophocles' *Oedipus Rex,* suggesting another typical Salon picture:

> Oedipus . . . has ripped out his eyes. He runs forward, bleeding and blind. The chorus shudders at the sight. He comes out of the palace, arms extended to feel his way along the wall.[2]

The same period — the late summer of 1858 — saw him doing drawings of Baroness Enrichetta Dembowski and her daughter; the baroness was

Bellelli's younger sister and the wife of the director of an astronomical observatory in Milan. But copies, Salon projects, and family portraits were not the only preoccupations of these weeks. Preceding and following the notes on the weeping Mary Stuart and the blind Oedipus, there are more than fifty sketches of horses or parts of horses. Although some are clearly derived from pictures (Van Dyck's *Equestrian Portrait of Charles V,* for example) and were history-painting studies, many were apparently done in the street, and two of them — a hint of the future — are accompanied by drawings of jockeys.

After a month, spent working and talking, the wait for Laura, Giulia, and Giovanna began to seem long. Moreau, who had renewed the master-disciple relationship begun in Rome, eventually moved on to Milan and then to Venice, where he settled down to copy Carpaccio. Delaunay deserted the Arno and Florentine drawing for the Grand Canal and Venetian color. Tourny did not appear. René-Hilaire died on August 31, and Laura prolonged her stay in Naples in order to attend the funeral and participate in the settlement of the estate. In the Uffizi and the Pitti one could still encounter friendly French artists, among them the painter John Pradier, who would become an academic *orientaliste,* and the sculptor Théodore Blard, who was already a Salon exhibitor. But Edgar did not think them very stimulating.

Aimlessly, he sketched Tuscan soldiers. On September 21 he wrote a long letter[3] to Moreau that reveals a disposition to succumb once again to familiar demons — to the goblin discouragement, to the old serpent procrastination, and to the see-yourself-seeing-yourself imp:

> I'm not amounting to much of anything. Since I'm all alone, I am rather bored. In the evening I am a bit tired from the day's work, and I would like to talk a little. I don't find an occasion to open my mouth. Pradier, who is here, does not set much of an example. Blard is surrounded by Englishmen whom I don't know. So after eating some ice cream at the Caffè Doney, I am in my room before nine o'clock. Sometimes I write. . . . Most often I read, before and after going to bed. . . . There are moments when I am so irritated by my loneliness and so worried about my painting that if the desire — which as you know is strong — to see my aunt and my little cousins again did not fix me here firmly, I would give up this beautiful Florence and the pleasure of your return.

He had been reading "with interest," he wrote, the section of Pascal's *Pensées* in which "regarding the 'me' as hateful is recommended." He had spent three weeks copying a Giorgione (perhaps the Uffizi's *Trial of Moses,* often merely attributed to Giorgione). He felt "up in the air," unable to begin a "work of my own," and gloomy about the future:

Great patience is needed on the hard road to which I am committed. I had your encouragement. Now, as if I lacked it, I am again beginning to despair a little, as in the past. I remember a conversation of ours here in Florence about the sadness that is the lot of anyone who takes up art. There was less exaggeration than I thought in what you said. The sadness is scarcely ever accompanied by compensations. It grows with age and the progress you make, and then youth is no longer there to console you with a few more illusions and hopes. . . . There is an emptiness that even art cannot fill.

An ironical flourish interrupted the solemnity: "Always me. But what do you want a lonely, abandoned man to say? He has only himself in front of himself, sees only himself, thinks only of himself."

In fact, he was not all that abandoned. The art collector Edmond Beaucousin, one of Auguste's friends, had been in Florence for a couple of weeks, and though "imagination," as Edgar reported to Moreau, was "not part of his charm," it had been amusing to go about town with a man whose "sole ambition" was to avoid buying *croûtes* (daubs). A week after the letter to Venice there was a visitor of more importance: a friend of Moreau's and the son of Léopold Koenigswarter, who was a powerful Paris banker and a deputy in the Corps Législatif — the lower but principal house of the Second Empire parliament. Degas organized a two-day expedition to Siena that provided the occasion, in the church of San Domenico, for an enthusiastic notebook comment on Sodoma's fresco *Saint Catherine in Ecstasy:* "A very youthful figure inflamed by faith, the whole body trembling and throbbing."[4] Koenigswarter *fils* summed up his companion, in a later account to Moreau, with a compliment and a hint of a businessman's condescension toward a fellow who would obviously never be able to meet a payroll: "A charming young man. It makes one feel good to encounter such naïveté and such freshness of feeling in the middle of our world of positivism."[5] Degas, in still another report to Moreau, described Koenigswarter, also with a hint of condescension, as "indeed a worthy lad."[6]

The days and weeks passed, the Tuscan summer cooled into a Tuscan autumn, and Laura did not arrive. The reading in bed seems to have shifted from Pascal on the hateful "me" to Shakespeare on unrequited womanly love, for the notebook in use at this time contains a French translation of Viola's lines on the subject in *Twelfth Night* (II, 4):

> And with a green and yellow melancholy,
> She sat like Patience on a monument,
> Smiling at grief. . . .[7]

Perhaps the image had suggested another possible Salon painting, but if it had, nothing came of the idea. Nor did anything on canvas result from the more specific projects that had been accumulating. All creative work was halted by the need to wait for Laura. At last some encouraging, if vague, news came up from Naples, and on October 25 Degas and Baron Bellelli went to Leghorn, the main port for Florence, to watch for ships from the Kingdom of the Two Sicilies. They watched in vain. When they returned to Florence they learned that there had been a delay in Naples because the wife of an émigré had to have an exit visa authorized by the king himself. A week later, on the strength of another message, Edgar went back to Leghorn, alone, and this time, after five more days of waiting, saw the familiar figure, in deep mourning, suddenly materialize on the gangplank, accompanied by the two children. Although he was undoubtedly affected by the reminder of his grandfather's death, in a later notebook entry he would recall, with a professional, appraising eye — the sort of eye Tintoretto may have had even while painting his dead daughter — the striking effect of "the black veil my aunt Laura wore so well."[8]

Now the demons vanished for a while, and he launched into some detailed preparatory studies for what he referred to, with an implied downgrading of all other projects, as simply "the picture." Although at times he may have considered doing separate portraits of the female members of the Bellelli family, one of the first sketches of the series was of a seated Laura with Giovanna and Giulia standing on either side. Then there were versions with Laura standing. He did careful drawings (at this time or somewhat later) of her face, of her coiffure, of the turban she sometimes wore, and of her right hand resting on Giovanna's pinafore — with a reminder to himself that "the hand makes a dent in the linen." These were accompanied by drawings of the girls' heads, of their ankle boots, and eventually of things in the family living room: a chair, a picture frame, and the clock on the mantelpiece. Several of the studies were elaborated, with touches of black chalk, gray wash, green pastel, or white gouache, and sometimes by being done on tinted paper, into little works capable of standing on their own. A notebook page was given over to a shaded sketch of the bearded baron, with an indication of a carved frame, but it is clear that for many weeks he was not thought of as being in "the picture."

While the long-nourished project was at last getting under way in Florence, a small torrent of exasperation, encouragement, art criticism, and fatherly advice was pouring from the Rue de Mondovi in Paris. On November 11, Auguste, vexed with an Italian tour that was already well into its third year, wrote to his son:[9]

In my last letter I asked you not to delay your return any longer. Today I repeat that request, and I even recommend that you pack your bags as soon as you get this letter.

The impatience was mitigated, however, by approval of the work samples Edgar had sent home from Naples and the Villa Medici:

> I have been very satisfied, and I can tell you that you have taken an immense step forward in art. Your drawing is strong, your color is right. You have got rid of that flabby, trivial, Flandrinian, Lamothian drawing style and that dull gray color. . . . My dear Edgar, you no longer have reason to torment yourself. You are on an excellent track. Calm your mind and, working quietly but with perseverance, without slacking off, follow this furrow you have opened for yourself. It belongs to you and to nobody else. Work calmly while sticking to this track, I tell you, and you can be certain you will succeed in producing great things. You have a beautiful destiny before you. Don't become discouraged; don't fuss and fret.

Further on it was made plain that the "beautiful destiny" envisaged was mostly a career devoted to painting portraits and making a good living:

> You speak of being bored with doing portraits. Later on you will have to overcome this feeling, for portraiture will be the finest jewel in your crown. . . . In this world the problem of keeping the pot boiling is so grave, so urgent, so crushing, that only madmen can scorn or ignore it. One should not diminish oneself because of it. One must simply learn to endure the boredom and annoyances that accompany it.

On November 25, having been informed by Edgar that the planned portrait of Laura (the girls seem not to have been mentioned) would take about a month to finish, the elder Degas pointed out that the picture had apparently not yet been roughed out in oil and that a month was not enough time for allowing each coat to dry safely before applying the next one. "So it seems to me," he concluded, "that you should limit yourself to doing a drawing instead of undertaking a canvas . . . and then hurry up and pack your belongings and come home." But he could not resist adding some questions concerning his beloved Primitives:

> Have you carefully examined, contemplated those charming fresco masters of the fifteenth century? Have you saturated your mind with them? Have you done crayon, or rather watercolor, copies so as to remember their colors? And Giorgione — have you analyzed his admirable tone values and colors, accompanied by such beautiful, elegant drawing? Have you soaked yourself in his work? [10]

Another letter, written five days later, has a tone of resignation: "I can see very well that the presence of Monsieur Moreau in Florence is going to detain you even longer." A warning about the danger in too much copying followed:

I'm pleased that you have studied Giorgione. Your colors, although exact, still need to be warmed up a bit. But beware of the gingerbread effect. That's what painters fall into when, after copying the Venetian masters, they want to reproduce from nature certain so-called hot colors they do not see. . . . You must learn the tricks of the great masters, and then escape from their control and reproduce nature by relying on your own inspiration alone.[11]

Edgar may have found the paternal complacency in such remarks a little hard to take. But he must also have noticed the evidence of genuine affection, and perhaps of frustrated ambition, of a banker father projecting the artist he might have been onto a gifted son.

Moreau, engrossed in Carpaccio, Titian, and the warm Venetian palette generally, remained on the Grand Canal longer than expected. On November 27 Edgar wrote to him again, suggesting that it was "time to come to Florence and do some drawing" and that there had been "enough indulgence of your penchant for color." The letter also referred to the portrait of Laura and in particular to her daughters:

The older one [Giovanna] is really a little beauty; the younger one has the wit of a devil and the goodness of a little angel. I am doing them in their black dresses and their little white pinafores, which suit them ravishingly well. There are backgrounds trotting around in my head. I want a certain natural grace, along with a nobility I don't know how to define. Van Dyck was a first-rate artist, Giorgione also, Botticelli also, Mantegna also, Rembrandt also, Carpaccio also. Make head or tail of that if you can.[12]

The eclectic list of possible influences implied both a stage of vague stylistic research and a lack of progress toward an oil version. And both implications were confirmed at the end of December in a note to Paris announcing that the picture would not be finished before the end of February.

In a reply[13] dated January 4, 1859, Auguste came close to losing his patience completely, partly because of a fear that the painting, in which he had begun to take a proprietary interest, would be spoiled by Edgar's attempt to meet a foolish, impossible deadline, and partly because of what looked to him, from his chair in the Rue de Mondovi, like an intolerable combination of dawdling and flightiness:

Since you wanted to undertake this picture, you must finish it, and finish it properly. . . . You overexcite your imagination too much, much too much, and then, when you descend toward reality, when you bump into that hard and inflexible reality, you fall flat. . . . I beseech you, Edgar, to put some lead ballast in your head.

His son, forgetting the Ingres dictum that drawing was the probity of art, had apparently ventured to say something in favor of Delacroix, and this provoked an Old Testament denunciation in which aesthetics and ethics were confounded and a liking for color was equated with sin:

> If an artist must have enthusiasm for art, he must also regulate his conduct wisely, under the threat of remaining a nonentity. You know that I am far from sharing your opinion of Delacroix. This painter has abandoned himself to the passionate element in his ideas and has neglected, unfortunately for him, the art of drawing — the Ark of the Covenant on which everything depends. He has totally ruined himself.

Here one guesses that a bit of unconscious jealousy sharpened the irritation, for Auguste probably suspected that the shift toward Delacroix and color was another result of the influence of Moreau, the rival father in Venice, who was partially responsible for Edgar's dawdling in Florence.

Moreau returned to the Tuscan capital early in January. One day at the Uffizi shortly after his arrival he did a drawing of his disciple that illustrates, to the point of a slight oddness, the nature of their child-and-father dialogue, for Edgar, wearing a long, Romantic cape and a big, floppy hat, looks astonishingly younger than in his self-portraits of these years — indeed, he looks closer to fourteen than to his real age, twenty-four. Another sign of intimacy and dependence is a notebook page on which imitations of Moreau's signature are accompanied by Degas's variations on his own name, as if he were trying to decide how to sign his pictures, or looking for the elusive "me" again. The next page, perhaps done in Paris the following April, makes the link with Romanticism via Moreau explicit. It contains imitations of the signatures of Delacroix and of Eugène Fromentin, Orientalist painter and art historian, follower of Delacroix's and friend of Moreau's, and later the author of *Les Maîtres d'autrefois*.

During the ensuing weeks, whenever the preparatory studies for "the picture" left some free time, the two artists worked together in Florentine museums and churches and occasionally in the surrounding centers of Tuscan art. In the Pinacoteca of Siena, Degas was particularly and unexpectedly seized with admiration for the *Paradise* of the naïve, mystical, irrational, reactionary, and tormented Giovanni di Paolo (the "El Greco of the Quattrocento," according to Bernard Berenson); and he seems to have been for a moment ready to renew the religious reverie of Assisi, for he would recall the presence of another Brother Pascal:

> The day I copied this painting there was a monk at my side, very tall, thin, and pale, and with eyes sunk in their sockets. He was praying, and his face was so radiant I involuntarily glanced up to see if there was a halo above his head.[14]

Degas at the Uffizi,
by Gustave Moreau, 1859

At Pisa in the Campo Santo he copied, among other things, some figures in Gozzoli's fresco cycle of scenes from the Old Testament. Somewhere, probably at the Uffizi, he found an occasion to study Rembrandt and Rubens, and on February 25 this fresh evidence of straying from the Ingresque path provoked Auguste, still attentively following his son's progress, into a mixture of halfhearted approval and grumbled alarm: "I can understand your consulting Rembrandt. . . . But Rubens — in order to do what?" [15]

Lamothe also, by way of reports from Edgar and probably with help from Paris conversations with Auguste, had been following the growing pro-Delacroix influence of Moreau and the consequent neglect of Ingres's precepts, and had been reacting with both a bitter sense of betrayal and a tiresome amount of argumentation — so much so that at one point during the winter professor and pupil seem to have been close to complete estrangement. Tourny, who had finally managed to spend a few days in

Tuscany on his way back to Rome, alluded to the trouble in a philosophical letter to Edgar, dated January 30:

> You told me about your quarrel with Lamothe. You are too frank and too sincere to put up with Jesuitism. But the older you get, and the more you learn about mankind, the more indifferent you will become.[16]

There was no dearth of epistolary advice during these months of research, experimentation, and alternating depression and euphoria.

Nor was there a lack of bright, youthful, loquacious companions whose talents could compete with Moreau's. (As Degas once reminded him, he had "a tongue that wagged very well.") One of the recent additions to the French community in Florence was Georges Lafenestre, a twenty-year-old poet from Orléans who would become an art historian, a contributor in 1866 to the historic anthology *Le Parnasse contemporain,* and in middle age a distinguished curator at the Louvre. His imminent connection with the Parnassian movement in contemporary verse implies that in 1859 he was, like Moreau, an admirer of the aestheticism of Gautier's poetry and of the splendidly cool, already somewhat post-Romantic style — more objective than emotional, and more visual than musical — of Leconte de Lisle. All of this suggests some effect on a Degas sensibility that was still in the process of discovering or inventing itself.

In this regard, however, a more important member of the local French colony was the painter Jacques-Joseph Tissot, who had recently changed his first name to James and had thus signaled an anglophilia, and a dandyism, that a dozen years later would help him to become a lionized depictor of fashionable life in London (what Ruskin, in an account of the artist's work, would call "vulgar society"). He had studied briefly with Lamothe and Flandrin, through whom he had probably met Degas, and had then, in Antwerp, come under the influence of Henri Leys, an archaizing Belgian painter of historical scenes. A shock of jet-black hair, a drooping Mongolian mustache, an excellent tailor, and a small private fortune made him, in the words of one of his many women friends in England, "a charming man, very handsome . . . nothing of artistic carelessness either in his dress or demeanour."[17] Yet he was not an ordinary swell. In 1859, at the age of twenty-two, he was already the possessor of a smooth, realistic technique that was like a camera with an infinite depth of focus. At the Paris Salon of the spring of that year he had five pictures accepted by the jury. Also, his inner life was more complicated than his appearance indicated: two of his Salon pictures, representing saints, were signs of a religious temperament that would finally lead him, after the death of an adored mistress, to desert the social glitter of London for Palestine and biblical compositions.

French influence was not the only up-to-date kind available. In the Florence of 1859 there was an unusual concentration of Italian painters from all over the peninsula, attracted partly by the city's cheapness and artistic atmosphere and partly — since many of the young men were veterans of the conspiracies and battles for national unification — by the Tuscan regime's persisting, though declining, reputation for tolerance. The most prominent and most audible were members of the group that, because of a fondness for simplifying the distribution of light and shade into contrasting spots, or *macchie,* would enter art history under the derisive label of the Macchiaioli, the "spot-painters." (The term was first used by a hostile critic in the local *Gazzetta del Popolo* in 1861 and was later improperly applied to almost any Italian painter who happened to rebel against traditional styles and subjects.) Telemaco Signorini, a cultivated, articulate bourgeois a year younger than Degas, was for the moment their leader, though his importance would shortly be reduced by the far more vigorous talent of a much less talkative artist, Giovanni Fattori. The budding theorist and ardent defender of the group was a twenty-year-old journalist, Diego Martelli, who had for his comrades the extra advantage of being the heir to a large country estate south of Leghorn, where one could stay for nothing and paint in rural peace. Signorini, looking back at this Florentine period, would remember Martelli as a *putto,* for he was as plump and round as an apple. But the *putto* could hold his own in an argument about politics or art, and his apple shape did not keep him from volunteering for the summer war of 1859, nor from fighting at the side of Garibaldi a few years later.

The regular meeting place of the Macchiaioli was the Caffè Michelangiolo, at 41–43 Via Larga (now the Via Cavour) near the Convento di San Marco and its collection of Fra Angelicos. The rooms were usually crowded, the walls were covered with frescoes executed by habitués, and the conversation was noisy. Representative talkers did not display much avant-gardism in their choice of heroes: they admired Corot, for example, the cow specialist Troyon, the Barbizon school, the *orientaliste* Decamps, and the now nearly forgotten but once very popular Auguste Raffet, who celebrated, mostly in lithography and in an otherworldly lucency, the glory and misery of the Napoleonic Old Guard and of the troops in Crimea. (Sizable samples of the work of these French artists were on view locally in the collection, recently opened to the public, of a wealthy Russian member of the foreign colony, Prince Anatole Demidoff.) In short, they tended like provincial painters everywhere to be one revolution behind. What gave their movement a real if short-lived vitality — and many of their pictures an unfading charm — was their violent opposition to the entire Italian art

Establishment, coupled with their insistence on the need to be realistic, contemporary, and unpretentious, even to the point of ingenuousness. They maintained that the past must not be allowed to kill the present, and guffawed at the religiosity and the highfalutin language that surrounded the masterpieces in the Uffizi. They made the Caffè Michelangiolo a sort of factory for caricature. They were especially vehement in their expressions of distaste for literary art critics. Meanwhile, without any very systematic use of the much discussed *macchie,* they painted family portraits, domestic genre scenes, vignettes of military life, and sunny little landscapes on slabs of wood, being careful to let the grain show through. They did not paint David and Goliath, nor weeping, eye-rolling Mary Stuart leaving France, nor blind Oedipus groping along the palace wall.

In his reminiscences Signorini mentions the presence of Lafenestre, Tissot, Degas, and Moreau at the Caffè Michelangiolo.[18] Perhaps Degas, in his fluent Italian, took part occasionally in the arguments about national unification, for during his long wait for Laura he had got into the habit of discussing politics with his uncle. ("I dispute frequently," he had reported to Moreau, "in a friendly way.")[19] In any event, he heard and observed what was going on. His notebooks for these months contain an unfinished copy of a lithograph by Raffet, many sketches of soldiers, and several caricatures (one of which seems to represent Tissot, rakishly smoking a cigarette). Later on he would become a tireless insulter of men of letters who ventured into art criticism. He would also manifest a warm regard, which probably began in 1859, for Signorini and especially for Martelli. The significance of all this should not, of course, be overestimated. There is very little evidence to suggest a specific stylistic influence emanating from the theories and practice of the Macchiaioli, and the little that can be discovered is open to being explained away as coincidence. But frequenting the Caffè Michelangiolo can nonetheless be counted among the seemingly minor deflections that ultimately resulted in a major change of course. For what was certainly the first time in his life the aesthetically right-thinking copyist of museum masterpieces heard educated people treat things like the *Apollo Belvedere* and Raphael's Madonnas with what the Italians called *coglionèlla,* a coarse, hard-to-translate term for a peculiarly Italian kind of deflating derision. Also for the first time, he encountered a band of painters of his own generation who, far from being co-opted by the fine arts system, were furiously opting out. (The fact that they were not opting out quite as definitely as they may have imagined does not alter the point.)

The Tuscan winter changed into a Tuscan spring, and "the picture" remained unfinished. By this time there were probably two oil sketches of figures, a pastel study for the whole composition, and a score or more of drawings, in addition to the notebook experiments. The baron had been incorporated into the scheme, and so had the dead René-Hilaire, in the form of a small, framed picture — a copy of the drawing done in Naples in 1856. But there could be little question of a final version executed in Florence, partly because Auguste was becoming more and more impatient and mostly because the canvas as now envisaged was to be two meters high and two and a half meters wide, which would make working on it in the Bellelli furnished rooms nearly impossible. Besides, Moreau was planning to leave soon, and his departure would make the city much less attractive. Edgar had already written an urgent letter to Paris mobilizing the entire family to search for an adequate studio, and he now at last began to pack. After two years and eight months of instructive experiences, he was finishing the Grand Tour.

During the final few days he returned to keeping a detailed record, often with his watch in his hand, of what he was doing, feeling, and thinking, and this time he talked, in a confessional counterpoint, both to himself in his notebook and to the absent Moreau, who consequently received a thick letter, dated April 26, from the Rue de Mondovi.[20] It was on the morning of March 30 that the older artist took the train for Rome; the younger man was in such an emotional state that it was decided he should not come to the station to say good-by. The next day it was his own turn to leave, and on this occasion the farewell, as described in the report to Moreau, was equally painful:

> I actually begged my aunt . . . to stay indoors. Poor woman, it was a hard moment for her. She tried to keep me from going, because of the strong wind. But I could not endure any longer the heartache over leaving, which had been constant for days.

In fact, Laura was right. at Leghorn the weather was so nasty that all sailings had been canceled. He spent the night in the port, and in the morning made the nineteen-kilometer journey to Pisa, where he found a small boat ready to put out to sea immediately. It was full of soldiers, who turned out to be a contingent of Garibaldi's volunteer Cacciatori delle Alpi, "Alpine huntsmen," moving north to join the Piedmontese army in preparation for an attempt to drive the Austrians from Lombardy and the south Tyrol — and make "Italy" something more than a geographical term:

> No more swaggering and blustering [he reported to Moreau]: I can assure you that these young fellows were firmly determined in their enterprise. . . . War is undoubtedly on the way. There is absolutely no danger for you and your family if you remain in Rome. Await events a little before going

to Naples. The king is going to die, if he is not dead already. If there is a revolution, it will be very short and very peaceful.

At six o'clock in the evening of April 1, he went ashore at Genoa.

The next afternoon he was standing in the showy seventeenth-century Palazzo Rosso, looking at Van Dyck's *Paolina Adorno, Marchesa Brignole-Sale,* thinking about the portraitist's relations with the sitter, and including the exact time in a notebook account of the picture:

> Two-thirty, April 2. Is it because I was predisposed by Van Dyck's adventurous love affair with the Marchesa Brignole or is it without predisposition that I find this adorable? One could not paint a woman, a hand, more supple and more distinguished. One is really taken. . . . She is as straight and light as a bird. Her face has blood and life in it, along with grace and subtlety. A firm little nose, a pinched, turned-up mouth . . . and of a great family.[21]

He also admired, in the same palazzo, Van Dyck's *Geronima Brignole-Sale and Her Daughter,* which he found both beautiful and sad. And in the letter to Moreau he continued to talk about the Flemish master's skill:

> There was more in this great artist than a natural aptitude, my dear friend, as you yourself once remarked. I think that he very often meditated over his subjects and penetrated them in the manner of a poet.

During this entire encounter with the work of Van Dyck he was evidently thinking of himself, of "the picture," and especially of Laura.

His next stopover was Turin, where he discovered more of Van Dyck in the local Pinacoteca and wound up in a pensive mood on the banks of the Po in the April-green Parco del Valentino, near the Castello built during the seventeenth century — in a style charged with reminiscences of Loire Valley châteaux — for Marie-Christine, the widowed French Duchess of Savoy. He described it to Moreau:

> It stands in the midst of trees, all alone. You can say that it is indeed the palace of a widow, sad after a brilliant girlhood, who often looked toward the snow-covered Alps that separated her from France. I sat down on the grass, rather tired after running around town since morning, and fell into one of those woolgathering daydreams of mine with which you are familiar. The place, it should be said, was very suitable.

During the train trip north he doodled a series of vague forms that at last shaped up into a pair of horsemen, and he added the remark that the shadows from the smoke of the locomotive created "an endless horde of nomads galloping endlessly up hill and down dale."[22] He crossed over the

Mont Cenis pass in darkness and suddenly began to hear people speaking French. He consulted his watch more and more often. At thirty minutes past noon, on April 4, he emerged from the snow and began to descend rapidly. By seven-thirty he was at Macon. At seven the next morning he was in the Rue de Mondovi.

He was "stunned," he informed Moreau, by the changes that had occurred in the family during his absence. His sisters, Marguerite and Thérèse, now respectively seventeen and nineteen years old and inclined to "impose themselves," made him feel "terribly diminished." Little brother René was now fourteen and "a young man, being very big for his age." Brother Achille, now twenty-one and a naval ensign, was at sea with his squadron. In the flux of time there seemed to be only one symbol of stability: "Papa is still the same."

Lamothe, encountered shortly after the return, was described as "more of an idiot than ever." This was one of several indications of how much Edgar himself had changed.

6. History, Horses, and Nudes

DURING THE FOUR YEARS since the Exposition Universelle, painting in France had been occasionally zigzagging toward an indiscernible future, occasionally backing up, and mostly marking time. In 1856 the fifty-eight-year-old Delacroix, an urban hermit working more and more feverishly in the nearness of death, had at last been elected to the Académie des Beaux-Arts (after six humiliating defeats by artists of the rank of Schnetz and Cogniet) and hence automatically to the powerful jury of the official Paris Salon. "I flatter myself," he had remarked, "with the notion that I may be useful, for I'll be pretty much alone in my opinions."[1] Ingres had received the news in rage and desolation:

> Today I am ready to break all relations with my century, so much do I find it ignorant, stupid, and brutish — a century that no longer burns incense except before the statues of Baal, and burns it shamelessly.[2]

Also in 1856 the young writer Edmond Duranty, a friend of Courbet's, had launched with an associate an influential if short-lived periodical, *Le Réalisme,* in which he had hinted that it might be a good idea to burn down the Louvre, urged painters to paint what they could see, defined Realism as simply "a rational reaction, stemming from sincerity and work, against charlatanism and laziness,"[3] and complained that, whereas the nineteenth century remained a forbidden pictorial subject, there was an abundance "of

Greek and Roman evocations, of medieval evocations, and of evocations of the sixteenth, seventeenth, and eighteenth centuries."[4]

In 1857 the Salon (which was biennial from 1855 to 1863, after which it became annual again) had displayed a large number of landscapes and so many Oriental scenes that a critic had observed that soon there would be "more camels than portraits" on view. Jules-Antoine Castagnary, a writer who became almost an official spokesman for Realism, had noticed, perhaps wishfully, that history painting seemed to be attracting fewer artists, and that "the human aspect of art" seemed to be replacing "the heroic and divine aspect."[5] Courbet had exhibited his *Girls by the Banks of the Seine,* without much gain for himself or for his cause: the conservative critic Maxime Du Camp had dismissed the picture as "a deflated balloon," and even the well-disposed Castagnary felt that the depicted working-class girls, who were apparently of easy virtue, constituted "a double insult to Paris and to the common people."[6] The suspicions concerning the solidity of the Realist leader's aesthetic and social convictions had been strengthened the following year by his going off to Germany to paint crowd-pleasing stags in forest glens and drink immense quantities of beer with wealthy admirers. And when the time had come to prepare for the next big Paris show, the jury, ignoring the protests of the new member, Delacroix, and apparently feeling that the antiacademics were on the run, had been unusually severe, so much so that the police had had to be called out to disperse a throng of disappointed artists booing under the windows of the Comte de Nieuwerkerke, Napoleon III's director of the fine arts. François Bonvin, a veteran, kind-hearted Realist, had organized, with some success, a small exhibition of rejected works in his studio in the Rue Saint-Jacques. But of course a Left Bank revenge was not a substitute for the entry to the art market provided by official recognition.

Thus the Salon of 1859, which opened on April 15 in the Palais de l'Industrie, a mammoth relic of the Exposition Universelle, found many people, for a multitude of reasons, in a bad humor. Moreover, it was not an exciting affair. Although there were eight pictures by Delacroix, all were small and none was provocative in subject matter, color, or handling. Courbet had not bothered to contribute anything. Another important abstainer was Ingres, who in spite of his interest in controlling the criteria of the jury had been boycotting the exhibition since 1834, when his huge *Martyrdom of Saint Symphorian* had been brutally, mockingly condemned as a piece of crypto-Romanticism. A third of the presented works were routine portraits. History painting still seemed to be descending from heroic actions and noble sentiments toward anecdotes and archaeology — toward what was often little more than nineteenth-century bourgeois genre painting tricked out with carefully reconstituted Greek or Roman costumes, palaces, beds, baths, lamps, and bibelots. Landscape was still dominated by Corot and the Barbizon school. Baudelaire, commenting on the show for the *Revue française,* was dismayed by the number of artists who had "raised stereotypes to the level of being honored as styles," and also by "the indolent, hard-to-stimulate minds" of the Realists, whom he preferred to call Positivists.[7] Paul Mantz, a respected critic on the staff of the *Gazette des Beaux-Arts,* was struck particularly by the vacuity of the religious pictures, which reminded him of the piously macabre story of how the mouth of the dying Louis XIV had gone on quacking meaningless prayers long after the onset of irreversible coma. Zacharie Astruc, a painter, sculptor, and writer who later became a supporter of the Impressionists, was so wearied by a walk through the *palais* that he entitled his review "The Fourteen Stations of the Salon." His cross had been somewhat lightened, however, when — alone among the critics — he noticed a little outdoor scene by Pissarro that had somehow escaped the jury's general rejection of fresh talent.

Degas reported to Moreau that two North African views by Fromentin made everything else in the show look like "brown sauce."[8] But in fact he also admired the Van Dyckish, Leonardesque, velvet-eyed women painted by the fashionable portraitist Gustave Ricard, and he used the assembled works of Delacroix as a point of departure for an important series of investigations into non-Ingresque tone, composition, and color. At the Salon itself, or at home from memory, he did carefully shaded copies in pencil or in pen and wash of the Romantic master's *Ovid in Exile Among the Scythians* and *The Entombment.* During the ensuing weeks and months he broadened his research with studies of eleven more of the artist's pictures: the *Massacre at Scio* and *Hamlet and the Two Gravediggers,* which were then in the Musée du Luxembourg; the *Combat of the Giaour and the Pasha, Christ on the Sea of Galilee,* and *Mirabeau Protesting to Dreux-Brézé,* which were in an exhibition staged by the dealer Louis Martinet in his gallery in the Boulevard des Italiens; the *Pietà* in the church of Saint-Denis-du-Saint-Sacrament; the mural *Attila Followed by Barbarian Hordes Trampling Italy and the Arts* and two other decorations in the library of the Palais Bourbon; the ceiling *Apollo Destroying the Serpent Python* in the Galerie d'Apollon of the Louvre; and *The Entry of the Crusaders into Constantinople,* which was then at Versailles in the Galerie des Batailles, a vast hall in the part of the château that Louis-Philippe had dedicated "to all the glories of France."

Auguste was certainly displeased with this evidence of an intense interest in an artist who had allegedly "ruined himself" by neglecting draftsmanship and yielding to "the passionate element in his ideas." And a

sufficiently sectarian Realist, informed of what was going on, might also
have disapproved, on the grounds that one should avoid imaginary subject
matter. (Confronted one day by an earnest, advice-seeking young man with
a drawing of the head of Christ, Courbet said, "Well, well, Christ. I assume
you have met Him.")[9] But the situation, as its final outcome would prove,
was much too complicated to be disposed of by paternal scolding or partisan
denunciations. Edgar was in the process of recapitulating the history of
nineteenth-century French painting, from Neoclassicism to Romanticism,
from David to Delacroix, and from Lamothe to Moreau, in a way that left
him excitingly, and sometimes paralyzingly, open to both the past and the
future. His notebooks show that he was fascinated by Ingres's Ariosto
illustration, *Roger Freeing Angelica* (then in the Musée du Luxembourg),
during the same period when he was going to a lot of trouble to copy things
like the *Attila* mural and *The Entry of the Crusaders,* and that, although
there is no sign of an awareness of the agitation in the Realist camp, he was
constantly sketching such contemporary material as soldiers, entertainers,
and horses. Moreover, Delacroix was a thoroughly ambiguous influence.
Although he was praised by modernist critics like Duranty and Astruc and
detested by die-hard conservatives like Du Camp, he was plainly not on
Courbet's side in the current artistic civil war; indeed, in his fondness for
literary and historical themes, for the grand manner of the seventeenth
century, and occasionally for the theatrical props of dated melodrama, he
was more of an anti-Realist than most of the Salon academics. Yet he was
not exactly a traditionalist either, for his storytelling bent was paradoxically
— insanely, according to his enemies — accompanied by a delight in attracting attention to the pictorial object itself: to its structure by means of
daring spirals and diagonals, to its surface by means of an inimitable
rugosity, and to its color by means of brilliant, loosely handled hues that
vibrated into unexpected harmonies. He himself objected even to being
called a Romantic, and that left him with no adequate label at all, except
possibly Dissenter.

The search for a studio, in which Prince Soutzo joined actively, eventually produced one on the Left Bank in the Rue Madame, near the apartment the Degas family had occupied during the Louis-le-Grand years, and
here Edgar installed himself, ostensibly to begin work on the final version
of "the picture." (He continued living at home in the Rue de Mondovi.)
His notebooks and letters do not, however, speak of any immediate progress
on the Florentine project. He dreamed of "doing the portrait of a family in
the open air, in the spirit and with all the boldness of [Rembrandt's] *Night
Watch,"* and then dismissed the idea with the comment that "for that one
must be a painter, really a painter."[10] He read Homer, Virgil, George
Sand, Musset's *Comédies et proverbes,* the Rousseauist Bernardin de Saint-

Pierre's *Arcadie,* and the eloquent, emotional, yet typically eighteenth-century maxims and reflections of the Marquis de Vauvenargues. He copied horses from pictures by Géricault and Alfred De Dreux. (The latter, in addition to being the most stylish of the Second Empire equine specialists, was a stimulating link with the English animal-painting tradition, of which Stubbs had been the eighteenth-century glory and Landseer the recent nadir.) He worried about the war in Italy, for he thought that the rapid French triumphs at Magenta and Solferino, on June 4 and June 24, 1859, were too costly. (Napoleon III thought so, too, and soon granted the Austrians an armistice, contenting himself with the annexation of Nice and Savoy and with leading a wildly applauded Paris parade of his victorious troops, drums rolling and bullet-torn battle flags flying.)

Plans for history paintings occupied the head in which backgrounds for the portrait of the Bellelli family were presumably still "trotting around." The *David and Goliath* that had been conceived in Italy was not yet abandoned, although it shortly would be. An idea that eventually reached the stage of being tried out in oil concerned Alexander the Great and the marvelous horse, Bucephalus. (This was evidently one of the reasons for the interest in Géricault and De Dreux.) Other projects, which remained in the state of notes and sketches, featured Hercules and Atlas supporting the globe; Andromache at the wall of Troy, bewailing the death of Hector; the legendary ancient bandit Sciron kicking his victims into the waves; Venus manifesting herself to Aeneas in some shrubbery; and "something with the figure of Vauvenargues."[11] At one point a project to be entitled *Nero Trying Out Poisons on a Slave* appeared to offer an opportunity for what would be greeted as an innovation in the Salon:

> Instead of a fat, bloated Nero, a real butcher, why not a Nero who is a young scoundrel, spruce and elegant? The busts of antiquity represent him as having been handsome, if a little stout.[12]

He dropped the notion perhaps because of second thoughts about its novelty, for in fact the Nero of Racine's *Britannicus* is a young scoundrel — in the dramatist's description, merely "an incipient monster," *un monstre naissant* — and was traditionally played as such by handsome actors. And as recently as 1857 Delacroix had painted, for the greenroom of the Comédie-Française, an imaginary portrait of a spruce and elegant Talma in the role.

Behind all the research there was a patent, naïve enthusiasm that may have softened the heart of Auguste, who was still waiting for his son to get started toward "a beautiful destiny." But there was an equally obvious tendency to forget the warnings of the talkers in the Caffè Michelangiolo against the past that could kill the present, and to absorb too much — too much of the Salon variety of erudition, too much of co-opting Italy, too much of Delacroix or some other hero, and too much of Moreau (whose own talent finally would be half smothered in too-muchness). And the danger ceased to be merely potential when Edgar, probably during the summer of 1859, went to work on a new project, *The Daughter of Jephthah*, whose genesis and execution rapidly turned into a kind of cautionary tale of nineteenth-century historicism.

The idea had emerged from a combination of direct sources with a miscellany of art works, cultural pressures, and other stimuli that may have been only on the fringes of the painter's awareness, without being for that reason less operative. The primary direct source, of course, was the Old Testament account (Judges 11:30–40) of how Jephthah, "a mighty man of valour" about to do battle with the Ammonites, rashly vowed that after his victory he would make a burnt offering to the Lord of "whatsoever cometh forth of the doors of my house to meet me":

> And Jephthah came to Mizpeh unto his house, and, behold, his daughter came out to meet him with timbrels and with dances: and she was his only child. . . . And it came to pass, when he saw her, that he rent his clothes, and said, Alas, my daughter! thou hast brought me very low . . . for I have opened my mouth unto the Lord, and I cannot go back. . . . And she said unto her father, Let this thing be done for me: let me alone two months, that I may go up and down upon the mountains, and bewail my virginity. . . . And it came to pass at the end of two months, that she returned unto her father, who did with her according to his vow . . .

The story, like that of Agamemnon and Iphigenia, mixed pathos, horror, sadism, sexual frustration, and echoes from a primitive tribal era of human sacrifice and jealous gods, in the right proportions for an enduring popularity. During the Renaissance it had been a frequent tapestry theme; in the seventeenth century it had been the subject of a celebrated oratorio by Carissimi and of a painting by Le Brun, Louis XIV's art director, which Degas may have seen at the Uffizi. In the eighteenth century it had inspired oratorios by Handel and a dozen other composers. During the Romantic period it had appealed to Byron, Vigny, Chateaubriand, the young Meyerbeer, and the Ingres disciple Henri Lehmann (whose picture had been condemned by Baudelaire for the absurdly long hands and feet, excessively oval heads, and sundry "ridiculous gewgaws").[13] As recently as 1858, in the form of a cantata, it had won a Prix de Rome for the composer Samuel David (later one of the Second Empire's many light-opera purveyors), and this event may have alerted Degas to the possibilities. Apparently he was already familiar, however, with Vigny's poetic — but very musical and

The Daughter of Jephthah, 1859–1860

visual — version of the tragedy, in which Jephthah, returning to the sound of trumpets and singing, is shattered by a glimpse of his daughter coming from the still distant city:

> *Sourd à ce bruit de gloire, et seul, silencieux,*
> *Tout à coup il s'arrête, il a fermé ses yeux.*

(Deaf to this sound of glory, and alone, silent, suddenly he stops, he has closed his eyes.)

The literary, musical, and pictorial mixture of subject sources was more than matched by a salmagundi of treatment sources. The figure and gesture of Jephthah were derived from the Attila in Delacroix's mural at the Palais Bourbon. Girolama Genga, a minor Renaissance artist from Urbino who had been among Degas's enthusiasms at Siena, supplied the bound, half-naked Ammonite prisoner cut by the frame on the far right, and also the straddling soldier with his back turned. The latter's helmet, however, was borrowed from a work by another now largely ignored Italian, Cesare da Sesto, in the Naples museum. The cloaked man in the foreground on the far left, carrying a banner, came from Mantegna's *Triumph of Caesar* in the Orangery at Hampton Court, via a reproduction. A plaster cast of a fragment from the Parthenon helped to shape the horse's head. Greek vases and Egyptian statuettes were transformed into the booty borne by the soldiers. A study for an early version of the painting carries a significant color reminder: "Almost no green, the hills in a half light as in Delacroix, with a gray sky." [14] Another note says, "For the red of Jephthah's robe remember the orange-red tones of the old man in Delacroix's picture." [15] Other notes refer to the tone values "of the heads in Veronese's *Feast in the House of Simon*," [16] which was then in the Louvre, and to a possible use of a Greek statue of Nike as a model for Jephthah's daughter or one of her companions. Poussin as well as Delacroix contributed to the general color scheme, to the relations between figures, and to the concentration or distribution of the action. In fact, Degas's eagerness to accept influences was such that finally the evolution of the composition did not leave proper occasions for all of them: at one stage, for example, Jephthah or one of his soldiers was to have a billowing cloak borrowed from the hero in *Roger Freeing Angelica,* and there was to be a fine stooping figure derived from a study by Ingres for *The Martyrdom of Saint Symphorian.*

After dozens of notes and some thirty-five preparatory drawings, the project began to become a reality on canvas. In its complexity and its size (nearly six square meters) it was the most ambitious painting Degas would ever undertake. And it was also, as things turned out, one of his biggest disasters. It seems to have advanced quite rapidly during 1859 and part of the following year, and then to have bogged down during a series of rescue operations that may have lasted until around 1864 or even, in a sporadic way, much later. In any event, it was never close enough to completion to be exhibited during its creator's lifetime. The colors, helped by time and reworking, evolved into a warm foreground tawniness that evoked Palestine, stood out vividly against the cool tones of the background, and permitted some agreeable dashes of refinement: the standard-bearer's pink mantle, for instance, and Jephthah's yellow turban and salmon shoe. But the horse never welded its various parts into a semblance of life; most of the borrowed forms continued to look borrowed; and the group of maidens remained floating in an operatic space that needed a printed program to be accepted as the outskirts of Mizpeh. Worst of all — and surprising in the product of an imagination drilled in the writing of coherent classical discourses at Louis-le-Grand — was the failure to correct an obvious, and rather medieval, lack of temporal unity, for the daughter, presumably the one in the white dress, continued to appear to lament a fate of which, at the moment depicted in the foreground, she was unaware. Jephthah alone, with his bowed head and closed eyes in the midst of his suddenly ironical victory parade, was left to express the savage absurdity of the story and its deeply pessimistic philosophical implications, and even he was finally abandoned in a partly botched state.

The wrestling with the Bible and Vigny, the attempt to combine Delacroix with Ingres (an operation now under the slight influence of Chassériau, which Degas reportedly once explained by remarking that he and Chassériau were "both Creoles"),[17] and whatever progress had been made on the Bellelli project were interrupted by a short trip to Italy, occasioned perhaps by a request to escort Thérèse and Marguerite home from a visit they had been making to Naples. Consulting his watch as usual, and recording events this time both in his notebook and for a letter to his brother René, Edgar sailed from Marseilles at ten-thirty in the evening of March 19, 1860. The weather was "magnificent" and his cabin very comfortable: "I really went to bed." At dawn there was nothing but sea and a distant strip of land. At four that afternoon he could make out the northern tip of Corsica. There was talk of something happening in the streets of Rome when Pope Pius IX excommunicated King Victor Emmanuel II of Sardinia for having annexed the papal territory of the Romagna: "It appears that a lot of curious Englishmen are filling the hotels and will rent the windows." (That bit of news, he added, was "for Papa.") At two the next morning he reached Civitavecchia, where most of the passengers disembarked for Rome. At nine he was sailing south again, and at eight that evening he was in the Bay of Naples. His report to René was full of affection for the members of the clan and of pleasure in their returned fondness:

> I was not able to go ashore until eleven o'clock. With my carpetbag in my hand I ran until I was out of breath toward Aunt Fanny's place, on which I fell like a bomb. They were in the hall getting ready to leave. Everyone is in good health. Although Thérèse has become thinner, Marguerite has gained what her sister has lost. Uncle Enrico alone was not there. When I got to his house I surprised him in bed, and "surprise" is not too strong, for he remained for a moment with his mouth open. The next day I went to see Aunt Rosa and [her daughter] Argia. Adelchi [Rosa's son] was in bed with a slight fever, the consequence probably of his excessive dancing. I am sleeping in Grandpapa's room. Poor man, he was not absent during my last visit, and when I arrived he was the first one I kissed. . . . On Wednesday I went out in a carriage with Thérèse and Marguerite, as far as Posilipo. The air was so pure you would have thought it was summer. . . . Marguerite sang last night at Aunt Fanny's, with a quite legitimate success.[18]

The letter was cut short, however, by his haste to get to the museum, where he again enjoyed the Roman mosaics and encaustic paintings.

View of Naples, 1860

During the next few days he sketched outdoors, painted a panorama of Naples in watercolor, and took careful notes on color. Although he tried hard to describe what he was actually seeing, he could not avoid seeing in terms of the pictures he had recently been copying in Paris:

> The sea, a little agitated, was of a greenish gray, with the froth of the waves silver. The sea vanished in vapor. The sky was gray. The Castello dell'Ovo rose in a mass of golden green. The boats on the sand were spots of dark sepia. It was a northern effect, but in it one could feel this country of sunshine, and therein lay all the charm. The gray was not the cold gray of the English Channel, but rather like a pigeon's breast. (How true is the tone of the sea in Delacroix's picture of Demosthenes {at the Palais Bourbon}! I recall that sea while looking at this one.) Through the masses of holm oak appeared the gaps of sea. I've never seen a green so powerful and at the same time so sober, nor a gray of sea and sky so rosy and limpid. It was all very suitable for an epic poem. [19]

On April 2 he left for Florence, where he copied the small Renaissance *Portrait of Barbara Pallavicino,* by Alessandro Araldi, in the Uffizi, and also some more horses, this time from Gozzoli's frescoes in the Palazzo Medici-Riccardi. His most important accomplishment, however, was to bring up to date his preparation for "the picture" by sketching Baron Bellelli, doing a general compositional study, and taking color notes for the family clock, Giovanna's hair, and the baron's beard, hair, and eyelashes.

The final version of what was now definitely *The Bellelli Family* was probably under way in the Rue Madame in Paris by mid-April, and probably finished by the end of the year. The qualifications in these assertions must be stressed, for the painting abruptly and mysteriously disappears from recorded sight after the spring of 1860. After that date the painter never explicitly refers to it in his notebooks and correspondence. He never, so far as is known, showed it to any of the friends with whom he was constantly discussing projects; nor did he ever submit it to the Salon jury, a venture that could have been expected in view of the work's size and quality and of his aspirations during the early 1860s. After his death, in 1917, the big, dusty canvas was discovered rolled up in a corner of his last Montmartre studio, a surprising Second Empire bourgeois relic among the little Third Republic dancers and the nudes in their tubs. It was then exhibited in public for the first time. What had happened during the previous fifty-seven years has of course been guessed at. Toward the end of July 1860, after the proclamation of an amnesty in the crumbling Kingdom of the Two Sicilies, Baron Bellelli was able to return to Naples. It has long been supposed that the picture was delivered to him some months later and remained with the Bellelli family, eventually becoming part of the inheritance of Giulia, until around the turn of the century. Then, reportedly, Degas noticed a hole burned by a lamp, took the rolled-up canvas back from Naples to Montmartre for repairs, and forgot about it.

At first glance all this seems plausible. But it does not fit very well with the fact that in 1918, although Giulia was still alive, the picture was sold as part of the artist's own estate. Nor does it adequately explain the swift oblivion to which the young Edgar of 1860 assigned a work in which he had invested years of dreaming in Naples and Rome, of waiting for Laura in Florence, of defying Auguste's wishes, and of laborious study and execution in Paris. The whole story suggests embarrassment.

Reasons for the embarrassment may have escaped the attention of the average contemporary outsider. The picture is in some ways as derivative as *The Daughter of Jephthah,* although without any traces of Romanticism. The composition is a Neoclassical frieze on a structure of horizontals and verticals formed by the glimpsed doorway, the flat wall, the picture and mirror frames, the table, the mantelpiece, the candle, the clock, and the reflections of another picture and another mirror. Laura and her daughters make a pyramid as Raphaelesque as anything the professors on the Salon jury could have desired. There are hints of the eighteenth-century group portraits the

The Bellelli Family, 1859–1860

English called conversation pieces, and of Ingres's early drawings. The sober colors, the domestic atmosphere, the little dog, and an implied silence broken only by the ticking clock reveal a Dutch genre influence — of which Degas was clearly aware, for he remarked many years later, "In our beginnings, Fantin, Whistler, and I were on the same path, the road from Holland."[20] This enumeration of debts could easily be extended. But it would be misleading, for here the borrowings, unlike those in *The Daughter of Jephthah,* do not remain borrowings. They function, along with nearly everything in the painting, as parts of a symbolic whole that understandably may have made everyone concerned feel uncomfortable. The objects that help to create the Neoclassical structure and the Dutch coziness also announce that the family is sandwiched socially between the upper middle class, specifically the Neapolitan *galantuomini,* and the lower Italian aristocracy, specifically the one invented during the Bonapartist occupation. When the portrait of René-Hilaire is identified, the Raphaelesque pyramid becomes a Degas-dynasty diagram, to which an invisible fifth person can be added, for Laura has become pregnant since rejoining her husband in 1858. When read from left to right the frieze is partly a record of the way the work grew by accretion, and evolved, as Degas's style matured, from formality toward informality. And it is also a series of other time notations: René-Hilaire is in the already dim past, Laura and Giovanna are immersed in the slow sequence of the generations, Giulia is stirring impatiently with personal life, and the baron, with his turning movement, his clock, and his newspaper, is of this moment in Florence. Finally, and most effectively, the layout yields a conversation piece without conversation and a remarkable example of psychological distancing, with the austere, unhappy Laura at one end of the symbolic space and the harassed baron at the other. Remove the charming little girls in their pinafores, and the picture will reveal itself as an image of a sadly unsuccessful nineteenth-century marriage of reason, with the guilty old arranger himself looking down on the scene from the flowered bourgeois wallpaper.

In sum, we are dealing here not so much with portraiture as with a brilliantly concise kind of history painting, devoid of action except for the husband's sudden pivoting to glare, perhaps not unjustifiably, in the direction of his remote wife. (Even pro-Laura viewers must grant that her long-suffering look and her romantic refusal to forget her young lover may have occasionally been exasperating.) Such an interpretation depends, of course, on knowledge beyond the visual information in the work, but a similar remark can be made about a full appreciation of *The Daughter of Jephthah* or any other history painting. You have to know the libretto, and in this instance the Bellelli and Degas families did know it.

Tissot was in Paris during the summer of 1860, and in spite of a bout of illness he was able to see a good deal of his painter friends before returning to Italy. On September 18 he sent Degas a voluminous letter from Venice that is evidence of a significant comradeship between the two artists:

> Dear friend, I wanted to write to you only from Florence, for I thought that only there would I be wonder-struck. But here I've found such things that for the past week I've been like Gastibelza. The wind that blows through the Carpaccio room [in the Accademia] makes me completely crazy. And then I did not want to wait any longer without telling you, better than by word of mouth, how much I thank you and how touched I was by your

warm kindness toward me during the last days, when I was ailing, and by your good-by, which moved me particularly. I'm more than ever pleased to have made the acquaintance of someone like you. But enough of that sort of sentiment. And Pauline? What is becoming of her? By now where are you with her? Is that pent-up passion of yours being spent only on Semiramis? I can't suppose that by the time I'm back your virginity in relation to her will still be intact, and you must tell me all about it. As for me, being a vagabond has many attractions, and novelty continues to please. At Milan the girls are pretty, but here they have an unusual shape. . . . I've met a Monsieur Schwiter, a very amiable baron, who shows you Venice and puts himself and his gondola at your service, with lots of affability.[21]

Gastibelza is the lovelorn, carbine-carrying chanter in Hugo's pseudo-Spanish ballad *Guitare,* which has as a refrain "The wind that blows across the mountain will make me crazy." Baron Ludwig August von Schwiter was a rich, German-born, thoroughly Gallicized art lover and artist, whose most interesting achievement was posing for an oddly Wordsworthian portrait-in-a-landscape executed in 1826 by his friend Delacroix. (At the end of the century the picture became part of Degas's private collection.) And the winking references to Pauline, Semiramis, and virginity were simply the skirt-chasing Tissot's way of mentioning two of Edgar's new works in progress.

The first of these works was a portrait of Princess Pauline von Metternich, whose husband had become the Austro-Hungarian ambassador to France in 1859. Possibly the reason for painting her was a hope that exhibiting the picture at the Salon would bring in wealthy clients for sittings and thus at last launch a career conforming to paternal wishes; more probably, however, as Tissot's letter hints, the reason was a sentiment of the kind Adelaide Ristori had once inspired, for the princess was an attractive woman. Although her snub nose and large mouth kept her from being conventionally beautiful, she was young, slim, witty, and elegant. She once referred to herself as "a monkey, but the best-dressed monkey in Paris."[22] At the Tuileries, at Saint-Cloud, at Compiègne, at Fontainebleau, at Biarritz, or wherever else the court of Napoleon III assembled to amuse itself, she was the principal animator of the fancy balls, amateur theatricals, charades, and occasional games of hide-and-seek. She played the piano expertly, defended Wagner's music against the stuffed shirts at the Jockey Club, sang café-concert songs with irresistible vulgarity, and sometimes smoked a pipe. Her willingness to pose for an obscure young painter she had never met (Auguste did not move in court circles) was, of course, unlikely, and finally unnecessary, for in 1860 she and her husband were portrayed, in the chic *carte-de-visite* format, by the high-society photographer André Adolphe Disdéri. Using the photograph — probably without shame, since the use of such pictures in place of live sitters was already common among painters — Degas had eliminated the husband and one of Pauline's arms. The eventual result, though left unfinished, along with much else during these years, was a candid little portrait with a strong period flavor and a number of implications for the artist's social and aesthetic future. (On stylistic grounds the work has been dated as late as 1875. But the stylistic argument is unconvincing; both Tissot's letter and Disdéri's photograph are evidence for 1860 or 1861, and it is hard to see why Degas would have painted the princess several years after the fall of the Second Empire and her departure from Paris.)

The second picture referred to in Tissot's sexual metaphor was an early state of *Semiramis Building Babylon,* which is commonly and imprecisely also called *Semiramis Building a Town* or *Semiramis Founding a City.* What had set Degas to thinking about the project was a revival of Rossini's thirty-seven-year-old *Semiramide* that opened at the Opéra in the Rue Le Peletier on July 9, 1860, in a French adaptation and with the addition of a wonderfully anachronistic ballet featuring the birdlike dancer Léontine Beaugrand in "La Polka des Niniviennes." The painting, however, was plainly

Semiramis Building Babylon, c. 1861

not meant, as is frequently supposed, to illustrate a scene in the opera. Rossini's Babylon is already in existence when the curtain rises, and his heroine, derived from a play by Voltaire and ultimately from medieval tradition, is a blend of Clytemnestra and Hamlet's mother who is too occupied with adultery, homicide, incestuous passion, and finally suicide to build anything at all. The very different Semiramis of the painting is an idealization of the legendary Assyrian queen mentioned by Herodotus and described in considerable detail by another Greek historian, Diodorus Siculus, as not only the builder of Babylon but also a creature "of surpassing beauty" and altogether "the most renowned of all women of whom we have any record."[23] Degas was undoubtedly thrilled, along with contemporary critics, by the sets in the Rue Le Peletier, which were gloomily monumental and, according to the program notes, based on careful research. He may also have been stimulated, more profoundly, by his own research and by the exciting newness of the archaeological material at his disposition. As recently as 1843 the discovery, by a French expedition at Khorsabad, of the palace of Sargon II had initiated the serious digging up of ancient Mesopotamia, provoked a Parisian mania for anything vaguely "Assyrian," and determined the creation, effective four years later, of the Département des Antiquités Orientales in the Louvre.

The notebooks for around 1860 reveal a deep burrowing into recent scholarly works on the Near East and a tendency, a compulsion, to copy whatever looked conceivably of use — Assyrian reliefs, Islamic Indian miniatures, Greek coins, Egyptian and Persian murals, and even lithographs of modern Greek and Javanese peasants. Surprisingly in view of such academic preparations, the finished painting (the nearly finished, for it too was abandoned) is a triumph of poetry over erudition, a dream of fair ladies in a never-never Babylon. A lovely, serene Semiramis is standing on a terrace that may be part of one of the two palaces Diodorus says she erected so that "she might be able to look down over the entire city and have the keys, as it were, to its most important sections."[24] Accompanying her is a suite composed notably of tall, willowy young women, though there is an old man in the background. With their pensive faces and their high-waisted white, brown, yellow, and red gowns, and despite a cuneiform scroll with which they are provided, the women look less Assyrian than pre-Raphaelite, both in the English nineteenth-century meaning of the word and in the exact sense referring to Auguste's fifteenth-century Italian Primitives. A chariot in which the queen has apparently just arrived is harnessed to a stiffly archaic horse that suggests the early Ingres, Greek vase painting, and the Neoclassicist John Flaxman's popular illustrations for the *Iliad*. (The influence of Delacroix is nowhere visible.) Far below the terrace the Euphrates flows through a vast metropolis of towers and temples that recedes into the misty distance and rises on the right toward patches that may be the embryonic Hanging Gardens, although Diodorus insists that they were the work of a later ruler. Across the river are indications of scaffolding, which remind the viewer that the picture was painted while Paris was being torn apart and transformed by the ruthless Baron Haussmann. The reminder is promptly annulled, however, by the strange airiness of the constructions, the even stranger absence of workmen, the liturgical gesture of Semiramis, and the kneeling maiden who, hand at mouth, contemplates the scene with half-fearful astonishment. Babylon, it appears, is being built mostly by enchantment.

While the painting was taking shape, the history of French visual art continued to zigzag toward the future. Edouard Manet, who in 1859 had failed in his first attempt to exhibit in the Salon, was among the accepted in the spring of 1861, and his energetic, modishly Hispanic *Spanish Singer,* soon nicknamed *Le Guitarrero,* was an immediate critical, official, and popular success. Gautier, reviewing the show in the half-governmental *Moniteur universel,* was particularly enthusiastic:

> *Caramba!* Here's a *Guitarrero* who does not come from the Opéra-Comique and who would cut a poor figure in a lithograph for a sentimental song. But Velázquez would greet him with a friendly little wink, and Goya would ask him for a light for his *papelito.*[25]

The Salon jury, after first "skying" the picture near the ceiling in the Palais de l'Industrie, felt obliged to move it down closer to eye level, and wound up by awarding it, possibly under urging from Delacroix, an honorable mention. Shortly after the opening of the exhibition a delegation of young artists, including Henri Fantin-Latour, Alphonse Legros, and Félix Bracquemond, called on the rising new star to express their admiration in flowery little orations, and eventually they brought around Astruc, Duranty, Champfleury, and Baudelaire. Thus Manet, after a single Salon appearance and certainly to his surprise, found himself annexed by, and even to some extent leading, a nuclear group in what was generally regarded as the opposition to the academic Establishment.

Actually, the group was not at all fierce in its opposition, nor very coherent in its outlook; and its members soon looked like merely transitional figures. Fantin was a scholarly craftsman best known at the moment for his copies of Louvre masterpieces; although never a *pompier,* he became a regular Salon exhibitor of flower pieces and Romantic fantasy scenes based on the music of Wagner, Schumann, and Berlioz. Legros was a pious Burgundian who specialized in low-keyed pictures of monks and peasants at prayer and who finally spent most of his life in England as a professor at the Slade School of Art. Bracquemond had studied under an Ingres disciple and shortly embarked on a successful career as a designer for china manufacturers. As painters, what these artists had in common was little more than the fact that none of them had experienced Italy and that they all liked Courbet, Delacroix, Zurbarán, Velázquez, Goya, and the seventeenth-century Dutch masters.

As good draftsmen, however, which they all were, they also shared an interest in prints, and this, besides making them slightly less dependent economically on the whims of the Salon painting jury, had the effect of strengthening their ties with the writers and reviewers who were partial toward Realism or Delacroix's kind of imagination or innovation in general. Fantin, though not yet at a very high level of professional accomplishment, had been involved with etchings since 1858, when his friend Whistler brought out in Paris the masterly series now known to collectors as the *French Set.* Legros had recently done four plates for Duranty's first novel and, at Baudelaire's suggestion, six scenes from Poe's tales. Bracquemond had worked as a boy for a commercial lithographer, had branched out into etching with the help of the article on the subject in Diderot's *Encyclopédie,* had made further progress by collaborating with Charles Meryon — the greatest etcher of the century, with the possible exception of Whistler — and had already ornamented some of Champfleury's books with frontispieces.

By 1861 they were all eager to launch a serious revival of the needle-and-acid art, which during the previous fifty years had suffered from the invention first of lithography and then of photography. And they were getting encouragement from several sources. Gautier, Baudelaire, and the art critic Philippe Burty offered eloquent journalistic support. A new class of dilettantes, well represented by the Goncourt brothers, offered a market for what was called the fine print, *la belle épreuve,* in order to distinguish it from an ordinary engraved illustration or reproduction. Auguste Delâtre, the expert if sometimes overly complicated printer of Meryon's and Whistler's etchings, supplied advice on inking plates and pulling proofs and allowed his workshop in the Rue Saint-Jacques to become a hangout for painter-printmakers. One of his business associates, the publisher Alfred Cadart, provided at a shop in the Rue de Richelieu, near the Cabinet des Estampes of the Bibliothèque Nationale, a place where prints could be exhibited and, with luck, sold. In 1862, on the initiative of Bracquemond, Delâtre, and Cadart, and with publicity from Gautier and Baudelaire, a Société des Aquafortistes was organized, and the first batch of etchings it issued included one, titled *Les Gitanos,* by Manet.

Degas, although not a member of the delegation that called on the creator of *Le Guitarrero,* had been friendly with Fantin since 1855, when they met in Courbet's nearly deserted Pavillon du Réalisme at the Exposition Universelle. He had become acquainted, perhaps through Fantin, with Bracquemond and Legros some time around 1860. Hence he was aware of the new developments, and clearly affected by them, if only at a distance at first. Without forgetting Italy, he began to show an interest in Velázquez. And without publishing anything, he embarked on a small print revival of his own. His notebooks for around 1860 to 1862 contain the address of Delâtre's workshop and copies of several Dürer engravings; and during the same period he produced eight etchings, with which he tinkered until there was a total of twenty states. Two of the works had as sitters the constantly available Marguerite and René. (Some sixty years afterward the latter could still recall the penetrating fumes of nitric acid in the kitchen in the Rue de Mondovi.) Two others were of a certain Mademoiselle Nathalie Wolkonska, who may have been a distant relative through the Italian branch of the family. The fifth was a copy of the Louvre's version of the *Infanta Maria-Marguerita,* which was then attributed to Velázquez and much admired by antiacademics in reaction against Ingres and Raphael. (Manet also copied it, and Renoir once maintained that "the entire art of painting is in the Infanta Maria-Marguerita's little ribbon.")[26] The three other plates, plus a study done with a lithographic pen, were all portraits of Manet. Although the exact date of the two artists' first encounter is not known, the second half of 1861 seems about right, and Degas recalled the circumstances with his usual precision. He had gone to the Louvre that day to do his etched copy of the *Infanta* and had started to work with his needle directly on the already grounded plate, without the aid of a preparatory drawing, when he was interrupted by a voice behind him, saying, "You have a lot of nerve, and with that method you'll be lucky if you come out with anything."[27]

The story implies, as do the four rapidly executed portraits and the absence of a reciprocal gesture of esteem, that the depth of the friendship in its early stages was not the same on both sides. Manet was not interested in earnest attempts to paint things like *The Daughter of Jephthah* and *Semiramis Building Babylon;* he was evidently pleased to acquire a cultivated, intelligent, well-dressed companion who belonged to the right social category, and that was about the extent of his initial reaction. Degas was obviously more generous and more inquiring; he was ready to admire and scrutinize his new acquaintance, and for good reasons. Manet, although only two years older, was already a Salon exhibitor and, in certain quarters, a hero who seemed capable of taking over the vanguard painting leadership from Courbet. He was also a fine, enigmatic subject for portraiture. With his carefully trimmed chestnut beard, frock coat, top hat, gaiters, cane, plaid vest, and light-colored trousers, he looked like a perfect example, except that he was a bit short, of the Second Empire *grand bourgeois* dandy. He appeared nearly every afternoon around five-thirty on the terrace of the "high-life" (pronounced "eeg-leef" by Parisians) Café de Bade in the Boulevard des Italiens, went to the races, and according to rumor — significant even if exaggerated — spent twenty thousand francs a year. But he worked hard at his art, and he lived soberly in the Rue de Clichy, on the northern edge of the Ninth Arrondissement, with a plump, motherly, musical Dutch mistress (who had been his piano teacher) and their nine-year-old son (who was introduced to visitors as the mistress's brother). After six years of study in the atelier of the conservative Thomas Couture, who dismissed both Delacroix and Ingres as daubers and Courbet as a drunken clown, he had emerged with a brilliantly heretical technique that combined

Edouard Manet, c. 1864

rich blacks with an otherwise light palette, and free handling with an unsettling (to academic sensibilities) indifference to the transitional tones used by conventional painters for modeling forms. The effect, in his most personal work, was like music that constantly skipped the expected intervals of the diatonic scale. Although he had traveled in Italy and never in Spain, he often looked toward the latter country for inspiration. He detested history painting but presumably suffered from his own version of the current crisis over historicism, for his contemporary subject matter was frequently of an exotic or theatrical sort that evaded period questions, and sometimes it was charged with enough reminiscences of the old masters to imply an intended pastiche or even a joke. He was charming, debonair, seemingly self-assured, and yet oddly inclined to arch, twist, or hunch his body into awkwardly boyish postures, to wring his hands, and to narrow his eyes as if to protect them from the light (a habit Delacroix also had). Openly and rather provocatively, he professed an ambition to win as many medals as possible at the Salon and finally the insignia of the Legion of Honor, but he showed no willingness to make his painting style conform to such a program. In this respect as in several others, his ambiguity made him amusingly different from the relatively straightforward comrades Degas had acquired at the lycée and in Rome and Florence.

Old friends, however, were not forgotten, and in September of 1861 he welcomed an invitation to abandon Paris, Mizpeh, and Babylon for a few weeks and visit the country estate of his Louis-le-Grand schoolmate Paul Valpinçon. The property was at Ménil-Hubert, a village east of Argentan, in the rich, rolling, almost overwhelmingly green middle of lower Normandy. Among the famous places in the immediate vicinity were the hamlet of Camembert, where at the end of the eighteenth century the most creamy of Norman cheeses had been created; the bourg of Nonant-le-Pin, where Alphonsine Plessis, destined to become the heroine of *La Dame aux Camélias* and *La Traviata,* was born; the town of Exmes, notable for its remains of ancient Gaul, its medieval church, and its apple trees; and above all the Haras du Pin, the most aristocratic of French stud farms. Here, in a setting of clipped lawns, white fences, forest avenues, and early-eighteenth-century architecture, some of it derived from designs by Mansart, were stabled several hundred stallions, carefully classified by coat and size and as Thoroughbreds, Norman Cobs, Norman Saddlebreds, French Trotters, and Percherons. In addition to all this, the trip offered a general sort of novelty, for though the Degas family had spent some holidays at Saint-Valéry-sur-Somme, a small port on the coast of Picardy, Edgar was not nearly as familiar with northwestern France as he was with Tuscany, Umbria, and the Roman Campagna.

He appears to have prepared himself by imagining, on the basis of British paintings and lithographs and with the help of Henry Fielding in a French translation, that he was going to something like an annex of the land of George Stubbs and Squire Allworthy; and some notes written during a carriage drive from Ménil-Hubert to the Haras du Pin show that — Exmes perhaps aside — he was not disappointed:

> We leave the Argentan road and with Paul move in a straight line toward Exmes. Exactly like England: little and big pastures, all enclosed with hedges; ponds, damp footpaths, green and umber. It's quite new to me, for at Saint-Valéry the countryside seems much less rich and thickly wooded. Up and down continually over green hummocks. We enter a roadway that is almost flooded. A steep path is blocked. I recall the backgrounds of characteristically English paintings. . . .
>
> At the moment I am reading *Tom Jones,* and nothing could be more suitable as an environment for all its personages. We are going up toward Exmes, a typical small town, clean, with its church and its brick houses, and the pastures below as a foreground. I think of Monsieur Soutzo and Corot: they alone could lend a little interest to this stillness. Exmes with its old church. How can anyone live here? On a hilly, wooded road. After half an hour we suddenly enter an alley of a park, with fences. Beginning of autumn. Dead leaves crackle underfoot. One expects horses. We arrive abruptly in a large avenue. . . .[28]

Although he was French enough to be reminded of the avenues at Maisons Laffitte and, when he got to the stud farm itself, of the stables at Versailles, his feeling of being across the Channel came back strongly when he reached the terrace of the main building, from which there was "a view of the countryside exactly like colored English racing and hunting prints."[29]

After his return to Paris he worked for a while on the small oil *Gentlemen's Race: Before the Start,* which is signed and dated 1862, and on at least three other pictures that have a similar subject matter. Eighteen years later, under the renewed influence of Delacroix's works, he reworked the *Gentlemen's Race.* By that time he probably felt equally dissatisfied with its three sister efforts. In 1862, in spite of his many drawings of horses in Florence and his copying of Géricault and De Dreux, he was not yet very certain about the finer points of equine anatomy, and he was still in the process of learning to depict movement. Also, though he was presumably inspired by the traditional October meetings at the Haras du Pin, he was at the moment inclined to see them through the eyes of English animal painters and printmakers, so much so that many art historians have mistakenly supposed that he had actually visited Epsom or one of the other British racing centers. But with all their defects these four canvases merit attention, for they are the first important examples of the long series of oils, pastels, watercolors, and sculptures that the mature Degas would devote to horses — to real, running, jumping, contemporary French horses, not to the stiff, legendary steeds of Thrace, Palestine, and Mesopotamia.

The 1860s were an excellent time and Paris a good place for getting started on such a series. After three centuries of lagging ignominiously behind England in the matter of breeding and racing horses, France was making determined and often spectacular efforts to catch up. In 1833, at a pigeon-shooting gallery in the Ninth Arrondissement, a dozen bankers and wealthy aristocrats had founded La Société d'Encouragement pour l'Amélioration des Races de Chevaux en France, which had quickly gained control of several major tracks and of a fine training establishment at Chantilly, and had then created the French Jockey Club as a social auxiliary. In 1838 the first volume of the *Stud Book Français* had appeared. During the July Monarchy the Société d'Encouragement had endowed several races that became classics, including the Prix du Jockey Club (the local equivalent of the Epsom Derby) and the Prix de Diane (the French Oaks); and in 1856 the City of Paris had ceded a strip of land in the Bois de Boulogne to a Jockey Club syndicate for the development of the instantly fashionable Hippodrome de Longchamp. The year 1863 would see the foundation of La Société des Steeple-Chases, under the presidency of Prince Joachim Napoléon Murat, with a track at suburban Vincennes, and the creation by the Duc de Morny, Napoleon III's half brother, of the Grand Prix de Paris, the winner of which would receive fifty thousand gold francs from the City of Paris, another fifty thousand from the five principal French railway companies, and an objet d'art from the emperor. Finally, in 1865, the years of promotion would pay off in one of the glorious events of the Second Empire: the French horse Gladiateur, after winning the Grand Prix de Paris at Longchamp, would cross the Channel and take the English Triple Crown — the 2000 Guineas, the Derby, and the St. Leger.

Unlike Géricault, Degas was not himself a horseman, and unlike such contemporaries as Courbet and Rosa Bonheur, he was too much of an urbanite to be fascinated by, or even very knowledgeable about, animals in their usual wild or domestic states. By 1862, however, he was already converting these apparent handicaps into aspects of a personal style. In the *Gentlemen's Race,* for example, he is visibly in the process of developing his role of nonparticipant into that of a seemingly casual observer, whose presence is connoted by the movement of some of the riders partway out of the composition. He was already concentrating almost exclusively, as he continued to do, on that specially bred horse, the racehorse. And he was also interested, as he continued to be, in horses as social symbols — and in this his attitude can be regarded as inevitable, given his class origins and the pervasive importance of equestrian affairs in the society of the period. Betting on the races was of course popular and, in a sense, democratically conducted: by the early 1860s pool organizers were competing with ordinary bookmakers, and in 1865 the parimutuel system was invented by an enterprising Parisian shopkeeper. But the races themselves were primarily the sport of the *grande bourgeoisie* and the Bonapartist aristocracy, and racehorse fanciers, in particular the members of the Jockey Club, were notorious for their exclusiveness. A classic at Longchamp ranked with a first night at the Opéra and a Salon opening as a Second Empire occasion; the return from the Bois de Boulogne converted the Avenue des Champs-Elysées into an in-group parade ground.

The lower end of this parade ground was not far from the Rue de Mondovi, and a notebook entry of perhaps the early summer of 1862 indicates a fleeting intention to paint two of the paraders:

> Calash returning from the Bois at six o'clock. On the Pont de la Concorde. Two women — a straw hat, gray like the fruit of the blackthorn, with a light blue feather. The other straw hat is of a burned, golden café-au-lait color, with a gray feather.[30]

Nothing materialized, however, from this rather Impressionist vision of harmonious, comestible hues; and another entry in the notebook reveals an impulse to forget hats and horses for the sake of another Salon subject: "Young girls and young boys wrestling in the plane tree grove, under the eyes of the aged Lycurgus alongside some mothers."[31] This time something did materialize, in the form of the oil the painter finally titled, in the catalogue of the Impressionist exhibition of 1880, *Young Spartan Girls Provoking the Boys.*

The project may have been in his mind a good while, for in the 1880 catalogue the picture is dated 1860, evidently on his authority. (It should be remembered, however, that he was frequently vague, and sometimes plainly mistaken, in the dates he later assigned to his early works.) The idea seems to have emerged from a blending of passages by several authors, all of whom he may have read at the Lycée Louis-le-Grand. Euripides, in one of the tirades in his *Andromache,* scolds Spartan girls for "leaving their homes and, with naked thighs and floating robes, sharing stadia and palaestrae with young men." Plutarch, in his life of Lycurgus, says that the girls wrestled with each other in obedience to a commandment from their legendary lawgiver, that they wore nothing except the traditional peplos open at the sides, and that they gibed at anyone who had not done his duty as a citizen. Pausanias, in his *Description of Greece,* refers to organized fights between boys in a grove outside the city of Sparta. The eighteenth-century Abbé Jean-Jacques Barthélemy, in his fictional, didactic, rambling but long-popular *Voyage du jeune Anacharsis en Grèce,* sums up:

> Spartan girls are not raised at all like those of Athens. They are not obliged to stay locked up in the house spinning wool, nor to abstain from wine and rich food. They are taught to dance, to sing, to wrestle with each other, to run lightly on the sand, to throw with force the discus or the javelin, and to perform all their exercises without veils and half naked in the presence of the kings, the magistrates, and all the citizens, without excepting even the young boys, whom the girls excite to glory by examples, or by flattering praise, or by stinging irony.[32]

To these literary sources one is tempted to add some pictorial material, because the general subject had interested other painters — including Delacroix, who had considered using it in his decoration of the Palais Bourbon and got as far as a robust preparatory drawing. But there is no convincing evidence that Degas was influenced by, or even aware of, the interpretations imagined by his predecessors.

The work in its present (not quite finished) state is in several ways the most intelligible of his history paintings. In the foreground the youngsters are lined up in a simple frieze composition, with a gap that allows Lycurgus and the group of mothers to appear as a second frieze in the middleground. The distant town is of course Sparta, and the great crag on the horizon — according to Degas himself, in a conversation around 1890 with his friend Georges Jeanniot — is the one from which the Spartans hurled malformed or sickly newborn infants. Another reminder of the attempts to improve the Dorian stock is the large number of babies with the mothers being lectured by Lycurgus; and there would have been still another had the artist added a row of pregnant women, which another friend reported he once contemplated doing. There is no sign, in the picture, notebooks, or conversations, of horror at a savage tribal custom, or even of mild disapproval. Nor is there any hint of the shocked indignation that was aroused in the Athenians (if Euripides is accepted as their spokesman) by the scanty attire and the unwomanly behavior of Spartan girls. On the contrary, the whole picture, when read in its broad lines, suggests that the young bourgeois painter, looking back from the unstable society of the Second Empire into this spacious, golden-lit Peloponnesian plain, was strongly attracted by the Spartan system of education and the Spartan sense of belonging to a closely knit community.

The intelligibility begins to waver, however, when, rather than viewing the work as a whole, we focus on the groups in the foreground. Here at first glance we may suppose that a challenge to physical combat is being delivered, and this impression is supported by the notebook reference to "young girls and young boys wrestling in the plane tree grove" and by the substituted title, *Young Spartans Practicing Wrestling,* given by certain museum curators. But the notebook entry obviously does not refer to the surviving final version, and the curator-endowed title cannot be traced back earlier than 1918, when it appeared in a list compiled for a sale of drawings and paintings found in Degas's studio after his death. Moreover, none of the known possible literary sources states explicitly that the Spartan girls wrestled with anyone except one another. So, in fact, we do not know what is going on between the two groups of adolescents, except that, according to the title chosen by the painter in 1880, there is a provocation. Perhaps the girls are taunting the boys for some failure in the Spartan games or trying to incite them into undertaking a glorious exploit. Possibly — and this interpretation has been favored by a number of modern art historians — the confrontation is an allusion to the war of the sexes, and thus in a sense is a remake of *The Bellelli Family,* with the female element once again on the left and the male on the right of the symbolic space.

Ambiguity in the meaning of the main incident is accompanied by ambiguity in the treatment, a stylistic wobble attributable to the fact that the artist is here attempting the nude for the first time, student work excepted, and is determined to renew a genre devalued as art by too many academic life classes, as symbol by too much eroticism of the slick *pompier* sort, and as a representation of reality by too much allegorizing and mythologizing. Although he has adopted the Neoclassicism of David and the young Ingres as his basic idiom, he has avoided the heaviness and the static poses of declining Neoclassicism by depicting Greek adolescents instead of ample Romans and by setting his groups into balletic motion. He has countered both the pompous idealism and the arch pornography of Establishment painters by employing warm flesh color, by putting one of the boys, for example, on all fours, and by equipping each of the girls with an absurdly un-Greek apron instead of a flowing peplos. (The anti-idealism is even more pronounced in the preparatory studies, in which the genitals of the completely undressed girls are drawn with an exactitude that would never have got past a Salon jury.) More subtly and more significantly, he has put expressive, anti-Classical faces on his people, who therefore tend to slip out of the universality of the nude into the specificity of the naked and to become highly individual human beings — irreverent, bare-rumped teen-agers who could just as well be from the alleys of nineteenth-century Montmartre or the suburbs of Naples as from ancient Sparta.

In short, this is a forward-looking picture. It contains hints of what will become a brilliantly idiosyncratic mixture of Neoclassicism and Realism, a passion for movement, and a peculiar way of advancing backward into modernism, with eyes fixed on the past. And Degas appears to have been more than a little aware of all this foreshadowing, for he cherished the painting all his life. In 1880 he was willing to risk hanging it in the contrasting and seemingly inappropriate context of the fifth exhibition of the Impressionists. Like a proud father with an unaccountably favorite child, he was apt in middle age to insist on showing it to studio visitors who had come to see more recent work. Ludovic Halévy's son Daniel, looking back at a long friendship with the painter, wrote, "I can still remember the tenderness he had during his last years for an old canvas, *The Girls of Sparta Challenge the Boys to Wrestle* [*sic*], which he had placed on an easel."[33]

But of course during the early 1860s, when the picture was being worked on (and frequently revised, according to x-ray evidence), contemporary viewers, including members of the Degas family,[34] could not see that it and the other history paintings constituted an apprenticeship for innovation. René, writing to the Musson family in New Orleans on March 6, 1863, reported merely that Edgar was industrious: "He is working furiously, and he thinks of only one thing: his painting. He is working so much he doesn't find time to amuse himself." Auguste, on November 21 of the same year, summed up for his American relatives the doubts he was beginning to have about his eldest son's career: "Our Raphael is still working but has not produced anything that is really finished, and the years are passing." Not until April 22, 1864, did the more generous René, in another report to New Orleans, display an inkling of the actual situation, and even then he could not resist adding, with the help of a tag line in English, an echo of his father's opinion of their Raphael: "What is fermenting in that head is frightening. For my part, I believe — I am even convinced — that he has not only some talent but even some genius. Will he, however, express what he feels? *That is the question.*"

7. Bonjour, Monsieur Degas

AUGUSTE WAS RIGHT about the years that were passing, and Edgar, seeing a thirtieth birthday on the horizon and comparing himself with his co-opted young contemporaries, must have understood his father's misgivings about the future. By 1863 Bonnat was a Salon regular, with two medals awarded by admiring juries and two large canvases purchased by the imperial government for provincial museums. Moreau was completing the first of his characteristic mythological fantasies, *Oedipus and the Sphinx,* which, after creating a sensation at the Salon of 1864, was bought for eight thousand francs by Prince Napoléon, the emperor's cousin and the owner of a spectacular new Pompeian town house in the Avenue Montaigne. Tissot was a rising portraitist and storytelling painter whose *Meeting of Faust and Marguerite* had been acquired for the Musée du Luxembourg. Delaunay was almost a pillar, well decorated, of the Establishment; and the sculptor Chapu, no longer the timid Monsieur l'abbé of the Villa Medici, was turning out caryatids for the façades of Haussmann's new Paris.

Meanwhile, the unexhibited, unsold, and frequently unfinished pictures were accumulating in the Rue de Mondovi and the Rue Madame. The exclusion from the academic fine arts system, and from the economic circuits of which it was the aesthetic and institutional superstructure, was plainly not accompanied by any of the satisfaction and motivation an artist may derive from being a committed outsider. And yet, as his family may have noticed, Degas was reluctant to do anything definite, such as submitting something for the official annual show, that might have helped him to become a committed insider. What was "fermenting in that head" often tended to substitute a vague elsewhereness for the average Second Empire painter's stark out or in.

A good example of the tendency occurred in the spring of 1863. In April the Salon jury, expressing a self-confidence that would ultimately become suicidal, rejected more than four thousand pictures and pieces of sculpture, some of which were presented by people who had won honorable mentions in previous exhibitions. Napoleon III, impressed by the volume of protests and eager to play the role of a protector of artists, thereupon decreed that the rejected works could be exhibited in another part of the Palais de l'Industrie, at the same time as the accepted ones, in order "to let the public judge the legitimacy of these complaints." The resulting Salon des Refusés opened on May 15 and quickly became an attraction for crowds of merry philistines, a target for wittily abusive critics, a theme for a comic revue at the Théâtre des Variétés, and, in spite of the mockery, an excellent thing for the antiacademic cause. Many young painters discovered the propaganda value of aesthetic shock and felt the excitement of belonging to an organized opposition. That the organization was an ad hoc one set up by a paternalistic dictator did not much matter. Manet provoked a useful scandal with his *Déjeuner sur l'herbe,* a translation of Giorgione and Raphael into modern French (and probably a spoof aimed at historicists), and emerged as the undisputed, if still somewhat unwilling, leader of what was beginning to look like a movement. Whistler attracted attention as well as laughter with the first of his "symphonies," *The White Girl.* Among the other noteworthy *refusés* were Fantin-Latour, Bracquemond, Legros, Camille Pissarro, the Dutch pre-Impressionist Johann Barthold Jongkind, the future Impressionist Armand Guillaumin, and the twenty-four-year-old Paul Cézanne, who was still working in the awkwardly Romantic Baroque idiom he later referred to as his *manière couillarde* (fat-head manner). Degas was of course not on the list, since he had sent nothing to the Salon jury. Nor, more surprisingly, does he seem to have been at all interested in the epochal event that was under way in the Palais de l'Industrie, only a few blocks from the Rue de Mondovi, for there is not a single reference to it in the notebooks he was filling during these months.

The elsewhereness was exemplified again the following winter, when Fantin-Latour produced his large, much noticed *Homage to Delacroix.* Although painted in an academic Dutch style that would win acceptance at the Salon in the spring of 1864, the picture was plainly intended as an anti-Establishment manifesto, for it showed Manet, Whistler, Baudelaire, the novelist Champfleury (an ardent defender of Courbet's Realism), Duranty, Bracquemond, Legros, the painter Albert Balleroy, the sculptor Charles Cordier, and Fantin himself assembled around a self-portrait of the great Romantic, who had died the previous August. Degas was not included, in spite of his now close relationship with both Manet and Fantin and his admiration for Delacroix. Evidently he was not thought of as counting in the current battles of the Paris art world.

That he was beginning, however, to have a certain reputation in that world is implied by one of Duranty's novelettes, *La Simple Vie du peintre Louis Martin,* which evokes, although not published until 1872, the period of the Salon des Refusés. In this oddly contrived semidocumentary the fictional Martin, a young Realist in love with the daughter of a *pompier,* meets many real, succinctly characterized contemporaries, among them the "professorial" Fantin, the "powerful," naïvely vain Courbet, and the equally self-assertive Manet, "flinging his ego in all directions, yet doing so with a gaiety, a liveliness, an optimism, and a desire to advance the new that made him very attractive." Degas, encountered by Martin in the Louvre copying and vehemently defending Poussin (which seems to date his version of *The Rape of the Sabines* to around 1862–1863), is portrayed both favorably and ironically:

> An artist of a rare intelligence, preoccupied with ideas, which seemed strange to most of his fellow painters. Because of a lack of method and transitions in his active, constantly boiling brain, they called him the inventor of social chiaroscuro.[1]

We are not told what the ideas were, nor are we given any examples of the lack of transitions, and it is probable that the story, given its publication date, condenses and places in the past some opinions accumulated by Duranty over several years. (He may not have been personally well acquainted with Degas before about 1865.) But both his praise and his adverse criticism are too consistent with the judgments of Auguste and René to be considered entirely anachronistic.

Clearly, then, Edgar in his late twenties was a disconcerting young man. From a number of family letters it is equally clear, however, that when the appropriate occasion presented itself, he could be charming and generous — generous in the rare fashion that involves giving one's time and self. And during this period the American Civil War presented, because of a series of Confederate disasters, such an occasion. In April 1862 New Orleans was captured by the Union fleet under Admiral David Farragut; in May the municipal administration was taken over by a stupidly ferocious Northerner, General Benjamin Butler; and for the next six months the normally easygoing city was subjected, if not quite to the reign of terror described by partisan Southern writers, certainly to one of the roughest, most humiliating régimes in local history. "Butler the brute," as he was called, was particularly eager to cut the high-toned ladies of the Vieux Carré down to size; so one of his many repressive orders, keenly resented by chivalrous citizens, was that if any female should "insult or show contempt for any officer or soldier of the United States, she shall be regarded and shall be liable to be treated as a woman of the town plying her avocation." By the end of the year, though Butler had just been replaced by a more civilized Northern general, the situation was such that Michel Musson, Célestine Degas's older brother and still a New Orleans cotton merchant, decided to send his wife, Odile, and two of their daughters, the nineteen-year-old Estelle and the twenty-four-year-old Désirée (Didy to the family), to Europe. (A third daughter, Mathilde, chose to stay home with a newly acquired husband.) Estelle in particular needed a change of atmosphere: in January she had married Lazare David Balfour, a young captain in the Confederate Army; on October 4 he had died at Corinth, Mississippi, in one of the bloodiest battles of the war; and three weeks later she had given birth to a baby girl.

After a delay of several months, apparently due to an illness that made it difficult for Odile to walk, the three women and Estelle's baby reached Paris, and Edgar immediately began to show the good side of his character. On June 24, 1863, he wrote to his uncle Michel:

> Your family arrived last Thursday, June 18, and is now entirely our family. One could not be on better or more simple terms. . . . Aunt Odile is walking extremely well. . . . Didy is completely her assistant. As for Estelle, poor little woman, one cannot look at her without thinking that in front of that head there are the eyes of a dying man. Greetings to good, pretty Mathilde.[2]

On the same day Didy wrote that her painting cousin, "who we had been told was very brusque," was in reality "full of attention and kindness."[3] He continued to be so during the following eighteen months, most of which the visitors from Louisiana spent, at the suggestion of Odile's doctor, in southeastern France at Bourg-en-Bresse. On December 31, 1863, Marguerite wrote from the Rue de Mondovi to New Orleans:

> Edgar left here the day before yesterday [for Bourg] to share the festivities of the new year [in fact, Twelfth Night] with them, and he is so gay that he'll amuse and distract them a little. He took with him a lot of crayons and paper in order to draw Didy's hands in all their aspects, for such pretty models are rare.[4]

Five days later Didy completed the news with a letter from Bourg:

> We had been expecting Edgar, who did not arrive, and we had lost all hope of seeing him when, around nine o'clock this morning, he arrived, loaded with packages up to his neck. Mother and I were still at Mass. He got out of his carriage and when the Mass was over came in and tapped Mother on the shoulder. I was in the front row and saw nothing, and so was very surprised on returning to our house to find Master Edgar busily emptying a little trunk full of gifts, toys, candy, marrons glacés, etc. . . . He has done several sketches of baby Joe [Estelle's daughter] but isn't happy with them, since it's impossible to make her hold still for more than five minutes.[5]

Plainly he had succeeded in his aim of amusing and distracting the three unhappy women.

Shortly after this expedition to Bourg, at the moment when several of his friends were manifesting their anti-Classicism in the *Homage to Delacroix,* he paid a third and last visit to Ingres, who was now eighty-three but still very active. The occasion was a one-man show organized by the artist himself in the studio on the Quai Voltaire; and Degas, reminiscing nearly fifty years later,[6] was able to recall vividly having seen, among other things, the *Homer and His Guide,* "the subject of which the master explained to us," then the *Portrait of Madame Moitessier Seated,* "that lovely Juno" (a reference to an ecstatic description by Gautier), and finally the *Turkish Bath,* which had been commissioned by Prince Napoléon, returned in 1860 as indecent, and recently changed from a square to a round format in imitation of the *tondi* of the Italian Renaissance. A companion during the visit, variously referred to in the later accounts as a friend, as someone who knew their host, and as "an idiot" (all of which suggests Lamothe), was profuse in congratulations for "having translated antiquity with so much perspicacity." The compliments were accepted "complacently" until the alleged idiot, having at last noticed the *Turkish Bath,* pronounced it "ah, another genre," whereupon Ingres stiffened and said, "Monsieur, I have several brushes." Degas seems to have greatly admired the paintings on view, and he found the remark about brushes "delicious."

By this time he was involved in another history project, a small work executed in a thin oil medium on paper and called, on its completion in 1865, *War Scene in the Middle Ages.* The project at one point in its evolution may have been more specific than this title indicates, for in the catalogue of the Degas post-decease sale of 1918 the picture is listed, presumably on the authority of a document found in the artist's studio, as *The Misfortunes of the City of Orléans.* There is no relevant misfortune, however, in the recorded medieval history of the French town, so, in the light of the visit of the Musson women to France, the suggestion has been made that the original title must have been *The Misfortunes of New Orleans.* The ingenious and not implausible hypothesis is that during the studio inventory in 1918 the words *la Nouvelle-Orléans,* which the painter in his correspondence sometimes shortened to *la Nlle Orléans,* were misread as *la Ville d'Orléans.* But this suggestion is also open to objection, for x-ray analysis of the painting has not produced any evidence of significant reworking, and the notion that the nineteenth-century American town was originally the setting is contradicted by the survival of preparatory drawings in which the soldiers are armed with the same bows and arrows and clad in the same roughly fifteenth-century costumes they have in the finished version. We are finally obliged, in speculating about the creative process that yielded this puzzling combination of images and titles, to be a bit more indirect than is customary in such matters — and at the same time to keep in mind Duranty's description of a young man whose "boiling brain" lacked "transitions."

The process appears to have begun, if such things can be said to have definable beginnings, on a day in August 1858 when Degas, copying Pontormo's *Visitation* in the entrance courtyard of the Annunziata at Florence, was impressed by one of Andrea del Sarto's neighboring frescoes, *The Miracles of San Filippo Benizzi,* in which men and women are distributed around a tree in various cowering, prone, and blindly fleeing attitudes after a stroke of lightning. The next element, at the Paris Salon of 1859, may have been a work called *The Evils of War,* painted by a Belgian artist, Joseph Lies, who was a close follower of the historicizing Leys by whom Tissot had been influenced. Degas undoubtedly saw the picture during his several visits to the exhibition after his return from Italy, and he may also have read Baudelaire's description that summer in the *Revue française:*

> *The Evils of War!* What a title! The vanquished prisoner, prodded painfully by the brutal victor behind him; the bundles of booty in disorder; the young girls insulted; a rush of unhappy people bleeding, crushed; the powerful cavalryman, red and hairy . . .[7]

In June of the same year there occurred the slaughter at Magenta and Solferino, the impact of which on Edgar's sensibility we have already noticed. In 1863 the reality of the evils of war was again brought home when Aunt Odile and her daughters, with their stories of the cruelty of General Butler and their memories of Estelle's dead husband, reached the Rue de Mondovi. At about the same time Degas was immersing himself in an ancient example of the military mistreatment of women by copying Poussin's *Rape of the Sabines;* and in 1864 he was supplied with a minor variation

War Scene in the Middle Ages, 1865

on the theme by his friend Tissot, who was at work — in the meticulous manner of Leys and Lies — on a supposedly sixteenth-century incident entitled *Attempted Abduction.* Admittedly, none of this, with the possible exception of Andrea del Sarto's fresco, was a source in the sense in which Mantegna, the Bible, Delacroix, and Vigny were sources for *The Daughter of Jephthah.* But that simply strengthens a suspicion, already warranted by the confusion over the title, that the normal methods of art history are largely irrelevant to a proper understanding of *War Scene in the Middle Ages.* Apparently we are dealing here with a fused, displaced response to many stimuli, and hence with a purely imaginary history painting, a symbolic apparatus in which looking for traces of medieval Orléans or of a Union rifleman would be like looking for a Heinkel bomber in Picasso's *Guernica.*

At the literal, storytelling level the picture is perfectly legible. In the upper left background smoke is billowing from a town that has just been sacked and set afire. In the foreground lie the naked bodies of four women who have evidently been raped and perhaps murdered. Riding away toward the right are three cavalrymen, one of whom has flung a woman across the front of his saddle, and another of whom has turned, like an ancient Parthian, to fire an arrow from his longbow into the naked, tortured body of a woman who has been attached by one arm to a tree. Near her are three more naked women, two of them attempting desperately to escape and the other bending over in agony. A lowering sky, a bleak plain, and the light from the blazing buildings add to the atmosphere of a Dantesque inferno. Arguably, one could not ask for a more straightforward piece of propaganda against war, and yet more than one modern critic, aware of the masquerading to which a sexual preoccupation may be prone, has wondered whether antimilitarism is the only, or even the main, subject of the painting. As in a dream or a phantasm, everything is overdetermined: the women are all young, lovely, soft, and unaccountably nude, and the soldiers are mysteriously, gratuitously savage. Again, the principal figures occupy the edges of the composition, with the left side female and the right side male; and now the implied alienation in *The Bellelli Family* and the playful provocation in the *Young Spartan Girls* have become open, sadistic aggression. Moreover, although in the picture at its literal level we are obviously supposed to sympathize with the female side, we cannot be quite sure of what, given the exciting excessiveness of the male cruelty, we are authorized to feel at other, more symbolic levels. Nor can we be certain that Degas did not sometimes think of reversing the situation, for in one of his preparatory drawings the archer is a naked woman. This may, of course, have been the

Study for *War Scene in the Middle Ages,* 1865

result of an impulse to make use of a model who happened to be in the studio, but that does not explain why he made this particular use of her. Indeed, his whole attitude toward these magnificent nudes seems to have involved transference, so much so that eventually they became merely a series of possibilities, transformable from war victims into dancers and prostitutes, or simply into housewives washing themselves and combing their hair.

During the first half of the 1860s, portraiture, though not of the commercial sort that might have stilled paternal doubts, was taking a growing amount of his time and providing him, as did his interest in horse races, with opportunities to escape from the academic past into contemporary reality. A pleasant example datable to about 1863 is a likeness of Bonnat wearing an elegant gray top hat and looking, Degas remarked, "like a Venetian ambassador."[8] (He probably meant the fifteenth-century kind painted by Gentile Bellini.) In the spring of 1863 Thérèse was engaged to marry Edmondo Morbilli — with special papal dispensation, since they were first cousins — and the event was marked by Edgar with a

Léon Bonnat, c. 1863

solemn, rather Spanish portrait in which she is wearing, as if about to take the train, a sensible gray skirt, a black lace shawl, and a little Second Empire hat secured by an immense pink ribbon tied beneath her chin. There is a reminder, in a Neapolitan panorama looming hazily through the window (a copy of the 1860 watercolor), of her destination and of her future as an Italian duchess. The subdued colors and somewhat stiff formalism of these two pictures can be seen yielding, around 1864, to something more warmly expressive in a small study of the mobile face of Enrique Mélida y Alinari, a Spanish genre painter who was Bonnat's brother-in-law. And then, with a suddenness that speaks of a leap from a plateau of learning, we come on a series of portraits that violates nearly all the conventions of the contemporary Ecole des Beaux-Arts — and also the more general rule that to be successful a portraitist should accept his sitters' opinions of themselves.

Perhaps the first in the series (the exact sequence is hard to determine, owing in part to Degas's cavalier handling of dates) is *The Lady in Gray,* in which the unknown, placidly good-natured subject, seemingly unaware that she is about to be immortalized in pigment, is caught with an incipient, self-depreciating grin on her face and in the process of shifting on her hips preparatory to rising from her sofa. In *Estelle Musson Balfour* and the watercolor *Madame Musson and Her Two Daughters,* both painted in Bourgen-Bresse early in 1865 as farewell gifts, witty offhandedness gives way to a compassion that unmasks dejection. Estelle, her bowed head silhouetted against a wintry background of barren trees, does indeed appear, as her observant cousin had noticed in 1863, to be looking into the eyes of her dying husband, and in the group portrait the three lonely exiles convey their sadness almost as poignantly by means of the sagging inertness of their bodies. They are literally weighed down by care.

Corporal expression is also prominent in *Manet Listening to His Wife Play the Piano,* which was completed probably in 1865. Here the urbane, snappily dressed habitué of Longchamp and the Café de Bade is represented in an extraordinarily inelegant position, with one foot drawn up on the white sofa he is occupying, one hand stuffed into a trouser pocket, and the other hand jammed through his beard into a corner of his mouth. All these nervous contortions, combined as they are with a definitely anguished look on his face, strongly suggest that he is not enjoying whatever his wife (and former mistress), Suzanne, in the right half of the composition, is playing, and this is supported by testimony that he was largely without taste in music and was usually bored by it. Also, the scene intimates that the household was less than tranquil, and this is also attested to by biographical fact, for Manet, though nominally a faithful husband, was a notorious flirt,

OPPOSITE: *Madame Michel Musson and Her Two Daughters,* 1865

Manet Listening to His Wife Play the Piano, c. 1865

and his overweight wife was not much competition for some of his women friends.

In sum, this whole double portrait is loaded with explosive innuendos. But presumably its principal subject at first found the image of himself amusing (it was uncannily lifelike, according to people who knew him well), since he accepted the picture as a gift and in exchange gave Degas a recent still life. And then the innuendos exploded. One day Degas walked into Manet's studio and saw that the right third of the portrait, including all of the piano and half of Suzanne, had been slashed out. He picked up the mutilated work, walked out without saying au revoir, and sent back his friend's still life with a curt note: "Monsieur, I am returning your *Plums.*" He also attached a new strip to the slashed canvas, with the intention of repainting the piano and the missing section of Suzanne. He

A Woman with Chrysanthemums, 1865

soon discovered, however, as he remarked later in telling the story, that "one could not stay vexed with Manet for very long,"[9] so he never got around to repairing the damage.

During these same eventful months of 1865 he completed *A Woman with Chrysanthemums,* which might be more appropriately called *Chrysanthemums with a Woman,* since the huge, luxuriant bouquet occupies the left two thirds of the composition and makes the musing, elfin sitter look as though she were there by accident, like someone in an uncropped photograph. Although she was apparently a certain Madame Hertel, nothing is really known about her except that Degas obviously liked her intelligent face and that, several years after doing her portrait, he jotted down two addresses for her, one in Montmartre and the other in Rome, where she was staying with a daughter, the Contessa Hélène Falzacappa. And the sources of the off-center presentation are equally uncertain, for although works by Van Dyck, Courbet, and Millet have been suggested, the first two (*Self-Portrait with Sunflower* and *The Trellis*) do not at all resemble *A Woman with Chrysanthemums,* and the third (*The Bouquet of Daisies*) appears to have been painted four years after Degas's picture. The only sure things about this bizarrely unconventional portrait are that the asymmetrical arrangement has the paradoxical effect of attracting attention to the woman and that this piece of subtlety was achieved in two widely separated stages. A deciphered date and a laboratory examination have revealed that the Baroque bunch of flowers was originally painted in Italy in 1858 as merely a still life (one of the two in Degas's entire career) and then reworked around 1865 for the sake of tucking in Madame Hertel. During the intervening seven years the academic frequenter of the Villa Medici had begun to have quite a lot of what Duranty called "ideas," and he had also begun to see that the unexpected positioning of images could be, like dissonance in music, a strongly expressive and even a signifying device.

Some of the ideas concerned himself. In an unfinished self-portrait of around 1863, plainly if somewhat surprisingly roughed out under the influence of Courbet's Romantic self-dramatizations (for example, the one called *The Man with a Pipe*), he looks as though he had intended to illustrate Pascal's comments on the "hateful me," or perhaps René's impression of a brother who was harboring "frightening" notions. In any event, he was evidently going through a psychologically difficult period, for he appears with his studio blouse unbuttoned on a bare chest, his hair and beard untrimmed, his head thrown back as if in pain or disgust, his eyes half closed, and what seems to be a film of sweat on his face. And the difficulty, whatever it may have been, lasted long enough to yield another version of the picture (which may have been a preliminary study), in a more frontal pose but with much the same air of mixed funk and defiance.

About a year later, in *Valernes and Degas,* he seems to have emerged from his funk, though not to have given up his defiance. Now he represents himself as a carefully trimmed, combed, and dressed *grand bourgeois,* seated in front of a view of Rome and staring straight at the viewer with an aggressive suggestion of being bored stiff. The only hint of self-doubt is the hand across the chin, and this can be interpreted in a variety of other ways — as a sign of mild astonishment, evidence of musing, a conversationalist's mannerism, or simply a trick for making a pose look informal. The Parisian critic Georges Rivière, who became well acquainted with the artist in the 1870s, later wrote of this picture:

> The portrait of Degas with his friend Evariste de Valernes . . . is extremely interesting, for it shows one of its author's habitual gestures. Very often

. . . reflecting on what he was going to say or do, Degas would put his hand on his chin in this fashion, as if he felt some hesitation about making a decision or formulating his idea.[10]

This is enlightening, but it overlooks the painter's use of almost the same gesture in the kneeling maiden marveling at Babylon, in Manet listening to Suzanne at the piano, in Madame Hertel, and in half a dozen other pictures. Apparently it could mean whatever he wanted. Or perhaps it was mostly a way of projecting himself into his work — a sly sort of signature.

In this double portrait the hand on the chin and the accompanying look acquire an extra psychological nuance from the personality of the second sitter and the nature of his relationship with Degas. Evariste de Bernardi de Valernes, the third son of a spendthrift provincial nobleman, was born in 1817 at Avignon. His eldest brother, a poet and a musician, had died young. The second brother, an actor and an opera singer, had married an American girl for love and lived on such a scale that finally the

Valernes and Degas,
c. 1864

ancestral seventeenth-century château had had to be sold. Evariste had then married the beautiful, consumptive daughter of the family concièrge and, with her and the small income left to them, had come up to Paris to study painting. By 1864, although he had worked for two years in Delacroix's atelier and made a début at the Salon of 1857, he was obviously in the process of squandering his life, much as his brothers and his father had squandered their inheritance. His talent was far from robust; his watered-down Romantic style was hopelessly out of date; and he himself was an incorrigible dreamer and procrastinator — a "seigneur," according to one of his close acquaintances, "for whom it was always six o'clock when it was really eight." [11] In brief, he does not seem to have been the sort of man who would attract the enduring devotion of the reputedly tough-minded Degas. Yet that is what he did. They appear to have met for the first time at the municipal museum of Lyons in 1855 and to have become close friends immediately, in spite of the seventeen-year difference in their ages. Shortly after his return to Paris that fall Edgar wrote to the older man:

> I very much believe that a new friendship between people chosen according to our hearts can make us better, which is to say more truly happy. One can derive an immense comfort from it. What a moving thing friendship is, in its mystery and its diversity! [12]

He had shared his enthusiasm for Rome with Valernes (hence the background in the painting), and nearly forty years later he wrote to him: "I think of you constantly, with the most affectionate feelings." [13] As the decades went by and their fortunes diverged, a touch of embarrassment and pity may have altered Degas's original attitude, but there were certainly reciprocal elements in such a long, unbroken association. The picture under discussion, then, with its noticeable contrast between an ambiguous tension and an oddly cheerful slackness, can be regarded as a kind of friendship-cult object, a votive offering by an ego to its alter ego.

Before the offering was finished, Degas was at work on the *Self-Portrait Saluting,* the personal importance of which is implied by the fact that he went on retouching it until apparently some time in 1865. Several critics have suggested that his idea was to produce a bourgeois Parisian reply to Courbet's rural *Meeting* of 1854, which had been nicknamed *Bonjour Monsieur Courbet* because of its trio of doffed hats. This, for a number of good reasons, is doubtful. The hat-in-hand pose was common in Second Empire photographs, and it had been occasionally used by painters and draftsmen since about the middle of the First Empire, when an early version of the eventually ubiquitous stovepipe began to replace the surviving wig of the ancien régime and the Napoleonic cocked hat as a symbol of masculine

Self-Portrait Saluting, 1863–1865

identity and status. Ingres's 1818 drawing of Turpin de Crissé, for instance, is very similar to the *Self-Portrait Saluting,* although its availability as a direct influence cannot be proved. Moreover, Degas was obviously quite capable of having thought up the pose and the accessory by himself, for he had been interested in headgear since adolescence, when he had noticed the delightful old hats worn by his father's art-collecting friends; and he had already portrayed himself in a soft hat, his brother Achille and their grandfather with seamen's caps, and Manet, Bonnat, and Valernes with their tall stovepipes.

Even so, a comparison of *The Meeting* with the *Self-Portrait Saluting* is instructive. Both pictures are author-starring theatrical productions that have to be approached warily as biographical documents; both are social studies; both are complex psychological revelations. But there are significant differences in the kind of theatricality represented and in the social and psychological content. The unsubtle Courbet, with his gaiters, knapsack, pilgrim's staff, and jutting Assyrian beard, vigorously hams the role of an itinerant limner, much as he hams other roles in the series of self-puffing works he painted after *The Meeting;* and he humorlessly presents himself as a still essentially Romantic artist accepting the homage of a patron. Degas is a suave man-about-town, saying *bonjour* to the world in general and to himself in particular. There is no hint of the sunburned woolgatherer who dreamed of retiring one day to the monastery in Assisi. Gone are the charcoal stick and other props that helped to provide the Edgar of 1855 with a personality borrowed partly from Ingres and Bronzino. Gone too are the trussed look and the formal pose; they are replaced by an up-to-date bagginess in the costume, by one hand resting on the hip and the other carrying gloves (a fashion that came in during the last years of the Second Empire), and especially by the hat-doffing gesture, which was made a bit more sweeping by some visible reworking. A viewer may still detect traces of spleen, boredom, and brusqueness in the unsmiling face; and he may remark the continuing presence of the see-yourself-seeing-yourself imp who had haunted the road from Rome to Tuscany and dictated some of the letters to Moreau from Florence. Most people, however, would probably agree that the strongest impression is that of irony. Unlike Courbet, Degas seems to be distancing his performance, to be an actor playing an actor. Indeed, he can easily be supposed to be making fun of himself in the glass, for he is mimicking a self-presentation common among the vaudeville entertainers and the café-concert singers of the period. A possible inference — in line with the theories of modern role psychology — is that after the ten years of anxious introspection recorded in his earlier self-portraits and his notebook entries, he has decided that the scrutiny is foolish and the thing to do is to act a self. Such an inference is not, of course, at all susceptible to proof, but it is significantly consistent with much of his future behavior, with a tendency toward intellectual dandyism widespread in the nineteenth century, and in particular with three facts that are hard to dismiss as being unrelated.

The first of these facts is that after the final retouching of the *Self-Portrait Saluting,* presumably early in 1865, he never again, in the remaining fifty-two years of his life, represented himself in a painting or drawing (though he did pose for photographs). The second is that at least by May of that same year he was out of the family apartment in the Rue de Mondovi and installed by himself in a studio at 13 Rue de Laval (later the Rue Victor-Massé), in the Ninth Arrondissement two blocks from Place Pigalle and the southern edge of Montmartre. The third is that after finishing the *War Scene in the Middle Ages,* also some time before May 1865, he never again attempted, or even projected in his notebooks, a history painting. Although one can think of a plausible separate explanation for each fact (and especially for the dropping of history painting, which will be discussed in the next chapter), the three taken together suggest the end of identity worries and the emergence, or invention, of an independent persona.

8. Into the Present

IN THE SPRING OF 1865 the Salon jury, whose membership had been slightly altered after the uproar over its severity in 1863, was relatively merciful, at least toward some of the future Impressionists and their fellow travelers. Although Cézanne was again a *refusé,* Manet, Pissarro, Fantin, Morisot, Monet, Sisley, and Renoir were among the accepted. So, for the first time, was Degas, who had emerged from his elsewhereness long enough to submit his *War Scene in the Middle Ages* for approval. The hanging committee, perhaps confused by the thin oil medium on paper, classified the work as a pastel and banished it among the miscellaneous drawings, where it was ignored by both the general public and the critics. The quality of the nudes, however, brought a compliment from Pierre Puvis de Chavannes, who was already on his way to becoming the best-known muralist of the century and was also, with an immense atelier in the Place Pigalle, a new neighbor. And there were things worse than silence to be feared from the reviewers. In 1864 Manet, because of his supposed artistic affinities and his address in the Batignolles quarter, had squirmed under the nickname Don Manet y Courbetos y Zurbarán de las Batignolas; and now he had to endure reading that his *Olympia,* a demythologized version of Titian's *Venus of Urbino,* was just a playing-card image of a "vile odalisque with a yellow belly." [1]

The submission and acceptance of the *War Scene* seem to demolish any supposition that discouragement was a principal reason for Degas's deciding, at about this time or only a little later, to abandon history painting.

"Seem" is used advisedly, because one can easily imagine moments when Jephthah, Semiramis, and the mass of notes and sketches concerning John the Baptist, David, Goliath, Dante, Virgil, Nero, Mary Stuart, Oedipus, Bucephalus, Alexander the Great, and King Candaules' wife, fished out, dusted, and poked over during the move to the Rue de Laval, suddenly looked embarrassingly incoherent and ingenuous. But the Salon début must have been an effective antidote for any such sinking spells, and a number of positive reasons for the big decision can be found. There were the examples provided by the resolutely if rather ambiguously modern Manet and, unexpectedly, by Tissot, who finished his pseudo-sixteenth-century *Attempted Abduction* at the same time as Degas finished *War Scene,* successfully submitted it to the Salon jury, and then also abruptly gave up painting the past. (One can imagine that the two friends consulted each other.) There was the return to the generally up-to-date musical, literary, painterly, theatrical, and sometimes bohemian world of the Ninth Arrondissement. There was the recognition that the irony implicit in the new hat-doffing persona, which went well with the visual wit of something like *A Woman with Chrysanthemums,* was not very compatible with even a mild sort of *pompiérisme.* And above all there was the cumulative effect of an important nineteenth-century trend toward contemporaneity.

A polemical awareness of the difference between past and present had been around since at least the reign of Louis XIV, when the *Querelle des anciens et des modernes* had agitated Paris. The slogan *il faut être de son temps* (one must be of one's time) had first been given wide currency among French intellectuals, however, in 1828 by the poet Emile Deschamps in the preface to his *Etudes françaises et étrangères,* which had become a manifesto of the new Romantic school of literature. The admonition had been in flagrant contradiction with the yearning of many Romantics for the past, with their diatribes against the Industrial Revolution, and with their frequent weakness for a primitive or rural lack of chronological precision. (Two generations earlier one of their precursors, Jean-Jacques Rousseau, had got rid of his watch in a quixotic gesture against modern time-obsessed civilization.) But they had never pretended to be very consistent, their love for the bygone had given some of them an acute sense of historical periods, and anyway the slogan had been a handy weapon with which to attack classicizing versifiers. So it had been repeated regularly, and eventually was picked up by those practicing the visual arts. It had encouraged Daumier's uncompromising pertinence and the Barbizon painters' rejection of academic landscape, and had acquired a sharper relevance as social and technological change widened the gap between then and now, stylistic revivals in architecture and furniture multiplied, and the Salon jury continued to proclaim the primacy of history painting. In his review of the Salon of 1846 the young Baudelaire had felt obliged to insist on the "heroism of modern life," on the challenge of painting frock coats and top hats with the same enthusiasm that was devoted to the cloaks of Achilles and Agamemnon, and in general on the "new beauty" available to urban artists: "Parisian life is fertile in its provision of marvelous, poetic subject matter. The marvelous envelops and drenches us, like the atmosphere. But we do not see it."[2]

The originally Romantic slogan had then been adopted by the Realists, whose doctrine had been explained by Courbet (with some help from Castagnary) in an open letter of 1861:

> I maintain that the artists of one century are fundamentally incapable of representing the look of a past or a future century. . . . Historical painting is in its essence contemporary. Each epoch should have its artists, who express it and reproduce it for posterity. An epoch that has not been able to express itself by means of its own artists does not deserve being expressed thanks to artists who come later. . . . I maintain also that painting is essentially a concrete art that can concern itself only with the depiction of real and existing things.[3]

During the early 1860s the campaign had been continued, with a growing optimism and an increasingly aggressive attitude toward the entire artistic past, by the young writers who were gravitating toward Manet. Astruc, for example, had written in his *Salon intime:* "The new school is emerging little by little. It must build on ruins. . . . Tradition is merely a pale principle for educators, Romanticism a soul without a body."[4]

Degas may have found some of the argument unconvincingly extravagant. He clearly did not think that the masterpieces in the Louvre were a pile of ruins, nor that the tradition represented by the precepts and practice of Ingres was simply pedantry, nor that Delacroix's kind of Romanticism was without substance, nor that an uncritical acceptance of the materialism of Courbet was the only possible philosophy for a modern painter. But by 1865 the demand for contemporaneity was in general very persuasive and very much in harmony with the zeitgeist, and during the next couple of years it was reinforced sufficiently to make unlikely any backsliding by a recent convert.

On the occasion of the Salon of 1866 the twenty-six-year-old Emile Zola, a boyhood friend of Cézanne's from Aix-en-Provence, launched himself, with a cockiness that immediately set the teeth of the Establishment on edge, into the career of a Paris art critic. His professional qualifications were meager, and his real vocation was already that of a novelist. (At the moment he was at work on the gruesome *Thérèse Raquin,* in which his scientism appears for the first time.) However, he had been frequenting the Louvre, the Salons, and artists' studios for several years, and through Cézanne and another friend, Duranty, he had become acquainted with Monet, Pissarro, Renoir, Manet, and — more remotely — Courbet. Also, he had the flair of a born journalist, an amusingly insolent if rather wordy style (critics were paid by the line), a good sounding board in the pages of a reasonably open-minded paper, *L'Evénement,* and a quickly apparent intention to use his position to defend his comrades and the notion that *il faut être de son temps.* In the first two articles of the series he had been engaged to write he devoted most of his space to the Salon jury, accusing it of criminal prejudice and rank cronyism. In the third he explained his personal aesthetic criteria and got in some further digs at the official exhibition:

> Paint truthfully, and I will applaud; paint individually and vividly, and I will applaud even more. . . . For it is laughable to believe that in matters of artistic beauty there is an absolute, eternal verity. . . . I do not want any returns to the past, any pretended resurrections, any pictures painted according to an ideal pieced together from fragments of an ideal picked up from past periods. I do not want anything that is not full of life, temperament, reality. And now, I implore you, take pity on me. Think of what a man with a disposition like mine must have suffered yesterday, lost in the vast and dreary nullity of the Salon. . . . Never have I seen such a heap of mediocrity.[5]

The fourth article was a panegyric of Manet, who had again been excluded by the jury; the fifth and sixth were roundups in which Courbet was scolded for having "sheathed his eagle's claws,"[6] Monet was singled out as "a man in the crowd of eunuchs,"[7] and the earlier theorizing was summarized in a definition of a work of art as "a corner of creation seen through a temperament."[8] Then the editor of *L'Evénement,* yielding to a flood of protests and threats from readers, decided to cut short the projected series, and Zola wrote a farewell piece in which he likened himself to a doctor who, "putting his fingers here and there on the body of the dying patient," suddenly provokes a scream of terror and anguish. "Now," he declared, "I know where the wound is."[9]

He need not have been quite so bitter, for he had certainly made an impact. The paper was the favorite daily of a large number of Second Empire authors, actors, artists, and frequenters of the cafés in the Boulevard des Italiens, and many of these sophisticated readers, although they did not take the trouble to write to the editor, were far from sharing the fury of the obscurantist defenders of the past. Moreover, some of the people most concerned were immediately and visibly grateful. Shortly after the series of articles was halted, Renoir, during an expedition to Fontainebleau with Sisley, painted *At the Inn of Mother Anthony,* in which *L'Evénement* lies prominently on the table amid the remnants of a convivial meal and appears to be the subject of an earnest discussion. At about the same date Cézanne, temporarily back in Aix, mischievously put a copy of the paper into the hands of his conservative father in an otherwise respectful portrait. In 1867 Manet began work on a warmly affectionate likeness of the new critic. Degas responded less explicitly, and later he disagreed violently with Zola's theories. But one can infer that in 1866 he was greatly impressed, because when *Thérèse Raquin* appeared a year later, he read it right away and began to plan a painting based partly on one of its incidents.

By the end of 1867 he was also reading Edmond and Jules de Goncourt's *Manette Salomon,* a book that was simultaneously an absorbing novel (especially for an artist), a piece of élitist, misogynic, and anti-Semitic propaganda, and an effective tract for the aesthetic times. Unlike Zola, the brothers were experienced critics, tourists, connoisseurs, and art historians, with Salon reviews behind them and a long study of French eighteenth-century painting in progress, and they were competent watercolorists and etchers. Their story was thus well documented and psychologically shrewd, so much so that it can still be profitably read as a parable of the history of art in Paris during the 1850s and 1860s. The hero, Coriolis, is a wealthy, elegant, talented young painter with an authentic nobiliary particle and an ancestry that is part Italian. He receives some conventional training at the Ecole des Beaux-Arts, decides to defy the Establishment, develops into a sort of pre-Impressionist, and then succumbs to Manette, a beautiful, illiterate Jewish model who enslaves him sexually and finally degrades him into commercialism. His close friends include Anatole, an engagingly Romantic bohemian who fails to cope with Second Empire reality and winds up as a concierge in the Jardin des Plantes; Crescent, a saintly landscapist who has a peasant wife and a small farm near Barbizon; Garnotelle, a cautious mediocrity who wins the Prix de Rome and returns to the Ninth Arrondissement to become a modish portraitist with a lilac-tinted studio in the Cité Frochot, almost next door to 13 Rue de Laval; and notably Chassagnol, a talkative vagabond who pops in and out of the lives of Coriolis and Anatole and on each appearance delivers a tirade somewhat in the manner of a caustic Shakespearean clown. He becomes violent when someone mentions the Villa Medici:

> Rome! Always their Rome! Rome! Well, let me tell you something, and so much the worse for you. Rome is the Mecca of the lovers of the stereotyped. Yes, the Mecca of the lovers of the stereotyped! And that's that.[10]

Although he spends a few days at Fontainebleau, he does so merely to study the work of Primaticcio in the château and to consult some books in the local library:

Oh, you know, me, the forest, I have a horror of that. . . . I am, you know, a real decadent. I like only what man has created. Cities, libraries, museums — that's all that interests me. As for the rest, as for that great expanse of yellow and green, that apparatus we have agreed to call nature, it's a big nothing for me, a badly colored emptiness that makes me feel sad in my eyes. Do you know why Venice is immensely charming? It's because it is the corner of the world with the least amount of soil with vegetation.[11]

On the entire current controversy over subject matter and stylistic innovation — over history painting, contemporaneity, ideal beauty, and the various kinds of realism — he is tireless and given to punctuating his remarks with "a mad, sneering, foolish laugh":

The modern, you know, the modern, that's all there is that is worthwhile. . . . Why, every period has within it a beauty, a beauty of some sort, more or less under the surface but seizable and exploitable. It's a question of digging. . . .

Ah, people think that this whole matter, this question of modernity, has been disposed of because we have had Realism, that caricature of the truth about our epoch, that attempt to startle the bourgeoisie. Because a fellow has made a minor religion out of the stupidly ugly. . . . I ask you if a Parisian woman dressed for a ball isn't just as potentially beautiful for a painter as a woman of no matter what civilization. . . . Ah, the leading strings, the examples, the traditions, the ancients, the heavy stone of the past on our bellies. . . . The nineteenth century incapable of producing its painter? It's inconceivable. I don't believe it. A century that has suffered so much, the great century of scientific restlessness, of anxiety about the truth. A failed Prometheus, but a Prometheus anyway, a Titan, so to speak, with liver trouble.[12]

It would be hard to overestimate the influence of all this on Degas. Although he later disapproved of the Goncourts' prose — of what they themselves called their *écriture artiste* — he once confessed in a studio conversation that *Manette Salomon* had been "a direct source" for his "new perception" of painting.[13] And he might have added that the book, with its remarkable though entirely fortuitous parallels (neither of the authors knew him in 1866) for his situation and evolution, had undoubtedly strengthened some of the nonartistic ingredients in his character and ultimate outlook.

It was one thing, however, to decide that *il faut être de son temps,* and another to put the decision into practice, with visible, distinguishable results. After all, in a sense one could not be, whatever one did, of any time other than one's own: the conservative Bonnat was just as much a mid-nineteenth-century artist as the provocative Manet. The *pompiers* could even maintain, since they had a clear majority in the Salon and the support of most of the public, that they were the true representatives of their epoch and that their enemies were out-of-phase agitators. In other words, the real challenge was not merely to avoid the pastness of Jephthah and Semiramis and the timelessness of the Classical nudes in the *War Scene;* it was also to give one's paintings a definite, recognizable aura of nowness. In the 1860s various artists were accomplishing this, with differing degrees of effectiveness, by doing on-the-spot landscapes, by depicting scenes of everyday Second Empire life, by portraying sitters in datable contemporary costumes, by rejecting, as Courbet had, the notion of an ideal beauty, and by imposing, as Manet had, a new, strongly personal style and technique — a temperament, in Zola's somewhat Romantic terminology — on motifs that were at times a mixture of the modern and the traditional. Proof that Degas had been thinking about, and toying with, such approaches to contemporaneity for a good while can be seen in his Italian landscape drawings, with their inscriptions giving the exact hour and minute of execution; his racing pictures and his many notebook sketches of observed incidents; his portraits, with their evidence of interest in hats, coats, and gowns; his having provided the youngsters of Sparta with the faces of modern Parisian or Neapolitan urchins; and his oddly off-center arrangement for *A Woman with Chrysanthemums.* Moreover, his acute, almost crotchety sense of time — combined with his see-yourself-seeing-yourself habit — had long been apparent in his tendency to consult his watch frequently during his travels and note precisely when he was doing or experiencing something. But he was nevertheless only occasionally a landscapist and a genre artist; his rejection of the dogma of ideal beauty was less forthright than Courbet's; and in the mid-1860s his stylistic arbitrariness was much less mature than Manet's. In short, he was still in many respects a Romantic Classical figure painter. And that did not make it very easy for him to find an adequate, fresh way of representing nowness.

Around 1865, almost simultaneously with the completion of the *Self-Portrait Saluting* and the decision to drop the past and move to the Rue de Laval, he had returned with renewed ambition to equine motifs, and in 1866 the Salon jury accepted his *Steeplechase: The Fallen Jockey.* This monumental oil, the largest of his horse pictures and the third largest, after *The Daughter of Jephthah* and *The Bellelli Family,* of all his works, asserts by its dimensions the artist's intention to elevate a contemporary mishap to the dignity of the big tragic compositions produced by history painters — to do for the riders of Vincennes and Longchamp what Courbet had done for the rustics of his native Franche-Comté. Unfortunately for any such aspiration, however, the completed painting lacks scale (as distinct from size) and suggests previous art more than present reality. In fact, it looks like what it may well have been at the start: a modified blowup of a detail from an English sporting print, possibly one of the many derived from the early-nineteenth-century paintings of the track specialists Henry Alken and John Frederick Herring. (Proof of his long familiarity with such prints is in the notes he made during the trip to the Haras du Pin in 1861.) The horses have the conventional flying look of the era before instantaneous photography; the figure of the injured man, for which Achille is said to have been cajoled into posing, has a hint of the awkwardness of popular imagery.

In agreeable contrast to this lack of firsthandedness, the Degas of the future — the alert looker, the incisive draftsman, and the laconic virtuoso of mise-en-scène — is already present in some of the studies of mounted jockeys and of turf spectators he began to accumulate during these years, both as a stock of persons and as poses for use in later paintings and pastels. Prominent among the spectators is a rather extramundane though fashionably dressed young woman, called "Lyda" in an inscription and otherwise unidentified, who appears in several squarely frontal, arresting little works,

Woman with Field Glasses,
c. 1865–1871

in each of which she is staring through field glasses with a directness that gives a viewer of the picture an almost disquieting sensation of the represented instant and of seeing, from the position of a Longchamp horse, himself being seen.

Several of the portraits Degas executed during this period of transition into sharpened contemporaneity — roughly between 1865 and 1867 — show a similar interest in exploring, with the help of gestures, accessories, or both, the psychopictorial crossroads formed by the personality of the subject, the self-awareness of the artist, and the implied presence of the viewer. Thérèse is now represented as the beardless mirror image of the Edgar of *Valernes and Degas,* with one hand holding her chin and the other resting timidly on the shoulder of the dominating Edmondo (space-dominating, at any rate); and her conventionally nineteenth-century, though apparently affectionate, submissiveness is accompanied by a daguerreotype composition lined up conventionally with the plane of the canvas. Victoria Dubourg, a painter who studied with Fantin and eventually married him, is depicted as an unpretentious, sturdy, warmly attentive young intellectual leaning slightly toward the viewer, as if during a pause in a conversation. Tissot, who by this time was prosperous enough to have a town house near the Bois de Boulogne in the swank Avenue de l'Impératrice (now the Avenue Foch), appears seated sideways in a studio corner, wearily holding a mahlstick and gazing out at the world with a look like that of the persona in the *Self-Portrait Saluting.* Near him are his top hat, a sixteenth-century portrait (formerly attributed to Cranach) that echoes his mustache, and some pictures — including an elaborately pseudo-Japanese one — that are apparently his but were in fact invented by Degas as characteristic theatrical properties. In *The Collector of Prints* the same method is used to make visible the inner life of the evidently secretive, even furtive, sitter, who has been interrupted in the private exercise of his passion by the inquisitive viewer standing directly over him. Although here we are reminded inevitably of Daumier, the parallel points to an important difference, for whereas Daumier's art lovers are types whose desired objects are unrecognizable, Degas's collector, although unidentified, is an individual whose principal interests are specified as wallpaper and patterned Japanese silk (in the frame behind his head), Chinese ceramics of the T'ang dynasty (in the cupboard), and the colored etchings and lithographs produced by the flower painter Pierre-Joseph Redouté at the beginning of the nineteenth century. Moreover, the painting has an autobiographical quality lacking in Daumier's work, for the used hat links the sitter to Auguste's connoisseur circle, and hence today's viewer to Edgar on Sunday leave from the Lycée Louis-le-Grand.

Edmondo and Thérèse Morbilli, 1867

Two other portraits that he painted at about this time reveal the persistence of a feeling for tradition beneath all the experimentation he was undertaking. One of them, a small masterpiece often compared with those of the sixteenth-century court artist François Clouet, shows an unknown snub-nosed young woman wearing the puffed-back hairdo of the mid-1860s and radiating a porcelain charm enhanced by the thinness of the paint, which lets the texture of the canvas produce a fine shimmer. (She is sometimes quite inexplicably identified as Rosa Morbilli, Edmondo's mother and Edgar's aunt, who was then past sixty.) The second, which exemplifies the enduring influence of Bronzino and Ingres, is a likeness of Joséphine Gaujelin, who was a ballet dancer at the Opéra in the Rue Le Peletier during part of the Second Empire and later an actress at the Théâtre du Gymnase, one of the Romantic Classical monuments on the Grands Boulevards. She is represented as a dark-eyed, tight-lipped, high-strung creature — a possibly bad-tempered Thoroughbred — seated on a cream-colored chair and a red paisley shawl in her dressing room after a performance, swathed to her chin in a black street costume, and crowned by a black bonnet strewn with tiny clusters of grapes. The artist, according to contemporary testimony, was vastly satisfied, and the sitter, on the evidence of her immediate and subsequent behavior, was furious. Although she had formally ordered the picture, she flatly refused to pay for it, on the grounds that it did not at all do her justice, and more than thirty years afterward she objected again when it was shipped off to an American collection. (A preparatory study in which she looks sparklingly seductive suggests that she was not being altogether unreasonable.) This was perhaps Degas's first experience with the commissioning of works — and also a stage in a long development that would transform much of modern portraiture into a battle between the artist and his model, between painting as an art and painting as representation.

The notebooks in use during these years reveal a preoccupation with the nature of man in society, with the difference between seeming and being, with the temptations of *arrivisme* and hedonism, and with the need to be an ironist while maintaining an unblinking, stoical respect for reality. Montesquieu is cited on the pleasures of detached observation: "I have no aversion at all to amusing my inner self with the men I see around me."[14] On the same page there is an unidentifiable quotation wrongly attributed to Byron and accompanied by what looks like a sketch of Valernes: "The heart of man is a cavern half lit by the rays of the sun. Where you see the light there is nothing. Where you see nothing there is everything."[15]

A poem by Degas himself sings the praises of one variety of the good Second Empire life:

> *Vive, sensible, un peu coquette*
> *Suivons la gloire et les plaisirs*
> *C'est à la fois la violette*
> *La rose amante du Zéphir*
> *Elle s'emporte elle s'apaise*
> *Elle pleure et sourit tour à tour*
> *En même temps elle est française*
> *Et constante dans son amour* [16]

(Animated, sensitive, a bit coquettish, let us follow [the goddess of] glory and pleasure. She is at once the violet and the rose in love with the breeze. She flies into a passion, she calms down. She weeps and smiles by turns. At the same time she is French, and constant in her love.) Five pages further on another poem is devoted to the eighteenth-century poet and playwright Alexis Piron, whose penchant for witty and sometimes obscene plain-spokenness is contrasted with Degas's own leaning toward understatement and allusiveness — in both conversation and painting:

> *Piron plus gai que délicat*
> *Sans nul préliminaire*
> *Dit partout qu'un chat est un chat*
> *Moi je dis le contraire*
> *Souvent un seul mot*
> *En dit beaucoup trop*
> *Mais qu'une gaze fine*
> *Sans cacher les traits*
> *Voile le portrait —*
> *Le reste se devine* [17]

(Piron, more gay than delicate, without any preliminaries at all, says everywhere that a cat is a cat. As for me, I say the contrary. Often a single word says much too much about something. But let a thin gauze, without hiding the features, veil the portrait — and the rest is guessed.) On the back of the sheet containing these lines there are some symbolic verses that read like the record of a dream, with the usual connotations of anxiety, condensation, displacement, and disguised wish fulfillment:

> *Au milieu du désordre affreux*
> *Que le choc a fait naître*
> *Cette rose frappe mes yeux*
> *Je crois vous reconnaître*
> *Je veux vous sauver et vous préserver*
> *De ce péril extrème*
> *Je cours vous sauver*

*Et j'ai le plaisir
De vous rendre à vous-même* [18]

(In the midst of the hideous disorder that the shock has created, this rose strikes my eye. I think I recognize you. I want to rescue you and save you from this extreme danger. I run to your rescue. And I have the pleasure of giving you back to yourself.) Toward the end of this section three staccato phrases, jotted down like a call to order, refer to some remarks by the seventeenth-century moralist Charles de Saint-Evremond:

> Fortunate would be the soul that could completely reject certain passions and could merely anticipate certain others. It would be without fear, without sadness, without hatred, without jealousy. It would desire without eagerness, hope without worry, and enjoy without transport. [19]

Although some of these entries were clearly intended for private meditation, others suggest preparation for public conversation — for the type of amusing, provocative, literate talk, ranging from persiflage to amateur philosophizing, that was still, as it had been ever since the wave of linguistic refinement in the seventeenth century, expected of a properly tutored Parisian. The scribbles include a considerable number of reminders of dinner invitations; the comparison with Piron, who had "rained *mots,*" according to a contemporary, in the Café Procope on the Left Bank (and whose works were reissued in 1866), hints at an ambition to perform similarly, if more subtly, on the slopes of Montmartre.

Elsewhere these notebook pages are a bit of everything from visual fantasies to some almost equally whimsical recordings of opinions and facts. There are sketches of a half-human weasel defecating and of a long, dappled serpent near an ancient temple, and caricatures of Napoleon III, Bismarck, and Louis-Philippe (or someone like him), the last with the pear-shaped head popularized by Daumier. A note on the eighteenth-century physiognomist Johann Kaspar Lavater indicates a growing interest in the problem of pictorial expression: "Goethe says somewhere that, strictly speaking, Lavater was a realist and was aware of the ideal only in its moral form." [20] The many addresses of models include those of Victorine Meurent, whose trim body and slightly cross-eyed gaze had become anonymously famous in Manet's *Olympia,* and of a Degas favorite, the pensive-faced Emma Dobigny, who lived up the hill in the Rue Tholozé, just below the Moulin de la Galette, and posed also for Corot and Puvis de Chavannes. Moreau's recent mythological paintings are described, in a symmetrical rhetoric that smells of the Latin class at Louis-le-Grand, as "the dilettantism of a man of feeling if one thinks only of the subject matter, and that of a man of wit if one sees only the execution." [21] (Manet was more forthright about these strange pictures: "He is taking a bad road. . . . He is bringing us back to the incomprehensible, whereas we want everything to be comprehensible.")[22] Other notes disclose that the Degas of this period owns ten thousand-dollar shares in the Indiana Southern American Railway (acquired probably through the New Orleans connection), that he has gone out to the Bois de Boulogne on a June morning, that he has bought a pair of women's gloves for use on the dressing table in the portrait of Joséphine Gaujelin, that he likes an aria in Bach's Kirchencantaten No. 11 (another hand wrote down the title in German for him), that he has received a hundred and ten liters of cider from Normandy and paid the shipping charges, that he is thinking of visiting the Pyrenees, that he has a seat in a ground-floor box at the Paris Opéra, and that he weighs exactly sixty-four and a half kilograms.

His taste in nineteenth-century literature was shifting away from the Romantic authors — Musset, Vigny, Gautier, and George Sand — who are referred to in earlier notebooks. In 1867 he read, in addition to the recent novels of Zola and the Goncourt brothers, some of Jules Barbey d'Aurevilly's aphorisms, and wrote one of them down: "At times there is a certain ease in awkwardness that is more graceful, if I am not mistaken, than gracefulness itself."[23] During the next couple of years he read or reread Baudelaire's pieces on art, some of them in collected editions he is known to have borrowed from Manet's private library. He also appears, on the basis of later and more external evidence, to have become interested at about this time in the work of Pierre-Joseph Proudhon, Charles-Augustin Sainte-Beuve, the Parnassian poets, Joseph de Maistre, Louis Veuillot, and (though here the interest was not entirely new) Duranty. The list as a whole was very heterogeneous but not without some perceptible separate motivations and finally a sort of subterranean coherence. Barbey d'Aurevilly was a disciple of Beau Brummell, a salon lion, a colorful novelist, and a militantly reactionary Roman Catholic who regarded his religion, to paraphrase one of his remarks, as a balcony from which to spit on the common people. His insolence and his irony were bound to fascinate a man-about-town who was already indulging in a fair amount of self-theatricalization. Baudelaire, if somewhat inclined to confuse the time of art history with time in dress fashions, was obviously a stimulating writer for a painter facing the problems of contemporaneity. The anarchist Proudhon, in spite of his famous banker-frightening phrase, "Property is theft," had the appeal of a remembered figure from the Louis-le-Grand past, of his posthumous portrait by Courbet at the Salon of 1865, and especially of his *Du Principe de l'art et de sa destination sociale,* which had been published in 1865. Degas in the future would often cite the attacks in this book on "the literary tribe"[24] who practiced art criticism, and he probably also liked such passages as the following:

> To paint men in the sincerity of their natures and their habits, in their work, in the accomplishment of their civic and domestic functions, with their present-day appearance, above all without pose; to surprise them, so to speak, in the dishabille of their consciousness . . . such would seem to me to be the true point of departure for modern art. [25]

In later years he also often said that "the finest mind" of the middle of the nineteenth century was that of Sainte-Beuve,[26] whose Monday morning critical essays, though still being written, were published in a collected edition during the 1860s, and whose characteristic outlook on life and literature was summarized in a private maxim:

> The good, the true, and the beautiful make a fine motto, and a specious one. . . . If I had a motto it would be truth and truth alone. And let the good and the beautiful look after themselves as best they can. [27]

A similar whiff of Positivism could be detected in the work of some of the new poets who contributed to the *Parnasse contemporain* in 1866, and an Ingresque draftsman with a nostalgia for the past of Rome and Pompeii could appreciate in particular the clearly focused, impersonal, but nonetheless evocative images of José-Maria de Hérédia:

> *Le temple est en ruine au haut du promontoire,*
> *Et la Mort a mêlé, dans ce fauve terrain,*
> *Les Déesses de marbre et les Héros d'airain*
> *Dont l'herbe solitaire ensevelit la gloire.* [28]

(The temple is in ruins on the top of the promontory, and death has mingled, in this tawny earth, the goddesses of marble and the heroes of bronze, whose glory is buried by the deserted grass.)

Joseph de Maistre, whose works may have been in the family library in the Rue Saint-Georges when Edgar was born, was a representative, during the early French Restoration period, of the clerical and Royalist backlash against the Revolution; but his loathing of democracy, his papistry, his belief in original sin, his fiery prose, and his harsh, rigorous logic were still finding a sizable audience during the Second Empire, and not only among *grands bourgeois* like Degas or dandyish Catholic snobs like Barbey d'Aurevilly. (Baudelaire, for instance, once confessed that "de Maistre and Edgar Poe taught me to think.")[29] Louis Veuillot was another savage advocate of an alliance between the altar and the throne, a believer in the natural depravity of man, and at the same time a talented journalist whose *Les Odeurs de Paris,* published in 1866, vividly evoked the daily life of a great city.

Edmond Duranty occupied a special place on this list, in part because he was only a year older than Degas and also because of his doctrine and personality. As a critic whose pieces appeared from time to time in such influential publications as *Le Figaro* and *La Gazette des Beaux-Arts,* he had long been advocating, in both literature and painting, a rejection of historicism and a focus on the daily life of ordinary people. As the author of three down-to-earth novels, he belonged to the inventorying, materialistic, populist school of literary Realism, which was more or less led by his old friend Champfleury, more or less in sympathy with the anti-idealism of Courbet and the social moralizing of Proudhon, and thoroughly contemptuous of the stylized bourgeois Realism of writers like Flaubert and the Goncourt brothers. (Flaubert responded in 1865 by dismissing "every word" of Proudhon's *Du Principe de l'art* as "filth.")[30] Duranty the man of theory was often, however, somewhat at odds with Duranty the man of sensibility. He admired Ingres's drawing and strong character, praised Delacroix's detachment "from the common herd," and maintained that Daumier was not only a fine deflator of the bourgeoisie but also an artist in the category of Poussin and Holbein. In contrast with the frequently sloppy contemporary writers of proletarian or peasant fiction (including Champfleury, who was notorious for grammatical howlers), he was the master of a crisp, correct prose style. It echoed the aristocratic language of the eighteenth-century Enlightenment and produced — like Flaubert's *mots justes,* the Goncourts' *écriture artiste,* and Degas's use, in both his writing and his painting, of a classical idiom — an impersonal, aesthetic effect that intimated membership in a dominant class. Indeed, Duranty was a marginal member of such a class, for he was the bastard son, by an obscure father, of a woman who had once been Prosper Mérimée's mistress, and this was enough to generate a romantic rumor (still current) that he was in fact Mérimée's offspring. Moreover, he had something of the air of a ruined nobleman, perhaps because of his awareness of his illegitimate birth but more probably because, though his intelligence and his talent were widely recognized, his literary ventures were nearly always unlucky. His periodical *Le Réalisme,* founded in 1856 with Champfleury, had collapsed after six issues. His first novel, *Le Malheur d'Henriette Gérard,* had been one of the successes of 1860, but only after he made the mistake of selling the rights to Poulet Malassis, Baudelaire's usually unbusinesslike publisher, for two hundred francs. He had then settled into the routine of a Paris intellectual journalist who wrote fiction when he could take time away from such tasks as reviewing an art exhibition, inventing a farce for the puppet theater in the Jardin des Tuileries, or turning out, for *La Revue libérale* in 1867, a long article on physiognomy. His fellow critic Armand Silvestre, who became well acquainted with him in the late 1860s, remembered him as a sum of understatements:

> He spoke rather slowly and very softly, with a kind of slight, almost imperceptible English accent. Nothing about him suggested money. . . . A likable, distinguished person, with a touch of bitterness. . . . One sensed a lot of disillusionment behind his quiet little jokes. His blond head was already almost bald; his blue eyes were at once alert and gentle. His life seemed to be written into his sometimes painful grin.[31]

It is not surprising that such a man should have rapidly become one of the closest friends of the self-aware, often atrabilious Degas.

It was another Realist critic, however, the generous Castagnary, who during the Salon of 1867 gave the painter, in a new daily called *La Liberté,* his first taste of seeing his name in the papers:

> The *Two Sisters* of Monsieur E. Degas, a remarkably gifted debutant, indicates that its author has an exact feeling for nature and life.[32]

The picture referred to may have been either a double portrait of Giovanna and Giulia Bellelli or one of Elena and Camilla Montejasi-Cicerale, Aunt Fanny's daughters. (The Salon catalogue deepens the mystery by listing two paintings under Degas's name, each with the unhelpful title *Family Portrait.*) Giovanna and Giulia are perhaps the better guess, for Elena and Camilla look mature enough in their picture to suggest that they were painted a bit later than 1867, at which date they were respectively only about eleven and ten years old. In any event both pictures are interesting mostly because of the oddly unrelated poses, which can be interpreted as studies in psychological contrasts, as not very successful attempts to modify traditional practice, or simply as confirmation of a suspicion — warranted by the graded tone values and the lack of detailed settings — that each work was based on individual photographs of the sisters, sent up from Naples and assembled rather arbitrarily in Paris. Since beyond that there is not much to say, one can see why Castagnary, having loyally decided to mention a member of the group around Manet, wound up by being disappointingly vague and too obviously dutiful. But of course it must have been pleasant, at the age of thirty-three, to at last have a press clipping to show to Auguste.

In fact the Salon of 1867 was in general disappointing. Although Fantin, Berthe Morisot, Whistler, and Degas were among the accepted, Sisley, Pissarro, Cézanne, and Renoir were thrust back into the anonymous ranks of the refused. Courbet, renewing his exploit of twelve years earlier, showed a hundred and forty of his paintings in a separate pavilion in the Place de l'Alma, near the part of the Palais de l'Industrie that still housed the official exhibition, and achieved a popular success at the cost of dismaying many of his former supporters. Manet, with eighteen thousand francs borrowed from his mother, also erected a separate little building, not far from the Realist leader's, and exhibited fifty of his works in it without provoking much of a reaction of any kind. The movement toward a new type of painting seemed, for the moment at least, to be running out of steam.

The Palais de l'Industrie itself was deprived of some of its usual annual éclat and fashionable varnishing-day hubbub, for it had to compete with a new Exposition Universelle, twice as big as that of 1855 and located this time across the Seine near the Ecole Militaire, on the eighteenth-century drill ground known as the Champ de Mars (now dominated by the Eiffel Tower). Among the distinguished summer visitors were Bismarck, the Prince of Wales, the Mikado's brother, the viceroy of Egypt, the queen of the Netherlands, the czar of Russia, the emperor of Austria, and the kings of Spain, Greece, Sweden, Prussia, Belgium, and Württemberg, each welcomed with parades, balls, and gala operatic or theatrical performances. Part of the old drill ground was transformed into a floral park and an international city, in which one could admire the vernacular architecture of a score of nations, listen to Gypsy rhapsodies, Neapolitan ballads, or risqué French café-concert songs, and drink Turkish coffee, Chinese tea, Spanish chocolate, Bavarian beer, or a sample of the dizzying eaux-de-vie of Eastern Europe. In the main hall the thousands of examples of scientific and technological progress included, as the principal contribution of the famous Krupp firm, a huge breech-loading steel artillery piece that made the standard French bronze muzzle-loader look like a relic from Waterloo (and may have reminded some visitors that less than a year before, while the France of Napoleon III was listening to Offenbach's latest hit, the Prussia of Bismarck and General von Moltke had taken only six weeks to defeat Austria decisively). For the art public there were brightly colored prints, fresh off the woodblocks, in the Japanese pavilion; a large sculpture section; a sizable number of English pictures; a commemorative selection — farther up the Left Bank at the Ecole des Beaux-Arts — of works by Ingres, who had died the previous January; and a panorama of European painting in which the stars were such Paris Salon favorites as Jean-Léon Gérôme (who showed a version of his already celebrated *Death of Caesar*), Ernest Meissonier (who delighted viewers with his minuscule imitations of Dutch seventeenth-century genre scenes), and Alexandre Cabanel (whose popular

Venus was dismissed by Zola as a *lorette* drowning in a river of milk). In short, the fair as a whole repeated, with some minor adjustments, the contradictions of its predecessor of 1855. It celebrated change in commerce, industry, and even war, encouraged an enjoyment of the fleeting present, and rewarded artists for refusing to be of their own time.

Degas spent part of his visit taking notes on the works of some typically mid-Victorian anecdotal landscapists: James Clarke Hook, John W. Inchbold, Charles Lewis, John Raven, Arthur Severn, Alfred William Hunt, Alfred P. Newton, and H. Brittan Willis. Although today most of these painters are either forgotten or judged to have been perhaps too much of their own time, in the Paris of the 1860s they and their fellows had a high reputation — helped by memories of Constable and by a certain amount of anglophile snobbery. Hook, for example, had been praised by both Baudelaire and Gautier. Moreover, during this period before the triumph of Impressionism, which the British long regarded as an aberration, French relations with the Victorian school in general were close — and often personal. Whistler and Legros had settled in London, and Tissot would soon join them. Fantin had had long holidays in Chelsea in the home of the etcher Seymour Haden, Whistler's brother-in-law, and also in Surrey, at Hook's country estate. Duranty was on friendly terms with the painter and engraver Edwin Edwards, who had a large house, a fine boat, and a printing press at Sunbury, on the upper Thames. Tissot was an admirer — as Delacroix had been a decade earlier — of John Everett Millais, whose *Eve of Saint Agnes,* a moonlit evocation of Keats's poem, was one of the sensations of the current Exposition Universelle. In London "the Paris Gang," so called because of its bohemian years on the Left Bank, included the *Punch* cartoonist George du Maurier, at one point a warm friend of Whistler's; the history painter Edward J. Poynter, a friend of Legros's and a future director of the National Gallery; and the young Anglo-Greek businessmen Luke and Alecco Ionides, whose wealthy father, Alexander Ionides, would become one of Degas's earliest collectors.

The Japanese pavilion must have been something of a disappointment, for the prints on view were the work of the last and least original epigones of the *ukiyo-e* masters of the eighteenth century and early nineteenth, and by 1867 *japonisme* in Paris was emerging from its uncritical fad phase. In 1862 a couple named Desoye had opened, under the arcades at 220 Rue de Rivoli, a shop called La Porte Chinoise and had begun to attract a group of sophisticated customers that soon included Bracquemond, Whistler, Fantin, Manet, Tissot, Baudelaire, Champfleury, Astruc, Zola, and the Goncourts. The last had devoted a chapter of *Manette Salomon* to a description of their painter-hero, Coriolis, lying on his belly on the floor of his studio and looking at Japanese prints:

The winter, the gray day, the poor, shivering sky of Paris were put to flight
and forgotten. . . . Before him unrolled a land of red houses, with painted
rooms and walls made of screens. . . . There were zigzagging branches . . .
a yellow door, a bamboo trellis. . . . Women with antennalike combs in
their hair, with pale, heavily made-up faces and eyes turned up at the corners
like smiles, were leaning on balconies with their chins on the backs of their
hands, silent, dreaming . . .[33]

Degas, according to the catalogue for the sale of his possessions after his
death, eventually owned a large number of such works, and probably he
acquired most of this collection from the Desoye shop in the second half of
the 1860s, for there is no pictorial evidence of an awareness of Oriental art
before his portrait of Tissot and *The Collector of Prints,* and in middle age he
was apt to scoff at *japonisme* as a vogue from a bygone era. Thus the
discovery of these exotic little drawings and woodcuts, with their frequently
arbitrary compositional tricks and their emphasis on such contemporaneous
subject matter as Kabuki actors and dancers, Tokaido travelers, Edo prostitutes, and unidealized women combing their hair or taking baths, appears
to have coincided significantly, quite apart from the Exposition Universelle,
with his transition from pastness into nowness.

By the spring of 1867, however, he was already at work on a fairly
large painting, titled *Portrait de Mlle. E.F., à propos du ballet de La Source* in
the Salon catalogue of the following year, that ranks as his first serious
venture into contemporaneity (if we except racing scenes and ordinary
portraits), his first exercise in *orientalisme,* and his first ballet picture —
though the represented time is mythical, the Orient in question is neither
Japan nor any other identifiable place, and there is no visible evidence,
aside from the title, of choreography. E.F. was Eugénie Fiocre, a dancer at
the Opéra whose plain little tilt-nosed face was more than compensated for
by a body that, in the opinion of Théophile Gautier, "managed to com-
pound the perfections both of the young girl and of the boy, and to make
of them a sexless beauty which is beauty itself . . . hewn from a block of
Paros marble by a Greek sculptor."[34] She also had an eye for bankers as
lovers, and would retire from the stage at the age of thirty with a private
fortune, a country estate, and a passion for shooting pheasants. The ballet
La Source (The Spring), which opened on November 12, 1866, was a
vaguely Islamic spectacle with dance numbers arranged by Arthur Saint-
Léon, on leave from his post of ballet master in Saint Petersburg; music by
Léo Delibes and the Hungarian composer Ludwig Minkus; and a fairy tale
scenario by Saint-Léon and Charles Nuitter, the archivist of the Paris
Opéra. A real horse took part in the action, and a spring of real water,
sparkling under gaslight, gushed from the rocks of a three-dimensional
mountain and flowed across the stage. Fiocre, in the role of a lovely, cruel

princess named Nouredda, seemed to some of the audience to be executing a sort of Oriental cancan part of the time, but she pleased the critic Paul de Saint-Victor, writing for *La Presse,* in one of the scenes of the first act:

> Wearing a bonnet in the form of a miter, with her body tightly laced into a Turkish officer's jerkin and her legs floating in trousers of gauze speckled with gold, she danced while holding in her arms a long lute. The number was a fairly exact copy of a painting one sees quite often on little Persian boxes.[35]

Shortly after this episode, handing her lute to an attendant and letting one of the horses of her caravan come up for a drink, she slipped into a filmy robe, took off her slippers, sat down on a cushioned rock near the spring, and struck a meditative pose while listening to one of Minkus's plaintive melodies and dangling her overheated toes in the cool water. Degas, who

Mademoiselle Fiocre in the Ballet La Source, 1866–1868

must have been in his ground-floor loge taking notes, decided that this was the moment he had been waiting for.

The resulting picture left Zola, who reviewed the Salon of 1868 for *L'Evénement illustré,* feeling both impressed and fretful:

> I would have preferred to call this painting *A Riverside Halt.* Three women are grouped on a bank, next to them a horse is drinking. The horse's coat is magnificent, and the women's dresses are rendered with great delicacy. There are some exquisite reflections in the stream. While looking at this work, which is a little thin and strangely elegant, I thought of Japanese prints and the artistic simplicity of their colors.[36]

One can see what upset him, though apparently he did not see it at all, for he made no mention of the Paris Opéra. One may indeed regard the picture as simply a waterside pause somewhere in the Middle East, painted with a poetic, unifying awareness of the play of light, shade, and reflections in a mountain defile and with a rich, mostly brown and green palette that calls to mind one of Courbet's forest scenes. (In the reference to Japanese prints Zola may have been merely displaying his up-to-date taste.) One may also regard it, with the help of a little more external information, as another in Degas's series of portraits with symbolic accessories, in this instance a musical instrument and ballet slippers. But in fact the mountain defile is the work of the set designer Despléchin and the chief machinist Sacré in the Rue Le Peletier; the halt is in part a pause for listening to the strains emerging from an orchestra pit; the portrait is of both Fiocre and Nouredda; and the women and the horse are where they are partly to structure the composition with some strong diagonals (influenced by Whistler's *Symphony in White No. 3,* of which there is a rough sketch in Degas's notebooks). In sum, the critic was confronted by a painter's juggling of the real and the simulated for which a straightforward Realist's criteria were inappropriate.

Work on, or planning for, such complex projects was interrupted early in 1868 by the painting of another portrait, as a gift for the sitter, of Valernes. The occasion apparently was a celebration in anticipation — badly mistaken, as things turned out — of a Salon triumph, for many years later (long enough for him to have forgotten Degas's exact street number) Valernes attached a note to the back of the canvas:

> My portrait, a study from the life, painted by my famous and intimate friend Degas in his Paris studio, 6 Rue de Laval, in 1868, during a period when I was reaching my goal and when I was close to becoming a celebrity.[37]

The goal referred to was of course success in general as an artist, but more specifically it was the completion of a picture that had become, after months of work, the bearer of all its author's hopes. Titled at first *The Narration of a Misfortune* and probably inspired by the Victorian vogue for images of fallen women (Alfred Elmore's *On the Brink,* for example, which was in the British section of the Exposition Universelle), it showed a melancholy young woman, half prostrate in an armchair in a bourgeois bedroom, telling the story of her sexual "misfortune" to a visiting woman friend. With the title changed to *A Poor Sick Woman* so as to avoid censorship, it was accepted by the Salon jury in the spring and praised, perhaps at Degas's suggestion, by Zola:

> Although the subject is nothing . . . Evariste de Valernes has managed to float some peculiarly sweet, clammy air into the room where his poor sick woman languishes. Everything holds together: the atmosphere, the figures, the walls.[38]

Other reviewers, however, ridiculed the picture with such hilarity that the painter, now past fifty, decided to give up trying to exhibit in Paris. Later that year his wife died and he returned to his native province in the south of France. He vegetated in poverty for several years near his family's lost château, and finally accepted a job as a part-time drawing teacher in Carpentras.

Degas, at the moment of the *Poor Sick Woman* disaster, was evidently in no danger of suffering a similar defeat at the hands of the Establishment. He had successfully negotiated his passage, via portraiture and the theater, from history painting into contemporary themes, had got past the Salon jury four times in a row, and had obtained two notices in the press — admittedly from friends of friends, but that was how favorable criticism, when not purchased from one of the many corrupt Second Empire reviewers, was usually procured by Palais de l'Industrie debutants. In terms of style and technique he had demonstrated that he could use an Ingresque kind of drawing for subjects as un-Ingresque as Longchamp jockeys and spectators, somewhat as Baudelaire had used the classical alexandrine to say something thoroughly unclassical, and the great Romantic Classical architect Claude-Nicolas Ledoux, two generations earlier, had employed the Doric column in ways that still look modern.

Color was a special problem. At a time when the impulsive Manet was slapping his characteristic yellows and browns directly onto the white canvas and frequently ignoring both scales of values and the contours of forms, Degas was still starting his oils in the traditional manner by laying in a coat of relatively dark underpainting, and still using color, as Poussin had, mainly to supplement tonal and linear expression. Also, unlike most of the future Impressionists, he continued to believe, as Ingres had done,

in "local" color — in the "real" color, that is, of an object, no matter what
sort of illumination or tinted reflection it may be subjected to. But a section
of a notebook in use around 1867 shows that he was not at all dogmatic
about such matters:

> Human skin is as various, especially among us Frenchmen, as the rest of
> nature — fields, trees, mountains, streams, forests. There is a good chance
> of finding as much resemblance between a face and a pebble as between two
> pebbles, since in two pebbles we often see two faces. (I am talking about
> colors, for there is no argument about shapes. We often find a lot of formal
> connection between a rock and a fish, between a mountain and a dog's head,
> between clouds and horses, and so on.) Therefore it is not unreasonable to
> say that in using color we should look everywhere for affinities between the
> animate and the inanimate and the vegetable. I remember easily the colors
> of certain kinds of hair, for example, because I think of hair made of var-
> nished walnut wood or of oakum, or of horse-chestnut bark, and yet real
> hair, with its suppleness and lightness, or its stiffness and weightiness.[39]

This is remote both from the doctrines of the Ecole des Beaux-Arts and
from the color theories of nineteenth-century scientists, but not far from
the Renaissance conception of the universe as a system of analogies, a vast
poem of visual metaphors.

He was encouraged to continue painting the present because the *fête
impériale* created by the reign of Napoleon III was at its height during the
second half of the 1860s, in spite of a falling industrial growth rate, a
growing political confusion, and some alarming clouds on the diplomatic
horizon. Theaters, vaudeville houses, indoor circuses, dance halls, opera
houses (of which there were three besides the one in the Rue Le Peletier),
and restaurants were crowded. In 1866 Meilhac and Halévy could write, in
their libretto for Offenbach's *La Vie parisienne,* a couplet that seemed to
many moralists a simple statement of fact:

> *Du plaisir à perdre haleine,*
> *Oui, voilà la vie parisienne.*

(Pleasure till you are out of breath, yes, there you have Parisian life.)

The city itself, still in the process of being transformed by the emperor
and Haussmann, was an important part of the pleasure. It was not to
everyone's taste; to the Goncourts it was a forewarning "of some American
Babylon of the future." But its combination of broad new avenues, sudden
ronds-points, surviving medieval lanes, relatively low buildings, and am-
bient river light made it one of the most agreeable places on earth for idle
strolling and gawking, for *flânerie.* And when the *flâneur* felt like resting
his feet, there was always a table at which he could sit indefinitely and

watch, with the close-up distancing of humanity that only a sidewalk café can provide, the spectacle offered by passing Parisians. Degas, who by now was a veteran first-nighter, stroller, and café man, clearly enjoyed the entire festival. Only occasionally does he seem to have worried about the difficulty of reconciling his relish for contemporaneity with his respect for the past — a difficulty that manifested itself in his art as the problem of making a break while preserving continuity. In the notebook discussion of color, however, he showed his awareness of the difficulty by pausing to apostrophize both the Italy of the great tradition and the stimulating modern French capital: "Ah, Giotto!" he wrote. "Let me see Paris. And you, Paris, let me see Giotto!"[40]

9. Talk and Music

B Y 1868 the principal future Impressionists and their anti-Establishment allies were well acquainted with each other and were beginning to form what can be called a group, though it lacked stylistic coherence and consisted mostly of overlapping circles. One of these circles had taken shape in Paris at the Académie Suisse, which encouraged individuality by offering, for a small fee, the services of a live model and no instruction at all; here Pissarro had met Monet in 1858, Cézanne in 1861, and Guillaumin in 1863. Monet, following his period in the army, had enrolled at the more serious Atelier Gleyre in 1862, had thus become friendly with a Gleyre circle composed of Renoir, Sisley, and Fréderic Bazille, and had then presented these new comrades to the Pissarro circle at the Académie Suisse. In the Grande Galerie of the Louvre the enthusiastic copyist Fantin-Latour had become acquainted with Manet in 1857, with Morisot in 1859, and with Renoir and Bazille in 1863. During the next three years the critics Champfleury, Castagnary, Astruc, Duranty, and Zola had been accepted by all the circles because of their articles and studio visits. In 1866, a surprisingly late date, Cézanne and Monet had been introduced to Manet — Cézanne by himself, and Monet by Astruc. During the winter of 1867–1868, Morisot, while copying a Rubens nude in the Grande Galerie, had also been presented, by Fantin, to the much discussed author of the *Déjeuner sur l'herbe* and *Olympia*. Degas in the meantime had become linked, although not always very closely, to most of these people through his own long frequenting of the Louvre and his friendship with Fantin and Manet.

What unity the group possessed was due largely to shared rebuffs from the Salon jury and derisive reviewers, and partly to age, for in 1868 the majority of the members were in their late twenties or early thirties. But a shift of the artistic population of Paris from the Left Bank to the Right and a tentacular extension of the city were also factors, without which the others may have had no effect. As far back as 1860, Philippe Burty, print fancier and art critic (and a close friend of the Goncourt brothers), had discovered that as one walked up the hill from the Rue Saint-Lazare toward Place Pigalle, one entered a sort of painters' paradise:

> A new quarter, a tranquil quarter, and one favorable to the arts. Not much noise, not much movement. Streets are bordered here and there by mysterious little town houses. Commerce is limited to shops selling what is indispensable for maintaining life. Fiacre drivers do not risk themselves on the steep slopes except when absolutely necessary. The itinerant dealer in painting materials peddles without difficulty his bundles of brushes and his piles of stretchers for canvases. And artists' models are always certain of finding employment.[1]

At the same date, this Eden had started to expand toward the north and the west when Paris moved its official limits from those of the eighteenth century, marked by Ledoux's string of tollhouses, all the way out to the ring of fortifications built under Louis-Philippe, and in the process annexed the villages of Montmartre and the Batignolles. By the mid-1860s the latter had become particularly attractive to painters and writers; it offered low rents, a lot of small houses surrounded by gardens, some new apartment buildings, a nearby supply of models in the slum area known as Little Poland, a rail line that took landscapists out to the country in a few minutes, and a cluster of good eating and drinking places that included the venerable Cabaret du Père Lathuille, founded in 1765, and the relatively modern Café Guerbois. A shortage of cheap studios at the lower end of the Ninth Arrondissement may have encouraged a migration toward the edge of the city, for in a study published in 1868 the social chronicler Gabriel Guillemot remarked that bohemians had become rare around their "former headquarters" in the Latin Quarter and were "swarming" in the neighborhood of Notre-Dame-de-Lorette.[2]

One result of this whole pattern of urban developments was to increase the overlapping of the circles created at the Académie Suisse, the Atelier Gleyre, and the Louvre. Degas was still at 13 Rue de Laval. Fantin was at various times during the 1860s installed temporarily in the Rue Saint-Lazare or the Rue de Londres, also in the Ninth Arrondissement. Renoir eventually settled for several years at 35 Rue Saint-Georges. Manet, after a period at 34 Boulevard des Batignolles, took an apartment early in 1867 at 49 Rue de Saint-Pétersbourg (now the Rue de Léningrad), where his widowed mother lived. Here he was a few minutes from the Rue de Laval and from Zola in the Rue Moncey; here also he was often the host of Berthe Morisot, who lived out in Passy but came across town regularly, at first to pose for his *Balcony*. He also had an atelier at 81 Rue Guyot (now the Rue Médéric), on the border of the recently annexed territory, and here his visitors, as documented in Fantin's new manifesto picture, *A Studio in the Batignolles Quarter,* included Astruc, Renoir, Zola, Bazille, and Monet. Astruc was by now living in the Rue Darcet, around the corner from Duranty in the Rue des Dames, the former country lane leading from the Batignolles to Montmartre. Bazille was also, by 1868, in the quarter, extending hospitality to his friends in a place at 9 Rue de la Paix (now the Rue de la Condamine), whose appearance is preserved in his painting *The Artist's Studio.*

Degas is as noticeably absent from Fantin's and Bazille's pictures of Batignolles ateliers as he is from the *Homage to Delacroix* of a few years earlier. Indeed, he was never painted by members of the group, though they were in general much addicted to doing amicable, informal portraits of each other. (Bazille even portrayed Monet in bed.) Nor did he paint them, with the exception of Manet and, much later, Duranty and a new member, Mary Cassatt. Although this does not prove that he was essentially an outsider, it suggests an association based more on career strategy and the stimulating exchange of ideas than on affection or on admiration for individual painting styles, and this suggestion accords with our knowledge that during the late 1860s relations often took the form merely of conversations at the Café Guerbois. Meeting places of this sort were, of course, standard features of nineteenth-century art history and art mythology. Romantic painters, poets, and *grisettes* had gathered on the Left Bank during the 1840s at the Café Momus, which figures prominently in the fiction of Champfleury and Henry Murger (and hence in Puccini's *La Bohème*). The Realists had held forth over their beer or coffee, the latter improved by the invention of the percolator in 1856, at the Brasserie Andler in the Latin Quarter, and also at the Brasserie des Martyrs, a block from 13 Rue de Laval. Degas himself was a veteran of the debates between Cald'arròsti at the Caffè Greco in Rome and of those between Macchiaioli at the Caffè Michelangiolo in Florence. But the Guerbois was exceptional in attracting so large a number of people who eventually became famous.

It was located a few doors from the Place de Clichy at 11 Grande Rue des Batignolles (which became 9 Avenue de Clichy in 1868), and it was thus almost exactly at the point where Montmartre, the Ninth Arrondissement, and the Batignolles came together. Duranty, in a novelette written around 1869, says there were two hall-like rooms, arranged lengthwise in a row like a palace suite and opening, by means of a large pane of glass, on a small garden planted with shrubs.[3] The front room, presided over by a pretty, prim woman cashier, was decorated in the Second Empire style of the cafés on the Boulevard des Italiens, "white and gold and lots of mirrors," mixed with provincial First Empire motifs; the back room, lower and darker, was a columned "temple" in which five billiard tables were lined up "like massive baptismal fonts," and a "bewitching, mysterious half-light" gleamed on red banquettes, the waiters' white aprons, and the bald heads of old men playing cards.

The charms of the place had been discovered as early as 1866 by Antoine Guillemet, a wealthy young landscapist who lived in the Grande Rue, had worked with Pissarro and Cézanne at the Académie Suisse, and knew Berthe Morisot (behind whom he is standing in Manet's *Balcony*). Two years later the habitués included, in addition to members of the circles already mentioned, Bracquemond, the photographer Félix Nadar, the musician and dilettante Edmond Maître (a friend of Bazille's), Whistler when he was in town, the Parnassian poet Théodore de Banville, Commandant Hippolyte Lejosne (a friend of Manet's), the painters Alfred Stevens and Giuseppe de Nittis (both friends of Degas), and the critics Burty, Silvestre, and Théodore Duret. Sometimes they dropped by in groups of two or three for coffee or a session at the "baptismal fonts" in the back room. (Manet remarks in a letter of this period that Duranty "will become a crack billiard player if he continues his studies.")[4] Something like organized meetings were held, however, on one or two evenings a week, with perhaps a dozen participants gathered around two tables reserved for them near the front door. The proprietor, Auguste Guerbois, seems to have had a good deal of sympathy for the struggles of young artists.

Unfortunately there was no secretary to compile minutes. Silvestre, in some later notes that mix confusingly the past and present tenses, indicates that Degas was generally liked, or at least not disliked, by the other talkers, and that the principal cause of this favorable sentiment was that he lacked any public reputation that could arouse envy:

> Among the silhouettes glimpsed there every evening, in the gaslight and amid the noise of the billiard balls, I want to mention the painter Degas, his very original, very Parisian face, and his humorous, extremely bantering expression. He never sat down for long. . . . The young school owes a lot to Degas, and the old school admires, if rather ill-humoredly, the quality of his drawing and of his artistic nature. He has the privilege of being challenged by nobody, not even by the fervent partisans of the school of Rome.

A renovator who works in private, he has been saved by his ironic modesty and his style of living from the hatred that a resounding success attracts. . . . This Degas has his nose in the air, the nose of a searcher, the sort of nose I imagine Rabelais's Panurge had. One day his works, which are too rare, will be furiously fought over by collectors.[5]

Manet, in London during the summer of 1868 and then at Boulogne-sur-Mer being bored by seaside society, reveals in a letter to Fantin that their mutual friend was inclined to develop a personal theory of painting (of which the notebook entry on color may be a sample), to adopt a *grand bourgeois* stance toward the question of the social function of art (in spite of being an admirer of Proudhon), and to advocate contemporaneity in terms of upper-class sophistication and the racetrack at Longchamp:

> I can see, my dear Fantin, that you Parisians have all the distractions to be desired, whereas here I have no one to talk to. I envy you your chance to argue with the great aesthetician Degas about the inopportuneness of an art made available to the poorer classes at the price of thirteen sols a picture. I haven't been able to discuss painting with a single one of the foreigners here since my arrival. . . . So tell Degas to write to me. He is about to become, I hear from Duranty, the painter of high life. That's the very thing for him, and I regret all the more, for his sake, that he did not come over to London. The movements of horses kept well in hand would have given him some ideas for pictures.[6]

These allusions are about the only specific indication we have of what was said at the Guerbois, and they are subject to discount because of Manet's habitually mocking, boulevardier manner. But his letter makes clear that the discussions were stimulating, even indispensable, to many of the artists concerned; and some thirty years later Monet, in a reminiscing interview, made the same point:

> Nothing could have been more interesting than these talks, with their perpetual clashes of opinion. You kept your mind on the alert, you felt encouraged to do disinterested, sincere research, you laid in supplies of enthusiasm that kept you going for weeks and weeks, until a project you had in mind took definite form. You always left the café feeling hardened for the struggle, with a stronger will, a sharpened purpose, and a clearer head.[7]

Degas also, walking back through the night across the Place de Clichy and down to the quiet Rue de Laval, must have often felt better steeled for the battle they were all committed to — the effort to break out of the mummery of the academic into an art of their own time and hence into what they considered a more authentic vision of the world.

The "perpetual clashes of opinion" were inevitable, given the vigor of the minds involved and the differences in class, education, temperament, and doctrine. Although Pissarro, the oldest of the painters and already the owner of a graying Jewish patriarch's beard, was one of the most amiable men on earth, his anarchist faith must have made him bristle at derisive remarks concerning art for the workers. Bazille, a well-to-do, cultivated representative of the Protestant *grande bourgeoisie* of Montpellier, would be remembered by Zola as "a bit like Jesus" and yet "terrible when he became angry."[8] Cézanne, whose genius was long unrecognized by the rest of the group (Pissarro excepted), defensively played the role of a Provençal yokel and denounced the others as a bunch of "notaries." Manet, who according to Silvestre had "a punching, cutting" way of arguing, got into a quarrel one night with Duranty that became a real duel with rapiers — an absurd, bumbling affair that ended in a complete reconciliation and a triolet of celebration composed by their friends at the café.

In addition to such personality conflicts there were disputes provoked by diverging artistic aims. Out at Pontoise, thirty-two kilometers north-west of Paris, Pissarro was evolving from an early dependence on Corot toward a personal landscape style of solidly structured yet airy greens and browns. What was more significant for the future, Monet and Renoir spent the summer of 1869 near Bougival, eighteen kilometers west of the capital, painting the sunlit Seine and the amateur boaters at a pleasure spot called La Grenouillère (The Frog Pond) with a flickering touch that can be called the beginning of Impressionism. Meanwhile, Degas and Manet remained studio painters (though the latter would eventually try his hand at the open-air method). They were also united by their upper-class backgrounds, their respect for the old masters, their indulgence in irony, their delight in the passing Second Empire show, and their love of *flânerie.* But they too had their differences, their rivalry, and even a sardonic, smoldering resentment of each other's qualities, which was always there without ever flaring up sufficiently to end their long friendship. Degas was often clearly envious of Manet's winning impulsiveness and natural charisma; Manet was sometimes irritated to the point of cattiness by Degas's brilliant artificiality. Although they obviously admired each other's work, neither could resist the pleasure of making malicious little critical remarks that were just fair enough to sting the other's ego.

Duranty and Degas formed a different and much less competitive pair, united by their astringent tempers and also, around 1868, by their interest in pictorial psychology — specifically, the question of how, in a wordless art like painting, to make the represented persons express something. (This did not, of course, seem at all important to Monet, who was moving toward a theoretically mindless attempt to record the impact of light and color on his retina; and it did not much interest Manet, whose enthusiasm for purely painterly qualities was such that in 1868 he was accused, by the friendly critic Théophile Thoré, of practicing an art "in which a head is esteemed no more than a slipper.")[9] The premise on which the question was based was not new: Aristotle and Plutarch had assumed that literature and the visual arts were sisters, and Horace had phrased the assumption as a famous simile, *ut pictura poesis* (as is painting so is poetry),[10] with which all graduates of Louis-le-Grand were certainly familiar.

Proposed practical answers to the question were also very old. In the sixteenth century Leonardo, for instance, had urged artists to study the necessarily expressive gestures of the deaf and dumb, whose afflictions put them in exactly the situation of people in a picture. During the reign of Louis XIV the artistic expression of emotions had been codified according to Cartesian principles by members of the Académie, notably Charles Le Brun; and copybooks containing expressive heads for the various "passions of the soul" had begun to circulate widely. In 1772 Lavater had initiated a fresh approach with the publication of his ostensibly scientific physiognomical "bible," which presented some five hundred plates of drawings of skulls and faces. Throughout the nineteenth century similar compilations had appeared: as recently as 1862 the physiologist G.-B. Duchenne had brought out a treatise that purported to be "an electrophysiological analysis of the expression of emotions" and added an important set of photographs to the collection of drawn and painted heads in the Ecole des Beaux-Arts. In the meantime François Delsarte, a professor of music and declamation, had been attempting a more practical solution in a series of lectures — aimed at actors and singers but of interest to painters also — that schematized the expressive possibilities in postures, gestures, countenances, and the movement of the eyes.

Both Duranty and Degas had already shown their familiarity with the problem in general, the first by his article of 1867 on physiognomy and the second by his notebook reference to Goethe and Lavater; and now, around 1868, Degas made his concern more explicit and personal in another of his pieces of advice to himself:

> Make of the *expressive head* (in the style of the Académie) a study of modern feelings — a sort of Lavater, but a more related Lavater, so to speak — sometimes with accessory symbols. Study Delsarte's observations on the emotional movements of the eye. Its beauty ought to be only that of a certain physiognomy.[11]

On the following pages of the notebook he moved, with his characteristic lack of transition, to a comment on artificial light, paused to recover from what seems to have been a return of his Florentine bouts of discouragement, and then circled back by way of portraiture to pictorial expression:

> Work a great deal on night effects — lamps, candles, and so on. The provocative thing is not always to show the source of the light but rather its effect. This sector of art can become immensely important today. . . . By getting up early in the morning, I can still save all of my extremely compromised life. Do portraits of people in familiar, typical attitudes, and above all give their faces and bodies the same expressions. [12]

Although all this is not as clear on paper as it undoubtedly was in his mind, it is evidence of his intention to avoid both the Cartesian formalism of Le Brun and the pseudoscientific reductionism of Lavater and to apply to the painting of "modern feelings" a combination of naturalistic miming and symbolic stagecraft. The basic idea was not, of course, a great novelty. Greuze had delighted a Rousseau-educated public with his tear-jerking melodramas and his maidenly ex-virgins equipped with such symbolic accessories as broken pitchers. A long series of British artists, from Hogarth to the Victorians at the recent Exposition Universelle, had produced anecdotal works that could be looked at as edifying little plays. Tissot was already embarked on the type of theatricalized high-society incident that would make his reputation in London. But Degas was neither a sentimentalist nor a moralist, and his mordant psychologizing was beyond the capabilities of Tissot.

The first result of his theories, apparently under way in 1868, was a stagy, somberly handsome picture destined to baffle critics and art historians completely for more than a century. Several viewers who had known the artist personally entitled it *The Rape;* others, also among his intimates, called it *The Quarrel, The Dispute,* or simply *Interior Scene.* Degas himself, in conversations during the 1890s, reportedly referred to it as *Interior,* or even more vaguely as "my genre painting." [13] Several experts confidently and mistakenly asserted that the picture illustrated an episode in Duranty's novel *Les Combats de Françoise Duquesnoy,* which in 1868 was not yet written. Some opted for Zola's *Madeleine Férat,* without being able to find a passage that exactly fitted the pictorial evidence. Not until 1972 was the principal literary source identified as a scene in another of Zola's early works, *Thérèse Raquin.* The heroine and her brutal lover, Laurent, have murdered her sickly, sexually inadequate husband and, after waiting nearly two years in order to allay any suspicion, have at last reached their wedding night. They are about to discover that their crime has made them psychologically incapable of resuming the wild, ruttish intercourse for which they had committed it. The bride has retired to their ironically cozy nuptial chamber, and now the bridegroom enters:

> Laurent carefully closed the door behind him and remained for a moment leaning against it and looking into the room with a worried, embarrassed expression. A bright fire blazed on the hearth, throwing out patches of yellow that danced on the ceiling and the walls. The room was thus full of a lively, flickering light, in the midst of which the lamp on the table seemed pale. . . . Thérèse was sitting on a low chair to the right of the hearth, with her chin in her hand and her eyes fixed on the bright flames. She did not turn her head when Laurent entered. . . . Her dressing jacket had slipped down, revealing a pink shoulder half hidden by a lock of black hair.[14]

There can be no doubt that this description influenced and perhaps even inspired the composition of what is now usually referred to as *Interior*. Yet the discovery is not nearly as helpful as it may seem at first glance, for there is plenty of evidence that Degas did not want the picture to be interpreted

Interior, 1868–1869

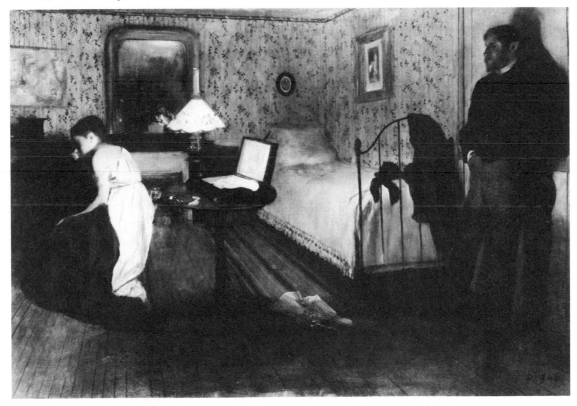

as an illustration of the scene in question. He obviously never told any of his speculating writer friends that the proper title was something like *Thérèse's Wedding Night*. One day in 1868 when he was away from the studio, Tissot dropped in and covered both sides of an old envelope with suggestions for improving the still unfinished work, all without giving an inkling of being aware of the novel as a source. Moreover, the assumption that the painting is a visualization of Zola's narrative becomes untenable when the viewer gets beyond a general first impression. The partly undressed woman is not staring into the fire; she is clutching a piece of her discarded clothing and half cowering on her low chair. The man has not just entered the room; his top hat is visible on the commode facing the woman. His fierce eye — a Delsarte touch — and Neanderthal scowl do not imply a "worried, embarrassed" state of mind, nor does his belligerent straddle. Tissot, for instance, assumed that the legs were intended to express possessiveness, and thought that they did not do so sufficiently in the version he examined. The sewing box on the table and the corset on the floor are prominent enough to be meaningful, and neither is derived from the novel. Finally, the bed, surely an important symbolic accessory in a wedding-night picture, is here a narrow, virginal affair manifestly for one person, whereas in the book it is wide enough for Laurent and Thérèse. (In the early 1900s the implications of the bed kept an American museum from buying the picture,[15] and Degas reportedly remarked, "But I would have furnished a marriage license with it.")

The only warranted conclusion is that *Interior* is a dumb show invented by Degas. (The actor who played the man was the painter Henri Michel-Lévy, portrayed by Degas in a similar pose ten years later.) Paradoxically, a literary source supplied part of the visual material but not the story line, so the viewer is authorized and indeed obliged to piece together the sense solely on the basis of physical attitude and mise-en-scène. A defensible interpretation might start with the premises that the setting with its single bed is the woman's room and that she has come in quite recently from outdoors, leaving her hat and cloak on the bed. Perhaps her intention was to spend the evening mending her clothes, for her sewing box is open and her pair of scissors are on the table. Enter the top-hatted villain, whom she obviously knows. He treats her in so rough a way as to rip her corset from her body, and what we see in the depicted moment is the immediate aftermath. Other interpretations are of course reasonable, if they properly exhaust the mute data. One can imagine a working girl ruined by a member of the gentry, or accept the rape hypothesis of the early critics, who had the advantage of a vision relatively unclouded by scholarship. One can also, moving from dramatic fable to extracted subject, easily perceive the strongly polarized symbolic structure that had been haunting Degas's sexual imagination, or his unconscious, for at least a decade. Again the figures are near the edges of the canvas, with the male on the right and the female on the left, and are separated and linked by a zone of push-pull tension, which is marked here by the strategically placed corset. And the resulting air of belonging to a recognizable department in the artist's mind is strengthened by a number of other analogies, each of which, minor when alone, draws significance from the existence of the others. The adolescent male bravado in *Young Spartan Girls Provoking the Boys,* although cheerful, is an anticipation of the sullen machismo of the man in *Interior;* the crushed, humiliated woman in the latter picture is a sister of the blindly fleeing nude on the far left in *War Scene in the Middle Ages.* The Delsartian gaze in *Interior* recalls the looks of Baron Bellelli, the Spartan youngsters, and the archer in the *War Scene,* plus the note on the sketch of King Candaules' wife, who when painted would have been looking toward the peeping Tom with "the eye alone burning with sexual modesty and the idea of revenge."

Although the phrase "my genre painting" implies that *Interior* is the only thing of its theoretically inferior kind in Degas's work, in fact it was shortly followed by another example, variously referred to by critics as *Distraction, Conversation, Pouting, The Bookmaker,* and *The Banker,* and now usually, although not very satisfactorily, called *Sulking.* No literary source has been found, and probably none exists, for the picture looks very much like an improvised playlet. And it is not an altogether successful one. The symbolic accessories work well enough. The racks with ledgers, the documents that litter the desk, and the little window for clients announce a business concern, in all likelihood Auguste Degas's bank in the Rue de la Victoire. Although the English sporting print behind the figures, which reproduces a work by John Frederick Herring titled *Steeple Chase Cracks,* may rather jarringly suggest a betting office, it need not do so, and anyway the banking and bookmaking professions have certain common features. The real trouble lies with the actors, who are recognizable as Duranty and the model Emma Dobigny, and with the stage direction. Duranty is miming furiously, like an amateur performing in one of the charades that were popular during the Second Empire, and Mademoiselle Dobigny is looking placidly toward the audience, or toward the painter-director, as if waiting to be told what to do next. The result is that the viewer has almost no notion of what is going on, beyond the evident fact that once again there is tension between male on the right and female on the left.

Apparently Degas himself realized that with this puzzler he had reached, and even passed, the limit to what could be done with his theory of wordless expression, for he abandoned contemporary narrative as abruptly

Emma Dobigny, 1869

Sulking, 1869–1871

as he had dropped history painting a few years previously. He continued, however, to apply his theory, enriched by his experiments with *Interior* and *Sulking*, to portraiture and to the representation of psychological situations that did not call for story lines, and he went on discussing his ideas at the Guerbois — most fruitfully with Duranty, as a pamphlet by the latter would one day reveal.

The café was by no means the only place where one talked. The witty, worldly Alfred Stevens, who had come down from his native Brussels twenty years earlier to sit at the feet of Ingres and had wound up earning a fortune as a painter of svelte Parisiennes in Worth dresses and neo-Rococo drawing rooms, often gave parties, usually on Wednesdays, at his house across the street from 13 Rue de Laval. His guests, in addition to some of the Guerbois habitués, included Tissot, Puvis de Chavannes, the three Morisot sisters and their parents, and occasionally the quintessentially Second Empire Charles Haas, a boulevardier and art expert. In the Rue de Saint-Pétersbourg Manet's mother organized Thursday soirées at which one was apt to find Degas, Fantin, Zola, Astruc, Stevens, Puvis, the Morisots, the young composer Emmanuel Chabrier, and the poet Charles Cros, future inventor (on paper) of the phonograph. The Morisot home, near the Place du Trocadéro at 16 Rue Franklin, was almost a permanent clubhouse for artists and intellectuals, presided over by the sharp-tongued, knowledgeable Madame Morisot, who was a grandniece of Fragonard, and by her daughters, Yves, Berthe, and Edma, all three of whom were painters. Here some of the familiars, besides the Manet coterie, were the journalist and future minister Jules Ferry, the celebrated Dr. Emile Blanche, whose clinic for mental patients was nearby, and Corot, with whom the Morisot sisters had studied. Filling in sometimes for these three centers were two others, both in the Ninth Arrondissement, with which Degas was certainly acquainted, though they seem to have been outside his regular circuit. At 17 Rue Chaptal the pretty, good-hearted Nina de Callias, former wife of an alcoholic art critic, maintained a slightly bohemian salon frequented mostly by poets; she appears, a few years older, in Manet's *Lady with Fans*. At 6 Avenue Trudaine Madame Lejosne, the wife of Manet's Guerbois companion and a cousin of Bazille's mother, received Cézanne, Barbey d'Aurevilly, Nadar, Silvestre, Bracquemond, Manet, Bazille, Monet, Astruc, and the republican leader Léon Gambetta, and the conversation often turned into vituperation of Napoleon III.

Alfred Stevens's brother Arthur was an art critic, old-master expert, picture dealer, and general impresario who operated in both Brussels and Paris, so successfully that, according to a letter of 1865 from Baudelaire to Nadar, he was regarded "in France as the king of the Belgians and in

Belgium as the emperor of the French." [16] (He had returned this esteem, and in July 1866 escorted the dying, half-paralyzed poet back to the French capital.) Although his taste in painting was not very advanced, he had been in touch with Manet, Fantin, and Bracquemond, and he now, through the parties in the Rue de Laval, became interested in the work of Degas — with an outcome related by Achille in a letter of February 16, 1869, to the Mussons in New Orleans:

> Edgar has come up to Brussels with me. He has met Monsieur Van Praet, one of the king's ministers, who had bought one of his pictures, and has seen himself represented in a gallery that is among the most celebrated in Europe. That has afforded him a certain pleasure, as you can well imagine, and has at last given him a bit of confidence in himself and his talent, which is genuine. He has sold two other paintings during his stay in Brussels, and a very well-known dealer, Stevens, has offered him a contract with a payment of twelve thousand francs a year. So he is definitely launched, and I think you will learn of his success with pleasure. He has merited it . . . [17]

Edgar must indeed have been gratified by an offer that would have made the impoverished Pissarro, Renoir, or Monet dance with joy. (Renoir was at the moment living partly on the charity of Bazille, and Monet was sometimes close to suicide.) But he finally, for unrevealed reasons, said no. Possibly he was dismayed by a close look at some of the dealer's specialties — genre scenes by local artists, miniature semipastiches by Meissonier, and pictures of dogs and monkeys by Joseph, the third Stevens brother (who was one of the Empress Eugénie's favorite painters). One may also suppose that he reflected on a climactic episode in *Manette Salomon* in which a commercial gallery owner negotiates successfully with the now completely degraded and will-less, though still faintly aristocratic, hero:

> Coriolis signed a contract by which he engaged himself to deliver a certain number of easel paintings each year, in return for a guaranteed annual income. It was his talent, his life, that Manette had just forced him to sell. [18]

The coincidence extended to the nationality of the fictional dealer; he was a Belgian, and not improbably an echo of Arthur Stevens himself, with whom the Goncourts were well acquainted through their activities as collectors.

Back in Paris the round of talk was resumed, and the Morisot sisters soon proved more interesting than an art merchant, partly because they were more vulnerable to ironic flirting and chaffing. Berthe was intelligent, talented, and almost melodramatically beautiful, with a helmet of black hair and the large, dark eyes of a potential femme fatale. She had exhibited her poetic, light-filled pictures — in some ways more modern than what the other members of the group were then doing — at the Salon and had won praise from the very serious critic Paul Mantz in the *Gazette des Beaux-Arts*. But in 1869 she was twenty-eight years old and still unmarried, and she was inclined, with perfect self-awareness, to become jealous or at least flustered when the men she liked and admired paid attention to other women. She called Manet's wife "fat Suzanne,"[19] resented Fantin's growing attachment to the demure Victoria Dubourg, and confessed that Eva Gonzalès, Manet's shapely, twenty-year-old model and disciple, irritated her profoundly. Her younger sister, Edma, had a milder form of the same competitiveness, complicated by a new situation: after years of painting alongside Berthe and sharing the stimulating company of male artists, she had recently married a naval officer, Adolphe Pontillon, and she now feared that she was sinking into provincial wifeliness. Yves, the oldest of the three, had married a certain Gobillard, an army officer too obscure for his first name to have survived, and was just beginning to emerge, a very late bloomer, from a habit of reticence acquired perhaps from living with her talkative sisters.

During the spring and early summer of 1869 all these traits and circumstances produced a set of family letters[20] that can be read as a little drama, half comic and half sad, of nineteenth-century feminine mentalities, with Degas frequently on stage, oddly remote and close up at the same time. Something about him impelled the sisters and their mother, even when writing to each other, almost always to call him Monsieur Degas, whereas they referred without any such ceremony to Fantin, Manet, and Puvis. Yet he was an intimate acquaintance, encountered regularly at Stevens's Wednesday parties and Madame Manet's Thursday salons, and he was sometimes around the house in the Rue Franklin nearly all day. Apparently part of their difficulty with him was his disconcerting way of addressing them rather as if they were men, without the conventional gallantry they had been educated to expect, and another part was his often multilevel and sometimes wicked sense of humor. For instance, shortly before her marriage he suggested to Edma that she should read Benjamin Constant's *Adolphe*. The play on her future husband's first name may have seemed obvious and harmless, but there was mischievousness in persuading an inexperienced young woman to prepare for her sexual initiation by studying Constant's pitilessly lucid analysis of emotional impotence.

On March 15 the newlyweds were temporarily established at Pau, in the Pyrenees, and Edma, already bored with the provinces and longing for her old life as a painter, sent off a melancholy note to Berthe:

> The snow has been falling in huge flakes all morning. The mountains have disappeared in the fog, and we are staying close to the fire. . . . I have

therefore bought *Adolphe,* which I found quite easily here, and I am reading a few pages of it when I am tired of doing nothing. The book rivets one's attention, as Monsieur Degas told me it would. . . . I am often with you, my dear Berthe, in my thoughts. I follow you around in your studio, and I should like to escape from here if only for fifteen minutes in order to breathe again that atmosphere in which we lived for so many years.

Berthe replied with an account of one of Stevens's parties:

Monsieur Degas seems very satisfied with his portrait [of Joséphine Gaujelin]. It is all he has done for the Salon. He talked about you the other evening. He finds you very strange, and from several things he said to me about you, I judge that he is quite observant. He laughed while thinking of you reading *Adolphe.* He came over and sat down beside me, pretending that he was going to court me. But the courting was limited to a long commentary on Solomon's proverb "Woman is the desolation of the righteous."

On March 19 she wrote again, clearly worried by Edma's rapid disillusionment with a dull marriage and saddened by her own recently mocked spinsterhood:

This painting and this work which you regret are the cause of many anxieties. . . . Come now, you have not chosen the worst of fates. . . . Remember that being alone is a great affliction. Whatever one may say or do, a woman has an immense need for affection. To try to make her retire into herself is to attempt the impossible.

Madame Morisot, in another letter to Edma, intervened more vigorously:

I have just found [Berthe] in bed with her nose against the wall, trying to hide her weeping. She is going to try to get up. We have finished with our tour of artists. They are brainless. They are weathercocks who play ball games with you.

On March 21 Edma, unconvinced by her mother's outburst, chose to reply to Berthe:

It's disheartening if one can no longer rely on artists! My infatuation with Manet is over. As for Monsieur Degas, that's different. I am curious, for example. I should like to know what he could have said to you about me, and what he finds strange in me. The commentary on Solomon's proverb must have been quite pretty and piquant. You can think I'm foolish if you want to, but when I reflect on all these painters, I say to myself that a quarter of an hour of their conversation is worth a lot of more solid things. . . . Here life is still the same. The fireplace and falling rain.

April was a difficult month for Berthe: she was harassed by an unsuccessful family attempt to find a husband for her and was too discouraged to work or to send anything to the big annual exhibition. In the meantime Degas was being cheered by the jury's acceptance of his portrait of Joséphine Gaujelin and was engrossed in a projected conversation piece involving a Madame Lisle and a Madame Loubens, two marginal members of the Manet circle whose large bodies and smooth, sluggish faces seem to have temporarily fascinated him. He reappears, however, along with other Morisot friends, on May 2 in an account of the Salon opening Berthe sent to Edma:

> I found Manet there, with his hat on in the sun and a dazed look on his face. He begged me to go look at his picture [*The Balcony*], saying he didn't dare. . . . [Fantin] cut a rather sorry figure with an insignificant little sketch hung at an unbelievable height. . . . Decidedly, I am afraid his abuse of the Louvre and of the company of Mademoiselle Dubourg is not good for him. Monsieur Degas looked contented. But can you guess for whom he abandoned me? For Madame Lisle and Madame Loubens! I must admit that I was a little nettled to see a man whom I consider very witty drop me and direct his amiability toward two female blockheads. This visit to the exhibition was beginning, I felt, to lack charm.

On May 5, after returning to examine the Gaujelin picture and other works, she reported:

> Monsieur Degas has a very pretty little portrait of a very ugly woman in black, wearing a hat and letting her cashmere shawl drop, the whole thing against the background of a very light apartment with a corner of a fireplace [*sic*] in half-tint. It's very subtle and distinguished.

A week later she had news of a more surprising kind, along with some comfort for Edma:

> On Wednesday we were at Stevens's place. Yves has definitely made a conquest of Monsieur Degas. He has asked permission to do her portrait. He still talks to me about you, wants to know how you are getting along, and becomes indignant at the idea that I am keeping you informed about his new admirations.

On May 23 Madame Morisot was able to announce that the promised likeness was under way:

> Do you know that Monsieur Degas has become mad about Yves's face? He has made a sketch of her — an odd way to do a portrait. He is going to transfer to a canvas what he does here in an album.

By this time Berthe was exasperated enough to drop the "monsieur" at least once, to enjoy some of Manet's maliciousness, and to pretend that Edma was the only one interested in the portraitist:

Yves Gobillard-Morisot, 1869

As for your friend Degas, I definitely do not think that he has an attractive character. He is witty, and that's all. Manet, in a very droll way, said to me yesterday, "He lacks naturalness. He is not capable of loving a woman, much less of telling her that he does or of doing anything about it." Poor Manet is sad; his exhibited pictures, as always, are not to the taste of the public. . . . Monsieur Degas has done a sketch of Yves, which I find mediocre. He chattered all the while he was doing it, making fun of his friend Fantin by saying that the latter would do well to go and draw new strength in the arms of Love, since painting was no longer an adequate inspiration. He was in capital mocking form, comparing Puvis to the condor in the zoo at the Jardin des Plantes.

With the approach of summer Edma and Berthe decided to get together in Brittany, and on June 26 Yves herself wrote a final report on the sittings:

As Mother must have told you, my dear Berthe, Monsieur Degas absorbed so much of my time at the end of my stay in Paris that my letter-writing

On the Channel Coast, 1869

was put aside. . . . The drawing he did of me during the final two days is really very pretty — both frank and refined. He could not stop working on it, and I am a little doubtful about his being able to transfer it to a canvas without spoiling it. He informed Mother that he would come back one of these days to draw a corner of the garden and tell her some thumping lies.

He finished the oil version of the portrait in his studio in July, and then he too left Paris for a vacation.

During the rest of the month and part of August he was at Boulogne-sur-Mer, where Manet was again spending the season, and also farther down the Channel coast at Etretat, Dives, and Villers-sur-Mer; the pictorial result was a series of forty-four pastel landscapes and seascapes that must have surprised the Guerbois talkers who thought of him as strictly a figure painter. In fact, these strange little compositions may still nonplus an appreciator. They do not fit easily into any such stylistic category as Neo-classicism, Romanticism, or Realism; they have no topographical value and none of the indulgence in the pathetic fallacy to be found in the work of the Barbizon school. Although they contain a scattering of boats, a few lonely houses, and some dark spots that may be human beings, they are mostly just nebulous studies of skies, seas, beaches, cliffs, and deserted slopes, made from a distance great enough to suggest sometimes a view of a hostile planet. Plainly, there was no question of planting an easel in the sand and communing with nature or catching the gaiety of a holiday crowd; these pictures were all painted from memory in hotel rooms or in the Rue de Laval. The only aspect they have in common with the exactly contemporary experiments of Monet and Renoir at La Grenouillère is an implied acceptance of the relatively new aesthetic of the sketch — new in the sense that sketches or impressions, long produced as preparation for finished paintings, were now being executed increasingly as valuable works in their own right, and were thus opening a breach in the academic tradition more important than the insistence on contemporaneity in subject matter. But there is a perceptible difference between a sketch filtered and simplified by memory and one that retains the complexity of on-the-spot vision, and in these Channel images Degas is often closer to a schematic nocturne by Whistler, who also worked from memory, than he is to Impressionism. Moreover, unlike the effort at La Grenouillère, they seem to have been largely just a summer's entertainment, for he was soon back in the Ninth Arrondissement, exploring other ways of being of his own time, especially those suggested by his interest in music.

The Second Empire was on the whole not very rich in great composers and not very appreciative of those it had. Hector Berlioz, hissed regularly in Paris, had to seek recognition of his genius in Germany and England. In the Rue Le Peletier the core of the usual season consisted of ballet and of such works from the 1830s and 1840s as Rossini's *Guillaume Tell,* Donizetti's *Lucia di Lammermoor,* Halévy's *La Juive,* and Meyerbeer's *Robert le Diable;* during the entire period from 1852 to 1870 only five new French operas entered the repertoire. Little was being written in the more abstract forms; for example, there was as yet no French piano sonata at all. Saint-Saëns, looking back forty years later, recalled:

> There was a universal cult, a positive idolatry, of "melody" or, more exactly, of the tune that could be picked up at once and easily remembered. . . . It was quite useless to try and get a symphony, a trio, or a quartet performed except by the Société des Concerts du Conservatoire or by one or two private chamber music societies.[21]

In the 1860s, however, the situation had improved measurably with the entrance of such composers as Charles Gounod, Bizet, and Saint-Saëns himself. And the last appears to have exaggerated the unresponsiveness of audiences, for there was certainly a lot of good, if not always immortal, music being listened to by a sizable public. Opera was available not only in the Rue Le Peletier but also at the Théâtre des Italiens, the recently rebuilt Théâtre-Lyrique (today the Théâtre de la Ville), and the Opéra-Comique. At the Bouffes-Parisiens, in the Rue Monsigny near the Bibliothèque Nationale, Offenbach went from success to success. On Sunday afternoons in the Cirque Impérial, the conductor Jules Pasdeloup organized low-priced orchestral and choral concerts at which audiences of up to five thousand heard Mendelssohn, Schumann, Saint-Saëns, Bizet, and even Wagner. Ostensibly more sophisticated and at any rate more affluent listeners were provided for by the semiprivate Société des Concerts du Conservatoire. Half a dozen chamber music societies were functioning, and musical soirées were frequent in the drawing rooms of the well-to-do.

This world of sound was linked in many ways to the visual world of what was often referred to by art critics as "the Batignolles group." Bazille played piano arrangements for four hands with his friend Edmond Maître, attended the Pasdeloup concerts, went to the funeral of Berlioz in March 1869, and adored Gluck, Mozart, and Wagner. Fantin, also one of the Sunday regulars at the Cirque Impérial, had already begun to paint his visionary evocations of *Tannhäuser* and of the music of Schumann, so assiduously that Champfleury had nicknamed him the Schumannist. Renoir as a boy had sung in the choir of the church of Saint-Eustache under the direction of Gounod, with such success that the composer had tried to persuade him to become a professional singer instead of a painter, and as part of the campaign had given the Renoir family a loge at the Opéra for a performance of *Lucia di Lammermoor.* (Ungratefully, the grown-up artist had shifted his admiration from Gounod and Donizetti to Offenbach and Wagner.) Between 1866 and 1869 Cézanne painted three pictures of a young woman playing the piano, each of them titled *Overture of Tannhäuser.* (At the time there were piano versions of nearly every popular opera and of many orchestral pieces.) Manet, besides listening to Suzanne at the keyboard, was friendly through her with the four Claus sisters, who formed the Sainte-Cécile String Quartet and performed at his mother's Thursday evenings; through his wife he was also acquainted with Chabrier, and through Commandant Lejosne with Offenbach, who had a town house in the Rue de La Rochefoucauld and sometimes showed up at Madame Lejosne's salon. (Jenny Claus stands next to Berthe Morisot in *The Balcony,* and Offenbach appears in another Manet painting, *Music in the Tuileries.*)

Degas participated in this cultural exchange between eye and ear very much on his own terms. Although he was in no sense a professional performer, he reportedly had a pleasant singing voice, a good musical memory, and a knack for picking out tunes on a piano. A notion of his musical tastes around 1869 can be pieced together partly from later evidence — and the operation is clearly quite safe, for there is no sign of evolution in his likes and dislikes. He enjoyed Gluck, Cimarosa, Weber, Meyerbeer, Verdi, Gounod, Chabrier, café-concert songs, ballads with guitar accompaniment, and the balletic works of composers like Delibes, Minkus, and Adolphe Adam. He found Beethoven a bit depressing, and he firmly, mockingly resisted Wagnerian religiosity. An important element in his pleasure was theatrical, in that he relished the visible presence of singers and instrumentalists. (If he had ever made the pilgrimage to Bayreuth, he would have certainly disapproved of the covered orchestra pit in the festival theater.) All this can be judged from several different angles. Generalizers about supposed national and racial characteristics may feel that he was typically French, or at least Latin, in his preference for intelligibility and sensuality over Germanic symbolism, idealism, and emotional content. From the Saint-Saëns point of view, he can be regarded as a Second Empire middle-brow who worshiped melody; from that of a psychosociologist, as an inverted snob given to musical slumming; from that of Wagnerian converts like Bazille, Fantin, Renoir, and Cézanne, as a hopeless reactionary; and in the long perspective of recurrent stylistic history, as a precursor of the sophisticated Parisian tastemakers of the 1920s who liked music hall jazz, praised Igor Stravinsky's return to the eighteenth century, and detested what they dismissed as Teutonic fog. In this context as in many others, about the only completely mistaken judgment one could make would be that he was uncomplicated.

He knew many musicians personally, some of them through his father and the Manets and others through his familiarity with the Opéra, where he had held a season ticket since he was twenty and had frequented the wings in the company of his old schoolmate Ludovic Halévy. Among the composers he knew were Bizet, who by 1869 had written *Les Pêcheurs de Perles* and *La Jolie Fille de Perth;* the brilliant, funny, voraciously vital Chabrier, future composer of *España,* eventual collector of Impressionist works, and already a close friend of several painters (Tissot had done a portrait of him as early as 1861); and Ernest Reyer, who was the composer of a ballet and three operas, a critic, and an intimate of the Halévys, the Manets, and the Lejosnes. The Restaurant de la Mère Lefebvre, in the Rue de La Tour d'Auvergne, within walking distance of both the Rue Le Peletier and the Rue de Laval, was a sort of Guerbois for musicians, with two large rooms that Degas referred to as the aquarium, because of its many mirrors, and the morgue, because of its slabs of marble. Here he was often in the company of members of the Opéra orchestra, and by around 1868–1869 he was particularly friendly with the burly, walrus-mustached Désiré Dihau, who played the bassoon, sometimes as a soloist at the Pasdeloup concerts, and composed songs and waltzes; the cellist Pillet (or Pilet), an apparently mild, scholarly man who was nevertheless known for his outspokenness during quarrels with the Opéra management about salaries; and the bald, faunlike flutist Joseph Altès, who was a professor at the Conservatoire and whose younger brother Ernest, a violinist, became musical director of the Opéra. Another new acquaintance of this period was Désiré Dihau's sister Marie, a talented, sweet-natured, rather plain young pianist and singer who lived in Lille but often came down to Paris to give concerts, and for whom Degas acquired a lasting affection. Somewhat outside the Mère Lefebvre circle, there was the Spanish tenor and guitarist Lorenzo Pagans, who had made his début in 1860 at the Opéra in *Sémiramis* (the French adaptation of Rossini's opera), had then transferred his activity to the Théâtre des Italiens, and now appeared frequently at private musicales, singing nineteenth-century serenades and eighteenth-century airs, particularly those of Rameau, with a charm that suggested Watteau. In a special category was Madame Camus, an excellent amateur pianist, a spirited, wistfully frail woman, and the wife of a prosperous physician who treated Degas, sculpted fake antique bibelots, and collected Meissen porcelain, fine glassware, and Japanese objets d'art. Edmond de Goncourt wrote of her that in the midst of her husband's fragile treasures "she looked, with her willowy figure and her aristocratic bloodlessness, like the goddess of the universe on the shelves," and added that she had never been seen eating anything.[22]

Auguste, now in his mid-sixties, with a white mustache and a faded, bony look, but with all of his old enthusiasm for music intact, organized little concerts in the Rue de Mondovi on Monday evenings, and he would be remembered circling up through the Ninth Arrondissement in a hackney coach to pick up Edgar, Marie Dihau, and her brother Désiré. Often the guests also included Pagans, Madame Camus and her husband, and Suzanne and Edouard Manet, the last sitting cross-legged like a Turk on the floor in front of the fireplace. If the conversation showed signs of being prolonged, the elder Degas would call everyone to order with a "come now, children, we are losing precious time,"[23] and the performances would get under way, reportedly with an emphasis on eighteenth-century Italian pieces in order to please the host, although Suzanne, in spite of having short, pudgy fingers, is said to have been an effective interpreter of Chopin.

A moment during such a Monday evening, probably in 1869, is exquisitely preserved in *Pagans and Auguste Degas.* Surprisingly, this is

Edgar's earliest portrait of Auguste; apparently the liberation indicated by the final self-portrait, the dropping of history painting, and the move from parental territory to the Rue de Laval had to occur first. But the picture is also, quite apart from its biographical interest, a lesson in economical mise-en-scène and one of the most affecting representations the nineteenth century has left us of the actual act, the inner psychological reality, of performing music and listening to it. To look at the eyes and hands of Pagans and then at those of Auguste is to be convinced that we are a long way from Puvis de Chavannes's pale muses and Fantin's vaporous echoes of Schumann and Wagner — and that Degas's dumb-show theory, when applied to something other than narrative, is thoroughly tenable.

To about the same date, give or take a year, can be assigned several other works related to the Opéra or the Monday evenings. Joseph Altès, bright-eyed, beaked, and a trifle seedy, is portrayed in a profile that sug-

Pagans and
Auguste Degas, c. 1869

gests the influence of one of Auguste's Italian Primitives, perhaps Pisanello. The grave, bulldog Pillet appears at his desk in the Rue Le Peletier at work on a composition or transcription he has been trying out on his cello; behind him hangs a lithograph, invented by Degas, in which a number of famous musicians, writers, and painters — among them Chopin, Liszt, Berlioz, Heine, Balzac, Gautier, George Sand, and Delacroix — seem to be welcoming him to their assembly. Marie Dihau is represented on one occasion looking back at us from her piano and score as if interrupted in her playing, and on another seated in the Restaurant de la Mère Lefebvre with her traveling bag, disconsolately ready for one of her trips back to Lille. (She was evidently a sympathetic subject to artists, for she was painted many years later by Toulouse-Lautrec, who was a distant cousin, and by Sargent.) Madame Camus also was favored with two portraits, both of which show her at home. In the first she sits next to her piano, wearing a black dress

*Marie Dihau
at the Piano,* c. 1869

with a plunging neckline and a blue bow, idly fingering the keys with her right hand, and looking neurotic; a lamp on the right outside the picture gently models her face and neck, glows in a flowery little mirror, and makes a porcelain figurine cast a shadow that resembles her own silhouette. In the second picture she is wearing a red dress, posing in profile against a red wall, and holding a Japanese fan; an invisible lamp supported by a statuette of a blackamoor is placed so as to leave the side of her toward the viewer in a deep shade. The intention to follow the notebook advice on hidden artificial illumination is plain, and so is the rejection both of academic diffusiveness and of the strong frontal lighting that flattens people and objects in many of Manet's paintings.

Madame Camus
at the Piano, 1869

In *The Orchestra of the Opéra,* which was perhaps begun in 1868, many of the ideas being experimented with during this period are summed up in a wonderfully complex, half-imaginary and half-veristic composition. The problem posed by the slogan *il faut être de son temps* is here solved with unusual precision: few pictorial motifs could be more indubitably in the Second Empire present, more a celebration of nowness, than this seemingly random glimpse of the stage, pit, and loges in the Rue Le Peletier, of swirling skirts and tripping legs, and of white-bibbed men sounding an orchestral tutti. An out-of-focus sketchiness in the handling of the dancers, combined with elimination of their heads and shoulders, adds to the effect

The Orchestra of the Opéra, 1868–1869

of an instantaneous rendering. (The cropping was probably borrowed from one of Daumier's lithographs, *The Orchestra During the Performance of a Tragedy;* other possible influences on the picture were Kiyonaga's prints showing instrumentalists accompanying Kabuki plays, and *The Théâtre du Gymnase,* by the German painter Adolf Menzel, whom Degas met at Stevens's house some time around 1867.)

Le Brun, Lavater, and Delsarte are relegated to the category of mere theorists by the expressive, carefully observed faces of the identifiable musicians — the cellist Pillet on the far left, the bassoonist Dihau in the center with the flutist Altès and the violinists Lancien and Gout diagonally to the right, and the double bass player Gouffé on the far right. Whereas in the picture of *La Source* Eugénie Fiocre is simply posing and the sets and lighting are realistic enough to have misled Zola into thinking of an actual landscape with figures, here the ballerinas, for the first time in Degas's work, are in tutus and in motion, the set is an almost abstract backdrop, and the scene — in line with the artist's new interest in artificial illumination from hidden projectors — is caught in the glare of gas footlights. The theatricality of this upper zone is strengthened, in the manner of the heavenly zone above the assembled hidalgos in El Greco's *Burial of Count Orgaz,* by the contrast with the realistic treatment of the orchestra men, who are bathed in a semiclarity produced by an unseen chandelier somewhere behind and above the viewer. (The Wagnerian theory of the theater of narcosis, which called for plunging an auditorium into total darkness during a performance, was not yet current, and the Opéra was essentially an eighteenth-century Italian house, designed and lit on the assumption that people came to see each other as well as the stage spectacle.)

But unreality does not completely cease in this supposedly factual area, for the orchestra itself turns out, after a second look, to be partly make-believe. Its seating arrangement is a musical absurdity, dictated by the demands of a group portrait and by such purely visual concerns as the effectiveness of Dihau and his diagonal bassoon in the center. Five of the violinists, for all their intent, score-following eyes and the exact unison of their bow movements, are simply friends miming their roles: from left to right above the heads of Pillet and Dihau, they are the singer Pagans (next to the harp), the ballet producer Gard (with white hair), the painter Piot-Normand (with a bald head), the composer Souquet (in full face), and the physician Pillot (looking up at the dancers). And this is not quite all of the amateur-theatrical aspect, for in the partly visible loge Chabrier, like a suddenly sprung jack-in-the-box, is playing the part of a spectator.

Although equally complex mixtures of observation, arbitrariness, verisimilitude, and aestheticized reality were of course not always possible or desirable, something of the sort can be found even in the racetrack scenes that reappeared toward the close of the 1860s and that often misled viewers into thinking they were reportage of actual events. None of these pictures was painted outdoors on the spot; all are mise-en-scènes fabricated in the studio with the aid of memory, notes, models, and already existing drawings. In only a few instances can the stands at Longchamp be recognized; the rest of the time we seem to be in vague reminiscences of the countryside on the Channel coast or around the Haras du Pin. Famous winners like Gladiateur and classic races like the Prix du Jockey Club or the Grand Prix de Paris are never represented. The pedigrees of the horses are discoverable not in the *Stud Book Français* but in the work of Parthenon artists, Uccello, Gozzoli, Van Dyck, Géricault, De Dreux, Meissonier, English designers of sporting prints, and perhaps the young animal sculptor Joseph Cuvelier,

Racehorses in Front of the Stands, 1869–1872

with whom Degas seems to have been on close terms at this time. (The notebooks covering the period from 1865 to 1870 contain addresses for Cuvelier in Paris and Fontainebleau and at Comines, in northern France.) The owners' colors worn by the jockeys are too imaginary to be of any interest to turf scholars, and sometimes the true "owner" is another painter: in *The False Start,* for example, the galloping horse in the foreground is a reversed copy of the one in the lower right corner of the Herring print that hangs back of Duranty in *Sulking* (and probably belonged to Degas or his father), and in *Racehorses in Front of the Stands* the horse on the left is a borrowing, again reversed, of the one in the center foreground of Meissonier's *The Emperor at Solferino.* (The latter painting and a tiny companion work had been purchased in 1864 for the Musée du Luxembourg for the sensational sum of fifty thousand francs.) This listing of debts is not meant to imply an academic approach, for in fact a picture like *Racehorses in Front of the Stands,* with its subtle contrasts between browns, reds, yellows, and blues, its cool light, and its pattern of late-afternoon shadows, is a remarkably fresh notation of a moment in a day at the track. It is, however, an additional example, like *The Orchestra of the Opéra,* of how Degas, though certainly a realist in one sense of the word, liked to work usually at a considerable psychic distance from raw data and often on material already processed by himself, by another hand, or by the methods and media of another art or discipline. Memory was a vital element in the processing. Indeed, he once suggested that for him memory was itself almost an artist, since it reproduced "only what has impressed you, which is to say only what is necessary."[24] But his love of the factitious was important too, and one explanation for his interest in turf motifs may be that racehorses are extremely unnatural animals, carefully processed for participation in a spectacle that is nearly as artificial as ballet.

He was winding up the decade in excellent shape. His relations with his family continued to be warm. Around 1869 he did an elegant pastel of Thérèse, standing in the drawing room in the Rue de Mondovi with a Rococo candelabra next to her and a work by Perronneau on the wall in the background — aristocratic accessories that remind us of her rank as a duchess and of her father's money and taste. Marguerite, who in 1865 had married an architect, Henri Fevre, and had settled down in the Boulevard Malesherbes to raise a large family, appears in a tender little oil that suggests the fondness Edgar had always had for her. His relations with the Morisots also continued; an item of evidence was a fan that he decorated with Spanish dancers and a portrait of Alfred de Musset and presented to Berthe, who treasured it all her life and copied it in several of her own paintings.

He was beginning, however, to move occasionally out of his own social class in search of subject matter, partly under the influence of writers like Duranty and Zola and partly because of his own penchant for observing Parisian manners and morals during his strolls about town, and one of the results was *Laundry Girl,* a pastel usually assigned to 1869. The theme was not a new one in the visual arts, Daumier and the lithographer Paul Gavarni having already treated it, but Degas — with the help of Emma Dobigny, who was again his model — brought to it an exact feeling for professional movement and an unsentimental matter-of-factness that were new. The picture turned out to be the first in a long, masterly series representing women ironing.

Laundry Girl, 1869

His self-confidence was now such that, in an open letter published by the *Paris-Journal* on April 12, 1870, he tried to explain to the Salon jury how it should go about organizing the annual exhibition. To get rid of the clutter and the "skying" that were the causes of chronic complaining by artists and visitors, he proposed that there be only two rows of paintings, hung at approximately eye level and reasonably spaced; that the resulting need for more walls be filled by some of the rooms normally reserved for drawings; and that the displaced drawings be hung on free-standing screens. (He had seen such screens in use in the English section of the Exposition Universelle of 1867.) Since many artists, evidently including himself, had misgivings about a picture or statue when they saw it out of the studio for the first time and found themselves in the position of the judging public, he thought that exhibitors should be given a few days of grace after the opening of the Salon during which they could withdraw a work if they wished. He also felt that big pieces of sculpture ought to be scattered around on the floor of the Palais de l'Industrie as if at random, and he concluded, "I could go on."

The jury ignored all his proposals. But it did accept for the exhibition his red portrait of Madame Camus with a Japanese fan, along with a pastel study of Yves Gobillard-Morisot that was one of the results of his visits in the Rue Franklin the previous summer. In fact, the so-called Batignolles group was on the whole favored: Manet, Berthe Morisot, Pissarro, Bazille, Renoir, Sisley, and Fantin were on view, all of them except Bazille with two pictures, and only Monet and Cézanne were among those totally refused. Berthe reported to Edma that the pastel of Yves was a "masterpiece," and that her own exhibited works brought compliments from nearly everyone, "with the exception as always of Monsieur Degas, who has a sovereign contempt for anything I may do."[25] (She was exaggerating.)

In *L'Electeur libre* Théodore Duret praised the portrait of Madame Camus; in *Paris-Journal* Duranty gently blamed the artist for having allegedly sacrificed the human being in the picture in favor of the effect of the luminous red background. But both the praise and the blame could be discounted, since *L'Electeur libre* was a small weekly representing the republican opposition to the imperial regime, Duret was a wealthy young cognac dealer just getting started as an art critic, and Duranty, in spite of his friendly intentions and frequently perceptive remarks, was after all a member of "the literary tribe" who thought in psychological and narrative rather than visual terms. And anyway, for a number of historical and personal reasons, Degas's career as a Salon exhibitor was now, like his attempt to become an Establishment history painter, permanently over.

10. Military Interlude

ON OCTOBER 30, 1869, Meilhac and Halévy had presented their new comedy, *Froufrou,* at the Théâtre des Variétés. The title, with its evocation of rustling silk and swishing crinolines, was an onomatopoeia for the entire *fête impériale,* the play was both droll and sentimental, and the public, including the empress, was enthusiastic. A visitor to Paris might have concluded that no important changes were impending in France, and his impression would have been confirmed on May 8, 1870, when, in a skillfully staged plebiscite, Napoleon III obtained a *oui* landslide of more than seven million against a *non* vote of only a million and a half. But in fact *Froufrou* and the plebiscite were the last notable successes of a Second Empire that was soon to collapse in a mishmash of jingoism, theatrics, inefficiency, heroism, and massacres.

On July 5 Europe was startled by the revelation that an obscure Hohenzollern princelet, a distant relative of King William I of Prussia, was a candidate for the vacant Spanish throne. The Quai d'Orsay feared a repetition of the sixteenth-century situation in which France had been surrounded by a Germanic empire, and hence made a stiff protest. Bismarck was delighted, because he was looking forward to a conflict with the French that would cement the unification of the still nominally separate German states into a single great power under the leadership of Prussia. But King William was past seventy, weary of war, and alarmed by the ambitions of his prime minister; and Napoleon III was gravely ill with a bladder complaint, preoccupied with liberal reforms at home, and acutely aware of being militarily unprepared for another Solferino. So a tactful arrangement for the withdrawal of the princelet's availability was soon at the point of being concluded. Then the French government, suddenly not satisfied with the extent of its diplomatic victory, blundered in a way for which Bismarck could scarcely have hoped. Egged on by chauvinistic newspapers and by a group of Bonapartists around the Empress Eugénie, it insisted on a Prussian promise never to renew the Hohenzollern candidacy. The worried King William, who was at Ems, temporized by politely refusing to see the French ambassador, and sent off a telegram to Bismarck in Berlin explaining the situation. The prime minister deleted the evidence of courtesy from the message and released the doctored version for publication, remarking to some friends that it would be "a red rag to the Gallic bull."[1] He was right. Swept into irrationality by what looked like an insult, by crowds singing the "Marseillaise," by a wave of hysterical patriotism in the press, and by the optimism of uninformed politicians, France declared war on July 19. It did so, Premier Emile Ollivier announced, "with a light heart."[2]

After a hasty, partly bungled mobilization, the imperial forces were assembled in Alsace and Lorraine, where they faced an enemy somewhat better at staff work, slightly inferior in infantry firepower, and vastly superior in numbers and in heavy artillery. In Alsace the Germans won a battle at Wissembourg on August 4 and another at the village of Froeschwiller two days later. At Reichshoffen the French cuirassiers, in bright red trousers and plumed shakos, spurred their horses across the hop fields with such impetuosity and allowed themselves to be slaughtered in such numbers that when the news of the engagement reached Paris, confused townspeople broke out flags in celebration of a victory — only to learn from another dispatch that the glorious charge was an incident in a major defeat at Woerth and that in fact the whole province was now lost. In Lorraine an army under Marshal Achille-François Bazaine was by mid-August bottled up at Metz and practically eliminated from the war (owing in part to the nearly treasonable lethargy of its commander). And meanwhile most of the remaining imperial troops in the region, under the command of Marshal Patrice MacMahon and the emperor himself, were being cornered near Sedan. On the morning of September 2 about two hundred and fifty thousand Germans launched a final assault on the hundred thousand trapped Frenchmen. At the village of Bazeilles, three kilometers southeast of Sedan, a group of infantrymen, most of them already wounded, held out to their last cartridge in a house that is today pointed out to tourists as La Maison de la Dernière Cartouche. Across a neighboring stretch of open ground French cavalrymen staged a series of futile charges and died with such panache that King William, on a nearby hilltop, was heard to murmur "Ah, the brave fellows."[3] Napoleon III, in agony because of his diseased bladder and heavily rouged to hide his pallor, galloped about the battlefield as if hoping to be killed. But at the end of the day he was unluckily still alive, and he and his surviving soldiers were prisoners.

The Germans were soon advancing, almost unopposed, toward Paris, and at this point in the story a flashback to the recent, frivolous past can throw some light on ensuing events. On the Sunday morning of March 27, 1870, Meilhac and Halévy were obliged to take a train trip up through the red brick towns of northern France to Brussels, where one of their plays was opening. Meilhac, unused to early rising, slept in a corner of their compartment during most of the journey. Halévy read, looked out the window, and took notes:

> *Ten o'clock. Tergnier.* Bricks, bricks, bricks. Meilhac has breakfast, but without waking up.

> *Eleven o'clock. Saint-Quentin.* At last, Meilhac can be considered approximately awake. He notices the houses of Saint-Quentin. "A town?" he says. "Away from Paris? What good is that? All towns should be forced to group themselves around Paris."

> *Eleven thirty. Maubeuge.* "Still another town!" Meilhac exclaims, completely scandalized. "What can people be doing in there?" I reply, "They are working for Paris."[4]

This sort of urbicentrism was not limited to badinage between sophisticates. Many plain Parisians, including workers, were close to tacitly assuming that France was a single metropolis surrounded by the suburbs and fields necessary for its maintenance, and there were substantial reasons for such an assumption. The capital was not only the center from which French highways, railroads, political decisions, and cultural activity radiated; it was also the place where within living memory much of French history had been made. Paris had toppled Louis XVI, Charles X, and Louis-Philippe, had created two republics, and during the Revolution — significantly in the present context — had organized the armies that cleared the country of invaders. A favorite author of Degas's, Louis Veuillot, could write with considerable justification that "since 1789 France has had only one king, Paris."[5] Moreover, in the autumn of 1870 both Parisian particularism and the Parisian sense of historical mission were heightened by the capital's vote in the May plebiscite — *non.* It was the régime of the peasants that had led to the disaster of Sedan, and now it was up to the republican center to save the nation. For the moment, on both the Left Bank and the Right, in both proletarian Montmartre and the bourgeois Ninth Arrondissement, patriotism, republicanism, and Parisianism were indistinguishable.

On September 4 a mob stormed into the Palais Bourbon, halted the deliberations of the still Bonapartist Corps Législatif, and then marched to the Hôtel de Ville, where the end of the Second Empire was voted by acclamation, a republic was proclaimed, and an exclusively Parisian "government of national defense" was formed and told to continue the war. All this was not quite as absurd as it may have looked to professional military men on the outside, and not quite an illustration of the Tocqueville adage that every historical event occurs twice, once as tragedy and once as farce. For the old municipal outer ring of fortifications, although in disrepair, was still usable, a sizable supply of artillery pieces, small arms, and ammunition was on hand, and a force of several hundred thousand more or less fit soldiers was available, at least on paper, in the form of local detachments of the regular army, some crack special units, and the rapidly expanding Parisian contingents of the National Guard. When the Germans, on September 19, finished encircling the city, they paused to consider the French defensive capability and finally decided on a siege instead of an attack. Moltke thought that it would take only about six weeks to starve the reputedly epicurean, morally weak inhabitants into submission.

The painters in the Batignolles group and their friends reacted to the war in a variety of ways. Bazille joined a Zouave regiment, wound up in the ragged, badly equipped Army of the Loire (created by Gambetta as part of a plan to relieve Paris), and died on November 28 in a useless little battle at Beaune-la-Rolande, near Orléans. Cézanne fled at first to Aix-en-Provence and then, when conscription officers appeared in the neighborhood, to the small Mediterranean port of L'Estaque, where he remained hidden for the duration. (After the successive French defeats, there were too many deserters, stragglers, and draft-dodgers wandering about for the authorities to be very serious about rounding them up.) Renoir cheerfully accepted military service, spent several months with a light cavalry unit training in southern France, and finally, after a bout of dysentery, found himself demobilized without having seen any action. Tissot volunteered for the Seine Scouts, a Parisian company of sharpshooters that included several artists, and when it was dissolved he switched to a special battalion of the National Guard called the Seine Skirmishers. Sisley, a British subject, remained with his family at Louveciennes, just outside the German lines, after the siege began. Monet and Pissarro took refuge in London. Fantin, in poor health during these months, stuck to his Left Bank studio. Stevens, Bracquemond, the sculptor Cuvelier, Manet, and Degas, all of whom were past the legal age for military service (or for whom fond fathers had earlier purchased exemption), seem to have done nothing during August — and of course there was not much that a civilian in Paris, however well intentioned, could have done while the Prussian blitzkrieg was rolling through

Alsace and Lorraine, several hundred kilometers away. But in September,
when the capital itself, their real *patrie,* was in danger, they all volunteered
for the National Guard. Stevens, now in his mid-forties and a Belgian
citizen, was assigned to a relatively inactive branch. Bracquemond entered
the artillery; Cuvelier the Seine Skirmishers. Manet was at first an artilleryman and eventually a staff lieutenant, serving, much to his displeasure,
under a colonel who turned out to be Meissonier. Degas joined an infantry
company, but when he was sent out to Vincennes for rifle practice he
rapidly revealed that he could not see a target clearly with his right eye. So
he too became an artilleryman, and finally a gunner in the outer ring of
fortifications.

The National Guard was a peculiar organization with a very up-and-
down history. It had been founded in the turbulent year of 1789, with
Lafayette as its first commander, in imitation of the burghers' militias of
the Middle Ages. Bonaparte, always distrustful of amateur soldiers, had
suppressed it and then, after becoming emperor, had allowed it to reappear
with the restriction that its officers were to be appointed by the government
and not, as had been customary, elected by the militiamen. The insecure
Louis XVIII had tried to flatter it; the reactionary Charles X, in 1827, had
dissolved it, on the grounds that it was a hotbed of liberalism. It had re-
emerged during the Revolution of 1830 and had developed under Louis-
Philippe into what was essentially a big riot squad of the conservative
bourgeoisie, to be mobilized whenever the lower classes showed signs of
getting out of hand. Napoleon III, as distrustful of the organization as his
uncle had been, and moreover thoroughly aware of the anti-Bonapartism of
many Parisians, had limited the number of battalions in the capital to
sixty, and had seen to it that only the more reliable ones actually received
arms.

But after Sedan and the fall of the Second Empire all the limitations
and restrictions, including the appointment of officers, disappeared, and by
the end of September the city had two hundred and fifty battalions, with a
total enrollment of close to two hundred thousand men. The units were
organized according to arrondissements, and since a certain competence was
required of the officers, especially in the artillery, the higher grades were
occupied by professionals. Well-to-do volunteers bought their own uniforms and served for nothing; the poor received their outfits and a salary of
thirty sous a day from the government. Everyone lived at home and could
do as he pleased when not called up for training, for service in the fortifications, or for one of the sorties that were staged from time to time in order
to test the German lines and give the inexperienced citizen-soldiers a taste
of combat. Admittedly, the whole thing was to some extent a comic-opera
militia. (There were embarrassing occasions when nearly an entire com-

pany, having spent its pay in bistros, showed up too drunk to fight.) It was also, however, a strongly politicized, surprisingly tenacious product of a levy en masse, rendered dangerous to its various enemies by its naïve confidence and its ignorance of the recognized rules of warfare. And it tended inevitably, as the battalions from the poorer parts of town began to outnumber those from the *beaux quartiers,* to become what French sovereigns had often feared the National Guard might become — a revolutionary army.

In the population at large, although the new, perfectly illegal, undemocratically formed government was not seriously challenged, the traditional division into five political groups persisted. There were the Bonapartists, who hoped that the dynasty might be preserved by a regency while the young Prince Imperial was growing up; the ardently Roman Catholic Legitimists, who now saw a chance to reinstall the senior branch of the Bourbons, ousted in 1830; the more liberal Orleanists, who supported the junior branch of the royal family, favored a constitutional monarchy on the English model, and possessed in old Adolphe Thiers a remarkably canny, statesmanlike leader; the moderate republicans, who were sometimes only slightly to the left of the Orleanists; and finally a miscellany of radical republicans, utopian socialists, fervent anarchists, and adherents of the First International.

It might be (and frequently has been) assumed, on the basis of some general data, that Degas leaned toward one or perhaps both of the two Bourbon factions. His family's anti-Jacobinism and his admiration for writers like de Maistre, Veuillot, and Barbey d'Aurevilly may have aroused in him a good deal of sympathy, if only of a romantic sort, for the Legitimists; membership in the Louis-Philippe *grande bourgeoisie,* his education at Louis-le-Grand, and his father's and grandfather's profession may have inclined him toward the Orleanists, who during the July Monarchy had been the party of financiers, industrialists, and prosperous tradesmen. His derisive remarks at the Café Guerbois about art for the workers certainly point toward political conservatism. All these indicators, however, turn out to have been misleading when, after recalling that nearly everyone in the Batignolles circle was both anti-Bonapartist and anti-Royalist, we look again at the evidence. On September 15, 1870, Manet, furious over the number of rich people who had deserted the capital as the Germans approached, wrote to Suzanne, who was in southern France with his mother:

> Even a lot of the men have left. But I think they will pay for that when they return. This evening I was at a meeting in Belleville with Eugène [Edouard's younger brother]. The names of the absent were read out, and it was pro-

posed to put these names up on posters around Paris and to confiscate the
wealth of their owners for the benefit of the nation. That is how we usually
spend our evenings. Yesterday Degas, Eugène, and I went to a public
meeting in the Folies-Bergère, where General Cluseret spoke. . . . The conversation is only about rifles and revolvers. I think we are ready to defend
ourselves energetically.[6]

Belleville was the reddest quarter of Paris. The Folies-Bergère was one of
several theaters being used for patriotic rallies and for declaiming Victor
Hugo's long-banned attacks on Napoleon III, especially the poem about
the boy killed during resistance to the coup d'état that had launched the
Second Empire:

L'enfant avait reçu deux balles dans la tête.
Le logis était propre, humble, paisible, honnête.

(The child had received two bullets in his head. The house was clean,
humble, peaceful, decent.) Gustave Cluseret was a French soldier-adven-
turer and occasionally shady trafficker who had fought in the Crimea and
Algeria, recruited a foreign legion for Garibaldi, risen to the rank of a
Union general during the American Civil War, and then returned to France
to work with the Russian anarchist Mikhail Bakunin in the International.
In short, there can be no doubt about the political orientation of the
meetings Manet refers to, nor about Degas's being a republican at this
time. Indeed, Madame Morisot, who was herself a very moderate anti-
Bonapartist, one day completely lost her always short temper and put him
in the same category as the ruffian, wild-eyed radicals of Belleville, which
was a gross exaggeration but an enlightening one. Thus the question is how
he resolved the contradiction between his political behavior and his evident
social and cultural toryism, and of course the answer is not difficult. He
was a Parisian and a patriot, and the new republican government, however
distasteful some of its elements might be to the upper classes, was defending Paris and stubbornly refusing to accept the humiliation at Sedan as the
end of the war.

By early October, obviously not well trained, he was taking his regular
turn of duty in the fortifications. They had been built during the 1840s on
the initiative of Thiers, at the time the Orleanist prime minister; and like
many things in the French military set-up they were a strange mixture of
the medieval and the modern. The main structure was a zigzagging line of
earthworks surmounted by a masonry wall ten meters high and four meters
thick, the whole constituting a rough circle with a circumference of forty
kilometers and the cathedral of Notre Dame as its center. A dry moat
fifteen meters wide protected the outer approaches to the rampart; along

the town side of the wall ran the Rue Militaire, which was used to supply the troops with food and ammunition (and is today the roadbed of the city's Boulevards Extérieurs). The heavy artillery was installed in a series of ninety-four projecting, specially reinforced bastions, spaced so as to catch an enemy in crossfire and furnished like little castles with grilled gates and drawbridges. The entire construction was on the average about two kilometers from the municipal limits traced before the annexations of 1860, but parts of it were almost out in the country: Bastion 84, for example, where Bracquemond was stationed, was near the village of Sèvres on the road to Versailles. Degas was assigned to Bastion 12, which was in the eastern segment of the fortified ring just north of the Bois de Vincennes and about halfway between the streets that led to the suburban localities of Montreuil and Bagnolet; he was therefore obliged to cross a good part of Paris on his journeys from and to the Rue de Laval.

He found an unexpected compensation for the inconvenience, however, in the fact that the captain in charge of Bastion 12 was a former schoolmate, Henri Rouart. During the siege the two men, who had long been out of touch, developed their adolescent comradeship into a lasting adult friendship. After leaving Louis-le-Grand, Rouart had attended the Ecole Polytechnique — then as now a producer of army officers, civil engineers, and pure scientists — and emerged to become an unusual representative both of the old, cultivated, leisurely Louis-Philippe *grande bourgeoisie* and of the new, up-and-coming Second Empire entrepreneurial class. He was a semiprofessional Sunday painter who had studied with Corot and worked alongside Millet in the Forest of Fontainebleau, and he owned an already sizable art collection. But he was also a student of higher mathematics, the holder of several patents for mechanical inventions, a pioneer in the manufacture of vapor-compression machines for artificial refrigeration, and the head of a prosperous metallurgical enterprise. (In fairness to Napoleon III it should be remembered that the *fête impériale* was accompanied by industrial progress.) In 1870, besides mounting guard in Bastion 12, he was converting his Paris factory so that it could participate in the production of artillery pieces more modern than the standard French muzzle-loaders, and he was thinking of opening, as soon as the war ended, a refrigeration plant in New Orleans, where the market for ice was still what it had been in the early years of Germain Musson.

For the moment the Germans showed no signs of activity on the eastern side of the capital, so the National Guardsmen in the casemates had little to do except to enjoy the Indian summer weather and the rural silence. In the center of town optimism was the rule. The danger of a food shortage seemed remote, partly because the local imperial authorities, shortly before

Sedan, had begun to prepare for the worst by filling the recently erected iron pavilions of Les Halles, the central markets, with sacks of wheat and flour and by bringing in livestock on the hoof to graze in Parisian parks and squares. The omnipresent Edmond de Goncourt (alone now, for his brother, Jules, had died the previous June) was particularly impressed by the spectacle of a Normandy transplanted to the capital:

> In the Bois de Boulogne, where there has never been anything except the colors of silk dresses and the green of the trees, I glimpse a large piece of a blue blouse. It is the back of a shepherd standing near a little column of bluish smoke. All around him sheep are nibbling, in default of grass, the leaves of abandoned brushwood. In the alleys reserved for carriages droves of huge, haggard, disoriented oxen are wandering.[7]

Café talk continued. For Degas one of the principal hardships was that the Opéra was closed for a while and then reopened merely for political lectures, the mass singing of republican hymns, and the inevitable recitation of Hugo's poetry. But there were days when the reality of the situation was suddenly made bitterly clear. On October 21 Tissot and Cuvelier were involved in an unusually large spoiling attack that got as far as Malmaison, where part of the French force was caught under heavy enemy fire in the walled park of the château and Cuvelier was killed. Tissot survived and brought back a drawing of his fallen comrade that put Degas, much affected by the death of the young artist, into a rage against art. "You would have done better," he said, "if you had brought back his body."[8]

The Thursday salon in the Rue de Saint-Pétersbourg was interrupted by the absence of Manet's mother and Suzanne, and Stevens was too busy in the National Guard to continue his Wednesday parties. But the Morisots, including Berthe, were still in town, in spite of scare talk by Manet designed to persuade them to leave, and toward the end of October there was an apparently unsuccessful attempt in the Rue Franklin to revive something of the old round of conviviality. Madame Morisot described the evening in one of her letters to Edma and Yves, who were waiting out the war together at Mirande, a small place west of Toulouse:

> Monsieur Degas was so impressed by the death of one of his friends, the sculptor Cuvelier, that he was impossible. He and Manet almost got to pulling each other's hair in an argument over our defense means and the employment of the National Guard, although each of them indicated he was willing to die in order to save the country. Stevens had rheumatism and did not come. The doctor played the languishing lover with Berthe. If one had not felt the seriousness of our situation, this little gathering would have been quite funny. Monsieur Degas has joined the artillery, and according to

him he has not yet heard a cannon go off. He says he is doing research on this noise in order to find out how he will support the detonations of his guns. . . . Hurricane weather adds to the gloominess of the state of affairs.[9]

The unidentified doctor was evidently one of the several suitors whom Berthe finally rejected — and also one of the several whom her mother could not stand.

Although the hurricane did not arrive, winter did, and it rapidly became one of the most severe in Parisian history. Within a few weeks the stock of coal ran out. Then the gas supply dwindled, kerosene lamps reappeared in homes, and bands of firewood marauders, often armed, began to roam the darkened city at night, chopping down the trees in public squares and the Grands Boulevards, ripping the fences from construction sites, and stealing any small article that looked burnable. On November 23 Manet informed Suzanne that sociability was also disappearing:

> The state we are in is so painful that nobody wants to see anyone else. Anyway, it is always the same conversation, the same illusions. The evenings are hard to get through. The Café Guerbois is my only resource, and even that is becoming very monotonous. . . . I would give all of Alsace and Lorraine to be with you.[10]

By the beginning of December the temperature was below freezing and staying there, and the ground was covered with a thick, dirty, frozen blanket of snow. The singing of the "Marseillaise" and the reciting of *L'enfant avait reçu deux balles dans la tête* had long since ceased. Conservative, peace-minded people were beginning to complain about the costly sorties of the garrison, which seemed to produce nothing except a series of supposedly morale-boosting governmental bulletins. Worst of all, the wheat and flour in Les Halles and the livestock on the hoof had vanished, partly because there was no effective rationing law, and the food shortage had become serious. Fiacres were getting scarce, for the horses were being eaten. The animals in the zoo in the Jardin des Plantes were slaughtered, but the price of an elephant steak, a tiger cutlet, or a fricassee of boa was beyond the means of an ordinary housewife. The poor dined on rat meat, when they could afford it. In the Rue de Saint-Pétersbourg the housekeeper's cat failed to show up one morning.

During the first week of January the Germans, with the obvious intention of delivering a finishing blow, massed their artillery on the plateau of the southern suburb of Châtillon and began an intensive bombardment of the outlying fortifications and the Left Bank, in particular the quarter around the church of Saint-Sulpice and the Théâtre de l'Odéon. A few days later Manet sent off a message (the mail was still getting out occasionally by balloon) to his wife: "No gas, black bread, and cannonades all day long and all night long."[11] The garrison attempted an all-or-nothing sortie in which a hundred thousand men participated, accompanied by rolling drums and yells of *vive la république*. They fought their way as far as Buzenval, on the road to Malmaison, and then retreated through the snow under the cover of darkness, with a long train of wagons loaded with the wounded and the dead. Among the killed was Henri Regnault, a promising young academic painter and friend of Degas's who had studied under Lamothe and Cabanel, won the Prix de Rome in 1866, and become the idol of a large number of writers and musicians.

The French high command decided that nothing more could be done. Violent protests from the still bellicose radical-republican battalions of the National Guard were ignored. Conservative townspeople, according to one of Rouart's sons, halted a quixotic demonstration presumably organized by Degas:

> When it was a question of turning Paris over to the Prussians, he and some members of his family started to march down the Grands Boulevards, carrying a large sign on which was inscribed in huge letters, "Don't give up our forts." Their troop was dispersed almost immediately and their sign torn to pieces.[12]

The cannonades continued, and on January 28 the city surrendered.

In the nationwide elections that were promptly staged (at the insistence of Bismarck, who wanted a legal government with which to negotiate), provincial France disavowed the heroic republican capital by voting overwhelmingly for the Legitimists, the Orleanists, Thiers, and peace. On February 27 Berthe Morisot wrote to Edma:

> Each day brings us a new sorrow, a new humiliation. . . . It seems to me that the Parisians are more in the right than the provincials, but if by chance I timidly advance that opinion, Father throws his arms in the air and treats me as a madwoman. . . . As you know, all our acquaintances have come out of this war without a scratch, except for poor Bazille, who was killed I believe at Orléans. The brilliant painter Regnault was killed at Buzenval. The others made a lot of fuss for a very small result. Manet spent his time during the siege changing uniforms. . . . Monsieur Degas is the same as ever, a little crazy but charming and witty.[13]

On March 1 some token detachments of the German army of occupation entered an almost completely silent Paris. The streets were deserted and the façades of the town halls of the twenty arrondissements decorated with black flags. On the locked shutters of cafés and shops the explanatory signs read: "Closed for national mourning." Although the spike-helmeted troops stayed only until March 3, their presence symbolized France's apparently total defeat; and while they were bivouacking in the Bois de Boulogne, the recently elected National Assembly, sitting in Bordeaux, provided another symbol by ratifying a treaty that ceded all of Alsace and half of Lorraine to the new German Empire and committed France to the payment of an indemnity of five billion francs.

Degas remained in town through February and early March, and the paintings and drawings of this period and of the immediately preceding months provide an indication of his wartime relations and sentiments that correct the somewhat waspish assessment by Berthe Morisot and her mother. There are likenesses of Rouart and of three other companions in Bastion 12, the gunners Jeantaud, Linet, and Lainé. The notebooks contain caricatures of Napoleon III, Thiers, and a pig-snouted Bismarck, and careful drawings, evidently done from photographs or engravings, of four prominent French general officers: the Marshals MacMahon, Bazaine, François Canrobert, and Adolphe Niel. Of particular documentary as well as aesthetic interest is a double portrait of Rabbi Elie-Aristide Astruc and General Emile Mellinet. Astruc, though only forty years old in 1871, was the chief rabbi of Belgium, an assistant to the chief rabbi of Paris, the chaplain of Louis-le-Grand and two smaller lycées, and an authority on the history of Judaism. Mellinet, who was seventy-three, had fought as a teenage lieutenant under Napoleon I during the Hundred Days, participated in the North African campaigns of the 1840s, commanded a section of the Imperial Guard in Italy in 1859, won a medal for valor at Magenta, and headed the Seine battalions of the National Guard in the 1860s. In spite of all this professional service to emperors and kings, he was a staunch republican and a strongly anticlerical, antiauthoritarian Freemason who from 1865 to 1870 had been grand master of the principal French lodge, the Grand Orient. During the worst days of the siege of Paris and the accompanying bloody sorties, he and Astruc, working together, had distinguished themselves in the ambulance service and the care of the wounded. They asked Degas to paint them together, to recall their fraternal effort. He responded with a little picture that is remarkable for its loose handling, its yellow, brown, and olive green harmony, its hint of El Greco, and above all its representation of two intelligent, humorous, humane, and unpretentiously brave men.

By mid-March, in answer to an invitation from the Valpinçons, he was at Ménil-Hubert, where the annual renewal of the opulent green of the Normandy countryside was proof that, whatever might happen in Alsace and Paris, the nation as a whole, *la France éternelle,* could not be beaten

Hortense Valpinçon, 1871

beyond recovery. To judge by the seasonal light in the paintings he produced (admittedly an unreliable indicator in the work of such a confirmed studio artist), he did nothing for several weeks except sketch, rest, and fill up on steaks, Camembert, and cider. By May, however, he was at work on some studies of horses in neighboring pastures, and especially on three portraits of the two Valpinçon children. In one of them, the baby Henri, rigid in his wagon like a bad-tempered little seigneur, dominates with his nurse the foreground of a domestic landscape in which his mother and his sister, Hortense, are almost dissolved by a dazzle of sunlight and bright green. Hortense alone, dressed like a small adult and provided with a slice of apple to get her to hold still, looks out at us inquiringly from a gaily artificial setting exactly right for a child. (Madame Valpinçon would remember being proud of the woolen covering on the low table, which she had embroidered herself.) In *Carriage at the Races* a landscape, although viewed as if by chance, is again important, so much so that only after concentrating on the centered, off-white parasol and following the lines of

Carriage at the Races, 1871–1872

sight of the dog, the top-hatted Paul Valpinçon, his wife, and her companion does a viewer realize that the whole elaborate composition is actually another portrait of Henri. Both this painting and the one of the baby in his wagon are similar in theme to many of the outdoor settings with figures produced by the mature Impressionists, but the brushwork is smoother and more unified, and the psychological emphasis, the spatial mise-en-scène, the elements cut by the frame, and the Bruegel-like trick of making a tiny, nearly unnoticeable figure the true subject are all marked by the sophisticated, well-stocked, ironic, and for the moment surprisingly tender mind of Degas. Evidently he was enjoying his escape from wintry, masculine Bastion 12.

In the meantime the predictable was happening in Paris. The townspeople, already embittered by the conclusion of what they regarded as a dishonorable peace and by the election of a monarchist National Assembly composed of alleged country bumpkins, were outraged by new laws that ended the wartime moratorium on debts and rents and cut off the salaries of citizen-soldiers. On March 18 Thiers, now the provisional "chief of the executive power" of the nation, tried to confiscate some artillery pieces parked on the Butte of Montmartre, and succeeded only in getting two of his generals lynched and provoking an ominous beating of drums that called out the National Guard all across the city. He then retired to Versailles with his government and concentrated on building up a sufficiently strong and loyal regular army. (Bismarck helped him by releasing thousands of Napoleon III's captured infantrymen.) On March 26 the capital defiantly held its own elections, and the radically republican municipal council that emerged called itself "the Commune of Paris," in memory of the urban rebels who had fought medieval monarchs and of the formidable Parisian organization that had supported Robespierre. (The resemblance to the word "communist" was apparently accidental.)

During the following weeks a visceral mutual hatred rapidly ended any hope of negotiations between the two camps. Troops from Versailles shot a group of National Guardsmen caught in the suburbs; the Communards retaliated by arresting a number of priests, including the archbishop of Paris, and holding them as hostages. Thiers reverted to the *grand bourgeois* mentality of the 1830s, when he had been a ferocious repressor of rioting workers; now, he felt, was the time to teach the lower classes a lesson they would not soon forget. The Commune, though it never got around to instituting a fundamental reform of the social structure, moved further and further to the left as its moderate supporters turned hostile and its tendency to play-act revolutionary history grew. It adopted a red flag as its emblem, demolished the Bonapartist column in the Place Vendôme, ordered the razing of the chapel erected to the memory of Louis XVI, and reinstated the republican calendar of the 1790s (which meant that punctilious patriots had to remember that April was partly the month of Floréal). Followers of the Socialist leader Auguste Blanqui dreamed of what he called "the Parisification of the whole of France." [14] At last, on May 21, Thiers felt that he was ready to strike, and what would be known in French history as the Bloody Week got under way.

The well-equipped Versailles regulars, indoctrinated by propaganda that represented the Communards as ruthless savages, poured through unguarded gaps in the ring of fortifications and advanced toward the working quarters of Paris, shooting anyone found at a barricade or in a National Guard uniform, and rounding up suspects for summary trial and execution or dispatch to a prisoners' enclosure. The Communards, as their desperation increased, were in fact transformed into savages. They resisted street by street, killed the archbishop and the other hostages, shot down monks and policemen under the shouts of maddened crowds, and burned, among other public buildings, the sixteenth-century Palais des Tuileries, the seventeenth-century Hôtel de Ville (in which Ingres's huge *Apotheosis of Napoleon I* was destroyed), the Conseil d'Etat, the eighteenth-century Palais de la Légion d'Honneur, the Cours de Comptes (the audit office), and a section of the Ministère des Finances in the Rue de Rivoli. The Louvre was saved by the timely arrival of the Versailles troops and firemen. Madame Morisot watched from the high terrace of suburban Saint-Germain-en-Laye, and on May 21 wrote to Berthe, who was at Cherbourg:

> Paris is on fire. It is unimaginable. Half-burned papers, some of them still readable, have been carried here all day long by the wind. A vast column of smoke covers the city, which at night is a red, luminous spot, horrible to look at, like a volcanic eruption. . . . If Monsieur Degas could be roasted a little in it, he would have what he deserves.[15]

At dawn on May 28 the last organized resisters were butchered with their backs to a wall in the Père Lachaise Cemetery. About a thousand of Thiers's soldiers were dead. At least twenty thousand Communards had been killed in the fighting or executed on the spot, and forty thousand were marched to Versailles to be sentenced to death, imprisonment, or deportation to the French penal islands. "They had seemed to think," MacMahon said, "that they were defending a sacred cause, the independence of Paris."[16]

Manet, who had been in southern France with Suzanne since the lifting of the siege, returned to the capital toward the end of the Bloody Week (in time to do some dramatic lithographs of the attacks on the barricades), and Degas soon joined him there. On June 5 Madame Morisot, back in Passy and more than ever a supporter of the Thiers government, wrote again to Berthe:

> I saw only the Hôtel de Ville on the morrow of my arrival. . . . It's a beautiful ruin. Your father wants to have the débris preserved as historical evidence and as a sacred reminder of the horror of popular revolutions. . . . At the moment when all the Communards were being shot, Tiburce {the Morisots' young son} ran into two of them — Manet and Degas! Even now, they blame the authorities for having resorted to energetic means of repression. I think they are insane. What do you think?[17]

Political disagreements did not, however, prevent the resumption of social relations, and two weeks later Edma received some comments from her mother on a party in the Rue Franklin:

> Men disgust me. I find them awful, and I am beginning to dislike everybody. That Madame Loubens spent the evening being amiable with Monsieur Degas, and instead of showing his contempt, as he should have, he was

charming with her. She has put on a lot of weight, which has not embellished her, in my opinion.[18]

By July 14 the Thursday evenings were being resumed in the Rue de Saint-Pétersbourg, and this time Madame Morisot's reportage was addressed to Berthe:

> I found the Manet salon the same as before. It's nauseating. If it had not been for the animation public disasters can provoke when described by individuals, I think very little would have been said. Suffocating heat, people parked in the single drawing room, warm drinks. However, Pagans sang, Madame Edouard [Manet] played the piano, and Monsieur Degas was present. I can't say that he flitted about: he looked completely asleep, and your father seemed younger than he. Mademoiselle Eva [Gonzalès] has grown ugly. Madame Camus had a sugary look; Tiburce found her ravishing. Champfleury put on airs, sat in the best chair with his legs stretched out, and didn't say a word to anyone. You can see the ensemble . . .[19]

Shortly after this soirée, Manet left for a summer holiday at Boulogne-sur-Mer, almost as if nothing had happened since his stay there in 1869.

He and Degas had not been the only members of their class to sympathize — up to a certain hard-to-define point — with the Communards. Courbet was in prison because of his supposed role in the demolition of the Vendôme column. (Actually his participation in that foolish gesture had been merely symbolic and was motivated partly by aesthetic considerations.) Tissot had let his house be used as a military hospital by the insurgent National Guardsmen, and fled to London when the roundup of suspects began. Duret, who had served as deputy mayor of the Ninth Arrondissement under the Commune, barely escaped execution by a Versailles firing squad and immediately decided to use his cognac money for a trip around the world.

But when the full extent of the arson and the killings was revealed, friends of the defeated became scarce. The young Anatole France found the captured Communards repulsive; Goncourt, recovering from a personal version of the Great Fear, brutally expressed a hope that enough of the Parisian lower classes had been exterminated to give the nation twenty years of stability. Zola complained that the repression had been too slow. George Sand, though a republican and in many ways a leftist, wrote that truly progressive people could be identified by their support of Thiers and "the indignation they vent against the infamous innovators of the Commune."[20] Manet himself, after a period of depression, repudiated extremism. Degas did not evolve in any such explicit fashion, undoubtedly in part because he never had been as radical as some of his remarks led Madame

Morisot to imagine. A more important and more subtle explanation, however, can be discovered in a double French ideological shift that left him about where he had been in September 1870, in terms of some deeply held convictions, and yet paradoxically at the other end of the political landscape. He was like an actor who stands still while a change in the stage scenery puts him in another place.

One part of the ideological shift concerned the nature of the régime that was to succeed the Second Empire. At the time of the Commune the Versailles government was still provisionally that of a republic, for Thiers and the monarchist majority in the National Assembly had not yet reached agreement on who — the heir of the senior Bourbon line or the representative of the junior branch — should become the new king of France. And as the weeks went by, the chances of such an agreement became more and more remote, in part because the Legitimists and the Orleanists could not patch up their policy differences and largely because the senior Bourbon pretender, the aging Comte de Chambord, refused to accept the throne except on his own terms, which included a return to absolute royal authority and the abandonment of the Tricolor, the national emblem since 1789, in favor of the white flag of Henri IV and Louis XIV. Meanwhile, in by-election after by-election, provincial voters were demonstrating their willingness to accept a republic as long as it was headed by a man like Thiers, was unconnected with the reds in Paris, and was as capable of putting down subversion as the present administration had shown itself to be during the Bloody Week. Finally Thiers himself, pragmatic as always, ended any hope of a Royalist restoration by abjuring his Orleanist faith and announcing his belief that a presidential system was what divided the nation the least. Republicanism had moved dramatically to the right, only a few months after having been associated, in the minds of a majority of Frenchmen, with intolerable Parisianism, Belleville radicalism, quixotic militarism, anti-Establishment artists and writers, and barbarous, seditious proletarians.

The other part of the ideological shift concerned nationalism. The French left, to use the term in a very general sense, had long been inclined to mix its humanitarian and liberal idealism with a good deal of flag-waving, and on more than one occasion it had been overtly a patriotic war party. The insurgents of 1830 and 1848 had dreamed of freeing the oppressed peoples of Europe and at the same time of re-establishing the country's pre-Waterloo frontiers. In the last days of the siege of Paris some of the National Guard battalions had reached mystical heights of belligerence. On March 1, during the National Assembly debate on Bismarck's peace terms, Hugo had insisted that the lost provinces would soon be recaptured, and wound up shouting, "Is that all? No, France will again seize Treves, Mainz, Coblenz, Cologne — the entire left bank of the Rhine!"[21] In reacting against all this, the right had often been made to look like a party of peacemongers and appeasers, and its loyalty to the nation had been rendered suspect by the tendency of its royal and aristocratic leaders to flee during crises and return with foreign military help.

But in the summer of 1871 there began a change of immense consequence for the future, and soon the left was far from alone in its chauvinism and militarism. On June 29 a hundred thousand of Thiers's smartly turned-out soldiers, many of them veterans of the campaign in Alsace and Lorraine, paraded before a cheering, weeping crowd, with the owlish little "chief of the executive power" in the reviewing stand, and the event marked the beginning of a veritable idolization of the army. Its patent inefficiency was overlooked and its undeniable courage remembered. A flood of books and pamphlets described in detail every engagement of the war. Academic artists answered the public demand for stirring, and inevitably sad, patriotic images: Alphonse de Neuville, for example, with *The Last Cartridge,* an evocation of Sedan that sold by the thousands in an engraved reproduction; François-Nicolas Chifflart with another very successful print, *The Charge of the Cuirassiers at Reichshoffen;* Etienne Berne-Bellecour with *The Seine Skirmishers at Malmaison,* in which the dying Cuvelier appears; Meissonier with *The Siege of Paris,* in which an embattled female allegorical figure, surrounded by wounded National Guardsmen, defies an approaching Prussian eagle and the specter of famine; and especially Edouard Detaille, who turned out a long series of photographically vivid scenes that transformed defeat into noble tragedy. Regnault became the favorite martyr-hero of the fine arts Establishment, exalted by inclusion in Meissonier's picture, by a bust in the Cour du Mûrier at the Ecole des Beaux-Arts, and by a monument at Buzenval near the spot where he was killed. (Bazille, whose death was a much greater loss for French painting, received honors only from his father, who in the winter of 1870–1871 journeyed to Beaune-la-Rolande, dug up his son's body from the snow-covered battleground, and hauled it back to Montpellier on a peasant's cart.) A climate was being prepared for politicians who, their eyes fixed on what they referred to as "the blue line of the Vosges," would shortly make *la revanche,* revenge, their sole program.

This whole evolution brought Degas out of his recent apparent ambiguity into consistency, with his republicanism, patriotism, and sociocultural sentiments comfortably together on the right. Although he was a little slower than George Sand to accept what would become the Third

Republic, he seems to have done so quite easily — with merely a hint, in a letter written early in 1873, of amused skepticism concerning Thiers's conversion from monarchism. In later years he was sometimes ironical also about the advocates of *la revanche* and the painters of battles. Confronted by one of Whistler's unusual hats, he remarked, "Yes, it suits you very well, but that won't get us back Alsace and Lorraine."[22] He once dismissed the chauvinistic Detaille (who went so far as to wear a uniform while painting) as "a furnisher of military equipment."[23] But he himself was by 1872 clearly fascinated by the army. His sympathetic study of General Mellinet — who had the merit of being a republican as well as a military hero — is part of the evidence, and so are his four drawings of French marshals, which suggest an unrealized project for a group portrait.

The decisive document, however, is a long notebook memo on publications he presumably intended to buy.[24] This shows him interested in a summary of the events of the war from German and the French points of view; a two-volume analysis of the fighting along the Rhine frontier; a two-volume history, by Veuillot, of the siege of Paris; an account of a secret mission to the capital during the Commune; a description, attributed to Moltke, of the German military organization; an inside view of the disastrous bottling-up of Bazaine's troops at Metz; some memoirs by a veteran who had served under General Chanzy, one of the most effective and most picturesque of the officers who had harassed the enemy in the provinces; a chronicle of the Army of the Loire, in which Bazille had fought; and a diary of the successful defense of Belfort, the only one of the great fortresses in eastern France to hold out after the collapse at Sedan.

To this list can be added, on the basis of later testimony, Ludovic Halévy's *L'Invasion,* a collection of articles, mostly rewritten interviews, on the events of 1870 that had appeared originally in *Le Temps,* the most important of the newspapers that had recently switched to conservative republicanism. The tone of the book can be caught in a first-person, present-tense description, by a participating officer, of a French cavalry attack at Gravelotte, a village near Metz, on a massed formation, a "wall," of German cavalrymen:

> We are approaching! We are approaching! I hear a thunderous shout of "Charge! Charge!" accompanied by frenzied hurrahs. . . . I am almost flat on the neck and withers of my horse, my boots jammed to the heels in the stirrups, my spurs digging into the animal's flanks, the reins pulled up short, my left hand grasping the mane and my saber, my right hand holding my revolver. I fire two shots into the wall of living flesh in front of me. I am hurled into that wall. . . . The ground is already covered with the dead and the wounded, men and horses. We gallop on corpses. . . .[25]

Degas was to recall this account — which could have served as a caption for a painting by Detaille or de Neuville — a quarter-century later, at a time when the country was sinking into another tragically divisive crisis. Plainly, after a short period during which his temporarily disarranged sentiments were settling back into their natural, class-determined pattern, one of the important personal consequences of the Franco-Prussian War and the Commune was that he was set on the path to becoming a typical old soldier, with all the sentimental militarism and idealistic nationalism, and also the inevitable intolerance, of the species.

Another important, and immediate, consequence permanently affected his morale as an artist. During the terrible winter of the siege of Paris he had discovered that the trouble with his right eye was becoming worse and was occasionally accompanied by acute physical discomfort, and he eventually concluded that the cold and the humidity in Bastion 12 (combined with his years in a damp room in the Rue de Mondovi) were the principal cause. He may have been partly right, although clearly at the moment of his rifle-practice fiasco at Vincennes in the previous September the ailment was already well advanced. It cannot, of course, be diagnosed at this distance in time, but from his various descriptions of the symptoms one can guess that it was some kind of lesion or chronic infection in the retina, and that in any event it was neither an incipient cataract nor one of the common sorts of deformation of the lens. He complained, for instance, that sometimes when he looked directly at a spot in his field of vision, he would see the surrounding area and not the spot itself, and that strong illumination or simply a prolonged period of close scrutiny produced a feeling of intolerable strain. His notebooks reveal that he consulted Dr. Camus and an ophthalmologist suggested by Manet, evidently without much result. He bought a pair of blue-tinted glasses; he acquired a habit of drawing random parallel lines in order to test himself. In a letter to Tissot, dated September 30, 1871, he mentioned what seems to have been a particularly frightening experience:

> I have just had and still have a spot of weakness and trouble in my eyes. It caught me at the château by the edge of the water in full sunlight while I was still doing a watercolor and it made me lose nearly three weeks, being unable to read or work or go out much, trembling all the time lest I should remain like that.[26]

Fortunately, he did not believe in the Guerbois landscapists' practice of finishing a picture outdoors. In fact, for many years he would manage, on most days, to work in a quite normal fashion. But from now on, the fear that he might become completely blind would never leave him.

11. Economics and Ballet

I N THE SUMMER of 1868 Manet, discouraged by the failure of his costly
one-man show at the Exposition Universelle and warned by his mother
that the family fortune was not inexhaustible, had written to Fantin-
Latour from Boulogne-sur-Mer:

> I've had enough rebuffs. What I want to do today is to make some money.
> And since I think, as you do, that there is not much to be done in our stupid
> country, in the midst of this population of government employees, I want
> to exhibit in London.[1]

At the moment Degas had not shared this attitude and had even rejected
the idea of crossing the Channel for an exploratory visit. But during the
next two years he gradually changed his mind. His successes at the Salon
were not very spectacular, and he was unhappy, as his open letter to the
Paris-Journal indicates, about the way his pictures were being hung. The
offer of a contract in Brussels finally looked unattractive. And it did not
take much of a survey to see that, with one possible exception, there was
only a vague hope of obtaining the promotional help of an important private
gallery in Paris.

At the end of the Second Empire the principal French art merchant
was Adolphe Goupil, whose firm dated back to 1827. He had won a
reputation as a publisher of reproductions, turned to the selling of originals,
and wound up with three Parisian establishments: a luxurious one at 2
Place de l'Opéra (the new Opéra, the construction of which had been

interrupted by the war), another at 19 Boulevard Montmartre near the art-auction center in the Hôtel Drouot, and a third in the Ninth Arrondissement at 9 Rue Chaptal, where the printing plant was also located. In addition there were branches in New York, London, Berlin, Vienna, Brussels, and The Hague (where in 1869 one of the employees was Vincent van Gogh). Goupil was not a hidebound conservative; he had once been interested in Courbet, and in 1861 he had been willing to exhibit, very briefly, Manet's *Boy with Cherries*. But he was the kind of retailer who sold reputations rather more than pictures, and at the beginning of the 1870s that meant concentrating on academic painters like Meissonier, Cabanel, William Bouguereau, and especially Gérôme, who had the extra advantage of being a Goupil son-in-law.

Louis Martinet was, or had been, another important dealer, and his recent adventures could be taken as a warning against the defying of prevailing taste. Oddly, he was himself a member, on the surface if not in his heart, of the Establishment: he had studied with Baron Gros, the great illustrator of the Napoleonic saga; made his début as a history painter at the Salon in 1833; and risen to the rank of inspector in the imperial fine arts administration. And then he had developed an impresario urge. In 1860, in some rooms at 26 Boulevard des Italiens rented from the British collector Richard Wallace, he had launched a permanent exhibition, partly revised each month, of Barbizon landscapes; during the next three years he had rapidly extended his activity by creating a magazine called *Le Courrier artistique*, organizing a Société Nationale des Beaux-Arts under the presidency of Gautier, adding several nonconformist painters and etchers to the organization, and staging concerts, at which gallery visitors could listen to Berlioz, Bizet, and Saint-Saëns. Eventually the list of exhibitors had included Manet, Legros, Whistler, Jongkind, and Bracquemond. Baudelaire had been delighted, but the public became thinner and thinner after an initial reaction of curiosity, and by the end of the decade Martinet was a ruined man.

Below the level of such spectacular operators as Goupil and Martinet the commercial opportunities of an uncelebrated painter shaded off rapidly from a few regular galleries to *courtiers* — art brokers without fixed places of business — and on down to shops that sold materials for artists and sometimes accepted a picture as payment, or simply agreed to put it in the window. In elegant quarters at 10 Rue Laffitte, Adrien Beugniet exhibited Stevens's studies of Parisiennes and occasionally commissioned the decoration of women's fans (at which Degas was becoming quite expert); at number 28 of the same street Gustave Tempelaere dealt in Corot, Courbet, and Fromentin and sometimes the work of lesser people. More useful, from the viewpoint of the Batignolles group, was the former *courtier* Pierre-Firmin Martin, who was referred to affectionately as Père Martin and with whom Degas, according to a notebook address, seems to have become acquainted shortly after his return from Italy. Martin was an alcoholic, rough-mannered, frequently dirty ex-saddler and ex-actor who had found his vocation by peddling objets d'art in Montmartre and had finally opened a small gallery at 52 Rue Laffitte, near the church of Notre-Dame-de-Lorette. His discernment, sharpened by long frequentation of painters' studios and the auctions at the Hôtel Drouot, had evolved with extraordinary historical prescience from Corot and the Barbizon school to the Realism of Courbet and Bonvin, the pre-Impressionism of Jongkind and Boudin, and then, beginning around 1868, the various tendencies of Pissarro, Manet, Cézanne, Monet, Sisley, and Degas. And the evolution would continue until it involved an appreciation of van Gogh in the 1880s. In Zola's novel of Parisian artistic struggles, *L'Oeuvre,* Martin is represented, under another name, as a savage, tricky haggler (in real life he sometimes paid only twenty francs and seldom more than a hundred for a picture) who was also a basically honest man and above all a born connoisseur:

> Beneath his thick layer of filth Père Malgras was a very subtle fellow with a taste and a flair for good painting. He was never misled by mediocre daubers. By instinct, he went straight to artists whose personal styles were not yet appreciated and whose great futures his flaming drunkard's nose could smell from afar.[2]

His principal defect in the eyes of the painters, and the reason for his hard bargaining with them, was that his clients were mostly of modest means (Henri Rouart was one of the exceptions). And a clientèle without much money became even more of a problem for painters who dealt with the furnishers of material. One of the most sympathetic of these was the minor landscapist Louis Latouche, who retailed frames, canvases, and tubes of paint at the corner of the Rue Lafayette and the Rue Laffitte, let his store be used as a meeting place by Renoir, Pissarro, and Monet, and did his best to sell some of their work. In about the same category, although more picturesque, was the Breton anarchist Julien Tanguy, whose shop was at 14 Rue Clauzel, two blocks from Degas's studio.

In this generally depressing situation the one faintly encouraging element — at the moment in its strongest form across the English Channel — was the Galerie Durand-Ruel, which during the previous forty years had developed from a Latin Quarter stationery shop into a prosperous Right Bank place exhibiting the work of Delacroix, Corot, Daumier, and especially the Barbizon landscapists. Paul Durand-Ruel, the son of the founder, had taken over the business in 1865, at the age of thirty-four, and had immediately launched into a daring, sometimes reckless expansion based on confidence in his own judgment (formed by many hours in museums), on loans from friendly bankers, and on massive buying, frequently of an entire collection or of everything in a painter's atelier. In 1869 he had moved his gallery from its old premises in the Rue de la Paix to a suite of rooms that ran from an entrance at 16 Rue Laffitte through the block to another entrance at 11 Rue Le Peletier, across the street from the Opéra; and during the year he began to publish, with the novelist Ernest Feydeau as editor, a periodical entitled *La Revue internationale de l'art et de la curiosité.* The Franco-Prussian War had not entirely interrupted all this activity, for the firm had shipped much of its stock to London and started to organize exhibitions of French painting at 168 New Bond Street — ironically, in space vacated by an enterprise called the German Gallery. In sum, Durand-Ruel was a plunger who combined audacity with a sense of strategy. (At twenty he had passed the entrance examination for Saint-Cyr, the French equivalent of Sandhurst and West Point, and throughout his life he wore a clipped mustache that made him look like a retired English colonel in the midst of the many bushily whiskered civilians of the Third Republic.) Moreover, although he was still primarily the merchant of such members of the older unacademic generation as Daubigny, Millet, Diaz, and Rousseau, he had shown a definite interest in the Batignolles group: his *Revue internationale* contained a favorable mention of Pissarro, Degas, Monet, and Manet in the spring of 1870, and early in the following year he met the self-exiled Monet and Pissarro in England and began to include them in the New Bond Street shows. Obviously, for a dissatisfied Parisian painter the thing to do was to take a close look at London.

Degas went over some time in October 1871. The only documentation of the trip is a note, requesting information, sent to Legros,[3] who by this time was an old hand in South Kensington. But it is not difficult to imagine a list of other people who may have been consulted. Whistler was giving regular parties in his half-Japanese house in Chelsea, exhibiting frequently at Royal Academy shows, and embarking on the period of his best nocturnes; he was also a link with the group of artists and writers around Dante Gabriel Rossetti, with such retailers as the Dudley Gallery, the Flemish Gallery, and the Berners Street Gallery, and with such collectors as Alexander Ionides and another art-minded British businessman, Louis Huth. Among the Frenchmen who had become political refugees in London after the collapse of the Commune were — in addition to Tissot — the printer Delâtre, the sculptor Jules Dalou, and Courbet's friend Bonvin. (The frequently published assertion that Degas broke off relations with former Communards in the 1870s is apparently just an inference drawn from the mistaken notion that he was an antirepublican during the siege of Paris; it

The Dancing Class (New York version), 1871–1872

is contradicted both by his correspondence and by his behavior at the time of the first Impressionist group shows.) The note to Legros mentioned a contact with a certain "Gambar," who was probably Ernest Gambart, a dealer well enough known to British painters to have been the subject of a limerick by Rossetti:

> There is an old he-wolf called Gambart,
> Beware of him if thou a lamb art . . .[4]

By the end of the summer Monet had moved on to Holland, and Pissarro had returned to Louveciennes, but there remained several people in town who could have taken the visitor from Paris around to 168 New Bond Street, where the Second Annual Exhibition of the Society of French Artists had been staged during the late spring. (The "society" was entirely Durand-Ruel's invention.)

During the next few months this prospecting brought results, though not at first in England. Durand-Ruel, leaving his London activities in the hands of an assistant, returned to Paris and devoted his energy to the gallery in the Rue Laffitte and the Rue Le Peletier. In January 1872 he pulled off

The Dancing Class (Paris version), 1872

one of his characteristic coups: partly at the urging of Stevens, he dropped in at Manet's studio and bought nearly everything in sight — twenty-four paintings in all, for which he paid thirty-five thousand francs. (This was not much in comparison with what Meissonier and Gérôme were getting from Goupil, but it was far above what Père Martin was offering.) At about the same time, he began to buy Degas's works, one of the first being what is now the New York Metropolitan Museum's *Dancing Class,* which had been painted during the winter of 1871–1872. From this point on Durand-Ruel rapidly became the Batignolles group's principal dealer, although he continued for a long while to count on the Barbizon landscapists for the bulk of his business. At the Fourth Exhibition of the Society of French Artists, which took place in the summer of 1872 in New Bond Street, Degas was represented by *The False Start* of 1869, presumably with the idea of getting the attention of wealthy British turf enthusiasts; his recent *Ballet from Robert le Diable* was also shown. In August another *Dancing Class,* the one now in the Jeu de Paume in Paris, was bought by Durand-Ruel, who entered it and the Ménil-Hubert *Carriage at the Races* in the fifth New Bond Street show, which opened at the beginning of November.

Pissarro had not been pleased by his stay in London. "Here," he wrote to Duret, "one encounters only scorn, indifference, and even boorishness."[5] His irritation was understandable, for his pictures were largely ignored by the British press and British collectors, as was the work of Monet, Manet, and Sisley. Degas, however, fared quite well. In the *Pall Mall Gazette* of November 28, 1872, his *Dancing Class* and *Carriage at the Races* were praised by the critic Sidney Colvin in terms that made the friendly reviews of Castagnary, Zola, and Duret look almost mealymouthed:

> If [young French painters] are to avoid commonness, it must be by extraordinary alertness of their perceptions as to common and unideal fact. That is just what Monsieur Degas exhibits, and in a really amazing degree. It is impossible to exaggerate the subtlety of exact perception, and the felicitous touch in expressing it, which reveal themselves in his little picture of ballet-girls training beneath the eye of the ballet-master, and his other picture of a bourgeois family in an open carriage at the races — the father on the box, within the mother watching her baby in the arms of its wet-nurse. Without the slightest pretension, these are both of them real masterpieces, and especially the former. It is a scheme of various whites, gauzes, and muslins, fluttering round the apartment, and the ballet-master in white ducks and jacket in the middle; and all the little shifts of indoor light and colour, all the movements of the girls in rest and strained exercise, expressed with the most perfect precision of drawing and delicacy of colour, and without a shadow of a shade of that sentiment which is ordinarily implied by a picture having the ballet for its subject.[6]

Ten days later *The Dancing Class* was bought by Louis Huth (perhaps at the suggestion of Whistler, who was about to paint a portrait of Mrs. Huth). That made three dance pictures sold by Durand-Ruel, for the Paris banker Albert Hecht, earlier in the year, had acquired *The Ballet from Robert le Diable,* and the French painter and collector Edouard Brandon — or possibly his father — had bought the other *Dancing Class,* the one now in the Metropolitan, in February 1872. Thus, both critically and commercially, Degas was well launched into the subject matter he would make peculiarly his own. During the rest of his career more than a third of his work in oil, pastel, and mixed media was concerned with ballet, and the proportion was considerably larger if drawings, etchings, lithographs, monotypes, and sculpture were counted.

Historically speaking, he was unlucky, for by the 1870s the art of the dance in Paris was thoroughly decadent, and it would remain so until the arrival of the Russians in the twentieth century. Saint-Léon's *Coppélia,* first presented three months before Sedan, and Louis Mérante's *Sylvia,* produced in 1876, turned out to be the last French choreographic creations for a long while that could stand comparison with such great Romantic productions as *La Sylphide* and *Giselle,* and moreover they owed much of their enduring success to the music of the innately balletic Léo Delibes (whom Tchaikovsky once rated above Brahms). Although brilliant foreign ballerinas continued to perform from time to time at the Opéra, there was no one in the noble category of a Taglioni or an Elssler, and the some sixty girls and young women in the permanent local company were often discouraged by low salaries or corrupted by wealthy boulevardiers, typically members of the Jockey Club, who regarded the stage in the Rue Le Peletier as less interesting than the backstage Foyer de la Danse, where they could dally with the little sylphs before a performance and perhaps arrange, sometimes with the help of a go-between mother, to take one to bed for the night. So-called balletomanes of this sort also had a bad effect on the repertoire, for they paid more attention to legs and bosoms than to *arabesques,* insisted on roles for their mistresses, and yawned at seriousness. In 1867 the critic Charles Yriarte had summed up the species:

> The man of fashion at the Opéra, with his box or his stall, his favorite dancer, his opera glasses, and his right of entry backstage, has a horror of anything which remains on the bills for a long time, of anything artistic, which must be listened to, respected, or requires an effort to be understood. [7]

The decay should not be overstated. There were still some honest, hard-working people at the Opéra, and the place was not quite what Berlioz had called it, simply "a house of assignation." But French ballets even at their best were tending to become minor entertainments, or mere episodes in operas, and were losing the poetic, life-enhancing, metaphysical content they had had during the July Monarchy and early Second Empire. At their worst they were little more than girlie shows with cultural trimmings. And one of the grave symptoms of the way things were going was a marked decline in the number and importance of parts for male dancers, plus the choreographers' inclination to assign such parts, when they did exist, to danseuses. In the 1870 première of *Coppélia,* for instance, the role of the young man, Franz, was taken by the excitingly androgynous Eugénie Fiocre — much to the satisfaction of the Jockey Club.

Given the situation, one can wonder why Degas was at all interested, let alone as fascinated as he evidently was. This is admittedly a little like wondering why he was Degas and not some other artist, since a complete answer would be a complex pattern of elements from his class, education, libido, talent, and so on. One can, however, put together a framework for speculation by noting how, over a relatively long period, he gradually took up ballet as a major subject matter, appropriated it for his own purposes, sharpened his observation of it, exploited its spatial, chromatic, tonal, kinetic, and temporal aspects, and integrated the whole enterprise into his personal social, aesthetic, and psychophilosophical outlook. He did not, of course, do all these things in exactly the chronological order corresponding to this list; in fact, he often did several of them in a single picture. But the order is not a very serious distortion of the inner logic of his evolution.

The precedents were of a mixed sort. During the eighteenth century, after the development of ballet from a court spectacle into a theatrical art, a number of celebrated danseuses, dancers, and choreographers had been depicted in oil or pastel by equally prominent portraitists — the influential precursor Françoise Prévost, for example, by the rather stately Jean Raoux; the brilliant Marie de Camargo and her poetic rival, Marie Sallé, by the Watteau disciple Nicolas Lancret; the great innovator Jean-Georges Noverre by one of Auguste Degas's favorites, Jean-Baptiste Perronneau; the durable Madeleine Guimard by her friend Honoré Fragonard; and the immensely popular Giovanna Bacelli by both Thomas Gainsborough and Sir Joshua Reynolds.

Although Neoclassicism had temporarily turned serious painters away from such allegedly frivolous models, it had not quite ruined the tradition. In 1834 the academic and normally uninspired Guillaume Lepaulle had painted a freshly Romantic oil showing Marie Taglioni and her brother Paul in the opening fireside-dream scene of *La Sylphide.* In 1841 Eugène Lami, whom Baudelaire would call a "poet of dandyism," had executed — as part of a series of watercolors devoted to ballerinas, *petits rats* (the girls still in dancing class), balletomanes, *coulisses, loges,* and the rest of the Opéra — his charmingly factual *Foyer de la Danse of the Rue Le Peletier,* in which Fanny Elssler is standing in the center of the already fashionable rendezvous room, Alfred de Musset is her nearest admirer, one of the waiting danseuses is having a sash tied, another is practicing her *pointes,* and another, seated beneath a bust of Madeleine Guimard, is adjusting a slipper. Ten years later Courbet painted, a bit too solidly, the Spanish *cachucha* expert Adela Guerrero. Also with an eye on the Second Empire market for *espagnolades,* Chassériau between 1852 and 1854 did several drawings, a watercolor, and an oil of the fiery Petra Camara, and Manet had followed suit in 1862 with his *Spanish Ballet* and his portrait of Lola de Valence.

Accompanying such firsthand works, and frequently reproducing them, there had been shoals of prints. For a long while the most popular had been lithographs of demure maidens with tiny feet and doll faces, and by the time of *Coppélia* these were numerous enough to warrant a suspicion that the art of painting and drawing ballerinas was becoming as decadent as French choreography. (Such imagery, or its Victorian equivalent, was probably what Sidney Colvin had in mind when he alluded disapprovingly in the *Pall Mall Gazette* to "that sentiment which is ordinarily implied by a picture having the ballet for its subject.") But there had also long been more respectable examples that catered to a legitimate admiration for virtuosity, or evoked supreme moments in terpsichorean history, or punctured balletic pretentiousness. Thanks to the engravers Francesco Bartolozzi and Benedetto Pastorini, one could have a good notion of what Auguste Vestris, idolized as "the god of the dance," looked like around 1780 when, beribboned hat in hand and one leg exactly perpendicular to the other, he had spun into one of his ovation-provoking pirouettes. With the help of a widely distributed color print by Alfred Edward Chalon, one could imagine the composition of the thrilling *Pas de Quatre* of 1845, which briefly brought together four of the finest ballerinas of the Romantic era: Marie Taglioni, Carlotta Grisi, Fanny Cerrito, and Lucile Grahn. (In the twentieth century Chalon's lithograph would be one of the sources for a reconstitution of the unrecorded choreography of this most famous of all *divertissements*.) At the debunking level Gustave Doré had included the little *rats* of the Rue Le Peletier in his satirical Parisian "menagerie" of 1854; and Daumier, during the 1850s and early 1860s, had caricatured such perennial figures as the young danseuse's meddling mother, the ogling bald-headed spectator from the provinces, and the aging dancer who refuses to retire.

The effect of the paintings and prints was echoed in a small body of mostly light literature. Prudent for once in his career, Voltaire had produced verses praising both Camargo and her rival, Sallé; and Musset, in a fanciful quintain of 1844, had implored the departing Taglioni to leave her shadow behind to perform for desolate Parisians. Gautier, in addition to writing reams of dance criticism and conceiving such celebrated ballets as *Giselle, La Péri,* and *Gemma,* had devoted some of the poetry in his *Emaux et camées* to danseuses — in particular to the Petra Camara who had captivated Chassériau:

> *Est-ce un fantôme? Est-ce une femme?*
> *Un rêve, une réalité,*
> *Qui scintille comme une flamme*
> *Dans un tourbillon de beauté?* [8]

(Is it a ghost? Is it a woman? A dream, a reality, that scintillates like a flame in a whirlwind of beauty?)

The more complicated Baudelaire had seen in Manet's portrait of Lola de Valence "the unexpected charm of pinka and black jewel,"[9] and in the general ephemerality of ballet a reminder of his old enemy the clock:

> *Le Plaisir vaporeux fuira vers l'horizon*
> *Ainsi qu'une sylphide au fond de la coulisse . . .*[10]

(Misty pleasure will flee over the horizon, as a sylph vanishes into the wings . . .)

In May 1870, in the periodical *La Vie parisienne,* Halévy had launched the serial publication of what in 1872 became his best-selling novel *Madame et Monsieur Cardinal* (thirty-three reprintings in ten years), a farcical, dryly ironical, often brutally realistic account of the adventures of two teen-age danseuses, Pauline and Virginie Cardinal, who become wealthy demimondaines with the connivance of their pandering, hypocritical, deadbeat parents. After the appearance of the first episode, the author had commented in his diary: "A bit violent perhaps, but the truth. Here, as I have seen them and as I know them, are these damsels of the Opéra . . . and their mothers."[11]

Degas was of course aware of this century and a half of visual and verbal material, and he was demonstrably, if not always consciously, influenced by some of it. He was also, however, plainly ready to react against much of it and to create his own approach. There is nothing in his notebooks that implies a transition from a Lancret or a Lami to the Metropolitan's *Dancing Class* of 1871–1872, nothing that is comparable to the copious evidence, long before his visit to the Haras du Pin in 1861 and his first racing oils, of his intensive study of the horses of Flaxman, Van Dyck, De Dreux, Géricault, Greek sculptors, and English printmakers. Nor is there any sign that the publication of *Madame et Monsieur Cardinal* at about the same time as his production of three important dance pictures was anything more than a coincidence, though there is plenty of proof that he was enthusiastic about the book. Clearly and quite uncharacteristically, he was not drawn to ballet as a subject matter by the achievements of earlier practitioners; he simply drifted toward it because of his personal familiarity with the Rue Le Peletier and his interest in equine movement, portraiture with signifying accessories, performed music, and the theater in general. The link is to be looked for in such works of his own as *The False Start, La Source* with Fiocre, *The Orchestra of the Opéra,* and the eloquent dumb show of *Interior.*

To that list of pictures one can add *The Ballet from Robert le Diable,* for it is significant both as a transitional work and as the end of a phase. Meyerbeer's grotesquely Faustian and neo-Gothic opera, first produced in 1831, owed much of its steady appeal to the scene in the third act in which lapsed nuns rise from their moonlit graves in a ruined convent and, led by their vicious abbess, waver into a ghostly, lascivious dance designed to complete the damnation of the already corrupted tenor. For the première, Taglioni had taken the role of the abbess, and the great Romantic set designer Pierre Ciceri had invented a vast, dimly gaslit, weirdly beautiful cloister that reproduced in part the galleries of a still intact sixteenth-century charnel house in suburban Montfort-l'Amaury. Degas saw a production of 1871 in which, although the leading danseuse was the reportedly mediocre Laure Fonta, the set — the real star of the proceedings — was splendidly close to the original one; and the result is a painting that functions, in terms of his biography, in three ways. It harks back to *The Orchestra of the Opéra* in its two-layer, light-dark structure and its distribution of figures in the lower zone. It recalls the tableau from *La Source* because it is the record of a specific theatrical event; in fact, it may have been inspired or at least influenced by a popular print showing a performance of *Robert le Diable* in the Rue Le Peletier. It is also, however, almost an evolutionary terminus, for in his entire output of the next half-century, a scene from *L'Africaine,* painted around 1879, and *Les Jumeaux de Bergame* (The Twins of Bergamo), staged in 1886, are the only other identifiable ballets. And one can push the argument a bit further by remarking that none of the fine paintings in question seems to have been conceived by Degas as a dance picture, since in *La Source* Fiocre was motionless, in *Robert le Diable* the movement was very unclassical, the scene from *L'Africaine* was centered on the singer, and *Les Jumeaux* was a mimed harlequinade.

An avoidance of the specific, the verifiable, and the namable is noticeable in other aspects of his balletic production. Although the stage in the Rue Le Peletier and some rehearsal rooms in both the old and the new Paris opera houses are recognizable in a few paintings, in general a given setting is wholly or partly invented, and sometimes it is simply one of the studios in the Ninth Arrondissement. Contrary to what is perpetuated in the titles used in many art histories, exhibition catalogues, and museum listings, there is no sign at all of the Foyer de la Danse that had become famous, and notorious, during the July Monarchy and the Second Empire. A window, a mirror, or a column may be placed arbitrarily, and even a costume may lack documentary exactitude: in the early dance class scenes, the brightly colored sashes and black throat ribbons are imaginary additions to the plain, longish skirts, flesh tights, and knickers worn by the girls for practice sessions. (The very short powder-puff tutu, devised by acrobatic Italians who wanted more freedom for their legs, did not come into use until the 1880s.)

Of the hundreds of danseuses represented, a mere dozen have been

The Dance Lesson, 1874–1875

definitely identified, and of these the only historically noteworthy ones are Fiocre, who faded rapidly after her successes in *La Source* and *Coppélia,* and the more gifted Rita Sangalli, a graduate of the flourishing Milan school who made a sensational tour of the United States in the late 1860s and danced the title role in the première of *Sylvia.* Although this scarcity of stars may be attributable to their unavailability for posing, it was also due to a predilection of Degas's for relatively inglorious models. He did three oil portraits and several dance drawings of the very minor Joséphine Gaujelin, for instance.

Although male performers, in keeping with their declining status, are completely absent from the paintings, two veterans of the Romantic era, Louis Mérante and Jules Perrot, appear as teachers. Mérante, in white ducks in the Jeu de Paume *Dancing Class,* had made his début as a dancer at the Opéra in 1848 at the age of twenty, and by the end of the Second Empire had assumed charge of the institution's permanent corps de ballet. During the next twenty years he arranged the choreography — not very imaginatively, according to contemporary critics — for *Sylvia* and for two later successes, *Les Deux Pigeons* (The Two Pigeons) and the Breton *La Korrigane* (The Goblin), in both of which the star was Rosita Mauri, a rapid, provocative Catalan who, after being discovered by Gounod at La Scala, reigned as prima ballerina in Paris until the end of the 1880s. Perrot, who is the squarely built, gray green man prominent in *The Dance Lesson* of around 1874 and half a dozen other pictures, was a direct link with the already legendary 1830s and 1840s and even with the eighteenth century; he had been one of the aging, deified Auguste Vestris's pupils. Taglioni had been his dancing partner, and Carlotta Grisi his mistress and eventually his wife. His powerful legs and feathery technique gave him an extraordinary capacity for elevation; Gautier called him "Perrot the aerial, Perrot the sylph, the male Taglioni." [12] As a choreographer and ballet master he had created such memorable works as *Giselle* (with Jean Coralli), *Ondine, La Esmeralda,* and the all-star *Pas de Quatre,* and had had a frequently stormy ten-year career at the Bolshoi Theater in Saint Petersburg. In 1859, though he was then only forty-nine, he left Russia in a fit of violent disagreement with the czarist aesthetic dictatorship and returned to Paris to become a retired celebrity who kept in touch with his old life by conducting occasional and always crowded classes at the Opéra. His principal defect was a streak of umbrageousness and absoluteness, especially in matters involving his art, and that was probably one of the several things Degas liked about him.

In a few of the dance pictures there is a return to the portrait tricks and play-acting of the 1860s. The bassoonist Dihau is near the center of

The Rehearsal, 1873–1874

The Ballet from Robert le Diable, and next to him, with opera glasses, is Albert Hecht, the future owner of the painting. In the Jeu de Paume *Dancing Class* the seated violinist, next to Mérante, has an elderly man's body and the singer Pagans's head. The motherly figure in *The Rehearsal,* painted around 1873–1874, is Sabine Neyt, Degas's housekeeper at the time, and her red plaid shawl may have been borrowed from the fictional Madame Cardinal, who is described in the book as "a fat, carelessly dressed woman with an old tartan on her shoulders." Much more common than such insertions, however, is his use and re-use, analogous to what is apparent in the horse pictures, of an accumulated stock of drawings of generally anonymous figures. In 1872, for example, he did a fine black-pencil study, accented with crayon and heightened with white chalk, of a buxom danseuse facing three-quarters front, and during the next two years he utilized it for the figure in the middle of the background of *The Rehearsal of the Ballet on the Stage,* of which there are three versions, and for the girl in front

The Rehearsal of the Ballet on the Stage, 1874

of the door in *The Dance Lesson.* The pair of ballerinas on the far right of
The Rehearsal of the Ballet on the Stage, Paris version, move up closer to us,
with flowers on their heads and tutus, in the *Two Dancers on the Stage* of a
few months later. A sketch of Gaujelin adjusting her slipper in 1873
reappears, with slight modifications, in *Three Danseuses* and *Danseuses at
Rest.* Sometimes the repeated figures are somewhat disguised by being
reversed, a procedure for which Michelangelo provided precedents in his
nude athletes, the *Ignudi,* for the Sistine Chapel; and here the *Ballet Lesson
on Stage* of around 1875 by itself furnishes enough examples, for it contains
mirror images of the Perrot of *The Dance Lesson* and the principal ballerina

of both *Two Dancers on the Stage* and the Paris *Rehearsal of the Ballet on the Stage.*

Thus the Degas who was his own horse-breeder and racetrack director was also largely his own ballet master and terpsichorean stage manager. And one of the advantages he derived from his control over his material was an opportunity to indulge fully in his taste for experimentation with pictorial space — space as an enclosed two-dimensional field, space as an extent or volume receding from the plane of the canvas, space as linear perspective, and so on. He began to favor relatively small formats: whereas *La Source* is 130 by 145 centimeters, the Metropolitan's *Dancing Class* is merely 19.7 by 27, and during the rest of his career there would be few works of any sort more than a meter high or wide. He continued to place figures asymmetrically and to allow some of them to be cut by the frame. One of his emerging stylistic trademarks was the use of a *repoussoir* (from *repousser,* "to push back"), a strongly defined person or object situated in the foreground of a picture, usually near the right or left edge, with the intention of deepening the illusion of depth, enhancing a principal episode, or simply deflecting a viewer's eye in a desired direction; in *The Orchestra of the Opéra* and several later paintings the *repoussoir* is the looming volute of a double bass, in the Paris *Dancing Class* it is the danseuse on the left, in *The Dance Lesson* it is the sprinkler used (before the advent of rosin) on slippery floors, and in the Metropolitan's *Dancing Class* it is again the watering can, reinforced by the pointing violin case. More dramatically, the *Musicians in the Orchestra* of 1872 offers, in the heads and instruments of the three men in the close foreground, a cluster of *repoussoirs* that pushes back everything. Sometimes in these works of the early 1870s the scene recedes diagonally from the picture plane and thus creates a kind of spatial counterpoint. Often the viewpoint is high enough to eliminate any suggestion of a "horizon" and to present almost a bird's-eye close-up. Often, too, there is a stimulating mixture of devices: in *The Ballet from Robert le Diable,* for instance, what can be called a macrospace moves back more or less parallel with the picture plane, breaks up on the stage into a collection of micro-spaces opening onto the yard of the cloister, and finally recedes on a diagonal in an accelerating perspective down the gallery on the left.

There are, of course, some faults. One may object that the vanishing points and orthogonal lines are frequently a bit askew, that the off-center compositions, cropped figures, and eccentric viewpoints now and then look arbitrary, and that some of the pictures come close to being merely playful spatial tours de force. In particular one occasionally finds a *repoussoir* that may seem too big and its pushing exaggerated, for although the retinal image of an object halves in size with each doubling of distance, the brain

Two Dancers on the Stage, 1874

usually compensates for the shrinkage by constancy scaling. Thus, nearby heads do not actually loom as much as those in *Musicians in the Orchestra,* and slightly distant girls do not actually dwindle as rapidly as those in the back of *The Dance Lesson.* (This tendency of Degas's to neglect size constancy is analogous to Monet's tendency to paint purely retinal instead of "local" colors.) But all these faults — if they are faults — are more than matched by a rare amount of spatiopsychological sophistication. The asymmetries, the apparently casual cuts, the odd angles, and the foreground elements indicate the presence of a space-controlling viewer (along with the artist, of course) in ways that are beyond the capacity of more conventional representations. In *The Dance Lesson* the floorboards, in addition to being lines of perspective, are a reality that runs out the bottom edge of the format to become a floor on which we ourselves are standing. Similarly, in other works we look down from a stage-side box or straight ahead from behind a huge double bass, doing our own visual pushing. Not since the Velázquez

*Musicians
in the Orchestra,* 1872

of *Las Meninas* had there been a painter with so much talent for a complex interplay between pictorial space and spectator space.

Critics, in a rather gleeful reductionist way, have suggested that photography was somehow the cause of all this virtuosity. Degas, they remind us, showed a keen interest in the new invention, eventually became an enthusiastic amateur photographer, and could scarcely have failed to perceive that the camera was apt to ignore both mental size constancy and traditional mise-en-scène. In two of his pre-ballet paintings, the *Princess von Metternich* and a study of Eugénie Fiocre's head, he is known to have worked from photographs, and on the basis of internal evidence — tone values, amorphous backgrounds, daguerreotype poses — we may assume that he did the same thing for a few other portraits. During the 1890s he also used photographs of a female nude, a danseuse, and some landscapes. In short, the argument can be quite persuasive, and indeed it does contribute to an understanding of certain pictures. Its defects, however, at least in the form it usually takes, are that it does not sufficiently distinguish photographs as simple substitutes for models from photographs as stylistic sources, that it tends to emphasize evidence from periods, like the 1890s, too late to be significant, and above all that it overlooks an impressive number of thoroughly possible and important nonphotographic influences. The Tuscan Mannerists of the sixteenth century had produced asymmetrical compositions; Mantegna, Raphael, Titian, Tintoretto, Van Dyck, Guercino, Callot, Daumier, Gavarni, and Meryon, among others, had cut figures with frames. The *repoussoir* had been a fairly common device ever since the Renaissance, with striking examples of the gesturing type in Tintoretto's *Presentation of the Virgin* and El Greco's *Burial of Count Orgaz,* and a recent variant in Gérôme's *Death of Caesar* in the form of the corpse of the dictator, which functions in exactly the same way as the violin case in the Metropolitan's *Dancing Class.* Japanese printmakers had long been expert manipulators of all these space indicators: Kiyonaga, for instance, had made poetic use of cut-offs in his narrow *hashira-e* (pillar pictures), and Hiroshige had invented huge *repoussoirs.* More generally, Parisian theaters themselves, with their mysterious depths and elaborate machinery, undoubtedly were sources. In this context a passage in the Goncourts' *Journal,* dated March 12, 1862, is relevant (though it was not published until more than twenty-five years later); it reveals that those who frequented the Rue Le Peletier in the middle of the Second Empire saw scenes similar to some of Degas's dance paintings of the 1870s:

We are at the Opéra, in the director's box above the stage. . . . And while talking I have my eyes on a coulisse opposite me. Next to a gas lamp, leaning against a wooden pillar, is [the danseuse] La Mercier, quite blond, radiant, loaded with golden trinkets and shiny necklaces. . . . She is modeled by light, absolutely like the little girl with the chicken in Rembrandt's *Night Watch*. . . . Then, behind the luminous figure of the danseuse, who is as erect as a desire, there is a marvelous tenebrous and glimmering background . . . with forms that disappear in shadows and in the smoky, dusty distance.[13]

Plainly, the best conclusion to be drawn from the whole mass of photographic and nonphotographic evidence, seldom specific, is that the influence of the camera, though real and at times important, was more reinforcing than formative. If Niepce and Daguerre had never existed Degas would probably still have been pretty much Degas.

His spatial experiments were accompanied by a rapidly evolving interest in light, color, and tone values. Whereas in the Jeu de Paume *Dancing Class* of 1872 the light is a diffused academic glow and the bright color is limited to three red accents in the dominant white and tan, two years later the *Danseuse Posing in a Photographer's Studio* is an exercise in strongly contrasting *contre-jour* in which wintry Paris sunshine bounces off rooftops, floods through the large window facing the viewer, glistens on grayish blue curtains, and transforms the ballerina's uplifted face into an unexpected patch of chiaroscuro. At about the same date, in the equally frontal *Rehearsal,* three windows are visible, a pair of cropped, back-lit legs is whimsically silhouetted on the spiral, space-pushing staircase, and a rather poisonous emerald green, intensified by the proximity of the ballet master's red shirt and the mother's tartan, is splashed onto the shoulders of a *rat* and into a trio of ribbons. An increasing sophistication in the use of artificial illumination is evident in the way the upward cast of the footlights half dissolves and half models the principal ballerina in the *Musicians in the Orchestra.* That such tonal effects were the result of on-the-spot documentation is shown by some notes, jotted down during a performance, that compare the actual scene at the Opéra with *The Ballet from Robert le Diable,* apparently still unfinished (and reveal incidentally that Degas was on a first-name basis with the orchestra conductor Georges Hainl):

Dark gray background . . . Georges silhouetted. . . . On the receding arcades the moonlight merely licks the columns. On the ground [of the cloister yard] the effect is pinker and warmer than I have made it. Black vault, indefinite arches . . . luminous blur around the arcades in perspective. Nuns more in a flannel color but more vague . . .[14]

On one occasion, for the Paris version of *The Rehearsal of the Ballet on the Stage,* he abandoned saturated hues altogether in favor of a semitransparent, subtly varied brown that captures admirably the subdued lighting, the shadow patterns, and the peculiar, unworldly isolation of an afternoon practice session in an otherwise deserted theater. Local color was by now forgotten.

Balletic movement was a far more difficult problem than theatrical space, light, and color, since the positions of classical dancing had long been codified with a precision that did not allow any approximation in their portrayal. Also, there were few imitable examples, aside from paintings and prints showing a Camargo or a Vestris with one leg raised, or a hovering Taglioni; and there was no handy, accepted artistic convention — nothing like the imaginary flying gallop favored by Géricault and British horse specialists — for representing *entrechats, cabrioles,* and other movements that were almost too fast to be caught even by the eye. Photographs of ballerinas had existed, of course, for years, but they were mostly straight portraits, and the rest were obviously posed tableaux that could be regarded as action shots only with the help of a lot of good will. (Although by the early 1860s plate exposures at a fiftieth of a second were feasible, Eadweard Muybridge's experiments in the late 1870s were the first serious attempts to employ "instantaneous" photography for an analysis of animal movement.) Understandably, therefore, Degas began his kinetic studies with little of the audacity he had manifested in his mise-en-scènes. The sketchy danseuses in *The Orchestra of the Opéra* are scarcely fluttering their legs; those in *The Ballet from Robert le Diable* are engaged, with authorization from the libretto, in a sort of ectoplasmic oozing. In the two versions of the *Dancing Class* the most noticeable ballerina is holding the preparatory position referred to technically as *quatrième derrière,* others are warming up at the bar, and no one is actually dancing. The dramatically lit star of *Musicians in the Orchestra* is doing a *révérence,* or curtsey, at the end of her solo; both of the only performing girls in *The Rehearsal* are teetering in *arabesques allongées.* Not until *The Rehearsal of the Ballet on the Stage* is there a danseuse on *pointes* and really in motion. And at this date her creator was still, as has been noted, unadventurous enough to use her several times.

One suspects, however, that something more complex than mere caution and an awareness of inexperience was involved in this evident reluctance to paint or draw rapid dancing. By the end of the Second Empire all of the more or less motionless elements in the classical ballet alphabet had evolved into clear, if unintended, examples of a concern for what Lessing, a century earlier in his influential essay on the Hellenistic *Laocoon* sculptural group in the Vatican, had called the "critical" or "fruitful" moment in a plastic representation of an action: the moment, that is, when a figure is poised intelligibly just before or just after a movement and is thus able to concentrate in itself, while remaining relatively unagitated, an implication of past or future movement. Degas may never have read the essay, but of course he did not need to in order to perceive that painting, a nontemporal medium, was not really very well adapted to depicting the human body in sequential action. Moreover, he was familiar, notably in the work of Poussin, with many classical instances of the effective employment of "moments." So the apparent timidity in these early dance pictures can be read partly as a deliberate aesthetic choice — and even as a prologue to one of the constants in his art, for though he would become expert at rendering fast movement, he would always display a marked liking for the eloquent "moment" of a *quatrième derrière,* an *arabesque,* an *attitude,* or a concluding *révérence.*

The treatment of movement contributes to the erection of a temporal structure that, in spite of the presence of vigorous touches of realism, frequently verges on the dreamlike. In general, to be sure, the viewer is made aware of the slogan *il faut être de son temps:* he is not apt to mistake *The Ballet from Robert le Diable* for a history painting. But this perception is quickly followed by a mixed sense of the vague and the precise. Since in most of the pictures an identifiable place, a known balletic work, and namable people are lacking, it is only within extremely broad limits that one can date the represented scene (as distinct from the canvas and pigment) by simply looking at it. When the light is artificial, as it frequently is, there is no way we can estimate the hour, as we can, often quite adequately, in a Monet that was executed outdoors in the middle of a sunlit morning. On the other hand, the spatial devices and unusual viewpoints, as already remarked, can give the viewer a lively sense of being present at a particular minute in the nineteenth century. The use of "critical moments" condenses and fixes the flowing temporal stream, and also provides it with arrows. In many compositions there are sudden, discrete images of sharply factual instants: a girl stretches her leg at the bar; Hecht looks around the house in search of an acquaintance; the violinist settles in his pelvis and waits for Mérante to complete an explanation. Sometimes, by squinting a bit and divesting ourselves of our habit of seeing paintings as literature — of looking *through* them, as Whistler once said, instead of *at* them — we can attain a state of aesthetic grace sufficient for scanning a work as a nonrepresentational object. Then the color and light become a splendid patchwork, the thick-thin contour variations take on a kinetic quality, and the movements of legs and arms arrange themselves into a rather Islamic pattern of lines on a flat surface. On such occasions the present ceases to be an imaginary flash in the nineteenth century or an infinitesimal point on a vector; it emerges as a psychological now, a temporal field comparable to what enables us to perceive a musical phrase as such and not as a mere succession of notes.

Once when he was asked by Mrs. Havemeyer why he painted the ballet, Degas replied, "Because, Madame, it is all that is left us of the combined movement of the Greeks."[15] In spite of its touch of affectation, the answer probably contained a good deal of sober truth. He was quite capable of seeing a Nike adjusting her sandal in the form of a *rat* tying her slipper,[16] much as in 1856 he had seen both a Parthenon figure and one from Attic pottery in the way Adelaide Ristori moved across the stage. Like the Greeks, he believed in the supreme importance of the human body as a source of art. Two of his history paintings, *Semiramis Building Babylon* and *Young Spartan Girls Provoking the Boys,* had subjects drawn mostly from Greek literature, and so did several of his projected works. His early notebooks contain many drawings based, usually by way of engravings, on the figures, costumes, and furniture represented on ancient vases; and of course much influence could have come by way of academic Salon artists, whose resurrections of antiquity were often meticulously documented. But when all this has been noted, the fact remains that an unprompted viewer of the dance pictures probably would not see any analogies with Greek Classicism. Indeed, if he felt like making any comparisons at all, he would be much more apt to think of Italian Mannerism. Nineteenth-century ballet itself, though the culmination of a long tradition, was to a considerable extent a product of the Mannerist era, and some of its postures were derived from mid-sixteenth-century painting and sculpture — the *attitude,* for example, from Giovanni Bologna's bronze *Mercury.* Spatial distortions, eccentric viewpoints, stylistic arbitrariness, and a tendency to proceed from other art rather than life were all characteristic of Mannerist painting. So in consequence were artificiality, theatricality, and subjectivism. The attitude of many Mannerists toward Raphael and the High Renaissance had a counterpart in Degas's ambiguous relationship with Ingres and Neoclassicism. Degas as a person, with his contradictory traits and regular attacks of angst, had something in common with such self-tortured Mannerists as Pontormo, Rosso, and Parmigianino.

Since most of the pictures show lessons, rehearsals, practice sessions, or at best hypothetical episodes from unidentifiable ballets, the dance steps represented can scarcely be said to express anything literary — certainly nothing like the narrative line of a *Giselle* or a *Coppélia.* They cannot even be assembled and arranged by the mental choreography of a viewer into a storyless, Balanchine kind of abstract ballet, an *Agon,* for they have almost no perceptible syntax: they are like dictionary words. Yet it would be absurd and impoverishing, in spite of the Mannerist aestheticism, to argue that these paintings are merely art for art's sake.

For one thing, they contain, without a trace of the sermonizing and sentimentality common in the contemporary Realist school, some recognizable social comment on the careers of nineteenth-century Paris danseuses, with which a frequenter of the wings and practice rooms at the Opéra was of course familiar. Most of the girls came from poor working-class families, since a wealthy bourgeois parent was unlikely to let a daughter enter such a reputedly wicked milieu. They arrived in the Rue Le Peletier — or after 1875 in the new Palais Garnier — around the age of seven or eight, sometimes in an older sister's worn-out dress, often with an empty stomach, and usually with an ambitious mother. At ten the presumably untalented ones were ruthlessly eliminated and the others given a chance to rise slowly and often haphazardly, by means of periodical examinations, from student *rats* to regular members of the corps de ballet, then coryphées (who danced in the relatively small groups), then *petits sujets* (irregular soloists), and so on up through the surprisingly military hierarchy to the generally unthinkable rank of a *première danseuse*. They spent their days and evenings in the opera house and had little in the way of a formal education except their dance lessons, although the quicker and prettier girls acquired a smattering of culture and a knack for repartee from being in the company of boulevardiers. After reaching adolescence they began to receive on the average nine hundred francs a year, which was about half the annual pay of a very minor government clerk and not enough to keep them from becoming the victims of constant insinuations about their morals: on one occasion the director of the Opéra cynically rejected a suggested salary increase on the ground that "these damsels . . . have the Foyer de la Danse."[17]

Degas, while delighting in their exacting discipline (to the point of mimicking their positions and movements), chose to paint them as they were, which is to say as members of an entertainment proletariat who did not pretend to be refined young princesses from the elegant parts of the city inhabited by their public. They scratch their backs with plebeian nonchalance while the ballet master discourses on the arcana of their art. Like kittens, totally free from the constraints of a superego, they yawn and stretch luxuriously. They sit with their legs apart, in the posture of slovenly boys. Often they have the bold stares and cheeky faces of gamines from the streets of Parisian suburbs — faces prefigured in the Montmartre mugs of the youngsters in the *Young Spartan Girls*. A modern viewer may minimize such details, for they are like musical expressiveness weakened by familiarity. But they surprised most of Degas's contemporaries and especially the critics in England, who were accustomed to the candy-box keepsake women usual in Victorian oils and lithographs. Whereas Colvin's article in the *Pall Mall Gazette* mentioned favorably an "extraordinary alertness . . . as to common and unideal fact," London reviewers of other Degas works during the next few years referred to "a vulgar awkwardness about some of the pink legs," [18] danseuses "scantily endowed with beauty," [19] a batch of "arch, sly, vain, and ugly ballet-girls," [20] and said of the artist that he "eschews graceful contours and regular features in a way really provoking." [21]

Frequently the proletarianization of the sylphs is incorporated in a more general tendency that may be called philosophical, though the word is too heavy for the attractiveness of these seemingly offhand paintings. Degas clearly relished the elaborate illusionism that was an important aspect of a production at the Paris Opéra in the nineteenth century; as a matter of fact, works like *The Orchestra of the Opéra,* the *Musicians in the Orchestra,* and *The Ballet from Robert le Diable* probably function for most museum visitors less as dance pictures than as marvelous evocations of backdrops, flats, gaslight, scenography, and miscellaneous theatrical magic. After the realistic landscape accompanying Fiocre in *La Source,* however, the illusionism is always represented as illusionism: the backdrops and flats are obviously pieces of cloth and wood daubed with color, the light is emphatically artificial, and even Ciceri's cloister is pure staginess. The spell is simultaneously cast and broken; we are asked to suspend our disbelief while not actually doing so. And this is true in relation to the danseuses as well as the sets and illumination. Degas certainly admired ballerinas when they were reversing the law of gravity, whipping through multiple *fouettés,* or effortlessly skimming the floor on *pointes.* But he also liked the occasions when they landed with an ignominious plop, waddled ludicrously, or stood still and suddenly revealed themselves as flat-footed, short-legged, pathetically earthbound creatures. Thus class-angling, décor, and action could merge — in the three versions of *The Rehearsal of the Ballet on the Stage,* for instance — to become unpretentious little comedies on the ancient theme of appearance and reality, with the implied spectator-author sitting in an upper box and, like an invisible *repoussoir,* distancing the scene spatially, socially, and aesthetically.

12. New Orleans

IN 1872 work on some of the dance pictures was interrupted by a departure for Louisiana that was a delayed and complex result of the trip made to France nine years earlier by Odile Musson and her two daughters, the widowed Estelle and Didy of the pretty hands.

When the three women and Estelle's little daughter returned to the United States in 1865, René de Gas (as he insisted on spelling his name) had accompanied them, with the intention of liquidating some inherited New Orleans property that had been in a legal muddle ever since his mother's death. But he found employment in the cotton-exporting firm in which his uncle, Michel Musson, was an associate, fell in love with Estelle, and liked the atmosphere of the still partly French city. Two years after his arrival, with his brother Achille as a partner and with the help of a large loan negotiated through the Degas bank in Paris, he set himself up in a local business of his own as a wine importer and commission merchant. (Old René-Hilaire's squeamishness in the 1840s about American investments appears to have been forgotten by everyone concerned.) In 1869 he married Estelle, with a special Episcopal dispensation for first cousins (equivalent to the papal permission obtained by Thérèse and Edmondo Morbilli) and against the strong opposition of her father, who was thinking less about consanguinity than about the possible consequences of the fact that the young woman, still tragically unlucky, had contracted ophthalmia in 1866 and become totally, incurably blind long before her wedding day.

During the summer of 1872 René returned to Europe on a commercial prospecting tour, and on June 26 he sent home a report from Paris on his older brother, who was now living in a flat at 77 Rue Blanche, a few blocks west of the Rue de Laval, and was evidently being well fed:

> At the station I found Edgar, more mature, fatter, more sedate, and with some gray streaks in his beard. Father and I had dinner at his place, and afterward we went to see Marguerite. Edgar is doing some really charming things. He has a profile portrait of Madame Camus in a garnet-red velvet dress, seated on a brown chair and silhouetted against a pink background; for me it's a pure masterpiece. His drawing is ravishing. Unfortunately his eyes are very weak, and he is forced to use them with the greatest caution. He has a good cook and a delightful bachelor's apartment; I have lunch there every day. Last night I had dinner there with Pagans, who sings to the accompaniment of a guitar and about whom Achille will give you some details. Edgar finds me very American . . .[1]

Apparently the Americanization was contagious, for on July 12 René wrote, "Although he is still the same, he has become crazy about learning to pronounce English and has been repeating 'turkey buzzard' for an entire week."[2] By July 17 the idea of a visit to New Orleans was taking definite shape, in the midst of inspecting pictures, eating good French food, doing some Paris-by-night musical slumming, and making patriotic excursions to the spots where, less than two years before this peaceful summer, National Guardsmen had been dying hysterically and uselessly in the snow:

> Edgar has got it into his head to go back with me and stay with us for a couple of months. I couldn't ask for anything better. He is pondering all sorts of things about the natives and is tireless in his questions about all of you. I really think I'll bring him along. Although his eyes are better, he has to take care of them, and you know how he is. Right now he is painting small pictures, the most wearying kind. He has done a charming ballet rehearsal [presumably the Paris *Dancing Class*], and I'll have a large photograph of it made. . . . He has an admirable cook named Clotilde, whose dream is to come to America, but she is too intelligent a girl not to drop us very rapidly, find a rich husband, and set herself up in a cook shop of her own. . . .
>
> After dinner I go down with Edgar to the Champs-Elysées, to a café-concert, to listen to idiotic songs. . . . Sometimes when he is in good form we dine in the country and visit the places made memorable by the siege of Paris. Prepare yourselves to welcome suitably the Grrrreat Artist. He insists on your not coming down to the station to receive him with a brass band, a company of militiamen, firemen, clergymen, etc.[3]

Around the beginning of October, after a delay caused by René's business activities, the brothers went to England to make final arrangements for passage to the United States.

Two letters to Tissot[4] written during the following months indicate that Edgar spent most of the waiting period in London actively looking into the local art market and also, slightly enviously, into the state of Victorian painting. As was natural, given his recently established connections, he visited the gallery of the French "society" in New Bond Street, where he found Durand-Ruel's knowledgeable secretary, Charles W. Deschamps, in charge. There are signs, however, of a greener-pasture mentality and a readiness to desert Durand-Ruel for the prominent British dealer Thomas Agnew: "I spoke about him [Agnew] casually to a few friends, and what they told me is absolutely fascinating. They urge me to place myself in his redoubtable hands." An expedition to Chelsea yielded the observation that "that fellow Whistler has really hit on something in those views of the sea and water that he showed me." (As the tone of this suggests, Degas's admiration for the American's work was always qualified by reservations about the histrionic personality of "that fellow.") Another remark reveals that the success of Millais's *The Eve of Saint Agnes* at the Exposition Universelle of 1867 was not forgotten: "If you see Millais, tell him I am very sorry not to have been able to see him and tell him of my appreciation for him." But finally there is an affirmation of confidence in the ultimate victory of the new French school:

> Our race will have something simple and bold to offer. The Naturalist movement will draw in a manner worthy of the great schools and then its strength will be recognized. This English art that appeals so much to us often seems to be exploiting some trick. We can do better than they and be just as strong.

Although the word "Naturalist" is confusing, the emphasis on drawing permits a guess that the reference was chiefly to one member of the Batignolles group.

René having completed his preparations, he and Edgar left London for Liverpool, where, on October 12, they embarked for New York aboard the paddle wheel *Scotia,* one of the prides of Cunard's Royal Mail Steam Packet Company. Edgar was soon sketching passengers, pelicans, and especially the voracious North Atlantic cormorants, and registering impressions preserved in a later letter to Lorentz Frölich, a Danish painter and engraver who was for a time a member of the Manet circle:

> The ocean! How big it is! How far away from you I am! The *Scotia* is a British ship. . . . A dull crossing! I didn't know English, I still don't, and on British territory, even at sea, there is a coldness and a conventional distrust you have perhaps already encountered.[5]

He felt better during the four-day train trip from New York to New Orleans, on which he reported to Dihau:

> You must have heard of the sleeping car, but you haven't used one, you haven't seen one, and so you can't imagine what a marvelous invention it is. You lie down at night in a real bed. . . . You even put your shoes at the foot of the bed and a nice Negro shines them for you while you sleep. Sybaritism, you say? No, it is simple necessity. Otherwise you couldn't make such a journey at a single stretch.[6]

At the station in New Orleans there was no brass band to greet him, but his cousins Estelle, Didy, and Mathilde, six of their children, and his uncle Michel were on hand, and he was soon a part of this large family.

The city in 1872 was a frightening political, social, and economic mess and a sign of the collapse of the idealism that, in some minds at any rate, had marked the start of the Reconstruction period. Many Confederate Army veterans had come home from their long ordeal intent on restoring rather than reconstructing; real power was often in the hands of Northern carpetbaggers and Southern scalawags; the emancipation of the slaves was turning out to have been largely nominal; and corruption was so common that the average citizen had been degraded to the point of being inured to it. Yet the letters Degas sent back to Europe might have been written in the 1840s, so little awareness of the current noisomeness do they show. The explanation, aside from a tourist's obliviousness and a guest's tact, may be that he did actually spend much of his visit in a sort of antebellum time capsule. In 1869 Michel Musson, though no longer very rich, had rented for himself and his extended family an immense mansion on Esplanade Avenue at the corner of Tonti Street. The avenue, which marked the northern limits of the Vieux Carré, was itself a fine relic of the old, more civilized way of life, with rows of palms, elms, live oaks, and magnolias, some truly palatial homes built by Creole dynasties during their boom (and sometimes bust) period, and a persisting allegiance to the French language at a moment when English was rapidly gaining ground in the quarter beyond Canal Street, now under Yankee influence. Michel's house had an ornamental cast-iron gate and fence, lawn planted with flowers and magnolias, and a columned two-story verandah vaguely reminiscent of both Steamboat Gothic and the Greek Revival. On the ground floor a central corridor opened on one side into the dining room and a series of salons, and on the other side into an apartment occupied by the unmarried Didy and her father. (Her mother, Odile, had died a year before Edgar's arrival.) Half of the second floor was assigned to Mathilde, her cotton-broker husband, William Bell, and their three children, and the other half to Estelle, René, their two young children, and Joe Balfour, Estelle's nine-year-old daughter from her first marriage. Above them a big unoccupied garret, usually littered with toys, was reserved for the children on rainy days. Edgar was given a spare bedroom in Michel's apartment and also the use, when he wanted to paint, of a second-floor gallery that ran along the front of the building.

He sometimes ventured beyond Canal Street to visit his brothers' offices on Common Street and those of his uncle's firm on Carondelet Street, and he renewed an acquaintance with Mathieu-Joseph Bujac, one of Henri Rouart's employees, who was in New Orleans to set up a refrigeration plant. On several occasions he got as far as the Terre-aux-Boeufs region, twenty kilometers out of town on the east bank of the Mississippi, where some members of the Millaudon family, whom he seems to have met in Italy, had a plantation. But he stuck mostly to the house on the Esplanade and its vicinity, where he enjoyed a stimulating exoticism combined with the atmosphere of a French village. (New Orleans at this time had a total population of less than two hundred thousand.) On November 27 he wrote, pell-mell, to Frölich:

> Everything attracts me here. I look at everything. . . . I like nothing better than the Negresses of every shade holding in their arms white, so very white, babies in front of white houses with wooden fluted columns and in gardens of orange trees and the ladies in muslin in front of their little houses and the steamboats with two chimneys as tall as factory chimneys and the fruit dealers with their crammed-to-bursting shops, and the contrast between the busy, well-arranged offices and this immense black animal force, etc., etc. And the pretty women of pure blood and the pretty quadroons and the well-built Negresses![7]

He even liked the new local street cars, which were steam-powered ancestors of the one named Desire.

Living in the large Musson household provoked a return of some of the velleities concerning marriage he had experienced after meeting the English couple in Assisi. In the letter to Dihau, on November 11, he exclaimed, "Ah, my dear friend, what a good thing a family is . . ." On December 5 he wrote to Henri Rouart:

> I am thirsty for order. I do not even consider that a good woman would be the enemy of this new way of life. Would a few children of my own, engendered by me, be too much? No. . . . Nearly all the women here are pretty, and many even include in their charms that hint of ugliness without which nothing works. But I'm afraid their heads are as weak as my own, and two such heads would constitute a peculiar guarantee for a new household.[8]

Once, in the style of a lovesick troubadour, he referred to Marie Dihau as *ma cruelle amie;* and to Tissot he confessed that he would like to be liberated from the need for being *galant,* in the French sense of "amatory."

Almost from the start of his visit, however, he began to have various sorts of small and large misgivings. One morning while he was still in his bed he suffered a severe attack of homesickness merely from hearing a workman on a neighboring building yell, "Ohé! Auguste!"[9] He worried about what Clotilde might be up to in the Rue Blanche, about being back in the Rue Le Peletier in time for one of Rita Sangalli's appearances, and about the state of the family bank in Paris. ("Papa," he told Rouart, "wants the world to come to an end, as if we weren't there to put things in order.")[10] A temporary lack of opera in New Orleans was for him a cause of "terrible suffering." The incessant talk about cotton, cotton, cotton, got on his nerves, and so did Southern work tempos, to the point of making him feel somewhat neurotically guilty about his own capacity for getting things done. (Actually, he was as industrious as ever.) He read Rousseau and, with himself as a similarly horrible example, twice referred — in the letters to Frölich and Rouart — to the following passage in the *Confessions:*

> I love to busy myself with doing nothing, to begin a hundred things and finish none of them, to go and come as it suits me, to change projects every instant, to follow a fly in all its movements, to uproot a rock to see what is under it, to undertake eagerly a task of ten years and abandon it without regret in ten minutes.[11]

On November 19 he wrote to Tissot, "Everything is beautiful in this world of the people. But one Paris laundry girl, with bare arms, is worth it all for such a pronounced Parisian as I am."[12]

The possible effect on his painting of having changed countries and climates was his principal concern, and portraiture his principal affliction, and both were stressed in the letter to Frölich:

> How many new things I have seen! How many projects, my dear Frölich, I have formed! I've given them up already. I no longer want to see anything except my own corner. I want to dig in it piously. You don't expand art; you sum it up. . . . My eyes are much better. True, I am working very little, although at difficult things — family portraits. You have to do them to the taste of the family, in impossible light, with many interruptions, with models who are very affectionate but a bit free and easy with you, and who take you much less seriously because you are their nephew or their cousin. . . . And then really it's only a long stay that can reveal the habits of a race, which is to say its charm. The instantaneous is nothing but photography.[13]

In the letter to Rouart, a much more intimate friend, the tone was more personal and resigned:

> Oh well, it's all an errand I will have run, and very little more. Manet, more than me, would have seen beautiful things here. But he wouldn't have made anything more out of them. In art you love and you produce only what you are used to. Novelty captivates you and then bores you.[14]

He added a remark on a desirable artistic career: "I dream of something well accomplished and as a whole well arranged (in the style of Poussin), and the old age of Corot."

A complaint about the brilliant light on the Mississippi suggests that he worked, or intended to work, outdoors, probably during one of the trips to the Terre-aux-Boeufs plantation. But if he painted any landscapes, they are either lost or unidentified, so the pictorial result of the whole visit is simply a series of portraits. Of these the most touching is a delicate, silvery pink image of Estelle in a tutu-thin muslin dress, sitting heavily (she was pregnant with René's third child) in the great house on the Esplanade and staring into her darkened world. Degas, whose sympathy was deepened by his worry about his own eyes, said of her in the letter to Dihau: "She accepts [her blindness] in the most extraordinary way, with almost no need for help when she is at home. She remembers the rooms and the positions of the furniture. . . . And there is no hope."[15]

In the *Woman with a Vase* there is a return to the decentralized composition of *A Woman with Chrysanthemums* of 1865, now given a tropical resonance by a jade green wall, a purple blue vase, and orange red flowers, and rendered more complex by devices that recall the early dance pictures: the vase is substituted for the volute of a double bass, and the unknown woman sits in a coulisse space created by the table and the back of the chair. (She has been identified, unconvincingly, as Estelle, and also as a Musson family friend, Madame Challaire.)

The masterpiece of the series, however, is unquestionably the *Portraits in an Office,* which is also sometimes titled, a bit less accurately, *The Cotton Market.* Here we are in the commercial Faubourg Sainte Marie quarter — more precisely at 63 Carondelet Street — looking into Michel Musson's sunlit, severely functional office at a moment when some samples have just arrived from a plantation. In the immediate foreground Michel himself, partly cut by the frame, is peering over his glasses at a piece of cotton whose tensile strength he is testing. Behind him René is reading the local *Times-Picayune,* and on the far left Achille is leaning cross-legged against a windowsill. (Apparently the brothers have been somewhat infected by Southern *farniente,* for they ought to be over in their own office on Common

A Woman with a Vase, 1872

Portraits in an Office, New Orleans, 1873

Street.) On the far right, in shirt sleeves, the cashier, John Livaudais, is examining his ledgers. Behind René, wearing a tan coat and sitting on a high stool, Michel's partner, James Prestidge, is talking to a customer who is taking notes; and William Bell, half seated on the long, fluff-covered table, is showing a double handful of cotton to another customer. The figures stand out with the unobtrusiveness of the kind of classicism that conceals art; the coats, shirts, newspaper, and cotton move across the mostly brown surface like a black and white ballet against a backdrop; the men and objects toward the back of the room recede with a photographic lack of constancy-scaling. Obviously this cool little work was intended by Degas as an example of the "simple and bold" French "Naturalist movement" and the strong draftsmanship that were meant ultimately to confound the supposedly trick-loving English school. He was even ready, he indicated in a letter to Tissot on February 18, 1873, to challenge the Victorians on their own terrain by turning the picture over to Agnew's gallery in London for possible sale to one of the new industrialists in Manchester. "If a textile manufacturer of cotton," he wrote, "ever wished to find his painter, I would make quite an impression."[16] (In fact, he continued to deal with Durand-Ruel.)

Probably several of the New Orleans paintings, including the *Portraits in an Office,* were finished in Paris, for their homesick author departed for New York and Europe around the middle of March without leaving as much as a preparatory drawing behind with the Mussons. At the beginning of April one of his two Parisian maternal uncles, Eugène Musson, reported to the family in Louisiana:

> Edgar has come back to us, enchanted with his journey, enchanted with having done some things that are new for him, and above all enchanted with having got to know all of his good relatives in America. As you say, he is a likable boy and one who will become a very great painter if God preserves his sight and puts a little more lead in his head.[17]

Fortunately the thirty-nine-year-old unballasted "boy" did not read this fresh evidence of the condescending attitude of some of his older kinsmen. But perhaps if he had read it he might not have minded it very much, for by April he was very busy at 77 Rue Blanche, which he referred to, in English, as "my home." He installed the motherly Sabine Neyt as a replacement for Clotilde, who he decided was really, as he had suggested to Frölich, "too young for a bachelor" and something of "a housemaid from a theatrical comedy."[18] He worked hard at his dance pictures and at a series devoted to the laundry girl with bare arms, who had become a memory talisman during the weeks on Esplanade Avenue. Apparently during the late spring (although his repainting habit makes the time problematical), perhaps after a visit to the Bois de Boulogne with Manet, he began *Racehorses at Longchamp,* in which a new sharpness in the observation of movement, a pattern of silky yellow, mauve, and blue, and some faint memories of Gozzoli's steeds in Florence merge to convey an extraordinarily serene sense of nowness.

The historic local event of the months after his return was the nearly total destruction by fire, during the night of October 28–29, 1873, of the Opéra in the Rue Le Peletier. The building was in any event about ready for a demolition crew; it had been erected in 1821 as a merely provisional structure, and its foundations were beginning to sink alarmingly. The Théâtre Italien was temporarily available, and soon the singers and dancers and their public would be in Charles Garnier's splendid new house, enjoying a vast stage, modern machinery, a monumental staircase, and expanses of colored Italian marble. But the catastrophe was nevertheless real: six thousand costumes, all the musical instruments, hundreds of orchestral scores, and the sets for fifteen operas and ballets were destroyed. And for habitués the era-ending shock was severe. Ludovic Halévy, after hearing the news the next morning, wrote in his diary:

> The Opéra! My old Opéra! This theater where I have spent my life, where I knew by heart every nook and corner. . . . How many hours I have whiled away on the red velvet banquettes in the Foyer de la Danse, in the midst of a wriggling and whirling little tribe of *petits sujets* and coryphées. . . . How gay and alive it was during the Second Empire! [19]

Degas, too, though not dependent on any particular locale in his dance pictures, and in any case supplied with drawings done in the old house, evidently felt the disaster as a personal loss, for in a letter to the baritone (and art collector) Jean-Baptiste Faure he said, "Here we are, both of us, without our theater." [20]

13. Organized Secession

AROUND THE BEGINNING of December 1873 Auguste left Paris for one of his periodic visits to Naples, this time with a planned stopover in Turin. After several days, during which the alarmed family was without news, he was discovered gravely ill in an obscure Turin hotel, and Edgar was sent to take care of him. The illness soon cleared up sufficiently, however, for the resumption of the journey to Naples, and Edgar returned to the Ninth Arrondissement, not realizing that he had just seen his father for the last time.

Art collectors were beginning to be aware of the studio at 77 Rue Blanche, and one of them was Edmond de Goncourt, who on February 13, 1874, made a long entry in his *Journal* that is worth quoting almost in full:

> Yesterday I spent my afternoon in the atelier of a strange painter named Degas. After many attempts, experiments, and thrusts in every direction, he has fallen in love with modern subjects and has set his heart on laundry girls and danseuses.
>
> I cannot find his choice bad, I who in *Manette Salomon* sang the praises of these two professions as furnishing a modern artist with the most pictorial models of the women of today. Indeed, pink flesh in white linen and a milky fog of muslin makes the most charming pretext for pale, tender colors. Degas showed me his laundry girls while speaking their language and explaining in technical terms the leaning on the iron, the circular movement, etc. . . . . Then it was the turn of the ballerinas. We were in their greenroom, with the legs of a danseuse descending a little staircase outlined

fantastically against the light from a window, with the bright splash of red on a tartan in the midst of all the ballooning white clouds, and with a ridiculous ballet master serving as a rascally foil; and there before me, caught from reality, was the graceful twisting of the movements and gestures of those little monkey girls. The painter presents his pictures to you while from time to time adding to his commentary the mimicry of — to use a danseuse's language — a choreographic *développement* or an *arabesque;* and it is really very amusing to see him, with his arms rounded, mix the aesthetic of a dance professor with that of a painter while talking about the delicate muddiness of Velázquez and the silhouetting talent of Mantegna.

This Degas is an original fellow, sickly, neurotic, and afflicted with eye trouble to the point of being afraid of going blind, but for those very reasons he is an excessively sensitive person who reacts strongly to the true character of things. Of all the men I have seen engaged in depicting modern life, he is the one who has most successfully rendered the inner nature of that life. One wonders, however, whether he will ever produce something really complete. I doubt it. He seems to have a very restless mind.[1]

The picture with the staircase legs and the figure in a tartan was clearly the recently completed *Rehearsal,* and the laundry girl studies must also have been fresh off the easel. But the mention of *Manette Salomon* (which was added in 1891) had no such basis in reality, for the novel, though certainly a general influence on Degas's use of contemporary material, contains only one reference to a laundress and nothing at all about ballerinas. Evidently Goncourt's memory was fogged a little by his desire to claim priority in a kind of art that deeply interested him.

Auguste died in Naples on February 23, 1874. One can imagine his last days as having been marked by a bitter sense of a failed life, for he had not become the painter or the musician he might have been, given his sensibility and talent, and the end of his career as a financier was a fiasco worse than what Edgar, in the letter to Rouart from Esplanade Avenue, had feared. The trouble was partly attributable to the recent history of capitalism. Small loan enterprises like the Degas bank, with their old-fashioned methods and rather sentimental investment policies, were becoming anachronisms in a France of the Rothschild empire and such giants as the Crédit Lyonnais and the Société Générale. Economic activity had slowed during the last years of Napoleon III; the siege of Paris and the Commune had interrupted all normal business; and toward the end of 1872 the first symptoms of a worldwide depression, with plummeting prices and swelling unemployment, had appeared. But Auguste had not been very provident. He had slowly eroded the assets of a hundred and fifty thousand gold francs with which he had been supplied in 1833. Some time before his death he had sold his Italian holdings to his brothers in Naples and had thus eliminated a potential recourse for a rainy day. (Although Edgar personally owned a bit of the palazzo in the Calata Trinità Maggiore, it could not, of course, be easily liquidated.) He had borrowed some forty thousand francs from the Bank of Antwerp, apparently in 1866 and hence presumably to help finance the De Gas Brothers wine-importing firm in New Orleans. All that was needed to provoke a collapse was a sudden loss of confidence among depositors — and that was not far off.

The disappearance of an affectionate if not always understanding parent, combined with worry about the family bank, came at a moment when Edgar was already harassed. By February he was inextricably involved in preparations for a sizable exhibition, a sort of anti-Salon, devoted to the work of the Batignolles painters and their friends. The specific proposal for such a show had come from Monet in April 1873. Pissarro, Renoir, Sisley, Degas, and eventually Berthe Morisot had been enthusiastic, and in December a legal-sounding organization, the Société Anonyme Coopérative à Capital Variable des Artistes Peintres, Sculpteurs, Graveurs, Etc., had been created with the declared aim of promoting "independent art." Now an opening date of April 15, two weeks before the start of the official Salon, had been fixed, and rent-free premises had been found in Félix Nadar's recently vacated studios and darkrooms on the second floor of 35 Boulevard des Capucines. The building stood at the corner of the Rue Daunou, in the middle of a quarter of theaters and cafés and only a block from both the new opera house and the fashionable Rue de la Paix; and a broad stairway led up directly from the boulevard sidewalk to the exhibition space. Furthermore, there seemed to be no problem about attracting the attention of potential visitors, for the redheaded, publicity-minded photographer had had the interior and exterior walls done in a rich russet red and a gigantic signature inscribed on the façade. Inspired by the address and eager to avoid a precise stylistic label, Degas had suggested, without winning the approval of the other organizers, that the group call itself La Capucine (The Nasturtium) and use the flower as an emblem on posters.

The general idea for the show was not new. In 1861 there had been a short-lived and relatively conservative Salon des Arts Unis, in which Ingres had participated and which had been praised by Charles Blanc, the editor of the *Gazette des Beaux-Arts*. In 1866 one of Cézanne's friends, the geologist and painter Fortuné Marion, had become exasperated enough with the Salon jury to suggest a rival exhibition that would be "deadly competition for all these half-blind old idiots."[2] A year later Bazille had described to his family a more detailed project, which because of a lack of money was never realized:

I am not going to submit any more pictures to the jury. It is much too ridiculous. . . . And a dozen young painters of talent think as I do. We have therefore decided to rent, once a year, a large atelier, where we'll exhibit as much of our work as we wish. We will invite artists who please us to send in pictures. . . . You'll see, we will be talked about.[3]

By 1873 the journalist and novelist Paul Alexis, one of the regulars at the Guerbois, could recall having heard many such proposals; and by that date a new sentiment of urgency was being added. The Salon jury, now influenced by conservatives like Cabanel, Gérôme, Meissonier, and Bonnat, was becoming more severe, more unpredictable, and more addicted to cronyism. Durand-Ruel was beginning to feel the pinch of the coming economic depression. Above all, the aesthetic gap between the Establishment and some of the more prominent members of the Batignolles group had widened. After several years of evolution out in the suburban countryside at such places as La Grenouillère, Pontoise, Louveciennes, and especially Argenteuil, the art of Monet, Pissarro, Renoir, and Sisley seemed destined never to satisfy academic tastes: it was impressionistic, even sketchy, rather than finished; painterly and loosely handled rather than linear and smooth; directly, sometimes rawly retinal rather than studio-cooked; unemotional and without ideas rather than expressive and intellectual; devoid of story rather than anecdotal; and objectively contemporaneous rather than imaginatively historical.

Degas may have surprised the other principal promoters of the exhibition by his decision to participate. After all, he had very little in common with them, either socially or stylistically, and he seemed to have none of their reasons for feeling dissatisfied with the existing situation. Although he had not appeared in the Salon since the war, he could scarcely blame the jury, for on the six occasions between 1865 and 1870 when he had submitted something, he had never had the humiliating experience of being a *refusé*. By 1873, largely through Durand-Ruel's London and Paris galleries, he had begun to acquire an impressive list of collectors and could hope that the process would continue in spite of the threatening business crisis. In short, he now looked, and not for the first time in his career, a bit capricious and unmotivated. He was known by his intimates to be worried about his family's financial predicament and somewhat overwhelmed by the sudden prospect of having to earn a living, and he was on record as disliking the way the hanging committee functioned at the big annual show in the Palais de l'Industrie. But such concerns were not enough to explain his joining — and to a considerable extent leading — a secession that was bound to provoke a hullabaloo.

Only after the enterprise was well under way did his more important motives reveal themselves, in his behavior, his letters, and his conversation; and they then turned out to be a sometimes disconcerting mixture of the tactical, the quantitative, and the moral. He believed that what he had called — with a significant emphasis on drawing — the French "Naturalist movement" had reached a point where it needed an institutional structure of its own, distinct from the official Salon, yet thoroughly respectable. Hence he intended, as he soon made abundantly clear, to obtain such a structure by transforming the original project of the Batignolles painters into something more conservative and less tainted by the presence of artists whom the general public might dismiss as chronic *refusés*. For himself he saw in the project an opportunity to present to critics and collectors a relatively large number of his recent works — in any event, more than the two to which each Salon exhibitor had been limited since 1864. (His notebook for around 1874 indicates that he had been planning a one-man show of ten of his dance pictures and had got as far as designing a poster that used three ballet slippers as an emblem.) And finally, informing his whole view of the planned anti-Salon, was his profound distaste, almost a physical loathing, for the pretentious phoniness of the fine arts Establishment and its system of rosettes, medals, and honorable mentions. In this respect he was still the Edgar who in 1856 had wanted "a thoroughly guiltless personality," and also the more recent Degas who had got rid of his bogus nobiliary particle.

Around the end of February 1874, he wrote again to Tissot, who had not returned to France from London since the Bloody Week of the Commune:

> See here, my dear Tissot, don't hesitate or try to evade the issue. You just have to exhibit on the boulevard. It'll do you good (it is a way for you to show yourself in Paris, which people say you are evading) and will be good for us, too. Manet seems to be obstinate in his decision to remain apart; he may very well regret it. . . . I am agitated and work quite hard and rather with success, I believe. . . . The realist movement no longer needs to fight with others. It *is*, it *exists*, it has to *show itself separately*. There has to *be a realist Salon*. Manet doesn't understand that. I definitely believe him to be much more vain than intelligent. . . . Exhibit. Stay with your country and your friends. . . . I have not yet written to Legros. Try to see him . . .[4]

By this time Tissot was very comfortably established near Regent's Park in a combined atelier and town house, with a garden, a colonnade, and liveried servants in silk stockings who served iced champagne to a stream of visitors; and he was not inclined to risk losing his Victorian clientèle by joining an artistic insurrection in Paris. Legros also refused to participate, as did both

Fantin and Manet, the latter because of his persisting belief that the official Salon was the place where the battle for recognition had to be fought and won. But Bracquemond, now the director of a porcelain workshop, was persuaded by the critic Philippe Burty to contribute a set of etchings; the veteran marine painters Eugène Boudin and Adolphe Cals were added to the list (probably by Monet); and in the end Degas was able to infiltrate the new *société* with enough artists of his own choice to make up a total in which the radicals of the Batignolles group were a minority. Among his typically half-Realist, half-traditionalist, and either aristocratic or *grand bourgeois* recruits were the Vicomte Ludovic-Napoléon Lepic, a painter, engraver, sculptor, balletomane, gentleman jockey, and greyhound-fancier who had studied with Cabanel and Gleyre; the financier's son Edouard Brandon, who specialized in anecdotal, conscientiously rendered scenes of Jewish life; Léopold Levert, a landscapist and etcher with a reputation as a designer of military uniforms; Henri Rouart, who was still strongly under the influence of Corot; and the Neapolitan Giuseppe de Nittis, who had worked with some open-air innovators at Portici, had moved into the orbit of the Macchiaioli at Florence, and in 1867, at the age of twenty-one, had arrived in Paris, where his smooth, slightly meretricious style, his lively intelligence, and his polished manners had rapidly won for him regular admission to the Salon, a contract with Goupil, and invitations to the house of the Princess Mathilde, Napoléon III's bluestocking cousin. Degas had known all these men for a good while: he had met Lepic at the Haras du Pin in 1861, Brandon at the Villa Medici in 1857, Levert at Rouart's dinners probably during the war, and de Nittis at the Café Guerbois around 1869, or possibly even earlier in Italy.

By the deadline for sending the exhibition catalogue to the printer, thirty exhibitors had been enlisted, with an average of a little more than five works per artist. Degas, however, had showed up at almost the last moment with a list of three dance oils, a pastel and an oil devoted to laundry girls, an oil racing scene, and four items described as drawings, all of which brought the total for the show up to a hundred and sixty-five. Today, identifying the pictures he presented has become something of a game for art historians, since the catalogue — prepared by Renoir's brother Edmond — has frequently vague titles, no dimensions, and no dates. But from information in reviews, letters, and Durand-Ruel's files, it has been pretty well established that two of the oils were the *Carriage at the Races* and the Metropolitan's *Dancing Class;* that one of the so-called drawings was *The False Start* (done in part by a process he invented, *peinture à l'essence,* which involved diluting the colors with turpentine after drawing out of them much of the oil with blotting paper); and that another was the Jeu de Paume version of *The Rehearsal of the Ballet on the Stage,* done in a combination of *essence* and bistre. Possibly the pastel of a laundress was the one for which Emma Dobigny had posed before the war.

After the excitement of the weeks of preparation, the exhibition itself was a dreary anticlimax. Fewer than two hundred people appeared for the inaugural on April 15; the daily number then dwindled rapidly; and at closing time on May 15, attendance had barely passed thirty-five hundred. (Roughly four hundred and fifty thousand attended the official Salon that spring.) An attempt to attract boulevard strollers by remaining open after dinner brought in only a few curiosity-seekers on an average evening. Many of the visitors burst into fits of uncontrolled laughter — the self-flattering sort of bourgeois-yahoo laughter that reverberates through all the avant-garde manifestations of the second half of the nineteenth century and through Zola's account of a Salon des Refusés in *L'Oeuvre:*

> Discreet at the entrance, the laughter became louder as [the hero] advanced. In the third room the women were no longer holding their handkerchiefs to their mouths, and the men were sticking out their bellies in order to laugh more easily. It was the contagious hilarity of a crowd that had come to amuse itself, that was exciting itself little by little, exploding over nothing, diverted by the beautiful as much as by the execrable. . . . They pushed each other with their elbows, they doubled up . . . [with] their mouths open from ear to ear.[5]

When the income from tickets, catalogues, and a 10 per cent commission on the sale of pictures and sculptures was added up, the operation was found to be deep in the red, so much so that at the end of 1874 the discouraged participants, after contributing a hundred and eighty-four francs apiece to meet the deficit, voted to dissolve the cooperative they had formed with such elaborate optimism only a year earlier.

Even the publicity value of the operation was debatable. The veteran Realist Castagnary, writing in the Voltairian daily *Le Siècle,* feared that a new kind of Romanticism was on the way. Silvestre, another Guerbois habitué, called the work of Monet, Sisley, and Pissarro "decorative," in a mildly favorable article in *L'Opinion nationale.*[6] The writer Emile Cardon, in *La Presse,* came out stoutly in praise of the principle of an "exhibition of rebels" and observed at the same time that the affair in the Boulevard des Capucines was much worse than the famous Salon des Refusés of 1863.[7] In *Le Rappel,* which was so far to the left that it was still using the Revolutionary calendar, an unsigned piece hailed the show as an "audacious enterprise" and then waxed heavily sarcastic about an art in which "a dozen yellow sticks" were supposed to represent a forest better than the detailed trees of Barbizon landscapists.[8] Marc de Montifaud — a pen name of Madame Marie de Quivogne, one of Villiers de L'Isle-Adam's intimates —

suggested in *L'Artiste* that the new painters should be called "the school of the eyes," and singled out Degas for a compliment that may have surprised him:

> The *Dancing Class* is a refined and profound work in which there is something one never finds among certain genre painters (who would blush at the idea of putting undraped figures on a canvas of a few centimeters); namely, the study of woman in her buxom nakedness and her thin or elegant anatomical shape. Monsieur Degas shows us bouncing buttocks and sharp, jagged shoulder blades, all with witty verve . . .[9]

In Gambetta's recently founded paper, *La République française,* an anonymous critic (who was in fact the Batignolles group's friend Burty) wrote perceptively of "the clearness of color, the plainness of the masses, and the quality of the impressions" in the works on view, admired especially the *Dancing Class* and *The Rehearsal of the Ballet on the Stage,* and asked rhetorically whether the time might not come when Degas would be considered a classic.[10] Beyond question, however, the most influential review, if it can be called that, was a long pleasantry written by the landscapist and professional humorist Louis Leroy, one of Halévy's favorite companions, for the satirical *Charivari.*[11] Inspired partly by Monet's sketchy *Impression: Sunrise* of 1872, Leroy referred to all the exhibitors as "Impressionists"; and his neologism, although intended derisively, rapidly established itself as an accepted critical term. He also invented a venerable, decorated *pompier,* Papa Vincent, who was represented as gradually losing his mind before the assembled "impressions," to the point of repudiating the gods of the Salon:

> I tried to reanimate his expiring reason by showing him Monsieur Rouart's *Pond Embankment.* . . . In vain, for the horrible attracted him. Monsieur Degas's badly washed washerwoman [*blanchisseuse si mal blanchie*] brought from him shouts of admiration.

At the end of the article Papa Vincent was doing a scalp dance and squealing, "Ugh! I'm a walking impression, an avenging palette knife. . . . Ugh! Ugh! Ugh!"

In the long run, Leroy's label was a good thing for the more innovative members of the former Batignolles group. It gave them — with the exception of Degas, who quite rightly never regarded himself as an Impressionist — a new kind of solidarity, a sense of being definably different from such older nonacademics as the Barbizon landscapists and Courbet's disciples, and the exhilaration of going forth to battle under a banner. But in the short run the word had two serious defects: it tended to conceal uniquely personal stylistic qualities (as it still does, to some extent), and it frightened Salon-conditioned speculative buyers at a moment when, given the decline of values at the Bourse, art was theoretically an attractive refuge. By the spring of 1875 a reluctance to invest in mere "impressions" was so strong that it was possible, in an auction at the Hôtel Drouot, to acquire a Monet for as little as ninety-five francs, a Morisot for eighty, a Sisley for sixty, and a Renoir for fifty. Although these prices were admittedly very exceptional and the bidding climate at this particular sale unusual, the effect on the money-measured reputations of the artists concerned was temporarily disastrous.

Degas was in a much more encouraging situation. Indeed, without seeming to be aware of his growing success, he was in fact in the middle of a four-year breakthrough. Seven of his ten pictures in the exhibition in the Boulevard des Capucines had been sold some time before the catalogue was printed. To such early buyers as Rouart, Huth, Brandon, and Hecht had been added the banker Jacques Mühlbacher, the textile merchant Ernest Hoschedé (whose wife shortly afterward became Monet's mistress), and the opera singer Faure, who in 1874 paid five thousand francs for another version of *The Dance Lesson* and during the same months, at Degas's request, bought back from Durand-Ruel for eight thousand francs six pictures that the artist wanted to rework. In November of 1874 a mysterious collector in Brighton, Captain Henry Hill, bought the *Two Dancers on the Stage,* and during the next two years he acquired a batch of six other Degas paintings that included *The Dance Lesson* and the Metropolitan's *Dancing Class.* Some time during 1875 the twenty-year-old Louisine Elder, who in 1883 became the second wife of Henry Osborne Havemeyer, the millionaire head of the American Sugar Refining Company, was brought into Durand-Ruel's Paris gallery by Mary Cassatt and persuaded to take back to New York with her the *Ballet Lesson on Stage,* which became the nucleus of the world's largest collection of the painter's work. (Most of these pictures, though not this first one, are now in the Metropolitan.) Years later Mrs. Havemeyer recalled with modesty her first reaction to this apparently slapdash image of abstract stage flats, light-speckled danseuses, a frame-cut *repoussoir* figure, and grumpy old Jules Perrot:

> I scarcely knew how to appreciate it, or whether I liked it or not, for I believe it takes special brain cells to understand Degas. There was nothing the matter with Miss Cassatt's brain cells, however, and she left me in no doubt as to the desirability of the purchase and I bought it on her advice.[12]

The advice must have been of a disinterested aesthetic sort, for in 1875 Degas was not yet the close friend of Cassatt's he would become.

Despite the sales, the goblin procrastination and the see-yourself-seeing-yourself imp came back to plague him. In return for the six pictures recovered for him from Durand-Ruel, plus an advance of fifteen hundred francs, he had agreed to supply Faure with four new paintings, and he found it excruciatingly difficult to get started on them. (In fact, he did not deliver the last of the four until thirteen years later, and then only after he had been sued successfully by the exasperated singer.) During the summer of 1874 he planned in detail, as if he had nothing else to do, a walking tour along the banks of the Seine as far as Rouen, and on August 8 he wrote to Rouart, who was already on a rural holiday and evidently enjoying it:

> You could not have done better, my dear friend, than to have sung the praises of the countryside, for if your peculiar correspondent did not quite burn down the Opéra, he has at least rented two rooms at Croissy. He'll go out there, like a strolling player, when he has recovered his peace of mind a bit, and he'll take his nature cure. . . . I cannot finish with the finishing of paintings, pastels, etc. How long it all takes! And how quickly my last good years are slipping away in mediocrity! I am very often ready to weep over my poor life.[13]

The two rooms were probably part of the Fournaise inn, a favorite of the Impressionists, on the Ile de Chatou near La Grenouillère, and it was perhaps during this trip that he did a fine drawing, later worked up into a painting, of Alphonsine Fournaise, the pretty daughter of the inn's owner and a frequent model for Renoir. (The drawing and the painting are usually dated 1861, which is much too early for Degas and his stylistic evolution and also for Alphonsine, who was then only fifteen.)

The state in which Auguste had left the family's finances was becoming worse as the world depression deepened. Achille returned from New Orleans and with the help of one of his Parisian uncles, Henri Musson, managed to negotiate enough fresh credit to keep the bank going for a while, in spite of what he described, in a later letter to his Louisiana relatives, as "an enormous uncovered balance."[14] Edgar spent part of March and April of 1875 in Naples, ostensibly to attend a funeral of one of the clan but mostly to discuss the predicament in Paris with his advisers in the palazzo. (He also found time on his way back to stop off in Florence and see his friend Signorini.)

The whole situation was rendered worse that summer by a little Far West melodrama that made the front pages of French newspapers and even became a brief sensation abroad. According to eyewitness accounts in *Paris-Journal* and *Le Figaro*,[15] the incident began, around two o'clock on the very hot afternoon of August 19, with Achille standing in the shade of the massive Corinthian columns that line the façade of the Bourse. A well-dressed man, eventually identified as an engineer named Victor-Georges Legrand, rushed up and began to beat him with a cane that had a heavy jasper knob. Achille thereupon pulled out a revolver, fired three wild shots, pursued his assailant through the crowd on the steps of the colonnade, and at last managed to graze him in the face with two more shots. Legrand was then taken away for first-aid treatment, and Achille was hauled off to spend thirty-six hours locked up in a neighboring police station. After a lengthy investigation the two men were both brought into court on September 24, and the whole story was revealed. In 1874 Legrand had married a former dancer named Thérèse Mallot, who, it turned out, had once been Achille's mistress and had had a child by him. The child had died; Achille had begun to see Thérèse again, to give her money, and allegedly "to make all sorts of insinuations" about Legrand. The latter had issued a challenge to a duel, but it was rejected, and he then decided to resort to a public caning. The judge took only a few minutes to decide that both men were guilty but not to the same degree, so he sentenced Achille to six months in prison and Legrand to a month. What became of Thérèse is not known, though perhaps she was the rather mysterious "Mademoiselle Malo" who sat for four portraits by Edgar around 1877, was mentioned once in his letters, and apparently danced at the Opéra. She is also recorded as having written to René.

For Edgar, the immediate effect of the scandal was to freshen his desire to do business in London. Three days after the shooting he sent off to Charles Deschamps, now completely in charge of the New Bond Street gallery, a letter that was a blend of money worries, brisk self-promotion, and gloominess: "As you can sense, now is the moment for me to leave no stone unturned in England. . . . Time marches on, one grows old, and eyesight weakens." [16] He also wrote of "many excuses" concerning a recently missed meeting with Whistler, "for whom I have so much admiration," and suggested — perhaps to Deschamps's surprise — that the gallery include in its group shows the slickly jejune Greco-Roman genre scenes of Lawrence Alma-Tadema, something by the Romantically medieval William Morris, and some of the slightly sentimental though realistic sculptures of the exiled former Communard Jules Dalou, who was not doing very well with the Victorian public. One could scarcely have asked for clearer evidence of a resolutely anti-Monet and anti-Renoir taste, oddly combined with sympathy for the survivors of the Paris antibourgeois political and social insurrection.

By the end of the year the former members of the cooperative in the Boulevard des Capucines had recovered their courage sufficiently to begin organizing a second exhibition, scheduled for the following spring in Durand-Ruel's temporarily available gallery in the Rue Le Peletier. Manet and Fantin again refused to join their friends, and thirteen of the 1874 participants, among them Bracquemond and Cézanne, withdrew from the enterprise. But the core formed by Degas, Monet, Renoir, Sisley, Pissarro, and Morisot remained loyal, and enough recruits eventually appeared to bring the exhibitors up to twenty and the number of works to two hundred and fifty-two. The relatively moderate faction was again represented by such artists as Rouart, Lepic, and Levert, and also by four newcomers: the aesthetically conservative but amusingly bohemian Marcellin Desboutin, whom Degas seems to have met in Florence; the landscapist Charles Tillot, who had studied with Millet and Rousseau at Barbizon; the pious Legros, who was now thoroughly anglicized (except for the language, which he never mastered) and whose contribution was mostly engravings; and Gustave Caillebotte, a young, wealthy, generous collector and artist who had worked with Bonnat, had known Degas, de Nittis, Pissarro, and Renoir for several years, and had developed a kind of pictorial Naturalism that had certain affinities with Duranty's literary Realism. Degas himself massively counteracted the Impressionist tendency by submitting twenty-four pictures, among which were the New Orleans *Portraits in an Office,* the recently completed *Absinthe,* half a dozen studies of danseuses, five of laundresses, and some portraits that included one of Manet's brother Eugène, painted to celebrate the latter's marriage in 1874 to Berthe Morisot.

The show opened on March 30, 1876, in the presence of a satisfying number of boulevardiers, artists, and journalists; and two days later an unsigned article in *Le Figaro* seemed to herald a change in the previously hostile climate of opinion:

> It is naturally difficult if not impossible for us to pronounce judgment on an art that situates itself quite outside the norms accepted up to now. To criticize it by ordinary rules would be unfair. So let us say merely that there is often something of value in this excessive originality. . . . Monsieur Degas has found some interesting effects in the illumination of coulisses. His danseuses, with their frail shoulders and their skirts lashed by electric light, are sometimes charming . . .[17]

On April 3, however, in the same newspaper, the influential critic Albert Wolff let fly with an almost unprecedented virulence:

> The Rue Le Peletier is ill-fated. After the burning of the Opéra, a new disaster has fallen on the quarter. In Durand-Ruel's gallery a so-called exhibition of painting has just opened. . . . Five or six maniacs, including a woman, and a group of unfortunates deranged by ambition have got together

to show their work. There are people who burst out laughing before these things, but I am sick at heart. . . . It is an appalling spectacle of human vanity gone astray to the point of becoming a mental deterioration. Try to explain to Monsieur Pissarro that trees are not violet and that the sky does not have the color of fresh butter. . . . Try to talk reason with Monsieur Degas, tell him that in art there are certain qualities called drawing, color, execution, control; he'll snort in your face and call you a reactionary. . . . Try to explain to Monsieur Renoir that a woman's torso is not a mass of rotten flesh . . .[18]

The stupidity of the attack was all the more sickening — and damaging — because Wolff was not actually a stupid man. Halévy found him in general "full of wit and common sense."[19] His trouble was a reckless sort of journalistic ambition combined with a desire, more usual among drama critics than art critics, to curry favor with complacently ignorant readers by playing the role of a vigorous public executioner. And in all this there was undoubtedly a lot of artistic, sociopolitical, and sexual compensation, for he was a very minor draftsman and book illustrator, a recently naturalized immigrant from Germany in a Paris still traumatized by the Franco-Prussian War, and a grotesquely ugly dandy notorious in the cafés on the Grands Boulevards for his mincing manners, tight corsets, and heavy use of cosmetics.

Other conservative commentators saw in high-keyed palettes, free handling, and unexpected viewpoints a recrudescence of the ideology of the Commune; and *Le Moniteur universel* warned the nation against "artistic intransigents hand in hand with political intransigents."[20] A heavily facetious critic in *Le Soir* echoed Wolff by likening the gallery in the Rue Le Peletier to an insane asylum. The supposedly more serious *Art* compared the exhibition with that of 1874 and discovered "absolutely nothing" new except "the worst increasingly being grafted onto the bad, the execrable, and the inexistent."[21] The articles that attempted to counter such wholesale condemnations were rendered relatively ineffective by the obvious friendship between reviewed and reviewer, or by puzzling qualifications, or simply by not appearing in the French language. Castagnary, in the review of the Salon he published independently each year, deplored the absence of the Durand-Ruel group from the official show and found Degas's dance pictures "superb."[22] Silvestre, in *L'Opinion nationale,* pronounced the group "interesting at least because of the warmth of its convictions," though he thought its "ideal" was "absolutely incomplete."[23] Stéphane Mallarmé, in a piece for the London *Art Monthly Review* devoted mostly to Manet (who had recently illustrated two volumes of the poet's work), praised the emerging school in general and Degas in particular:

A master of drawing, he has sought delicate lines and movements exquisite or grotesque, and of a strange new beauty, if I dare employ towards his works an abstract term, which he himself will never employ in his daily conversation.[24]

Zola, reporting on the exhibition in the Rue Le Peletier for a Saint Petersburg literary magazine *Viestnik Evropy* (The Messenger of Europe), began by informing his Russian readers that the Impressionists and their allies had "heard the murmur of the future." But he then rapidly moderated his enthusiasm:

> Degas has a curious mind that often finds original and exact material. His laundresses are particularly striking in their truthfulness — the great, marvelous kind of truthfulness that is not banal and that in art simplifies and glorifies everything. His dance room, with the students in short skirts doing their steps, is also extremely original. This painter is very fond of depicting present-day reality, the inner life of people, and ordinary types of humanity. Unfortunately he spoils everything with his embellishments. His best things are his sketches. When he begins to niggle, his drawing becomes feeble and pitiful: he does pictures like his *Portraits in an Office* (New Orleans), which is somewhere between a seascape and an engraving for an illustrated newspaper. He has excellent aesthetic ideas, but I am afraid his brush will never be creative.[25]

If the victim of these oddly unperceptive remarks ever knew about them, his dislike for the art criticism of "the literary tribe" must have been confirmed. And possibly he did know about them, for there is evidence that at least some of Zola's reports to *Viestnik Evropy* filtered back to Paris and, after a retranslation from Russian into French, circulated among the people concerned.

Duranty was temporarily without a journal for which to write a review. He could not, however, stay out of the controversy, so in mid-April of 1876 he published, at his own expense and in an edition of only seven hundred and fifty copies, a thirty-eight-page pamphlet, *The New Painting: Concerning the Group of Artists Who Are Exhibiting in Durand-Ruel's Gallery.* As the title suggested, his intentions were partly historical, partly theoretical, and largely polemical. And in fact what he did was to update and apply to painting a doctrine of literary Realism he had been advocating for more than twenty years. He began his essay by attacking the Ecole des Beaux-Arts and Gérôme's "atelier of anecdotal archeology,"[26] and then went on to show that the origins of the modern school lay in the work of such artists as Constable, Courbet, Millet, Corot, Boudin, and even Ingres. He analyzed, with a scientific touch, the light and color of the new landscapists, whom he carefully refrained from calling Impressionists. But his principal emphasis was on recent innovations in drawing, mise-en-scène, and pictorial expression, and this led quite naturally to an emphasis on the contribution of a particular artist:

> Thus the series of new ideas was formed above all in the mind of a draftsman — a member of our group, one of those who are exhibiting in the gallery, and a man of the rarest talent and the rarest intellect. Enough people have profited from his conceptions and from his artistic unselfishness for justice to be done to him . . .[27]

Any doubts a knowledgeable reader may have had about the identity of this unnamed head of the movement were dispelled in the next paragraph:

> And since we are sticking closely to reality, we can no longer separate a figure from an accompanying apartment or street. In real life a person never appears against an empty, vague, or neutral background. Around him and back of him are furniture, fireplaces, tapestries, a wall that reveals his income, his class, his profession. He sits at his piano, or he examines a sample of cotton in his office, or he waits behind a décor for the moment to come out on the stage, or he applies the iron on an ironing board . . .[28]

He devoted an important part of the following pages to scolding the group for having admitted too many visionaries, eccentrics, and dunces to its ranks. The conclusion was an elaborate nautical metaphor that implied something less than serene confidence in the future:

> I wish fair winds for the fleet, and I hope it reaches the Fortunate Islands. I urge the pilots to be attentive, resolute, and patient. The navigating will be dangerous, and they should have embarked on larger, more solid vessels . . .[29]

Understandably, the more ardent Impressionists, in particular Monet and Renoir, were profoundly irritated by this strange defense of their new aesthetic, and much of their anger was directed at Degas, whom they suspected — perhaps rightly — of having urged or at least encouraged the writing of the pamphlet.

In spite of such suspicions the cooperative association held together and soon began to organize a third brave attempt to penetrate the hostility of a derisive press and a crass public. Degas protested vigorously when the other members of the core group voted to announce the new enterprise as an exhibition of Impressionists, for he felt that the neologism was mostly meaningless and in any case not applicable to himself. He was mollified, however, by the adoption of a rule stipulating that a participant could not submit a work to the jury of the official Salon: from now on the secession from the Establishment would be perfectly clear, and there could be no slighting talk about a show of disgruntled *refusés*. The choice of a locale was a worry for a while, since Durand-Ruel's gallery was no longer available and the association's treasury was almost nonexistent. But finally a large, well-lighted, empty apartment was discovered on the third floor of a building at 6 Rue Le Peletier, about where the old opera house had stood, and Caillebotte, who knew the owner, was persuaded to make the necessary arrangements and advance the money for the rent.

The exhibition opened on April 4, 1877, in the presence of what a reporter for *Le Siècle* described as a "considerable number of elegantly dressed visitors."[30] Although this time the number of exhibitors had been reduced to only eighteen, there were two hundred and thirty-one works on view, and among them were many that are today widely recognized as masterpieces. Monet, for instance, contributed seven of his studies of the Saint-Lazare railway station, Renoir *Le Moulin de la Galette* and *The Swing,* Sisley *The Flood at Port-Marly,* Cézanne a small version of his *Bathers* of 1876, and Pissarro a series of the landscapes painted at Pontoise and Auvers. Degas had a room almost to himself at the far end of the apartment, and here he presented twenty-five of what, in the language of French tradesmen, he referred to as his *articles.* Among them were *Women on the Terrace of a Café, Beach Scene,* the *Portrait of a Young Woman, Henri Rouart in Front of His Factory,* probably *End of an Arabesque,* perhaps *The Café-Concert at Les Ambassadeurs,* and a miscellany of monotypes, portraits, and ballet pictures, hard to identify from our distance.

A few journalists resumed the tedious references to bumbling, insanity, and putrefaction; and a cartoonist for *Le Charivari* depicted a policeman waving a pregnant woman away from the entrance to 6 Rue Le Peletier. On the whole, however, the critical reaction was more serious, more selective, and less unfavorable than it had been during the first two exhibitions. In *Le Petit Parisien,* Alexandre Pothey, a familiar of the Café Guerbois, admired the "frightful realism" of *Women on the Terrace of a Café:*

> These wilted, rouged creatures, exuding viciousness and recounting cynically the day's doings and exploits, are women whom you have seen, whom you know, and whom you will shortly see again on the boulevard.[31]

A writer who signed himself "Baron Schop" told the readers of *Le National* that Renoir, Degas, and Caillebotte apparently had some talent and that Pissarro and Cézanne had none at all. The loyal Burty, in *La République française,* also preferred the work of Renoir and Degas to that of the landscapists in the group. In *Le Temps* Paul Mantz made an earnest attempt to define the new tendencies and then concluded that in art "ignorance will

End of an Arabesque, c. 1877

Women on the Terrace of a Café, 1877

never become a virtue.''[32] Zola, reporting this time to *Le Sémaphore de Marseille,* praised everybody, Degas included:

> He has some stupendous danseuses, caught in the middle of their movements, and some astonishingly truthful café-concert scenes, with the "divas," their mouths open, bending forward above the smoky footlights. Monsieur Degas is an admirably precise draftsman . . .[33]

Frédéric Chevalier, for the monthly *Artiste,* noticed the *Beach Scene* before moving on quickly to the urban subject matter: "Monsieur Degas sometimes inhales the strong breezes of the ocean, although the dust of a theater and the fuming atmosphere of a café are more salutary for him."[34] In *Le Figaro* a certain "Baron Grimm," who was probably Wolff, blasted the exhibition in general as a "museum of horrors" and a "mystification," but granted that Degas, with just a little more hard work, might become worthy of an honorable place in the official Salon:

> In his pictures, which are numerous, there is often at least a funny idea, and always a reality captured from life. His café-concert is absolutely delicious: the pose of the prima donna in a red dress, her salute, her smile. . . . The whole thing is soberly colored. Perhaps the drawing is a little slipshod, a bit roughly sketchy, but Monsieur Degas was yielding to an impression and being faithful to his school.[35]

Commenting for *Le Courrier de France* on the evident evolution of opinion since 1874, the open-minded Oscar-Charles Flor remarked that possibly "the hostility encountered by the Impressionists at their début was merely a slightly savage, maladroit expression of a deep amazement."[36]

During the month the show lasted Georges Rivière, a twenty-two-year-old free-lance critic who was a close friend of Renoir's, published, edited, and largely wrote a little weekly boldly entitled *L'Impressionniste: Journal d'Art.* Although not a very professional journalist, Rivière effectively ridiculed the hooting viewers and pretentious "connoisseurs" of the *Figaro* sort, did his best to explain the intentions of the exhibitors, defended Cézanne, and helpfully analyzed Degas:

> He does not pretend to have a naïveté he does not possess. On the contrary, his prodigious knowledge is everywhere brilliantly evident. With a very special and very attractive sort of ingeniousness, he arranges his figures in a way that is thoroughly unexpected and thoroughly amusing and at the same time always true and always normal. What Monsieur Degas hates the most is romantic intoxication, the substitution of dreams for life — in a word, panache. He is an observer . . .[37]

Unfortunately the journal, though energetically hawked on the Grands Boulevards, was generally dismissed as simply a publicity tract; when the exhibition closed, there were stacks of unsold copies in the Legrand Gallery, a shop at 22 Rue Laffitte that had been recently opened by one of Durand-Ruel's former employees and had been used by Rivière as an editorial office.

The improvement in press relations was not accompanied — at least not for most of the members of the group — by an improvement in the market. On May 28, 1877, Caillebotte, Renoir, Pissarro, and Sisley optimistically staged another auction at the Hôtel Drouot, this time with forty-five pictures that had been recently exhibited in the Rue Le Peletier, and the result came close to being as disastrous as the sale of 1874, with some of the Renoirs and Pissarros going for as low as fifty francs per work. Three months later Cézanne, who received a regular if small allowance from his father, wrote to Zola, "I am not too unhappy, but a profound desolation seems to reign in the Impressionist camp. The Pactolus is not exactly flowing through their pockets, and their studies are drying in their studios. We are living through a very troubled time."[38]

Although Degas was in better financial shape than men like Pissarro and Sisley, who were almost hopelessly poor, for the moment King Midas' golden river was not exactly flowing through his pockets either. Durand-Ruel, plagued by the economic depression, worried by a decline of interest in the Barbizon school, and afraid of weakening the confidence of his conservative customers, had temporarily stopped buying unconventional work. In London, where during the spring of 1876 the dance pictures had had a gratifying success with local critics and with Captain Hill, the Brighton collector, the glowing prospects had abruptly faded when, later in the year, Deschamps felt obliged to close the gallery in New Bond Street. Buyers still existed in France, of course; the catalogue for the 1877 show reveals that three of the twenty-five works by Degas belonged to Caillebotte, two to Henri Rouart, another to Monsieur H.H. (perhaps the banker Henri Hecht, a brother of the owner of *The Ballet from Robert le Diable*), another to Monsieur V. (perhaps Paul Valpinçon), and another to Monsieur C.H. But the collapse of the family bank meant that what money was coming in was rapidly going out. On August 31, 1876, Achille had written to Michel Musson:

> It was at last necessary to call a halt. Fortunately we have been able to avoid a worse catastrophe and to make arrangements on an amicable basis with our creditors. But payments to come in depend in large part, not to say entirely, on the remittances that René will have to make to us to put an end to his debt to his father's firm. This cannot be done immediately, because he has [other] commitments. . . . We are obliged, Edgar, Marguerite, and I, to live altogether on a bare subsistence in order to honor the promises we have made. I am trying to find another business for myself, but you know how slow and difficult that is.[39]

To be sure, among members of the *grande bourgeoisie* the phrase "a bare subsistence" did not mean dire poverty. Edgar continued to have his bachelor's quarters, his housekeeper (still Sabine Neyt), his café conversations, his evenings at the Opéra, and his holidays in Normandy. Even so, the crisis was real. In a report to New Orleans, written early in 1877, Henri Musson said, "Fevre [Marguerite's husband] and Edgar, cornered by the Bank of Antwerp, pay with the greatest trouble by monthly installments."[40]

The financial crisis was soon followed by a series of events that shattered forever the extended Musson-Degas family and the antebellum time capsule on Esplanade Avenue. Justifying the Neapolitan patriarch's ancient warnings against American investments, René shortly demonstrated that he was unable, or unwilling, to pay his debt to the Paris bank. On April 13, 1878, in a fit of what appears to have been a combination of panic and caddishness, he suddenly abandoned Estelle and their six children and left New Orleans with a clear-eyed local woman named Mrs. Léonce Olivier (whom he eventually married). A month after his departure, the youngest of the children died, and six months later an epidemic of yellow fever carried off another. Achille returned to take care of René's business, and soon quarreled with Michel Musson, who was now partly paralyzed and living mostly on an insurance company pension. Then two more of Estelle's children — one of them the teen-age Joe Balfour — died. Michel adopted the two survivors, changed their names to Musson, and broke with all of his Parisian nephews. Somehow, the blind Estelle went on living.

This whole economic, ethical, and existential drama obviously distressed Edgar, though in ways that, owing to his fierce reticence about such matters, often have to be surmised. His ironical references to his pictures as *articles* suggest a bitter awareness of his no longer being an entirely free artist — indeed, no longer being exactly a gentleman. In undated letters written apparently between 1876 and 1879 he mentions an urgent need to finish "some little pastels"[41] in order to earn "my bitch-dog of a living,"[42] and states flatly, "You cannot imagine the troubles of every sort with which I am overwhelmed."[43] For a man who had always been warmly attached to his family and his clan, the rupture with the Mussons of New Orleans must have been extremely painful, all the more so because he himself was totally innocent in the affair and undeserving of Michel's rancor. Undoubtedly dominating everything else was sympathy for Estelle, who seemed to be pursued by Furies as absurdly savage as Jephthah's Jehovah. Although letters to her from Paris were returned unopened, Edgar made his attitude explicit by refusing to see René when the latter reappeared in France. They were not reconciled until some time in the 1890s.

14. The Celibate

IN ANCIENT LACEDAEMON the Spartan women ceremoniously spanked an unmarried man once a year. Although in the France of the second half of the nineteenth century there were no such rituals, in many sectors of the bourgeoisie a bachelor was similarly classified as an undesirable (and Madame Morisot would certainly have enjoyed smacking the backsides of some of the eligible young men who had not proposed to Berthe). He was thought of as a retarded adolescent who refused to accept an adult male's obligation to found a household, beget children, and thus continue the established order. In short, he was something of a traitor to his class. He was apt to be suspected of secretly being a homosexual, a masturbator, an impotent syphilitic, or a libertine ready to prey on innocent females. In 1872 a booklet by a well-known medicolegal specialist, Dr. Auguste Tardieu, vindictively denounced abstention from marriage as "an incessant cause of nervous disorders, desperate actions, and moral depravity" and proposed that it be punished by a special tax.[1] During the debate in 1875 over the constitution of the Third Republic there were attempts to deprive bachelors of the right to vote. A few years later a series of statistical inquiries purported to prove that wifeless men were far more disposed than husbands to go mad, become criminals, or commit suicide. Most people, of course, did not take such a dramatic view of the celibate status, but even the more permissive tended to consider a bachelor an odd duck, *un marginal*.

By the time of the third exhibition of the Impressionists and their allies, Degas, now well into his forties, was clearly such a marginal person, and among his close acquaintances his celibacy had long been the subject of speculation. He remained unmarried, however, for the rest of his life, and the speculation continued, so a discussion of the questions raised by his abstinence — aesthetically relevant questions, since he was a painter of women — cannot be properly based on evidence drawn from only a part of his career.

One can imagine that the years of his adolescence, spent in contact with a widower father, two widower grandfathers, and four bachelor uncles, did not encourage any latent inclination to marry. Nor did his awareness, when he was young, of the quarrels between Célestine and Auguste, heightened in 1858 by intimate knowledge of the tension between Laura and Baron Bellelli, and reinforced in 1878 by the shock of the dénouement of René's idyll with Estelle. But there were of course some examples of conjugal happiness at hand, and Degas was not unaffected by them. His notebook entry at Assisi about finding "a good little wife"[2] and his longing in New Orleans for "a few children of my own"[3] are parts of a recurring theme, accompanied more and more often by melancholy overtones. On May 25, 1896, in a letter to Rouart, he remarked, "I have been reflecting, with a cold in my head, on celibacy, and three quarters of what I've been saying to myself is sad."[4] Around the same date, in a conversation with the dealer Ambroise Vollard, he suddenly said, "You must get married. You have no idea of the loneliness you will feel as you grow older."[5] Rivière, referring mostly to the period of the 1870s and 1880s, recalled:

> [Degas] was unhappy about living alone, and at the same time he realized that, because of the conditions under which he lived, he was not at all cut out for the worries of family life. He envied, he said, the lot of some of his friends who were surrounded by happy families, but his imagination would raise a hundred objections against any slight wish to marry — if ever his thoughts went farther than a vague sadness over being deprived of joys not made for him.[6]

Although this is indefinite enough to mean several things, it does not imply an attitude derived from the influence of single relatives and observation of wretched couples.

In any event a more important incentive to bachelorhood may be found in the notion, widespread among French antibourgeois intellectuals by around the end of the Second Empire, that a wife was likely to weaken physically an artist's creative powers, or hamper them by trivial, henpecking criticism, or divert them into remunerative but disastrously safe channels. As early as 1846 Balzac had advanced a chilling version of the idea in

La Cousine Bette, which describes the destruction of a talented sculptor by conjugal indulgence and contains an analysis of the effect of the honeymoon in the arts.[7] Two decades later in *Manette Salomon* the Goncourts had ostensibly demonstrated that a legal status immediately metamorphosed Eros into a vulgar capitalist slave-driver. In their characterization of Coriolis — before his enslavement by Manette — the brothers had inserted a detailed warning of the peril:

> According to him, celibacy was the only state that left artists with their liberty, their strength, their brains, and their consciences. He had a feeling that it was because of wives that so many artists slipped into weaknesses, into complacent modishness, into concessions to profit-making and commerce, into denials of aspirations, into sad desertion of the disinterestedness of their vocation, and into a hasty, botched sort of industrial production for the sake of the money that so many mothers of families shamefully sweated out of talented husbands. And marriage eventually involved paternity, which he considered harmful to artists because it turned them away from things of the mind, attached them to an inferior kind of creation, and degraded them into bourgeois pride in fleshly property. . . . In sum, he thought it wise and reasonable to seek only a sensual satisfaction from a woman, in a liaison without attachment.[8]

Such sentiments were not confined to fictional artists. "A married man," Courbet had asserted, "is a reactionary in art."[9] Corot had pronounced good landscape painting incompatible with marriage. The usually reserved Delacroix had once lost his temper with a young disciple who was thinking of taking a wife: "If you love her and she is pretty, then the whole situation is worse. Your art is dead. An artist must have no passion except for his work and must sacrifice everything to it."[10]

All of the more prominent male members of the Batignolles group noticeably dragged their feet on the way to the altar. In some instances there were practical reasons, but the record as a whole suggests a resistance to the idea of wedlock. Manet did not marry Suzanne Leenhoff until 1863, by which time their son was eleven years old. Renoir lived with the model Lise Tréhot from 1865 to 1872, had a series of mistresses during the next few years, took up with another model, Aline Charigot, around 1879, and finally married her in 1890, when he was forty-nine and their first son was five. The anarchist Pissarro began an affair with his mother's maid, Julie Vellay, in 1858, had a son by her in 1863 and a daughter in 1865, and made her his legal wife in London in 1870, when he was thirty-nine and shortly before she gave birth to their third child. Monet began a liaison with the model Camille Doncieux in 1865 and married her just before the outbreak of the Franco-Prussian War, when their first son was three years old. Cézanne met a young Parisian bookbinder, Hortense Fiquet, in 1869, had a son by her in 1872, and did not marry her until 1886.

Thus, at least up to a certain point, there was nothing very extraordinary about the reluctance of a nineteenth-century French artist to become a husband. Moreover, Degas was on occasion quite explicit about his exclusive sense of vocation, his general agreement with the views of the pre-Manette Coriolis, and his qualms at the prospect of getting adverse criticism or frivolous appreciation from a meddling spouse. "There is love, there is our art," he argued, "and we have only one heart."[11] Late in life, after one of his warnings to Vollard about the loneliness of bachelors, he was asked pointblank why he himself had not married. The reply was one of his frequently revealing conversational pirouettes: "Oh, with me things were different. I was too afraid that after I had finished a picture I would hear my wife say, 'What you've done there is very pretty indeed.' "[12]

There were obvious limits, however, to the adequacy of the explanation suggested by such remarks, since the supposed hostility of Hymen to the muses had never been interpreted as condemning writers and painters to chastity. Balzac, though single until shortly before his death, had been a notorious womanizer. Coriolis had recommended casual "sensual satisfaction," and the Goncourt brothers had shared not only the writing of the novel but also the favors of a strapping midwife named Maria. Both the Pygmalion myth and the actual practice in Parisian studios condoned the idea that an artist was entitled to take physical possession of a woman after sculpting or painting her. During their long periods of resistance to wedlock the members of the Batignolles group were not at all hesitant about acquiring mistresses, usually models, and fathering a flock of illegitimate children. In striking, mysterious contrast with these accepted patterns of masculine bohemian behavior, Degas lived, as far as even his close acquaintances could tell, utterly without sexual gratification. He was concubineless as well as wifeless. He was therefore an irritating provocation to the openly adulterous, nonconformist artistic community almost as much as to the antibachelor bourgeoisie, and he has remained in this respect a riddle for art historians.

The possibility that he was a repressed homosexual has to be considered, partly because of his bristling attitude toward known or suspected homosexuals. He met Oscar Wilde in 1885, probably at Dieppe, and disliked him instantly. "He looks," he said to Walter Sickert, "like an actor playing Lord Byron in a suburban theater."[13] During the winter of 1891–1892 Wilde appeared in various salons in Paris, and the conversation with Degas, as reported by Ludovic Halévy's son Daniel, went like this:

WILDE: You know, you are very well known in England.
DEGAS: Fortunately, not as well known as you are.[14]

The attitude also manifested itself in regard to the young André Gide and the dandy Comte Robert de Montesquiou-Fezensac, whose reputations were not very good, and it became increasingly violent with the spread of the various ingredients — Symbolism, Decadence, Rosicrucianism, Art Nouveau, and the cult of the "unutterably precious" — that constituted fin-de-siècle aestheticism. When the London fabric designer Arthur Lazenby Liberty, one of the pioneers in the movement, opened a shop in the Avenue de l'Opéra in 1889, Degas inspected the place and commented, "That much taste will lead to prison."[15] He again linked pederasty with aestheticism when, five months after Wilde was sent to jail, the dealer Samuel Bing opened a shop in the Rue de Provence called La Maison de l'Art Nouveau. But of course the evidence in such remarks is meaningless without some external clue, and in this instance there is nothing of the sort, nothing that even remotely hints at homosexual relations. If there was indeed any repression of feelings, it was so thorough as to be indistinguishable from their complete elimination. And so by the mid-1880s Degas was being accused, as he still is by many critics, of simply a peculiarly vicious form of misogyny.

Some historical reminders are helpful as one thinks about this accusation. The society of the period was male-dominated, quite patriarchal, and generally intolerant of differences. Although the facts about ovulation had gradually become known during the first half of the century, women were still regarded as passive, uncreative partners in the reproductive process — as mere vessels, to use Shakespeare's word, for the male fecundating fluid. Sexual bipolarity, in a bizarre anticipation of the reactionary Freudian dictum that "anatomy is destiny," was being emphasized to a degree unprecedented in the history of costume: trousers, frock coats, and phallic hats on one side, and petticoats, corsets, crinolines, and bustles on the other. Moreover, the supposed biological inferiority was accompanied by real sociocultural deficiencies. In 1859 the distinguished historian Jules Michelet could write:

> Everyone can see the capital fact of our time, which is that, because of a strange combination of social, religious, and economic circumstances, men and women now live separate lives. . . . Men, however weak they may be morally, are embarked on an express train of ideas, inventions, and discoveries, so rapid that the burning rails throw out sparks. Women are inevitably left behind, in a furrow of the past of which they themselves are scarcely aware. They are outdistanced, for our misfortune.[16]

In nineteenth-century France a woman, unless she was very exceptional and very lucky, had to be content with an assigned rather than an achieved role. A legal code derived from ancient Rome deprived her of the right to vote or to manage her affairs, and thus put her in the same juridical category as children and congenital idiots. Poor girls were practically without schooling and were constantly tempted to become professional or at least amateur prostitutes; the daughters of the well-to-do were educated mostly to become empty-minded parlor ornaments and status symbols for husbands.

All these factors contributed to the proliferation among men of a taken-for-granted, sometimes contemptuous, more often ironical antifeminism. It could manifest itself at an appallingly low level; popular satirical prints, for instance, multiplied images of women urinating, which for some reason was regarded as proof of inferiority when it was done crouching instead of standing. A long list of current folk sayings, many of them inherited from the Middle Ages, castigated alleged feminine prurience, vanity, talkativeness, faithlessness, avarice, envy, and irrationality. Further up the social scale, among men who would have been surprised by the charge of misogyny, women were regularly the targets of brutal metaphors, snickering condescension, and jokes that could wound a sensitive life companion. There was even something like a period style in such verbal aggressions, much as there were period houses, chairs, and haircuts. In the prose poem *Portraits of Mistresses,* Baudelaire introduced a veteran roué who meditates for a moment on the possibility of complete sexual satisfaction and then confesses:

> But all my life, except at the age of [Beaumarchais's] Chérubin, I have been very sensitive to the nerve-racking stupidity and the irritating mediocrity of women. What I like above all in animals is their guilelessness.[17]

Manet, after being introduced to Berthe and Edma in the Louvre in 1868, wrote to Fantin:

> I agree with you: the Morisot damsels are charming. It's a pity they aren't men. But as women they might serve the cause of painting by marrying members of the Académie des Beaux-Arts and sowing discord in the camp of those old dotards.[18]

Zola, in his art criticism, constantly implied that women were congenitally incapable of judging serious painting and sculpture. Cézanne said that Hortense appreciated "nothing except Switzerland and lemonade."[19]

Degas indulged in this kind of period antifeminism, and often he did so with an asperity that the victims of his sallies apparently found hard to forget. He said that Berthe Morisot painted pictures "the way one would make hats."[20] He explained that his etching of Mary Cassatt in the Etruscan room of the Louvre was intended to illustrate "that bored and respectfully crushed and impressed absence of all sensation that women experience in front of paintings."[21] After examining Cassatt's aquatint *La Toilette* at Durand-Ruel's gallery, he commented, "I am not willing to admit that a woman can draw that well."[22] During a dinner with the Halévy family he went on and on about supposedly feminine mental operations:

> Women think in little packages. I understand nothing in the way their minds work. They make an envelope for each subject, attach a label to it, and that's the end of the matter. Little packages. Little packages.[23]

He referred to the women in some of his pictures as animals. On other occasions he implied that they were simply objects, without wills or even existences of their own. The engraver and illustrator Georges Jeanniot recalled a day around 1881 when a *petit rat* appeared at the studio door for a posing session; Degas let her in, looked her over, and discussed her fine points exactly as if she were a little horse: "Quite fresh and pretty, isn't she? A real find. With a first-rate back. Come now, show your back."[24] When a wealthy amateur painter deprived him of the modeling services of a favorite ballerina, he accosted the miscreant at the Opéra and said, "Monsieur, you have no right to take our tools away from us."[25]

The damaging inferences to be drawn from such remarks can be easily countered, however, by other evidence. Denis Rouart, a grandson of Henri Rouart and of Berthe Morisot, reported that during an exhibition in 1892 Degas gave Berthe "the greatest pleasure he could have given her by telling her that her rather airy painting concealed drawing of the most unerring kind."[26] The heavy-handed joke about "absence of all sensation" in the presence of art was somewhat palliated by a letter to Lepic that referred to Cassatt as "a good painter" and "this distinguished person by whose friendship I am honored,"[27] and also by a note to Pissarro that called her engravings "delightful."[28] In a letter to Halévy, he remarked in passing that "women are good in situations in which we men are worthless."[29] That young danseuses were not always treated as lower mammals is seen in an account by the dilettante Albert Boulanger-Cavé, recorded by Daniel Halévy, of an afternoon ballet rehearsal in 1891:

> Cavé told us how droll was the attitude of Degas toward these little creatures, and also their attitude. Degas found them all charming, treated them as if they were his own children, excused everything they did, and laughed at everything they said. They in turn had for him a genuine veneration. The *petits rats* were ready to do anything to please him.[30]

An affectionate message to Emma Dobigny from the Rue de Laval, probably written in 1869, disposes of any idea that the reference to mere "tools" should be taken very seriously (and incidentally shows Degas already playing the role of a tradesman):

> You have stopped coming to see me, my little Dobigny. Yet I haven't buried my street sign, the notice on the door still says "Bubble Factory," and I am not going out of business. This evening I'll keep the shop open until six-thirty. Try to give me a posing session or two.[31]

Another indication of his attitude toward models was his practice of aiming some of his habitual persiflage in their direction. To one of them he said, "You are a very rare case; you have pear-shaped hips. Like Mona Lisa."[32]

Into a more general section of the dossier can be put his well-attested admiration for a large number of actresses, ballerinas, divas, and café-concert chanteuses, beginning with Adelaide Ristori in 1855; his long and often close relations with some of the most intelligent women of his time, including Morisot and especially Cassatt; and his evident pleasure in observing feminine demeanor, occupations, and amusements. Rivière, whose objectivity in this context can be credited, since he was particularly friendly with Renoir, wrote:

> Degas loved the company of women. Although he often painted them with real cruelty, he liked being with them, enjoyed their idle talk, and said flattering things to them. This attitude was in curious contrast with that of Renoir, who depicted women seductively, lent charm even to those who did not have any, and yet in general derived no pleasure at all from what they valued. He liked women, with a few exceptions, only if they were capable of becoming his models.[33]

A confirmed misogynist, of course, can always assert that some of his best friends are female. Even so, a fair balancing of the available information on Degas as a person, with the artist and his supposed "cruelty" left aside for the moment, must lead to the conclusion that in fact he did not dislike women and did not regard them as inferiors.

Some other reason for his celibacy must therefore be sought, and there can be little doubt that this other reason was impotence — either psychic or physical impotence, and perhaps, as is often the case, a combination of the two. In 1869 Manet had hinted at such an infirmity in what Morisot had called a "very droll" observation: "He is not capable of loving a woman . . . or of doing anything about it." A few years later something a bit more definite was learned by a group of café talkers, led by Manet, who thought that Degas might be sleeping with his maid. "Monsieur?" she said to their committee of inquiry. "He isn't a man. I once went into his bedroom while he was changing his shirt, and he said, 'Get out of here, you wretched girl.' "[34] The time of the incident and her implied age indicate that she was Clotilde, and her scornful comment fits in with her employer's decision, shortly after his return from New Orleans, to replace her because he thought she was "too young for a bachelor."

In 1874 Edmond de Goncourt, recounting his visit to 77 Rue Blanche, had again approached the matter: "This Degas . . . is sickly, neurotic." During the 1880s the rumored deficiency became a topic in Vincent van Gogh's correspondence. In the early 1890s the journalist and collector Thadée Natanson got the impression that the whole problem was due to an early "disappointment" and "possibly to causes of a special kind — the state of his health, for example."[35] On December 2, 1894, the still tirelessly gossiping Goncourt recorded in his *Journal* something like a confirmation, gleaned during an evening with the painter Jean-François Raffaëlli and the novelist Léon Hennique:

> Raffaëlli began to revile Degas. . . . This led Hennique to say he had once had a mistress whose sister had slept with Degas and that the so-to-speak sister-in-law had complained about the insufficiency of Degas's amorous capabilities.[36]

Buttressing information of a less explicit sort can be found. A notebook used by the young Edgar in the spring of 1856 contains a partly scratched-out allusion to a sexual adventure that seems to have revolted as well as enraptured him:

> I find it impossible to say how much I love that girl, since for me she has . . . Monday, April 7. I cannot refuse to . . . how shameful it is . . . a defenseless girl. But I'll do it the least often that is possible.[37]

In later notebooks there are bits of material that suggest a preoccupation with the virile reflex. Datable to around 1876–1877 are three sketches of a penis transformed into a cannon, two drawings of the male organs changed into a cat with its tail lifted, and an imitation of the composer Ernest Reyer's signature in which a flourish becomes a penis and a pair of testicles. (There was perhaps much more of this sort of thing, for René is known to have destroyed a stock of pornographic drawings after Edgar's death.) Several pieces of doggerel from the same period evince a similar concern; one of them, for example, comments on the amorous exploits of the actor Alphonse-Emile Dieudonné, who was long a mainstay of the Théâtre du Vaudeville and was about Degas's age:

> *A quarant'deux ans Dieudonné*
> *de ses succès est étonné.*
> *On le dit même convaincu*
> *que son arme est d'acier fondu.*[38]

(At forty-two Dieudonné is amazed by his successes. He is reportedly even convinced that his weapon is of cast steel.) Such evidence is of course open to the objection that it merely corresponds to a preconception and therefore leads to a circular argument. But there is a good deal of it.

The pictures remain to be considered. Many of them need not be discussed in the present context, for, though nearly everything is grist for the depth-psychology mill, it would take a very determined analyst to discover signs of misogyny or impotence in landscapes and horse races. Most of the dance items can also be set aside, since we are no longer apt to see in their social comment and their often quite tender realism the cruelty toward women sometimes imagined by nineteenth-century critics. That leaves three important groups to be examined for the light they may throw on their author's celibacy: first, the series of relatively early paintings in which a sexual bipolarity is evident; second, a series of brothel scenes that began to appear around 1876; and third, a series of bathroom or related scenes that also got under way around 1876. This choice need not, of course, rule out an occasional look at other works that seem pertinent.

The principal compositions in the sexual-bipolarity series, all of them executed or at least undertaken between Degas's return from Italy in 1859 and his participation in the Franco-Prussian War, are the already discussed *Bellelli Family, Young Spartan Girls Provoking the Boys, War Scene in the Middle Ages, Interior,* and *Sulking.* Each of them has the same construction: female on the left, male on the right. None of them can be legitimately interpreted as evidence of egregious, vulgarly masculine nineteenth-century misogyny, for Laura is represented as a deeply poignant figure, the Spartan maidens as ingratiating hoydens, the medieval war victims as tortured innocents, the desolate woman in *Interior* as certainly the injured party, and the enigmatic one in *Sulking* as apparently not the cause of whatever is going on. Moreover, we know that in real life Degas was fond of his aunt, young girls generally (perhaps because they were reassuringly inaccessible), the unhappy refugees from New Orleans, and the "little Dobigny" who posed for *Sulking.* Yet this group of pictures, when taken as a whole, unquestionably implies some sort of sexual anxiety, both by the obsessive repetition of a compositional device and by the figural content: the playful, sunlit confrontation of the Spartan adolescents and the estrangement of the Bellelli couple become, with the nubile nudes and the sadistic archers of the *War Scene,* an infernal blending of the human libidinal and destructive drives — a symbolic union of Eros and Thanatos — and finally, in *Interior* and *Sulking,* two extremely ambiguous, but clearly not Darby-and-Joan, dumb shows. Although it may seem facile to say that in the 1860s one might have predicted lifelong bachelorhood and nearly uninterrupted chastity for the creator of such images, in fact one might have.

The brothel series, nearly all of which was produced in the late 1870s and early 1880s, consists of some fifty monotypes, a smaller number of pastels (many of them reworked monotypes), and a few drawings. The subject matter was an obvious one for a realist who wanted to depict contemporary life. By the end of the Second Empire there were probably forty thousand prostitutes in Paris, far more than in any other European capital,[39] and several thousand of them were in the officially tolerated and police-inspected establishments euphemistically referred to as *maisons de tolérance.* Such houses, often elaborately if garishly furnished and decorated, were both bordellos and something like clubs to which Frenchmen of all classes resorted for relaxation and an escape from family stuffiness, as naturally as they went to cafés. (A Flaubert character says of one of them, "That's the only place where I have been happy.") In 1863 Baudelaire, commenting on Constantin Guys's drawings and watercolors of these enterprises, had described the waiting women with detachment and sympathy:

> Sometimes they find, without effort, bold and noble poses that would enchant the most delicate sculptor. . . . At other moments they exhibit themselves prostrate in desperate attitudes of boredom, in a barroom apathy, killing time by smoking cigarettes with masculine cynicism and the resignation of Oriental fatalists; or they roll and sprawl on sofas, their skirts rounded out behind and in front like double fans; or they balance themselves on stools and chairs, heavy, dejected, stupid, extravagant, their eyes glazed by alcohol.[40]

Other painters besides Guys had treated the general theme, although somewhat allusively: Courbet in 1857 with his *Girls by the Banks of the Seine,* Manet in 1863 with *Olympia,* and the academic Couture in 1864 with *The Modern Courtesan,* in which a draped nude is riding in a carriage and holding a whip over a team composed of a youth, an old man, a warrior, and an artist. By the time Degas was at work on his series, several French novelists in the more or less Naturalist school were exploiting the market that seemed to be opening up. Joris-Karl Huysmans's *Martha, a Girl of the Streets* appeared in 1876, Edmond de Goncourt's *The Prostitute Elisa* in 1877, Zola's *Nana* in 1880, and Guy de Maupassant's shorter and very funny tale, *The Tellier Establishment,* in 1881.

Unlike Guys's crinolined fatalists, Courbet's suburban hussies in their Sunday splendor, Manet's successful demimondaine, and Couture's allegorical figure, Degas's prostitutes are ordinary, hard-working whores, sometimes comic, frequently depraved, usually as naked as grubs, and about as erotic as cold mutton. In *The Party for Madame's Name Day* they are robust, carefree, peasantlike women, lining up to beflower and buss their employer with an effusiveness that recalls the sentimentality of Madame Tellier's hilarious harlots, who temporarily recover their girlish purity of heart by attending a celebration of a first communion in a Norman village. (Degas once accepted a commission to illustrate Maupassant's story, and then did nothing about it.) In *Waiting* and *In the Salon* they are dimwitted bawds who slump and wallow on long sofas, their crotches exposed, in postures that parallel Baudelaire's description and also the passage in Huysmans's novel in which Martha enters a *maison*:

> She felt nauseated and exhausted. . . . Then she looked with stupefaction at the strange poses of her companions, who were queer and vulgar beauties, irritating chatterboxes, some of them mannishly solid, others skinny,

The Party for Madame's Name Day, 1878–1879

stretched out on their bellies, crouching like bitch-dogs on stools, hooked like cheap finery to the corners of divans.[41]

A particularly arresting and gloomy print reveals one of them in her room servicing a lesbian customer.

The habitual Degas cut-offs, arrested movements, eccentric viewpoints, and lack of *pompier* symmetry, plus a few apparent borrowings from *ukiyo-e* artists, contribute to an initial impression of instantaneousness and authenticity. After another look and some thinking, however, one doubts that very much actual brothel experience lay behind these seemingly realistic snapshots. Many of them imply an intent reading of contemporary fiction. In several there are imaginary elements that suggest a nightmare pendant for the Babylonian dream of fair ladies; the obscene nakedness on the long sofas, for instance, is a straight invention, or a sexual phantasm, for in fact the women in these establishments, if often licentious in their posture and talk, were at least partly and sometimes fully dressed when they exhibited themselves in the visitors' salon. There are no allusions in the prints and pastels to identifiable places, nothing even remotely approaching the pictorial specificity of the luxurious whorehouses in the Rue d'Amboise and the Rue des Moulins which Toulouse-Lautrec painted a little more than a decade later (and into which he vanished for days at a time). Monotypes were of course necessarily executed in the studio, and no preparatory on-the-spot drawings and notes have survived, as they have by the dozen for the home-assembled dance and racing pictures. (Some existing notebook pencil sketches of courtesans are not relevant here, for they were intended as illustrations for Goncourt's *The Prostitute Elisa* and were mostly drawn in Halévy's dining room.) To such facts can be added some softer, more insinuating evidence in the form of a Chaplinesque little man in a derby who is one of the few males in the series and who can be regarded as representing the attitude of Degas himself, in the way a character in a play or novel can be supposed to speak for the author. In *The Client* the little man is resisting a woman who is trying to pull him out of the downstairs salon. Another print depicts him as a ghostly, indecisive presence in a mirror near a bed. In *Admiration,* he has ventured into a room where a prostitute is taking a bath, but he seems to have come upstairs merely to look.

By the time of *Admiration,* probably around 1880, the artist was well into the series of scenes he once summarized in an exhibition catalogue as "women bathing, washing themselves, drying themselves, rubbing themselves down, combing their hair or having it combed,"[42] and he was still turning them out more than twenty years later, by which time they consti-

The Client, c. 1879

Admiration, c. 1880

tuted a section of his life work only slightly less important than the dance pictures. Two particularly fine preludes to the series, both painted between 1875 and 1877, are the sketchy *Women Combing Their Hair,* in which the same figure is repeated in a composition that hovers between a Classical frieze and a modern film sequence; and the more spacious, more carefully finished, more Manet-like *Beach Scene,* in which the foreground figures and scattered pieces of clothing and equipment create a flat pattern of white, brown, and green that is as shadowless as a Kiyonaga print. (The Impressionistic seaside setting in this second picture is verifiably fictional, for the background is mostly a re-use of the pastel *On the Channel Coast,* executed in 1869, and Degas is on record as explaining that the models sat on "my flannel vest spread out on the floor of the studio.")[43] Other relatively early examples, from between 1879 and 1886, are the monotype *Woman at Her Toilette,* which may be a brothel scene, the etching *Woman Leaving Her Bath,* and the pastels *Nude Drying Her Arm, The Cup of Tea,* and *The Tub.*

There was a sizable network of historical, aesthetic, technological, social, and symbolic justifications for the production of these works. Depicting cleaning and combing had long been an accepted pretext for representing the female nude. Among the predecessors of whom Degas was certainly aware were such masters as Bellini, Tintoretto, Rubens, Rembrandt, Boucher, Fragonard, and especially Harunobu, Kiyonaga, and Utamaro. The first half of the French nineteenth century had not neglected the opportunities: Ingres had painted his *Valpinçon Bather* as early as 1808, Chassériau his *Toilette of Esther* in 1841, and Courbet his *Bathers* in 1853. More recently the tradition had been continued in the Ninth Arrondissement and the Batignolles quarter by Stevens with *The Bath,* Puvis de Chavannes with *The Toilette,* Bazille with another *Toilette,* Manet with *The Tub,* and Renoir with the first of his many *baigneuses.*

In the meantime, partly as a result of improvements in gas heating, the reality of washing one's body had been changing, and by the late 1870s the separate bathroom was becoming fairly common in up-to-date Parisian apartments and houses, often as an annex to the older *cabinet de toilette* with its small, portable tub, disguised bidet, overstuffed and quilted chair or chaise longue, cheval glass, and arsenal of powders, creams, and perfumes. The good long soak that had once been the luxury of sinful women like the royal mistresses at Fontainebleau was now being regularly enjoyed by decent bourgeois housewives (with the help of a servant and large pitchers, for running water was still mostly in the future). Progress had not, however, diminished the age-old sexual excitement associated with feminine grooming and hygiene. Undone hair, the longer the better, was one of the great erotic symbols of the period: Baudelaire was ready to compare his mistress's locks to "languid Asia and blazing Africa,"[44] and Zola was excited simply by the sound of hairpins falling from loosened tresses into a metal wash basin. Water, in addition to retaining many of its ancient, half-subliminal connotations of initiation, purification, and regeneration, was apt to acquire special arousal overtones at the beach and in the intimacy of a *cabinet de toilette*. Sea water, in particular the cold variety along the Channel and Basque coasts, was supposed to be an aphrodisiac.[45] Mallarmé dreamed of lukewarm water shamelessly exploring, "naked in its promenade,"[46] the most secret recesses of a bather's body, and felt that being in love was somehow an aquatic, or at least a very humid, kind of ecstasy.

In spite of this justifying, acceptance-provoking context, Degas's series shocked many of his conservative contemporaries and made some of his admirers feel uneasy. One very probable reason was the contrast between an idealizing idiom and a realistic content — the use, once again, of a

Woman Leaving Her Bath, c. 1879

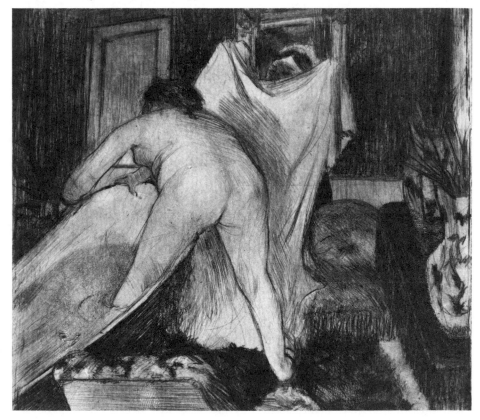

Classical or at least a traditional language to say something un-Classical. Art historians have noticed evidence of the painter's wide-ranging visual culture: in *Woman Leaving Her Bath* the figure has the simple, clearly related structural blocks and the weight-carrying columns of a Doric temple; *The Tub* contains reminiscences of a Hellenistic crouching Venus, of Rubens's *Diana and Callisto,* and of Harunobu's high viewpoints; *A Woman Having Her Hair Combed* recalls Rembrandt's *Bathsheba,* which the young Edgar may have seen when it was in the La Caze collection; and a large number of the bathers have the plastic energy of Michelangelo's nude soldiers in the *Battle of Cascina* cartoon. But these women are obviously, emphatically not Venuses, Bathshebas, exotic geishas, or Renaissance athletes; they are the sisters and wives of middle-class Third Republic Frenchmen. Most of them are faceless; they are backs, buttocks, and masses of cascading hair. They comb and comb, or allow themselves to be combed, with a physical satis-

The Tub, 1886

faction evident enough to connote a very pleasurable if mild sexual aberration. Blissfully intent on cleaning, rubbing, and drying every accessible patch of their skins, they contort themselves into postures that are the opposite of the modest shrinking and the locked thighs of academic nymphs. Sometimes they are astride bidets. The viewer is permitted to slip up behind them, or often directly over them, close enough to be trespassing into the normally inviolable buffer zone, the psychic bubble of portable personal territory, with which spatially sensitive people surround themselves. Even the professional models of Montmartre and the Little Poland quarter were troubled, and perhaps humiliated in their femininity, by the artist's persistent preoccupation with their supposed crowning glories and with the most private sector of a woman's daily life; and their reaction became part of Parisian atelier talk. One of them remarked to Raffaëlli about Degas, "He is an odd monsieur — he spent the four hours of my posing session combing my hair."[47] Another said to the critic Gustave Coquiot, "Can you imagine what we pose for with Degas? Well, it's for females climbing into tubs and washing their hind ends."[48]

The artist could have pointed out that most of the women in the series are pretty, that they are not represented satirically, that the depicted space is without the usual anguish of human existence, that many of the prints and pastels are quite extraordinarily beautiful, and that the average *pompier* nude was salacious. But he chose instead to play the role of the jocular naturalist and to advance a defense theory that, while sound in some respects, almost certainly revealed more about the inner workings of his imagination than he intended. Showing one of his bathroom scenes to the Irish writer George Moore (perhaps in the mid-1880s, though the conversation was not published until 1891), he commented:

> It's the human animal taking care of its body, a female cat licking herself. Hitherto the nude has always been represented in poses which presuppose an audience, but these women of mine are honest, simple folk, unconcerned by any other interests than those involved in their physical condition. Here is another; she is washing her feet.[49]

His "hitherto" was an exaggeration: Ingres's Valpinçon bather, for instance, does not indicate that she knows she is being inspected, nor do the odalisques in the *Turkish Bath,* with the exception of the one on the far right with raised arms (whose inviting gaze is explained by the external detail that the model was the painter's wife), nor do the Eves, goddesses, and heroines in a lot of Gothic, Far Eastern, and Islamic art. Still, it is generally true that the female nudes in Western painting since the Italian Renaissance suggest — by their postures, by their eyes, and not infrequently by their smiles — an awareness of being looked at and of being in a sense the visual property of the viewer, who is always assumed to be a man. A militant feminist might therefore be confronted by the argument that Degas's combers and tubbers are exactly what is wanted: here at last are women as they really are, as independent beings, not as man-pleasing objects in abasing provocative poses and with foolish come-hither stares.

There is, however, an obvious catch in the argument, for of course these happy, intent, liberated creatures are actually being examined very closely by a prying male eye, and their manifest obliviousness of the fact can be considered an aggravating circumstance. Indeed, there is probably no way to keep a depicted naked woman from losing part of her human dignity and becoming to some extent a mere sight for men, unless or until one is prepared to foment a rebellion against male dominance, change the economic organization of Western society, and drastically reform the education of girls. And though Degas may not have reflected on all the complex psychological and social problems raised by his bathroom pictures, he was clearly conscious of the catch in his defense case, for he wound up his talk with Moore by saying, "It is as if you looked through a keyhole." [50]

The voyeurism implicit in this concluding remark has been frequently noted and, largely because of a failure to define and situate historically the deviation in question, seldom treated seriously. Surveying an undressing mistress or enjoying a pornographic show is not necessarily an instance of voyeurism, whereas peeping through a closed bedroom window or simply eyeing feminine underwear on a clothesline can be easily and properly classified as such. The true voyeur, who is apparently never a woman, does not indulge in his characteristic activity as a kind of visual foreplay, as a preliminary to actual or desired intercourse; to him, looking is itself the sexual act. Far from being a potential rapist, he is a relatively harmless, if not very respectable, dreamer and compensator, a Walter Mitty of the libidinal realm, who achieves feelings of potency and of revenge for sexual shyness or inadequacy by merely violating, unseen, the seclusion and modesty of the female being watched. Along with other deviations, voyeurism exists to a degree in every type of social organization and among all the members of a statistically normal male population. But since it is rendered more exciting by obstacles, restrictions, and repression, it is apt to flourish in societies where women are overdressed and taught from childhood to conceal themselves, where the moral code is ostensibly puritanical, and where young men are afflicted with a good deal of frustrated sexual curiosity. And so it was very prevalent in nineteenth-century France. Like the period antifeminism, with which it was psychologically meshed, it had its ribald and its taken-for-granted aspects: in 1862 a Paris judge convicted a merchant of obscenity for selling chamber pots that had eyes painted in their bottoms,[51] and a generation later an unusually likable and energetic Paris prefect of police, Louis Lépine, tried in vain to reform the local *maisons de tolérance* by plugging the traditional peepholes.[52] At more acceptable levels of behavior middle-aged gentlemen adjusted their top hats in order to gape surreptitiously at exposed ankles on the steps of omnibuses, boys pushed girls to indecent heights on the swings in the Jardin du Luxembourg, Gérôme painted King Candaules' wife, Nyssia, in her half-Oriental bedroom being spied on by the suborned Gyges, and Gautier, in his prose version of the story, breathlessly described the emotions of the hidden spectator:

> She undid the clasp that pinned her peplos on one shoulder, and there remained only her tunic to be let fall. Gyges, behind the door, felt his veins hiss in his temples. His heart was beating so loudly he thought it could be heard in the bedroom, and in an attempt to calm it he put his hand on his chest. When Nyssia, with a movement of nonchalant grace, untied the belt of her tunic, he felt that his knees were going to give way beneath him.[53]

One of the popular pictures in the Louvre was Tintoretto's *Susannah and the Elders,* which provides the presumably male and almost if not quite statistically normal viewer with a whole series of interesting possibilities. Since Susannah has the Western nude's come-hither stare, he may feel invited to possess her, visually at least. He may be self-righteous about the nasty old men who are peeking at her through the window. At the same time, since she is evidently unaware of them, he may feel free to identify with them and become a voyeur by proxy. Or, more subtly and perhaps more titillatingly, he may enjoy watching the unconscious watchers watching and thus become the ultimate refinement, a voyeur of voyeurs, a patron of sexual theater within sexual theater.

Speculating about such a matter is as hazardous as trying to think straight about an alleged case of misogyny, a rumored physical or psychic sexual insufficiency, a merely repeated bipolar pictorial structure, and some brothel scenes, perhaps mostly fictional; but it is not an entirely hopeless operation. For there is a discernible pattern in the evidence, a drift toward a meaningful order, however slight each indication may be. Some time around 1890, in the presence of Daniel Halévy, Degas said, concerning his bathroom pictures, "It's odd to think that in another era I would have painted Susannah and the Elders."[54] His intention may have been simply to suggest, ironically as usual, that he was continuing the central tradition in European art by updating it. But it is easy to go beyond his intended point. The supposed impotence — which is finally the most adequate single explanation for his mysterious celibacy — and the "through a keyhole" confession to Moore both imply the possibility of a furtive identification with the peeking elders. So do the scores of unaware women combing their hair and washing their bodies, the little man gazing at the prostitute in *Admiration*, and the early plans to paint King Candaules' naked wife climbing into bed under the hidden eyes of the boiling Gyges. (There is plenty of proof that the twenty-two-year-old Edgar had read Gautier's version.) After finishing the etching *Woman Leaving Her Bath*, which was done from memory with the help of imagination, the artist slyly remarked to Henri Rouart's brother, Alexis, that one of their matronly acquaintances "must be like that when she gets out of her tub."[55] The desire to see into the intimacy of women frequently manifested itself in a more overt form as a fascination with milliners' shops, couturier's salons, and normally concealed items of feminine attire. Several of the sprawling courtesans in *In the Salon* call attention to their undressed state by wearing stockings and skimpy shifts. The corset on the bedroom floor in *Interior* is not only a signifying dramatic prop; it is also something of a personal fetish and a sign of a recurring tendency to substitute spectator for participant eroticism. A notebook entry for around May 1879 reads, "Do all sorts of objects in use, placed and accompanied so as to have life . . . corsets, for instance, that have just been taken off and that seem to retain the shape of the body, etc., etc."[56] In 1878 the successful young academic painter Henri Gervex made the mistake of showing his nearly finished *Rolla*, an anecdotal nude inspired by one of Musset's poems, to Degas, who insisted that a corset should be added to a pile of discarded petticoats and fluffy linen near the woman's rumpled bed. Gervex followed the advice, and the Salon jury promptly rejected the picture as unseemly.

There is no warrant, of course, for supposing that Degas sneaked through the darkened streets of Paris in search of a lighted bedroom window or an accessible door to a *cabinet de toilette*, nor is there reason for becoming morally indignant about his spectator eroticism. The bathrooms are mise-en-scènes in a Ninth Arrondissement studio; the keyholes are supplied by the painter's eye and mind; and in the ambiguous psychological realm of great art, with its innumerable symbolic condensations and displacements, a sublimated voyeurism is every bit as legitimate, and admirable, as Michelangelo's heroically sublimated homosexuality or Cranach's sublimation of participant goatishness. Moreover, we cannot censure Degas's covert sexual theater and what might be called his Actaeon complex without risking the failure to perceive the stimulating consistency of his work as a whole. A large part of his output is explicitly concerned with the professional world of spectacle, and much of the rest may be interpreted as exercises in uncommitted looking, although not only as that.

In the racing scenes there is no hint of an impulse to ride the horses or even to bet on them; in the landscapes there is no communing with nature. The bedroom of *Interior* is almost as theatrical as the set for *Robert le Diable.* In many pictures the presence of hidden viewers, of ourselves along with the artist, is implied so strongly by the sophisticated perspective that we cannot help becoming voyeurs. We violate visually the nonpublic space of coulisses and danseuses' practice rooms; in *The Rehearsal,* like the boys under the swings in the Jardin du Luxembourg, we peek at silhouetted feminine legs coming down a staircase. Often there is the special bonus pleasure of being the concealed spectators of spectators: we are permitted to watch the absorbed Cassatt inspecting the masterpieces in the Louvre, the Opéra audience responding to a ballet while Hecht peers around the house in the Rue Le Peletier, and the little man eyeing the whore in the tub. The objects of our scrutiny rarely look back at us, and when they do there is no insinuated invitation: Emma Dobigny questions us, Degas

The Baker's Wife, c. 1886

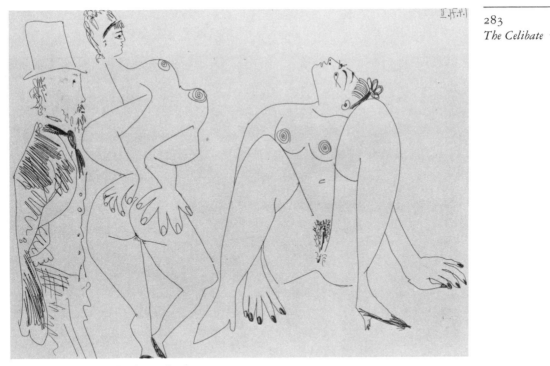

Degas and Two Nudes, by Pablo Picasso, 1971

ironically salutes himself, and Lyda glowers through field glasses that break through our own psychic bubbles of personal territory and transform us, in our turn, into watched animals.

A renunciation of statistically normal love was perhaps a necessary condition for the creation of this brilliant universe of looking. Such at least appeared to be the opinion of the ninety-year-old Picasso, who in 1971 produced a series of some two hundred erotic engravings that one may interpret as another of his many comments on the artist-and-model relationship and also as a long, furious lament for a lost potency. About half of these prints are baroque variations on Degas's brothel and bathroom scenes, and in many of them Degas himself appears, grave, uncommitted, just looking.

15. Life and Art

B Y THE LATE 1870S references to "the Batignolles group" were completely out of date, and not only because of the growing currency of the term "Impressionists" among journalists and some of the painters concerned. Manet's atelier in the annexed former village had been wrecked during the Commune and finally given up by the artist in favor of workplaces closer to his Rue de Saint-Pétersbourg apartment, at first in the same street and after 1878 in the nearby Rue d'Amsterdam. Fantin-Latour had married Victoria Dubourg in 1876 and settled down on the Left Bank in the Rue des Beaux-Arts, remote both physically and stylistically from the anti-Establishment movement he had publicized in his manifesto picture, *A Studio in the Batignolles Quarter.* After the Franco-Prussian War Monet had resided and painted mostly at Argenteuil until 1878, when he had rented Parisian lodgings near the Gare Saint-Lazare for a few months and then moved out to Vétheuil, a small town on the Seine halfway to Rouen. Sisley was at suburban Marly-le-Roi for a while and then at Sèvres; Renoir was still in the Rue Saint-Georges, where he would remain until 1884. Between 1875 and 1880 Cézanne lived at three different addresses on the Left Bank, at three in the Parisian environs, and also at L'Estaque and Aix-en-Provence. After a short period at Louveciennes Pissarro had returned to Pontoise, and though a frequent visitor to Paris he had long since given up the Batignolles flat he once shared with his mistress, Julie Vellay. Degas, whose own nomadic impulse was strictly circumscribed by the frontiers of the Ninth Arrondissement, had moved in 1876 from the Rue Blanche to number 4 of the Rue Frochot, a block-long link hanging southward from the Place Pigalle and joining the entertainment world of Montmartre and the network of lanes that led down the hill to Notre-Dame-de-Lorette. Rivière later remembered the building with amusement at its old-fashioned, provincial air and its lack of the exotic bric-à-brac and self-expressive decoration usual in painters' domiciles:

> A pavilion preceded by a small garden in which a vigorous acacia flourished and, when the springtime came round, darkened the house with its abundant foliage. The artist lived there alone, served by an aged housemaid and guarded, so to speak, by a peevish, snappy little dog. The interior, with its absence of fantasy and its Louis-Philippe furniture, was rather dismal.[1]

Alfred Stevens and Désiré Dihau had been living in the street for some time, and the *pompier* Garnotelle of *Manette Salomon* was a fictional neighbor.

Another reason that the Batignolles label was obsolete was that the Café Guerbois, where a new generation of billiard players had become more and more noisy, had been gradually abandoned, beginning around 1875, by many of its old habitués in favor of the Café de la Nouvelle-Athènes, a smaller, quieter eating, drinking, and talking establishment in Place Pigalle. George Moore, who began to come to the new center in 1877, when he was twenty-five, recalled it with immense nostalgia — and perhaps a bit of imaginative embellishment — in his *Confessions of a Young Man:*

> I can hear the glass-door of the café grate on the sand as I open it. I can recall the smell of every hour. In the morning that of eggs frizzling in butter . . . and as the evening advances, the mingled smells of cigarettes, coffee, and weak beer. A partition, rising a few feet or more over the hats, separates the glass front from the main body of the café. The usual marble tables are there, and it is there we sat and aestheticized till two o'clock in the morning.[2]

The evocation continues with descriptive notes on three of the principal figures among the aestheticizers:

> Manet entered. Although by birth and by art essentially Parisian, there was something in his appearance and manner of speaking that often suggested an Englishman. Perhaps it was his dress — his clean-cut clothes and figure. That figure! those square shoulders that swaggered as he went across a room and the thin waist. . . . He sits next to Degas, that round-shouldered man in suit of pepper and salt. There is nothing very trenchantly French about him either, except the large necktie; his eyes are small and his words are sharp, ironical, cynical. . . . Duranty, an unknown Stendhal, will come in for an hour or so; he will talk little and go away quietly; he knows, and his whole manner shows that he knows, that he is a defeated man.

Degas's *Women on the Terrace* shows the glass front of the café; some of the marble tables appear in *Absinthe*, along with two of the newspapers the waiters were in the habit of calling to the attention of painters and writers concerned about reviews. Moore himself, looking scatterbrained and youthfully eager, is represented in a pencil drawing, datable to about 1879, that could have been used to illustrate his own ironical account of his years of Parisian avant-gardism and great-man idolatry:

> I was as covered with fads as a distinguished foreigner with stars. Naturalism I wore round my neck, Romanticism was pinned over the heart, Symbolism I carried like a toy revolver in my waistcoat pocket, to be used in an emergency.[3]

He was also portrayed by Manet, who enjoyed his inquiring mind, enthusiastic francophilia, atrocious French, and crooked Irish face.

Degas and Manet, both of whom lived nearby, are said to have showed up nearly every evening for several years, Degas usually around ten o'clock. Renoir came quite often, Caillebotte now and then, Pissarro when he was not out in the suburbs, Cézanne very occasionally, and Monet and Sisley almost never. Gervex and de Nittis, both Salon exhibitors, sometimes gave the conversation a conservative, worldly flavor. Among the writers, in addition to Duranty and Moore, were Rivière, Burty, Silvestre, Villiers de l'Isle-Adam, and Zola, although the last could scarcely have been an assiduous visitor in the Place Pigalle, since he was now installed in a house on the Seine at Médan, forty kilometers out of town.

The most picturesque and most popular talker was Marcellin Desboutin, who wore arty jackets and battered soft hats, smoked a clay pipe incessantly, convincingly posed for the down-and-out drunkard in *Absinthe,* and charmed everyone with a bumpy, scarlet countenance that looked, according to Goncourt, "as if a thunderbolt had hit him."[4] In fact he was a sober, talented painter, strongly influenced by Dutch realism, and a gifted printmaker who excelled especially in the drypoint medium. At the time of his appearances in the Nouvelle-Athènes, when he was in his fifties, he was already the possessor — one might say the survivor — of a remarkably varied and romantically unlucky career. As a young man, well supplied with money by wealthy, indulgent parents, he had studied with Couture and had traveled in England, Holland, and Italy. In 1854 he had purchased a palatial villa, L'Ombrellino, in Florence, and there for several years he had lived like a Renaissance prince, entertaining his friends, collecting the works of Italian artists, and dabbling in painting and engraving. Convinced that Florence would become the capital of a unified Italy, he had invested heavily in local real estate, and the value of his holdings collapsed after

Rome was chosen as the seat of the new government. In 1868 he had made his début at the Paris Salon, without any appreciable effect on his financial condition. He had translated into French the whole of Byron's *Don Juan,* without being able to find a publisher. A poetic history drama, *Maurice de Saxe,* had been accepted by the Comédie-Française and seemed on the way to a satisfactory run when the outbreak of the Franco-Prussian War closed the theater. In 1872, his fortune exhausted, he sold L'Ombrellino, settled in the Batignolles quarter with his wife and eight children, and set out to earn a living as a completely professional artist.

A special category at the café comprised the painters Jean-Louis Forain, Federico Zandomeneghi, and Jean-François Raffaëlli. They were relatively young — Forain and Raffaëlli were still in their twenties — and only moderately modern in their work, and they were generally regarded as Degas's "disciples," which was another way of saying that they were fresh instruments in his already evident determination to infiltrate and perhaps eventually control the series of exhibitions originally proposed by the pure Impressionists. Forain, by far the liveliest and most gifted of the three, had been one of Gérôme's pupils, a caricaturist for satirical journals, and a close friend of Arthur Rimbaud's; his style was a blend of a slightly academic dryness with something from Manet, Daumier, and the Japanese, and a good deal from Degas, who said of him, "The little Forain is still hanging to my coattails, but he'll go far if he lets go of me."[5] Zandomeneghi, born in 1841 in Venice into a family of sculptors (his grandfather and father had created the Titian monument in the church of the Frari), had studied painting in the Accademia di Belli Arti on the Grand Canal, fought under Garibaldi for the unification of Italy, spent several years in the Florence of the Macchiaioli, and joined the Parisian Italian colony in 1874; by the time of the sessions at the Nouvelle-Athènes he had picked up a smattering of French subject matter and mise-en-scène without losing his sculptural draftsmanship, his apparently innate heaviness of mind and handling, and a somewhat factitious feeling for color derived more from the Macchiaioli and the Venetian old masters than from the banks of the Seine. Raffaëlli, who came from an Italian milieu in Lyons, was another former pupil of Gérôme's and also, because of a need to earn money while still an adolescent, a former shop boy, bit-part actor, and itinerant singer. After painting for several years in a flashy academic manner, he had switched to a sweetish, dulled Impressionistic technique to represent ragpickers, street cleaners, jobless old men, and messy, melancholy Parisian suburbs. Duranty, Zola, Huysmans and other Naturalist writers were enthusiastic; the habitually hedonistic Impressionists were irritated by a success they had never enjoyed, by the artist's often ludicrous vanity and pushiness, and by what they regarded as a counterfeit, excessive *misérabilisme*. "Everything," Renoir once remarked, "in Raffaëlli's landscapes is poor, even the grass."[6]

According to Rivière, the café discussions took place on the glassed-in terrace and had a rather formal organization at the start of an evening:

> Two marble tables were pushed together for our use. Marcellin Desboutin had his immutable place on the moleskin banquette with its back against the partition separating us from the interior of the establishment; and Manet, Degas, Armand Silvestre . . . took their places next to him or on chairs, depending on their times of arrival. In fact, with the tacit agreement of everyone, Desboutin was a sort of presiding officer for our meetings. No one could have been as skillful as that excellent man at directing the talk and keeping it on a level of cordiality.[7]

Sometimes the conversation veered into personal confession. Moore remembered Duranty, for example, bitterly explaining his failure to write another novel: "What's the good, it would not be read; no one read the others, and I mightn't do even as well if I tried again."[8] Sometimes, too, in spite of Desboutin's efforts as chairman, clashes of temperament occurred, and one of them in particular amused Rivière:

> When Cézanne and Degas explained their views on art, they were both extremely categorical. Cézanne, however, expressed himself with a vehemence that wound up in an Olympian storm, whereas Degas darted cruel little scratching blows at his opponent with feline dexterity.[9]

The same source reported that Degas "did not always have the warmest of feelings" toward Renoir and that the latter "maintained that Degas could not pardon his [Renoir's] prettifying of female models."[10] Degas himself, about a dozen years later, recalled disagreeing profoundly with Zola — and with critics and novelists generally — and added a self-justifying comment that can be taken as an echo from the Nouvelle-Athènes:

> We argued about things endlessly. Zola's conception of art, which is to stuff everything about a subject into one volume and then go on to another subject, seems to me childish. . . . We painters do not have synthesizing minds. And yet in a way we do, more than we seem to. In a single stroke of the brush we can say more than a literary man can in a volume. And that's why I shun phrase-making art critics.[11]

Another echo can be heard in a remark to Moore: "I have spoken to the most intelligent people about art, and they have not understood . . . but among people who understand, words are not necessary; you say humph, he, ha, and everything has been said."[12]

Presumably the painters seated around the marble tables often discussed such topical issues as outdoor versus studio work, sketching versus finishing, color versus drawing, and tinted shadows versus black ones. One supposes that something more specific than humph, he, ha was said. But what all the memoir writers stressed as the principal attraction of these evenings was a running debate between Manet and Degas. Moore represented Manet as saying that he was painting "modern Paris" when "Degas was painting Semiramis," and Degas as riposting, "Manet is in despair because he cannot paint atrocious pictures like Durant [Carolus Duran], and be fêted and decorated."[13] In 1878 de Nittis became a member of the Legion of Honor and thereby inadvertently provoked a particularly sharp oral duel at the café:

> My friend Degas's disdain was without limits. Manet listened to him . . . and said: "Little man, all this scorn is just flummery. . . ." Degas replied with a series of tart remarks without for a moment affecting the composure of Manet, who went on: "My dear fellow, if there were no recompenses, I would not invent any. But there they are. And we must take anything that can distinguish us from the mass of the others. It's a sign of progress. It's one more weapon. In this hard life of struggle that is ours we are never too well armed. I am not decorated. But that's not my fault, and I assure you that I'll be decorated if I can — that I'll do everything necessary." Degas, shrugging his shoulders furiously, interrupted him: "This is not the first time I've realized how bourgeois you are."[14]

Gervex remembered that on another occasion the younger of the two rivals said, "After all, what are you complaining about? You're as famous as Garibaldi."[15] And in a very unwelcome sense the sally was true, for Manet was constantly the butt of caricaturists and professional humorists.

The debate, in spite of the comic element in the use of "bourgeois" by one *grand bourgeois* to insult another *grand bourgeois,* was based on real differences. Manet honestly believed that an innovating painter had to fight according to the rules laid down by the Establishment and that the future lay with the Salon. He was, of course, completely mistaken, for in fact the official Salon, already seriously if not yet patently weakened by the secession of the Batignolles group in 1874, would be rapidly reduced to historical insignificance by the influence of dealers on the art market, by the creation of the juryless Salon des Indépendants in 1884, by the organization of the conservative but schismatic Salon de la Société Nationale des Beaux-Arts under the leadership of Meissonier and Puvis de Chavannes in 1890, by the advent of the resolutely avant-garde Salon d'Automne in 1903, and more generally by a growing number of collectors who were willing to — or afraid not to — speculate in modernism.

Degas was equally honest in his belief that what he had called "the realist movement" in writing to Tissot had "to show itself separately."

Manet was perfectly aware of the streak of childish vanity in his desire for public recognition, to the point, according to Moore, of once confessing:

> You, Degas, you are above the level of the sea, but for my part, if I get into an omnibus and some one doesn't say "Monsieur Manet, how are you, where are you going?" I am disappointed, for I know then that I am not famous. [16]

Degas, if not always above sea level in his independence of spirit, certainly had a large portion of the feigned modesty of the secretly proud and a genuine hatred of being soiled by recognition from people he considered incapable of appreciating him: he told Alexis Rouart that he wanted to be "illustrious and unknown," [17] and in a notebook used around 1879 he wrote that there was "something shameful about being known." [18] He must have relished the passage in *Manette Salomon* in which Coriolis, offered the red ribbon of the Legion of Honor, finally summons up enough "arrogant dignity" to refuse the distinction. [19] And yet it would be a mistake to conclude from all this that the nightly performances in the Nouvelle-Athènes were manifestations of mutual dislike. Moore says that Manet was "the friend of [Degas's] life." [20] During one of the arguments about being decorated, the older artist temporarily disarmed his adversary by suddenly saying, with obvious sincerity, "We have all, in our minds, awarded you the medal of honor, along with many other things even more flattering." [21]

Often there may have been a tone to the exchanges that took the bite out of what may look like acerbity on a printed page more than a century later, for both men were inveterate Parisian *blageurs,* mockers, who enjoyed an ironical sort of gamesmanship — especially when it was practiced on each other. Forain remembered a studio visit made by Degas to inspect some recent work with which Manet seems to have been particularly pleased:

> Degas looked at the drawings and pastels. He pretended that his eyes were fatigued and that he could not see very well. He made almost no comment. Shortly afterward Manet met a friend, who said, "I ran into Degas the other day. He was just leaving your atelier and he was enthusiastic, dazzled by everything you had shown him." Manet said, "Ah, the bastard . . ." [22]

De Nittis noticed that while listening to one of Degas's scoldings Manet had "that youthful smile, that street urchin's grin, slightly bantering, which turned up the corners of his nose." [23]

One of the few women who occasionally took part in the discussions was the former model Victorine Meurent, now no longer the seductress of Manet's *Olympia* and herself a painter, skillful enough to be admitted several times to the Salon. (Her frequenting of cafés eventually, however, was her undoing; she became a hopeless alcoholic, playing the guitar in Montmartre dives for drinks and a few francs.) Another may have been Ellen Andrée, who posed for the weary slattern in *Absinthe* and thus helped to make the picture a double portrait as well as a pseudo-Realistic genre scene and an example of Degas's dumb-show procedure. In fact, of course, she was no more a slattern than Desboutin, her depicted companion, was a lush. An article in *Le Courrier français* described her as "a lovely demirep," *une cocodette exquise,* who was naturally endowed with *chien,* with "dog," that did not have to be put on, and whose stated ambition was to become an actress "like Réjane" on the Grands Boulevards.[24] Her piled-up mass of blondish hair and her small, fine-featured, usually smiling face appear in a score of very Parisian paintings by Manet, Renoir, de Nittis, Stevens, and Gervex, and also in photographs of Worth fashion creations. Although she complained that Degas had "massacred" her in *Absinthe* and had maliciously placed the degrading glass of green liqueur on her corner of the table instead of on Desboutin's,[25] she posed again for several of his prints and drawings, notably, around 1879, as the trim, droopy-hatted young woman on the far right of his chalk-and-pastel *Project for Portraits in a Frieze;* and she sometimes let him take her to lunch at the Café La Rochefoucauld, which was something of a gourmets' rendezvous down the hill at the corner of the street of the same name and Notre-Dame-de-Lorette. Her desire to equal the sensational Gabrielle Réjane was never realized, but she became a player at the Théâtre des Variétés, where Degas often went expressly to see her, and in the late 1880s was a member of André Antoine's vanguard Théâtre-Libre company, which helped to introduce Ibsen and Strindberg to French audiences. The role in *Absinthe* was thus not her only experience with stage naturalism.

The two figures on the left in the *Project for Portraits in a Frieze* are often listed as unidentified, and in fact there is no clue at all to the identity of the standing one. The seated one, however, with her crabapple face, her characteristic tilt of the hips, and her equally characteristic furled-umbrella pivot, is clearly Mary Cassatt, with whom Degas was at this time in the early stages of a close friendship that would last, in spite of rather long breaks, for some twenty years. She was socially, artistically, and temperamentally almost his exact feminine counterpart, though ten years younger. Her father had been a stockbroker and real estate speculator in the Pittsburgh suburb where she was born and, later, in Philadelphia; her older brother, Alexander, became the president of the Pennsylvania Railroad. The family, if not quite in the Neapolitan palazzo category, was well enough off, and culturally ambitious enough, to spend long periods in Europe, like characters in a Henry James novel, and she was intimate with

the generation of wealthy art lovers whose treasures would become the cores of American museums. (For many years she was the adviser and agent of such collectors, and thus herself aided in enriching public galleries in the United States.) She had endured four dull years at the Academy of the Fine Arts in Philadelphia, studied briefly with the modish but essentially *pompier* Charles Chaplin in Paris, copied the old masters in France, Holland, Belgium, Italy, and Spain, acquired the rudiments of printmaking from the engraver Carlo Raimondi in Parma, learned to admire the Japanese, and emerged as a solidly professional artist with a crisp drawing style and a growing impatience with academic painting. She had made her début in the official Paris Salon in 1872, exhibited there regularly until 1877, and in the meantime decided to settle permanently in the French capital with her parents and her older sister, Lydia, who eventually took an apartment in the Ninth Arrondissement at 13 Avenue Trudaine, three blocks from the Rue Frochot.

In 1873 she had what she later described as a revelation:

How well I remember . . . seeing for the first time Degas's pastels in the window of a picture dealer on the Boulevard Haussmann. I used to go and flatten my nose against that window and absorb all I could of his art.[26]

The following May Degas returned the compliment by inspecting one of her realistic Salon portraits and remarking to the "old Roman" Joseph Tourny, "That is authentic. There is someone who feels as I do."[27] In the summer of 1877 Tourny, who had met Cassatt while she was copying Rubens in Antwerp, introduced her to Degas, who promptly invited her to join the group of secessionists from the Salon. Forty years later she told her first biographer, the French critic Achille Ségard, "I accepted with joy. Now I could work with absolute independence without considering the opinion of a jury. I had already recognized who were my true masters. I admired Manet, Courbet, and Degas. I took leave of conventional art. I began to live."[28]

Although Degas at first was probably intent on recruiting another infiltrator for the Impressionist exhibitions, he soon came to have other reasons for cultivating his new acquaintance. Her integrity and her intelligence were evident, and there was a certain charm even in her sharp tongue and her ability to withstand, more than most women did, his caustic humor. During the late 1870s and early 1880s they were seen everywhere together. For a while, before developing her own linear manner and turning, partly at his suggestion, to the mother-and-child theme with which she is now popularly identified, she adopted some of his spatial devices and theatrical subject matter. They worked side by side on prints, and at her

OPPOSITE: *Absinthe,* c. 1876

At the Milliner's, c. 1882

request he repainted some of the background of her *Little Girl in a Blue
Armchair* — which was already quite Degas-like in its use of *repoussoirs* and
cut-offs. Since she was aware of not being conventionally pretty ("It wasn't
my fault though," she remarked to her friend Louisine Havemeyer),[29] she
took a lively interest in clothes, and she permitted him to accompany her
to millinery shops. When he could not persuade his professional models to
adopt the bodily attitudes and properly grave facial expressions of women
trying on hats, she was willing to pose for him.[30] All her life she adored
the pushed-in, disheveled, clownish look of Belgian griffons, whereas he
disliked dogs in general. (The spiteful little animal Rivière noticed in the
Rue Frochot was exceptional, and it may have been one of Cassatt's griffons
being sheltered while she was absent from Paris.) Yet when one of her pets
disappeared, he rose, manfully, elaborately, ironically, to the occasion and
immediately sent off a letter to Lepic, who raised griffons as well as greyhounds on his Channel coast estate:

In your kennels or apartments, or among your friends and acquaintances, could you find me a little griffon, purebred or not (a male, not a bitch), and send it to me here in Paris at your convenience or by parcel post? I won't look at the price. . . . I think it is in good taste to inform you that the person who desires this dog is Mademoiselle Cassatt and that she has addressed herself to me because I am famous for the quality of my dogs and my affection for them as well as for my old friends, etc., etc. . . . She wants a young dog, a very young one, that will love her.[31]

Possibly the tender, dashingly brushed, wittily angled *Woman with Dog* is a souvenir of the arrival of the new griffon in the Avenue Trudaine, although the woman seems to be Lydia Cassatt instead of Mary.

Among the several studies of Mary executed just before or just after 1880, the closest to a straight portrait is the one often entitled *Miss Cassatt Holding Cards,* in which she sits hunched forward on her chair in a posture that recalls Auguste Degas listening to Pagans, and the collector of prints

*Miss Cassatt
Holding Cards,*
1880–1884

engrossed in his pleasure. (In fact, what she is holding may be small prints or photographs instead of cards.) The blue eyes seem to be focused on her thoughts. The face has been variously interpreted as expressing a humorous, logical, or withdrawn state of mind, and it can also be read, with the usual wariness about such readings, as anticipating the self-depreciation and moral severity she indulged in as she grew older. Vollard remembered her as working with "a sort of frenzy" for the success of Renoir, Pissarro, and the other artists in the group, and as saying "Ah, bah" when told she was "a painter whom Degas places very high."[32] The American critic Forbes Watson wrote of her during her last years:

> The elegance that was Mary Cassatt's had its limitations. This was due to a fierce love of truth which made it impossible for her to say a gracious word to the conniving or to flatter the painter who had been untrue to himself. Miss Cassatt sent more than one inelegant message to those of her contemporaries who allowed their gifts to become tainted by worldliness.[33]

One hopes that some of the victims of these puritanical scoldings had the courage to reply that being an artist untainted by commercialism was a bit easier with the help of a stockbroker father and a railroad-president brother.

But it is more agreeable to look at the series of spectacularly effective images of Cassatt at the Louvre that Degas turned out around 1879–1880. In a pastel she is a neatly tailored silhouette advancing on a waxed parquet floor against a background formed by the marble dado and the paintings in the Grande Galerie, while Lydia pretends to be consulting a guidebook. In a narrow etching that resembles a Kiyonaga pillar print the sisters are still in the Grande Galerie, but now Lydia is partly hidden by a large door jamb. In another etching they are in the Etruscan Gallery. Mary looks at the paintings or at the polychromed terra-cotta effigies of a smiling Etruscan husband and wife reclining on the lid of a sarcophagus. Lydia peeks out from behind her book at Mary. The dead Etruscans look back at the sisters and smile and smile, while we and the artist, concealed cultural voyeurs,

OPPOSITE:
At the Louvre: Mary Cassatt in the Etruscan Gallery, 1879–1880

At the Louvre: Mary Cassatt in the Picture Gallery, 1879–1880

look at Lydia looking at Mary looking at centuries of European art history. The light glistens on the polished floor and marble dado, on the picture frames and the Etruscans' glass case, and on Mary's sharp shoulderblades and corseted hips. Lydia's turned head reinforces the sense of receding space created by tonal contrasts and diagonal lines. Mary is not so much advancing as hovering, with the aid of her umbrella, on one leg in a sort of incipient *quatrième derrière* or *arabesque allongée,* a "critical moment." (The museum's rule against visitors with pointed accessories was apparently not then in force.) Although no faces except those of the Etruscans are visible, the sisters are characterized by their postures. Mary's eloquent back is a reminder both of how the adolescent Edgar had seen Proudhon on a Seine quay as "a large frock coat, a crease in the back" and of how Duranty had argued, in his pamphlet *The New Painting,* that a properly depicted back was enough to reveal "a temperament, an age, a social position." In fact, the whole series, which comes to at least thirty-three pictures when all the pastels, drawings, and subtly modified etching states are counted, is so full of reminders as to constitute a kind of summa on the aesthetic principles Degas had accumulated by the time he was forty-five.

His long and close friendship with Cassatt inevitably inspired rumors that they were sleeping together. And the rumors were almost certainly false. Their intimacy, though biased and spiced by their being a man and a woman, was obviously based on a shared devotion to their art, on admiration for each other's talents, on common social origins, and on the hard-to-define dialectical tension that always accompanies a lasting relationship between two strong personalities. He had his own vocational, temperamental, and physical or psychic reasons for remaining relatively chaste, and they went too deep to permit a supposition that he could have altered them for the sake of an affair when he was approaching middle age. Long afterward Forbes Watson heard him say, bizarrely and cryptically, "I would have married her [Cassatt], but I could never have made love to her."[34] She too seems to have been chronically chaste, for when they met in 1877 she was already an old maid of thirty-three. She never married, apparently never took a lover, and firmly disapproved of adultery among her acquaintances. It is nearly impossible to imagine a woman with her moral fastidiousness and conservative upper-class background becoming a painter's mistress, like a vulgar model from Montmartre. Moreover, she was too proud to have easily played the role of a sexually submissive female, and too opinionated to have endured being disadvantaged by caresses in an argument with the equally opinionated Degas. She later told Mrs. Havemeyer:

Oh, I am independent! I can live alone and I love to work. Sometimes it made him furious that he could not find a chink in my armor, and there would be months when we just could not see each other, and then something I painted would bring us together again and he would go to Durand-Ruel's and say something nice about me, or come to see me himself.[35]

Late in life, asked by a relative whether she had ever had an affair with him, she flew into a snob's tantrum: "What, with that common little man; what a repulsive idea!"[36]

She did, however, behave strangely on at least two occasions after 1900. She burned all of his letters. Toward the end of 1912 she wrote to Durand-Ruel concerning the picture of her holding cards or prints, which she had then owned for some thirty years:

> I particularly want to get rid of the portrait Degas made of me. . . . It has some qualities as a work of art but it is so painful and represents me as such a repugnant person that I would not want anyone to know that I posed for it. . . . I should like it sold to a foreigner and particularly that my name not be attached to it.[37]

Since the work does not represent her as a repugnant person, one suspects that what she really wanted to get rid of was a constantly present suggestion (it was hanging in her studio) of what might have been and her memories of the splenetic, fascinating man who had looked at her so closely while he was painting it. Perhaps there was, after all, a chink in her armor.

Degas himself, as he looked and comported himself around the time when the nightly sessions began at the Café de la Nouvelle-Athènes, is drawn in a prose portrait by Rivière and a more vivid, more psychological etching by Desboutin. Rivière wrote:

> Edgar Degas was of rather medium height, with good proportions and a distinguished air. He carried his head high without affectation, and when talking with someone while standing up he kept his hands crossed behind his back. He dressed without studied elegance but also without eccentricity or negligence. Like all the bourgeois of his time, he wore a top hat, although his was flat-brimmed and pushed back a little on his head. On most days he protected his ailing eyes against bright light with tinted glasses or a pince-nez perched on his nose, which was a bit short. His face was almost colorless and framed by dark brown side-whiskers that were closely trimmed, as was his hair.[38]

The etching presents a Degas who is visibly still the persona of the *Self-Portrait Saluting* of 1865, now about a dozen years older, slightly heavier, and possibly more aggressive and sure of himself.

In 1877 he was also represented — or at least some of his ideas were represented — in *La Cigale* (The Grasshopper), a comedy by Meilhac and Halévy satirizing avant-garde artists and exploiting the interest aroused by the controversies over the first Impressionist exhibitions. The set for the

Ludovic Halévy and Albert Boulanger-Cavé, 1879

third act of the play was the "Intentionist" painter Marignan's studio, in which there were caricatures of well-known pictures by Manet, Monet, Degas, Cézanne, Renoir, Sisley, and Pissarro. In one scene Marignan set up a washtub in the studio and had his model, Catherine, pose as a laundress scrubbing linen in a froth of suds. In another he brought out a picture that consisted of two equal bands of color, like some of the Whistlerian seascapes Degas had painted on the Channel coast in 1869, and solemnly explained that with the blue band below and the red band above, you had a magnificent sunset at sea, whereas with the thing turned upside down, you had a splendid blue sky above the burning sands of a desert. (When *The Grasshopper* was produced in English in London, the same gag was used to make fun of Whistler's nocturnes.) Elsewhere the Intentionist master went into ecstasies over a nose that was Parisian and modern instead of being Greek and old-fashioned. Degas was generally supposed to have supplied the authors with many of the jokes, including some that were obvious thrusts at Monet's retinalism. And he may also have had something to do with the design of the third-act set, for in a letter to Halévy, written a couple of weeks before the dress rehearsal, he said:

> You know . . . that I am at your disposition for the studio of Dupuis [the actor who had the part of Marignan]. It's no use my finding fault with the idea; doing the thing pleases me a lot, and I will do it. A word from you and I'll cover with a beautiful laundry lather the arms of Mademoiselle Baumaine [who was Catherine].[39]

The whole business, played in the rapid-fire style of boulevard comedy, must have been more amusing on the stage than it is on paper, for on the opening night at the Théâtre des Variétés the audience, Degas included, is said to have roared with laughter.

The series of portraits continued, usually with signifying backgrounds or accessories and often with unexpected angles and croppings that suggest the presence of the artist and ourselves. In *At the Bourse* the banker, speculator, and art collector Ernest May is caught in the midst of his professional activity on the steps of the Paris stock exchange (about where Achille was waving a revolver in 1875), with a friend whispering a tip into his ear. An exceptionally solemn Halévy talks in the wings of the new Opéra with the dandy Boulanger-Cavé, who is half-hidden by a stage flat. (Halévy commented in his diary, "Myself, serious in a frivolous place: that's what Degas wanted to represent.")[40] Rows of books and stacks of manuscripts, combined with hunched shoulders and fingers drilling into a temple (a gesture derived perhaps from a Pompeian mural by way of Ingres's *Madame Moitessier*), characterize the disenchanted Duranty as a writer about ready to give

Place de la Concorde, c. 1876

up. In *Place de la Concorde* a debonair Vicomte Lepic, his lively daughters Janine and Eylau (the latter named after the battle of 1807, because her father was a Bonapartist aristocrat), and one of his greyhounds animate a street scene that resembles the stereoscopic snapshots of Paris popular in the 1870s; and all the figures except the dog seem totally unaware of being stared at by the passerby on the left, who is evidently a psychological cousin of the little man with the derby in the brothel monotypes. The critic Diego Martelli appears in shirt sleeves in his Paris apartment, accompanied by his work and his red-lined slippers and seen from a high viewpoint that drastically foreshortens his compact, rotund body. He was at this time — roughly early 1879 — a correspondent in the French capital for several Italian newspapers and had been taken to the Nouvelle-Athènes by Desboutin and Zandomeneghi, both of whom he had known in Florence. In a letter of December 1878, he referred pleasantly to "running the risk of becoming a friend of Degas's,"[41] and toward the end of 1879, in a lecture at Leghorn, he made clear his growing conviction that the ideas of the

Diego Martelli, 1879

Macchiaioli had been outmoded by the work of Monet, Pissarro, and especially Degas.

Probably none of these portraits was commissioned, although May in time acquired *At the Bourse.* But it is not true, as it is often stated, that Degas rarely accepted commissions. In a letter of the late 1870s to Bracquemond he wrote, "I am seldom in my studio in the afternoon, for I go into town nearly every day to do a large portrait."[42] And around 1879 he got into trouble over a likeness ordered by Madame Dietz-Monnin, about whom little is known except that she was an extravagantly dressed fortyish woman and the mother-in-law of an animal-hide dealer whose artist-brother Degas knew. She sat for three studies or possible versions, in two of which she is wearing a huge, floppy bonnet and a boa that crisscrosses her body and falls below her knees. She then wearied of the sittings and proposed that they be continued for a while in her absence with nothing but the principal elements of her costume as models. Degas, who evidently was interested in her expressive if plain face and was in any case not willing to be reduced to the status of a painter of flattering frippery, drafted a blunt reply:

> Please, let's drop the portrait. I was so surprised by your letter proposing that it be reduced to a boa and a hat that I won't answer. . . . Need I tell you that I regret having begun something in my fashion in order to see it transformed entirely into something in your fashion? Explaining all that would not be very polite. . . . But I can't say any more, dear Madame, without revealing that I remain extremely hurt. My unfortunate art aside, accept all my compliments.[43]

He seems to have had second thoughts, for his letter was found unmailed in his studio after his death. But none of the versions of the portrait was ever finished or delivered.

By the time of this contretemps he was thinking more and more of series, and in doing so he was neither alone nor very innovative. In the 1830s Hokusai had done his *Thirty-six Views of Mount Fuji* and Hiroshige the first of what would become forty versions of his *Fifty-three Stages Along the Tokaido.* French Romantic painters, beginning with Géricault, had frequently dropped their attempts to create huge Salon stunners and turned to cycles of stallions, maniacs, lions, Faust, and Hamlet. In 1876 Monet had begun his Gare Saint-Lazare series, and he later concentrated on multiple representations of haystacks, Rouen Cathedral, poplars, the Thames at London, and water lilies. Cézanne had started his many bathers in 1873, and by the early 1880s he was finding in the Mont Sainte-Victoire of his native Provence a personal equivalent for Hokusai's spectral Fuji.

In Europe the sensibility behind the whole phenomenon was undoubtedly linked, though perhaps not as closely as economic determinists would like to believe, to the spread of mass, repetitive production in industry and a consequent erosion of the old élitist notion of the unique work produced by the elaboration of a single flash of inspiration. But Degas was nevertheless exceptional in his addiction to repeated motifs, so much so that they finally became the bulk of his life's output and part of the essence of his creative process. His series of such subjects as racehorses, ballerinas, musicians, laundresses, prostitutes, and women washing their bodies or combing their hair were on the average far longer than the series of his contemporaries. He maintained that "the same subject must be done ten times, a hundred times over";[44] he said that his idea of a genius was "a man who finds a hand so lovely . . . he will shut himself up all his life, content to do nothing else but indicate fingernails";[45] and when questioned by Moore about the personality people saw in his paintings, he replied, "It is strange, for I assure you no art was ever less spontaneous than mine."[46] Moreover, the quantitative superiority of his series over those of his fellow artists was accompanied by an important if subtle procedural and qualitative difference. In their historically most significant series Monet and Cézanne took as their respective points of departure the real lily pond at Giverny (eighty kilometers west of Paris) and the real Mont Sainte-Victoire; they then pursued their variations on these given themes until the water lilies and the mountain almost vanished in pictures that are now generally regarded as heralding twentieth-century lyrical abstraction and the first phase of analytical Cubism. Degas, on the contrary, seldom began with a unified, on-the-spot reality. He worked from disparate sketches, from pre-existing art, and from fragments transformed by memory, and these he welded into analogues of reality. His themes, like many of those in Beethoven's late works, had an emergent rather than a given mode of existence. He reversed the dissolution of form and explicit meaning to which repetition often leads.

Three particularly splendid examples of the many first-rate dance pictures he painted between 1876 and 1880 are *Dancers Practicing at the Bar,* in which legs, bar, floorboards, the familiar watering can, and even the signature join in a daringly simple sweep, a single chord, of diagonals; *The Ballet,* in which we look down across a looming fan at a bright stage that is the quintessence of theatrical artificiality; and *The Ballet Class,* in which a group of *petits rats* attempts a *pas de trois* in front of a mirror and a window while other students walk casually out of the frame and a dowdy, bored mother or sister reads a newspaper. (Mary Cassatt once owned this third picture.) He appears to have had balletic patterns and straining balletic

Dancers Practicing at the Bar, 1876–1877

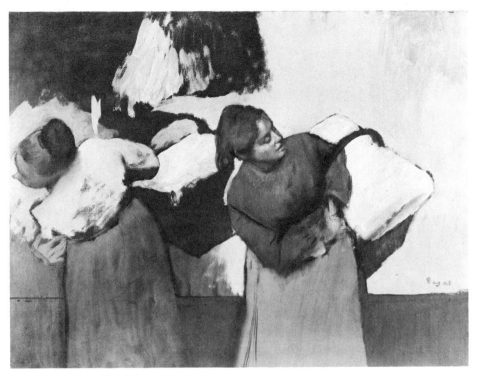

Laundresses Carrying Linen, c. 1878

muscles much in mind during these years, for in his *Laundresses Carrying Linen* the two women, despite their laden baskets, perform a stately back-to-back *pas de deux*, a proletarian pavane, that parallels the symmetry of the stretching girls in *Dancers Practicing at the Bar*.

After a period of relative neglect of racing scenes, he returned to them with éclat in *Jockeys Before the Start*, which is sometimes cited as an instance of the influence of photography on his art and is more instructively regarded as an example of his way of creating something new out of old and originally unrelated elements. All the jockeys and horses existed as part of the stock of pencil drawings he made during the 1860s in the Rue de Laval. Around 1868 the man in the center was promoted to the dignity of oil in *Jockey: The Red Cap*. (He reappears as a reversed mirror image in a painting of the mid-1880s.) Also around 1868, everyone was brought together in the oil *Racecourse Scene* and combined with a Channel coast landscape, the disquieting woman with field glasses, and an accompanying spectator who in one of the drawings had been Manet and in another Achille and had become Achille with Manet's beard. At some point after the Franco-Prussian War

Jockeys Before the Start, c. 1879

the woman with field glasses was painted out, the landscape, the horses, and the Achille figure were reworked, and the picture was finally abandoned as a mess. (It was cleaned and restored to a rather bleary version of its first state after an auction in 1959.) Around 1878, still haunted by the composition and what might be called its archaeology, the artist, now far more mature, took a fresh sheet of paper and went to work — this time in oil and *essence* with touches of pastel — on the present version. He eliminated the escort of the woman with the field glasses and one of the jockeys, tightened the drawing, accentuated the lack of symmetry, inserted a watery sun, transformed the landscape into a misty nowhere, pushed one horse partly out of the frame, deepened the space by adding a flagpole to the foreground, and came up with another of his convincing simulacra of glimpsed reality. And in the whole process a debt to nineteenth-century photographers is not very evident.

At about this time, however, he seems to have become more aware of what the camera could contribute to the study of movement. A notebook entry shows that he knew of an important illustrated article, written by the scientist Gaston Tissandier and published in the learned journal *La Nature* on December 14, 1878, that recounted the successful outcome of Eadweard Muybridge's recent attempts in California to photograph galloping and trotting horses. (The notebook reference may also indicate familiarity with another animal-locomotion piece, by the eminent physiologist and photographer Etienne-Jules Marey, which had appeared in the October 5 issue of *La Nature*.) Muybridge had been fascinated by the problem for several years, but his investigations had been interrupted by a series of equipment failures and by his trial, which had ended in acquittal, for the murder of his wife's lover. On the sunny morning of June 19, 1878, with a row of apparatuses activated by trip wires, he at last managed to produce a sequence of shots of the mare Sally Gardner, silhouetted against a white background, in various phases of rapid motion. The resulting pictures demolished a pictorial convention, for they showed the horse with its four feet quite close together when off the ground. Géricault disciples, racecourse lithographers, battle specialists, and other members of the outstretched-legs school were now told to mend their unscientific ways, and the force of nineteenth-century Positivism was such that only a few artists (Rodin was one of them) thought of pointing out that in art an illusion of equine speed might be better than photographic accuracy. Degas used the flying gallop once more, in his 1880 pastel *The Trainers* (probably on the basis of an older drawing), and then gave it up for good.

His notebooks for the second half of the 1870s reveal that he was far from spending all of every evening at the Café de la Nouvelle-Athènes.

There are reminders of dinner dates with the Rouarts and the Halévys and of the reservation of loges at the Opéra-Comique. Drawings of boxes and the stage curtain in the Palais Garnier indicate a successful transfer of affection from the old Opéra in the Rue Le Peletier to the new house, which had been inaugurated on January 5, 1875, with a potpourri obviously designed to assure conservative habitués and members of the Jockey Club that things were much as before: there was one act from Fromental Halévy's *La Juive* of 1835, a scene from Meyerbeer's *Les Huguenots* of 1836, and Eugénie Fiocre in a revival of the 1866 production of *La Source.*

Snatches of doggerel in the notebooks refer to several actors and actresses, including Réjane, at the Théâtre du Vaudeville and the Théâtre des Variétés, both of which were within walking distance of the Rue Frochot. Apparently the famous Comédie-Française actor Ernest Coquelin, called Coquelin Cadet because of an older brother, was also an acquaintance, for around 1878 he bought the *Laundresses Carrying Linen.* A large pencil sketch shows that Degas attended the literary salon of Madame Charles Hayem (a sculptor and the wife of a fashionable shirtmaker) in the company of Barbey d'Aurevilly. Two drawings of clowns are evidently souvenirs of a visit to the Cirque Fernando (renamed the Cirque Médrano at the end of the nineteenth century), which had opened in 1875 in a permanent amphitheater at 63 Boulevard Rochechouart, a block from Place Pigalle, and rapidly attracted a clientèle of Montmartre and Ninth Arrondissement painters, among whom Renoir and Degas were particularly fervent. Easily the most noticeable, however, of the many jottings and hasty images are more than thirty references to café-concert singers. And these were the accompaniment to a handsome, funny, astonishingly modern series, with new and slightly gamy subject matter, that got under way perhaps as early as 1875, existed in several media, and continued into the mid-1880s.

According to a tradition, the Parisian café-concert, or caf'conç', was born one night in 1770, when the proprietor of the Café d'Apollon, on the Boulevard du Temple not far from the Bastille, invited indoors a group of singers performing in the street. The formula of the future — a combination of low-priced drink with lowbrow entertainment — was present in that simple gesture. The institution really began to flourish, however, during the Second Empire, when it was encouraged by the carefree atmosphere of the *fête impériale,* by the patronage of chic slummers like the Princess von Metternich, and by the lifting of legal restrictions originally intended to protect the legitimate theater from possibly ruinous competition. In the last third of the nineteenth century, the French capital had, if one counts everything, perhaps two hundred café-concerts.

At the lower end of the scale were sinister little bars, referred to as *beuglants* (from *beugler,* to bawl in a bovine manner), that presented usually excruciating singers perched on a few planks. More respectable, in Belle-ville and other working-class quarters, was a type of caf'conç' that had something of the informality of a village inn. In the top category were fancy establishments like Les Ambassadeurs, the Alcazar, the Eldorado, and the Bataclan (named after one of Offenbach's early successes), which had stages and sizable orchestras and differed from music halls in having tables at which the customers could sit and nurse a mug of beer or an eau-de-vie with a cherry in it. The most fashionable were Les Ambassadeurs, which was housed in a Greek-columned pavilion in the gardens of the Champs-Elysées (the building is still standing), and the Alcazar — or rather the double enterprise so designated, for there was a warm-weather Alcazar d'Eté next door to Les Ambassadeurs and a cold-weather Alcazar d'Hiver in the Rue du Faubourg-Poissonnière on the eastern edge of the Ninth Arrondisse-ment.

Even in the top places the amusement was apt to be crude, the audience rowdy, the din nerve-destroying, and the ventilation almost non-existent: the young literary critic Jules Lemaître was struck by the "elemen-tary pleasantries, grimaces, contortions, and buffoonish mouthing,"[47] and the odor-conscious Louis Veuillot by the smell of "old tobacco pipes, leak-ing gas, and the vapor from fermented liquors."[48] It is clear, however, that there were sometimes compensations in the form of a raffish vitality, a disarming show-biz professionalism, and — if one had the appropriate sophisticated taste — a blend of vulgarity and silliness that transformed kitsch into irony. In the crowd there were usually some bourgeois top hats, and Lemaître was willing to enjoy "a salutary belly laugh" and a sense of "communion in the universal stupidity." As René had noticed in 1872, the songs were in general deliberately idiotic; some were sentimental ballads sung to waltz tunes, others were patriotic numbers that catered to the chauvinism that followed the French defeat of 1870, and the majority were comic ditties loaded with risqué connotations and punctuated by nonsense refrains. Among the enduring favorites of the period from the 1860s into the 1880s were "La Fleur des Alpes" (The Alpine Flower), "En revenant de la revue" (On Returning from the Military Review), "La Soeur du Pompier" (The Fireman's Sister), and "La Chanson du Chien" (The Song of the Dog), which the singer rendered while pawing the air in front of her breasts. Although Veuillot spoke of "small yelping voices and caterwauling," a writer in the magazine *La Vie parisienne* described a typical caf'conç' diva of 1878 as talented in other ways:

> [She is] very *female,* underlining indelicate passages with a gesture and a look and pretty movements of the arms. She has a special way of holding herself, a bit like a bird, her body leaning forward and seeming to offer itself.[49]

Many of these off-color canaries obviously had enough voice to belt out a melody above the clatter and chatter in the hall, and some had authentic musical talent. The soprano Marie Sass, for instance, began her career with double-entendres in the Café du Géant (so called because a nonsinging retired circus giant was long one of the attractions) and went on to triumph at the Opéra as the Elisabeth of Wagner's *Tannhäuser,* the Selika of Meyerbeer's *L'Africaine,* and the Elizabeth de Valois of Verdi's *Don Carlos.*

In his notes, sketches, and letters, Degas referred to four of the women singers: Dumay, Faure, Bécat, and Thérèsa. "Dumay" may have been Victorine Demay, though the identification is a bit shaky. Not much is known about Faure except that, according to a journalist, she had "a severe profile" and during the summer of 1879 sang "The Fireman's Sister."[50] Emilie Bécat was a girl from Marseilles who made her début at Les Ambassadeurs in 1875 and later appeared at the Alcazar d'Hiver; she is described in memoirs of the period as having created a sensation with an unusually inane marine ballad, "Le Turbot et la crevette" (The Turbot and the Shrimp), and as having inaugurated "the epileptic genre," which featured jumps, twists, convulsive arm-waving, and "wheedling, coarse gestures that always hit the mark."[51]

Thérèsa was one of the great representative figures of nineteenth-century France, a miracle of popular art, and a precursor of such music hall idols as Yvette Guilbert and Mistinguett. She arrived in Paris from her native Normandy in 1860, when she was twenty-three, worked for three years as a milliner under her real name, Emma Valandon, began to sing things like "The Alpine Flower" at the Café du Géant, switched to comic numbers at the Alcazar, and rapidly won an enthusiastic following, at all social levels, with her huge mouth, caressing voice, energetic plumpness, and such absurdities as "La Femme à Barbe" (The Bearded Lady), "C'est dans l'nez qu'ça m'chatouille" (It's in the Nose That It Tickles Me), and especially "Rien n'est sacré pour un sapeur" (Nothing Is Sacred for a Sapper). In Offenbach's hit operetta of 1866, *La Vie parisienne,* a Swedish tourist sings to the guide at the railway station:

> *Je veux, moi, dans la capitale
> Voir les divas qui font fureur,
> Voir la Patti dans Don Pasquale,
> Et Thérèsa dans le sapeur.*

(As for me, in the capital I want to see the divas who are all the rage, see Patti in *Don Pasquale,* and Thérèsa in "The Sapper.") The Second Empire had collapsed, the Prussians had bivouacked in the Bois de Boulogne, and Thérèsa, a little stouter and more insolent each year, sang on and on. "She is beautiful," Banville wrote, "in her ardor, her mettle, and her violence, and as far as possible from the adorable type."[52] Even Veuillot, the foe of caf'conç', was impressed, though he had reservations about her repertoire:

> She knows how to sing. As for her voice and her way of singing, they are impossible to describe, and so is what she sings. You have to be a Parisian to grasp the charm, a refined Frenchman in order to relish the profound, perfect ineptitude.[53]

In 1883 she returned to the stage after a short absence that had provoked demonstrations approaching riots, and Degas sent off an urgent note to the painter, collector, and violinist Henry Lerolle, who at the moment was lining up singers for a production of the French version of Gluck's *Orfeo ed Euridice:*

> My dear Lerolle, go right away to hear Thérèsa at the Alcazar, Rue du Faubourg-Poissonnière. It's near the Conservatoire. . . . Someone — I don't know what man of good taste — said long ago that she should be used in Gluck. . . . She opens her big mouth and out comes a voice that is the most roughly, the most delicately, the most wittily tender that exists. With soul, with taste. Where can one find anything better? It is admirable.[54]

In 1893 she made her last appearance before her still faithful public and retired to a farm she had purchased in Normandy; she felt that there was a time for everything.

The initiator of "the epileptic genre" is represented in action in *At Les Ambassadeurs: Mademoiselle Bécat,* with a high viewpoint provided by the balcony restaurant of the establishment (where the food was reportedly quite good) and with a poetic pattern of tonal values furnished by the grays and blacks of the lithographic medium, by the glare of footlights, and especially by the gas fixtures, called *globes lumineux,* which were one of the technological novelties of the late 1870s and were much appreciated because of the romantically diffused glow they produced. (Electric illumination was coming in only gradually, largely because of a lack of adequate power sources and partly because of a fear of sudden failure. The stage of the Opéra, for instance, was not equipped with it until 1887.) She appears again in *Two Studies of a Café-Concert Singer,* in which she can be easily imagined as making one of the indecent insinuations that in 1875 provoked the minister of fine arts, who at the time was the future premier Jules Simon, into a Comstockian diatribe against "these spectacles that are selling and distributing poison."[55] (A battalion of writers and painters immediately took up the defense of the caf'conç', and Simon quieted down.) Both works, along with a notebook sketch and a contemporary photograph, show her wearing the same Tyrolean outfit with ribbons around flared sleeves. Apparently she believed in repetition not only of mind-numbing nonsense refrains but also of image-creating costume and accessories — and by doing so she helped to launch a tradition that would include Yvette Guilbert's black gloves, Jane Avril's underwear, Maurice Chevalier's straw hat, and Edith Piaf's little black dress.

Few of the performers in Degas's series, however, can be identified as readily as Mademoiselle Bécat; and *Café-Concert Singer Wearing a Glove* is a warning against too much art-history factual explication. Although in a variant, or perhaps a preliminary version, of this extraordinarily cinematic painting there is a trellis that leads the viewer to think of an outdoor summertime performance at Les Ambassadeurs or the Alcazar d'Eté, in the present picture the realistic background has been eliminated in favor of a pattern of black, gold, gray, green, and red verticals that anticipates twentieth-century Abstractionism and reduces the setting to a brilliant nonspecificity. The open mouth, the distorting glare of the footlights, and the

Café-Concert Singer Wearing a Glove, 1878

OPPOSITE:
At Les Ambassadeurs: Mademoiselle Bécat, 1875–1877

The Café-Concert at Les Ambassadeurs, c. 1876

low viewpoint suggest an instantaneous close-up from a table pushed against the rail of the stage; the black glove, prophetic of Guilbert and Toulouse-Lautrec, could easily send a researcher off to the library to check in the periodicals of around 1878 for the name of the owner of such a definite image-making accessory. But in fact the view is from the floor of the studio in the Rue Frochot, and it is no use looking through the light-amusement literature of the period, since the model was Mademoiselle Alice Desgranges, a serious singer who evidently found posing as a caf'conç' diva good fun. We are in a universe of closely observed and imaginatively, ironically distanced reality.

In the quite different but equally fine *Café-Concert at Les Ambassadeurs,* the procedure at first glance looks simpler and more direct, partly because the setting is more detailed and hence presumably more real. Here the viewpoint has shifted from the bourgeois balcony used in the Bécat picture to the lower-class ground floor, where the artist-spectator looks across a group of loutish Daumier heads and a Degas double bass at a singer whose extended arm prolongs a diagonal of *globes lumineux* and whose nearest seated companion is flirting with someone in the audience. The identity of the singer raises a problem. Her dress, hairdo, round face, and substantial silhouette make her look like the Thérèsa of contemporary photographs and posters, but she is not named in the title or in comments on what was probably this picture at the third secessionist exhibition. And Thérèsa sang at the Alcazar, not Les Ambassadeurs. The same problem recurs, but in reverse form, in the diaphanous, light-drenched, superbly lowbrow, solemnly foolish *At the Café-Concert: The Song of the Dog.* Here, the woman, on the basis of the silhouette, has long and confidently been referred to as Thérèsa, though there is no record of Thérèsa's having sung "The Song of the Dog," and the beaked nose and horsy coiffure are not those of the Thérèsa of photographs and posters. One might guess that the woman is the Mademoiselle Dumay who is supposedly the subject of some notebook drawings and of four pastels, except that the silhouettes do not correspond and there is no documentary proof of the existence of a café-concert singer named Dumay. If we accept the hypothesis of a spelling error for Victorine Demay, who did exist, the silhouette discrepancy disappears, since, according to a critic, Victorine was a "copious person" who was "vast and cordial, opulent and gay."[56] But otherwise we are still in trouble, for Victorine reportedly had a button nose, not a beak, and she did not become prominent until the late 1880s, more than ten years after the painting of *At the Café-Concert: The Song of the Dog.* Thus the contradictory realities and the glinting ambiguities accumulate, until it becomes plain that Degas was an impresario who managed his own café-concert world, just as he managed his own racetrack and his own ballet. In the process the real Thérèsa became simply an archetypal figure, a Platonic idea of the caf'conç' diva, capable of assuming several different forms in his work.

The nearness of the new circus to the Rue Frochot might have led to another important series of pictures devoted to the flourishing realm of Parisian spectacle, but it failed to do so. Perhaps there were simply too many subjects on hand, during these years, in the form of horses, danseuses, prostitutes, bathers, laundresses, and singers. It did, however, stimulate Degas to do several drawings, a lithograph, and in particular a sizable oil, *Miss La La at the Cirque Fernando,* which is among the artist's most striking and complex achievements. With Renoir's *Two Little Circus Girls* of the same year, it is also an inviting prelude to the many acrobats and clowns painted around the turn of the century by Toulouse-Lautrec, Seurat, Bonnard, Picasso, and Van Dongen. Miss La La, whose family name may have been Kaira, was a pretty, curved mulatto performer who was billed as "the Black Venus" and "the Cannon Woman" and whose feats were dependent on the astonishing strength of her teeth and jaws. In one of her numbers she hung by her legs from a flying trapeze and held in her mouth a long chain, on which a small but real cannon was ceremoniously suspended and then fired. In another she grasped the end of a pulley rope between her teeth and allowed herself to be hauled and whirled up into the dome of the building, three stories above ground level, to the accompaniment of an exciting drum roll from the Fernando band.

Degas chose to depict her near the climax of this second stunt. From notebook pages and dated drawings it is evident that he watched her intently on the evenings of January 19, 21, 24, and 25, 1879, and that he had trouble finding the pose that would convey her soaring movement and the strain on her jaws: in one sketch she turns toward the viewer, and in another, a variant of which he adopted for the painting, she gyrates into a *profil perdu,* with most of her face invisible and her legs and arms indicating a leap from one of the classical ballet starting positions. The architectural setting — a stone, iron, and glass polygon that mixed Baroque columns and brackets with something like Gothic vault ribs — raised additional problems for him, not only because of its complicated pattern of shapes and lines but also because, though he had seen many decorated ceilings in Rome, he had no practical experience with the type of neck-stretching, frog's-eye perspective the Italian old masters had called "from below upward," *sotto in sù.* He therefore did a number of studies without La La, warned himself on one of them that "the trusses are more inclined," and at last felt obliged (as he later confessed to his friend Walter Sickert) to call in one of the professional mathematical *perspecteurs* who were available for

At the Café-Concert: The Song of the Dog, 1875–1877

Miss La La at the Cirque Fernando, 1879

consultation by perplexed painters. All these preparations included notes on color, some of which were probably inspired by the contemporary French chemist Michel-Eugène Chevreul, whose "law of simultaneous contrast" stated that adjacent complementaries enhanced each other. In any event, the completed oil obeys this "law"; La La's costume pairs yellow with violet, and in the gaslit background a cool greenish blue helps to intensify a warm, roughly complementary reddish orange. (That current scientific color theory was sometimes a topic at the Café Guerbois and La Nouvelle-Athènes can be inferred from Duranty's remark, in his review of the Salon of 1870, that the red portrait of Madame Camus "would make a very appropriate frontispiece for Monsieur Chevreul's treatise.")

The outcome of the whole extremely deliberate process of looking, sketching, annotating, remembering, and elaborating is a seemingly instantaneous image that updates the *sotto in sù* illusion of the Ascensions and Assumptions in the domes of seventeenth-century Italian churches and at the same time irreverently breaks the illusion, since an instant of concentration on the prominent rope transforms the aerial divinity into a pathetic human mackerel, flapping on a hook. Once again, as in many of the dance pictures, an underlying theme is the eternal comedy of appearance and reality. That Degas liked circus mummery, that he admired the skill of the performers, and that he saw in their frequent acceptance of a dangerous equilibrium an analogy with his own discipline cannot be doubted. One day at the Cirque Fernando, as reported by Moore, he said to a landscape painter, "For you, natural life is necessary; for me, artificial life."[57] But he was far too sophisticated to overlook the paradox that the artificial had to reveal itself as such in order to yield the characteristic pleasure of the artificial, and so he was always alert to the giveaway detail — the obviously daubed stage flat, the ludicrously earthbound ballerina, and Miss La La's rope.

16. Defections and Quarrels

UNDAUNTED BY IMBECILIC LAUGHTER and unfair press notices, some of the veterans of the group exhibitions of 1874, 1876, and 1877 decided early in 1879 to stage a fourth display the following spring. A suitable location was discovered around the corner from the Théâtre des Italiens at number 28 of the still new Avenue de l'Opéra, April 10 and May 11 were fixed as the opening and closing dates, and the *courtier* Alphonse Portier, whom both Monet and Degas liked and trusted, was engaged to give the enterprise a professional business management. Caillebotte again proved generous with his time, energy, and money. The old question of a label provoked merely a mild discussion before being settled by the substitution, at Degas's insistence, of the neutral term "Independent" for the provocative "Impressionist" that had been used to announce the 1877 show. The usual atmosphere of the planning sessions was altered, however, by the absence of Morisot, who was pregnant, and by the decision of Cézanne, Sisley, and Renoir to abandon their comrades and return, if possible, to the official Salon. Degas and Monet were still unshakably attached to the group's rule against exhibiting simultaneously with the Establishment and with the secessionists.

The defection of Cézanne was not particularly surprising; he had always been something of an outsider. He had preferred the literary and musical evenings arranged by the bohemian Nina de Callias to the arguments of the aestheticians at the Guerbois, and he sometimes, as described disapprovingly by Duranty in a letter of 1878 to Zola, turned an appearance at La Nouvelle-Athènes into a piece of individualistic bravado:

> If it interests you, Cézanne showed up recently at the little café in Place Pigalle in one of his olden-time costumes — blue overalls, an ancient bashed-in hat, and a white linen jacket covered all over with blobs of paint from brushes and other instruments. He had a great success. But such demonstrations are dangerous.[1]

In 1874 the author of "such demonstrations" had been accepted by the organizers of the first exhibition only because of Pissarro's warm advocacy; in 1876 he had abstained because of a sudden (and temporary) ethical objection to exhibiting in a place owned by a dealer; and in 1877 his participation had been a principal cause of hoots from visitors and of exasperation from critics. By 1879 his tendency to be apart from the group was strengthened by the first signs of a stylistic evolution that would lead him into an ever deeper rejection of Monet's flickering luminosity in favor of an essentially French classical — although modern — art of structures, forms, planes, and deep color harmonies. And to all these reasons for a break with the Impressionists can be added a growing confidence in his powers that was the inner counterpart of his external eccentricities, his Olympian rages, and his frequent surliness. As early as 1874 he had written to his mother, "I know that [Pissarro] has a good opinion of me, and I have a very good opinion of myself. I am beginning to find myself stronger than everyone around me."[2]

Sisley, unlike the relatively well-off Cézanne, had purely economic motives for defecting. His family's fortune had vanished in the maelstrom of the Franco-Prussian War and the Commune, his sales to Durand-Ruel had almost ceased since 1877 because of the merchant's own financial difficulties, and efforts to earn a living through the small gallery of Père Martin and auctions at the Hôtel Drouot had produced a drastic lowering of prices. On March 14, 1879, the unhappy artist explained his situation in a letter to Théodore Duret (who had become the apologist for the avant-garde by publishing a pamphlet entitled *The Impressionist Painters*):

> I am tired of vegetating in the way I have been doing for such a long while. The moment has come for me to make a choice. It is true that our group exhibitions have served to make us better known, and in that respect I believe they have been very useful for me. But we must not, I think, isolate ourselves any longer. The time is still distant when one will be able to do without the prestige of the official exhibitions. I have therefore decided to send something to the Salon. If I am among the accepted — and there is a chance this year — I think I'll be able to do some business.[3]

The hope of being able to do some business was based in part on the increasing activity of Georges Petit, a young art dealer who in 1878 had taken over a family enterprise dating back to the reign of Louis-Philippe and had shown a disposition to wean the Impressionists away from the temporarily embarrassed Durand-Ruel, provided that the painters first went through the reassuring ritual of being accepted by the Salon jury.

Renoir had left the secessionist camp shortly after the third group exhibition and had managed to get one of his portraits into the Salon of 1878. In a later letter to Durand-Ruel he indicated that his desertion had not troubled his conscience:

> In Paris there are scarcely fifteen collectors capable of liking an artist who is not in the Salon. There are eighty thousand who will not buy a nose if its painter is not in the Salon. . . . Ah, if one could accuse me of neglecting my art, of sacrificing my ideas because of a stupid ambition, I would understand the criticism. But since I cannot be accused of such things, there is nothing to be said against me. . . . My sending a work to the Salon is entirely a commercial operation. And in any event it's like certain medicines: if it doesn't do any good, at least it doesn't do any harm.[4]

The explanation was short on candor, for it failed to point out that its artisan-class author was at the moment in the midst of a flattering, remunerative, nearly irresistible embrace by the current version of the cultivated *grande bourgeoisie.* In 1875 after a sale at the Hôtel Drouot he had met the publisher Georges Charpentier, whose firm supported the Naturalist school of novelists and whose wife, Marguerite, the daughter of a prominent Second Empire jeweler, maintained a brilliantly unconventional salon at which one was apt to encounter the Comédie-Française actress Jeanne Samary, the stag-hunting Duchesse d'Uzès, the politicians Clemenceau, Ferry, and Gambetta, and the writers Maupassant, Zola, Goncourt, Flaubert, Alphonse Daudet, and Huysmans. At the beginning of 1879 Madame Charpentier, with her husband's aid, had launched an illustrated weekly, *La Vie moderne,* and an art gallery of the same name situated at the corner of the fashionable Passage des Princes and the Boulevard des Italiens. By this time Renoir had become what he called, in an ironical play on seventeenth-century court terminology, "the Painter in Ordinary" of the Charpentiers and their circle, with a steady flow of commissions for portraits, fancy mirror frames, interior decorations, and special dinner menus.

In spite of the defections, what was billed as "A Group of Independent Artists" opened the exhibition in the Avenue de l'Opéra on schedule, with fifteen painters listed in the catalogue: Bracquemond, his wife, Caillebotte, Cals, Cassatt, Degas, Forain, the Seine specialist Albert Lebourg (invited by the business manager Portier), Monet, the landscapist Ludovic Piette (a recently deceased friend of Pissarro's), Pissarro, Rouart, the illustrator Henry Somm, Tillot, and Zandomeneghi. At the last minute, too late for the printed catalogue, a sixteenth exhibitor was added when the thirty-year-old Paul Gauguin, recruited by Pissarro and Degas, showed up with a statuette. Degas himself, according to the catalogue, contributed twenty-five items, including *Miss La La at the Cirque Fernando, Laundresses Carrying Linen, At the Bourse, Jockeys Before the Start, Café-Concert Singer Wearing a Glove, Danseuse Posing in a Photographer's Studio,* and the portraits of Martelli, Duranty, and Halévy with Boulanger-Cavé. One wonders, however, whether all the things listed were ever actually seen by visitors, for at the end of the first day Caillebotte reported to Monet, who had not come into town from Vétheuil for the opening ceremonies:

> No need to tell you that there were some pieces of insane behavior. Don't believe, for example, that Degas sent in his twenty-seven or thirty items. This morning there were eight canvases by him on hand. He is indeed vexing. But you have to admit that he has a lot of talent.[5]

Although Pissarro showed thirty-eight works and Monet twenty-nine, Impressionism was very much a minority tendency in the exhibition as a whole. Moreover, there were enough items other than paintings on view to give the proceedings something of the flavor of an arts-and-crafts section at a county fair: Marie Bracquemond, for instance, exhibited a colored faience plate, her husband four etchings, Caillebotte a series of decorative panels for small boats, Degas five decorated women's fans, Gauguin his statuette, Pissarro eleven fans, and Somm an engraved calendar.

The total of paying visitors for the month came to nearly sixteen thousand, which constituted a record and also meant that each member of the cooperative emerged with a profit of 439.50 francs instead of the expected deficit. Press comment was mostly of the usual hostile or merely lukewarm sort, but with a few variations. In *Le Figaro,* Wolff added a patronizing tone to his denunciation:

> In the past these raging maniacs called themselves Impressionists. They have changed the word without changing the thing. . . . As for Monsieur Degas, he once had some talent. His sketches are certainly not the work of a mere nobody. If a young man of twenty had signed them, one would predict a future for him. But now Degas is in the declining years of his career without having taken a step forward. . . . The misfortune of this school is to refuse to learn anything — to elevate ignorance to the level of a principle.[6]

In a new letter from Paris, published in Russian in the Saint Petersburg *Messenger of Europe,* Zola pointed out the growing influence of the Impressionists' brushwork and high-keyed palette on Salon painters and then commented briefly on the exhibition in the Avenue de l'Opéra: "We saw there the work of Degas, who paints with astonishing truthfulness the people of our contemporary world, and that of Pissarro, whose conscientious research sometimes produces the effect of a veritable hallucination of verity."[7] Huysmans, in an essay that eventually appeared in his volume *L'Art moderne,* noticed above all Degas's technical virtuosity:

> A remarkable, intrepid kind of painting that addresses itself to the imponderable, to the breath of air that lifts the gauze on a danseuse's tights. . . .
> A kind of painting that is learned and yet simple, that is interested in the boldest and most complex bodily postures . . . and that, in order to give the exact sensation of the eye following Miss La La as she climbs to the top of the Fernando by the strength of her teeth, dares to make the circus ceiling lean wholly to one side.[8]

In the third issue of *La Vie moderne* Silvestre praised the *Laundresses Carrying Linen* and *Jockeys Before the Start,* and announced that, with the exception of Degas, everyone in the show was at "the stammering stage" of artistic development.[9]

The Salon jury rejected the pictures submitted by Cézanne and Sisley and left the latter feeling, as he told Charpentier, "more isolated than ever."[10] Renoir, however, pleased the academics with his monumental, carefully pyramidal, uncharacteristically sober *Madame Charpentier and Her Children,* and promptly found himself being welcomed back into the Establishment as a returning — and properly repentant — prodigal son. In the conservative *Revue bleue* the critic Charles Bigot spoke of a sinner who "has been converted,"[11] and in *L'Art* Charles Tardieu commented, "Impressionism is cleaning itself up; it is putting on gloves. Soon it will be dining in town."[12] The welcome was followed by a one-man show in the Charpentier gallery, an enthusiastic article in *La Vie moderne* written by Renoir's brother Edmond, an invitation to a château in Normandy, and a number of commissions for portraits. Monet thereupon decided in his turn to desert the band of secessionists and rejoin the Salon; and on March 8, 1880, he sent off the ritual letter of explanation to Duret:

> I'll be running a big risk, not to speak of the fact that I'm now being treated as a quitter by the entire group. I think it's in my interest to take the chance, for I am almost certain of doing some business, notably with Petit, if I can force the door of the Salon. But none of this is to my taste. It is indeed regrettable that the press and the public have failed to take seriously our little exhibitions, which are much to be preferred to the official bazaar.[13]

As if to underline the risk he was running, he added that at the moment, in the hope of being accepted by the jury, he was working on a picture that was "more discreet, more bourgeois" than the kind of painting he really wanted to do. [14]

Although this new defection left only three members of the core group of 1874 — Pissarro, Degas, and Morisot — in the battle against officialdom, plans went ahead for a fifth exhibition of "Independent Painters," which was scheduled to open on April 1, 1880, in an apartment at 10 Rue des Pyramides that offered a possibility of drawing visitors from the nearby Louvre. In a letter to Bracquemond, evidently written around the middle of March, Degas accused Monet of contemplating a campaign of "frantic self-puffery" with the help of *La Vie moderne,* and revealed that even among the secessionists there was a weakness for personal publicity:

> The posters will be up tomorrow or Monday. They are in bright red letters on a green background. There was a big struggle with Caillebotte over including names. I had to give in to him and let them appear. When will we stop playing at being star actors? . . . It's idiotic. Taste and every kind of solid reason were completely unavailing against the inertia of the majority and the stubbornness of Caillebotte. . . . Next year I'll certainly see to it that this sort of thing does not continue. I feel stricken, humiliated. [15]

Such a passionate opposition to what was, after all, a normal practice in the announcing of exhibitions may have looked like sheer contrariness to Caillebotte. But Degas was being consistent with his love of privacy, his feeling for the dignity of art, and his frequently expressed contempt for every sort of *arrivisme.*

Finally eighteen artists agreed to take part in the show. Impressionism, or something fairly close to it, was represented by Pissarro, Caillebotte, Gauguin (who had not yet developed his personal aesthetic), Guillaumin, Lebourg, and Morisot. The relatively conservative faction comprised Bracquemond, his wife, Cassatt, Degas, Forain, Levert, Rouart, Tillot, and Zandomeneghi, to whom were added three recruits: Raffaëlli, the Corot disciple Victor Vignon, and the portraitist Eugène Vidal, who was a pupil of Gérôme's and a friend of Lebourg's. Tactlessly, for a newcomer to the group, Raffaëlli — Gafferelli to his enemies — took over a large section of the available wall space with no fewer than thirty-five oils and watercolors. Degas went on record as contributing twelve items, among which were some dance pictures and several clustered drawings and etchings. But he seems to have been caught unprepared once more by the opening date, for one of his entries — strange, in a presumed display of vanguard tendencies — was the twenty-year-old and still unfinished history painting *Young Spartan Girls Provoking the Boys,* another was a mysterious wax statuette, titled *Little Dancer of Fourteen Years* in the catalogue,

Edmond Duranty, 1879

which materialized as merely an empty glass case, and another was *At the Bourse,* which had been shown, or at least listed, in the Avenue de l'Opéra in 1879. Later the portrait of Duranty was also put on view again — this time as a last tribute, for he died shortly after the start of the exhibition.

Although attendance was down from the year before, the visitors laughed a bit less, the critics showed more selectiveness in their comments, and Degas emerged with his reputation considerably solidified. Huysmans, in one of the essays collected in *L'Art moderne,* remarked that "this artist is the greatest we have today in France," likened him to Baudelaire, Flaubert, and the Goncourts, and praised the portrait of Duranty in terms that echoed the dead Realist's pamphlet of 1876:

> Needless to say, Monsieur Degas has avoided the stupid backgrounds painters love — the scarlet, olive green, adorable blue curtains, or the spots of purplish red, greenish brown, and ash gray that are such monstrous tatters of reality. For a person should be portrayed at home, in the street, in an authentic environment, anywhere except in a glossy layer of meaningless colors. Monsieur Duranty is there, in the midst of his prints and his books, seated at his writing table. And as I look at this canvas . . . his tapering, nervous fingers, his keen, mocking eye, his sharp, searching expression, his pinched look of an English humorist, and his dry little laugh into the stem of his pipe all come back to me.[16]

Charles Ephrussi, a thirty-year-old banker, boulevardier, collector, and art expert who had recently become acquainted with the Impressionists (he is the top-hatted man in the far background of Renoir's *Luncheon of the Boating Party*), wrote in the *Gazette des Beaux-Arts* (of which he would become the owner in 1885):

> Consider Monsieur Degas. He chooses typically skinny little danseuses with uncertain shapes and disagreeable, repulsive features; he gives them movements without harmony. Over these bizarre subjects he spreads subtle colors and a delicate light that covers the floor and the stage sets. His tone values are of an astonishing exactitude that puts each thing in its plane, in spite of a frequently whimsical perspective. . . . The painter remains distinguished in the midst of the ugliness of his figures. . . . And one has only to look at the drawings on yellowish paper of busts of women, and at a study of a head, to see that Monsieur Degas is both an estimable draftsman and a pupil of the great Florentines, of Lorenzo di Credi and Ghirlandaio, and above all of a great Frenchman, Monsieur Ingres.[17]

In a new pro-Gambetta daily, *Le Voltaire,* Zola analyzed with sympathy the defections of Renoir and Monet and decided that Degas alone had profited from the secessionist shows:

He was never one of the persecuted in the official Salon. His efforts were accepted and relatively well displayed. However, he has a delicate artistic temperament, he does not impose himself with great power, and so the public walked past his pictures without seeing them. Quite legitimately irritated, he saw how much he would gain from a little chapel in which his subtle, carefully wrought works could be viewed and studied separately. And in fact, now that he is no longer lost in the Salon mob, he has become very well known. A circle of fervent admirers has gathered around him. [18]

Even the unscrupulous, toadying Wolff, again using the columns of *Le Figaro* to dismiss most of the exhibitors as fools and charlatans, managed to deliver a backhanded compliment by inquiring, "Why does a man like Monsieur Degas linger in this collection of nonentities?" [19]

Unlike Renoir, Monet did not gain much from his return to the Establishment fold. Only one of the pictures he submitted to the Salon jury was accepted, and it was the almost academic *Lavacourt,* which he himself had described as bourgeois and which violated his Impressionist principles, having been executed in the studio on the basis of earlier works. Shortly after the closing of the Salon he exhibited eighteen canvases in a one-man show at the Charpentier gallery (arranged probably with the help of Renoir) and made a single sale — to Madame Charpentier. But these setbacks did not shake his conviction that he was on the right aesthetic path, nor did they contribute to an improvement in his extremely strained relations with his former comrades in the secessionist camp. Asked by a reporter from *La Vie moderne* whether he had ceased to be an Impressionist, he replied:

> Not at all. I am still an Impressionist, and I intend to remain one. . . . But I now see my colleagues, both men and women, only very rarely. Today the little church has become a commonplace school that opens its doors to the first dauber who comes along. [20]

One of the "daubers" he had in mind was evidently Raffaëlli, and another was possibly Gauguin, whose ego was becoming rougher and rougher as his talent matured.

When the time came round to think about a possible sixth exhibition of the Independents, Caillebotte decided that the infiltration by second-rate painters had to be stopped, that the original exhibitors had to be persuaded to take part again, and that it would be necessary to call a spade a spade and a factionalist a factionalist. On January 24, 1881, in a long letter to Pissarro, [21] he boiled over:

> Degas has brought disorganization among us. Unfortunately for him, he has a bad character. He spends his time orating at the Nouvelle-Athènes, when he would be much better occupied in turning out a few more pictures. No one denies that he is a hundred times right in what he says and that he talks

about painting with infinite wit and good sense. (And isn't all that the clearest part of his reputation?) But it is still true that the real argument of a painter is his painting. . . . Today he says he needs to earn a living, and he will not grant that Renoir and Monet have such a need. . . . No, this man has gone sour. He does not have the high rank his talent entitles him to, and he blames the entire earth, although he will never admit that he does. He pretends that he wanted to have Raffaëlli because Monet and Renoir had defected and we had to have someone. But he has been tormenting Raffaëlli to join us for the past three years. . . . In 1878 he brought in Zandomeneghi, Bracquemond, Madame Bracquemond. . . . What a phalanx of fighters for the great cause of Realism!

The letter went on to accuse the alleged factionalist of having "almost a persecution mania" and of attacking "everyone in whom he sees some talent," and concluded sadly:

> All this profoundly grieves me. If art were the only matter at issue between us, we would always be in agreement. Degas is the one who has raised a question on another terrain, and it would be stupid to allow ourselves to be troubled by his madness. True, he has an immense talent. I am always the first to proclaim myself his great admirer. But that's all. As a man, referring to Renoir and Monet, he has gone so far as to ask me, "Do you invite such people to your home?" As you can see, although he has a great talent, he does not have a great character. And now let me sum up. Do you want an exhibition that is simply artistic? . . . If Degas wishes to join us, let him do so, but without all those people he drags along with him.

Predictably, Degas refused to drop Raffaëlli and the other infiltrators, Pissarro balked at the idea of dropping Degas, and anyway Cézanne, Sisley, Renoir, and Monet showed no intention of rejoining the secessionists. So the only practical result of the incident was that Caillebotte in his turn became a defector.

His diatribe nevertheless calls for some corrective comment. The assertion, for example, that Degas spent most of his time talking instead of painting was demonstrably false, and irrelevant to boot. The allegation that he alone had "brought disorganization among us" was also easy to rebut, for though he had certainly done his best to persuade relatively conservative non-Impressionists to join what had been the Batignolles group, their participation in the exhibitions was not the real, nor at first even the ostensible, reason for the departure of four of the original members. Moreover, the moral indignation in the letter was somewhat misdirected, since, in spite of the difficult financial situation created by the failure of his family's bank and the vanishing of his expected inheritance, Degas had not been one of those who had lost their nerve, deserted their comrades, and compromised themselves artistically by defecting to the *pompiériste* Establishment. He had not run off looking for a handful of silver and a ribbon to stick in his coat, nor had he descended to planting homemade self-glorification in the pages of *La Vie moderne* and making snide remarks about daubers for the amusement of the journal's more conservative readers.

In short, what he had been guilty of was mostly an extreme kind of cantankerousness. To a degree, of course, he had long had this fault, or at least something like it. In Rome in 1858, when he was only twenty-four, he had been for the Tournys "a little bear" and "the Edgar who growls," and by 1863, according to Didy Musson, he had acquired a reputation for being "very brusque." From Caillebotte's explosion and from the quarrel over the posters, however, it seems that the rather amusing morosity and the Romantic spleen of the young Edgar had become, in the Degas of the 1880s, something far more serious and exasperating — a combination of irascibility, touchiness, and obstinacy that does indeed suggest a personality "gone sour." Confronted by the spectacle of Renoir and Monet seduced by the phoniness of the official Salon, he could not bring himself to be charitable, and when sufficiently provoked he lapsed into the ready-made scorn of a *grand bourgeois* for "such people" (though it should be noted that he remained on good terms with the anarchist Pissarro). Extravagantly, he declared himself "stricken" and "humiliated" simply because his fellow exhibitors liked seeing their names in red letters on the walls of Paris, and in the argument over the participation of Raffaëlli he indulged in what was close to mulishness for its own sake.

A bad disposition (which is what the French expression *un mauvais caractère* usually means) is nevertheless not the same thing as a bad character, and Caillebotte was unfair in failing to make the distinction. Degas, in a phrase of Pissarro's, was "a terrible man, but frank, upright, and loyal."[22] He was also generous, in spite of his need to watch his purse, and both his loyalty and his generosity were evident during these months of bickering between former allies. Having been named the executor of Duranty's will, he participated actively in the organization of an auction at the Hôtel Drouot for the benefit of the widow, who had been left nearly destitute. Monet, Cassatt, Pissarro, Cazin, Desboutin, Forain, and Fantin-Latour eventually donated works for the sale, and Zola furnished an introduction for the catalogue, praising Duranty as "one of the direct continuators of Stendhal." Degas, besides writing letters to drum up interest in the enterprise, made the most substantial of the concrete contributions — a pastel study for the large portrait of Duranty, a drawing and a pastel of danseuses, and one of the versions of the woman looking through field glasses, all of which meant a thousand francs in cash for Madame Duranty.

During these months he was also putting the finishing touches to his

Little Dancer of Fourteen Years, the statuette that had failed to appear in its waiting glass case at the exhibition of 1880. The model was a Belgian girl named Marie Van Goethen (or perhaps van Goethem) who performed as a *petit rat* at the Opéra, frequented the Nouvelle-Athènes, and lived at 36 Rue de Douai, in the Ninth Arrondissement a few blocks from the Place Pigalle café. Since she is recorded as having been born on February 17, 1864, Degas presumably began work on the sculpture — or on the preliminary studies for it — some time during 1878 or very early 1879. Following established academic procedure, he first made a series of drawings from the nude, and with these as a guide he modeled in red wax a small maquette he seems to have altered for a good while: cracklike lines and an imprint still visible in the bronze version reveal, for instance, that he tilted the head farther back, pulled the arms and clasped hands away from the hips, and changed the position of the turned-out right foot. After calling in the model for a dozen more drawings, this time in her dance costume, he

Little Dancer of Fourteen Years,
1880–1881

produced a final wax version about two-thirds life-size, painted the imitation flesh, and provided the figure with real ballet slippers, real silk stockings, a real tutu of white gauze, a real bodice of white linen, and real hair braided into a pigtail tied with a green satin ribbon. (The real Marie prided herself on her black hair and insisted on wearing it hanging down her back during classical numbers at the Palais Garnier.)

There were precedents for nearly all of this. Painters, among them Tintoretto, Poussin, and Meissonier, had frequently resorted to wax figurines as aids in working out complex compositions, and sculptors had long employed wax as an auxiliary substance in the making of preliminary sketches for carving or of models for casting. Since at least the fourth century B.C., according to Pliny, this humble material, theoretically less noble than marble or bronze and yet marvelously suitable for reproducing delicate anatomical details and skin transparencies, had also been used for relatively permanent works, especially those in which the intention was not so much to create art as to simulate the appearance of life — death masks and royal funeral effigies, for instance, and eventually the personages in waxwork museums of the Madame Tussaud sort. An equally respectable tradition, strong in both Classical Greece and Gothic Europe, sanctioned polychromed sculpture and the addition of real accessories, and among nineteenth-century artists the tradition had occasionally reappeared: the Neoclassical John Gibson, for example, provoked Londoners in 1862 with his *Tinted Venus,* the Salon regular Jean-Baptiste Clésinger loaded his painted marble *Cléopatre* of 1869 with real jewelry (designed by the imperial goldsmith, Emile Froment-Meurice), and Gustave Moreau, experimenting in three dimensions during the late 1870s, wrapped a wax Salomé in a real linen mantle. Even the choice of a teen-age subject, though not very common, had some historical and contemporary justification, notably in Donatello's *David,* which Edgar had sketched during his Italian tour, and in Paul Dubois's Second Empire — and charmingly neo-Renaissance — *Florentine Singer of the Fifteenth Century,* which, after winning a medal at the Salon of 1865, became one of the sculptural best sellers of the century in the form of bronze, terra-cotta, wax, and Sèvres porcelain reductions.

None of these precedents, however, could have been of much help to an ordinary Third Republic viewer of the *Little Dancer of Fourteen Years,* for Degas had given everything in the tradition an extra turn of the screw. He had smeared his figure's real slippers, stockings, and bodice with a thin layer of hot wax, which after hardening had partly integrated the disparate substances in the work and at the same time had set up a characteristic play between appearance and reality, since the actual cloth was visible through the film of wax, and the hair, tutu, and green ribbon were left unsmeared.

A sufficiently lively and philosophical imagination could extend the ambiguity into one concerning art and life, for the obviously real costume implied that the rest of what was beneath the wax surface was also real. Thus the ancient sculptural rule of truth to material was turned inside out, nineteenth-century Naturalism was transformed into a prenotion of twentieth-century psychological Hyperrealism, and appreciators, the hostile ones included, were led quite naturally into the use of "she" instead of "it" when referring to the statue.

And "she" was as equivocal as her raiment and flesh. Her bony body, made almost disjointed by balletic exercises, was no longer that of a girl and not yet that of a woman; her pose was at once snooty, awkward, adolescent, and beautifully taut, like a wound-up crossbow ready to be fired. The rigid arms and locked hands, forced into a position hard to hold for more than a few seconds, added to the impression of an emotional strain or a partly repressed paroxysmal excitement. The uplifted, thrusting, strangely Cro-Magnon face and the half-closed eyes implied aggressiveness, anguish, sexual hunger, and several other supposedly unmaidenly feelings, in addition to evoking the age-old association of wax modeling with death masks and funeral effigies. (It should be remembered that some of this expressiveness is lost in the bronze casts now exhibited in European and American museums.) In short, Eros and Thanatos were once again united, and the result could scarcely have been farther from Dubois's sweetness or Donatello's relaxed, meditative heroism.

Since this startling, perverse masterpiece is unique in Degas's output (and in the history of sculpture), guessing at the psychic process behind it involves accepting a narrow time span along with the usual restrictions on such operations. A possible although very general stimulus was Daumier, part of whose brilliantly unconventional achievement as a sculptor was revealed in a retrospective exhibition at Durand-Ruel's in 1878, shortly after Marie Van Goethen's fourteenth birthday. Delacroix may also have counted, in some inadmissable, darkly Freudian, Eros-and-Thanatos fashion; during that same season the gallery put on view his fifty-year-old *Death of Sardanapalus,* in the foreground of which a nude about to have her throat cut is arched into a pose faintly similar to that of the *Little Dancer.* Speculating about such hints, however, is less pertinent than noticing that Degas during this period seems to have been thinking a good deal about fresh females and artists' puppets or lay figures. His surprising decision to enter the *Young Spartan Girls Provoking the Boys* in the group show of 1880 is part of the evidence, and another part is his portrait of the painter Henri Michel-Lévy, which was begun in 1878 and was scheduled for the secessionist exhibition of the following spring, though it was not done in time to be hung. Michel-Lévy, who was a wealthy publisher's son, a collector of eighteenth-century art, and the possessor of an extremely modest, vaguely Rococo talent, is represented as an introvert with his back to the wall, both figuratively and literally, in the posture he had adopted for *Interior* ten years earlier, and his evident disillusionment is projected into a fully clad, nearly life-size female dummy slumped grotesquely next to him after having served as a model for one of his partly visible pictures — and perhaps as a studio companion. Degas was in an entirely different situation in terms of gifts and career, but he clearly had his own sort of projection impulse, for during the long months when he was patting and smearing the *Little Dancer* into a simulacrum of reality, and attentively dressing her naked adolescent body, she acquired perceptible echoes of his sexual preoccupations, his troubled "me," his growing misanthropy, and even his recorded physical persona, with its nose-in-the-air imperiousness, its veiled glare, and its chest-forward, arms-back stance. Possibly she was not quite, as a depth psychologist might imagine, his ersatz mistress. But she was unmistakably his daughter.

While the patting and smearing were proceeding, obviously not without difficulty, the planning for a sixth group show was advancing, in spite of the absence of Sisley, Cézanne, Renoir, Monet, and Caillebotte, and space was being prepared in an annex to Nadar's old headquarters at 35 Boulevard des Capucines, where the historic first display of Impressionism had been staged seven years earlier. The new exhibition opened on April 2, 1881, with the thirty participants of 1874 now reduced to thirteen — Cassatt, Degas, Forain, Gauguin, Guillaumin, Morisot, Pissarro, Raffaëlli, Rouart, Tillot, Vidal, Vignon, and Zandomeneghi — and nearly all of the original esprit de corps dissipated. The incorrigible Raffaëlli, with thirty-four oils, pastels, and watercolors, did his best to convert the affair into a one-man spectacle. Gauguin, increasingly drawn toward a career as an artist, though continuing to speculate actively and for the moment very successfully at the Paris Bourse, appeared with eight paintings, one of which was owned by Degas, and two small pieces of sculpture. Cassatt, now in her stride, sent in some fetching variations on the mother-and-child theme that suggested a frustrated personal interest in maternity. Degas contributed, according to the catalogue, a picture of a laundress, two studies of criminals' heads (evidently inspired by a still lively fascination with pseudoscientific physiognomy), four portraits of unidentified sitters, and the *Little Dancer,* but once again he failed to meet the organizers' deadline.

Three days after the opening the columnist Jules Claretie reported in *Le Temps:*

Henri Michel-Lévy, c. 1878

Monsieur Degas . . . was supposed to exhibit a danseuse modeled in wax. Up to now we have seen only the glass cage destined to receive and protect the statuette, which is said to be charming. He has delivered some curious drawings, but we are lying in wait for his sculpture. And he is enough of a teaser not to send it.[23]

Five days later in *Le Figaro* Wolff resumed his patronizing compliments of the year before, added a few new insults, and finally dismissed Degas as merely the *dieu des ratés,* the god of failures, all without giving any sign of having seen the *Little Dancer:*

> He is the standard-bearer of the Independents. He is the leader, he is fawned upon at the Café de la Nouvelle-Athènes. And thus, to the end of his career, he will reign over a little circle. . . . Frankly, he could have aspired to a higher destiny. However.[24]

An anonymous reporter for *La Chronique des Arts et de la Curiosité* had already noted, the year before, that the glass case was "admired . . . for its magnificent simplicity."[25]

At last, like a stage star delaying an entry for the sake of the effect, she appeared, and she did produce an effect, even on those who did not like her. "Artistic Paris," Mrs. Havemeyer recalled, "was taken by storm."[26] The critic and caricaturist Charles Bertall told the readers of *Paris-Journal* of having found "groups of adepts, of male and female nihilists, fainting with rapture in front of this danseuse and her muslin skirt."[27] Forty years later the painter Jacques-Emile Blanche remembered having seen Whistler among the enraptured: "He was wielding a painter's bamboo mahlstick instead of a walking stick; emitting piercing cries; gesticulating before the glass case that contained the wax figurine."[28] In *Le Temps* Claretie, after a second visit to the exhibition, announced, "The vicious muzzle of this little, barely pubescent girl, this little flower of the gutter, is unforgettable." In the same newspaper two weeks later Paul Mantz, who as a fine arts administrator and a mainstay of the *Gazette des Beaux-Arts* was among the most influential critics of the nineteenth century, published a long article that mixed profound distaste with grudging admissions of quality:

> She is frightening because she is mindless. With bestial effrontery, she thrusts forward her face, or rather her little muzzle, and the word is entirely appropriate, for this poor little girl is an incipient *rat*. Why is she so ugly? Why is her brow, half covered by her hair, already marked, as are her lips, by such a deeply vicious character? Monsieur Degas is without doubt a moralist. Perhaps he knows things about the danseuses of the future that we do not know. He has plucked from the espalier of the theater a flower of precocious depravity, and he shows her to us, faded before her time. The intellectual result is there. The bourgeois citizens allowed to contemplate this wax creature remain stupefied for a moment, and one can hear fathers

shouting, "Heaven forbid that my daughter should become a danseuse!" There is, however, something in this disagreeable figurine that comes from an observant and sincere artist. . . . Monsieur Degas has dreamed of an ideal ugliness. O happy man! He has realized his dream.[29]

The more ferociously conservative Elie de Mont, writing in *La Civilisation,* likened the figure to a real rat, a monkey, an Aztec (which in colloquial French has the pejorative connotation of "a little shrimp"), and an expelled fetus, and concluded, "If she were smaller, one would be tempted to pickle her in a jar of alcohol."[30] In *Le Constitutionnel,* a daily with a lingering prestige derived from having once published Sainte-Beuve's articles, Henry Trianon decided that Degas had fallen ill with "the modish malady" of Naturalism and would soon recover.[31] In a new evening paper, *Le Courrier du soir,* Nina de Villars warmly defended both the danseuse and the sculptor:

> You have to suffer to acquire the aerial lightness of the sylph and the butterfly. Now here is the sad reality of the métier. The grubby, sickly face is contorted with effort. . . . Before this statuette I experienced one of the most violent artistic impressions of my life — and something of which I had long dreamed. Seeing in village churches the Virgins and saints in painted wood, covered with ornaments, fabrics, and jewels, I had asked myself why a great artist had not had the idea of using these charming, naïve procedures to produce a powerful modern work. Now I find my notion realized, and it's a real joy.[32]

Huysmans, recording his reactions for his *Art moderne,* took much the same leap from medieval or folk artlessness to nineteenth-century artfulness, and added a few cuffs for Neoclassicism and academicism:

> The terrible reality of this statuette produces an evident uneasiness in spectators. All their ideas about sculpture, about cold, lifeless whiteness, about memorable clichés copied again and again for centuries, are upset. The fact is that, with a first blow, Monsieur Degas has knocked sculptural tradition head over heels, in the same way that he has long since jolted painting conventions. . . . Like certain colored and dressed Madonnas, like the Christ in the cathedral of Burgos, whose hair is real hair, whose thorns are real thorns, whose drapery is a real fabric, Monsieur Degas's danseuse has a real skirt, real ribbons, a real bodice, real hair. . . . At once refined and barbarous, with its tinted, throbbing flesh marked by the movement of the muscles, this little statue is the only truly modern attempt I know of in sculpture.[33]

That such appreciation was not limited to a few avant-garde intellectuals is clear in a complaint in *La France nouvelle* of May 2 about the number of "idiots in ecstasy" before the "little Nana."[34]

Although no buyer appeared for the work, Degas seems to have benefited immediately in his other activities as an artist. His sister Thérèse, in Paris on a long visit during the summer of 1881, reported back to the palazzo in Naples that "Edgar has become a celebrated painter whose pictures are being snapped up."[35]

Success did not make him any more tractable when, toward the end of the year, negotiations were opened on the possibility of a seventh group exhibition. Caillebotte, after failing in an attempt to use the good will of Rouart, wrote to Pissarro, "Degas will not drop Raffaëlli, for the sole reason that he is being asked to drop him."[36] Gauguin came to the same conclusion, and on December 14 wrote to Pissarro (who during this period was usually at Pontoise):

> [Because of Degas] the situation has been getting worse and worse: each year an Impressionist has left the group and been replaced by a cipher or a product of the Ecole des Beaux-Arts. In another two years you will be alone in the midst of phonies of the worst sort. All your efforts will be ruined, and Durand-Ruel along with them. In spite of my good will I cannot go on being made a fool of by Monsieur Raffaëlli and company. So please accept my resignation from the group. . . . I think Guillaumin intends to do likewise, but I don't want to influence him.[37]

At last, very reluctantly, Pissarro agreed to proceed without Degas, and Caillebotte set about organizing a show that would by-pass the rule against sending something to the Salon and could therefore include Monet and the other recent defectors. But then it immediately became apparent that Degas and his infiltrators had not been the only problem. At the beginning of 1882 Eugène Manet wrote to Berthe Morisot, who was at Nice, "I have just had a visit from the terrible Pissarro, who talked to me about your next exhibition. These gentlemen do not seem to be in agreement. Gauguin is playing dictator."[38] By the end of January, Caillebotte was ready to abandon the project.

Durand-Ruel thereupon decided to attempt to organize the exhibition himself, partly in order to end the bickering among his artists and largely for imperative personal reasons. In 1880 he had resumed his massive buying of paintings, Impressionist ones included, with the help of loans from his friend Jules Féder, a director of the rapidly expanding Union Générale bank. On January 19, 1882, in one of the most resounding *krachs* of a period well supplied with financial scandals, the Union Générale collapsed, the police started to look into Féder's affairs, and Durand-Ruel suddenly found himself obliged to pay back his borrowings. His situation was rendered all the more dangerous by the activities of his most enterprising rival,

Georges Petit, who was preparing at this very moment to open (with encouragement from Jules Grévy, the president of the Republic) a palatial new gallery near the church of the Madeleine, in the center of the new quarters à la mode. The gallery of La Vie moderne in the Boulevard des Italiens was also very active, and it was using effective, if not exactly élitist, promotional methods: it had recently, for example, put on a show of Easter eggs painted by Madame Charpentier's favorite artists, presented some of Manet's oils and pastels against a background of rare Oriental wall hangings (borrowed from a friendly rug merchant), and staged, for the benefit of flood victims in Spain, an exhibition of tambourines decorated by Renoir, de Nittis, Manet, Lepic, Carolus Duran, Giovanni Boldini, and Sarah Bernhardt.

Pissarro, with his usual sensitivity and loyalty, responded immediately to his merchant's predicament. "For Durand-Ruel," he told Monet, "and even for us, the exhibition is a necessity. And for my part I would be very unhappy if I could not answer his request. We owe him too much to refuse him this satisfaction."[39] But some of the other potential exhibitors were much less generous in their reactions. Cézanne pretended that he had nothing on hand worth showing. (In fact, he had in mind the possibility of getting into the Salon with the help of his friend Guillemet, who was now a member of the jury.) Degas automatically excluded himself by continuing to insist on the participation of the rejected Raffaëlli. Cassatt and Rouart refused out of allegiance to Degas. Monet did not want to exhibit alongside Gauguin, Guillaumin, and Vignon, whom he detested. Morisot was reticent because she thought Monet would back out. Manet, who in the Salon of 1881 had at last won a medal, was in no mood to join an anti-Establishment operation. The usually good-natured Renoir, suddenly fearful of compromising himself with his new bourgeois patrons by being seen in the company of the anarchist Pissarro and the socialist Guillaumin, composed a nasty letter (but perhaps did not mail all of it) to Durand Ruel, mixing rightism with anti-Semitism and a neurotic dread of becoming the victim of a conspiracy:

> The public doesn't like what smells of politics, and at my age I don't want to be a revolutionary. To remain with the Jew Pissarro is to join the revolution. Also, these fellows know that I have made a lot of progress because of the Salon, and their idea is to hurry up and make me lose what I've gained. They will neglect nothing for that, and then abandon me when I am down.[40]

Patiently, Durand-Ruel worked to overcome the hesitations. Monet eventually came down off his high horse, and Gauguin stopped playing dictator. Renoir, apparently a little ashamed of himself, recovered his sunny disposition, accepted Pissarro, and even suggested, in vain, that "the elusive Degas" should be included in order to round out "an interesting artistic display."[41] Space was rented at 251 Rue Saint-Honoré on the site of the vanished Bal Valentino, where the eighteen-year-old Edgar had danced in the costume of Pierrot; and at the beginning of March the show was inaugurated with the participation of Caillebotte, Gauguin, Guillaumin, Monet, Morisot, Pissarro, Renoir, Sisley, and Vignon.

In an odd play-acting way it was the seventh and most coherent, most successful exhibition of the originally cooperative "society" of anti-Establishment secessionists. Durand-Ruel remained discreetly in the background (partly in order to avoid alarming his conservative clients by flagrant association with radicalism); Alphonse Portier again assumed the role of business manager, at least ostensibly; and the posters and catalogue, in spite of some scattered protests, again called the artists *les Indépendants*. Degas, although not exhibiting, insisted on keeping up the fiction of solidarity by paying his dues to the "society." The critics, Wolff included, were less hostile than usual, and a few new buyers were unearthed. But the commercial-gallery aspect of the event was perfectly evident, since most of the pictures on view were from Durand-Ruel's large stock of Impressionist works, and no one was under any illusions about the durability of a unity recovered mostly because the dealer was in trouble.

17. Media

T HE *Little Dancer of Fourteen Years* was the only sculpture by Degas
that was exhibited during his lifetime. Nevertheless his friends
were aware that he did a good deal of modeling, mostly in wax,
and in 1917 after his death about a hundred and fifty dusty,
crumbling little pieces, or fragments of pieces, were extracted from the
clutter of his last studio. Seventy-four of them, the only ones that appeared
salvageable, were entrusted to the founder Adrien Hébrard, who during
the next few years produced twenty-three remarkably exact bronze casts of
each piece. It was long assumed that the originals had been destroyed in
the casting. In 1955, however, nearly all the waxes, the *Little Dancer*
included, were discovered in the cellar of Hébrard's house on the Ile de la
Cité in Paris, and it became clear that the foreman of the foundry, an
ingenious and conscientious Italian craftsman named Albino Palazzolo, had
used duplicates during the *cire-perdue* (lost-wax) process. Thus, owing to
the concern of outsiders and not at all to that of the artist himself, at least
some of what was probably a large sculptural output was rescued for pos-
terity and given a relatively permanent form.

Critics and the official art world were slow to see the importance of
this three-dimensional achievement, partly because Degas was thought of
as a painter merely amusing himself with sculpture and because of the sizes
of the samples, for although the *Little Dancer* is a quite respectable ninety-
nine centimeters high the average for the other statuettes is well under fifty

centimeters. In 1946 the *Bulletin* of the Metropolitan Museum of New York, reverting to the criteria of the Ecole des Beaux-Arts of the 1870s, dismissed the bronzes as "unfinished sketches" that could not be regarded "as serious works in sculpture in the academic sense of the word."[1] During the following decades appreciation became considerably warmer, and by the 1970s it was not uncommon to find an art historian classifying these "sketches" with the work of Auguste Rodin and Medardo Rosso as examples of protomodern modeling. But this approach had the defect of underplaying some affinities with the Classical tradition and with the Romanticism of the age of Barye, Carpeaux, Daumier, and Dalou; and so today the tendency is simply to recognize that Degas was a great nineteenth-century sculptor with an extraordinary inclination to experiment.

Thirty-eight of the seventy-four surviving pieces are danseuses, fifteen are horses, two are jockeys, fourteen are more or less bathroom scenes, three are portraits, and two can be put in the genre category, so the scarcity of documents for dating might seem compensated for by analogies with datable paintings. The *Arabesque Over the Right Leg, Left Arm in Front,* for example, goes reasonably well with a picture like *The Rehearsal,* which Goncourt saw during his studio visit of 1874; *The Tub* recalls a pastel of around 1886; and the *Horse at Trough* looks like something from about 1866–1868, when Fiocre in *La Source* was being painted. Dates based on such analogies are rendered extremely shaky, however, by occasionally contradictory collateral information, by the lack of any indication that Degas used his figurines as aids in his painting, and above all by his habit of repeating, sometimes at intervals of many years, a set of motifs accumulated in the form of drawings. The chronology of the supposed early pieces is particularly uncertain, for there is no reliable external evidence of a date prior to 1878 and Marie Van Goethen's fourteenth birthday. In fact, it is not altogether improbable, although the majority of scholars have assumed otherwise, that the *Little Dancer* was his first serious attempt at sculpture. The large number of preparatory drawings, the signs of fumbling and revision in them, the existence of an altered nude maquette (left slightly botched in the pelvic area), and the three years devoted, off and on, to the project all suggest a lack of previous experience. So does Huysmans's remark about having knocked down sculptural tradition "with a first blow." The frequently published assertion that statuettes of horses preceded those of human beings gets some support from the parallel with the steed in *La Source* and from Degas's friendship before 1870 with the animal specialist Cuvelier. But it is finally just one more undocumented guess, and it is weakened by a letter of around 1882 to Pissarro from Gauguin in which the latter implies a very recent turn toward equine subject matter. "Decidedly," he writes, "the craze for sculpture is growing. Degas, it seems, is doing horses."[2]

Although "craze" may have been too strong, there was certainly a lot of interest in sculpture among French painters in the late 1870s and early 1880s. During these years Moreau executed a dozen characteristically ornamented and strangely decadent statuettes. Renoir began modeling around 1878 and within a couple of years became proficient enough to turn one of his plump women into a medallion for Madame Charpentier, who displayed it as part of a mirror frame in her apartment across the street from the Louvre. By about 1881 Pissarro was doing three-dimensional cows. Gauguin exhibited marble portraits of his wife, Mette, and their son Emil in the secessionist show of 1880, a terra cotta of a woman in street costume in 1881, and a polychromed wax and wood bust of his three-year-old son Clovis in 1882. A similar urge manifested itself even among academic painters: Gérôme, for example, surprised his clientèle by displaying at the Salon of 1878 a plaster *Anacreon with the Child Bacchus and Cupid,* and he then embarked on a series of horses, nymphs, and goddesses, in some of which he attempted to revive the chryselephantine technique of Phidias by using ivory for flesh, marble for garments, and bronze mounts for attached jewelry. The whole trend was reinforced, in radically different ways, by retrospective exhibitions of the work of Barye and Carpeaux, both of whom died in 1875, by the revelation of the sculpture of Daumier, by the appearance at the Salon of 1878 of Rodin's scandalously lifelike *Age of Bronze,* and by the return of Dalou from London to Paris in 1880, after the new French government's proclamation of an amnesty for former Communards.

Many of the recent pieces were rather unsculptural compromises between a desire for contemporaneity and a conflicting traditional notion of what sculpture was and did. The various shades of literary or pictorial Realism and the slogan *il faut être de son temps* had not proved compatible with the implications of eternity in monumental marbles and bronzes; sculpted frock coats and crinolines, in spite of Baudelaire's talk about the heroism of modern life, tended to look silly in competition with the universality of the nude statue, and the specificity of portrait busts and genre groups seemed to point inevitably toward painterly effects and *tableaux vivants.* When Dalou, at the Salon of 1870, had exhibited his *Embroiderer,* which represented a woman in contemporary dress seated on a Second Empire chair, even the pro-Realist Castagnary had had a moment of uneasiness: "Is this sculpture? Or is it rather to be looked at as a painting? Sculpture, I have said, is nourished on general ideas, and here we have only a particular idea."[3]

An obvious answer to such conflicts and misgivings was to avoid being big and pretentious. This course was especially advantageous because of a flourishing bourgeois demand for bibelots, so-called *bronzes d'art,* and other portable works of indoor sculpture. In fact, the market was such that the most important people in the history of French sculptural taste during the second half of the nineteenth century were not creative artists at all but entrepreneurs of a sort brilliantly represented by the founder Ferdinand Barbedienne, who made a fortune and became a commander of the Legion of Honor by specializing in editions of reductions of Renaissance, eighteenth-century, and contemporary statues — in almost any material the customer was willing to pay for, from gold down to lead or terra cotta.

In 1874 the sensibility that had created the market received a well-timed fillip from Hellenistic Greece in the form of the discovery at Tanagra, in northern Boeotia, of a large cache of terra-cotta figurines dating mostly from the early third century B.C. The best of them, executed in a flowing, sensuous style that showed the lingering influence of Praxiteles, were colored effigies of smartly draped girls and young women captured in moments of light reverie, of passing melancholy, of domestic puttering, or of flirtatious sauntering under parasols and little pancake hats. They were delightful Attic sisters of Kiyonaga's Edo courtesans and geisha and of the typically Parisienne belles and *cocodettes,* the Ellen Andrées, who had become popular during the Second Empire, and so they had been rapidly, enormously successful in the France of the Third Republic. The word *tanagréenne* had been added to the vocabulary required for up-to-date café and drawing room conversation, and within a few years the figurines had begun to be extensively and expertly forged (in ways often hard to detect, since the originals had all been manufactured with molds).

By the late 1870s Degas had long been sensitive to this cultural pattern of multiple copies, parlor statuary, middle-class naturalism, and the attractiveness of the antique, and he continued to be so during the following decade. Immediately after his return from his Grand Tour of Italy he had jotted down the address of Barbedienne's Paris ateliers, in the Rue de Lancry near the Boulevard de Magenta, and he eventually acquired several Barbedienne bronze reductions of Barye's animal sculptures. The correspondence of 1875 concerning the exhibitions in the New Bond Street gallery in London is evidence of his friendly relations with and warm admiration for the exiled Dalou. A notebook in use in Naples during the spring of 1860 contains a surprisingly non-Phidian comment on a visit to the local museum: "How can one forget that the art of antiquity, the strongest of the arts, is also the most charming?"[4] And when the Rouart brothers, some time around 1880, began to collect *tanagréennes,* Degas quickly became an enthusiast: he planned and partly executed a double portrait of Madame Henri Rouart and her daughter Hélène centering on one of the figurines and showing Hélène in a Tanagra-type costume and pose — which would have repeated the visual conceit of the 1869 picture in which a shadow cast by a porcelain statuette was made to resemble the willowy silhouette of Madame Camus. He even managed to use the Hellenistic figures as examples of what he meant by Greek Classicism in general, and he sometimes did this in ways that seemed deliberately provocative and paradoxical. "Daumier," he once remarked when he was in the mood, "had a real feeling for the antique. He understood it to such a point that when he depicted Nestor [it was actually Mentor] pushing Telemachus, he drew as they would have at Tanagra."[5]

A sharing of period taste did not, however, keep him from projecting his own vision of humanity, movement, time, space, and sex into the sculptures he began to turn out in considerable quantity after the success — the *succès de scandale,* at any rate — of the *Little Dancer of Fourteen Years.* In *The Schoolgirl,* which he probably executed or at least began during the summer of 1881, the alert, tilted, softly hatted head resembles that of Ellen Andrée (who may have been the model) in the right side of the *Project for Portraits in a Frieze;* the shifting of the weight of the body to one leg recalls, despite the absence of the furled-umbrella pivot, the poised disequilibrium of Mary Cassatt in the Louvre; the hand behind the back comes from Degas himself; and the whole image of pigtailed, awkward, assertive female adolescence suggests a Marie Van Goethen dawdling and dreaming of unmentionable activities on her way to her dance class in the Palais Garnier.

A characteristic interest in the complexities of animal locomotion appears in *Horse Galloping on Right Foot,* which is clearly related to Muybridge's photographs and may be one of the pieces referred to by Gauguin in the letter to Pissarro. (Muybridge himself visited Paris in 1881 and 1882 and presented his studies at receptions arranged in part by Meissonier.) In the *Arabesque Over the Right Leg, Left Arm in Front,* which, in spite of the analogy with the two-dimensional *Rehearsal,* is impossible to date with any certitude, the idea of the critical or fruitful moment, of the arrested posture that concentrates implications of both past and future action, is combined with a fanlike occupation of space that could only be hinted at in the comparable oils, pastels, and drawings. The artist's familiar fascination with unusual viewpoints that insinuate the presence of a hidden spectator reaches a rare pitch of voyeuristic delectation, datable to about 1889, in *The Tub,* which is one of the few pieces of nineteenth-century sculpture,

Horse Galloping on Right Foot, c. 1882

The Tub, c. 1889

tomb slabs aside, that has to be looked at from directly above instead of being faced or circumambulated.

In the decade between the *Little Dancer* and *The Tub* there were two particularly memorable sculptural disasters. The first involved a clay bas-relief, about half life-size, that represented some young girls picking apples and that at one stage must have been very promising, for Renoir remembered it many years later as having been "as handsome as the antique."[6] Degas worked on it during part of the summer of 1881, using as models his niece Anne Fevre — one of Marguerite's five children — and his Neapolitan cousin Lucy de Gas, who had come up to Paris on a visit with her guardian, Thérèse Morbilli. During the following winter months, when Anne and Lucy were no longer available, he tried to keep the clay in a plastic condition by moistening it regularly with a syringe; but he had other tasks, so he eventually stopped squirting and let the whole thing dry out and disintegrate. Today all that remains of the project is a small wax sketch (plus the bronze casts of it by Hébrard), in which it is difficult to make out either apples or girls.

And the second disaster is even sadder to contemplate, for from it nothing at all has survived. The affair began around the beginning of September 1884, in Paul Valpinçon's Norman château at Ménil-Hubert, where Degas had been making one of his usual summer visits. Madame Valpinçon, partly as a trick to get him to prolong his stay, urged him to model a portrait of her daughter, Hortense, now grown up and about to be married. He accepted the challenge, began a head in clay, and soon found himself struggling with a life-size, half-length statue. A few days later he wrote to Henri Rouart:

> I shall eventually return to Paris, my dear friend, bursting with health after one of the longest periods in the country I can remember. The reason is a huge bust of the young Hortense, with arms, which I have undertaken and which I am finishing very patiently and painfully. The whole family and their friends are watching me. . . . My God, how I floundered at first! We know very little what we are about when we don't let a bit of métier intervene. It's no use telling ourselves that with naïveté one can do everything. Perhaps one can, but very messily.[7]

The next report went to Ludovic Halévy, who had been expecting Degas to join him for a holiday at the Halévy family's seaside villa in Dieppe:

> I am being kept here until the end of the week, or rather I am keeping myself here, in order to finish a bust with arms. It's a long job, although extremely amusing. And the interest manifested in what I am doing strongly resembles malignant curiosity, which makes me go at it tooth and nail to produce a good likeness, and even something more.[8]

On September 15 the now thoroughly engrossed modeler wrote to the painter (and future sculptor) Paul-Albert Bartholomé:

> In order to keep busy I began to toil at a big bust with arms, in clay mixed with little pebbles. . . . In short, one amuses oneself only with what one doesn't know how to do, when one is as badly balanced as I am.[9]

On October 3 another letter to Bartholomé revealed that the piece was coming along:

> There are two arms, as I have told you; and it should be enough for you to know that naturally one of them, the one of which the hand is visible, is behind the back. I am perhaps the only person to whom this seems a very good idea.[10]

The dénouement, as recounted long afterward by Hortense herself, took place during the last week of October. Having finished the modeling, Degas decided to make a cast with ordinary local plaster instead of waiting for special sculptor's material to arrive from Paris — and he wound up by shattering both the clay bust and the cast. He kept a fragment of the figure in his studio for a while, but finally it too fell apart.

Although such mishaps could be attributed partly to ordinary negligence and partly to the exasperating friability of unfired clay, behind them there was also the stance of an accident-prone *bricoleur* — a word for which such usual English translations as "jack-of-all-trades" and "handyman" are not quite adequate. The true *bricoleur* does not just make do; he prefers to make do. He enjoys turning materials and devices to uses for which they were not intended; he rejects the easy, orthodox approach. Since he is often more interested in the process, in the *bricolage* itself, than in the product, he has an irresistible itch to tinker, repair, modify, and metamorphose. He is a problem-solver, to the point of creating problems for the pleasure of solving them. And in all these respects Degas (along with many other great artists) was an inveterate *bricoleur.*

In order to be able to work rapidly and to alter poses at will, he built up his smaller pieces of sculpture over flexible armatures made of wire, hemp, and metal rods, and when arms and legs, after much yanking to and fro, began to show signs of cracking and sagging, he reinforced them with matchsticks that merely postponed the final collapse of the whole structure. He liked plasteline, a slow-to-harden modeling material made from clay mixed with wax or oil, but because of its cost he usually employed it in combination with ordinary wax; and the different drying rates of the two materials hastened deterioration. Frequently, in the hope of creating bulk and tensile strength cheaply, he filled out a mass of wax and plasteline with corks, which ultimately worked their way to the surface and left holes behind them. Sometimes he also incorporated string, cloth plugs, and bits of sponge. When such methods did not prove fatal, his impulse to revise might assert itself. Vollard recalled a typical example of its destructiveness:

> One day he said to me of a *Danseuse* that was in its twentieth transformation: "This time I've got it. One or two more short posing sessions and Hébrard can come." The next day I found the *Danseuse* again reduced to the state of a ball of wax. Confronted by my astonishment, Degas said, "You think above all, Vollard, of what it was worth. But if you had given me a hatful of diamonds, my happiness would not have equaled what I have had from demolishing that work for the pleasure of starting over."[11]

Everything considered, perhaps we should be surprised by the survival of any figurines at all.

The turn toward sculpture in the 1870s and 1880s was accompanied by a burst of interest in the production of monotypes, etchings, drypoints, and lithographs. This too was in line with a trend among painters: Pissarro, Cassatt, and Fantin-Latour, among many others, were experimenting with printmaking during these years. The movement became an organized one in 1889 with the foundation of the Société des Peintres-Graveurs Français. (Throughout the second half of the nineteenth century French artists were extraordinarily addicted to the creation of *sociétés,* so much so that one can imagine some sort of separation anxiety provoked by the breakup of the old system of centralized, paternalistic patronage and the need to face the new reality of the free-market system.) Degas, however, was exceptional in being able to combine an enthusiasm for reproduction media with a growing taste for the serialization of subject matter and an already existing delight in the arcana of all sorts of professions, from ironing shirts to executing *entrechats* and singing double-entendres.

Although monotype had been explored ("invented" is a bit fancy for such a simple technique) in the middle of the seventeenth century by the Genoese painter and etcher Giovanni Benedetto Castiglione, about the only major artist attracted to it during the intervening two hundred years had been the very unconventional William Blake. A common procedure called for drawing on glass or smooth metal with oil paint and pressing a sheet of absorbent paper onto the plate by pushing with one's hand or sitting on the joined elements. (Usually there not being enough pigment left for a second impression justified the term "monotype.") Degas employed a variant of this method for some colored landscapes he produced in the 1890s, but for the rest of his two hundred catalogued monotypes he laid down the designs in black or brown ink on copper or zinc and then ran plates and paper through a roller press of the type used for etchings. Sometimes he covered a plate with greasy printer's ink and roughed out images in white or gray by wiping with a brush, a rag, or a finger; sometimes he resorted to line-drawing directly on the bare metal in india ink; and more often than not he mixed the reverse and positive, the dark-field and light-field, techniques. His papers ranged from ordinary white stock through cream, light beige, brownish gray, and sepia, and also through several varieties — laid, rice, wove, Dutch, Chinese, and Japanese. At some point in his career, perhaps in the 1870s, when he was at the peak of his fascination with all kinds of printmaking, he acquired his own etcher's press, an old-fashioned mostly wood mangle set on a Tuscan colonnade and equipped with a massive spider-wheel for forcing the traveling bed and plate through the rollers. (The whole apparatus, in what looks like working order, is preserved in the Musée de Montmartre, at the top of the Butte, along with a similar press used by Auguste Delâtre in the 1860s.)

He executed his first monotype, a study of Jules Perrot during a ballet rehearsal, in 1874 in collaboration with Lepic (both artists signed the plate), and during the next few years he turned them out in clusters — sometimes at the rate of half a dozen a day — on such expected themes as the dance, the theater, the brothel, the café-concert, the bathroom, and the unending spectacle of Parisian street life. By July of 1876 he was so caught up that Desboutin, himself mostly a drypoint fanatic, reported from the French provinces to Madame de Nittis, who was in London:

> I'll give you only a bit of news about our friends, about those who were still in Paris when I left. . . . Degas was the only one I saw every day, and he is no longer exactly a friend, he is no longer a man, he is no longer an artist. He is just a zinc or copper plate blackened with printer's ink, and this plate-person is laminated by his press to the point of disappearing entirely between its rollers. The infatuations of this man are really phenomenal. He has reached the metallurgical phase in the reproduction of his drawings by means of the rollers and is running all over Paris (in this heat!) in search of the branch of industry that suits his obsession. It is altogether poetic.[12]

In many of the most effective of the brothel scenes the influence of Ingres and of Neoclassicism has receded to such an extent that the viscous ink and the slippery, unretentive plates are allowed to produce foretastes of the harsh inchoateness of German twentieth-century Expressionist work and Georges Rouault's hideous strumpets. But the irony excludes anything like the German sociopolitical angling or Rouault's religious moralizing, and much of the same sort of irony permeates another first-rate series, the twenty-seven monotypes pulled toward the end of the 1870s and intended as illustrations for an edition of Halévy's account of the adventures of Monsieur and Madame Cardinal and their dancing daughters in the Paphian world of the Paris Opéra. The prints were not used in the book until nearly sixty years later, and probably the principal reason for the initial refusal was that Halévy thought them too unrelated to specific incidents in the story. But he may also have found their Daumier-like quality a little too strong, for at the moment he was in his own work moving away from satire. And when he published the first part of a moralizing, sentimental novel, *The Abbé Constantin,* in the *Revue des Deux Mondes* in 1882, he remarked in his diary concerning his friend:

> He is disgusted with all that virtue, all that elegance. He was insulting to me this morning. I must always do things like *Madame Cardinal,* dry little things, satirical, skeptical, ironic, without heart, without feeling. He called me "Father Halévy." [13]

At the third secessionist exhibition, in 1877, Degas showed three monotypes, which were listed without titles as "drawings done in greasy ink and printed." [14] (He disliked the term "monotype.") In general, however, the results of this branch of his activity were reserved for a small number of acquaintances, who were often printmakers, or for his own pleasure. He obviously relished the unusual textures, the dashed-off look, and the rich variety of gradations of tone from light to dark that sometimes emerged when he gave the big spider-wheel of his press a heave. And the *bricoleur* in him probably also liked the fact that the whole operation was as aleatory as making a soufflé. Moreover, the possibilities did not end with the first print: often he ran a plate through the rollers a second time or even a third, and many of the proofs served as foundations for works that are usually appreciated as examples of other media. His *Ballet Lesson on Stage,* for instance, is a combination of monotype, pastel, and gouache, and *The Café-Concert at Les Ambassadeurs* is a pastel that owes part of its vigor and nonchalance to its having been built up over a monotype.

Between 1856 and about 1863 he had produced twenty-three etchings, at first with Prince Soutzo in Paris, then with Tourny in Rome, and then on his own in the kitchen in the Rue de Mondovi. After that he had lost interest in needles and acid. During the winter of 1875, however, he did a drypoint portrait of Alphonse Hirsch, and this marked the start of another spell of intermittent engraving that lasted until shortly after 1880 and yielded twenty-one works (plus many states) in half a dozen intaglio techniques. Hirsch was a young painter and etcher who had a knack for getting along with everyone: he was a loyal former pupil of Bonnat's, an intimate of Wolff's, a frequenter of Impressionist circles, and a half-professional *courtier* who specialized in helping — for a commission of 10 per cent, according to Goncourt — busy speculators at the Bourse who yearned to become art collectors. He had a house in the Rue de Rome near the Gare Saint-Lazare, with a pleasant garden in which Manet had posed Victorine Meurent and Hirsch's little daughter while painting *The Railroad.* Degas is said to have done the drypoint on February 20 during something like a copper-plate portrait-making competition between himself and Hirsch, Desboutin, and de Nittis, organized by Desboutin and the critic and print-fancier Philippe Burty. There is no record of who won.

Drypoint had long been favored by painter-printmakers and other semiprofessional engravers, since in principle it is the simplest and most direct of the intaglio processes: you scratch the bare sheet of copper with a steel or diamond-tipped tool, and that's that — there is no biting with acid. Moreover, as some of the details in the portrait of Hirsch reveal, when the plate is sufficiently scored the point throws up a metal burr that holds the ink and prints a warm, rugged, velvety line well calculated to appeal to a painterly sensibility. Degas, however, was much too aware of the poetry in crafts — of *poiesis* in the original Greek sense of the making of something — to limit himself to a single method. In a second state of the portrait (notably for the cravat and the jacket) and in thirteen other prints produced during this period, he resorted to aquatint, a process in which transparent tones, similar to those in a wash drawing, are obtained by biting the plate with acid through a porous ground of granulated resin.

After the mid-1860s he did just one work that is only in the classical hard-ground etching technique, the kind in which a needle produces something comparable to a line drawing by cutting through a resist and exposing the copper to the bite of a mordant. But there are many examples of his use of this method in conjunction with others, and there are several instances of soft-ground etching, in which the acid-resist is left in a tacky condition and can be removed in the desired areas simply by being pressed with a drawing instrument or, if texture is wanted, with fabrics, leaves, and so forth. Some time around 1879 he supplemented these traditional processes with a personal one, which he invented, or improvised, at Alexis Rouart's house in the Boulevard Voltaire, a thoroughfare opened during the Second Empire in what was then an industrial suburb on the easternmost side of Paris. Degas had come for dinner and stayed the night because of suddenly icy streets that made returning to the Ninth Arrondissement in a horse-drawn conveyance nearly impossible. The next morning, eager to get some work done, he turned out a sort of etching, *Woman Leaving Her Bath,* with the aid of a carbon rod from an arc lamp he discovered in Rouart's factory next door. (The lamp was probably one of the efficient new ones, called Jablochkov candles from the name of their Russian inventor, that in 1879 were beginning to be used for street lighting in the French capital and other European cities. One of Degas's letters suggests their use also in the secessionist exhibitions.) Pleased by the silvery tonality and the brushed texture that resulted from this piece of *bricolage,* he adopted what he called "electric crayon" as one of his regular media.

One of the few prints, however, in which this novel medium remained untouched is a small study of Ellen Andrée derived from *Project for Portraits in a Frieze* and related to the statuette *The Schoolgirl.* The plate for *Woman Leaving Her Bath* eventually went through at least thirty-nine states, and possibly forty-nine, involving drypoint, aquatint, and hard-ground etching in addition to the first-state electric crayon, and incorporating changes in the bathroom rug, the fabric hanging in the background, and finally some sections of the woman's body. (In spite of all this devoted, manic attention to detail, Rivière saw in the work merely "the bitterness of a disappointed bachelor.")[15] A similar zeal led to the transformation of *On Stage,* which went through five states marked by the use of drypoint, hard-ground etching, and a toothed wheel or roulette in a composition that was basically a soft-ground etching, possibly with a piece of pebbled paper pressed into the sticky acid-resist to produce the grainy texture of the dark forms along the upper half of the design. The twentieth (though perhaps not the final) state of *At the Louvre: Mary Cassatt in the Picture Gallery* shows the addition of drypoint and electric crayon and the modification of a score of details — floorboards, door jamb, background paintings, Mary's hat, Lydia's foot — in what was at the start a simple hard-ground line etching with a light grain of aquatint.

Although none of the engravings was published during their author's lifetime, there was at one stage a fairly elaborate publication project, an explicit indication of which is in an entry in Halévy's diary for May 16, 1879, five days after the closing of the fourth Exhibition of a Group of Independent Artists in the Avenue de l'Opéra:

> Visit to Degas. I find him in the company of the *independent* Miss Cassatt, one of the exhibitors in the Rue de la Paix [*sic*]. They are very excited. Each has a profit of 440 francs from their exhibition. They are thinking of founding a journal; I ask to write for it.[16]

From other sources we learn that the publication was to be called *Le Jour et la nuit,* was to appear every month, and was to consist mostly of engravings by Degas, Cassatt, Bracquemond, Pissarro, Desboutin, Raffaëlli, and Henri Rouart, with perhaps, as Halévy's account implies, some literary contributions. On May 13 Degas had written to Bracquemond, who was the only professional printmaker in the group (and was still living in suburban Sèvres):

> I have spoken to Caillebotte about the journal. He is ready to stand surety for us. Come and talk about all that with me. There is no time to lose. This morning I went . . . to see a certain Geoffroy, a first-rate photoengraver, Rue Campagne-Première. A strange man, an inventor with ailing eyes. We must profit quickly from the gains we have made. Courage, courage as we attack the poor old world. . . . So find the time to spend a day with me. There are a lot of things to decide definitely for our journal so that we can present something like a program to our capitalists. [17]

Associated with Caillebotte as a "capitalist" in the enterprise was the young banker Ernest May, who by this date owned paintings by Manet, Pissarro, Monet, and Sisley, in addition to the portrait of himself in *At the Bourse,* and concerning whom Degas wrote again to Bracquemond:

> I'll be seeing him soon. He is getting married. He is going to acquire a small town house, I believe, and arrange his little collection in one of its galleries. He is a Jew. . . . As you can see, he is a man who is launching himself into the arts. [18]

The letter added that Pissarro, who was "marvelous in his ardor and faith," had just sent in from Pontoise a batch of soft-ground etchings.

During the following months the project continued to have every appearance of life. Degas plied all concerned with compliments and advice, and filled notebook pages with printmaking recipes, with the addresses of suppliers and with lists of possible print subjects, under the heading "for the journal":

> Cut a lot. Do the arms or the legs or the back of a danseuse. Do the shoes, the hands of a hairdresser. . . .
>
> Series on instruments and instrumentalists, their shapes, the twisting of a violinist's hands and arms and neck, for example. The swelling and deflation of the cheeks of bassoonists, oboists, etc.
>
> Do in aquatint a series on mourning, different blacks, black veils of deep mourning floating on the face, black gloves, carriages in black, equipment of the Compagnie des Pompes Funèbres, carriages like Venetian gondolas.
>
> On smoke. Smoke of smokers, pipes, cigarettes, cigars, smoke of locomotives, of tall chimneys, factories, steamboats, etc. Smoke flattened under bridges. Steam.
>
> On evening. An infinite number of subjects. In cafés the different values of light globes reflected in mirrors.

On bakeries. . . . Lovely curves of dough. Still lifes with the different sorts of loaves, big, oval, fluted, round, etc. Color essays on the yellows, pinks, grays, whites in bread. Perspectives of lined-up loaves. Delightful arrangements of bakeries. Cakes, wheat, mills, flour, sacks, the market porters in Les Halles. [19]

This detailed expansion of his universe of looking was accompanied by plans for unusual viewpoints that would intimate the presence of the invisible looker. Since French bakers frequently worked in a basement below the shop, he suggested depicting them as if they were being peeked at through one of the air vents at street level. He thought of installing a stepped series of seats, a small grandstand, in his studio "in order to get used to drawing things from below and from above." [20] He sketched the Paris Pantheon with a marked tilt and observed, "No one has ever done monuments or houses from below, from beneath, up close, as one sees them going by on the sidewalks." [21]

In March 1880 Bracquemond, Cassatt, Degas, Pissarro, and Raffaëlli all listed etchings in the catalogue for the forthcoming secessionist exhibition in the Rue des Pyramides, and Pissarro specified that some of his were "part of the first issue of the publication *Le Jour et la nuit*." [22] In one of his letters of these weeks Degas warned Bracquemond that the printer's deadline was approaching, and in another he informed Pissarro, "I am beginning to announce the journal here and there. Several collectors of engravings have told me we are going to cover our expenses with our *avant la lettre* sales." [23] (An *avant la lettre* proof is one pulled before the addition of an inscription to the plate.) But then something suddenly went wrong, and a letter written by Mary Cassatt's mother on April 9 offers an explanation:

> Degas who is the leader undertook to get up a journal of etchings and got them all to work for it so that Mary had no time for paintings and as usual with Degas when the time arrived to appear he wasn't ready, so that *Le Jour et la nuit* . . . which might have been a great success has not yet appeared. Degas never is ready for anything. This time he has thrown away an excellent chance for all of them. [24]

The implication of the "not yet" was merely that the "excellent chance" provided by the inauguration of the Rue des Pyramides exhibition on April 1 had been missed. In fact, however, the journal never came out at all, so something besides Degas's delays seems to have been involved. Georges Rivière thought that the real trouble was that Caillebotte and May became much less generous after learning that Charpentier's year-old art periodical, *La Vie moderne*, was deeply in the red.

Original lithography, as distinct from the commercial reproductive sort, was at this time in an uninspiring state in France, a trough between the achievements of Géricault, Delacroix, and Daumier and the new wave toward the end of the century that would be marked by the brilliant color work of Toulouse-Lautrec, Bonnard, and Vuillard. But there were some exceptions to this generalization: Manet did a fine set of illustrations for Edgar Allan Poe's *The Raven* in 1874; Fantin-Latour began to turn out his series of flower pieces and musical evocations at about the same time; and in 1879 Redon executed *The Dream,* the first of his sets of strange, visionary, half-Symbolist and half-Surrealist prints.

Initially Degas may have found the medium less interesting than the intaglio processes, for much of the technical work had to be left to the professional lithographic printers. But between 1876 and 1880 he produced ten lithographs that included such a masterpiece of light and shade as *At Les Ambassadeurs: Mademoiselle Bécat,* and in many of them he managed to complicate matters to a degree that must have astonished his fellow painters and printmakers, who were inclined to brush or draw a design onto lithographic transfer paper and never go near a lithographic stone. Often he began by doing what was mostly one of his regular monotypes, except that he used the special lithographic ink called tusche and ran the copper plate through the rollers of his press with a sheet of transfer paper; then, after the design had been transferred in a workshop, he went to work on the stone, splashing, sprinkling, and modifying with a litho crayon or a brush and using a scraper to pick out patterns of bright light, like those behind Mademoiselle Bécat. Sometimes, after inspecting a proof, he added a few touches of pastel and then, carried away, went on to metamorphose the whole composition into a pastel. He was clearly not interested in lithography as a duplicating process; what fascinated him were the opportunities to experiment and the quality of the tone values in a single print. "If Rembrandt," he said, "had had lithography, God knows what wonderful things he might have done with it."[25]

Although the artisan aspects of sculpture and printmaking offered particularly tempting opportunities for *bricolage,* they cannot be regarded as having been in any sense a cause or even an important conditioning factor. For in his drawings, oils, and pastels the artist-artisan manifested much the same delight in materials and methods, the same tendency to improvise, the same impulse to transform, and the same chronic, often fatal dissatisfaction with results. Well enough aroused in him a raging desire not to let it alone.

In his early drawings, of which the portrait of the twelve-year-old Marguerite in 1854 is a good example, he used a hard, carefully sharpened pencil of the common type usually referred to as a lead pencil, although in fact the marking material is graphite compressed with very fine clay. When he was in form, his lightly traced lines resembled those produced by his adored sixteenth-century masters with a silver point on coated paper. By the mid-1860s, notably in some of the studies for *War Scene in the Middle Ages,* he favored black chalk, frequently rubbed into delicate transitions of tone with the help of the cigar-shaped roll of paper called a stump or a tortillon. (This last technique was undoubtedly a relic from his years with Lamothe; stumps were much used by academic drawing teachers as instruments for imitating the modeling of plaster casts.) As he grew older he turned increasingly to black crayon and finally almost exclusively to charcoal, perhaps because it was less tiring for his eyes and quite certainly because with it he could obtain the relatively thick, vibrant lines and vigorous forms evident around 1882 in his *Jockey,* which is a long way from the Ingresque universe of the 1854 portrait of Marguerite.

He also resorted more and more to tracing a drawing through transparent paper in order to be able to modify it without affecting the original. Sometimes, seized by his revision demon, he went on making tracings of tracings until he had accumulated the equivalent of a series of states of an engraving (with the important difference that each tracing, for reasons that are not clear, tended to be larger than the preceding one), and many of the tracings, like many of the monotypes and engravings, wound up serving as foundations for pastels. Another of his favorite devices was the taking of a counterproof, an imprint with the composition in reverse, by pressing a charcoal drawing face down on a clean sheet of dampened paper. This sometimes was the start of a series of operations ending up in pastel: there is a left-facing version of the *Nude Drying Her Arm,* for instance, and a number of preliminary studies in each direction, all apparently done around 1884. Such Janus-like evidence makes it difficult to apply to Degas any of the various theories about the psychological significance of left and right in pictorial space.

He found watercolor a "meager"[26] medium and seldom used it, which is surprising, in view of what he might have achieved with it in the sheer-muslin and pink-satin realm of the ballet. But there was nothing in French art history comparable to the line of great English watercolorists, and he was enthralled — often in a characteristically contradictory way — by the prestige, the romantic lore, and the difficulty of oil painting. He talked about the old workshop practices of the guild system in language that recalled the common derivation of such words as "métier," "ministry," and "mystery"; when he admired a well-made picture he might remark that it was "painted like a door."[27] Although he had inherited the Florentine linear emphasis through Lamothe and Ingres, and had never gone as far as the Grand Canal during his Italian travels, he affected an immense respect for the Venetian painterly tradition and studied the examples of it he found in the Louvre. He believed, or pretended to believe, that "Van Dyck got from an old maid he had known in Genoa some secrets confided in her by Titian."[28]

Impressionism, with its reliance on a retinal response to the motif and its neglect of preparatory drawing and careful underpainting in favor of a direct, *alla prima* approach, seemed to him both sacrilegious and wildly mistaken:

> Beauty is a mystery, but the fact is no longer realized. The recipes and the secrets are forgotten. A young fellow is planted in the middle of the fields and told, "Paint!" And he paints a sincere farm. It's idiotic.[29]

Much of his own early work in oil was done in what passed for a traditional technique at the Ecole des Beaux-Arts and the Villa Medici, and as late as 1881, according to an account of a studio visit by Georges Jeanniot, he might be found proceeding as sagely as a sixteenth-century apprentice — in a costume that contrasted with the bourgeois gentleman's dress worn by contemporary *pompiers* in their ateliers:

> He came to the door in a house painter's long smock and a crushed felt hat. He was working on a racehorse picture. . . . The jockey in the foreground was facing to the right, and his jacket was painted a pure white with some gray shadows. Degas was hesitating between yellow and pink as the color in the glaze to be added to the shadows — for this so-called Impressionist loved the old methods and thought they were still the best. . . . He mixed some tones, wiped with a rag, dipped the tip of his brush into a saucer, paused. At last he made up his mind, and with a light, rapid, scumbling action he put some pink on the gray.[30]

He was not always old-fashioned, however, in his practice, nor always prudent. A modern laboratory analysis of one of his palettes has revealed, along with such traditional pigments as white lead, yellow ochre, and iron-oxide red, the presence of several relatively recent synthetic colors: barium yellow, for instance, which came into use in the 1830s; chrome yellow, which appeared on the market in 1818 and did not attract many painters (with the important exception of Turner); and Prussian blue, which was invented in Berlin in 1704 as a substitute for the rare and expensive lapis lazuli. One of his technical discoveries, used in *Dancers Practicing at the Bar* and half a dozen other fine pictures, was *peinture à l'essence.* The thin turpentine medium resulted in a matte, chalky look that, because there was so little oil left in the paints, was resistant to yellowing. Another, much less brilliant, experiment consisted of painting with oil colors on paper previously rubbed with oil: he enjoyed the way a brush glided over the slippery surface, and it took him a while to realize that too much oil would eventually darken the paper into a brown fog. Almost as risky was his tendency to mix media in an attempt to obtain a more convincing equivalent for the variety of visual effects in the real world. Although he detested the Salon kind of illusionism, and did not yearn to paint sincere farms, he had some notions of his own about the need to represent things as they were.

The late 1870s were a watershed in his attitude toward materials and methods. Before that period nearly all of his easel pictures, with the exception of the 1869 series of Channel coast landscapes and a few portraits and preparatory studies, were oils. After that period more than 80 per cent were pastels, though he continued to experiment in oil and to talk a good deal, as did most of the French artists of his generation, about the supposedly lost secrets of the Renaissance masters. (In fact, the recipes in question had never been very secret and were not actually lost.) Undoubtedly an initial reason for the change was that during the difficult years immediately after the collapse of the family bank, oil paintings seemed to offer him less chance to make some money quickly than did pastels, which he could produce with relative ease and sell at moderate prices. But other reasons are not hard to find. After a severe decline in the first half of the nineteenth century, pastel was going through a general revival in both France and England: in 1870 the Société des Pastellistes was founded in Paris, and in 1880 the first exhibition of the Pastel Society was held in London. Manet, Renoir, Cassatt, and Whistler were interested in the medium. Degas had learned to admire it as a boy at home, where the work of such eighteenth-century virtuosos as La Tour and Perronneau was constantly on view, and he had seen many other splendid examples in the collections of his father's art-minded acquaintances (in particular the eccentric Dr. La Caze and the "gaffer," François Marcille). And, too, it was well suited to the nature of his talent and the evolution of his sensibility. It extended drawing into the realm of painting in ways that were impossible with oil; it satisfied his liking for matte, dry, chalky surfaces, which was evident also in his use of *peinture à l'essence;* it offered pure, unchanging color; and it presented him with good opportunities for experimentation.

In such relatively early performances as the 1869 Channel coast landscapes and the portrait of Thérèse in the Rue de Mondovi apartment, which was probably executed that same year, the technique was pretty much the standard eighteenth-century one: the artist merely laid the colors on the paper with the crayons and then blended them together by rubbing with his finger or a stump. Four years later, in one of the Metropolitan Museum's versions of *The Rehearsal of the Ballet on the Stage,* he used much more

complicated methods: he began with a pen-and-ink drawing intended for publication in the *Illustrated London News,* which rejected it on the grounds (according to George Moore) that French ballet was not a proper subject for readers in English rectories; he thereupon launched into one of his prolonged processes of revision and wound up with a mixture of pastel, ink, watercolor, and *peinture à l'essence* on paper mounted on canvas. During the following decade he devised a method of blowing steam from a boiling kettle onto a fresh layer of pastel; sometimes he let the wet pigment settle into a vaporous film on the surface of the picture; on other occasions he melted the powder into a paste thick enough to retain brush marks. One of his notebooks mentions "mixtures of water-soluble colors with glycerine and soda; one could make a pastel-soap."[31] In one of his finest studies of theatrical appearance and reality, the *Dancers Behind a Stage Flat* of around 1880, he seems to have begun by rendering the girls' flesh, hair, and tutus in ordinary pastel, then worked over the floor and stage flat with a powdered color steamed or perhaps simply diluted in water, and retouched the background foliage and the girls' flowers in either tempera or gouache. At this time he was visibly beginning to abandon the rubbing and blending of colors in favor of juxtaposed strokes of the pastel crayons, a technique that by the mid-1880s he would use for producing the vaguely Impressionistic textures of pictures like the *Singer in Green.*

The number of oil paintings ruined by his technical experiments and his impulse to revise was appallingly large, and some of his most interesting works appear to have had narrow escapes. His representation of Fiocre in *La Source* had to undergo major repairs in the 1890s, because in 1868 he had had it varnished on the spur of the moment and had then damaged part of the paint surface in an unsound attempt to remove the varnish. The head of the man in *Interior* had to be redone some twenty-five years after its creation, apparently because of an amateurish procedure followed in the original underpainting. Disaster in pastel was rendered less frequent by the nature of the medium, but that it was always hovering over the atelier is evident from a story told by Henri Rouart's son Ernest, who was himself a painter keenly interested in technique:

> When he came across one of his old pictures, he always felt like putting it back on the easel for a revision. Thus, seeing constantly at our house a delightful pastel my father had bought and of which he was very fond, Degas was seized by his usual imperious urge to retouch. He talked about the matter incessantly, until finally my father, out of sheer weariness, let him take the picture away. We never saw it again. My father often asked for news about his beloved pastel, and Degas would answer evasively. But at last he had to confess his crime: he had completely destroyed the work

OPPOSITE: *Dancers Behind a Stage Flat,* C. 1880

entrusted to him for some simple retouching. . . . He thereupon, as a way of making good the loss, sent my father the famous *Dancers Practicing at the Bar.* And the comical part is that after that, for many years, every time Degas passed these danseuses we heard him say to my father, "Decidedly, that watering can is idiotic. I really must get rid of it." In my opinion he was right: the removal of that utensil would have improved the picture. But my father, instructed by experience, would not agree to another revision.[32]

A report that Henri Rouart had the painting fixed to the wall in his house in the Rue de Lisbonne with a chain and a padlock was probably an exaggeration. But that it made the rounds of Paris studios is an indication of the notoriety Degas eventually acquired as a compulsive *bricoleur.*

Several people who knew him thought that his attitude toward his craft resembled that of Leonardo da Vinci, whose reputation as an experimenter and an inventor was growing rapidly during the second half of the nineteenth century. And it is true that the two men had much the same sort of curiosity about media, the same willingness to run risks, and sometimes the same romantic impracticality. (They also had the same habit of talking to themselves in notebooks.) But whereas Leonardo combined to a remarkable degree the outlook of an artist with that of a scientist, Degas had in him almost nothing of the scientist. His mind, which both his friends and his enemies agreed was exceptionally sharp, functioned more often than not at the prescientific, prelogical level of poets, alchemists, and tribal man; he "thought-felt" in terms of transubstantiations, analogies, found objects, physical synecdoches, and visual metaphors — wax and flesh, Madame Camus and the shadow of a figurine, human hair and varnished walnut wood. Reality was for him inseparable from make-believe; it was the back of a stage flat. He had little capacity for scientific externalization; he tended to regard a work of art as an extension of the artist's own psychophysical substance. Hence he felt free to alter his *articles,* even after they were sold. Yet at the same time he furiously condemned any tampering with pictures by outsiders, like museum curators and restorers. When the Louvre cleaned one of its Rembrandts he reacted, in a tirade aimed at the innocent young Daniel Halévy, as if to a torturer's hot poker:

> Touch a painting! A painting should be left for time to roll over it, as over all things. That becomes part of its beauty. A man who touches a painting should be deported. Touch a painting! You've no idea of the effect that has on me.[33]

He obviously saw nothing paradoxical in the fact that at the moment he was still hoping for an opportunity to commit some kind of mayhem on *Dancers Practicing at the Bar.*

18. Victory and Disbandment

AFTER WINNING HIS MEDAL at the Salon of 1881, Manet also obtained, through the political influence of a former schoolmate, the ribbon of the Legion of Honor. But the decorations he had desired with such stubborn credulity and candor came too late, for he was already afflicted with the nervous disorder, probably a form of tertiary syphilis, that would shortly kill him. At the Salon of 1882 he exhibited his last major work, the luminous, melancholy *Bar at the Folies-Bergère.* (Degas found it "tedious and artful,"[1] probably because of the difficulty a viewer may have had when trying to situate bottles, barmaid, client, audience, and himself in the partly mirrored space.) Then the ailment worsened rapidly, to the accompaniment of hydropathic, homeopathic, and herbalistic proof that the medical science of the Third Republic was in many respects not much more advanced than that of Hippocrates' Greece. The boyish swagger became a hobble supported by a cane. At the beginning of April 1883, Degas wrote to Paul-Albert Bartholomé:

> Manet is done for. Reportedly that Dr. Hureau de Villeneuve has poisoned him with doses of ergotized rye. Several newspapers have taken the trouble to inform him of his approaching death. I hope his family can get to these articles before he does, for he has no inkling of his real condition. He has gangrene in a foot.[2]

The brutal amputation of a leg merely postponed the inevitable outcome until April 30. In *Le Figaro* Wolff played Tartuffe enough to write "God knows how much I loved Edouard Manet."[3] Zola, Monet, Fantin-Latour, Stevens, Duret, and Burty were pall-bearers. "He was greater," Degas said, "than we thought."[4] Many friends mourned especially the man of whom Banville wrote:

> *Ce riant, ce blond Manet*
> *De qui la grâce émanait*
> *Gai, subtil, charmant en somme,*
> *Sous sa barbe d'Apollon*
> *Eut de la nuque au talon*
> *Un bel air de gentilhomme.*[5]

(That laughing, that blond Manet, from whom grace emanated, gay, discerning, charming in sum, under his Apollo's beard had from head to heel a fine air of a gentleman.)

The meetings at the Café de la Nouvelle-Athènes, deprived of their principal animator's boulevardier style and gamin's grin, became less frequent. And there were other signs of the coming end of an era. By 1883 the twenty-four-year-old Georges Seurat had developed a conception of painting that combined Poussin with Chevreul and would soon blossom into the classicism and systematic optical mixtures of Pointillism. In 1884, after some historic struggles in which the post-Impressionist Seurat and the pre-Symbolist Redon were allies, an anti-Salon salon was put together by the recently founded Société des Artistes Indépendants, an organization that loudly announced the abolition of juries, medals, cronyism, and corruption and made the little band of secessionists formed in 1874 look halfhearted. Renoir, after an Italian tour that had made him aware of the merits of Ingres and Raphael, was destroying some of his Impressionist pictures and sinking into a crisis he would describe as the most severe in his career:

> Around 1883 something like a fracture occurred in my work. I had gone to the end of Impressionism and had reached the conclusion that I did not know how to paint and did not know how to draw. In short, I was in a blind alley.[6]

In May of that year Pissarro had a one-man show in Durand-Ruel's recently rented rooms at 9 Boulevard de la Madeleine (within competing distance of Petit's glittering new gallery) and emerged with his self-confidence shaken by the lack of sales and subtly undermined by the nature of the compliments he had received. "The most precious to me," he wrote to his son Lucien, who was now settled in London, "were those from Degas, who told me he was happy to see me purifying my manner more and more. . . . Actually I can see only vaguely whether what I'm doing is good or not."[7]

Some eighteen months later his faith in his empirical kind of Impressionism was further weakened by talks with the scientific Seurat and the latter's principal disciple, Paul Signac.

Degas had reasons for facing the future with more serenity. The complex, sophisticated kind of art to which he was committed had enough intellectual content, enough métier, and enough potential for variation and evolution to resist for a good while the malady of satiation to which a relatively simple, sensuous, iterative style like Impressionism was peculiarly susceptible. Moreover, he did not lack evidence of appreciation. His picture of Michel Musson's cotton office in New Orleans was now hanging in the Musée des Beaux-Arts in provincial Pau, which was not quite like being in the Musée du Luxembourg in Paris, alongside the Delaunays and

Waiting, c. 1882

the Bonnats, but was nevertheless a sort of consecration. He was selling regularly, at prices that sometimes reached five thousand francs. In the spring of 1883 he repeated his early British successes, this time in the course of an exhibition of contemporary French painting arranged by Durand-Ruel at Dowdeswell's Galleries in New Bond Street. On April 25 the London *Standard* complained:

> Degas, the master of the Impressionist school, the man of genius, the inspirer of the whole party, is not represented with quite enough of amplitude. . . . We could have borne more of him, for on him the vitality of the Impressionist movement depends.[8]

On April 28 the critic for the *Academy* decided that the seven works on view, which were a sampling of the racehorse, milliner, and ballet series, would be largely sufficient "to prove to all who are open to be convinced that the chief painter of the Impressionist school has rare gifts of observation, and that his skill and agility of hand are not less remarkable than his quickness of sight."[9]

Pissarro, whose usual irony was unaffected by the bad reception of his own work in the show, wrote to Durand-Ruel, "My son has sent me two articles . . . on the exhibition. If Degas knew that he has been designated the chief of the Impressionists! Anathema!"[10] (In fact, Degas eventually saw the piece in the *Standard* and remarked merely that he had been "caressed with a few courteous and supercilious lines.")[11]

Financial gains and a growing reputation did not prevent the onset of an acute attack of fiftieth-birthday blues. On August 16, 1884, the new quinquagenarian wrote to Bartholomé from Ménil-Hubert:

> Ah, where is the time when I thought myself strong, when I was full of logic, full of projects? Very soon I'm going to descend the slope and roll I don't know where, wrapped up in a lot of bad pastels . . .[12]

On August 21, still in Normandy, he wrote to Henry Lerolle, who had recently paid three thousand francs for *Before the Race* and who seems to have had a reason for being vexed by Degas's negligence in a matter of sweetmeats for a baptism:

> If you answer this letter, my dear Lerolle, you can say that I am a queer stick. I don't know why I didn't get the box of sugared almonds and write before your departure. If you were a bachelor and fifty years old (a month ago), you would have moments like that. One shuts oneself like a door, and not only against friends. One eliminates everything around oneself and then, all alone, one kills, annihilates oneself, out of disgust. I have had too many projects, and now I'm blocked, impotent. I've lost the thread. I thought I would always have time: in the middle of my troubles and in spite of my

weakening eyesight, I never despaired of being able, one fine morning, to get going on what I had not done, what I had been kept from doing. I piled up my plans in a cupboard for which I always had the key with me. And I've lost the key.[13]

In a letter to Rouart the next day he again cited, as he had repeatedly in New Orleans, the passage in Rousseau's *Confessions* about starting ten-year undertakings and then dropping them in ten minutes "without regret."[14] On December 19 he remarked to Bartholomé, "At bottom the trouble is that I don't have enough heart."[15]

Such spells of loathing for the Pascalian "me" were incidents, however, in an existence that rolled along very agreeably in a France in which the class structure was still rigid (with an estimated 90 per cent of the wealth in the hands of 10 per cent of the population), the tax-collection system was almost a joke, the entertainment industries — despite a continuing economic stagnation — were prosperous, and the holidays of the well-to-do were transfers of entire households to *résidences secondaires*. At Dieppe during the period of 1884 to 1886 the Halévys had a large summer home perched on a strip of pebbled beach between the chalk cliffs and the sea, and here Degas became a frequent and long-staying guest. One of Madame Morisot's old friends from the years in the Rue Franklin, Dr. Emile Blanche, owned the next-door villa, to which he had added a studio for his son Jacques-Emile, who, after studying with Gervex, was becoming a competent, if rather flashy and derivative, portraitist and landscapist. The charmingly idle Boulanger-Cavé, whose taste and "indifference" Degas admired, was usually around, and so was the young English painter Walter Sickert, whom Whistler had presented to Degas in Paris. Whistler himself often crossed the Channel, and during one visit, at the Dieppe villa of British acquaintances, he repeated his much discussed London lecture on art, the "Ten O'Clock" (so titled because of the afterdinner hour of delivery). The evening promenades on the seafront Boulevard Maritime were given a flavor of Proust's Balbec, or of Tanagra, by a group of young women, among them the aristocratic Olga Carracciolo, who had the Prince of Wales for a godfather (and reputedly for a father), and the three daughters of John Lemoinne, who was an editor of the *Journal des Débats* and a member of the Académie Française. An English photographer named Barnes, who seems to have been down on his luck, was often on hand with his camera.

On fine days, long rambles through the surrounding wooded, farm-dotted countryside were organized. Degas was by now a fanatical stroller whose motto, he said, was walk after work, *ambulare postea laborare*. On rainy afternoons when the conversation lagged he amused the young people with tales from *The Thousand and One Nights,* which he had been reading all his life in Antoine Galland's elegant eighteenth-century translation. Sometimes he would start a musical session by singing, with a *bis,* the refrain of one of Thérèsa's more sentimental successes: [16]

> *Là-bas dans la vallée*
> *Coule claire fontaine.*

(Down there in the valley flows the clear fountain.) In 1885 he arranged for Barnes's apparatus a photographic parody of Ingres's chilly *Apotheosis of Homer,* with himself in the role of the blind poet, the young Elie and Daniel Halévy as the allegorical figures representing the *Iliad* and the *Odyssey,* and Rose, Catherine, and Marie Lemoinne as three muses. During that same summer, in Jacques-Emile Blanche's studio, he executed his pastel *Six Friends at Dieppe,* in which Sickert, his coat collar inadvertently turned up, stands with his back to a totem-pole composition consisting, from the bottom, of Boulanger-Cavé, Gervex, Blanche, and Ludovic Halévy, with the thirteen-year-old Daniel Halévy, in a straw hat, nearly lost between his father and Blanche. Glancing at Sickert's turned-up collar during the posing session, Halévy said, "Degas is always looking for an accident." [17] In September, from Paris, the portraitist sent his host a letter full of affection and postvacation nostalgia and accompanied by some vacation snapshots:

> Here in three envelopes, my dear friend, are the photographs for the young and handsome Sickert. . . . This morning the young Blanche sent me, with a charming *bonjour,* his study of a group. . . . He has begun posing sessions again with the little Carracciolo, and I envy him. What a change, what a pleasure it would be for me to draw that grace! . . . I gather that Barnes is no longer quite in despair. How are my dear little comrades? Greetings to them and the Sickerts. [18]

Looking back sixty years later at this avuncular Degas and the Dieppe of the 1880s, Daniel Halévy wrote, "I think he was happy there." [19]

He was also happy, very clearly, when settled in his season-ticket seat at the Palais Garnier. His letters of these years show him organizing opera evenings in the company of Raffaëlli, Clemenceau, and other friends, and contain references to Gounod's *Faust* (then setting box-office records in Paris), Gluck's *Orfeo ed Euridice,* Meyerbeer's *L'Africaine,* and Verdi's *Simone Boccanegra,* the last in its new version with the libretto revised by Arrigo Boito. On June 11, 1885, with Ernest Reyer, Albert Boulanger-Cavé, and Ludovic Halévy, he was present at the *répétition générale,* the final dress rehearsal attended by critics and Opéra insiders, of Reyer's *Sigurd,* a thoroughly French and non-Wagnerian work, in spite of its title, some Germanic orchestration, and a libretto based on the Nibelung legend. (Reyer had composed it, in fact, before the première of Wagner's *Ring* and had then run into production problems.)

During this period his favorite singer was the French soprano Rose Caron, who had made her début in 1884 in Brussels as the Alice of Meyerbeer's *Robert le Diable,* had created the part of the Brunehilde of *Sigurd,* and in Paris would go on to sing principal roles in Fromental Halévy's *La Juive,* Weber's *Der Freischütz,* and — with the great Polish tenor Jean de Reszke — Massenet's *Le Cid.* Through Reyer she became personally acquainted with Degas, who admired her voice and especially her sculptural acting style, which reminded him of the noble Rachel of the Comédie-Française of his youth and appealed to the consciousness of arms that he had been manifesting in such works as *The Café-Concert at Les Ambassadeurs,* the *Little Dancer of Fourteen Years, The Schoolgirl,* and the shattered bust of Hortense Valpinçon so insistently described as "with arms." In the autumn of 1885 he attended another performance of *Sigurd* and reported to Halévy, who was lingering at Dieppe:

> Madame Caron's arms are still there — those thin and divine arms, which she knows how to leave in the air for a long time, a long time, without affectation, and then lower without haste. When you see them again you'll exclaim "Rachel, Rachel," as I do.[20]

In a letter to Bartholomé of about the same date he referred to himself, with an echo of his Louis-le-Grand Ovid, as a "bear . . . habitually sucking the honey of Mount Hymettus at the Opéra," and added, "Divine Madame Caron! In a conversation with her I compared her to the figures of Puvis de Chavannes."[21] With allowances for the replacement of Phidias by Puvis, he was still pretty much the Romantic Classical Edgar who had likened Adelaide Ristori to the Nike on a Parthenon pediment.

His relations with the ballet generation that had followed that of Eugénie Fiocre and Rita Sangalli were close and often pleasantly informal. Georges Jeanniot, in his *Souvenirs,* tells of spending an afternoon of 1881 in Lepic's studio sketching Rosita Mauri, another ballerina, who was perhaps Marie Sanlaville (Jeanniot, or his printer, calls her "Sauleville"), and two Opéra *rats.* Degas appeared, received a warm welcome, showed the other men exactly how to draw a ballet slipper, and then, humming the refrain of the song "A table, à table," led a parade to the buffet — cherry pie, sponge cake, and wine — Lepic had prepared.[22] Evidently such sessions were not uncommon; in an undated note of this period Degas referred to "lunch with some Italian and French danseuses Sunday at Boldini's place."[23] Among his favorite ballerinas during the 1880s were Mauri, who was the star of *La Korrigane* and *The Two Pigeons;* Alice Biot, who was the Harlequin Junior in *Les Jumeaux de Bergame;* and Sanlaville, who was the Harlequin Senior in *Les Jumeaux.* In August 1885, after visiting lower Normandy and going on into Brittany as far as Saint-Malo, he told Halévy that Mont-Saint-Michel and Madame Poulard's inn at the foot of the abbey had made an impression on him "second only to that made by Mademoiselle Alice Biot."[24]

There is no firm evidence, however, that Biot or Sanlaville posed in person for any of the Harlequin pictures (which would influence Picasso) presumably inspired by *Les Jumeaux de Bergame,* and no work that can be said to represent Mauri. He continued to prefer models who were not stars, and one whom he liked particularly was Mathilde Salle, who rose from the rank of *petit sujet* to become an excellent mime, and whose plump, intelligent face appears in a three-mood pastel of 1886. Marie Van Goethen and her long pigtail return in several pastels of around 1885, one of which, *The Pink Danseuses,* was bought by Henry Lerolle. Among the youngest of the *petits rats* to pose was the nine-year-old Suzanne Mante, who appears in her new tutu with her sister Blanche and their mother in *The Mante Family,* datable to around 1882, and who in the 1950s would remember Degas as a quiet, kind man in blue spectacles who used to stand at the top or the bottom of one of the many staircases in the Palais Garnier, sketching the girls as they rushed up and down and sometimes asking one of them to pause for a moment. And that he was in fact kind can be felt in a letter of November 1883 in which he tried to get Halévy, who had influence in theatrical circles, to help a danseuse named Joséphine Chabot with the renewal of her engagement:

> You must know what it's like when a ballerina wants someone to intervene in her favor. . . . If you have the courage or the strength, send a note to Vaucorbeil and to Mérante . . . on her dancing, her experience, and her future. I had no idea that such a wild woman could exist. She wants everything done right away. If she could, she would wrap you in a blanket, take you in her arms, and carry you to the Opéra.[25]

When Vaucorbeil, who was the director of the Palais Garnier, and Mérante, who was still the ballet master, agreed to an extension of the engagement, Degas renewed his effort and insisted that "the little Chabot" be given a three-year contract, with stipulated annual increases in salary.[26]

Although he remained attached to the Ninth Arrondissement, he enjoyed changing his workplace and residence from time to time. At least by 1879, while still living in the little pavilion under the shade of the acacia in the Rue Frochot, he had acquired a separate studio at 19 bis Rue

Fontaine-Saint-Georges (today simply the Rue Fontaine), around the corner from a house the Halévys occupied when they were not at one of their summer places. At its top end the Rue Fontaine-Saint-Georges opened onto the Place Blanche and some of the cabarets and music halls that were being advertised in Jules Chéret's dynamic, brilliantly colored posters; at its lower end the street offered a view of the Café La Rochefoucauld — "La Roche" to a large and extremely varied collection of habitués that included Moreau, Reyer, Forain, Stevens, Renoir, Gérôme, and Gervex. On October 16, 1883, a letter from Degas to Henri Rouart, who was on a holiday in Venice, provided evidence that the long train of talk that had begun in the Guerbois and moved on to the Nouvelle-Athènes was continuing in the slightly more bourgeois environment down the hill:

> You love both nature and wetness. Do me the favor of leaving for a moment your two loves in order to enter, dry, the Palazzo Labia and see, partly for yourself and partly for me, Tiepolo's frescoes. Last night on a table at the Café La Rochefoucauld, Forain — yes, Forain — gave me a general sketch of them, which he completed by comparing them to one of Chéret's posters. That's his way of admiring, and perhaps it's no worse than any other way.[27]

At some unspecified earlier date, probably in 1882, the tourist-by-proxy had wound up his downhill shift by leaving the Rue Frochot for bachelor's quarters (still managed by the motherly Sabine Neyt) at 21 Rue Pigalle, across and up the street from the town house and patch of greenery where Célestine Musson had fallen in love. In one of the house-warming invitations he sent, he described his new place as "the handsomest third-floor flat in the neighborhood," and in another he promised that his guests were to be "few but merry."[28]

Such a way of life, though not exactly *grand bourgeois,* called for a regular income, and this was provided by Durand-Ruel, who in theory had exclusive rights to all of Degas's production, advanced funds somewhat in the manner of a banker, and from time to time drew up a balance sheet to show who owed what. Degas, unlike several other artists in the dealer's stable, usually resisted temptations to sell to collectors directly or to other merchants. But the temptations were often irresistible, since there was more than one occasion during the mid-1880s when Durand-Ruel did not have any money to advance. For a while Mary Cassatt seems to have tided him over. In 1884 his debts rose to a million gold francs. His competitors were constantly on the watch for a chance to finish him off: in 1885 he was falsely accused in an affair involving a fake Daubigny, and at about the same time there was a plot — which fell through because Petit refused to participate — to wreck the Impressionist market temporarily by means of a dumping operation. It was largely through small shows in London, Boston, Rotterdam, and Berlin that Durand-Ruel managed to keep his Paris gallery, now temporarily back in the Rue de la Paix, where it had been during the Second Empire, halfway afloat. But new menaces were constantly appearing: the Goupil empire, for instance, under its changed name of Boussod and Valadon, was beginning to take a discreet interest in the Impressionists because of the presence of Theo van Gogh as director of the firm's branch in the Boulevard Montmartre. In a note of around 1885 to his faithful merchant the usually faithful Degas wrote, "If there is not a lot of money, send me a little. . . . Damned life. I'm finishing your diabolical pictures." [29]

Money was the reason for a trip to Naples in January 1886. As a result of a series of deaths and wills, Lucy de Gas had become a joint owner with her Parisian cousin Edgar of part of the estate left by their grandfather, and since she was nearing the age of marriage and in need of an unattached dowry, she wanted to buy the other part of the inheritance. Degas was willing to sell but uncertain about how much to ask, and so he was soon at a disadvantage with the Italian lawyers he had to face. On January 7 he wrote to Bartholomé:

> I am already eager to be back in Paris. Here I'm nothing but a Frenchman who is in the way. The family is disappearing; everyone is more or less divided. Like a Valkyrie, I long for my palace of flame — for my studio heated by a good stove. Here Hagen is a lawyer. [30]

(The references were to Reyer's *Sigurd,* not to the *Ring.*) He planned tours along the coast to the Roman amphitheater and market at Pozzuoli, to the ancient bathing establishment at Baia, and to the eighteenth-century royal pavilion in the middle of the Lago del Fusaro — but because of rain did nothing except take the new Belgian street car to Posilipo. As the days passed, he became more and more depressed by the legal arguments, the lack of the clan solidarity he had known in his youth, and his sense of getting nowhere. On January 17 he reported again to Bartholomé:

> All I've done is to lose a month. . . . I feel that everything in me, aside from the heart, is growing old together. And the heart itself is rather artificial. The danseuses have sewed it up in a sack of pink satin, of pink satin a little faded, like their ballet slippers. [31]

A few days later he returned to the Rue Pigalle with a stack of documents and a firm intention to seek the advice of Rouart or some other businessman before concluding the debate with Lucy's attorneys.

In Paris a more familiar kind of argument was under way. Toward the end of 1885 Pissarro had proposed another group exhibition, and after the usual discussions the project had bogged down because of what Berthe Morisot had described as "Degas's bad disposition" and the "clashes of vanity" among the other possible participants. "It seems to me," she had told her sister Edma, "that I'm about the only one without pettiness of character, and that compensates for my inferiority as a painter."[32] By the following February, however, she and her husband, Eugène Manet, were working hard to organize some sort of show, and they were not without hope. Raffaëlli had eased the situation by deciding to abstain. Degas was still insisting on the rule against exhibiting at the same time in the Salon, but that did not much matter, since in any event Monet and Renoir would not join the secessionists. (Both men intended to take part in an Exposition

Women Ironing, c. 1884

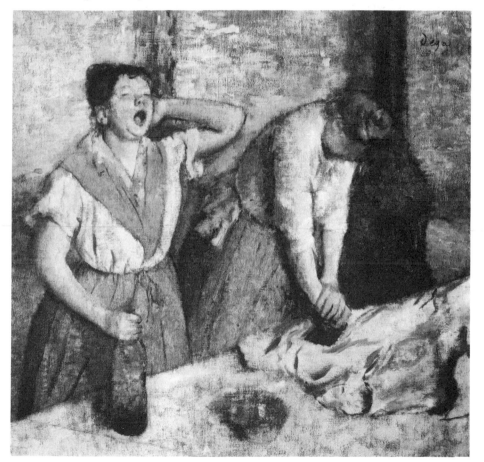

Internationale being staged by Petit.) Surprisingly, the only important obstacle was the normally gentle and cooperative Pissarro, who had just been converted to Pointillism and was now determined to get Seurat and Signac into the exhibition. The idea was opposed by several members of the group on aesthetic grounds, and by others on a practical basis, for one of the pictures Seurat planned to show was his *Sunday Afternoon on the Island of La Grande Jatte,* which was more than two meters high and three meters long. At the beginning of March, Pissarro wrote to his son Lucien:

> Yesterday I had a rough set-to. . . . I explained to Monsieur Eugène Manet, who probably didn't understand anything I said, that Seurat has brought in a new element that these gentlemen cannot appreciate, in spite of their talent. . . . Monsieur Manet was beside himself. I didn't calm down. They are being underhanded. But I won't give in. Degas is a hundred times more sincere. I told him that Seurat's picture was very interesting. "Oh," he said, "I would have noticed that myself, Pissarro. It's just that the thing is so big." [33]

Finally Seurat, Signac, Pissarro, and Lucien, who was also something of a Pointillist, were admitted, with the understanding that they would be quarantined to a room of their own. The other exhibitors, in addition to Degas, were Gauguin, Guillaumin, and Morisot, whom Pissarro now referred to as "Romantic Impressionists";[34] Emile Schuffenecker, a pupil of several academic masters and a former colleague of Gauguin's at the Bourse; the Corot disciples Rouart and Vignon; the Millet disciple Tillot; the still somewhat Ingresque Marie Bracquemond; the Degas disciples Cassatt, Forain, and Zandomeneghi; the approximately Symbolist Redon; and a mysterious Comtesse de Rambures, whom Gauguin had insistently recommended. Since the Salon des Indépendants had appropriated the group's recent label, and since the term "Impressionist" was obviously inappropriate for such a mixture of styles, the display was billed simply as "Eighth Exhibition of Painting."

May 15 was chosen as the opening date, because Degas, against the wish of the other organizers, wanted the inauguration to coincide defiantly with that of the official Salon. Space was found on the second floor of an amusingly ornamented building (which still stands) at the corner of the Rue Laffitte and the Boulevard des Italiens. Stretching back up the Rue Laffitte toward the tall Corinthian portico of Notre-Dame-de-Lorette was a file of antique shops and commercial art galleries; on the ground floor directly beneath the exhibition rooms was the Restaurant de la Maison Dorée, admired for its massive balcony of gilded cast iron and frequented by publishers, theatrical people, and wealthy visitors from Central Europe; and just across the street, at the corner of the Rue Taitbout, was the Café

Tortoni, famous for its apéritifs, its terrace, its three-stepped perron, and a clientèle of *élégantes,* boulevard wits, and art critics (including especially Wolff). Perhaps thinking of the fashionable and sophisticated public of the quarter, Degas showed a small hat picture and the *At the Milliner's* for which Mary Cassatt had posed; three items catalogued as portraits or studies for portraits; and a series of ten pastel bathroom scenes, among which were almost certainly, though no titles were listed, *A Woman Having Her Hair Combed, Woman Bathing in a Shallow Tub, Woman Drying Her Foot, After the Bath,* and *The Tub.* Seven of his fifteen entries were on loan from collectors.

This time the visitors laughed mostly at the work of the Pointillists and in particular at the monkey and the stiff Parisians in *La Grande Jatte.* On the afternoon of the first day, according to Signac's memoirs, the usually open-minded Alfred Stevens

> shuttled constantly between La Maison Dorée and the neighboring Café Tortoni, picking up members of the band of sippers around the celebrated perron and leading them up to Seurat's picture in order to show them that his friend Degas had become so abject as to admit such horrors to the exhibition. In his haste to conduct new batches of viewers, he threw pieces of gold on the turnstile and did not wait for his change.[35]

Degas's bathers and combers, however, also received some attention. For the avant-garde literary review *La Vogue* a rising young critic, Félix Fénéon, described them in a long burst of up-to-date Alexandrian prose:

> Women fill with their cucurbitacean squatting the shells of the tubs. One of them, her chin on her chest, scrubs and rasps her nape; another, in a torsion that causes her to slew around, with one arm stuck to her back, employs a soap-frothing sponge to work on her coccygeal region. A bony spine becomes taut; forearms, leaving the fruity, pearlike breasts, plunge straight down between the legs to wet a washcloth in the tub water in which the feet are soaking   . In Monsieur Degas's work (and in what other?) human skin is alive and expressive. The lines of this cruel and alert-minded observer elucidate, amid the difficulties of madly elliptical foreshortenings, the mechanism of every movement; they register not only a budging being's essential gesture but also the action's smallest and most distant myological repercussions . . .[36]

Huysmans, in comments published later as part of the volume entitled *Certains* (Certain People), began with a moralistic and misogynous shudder and then switched to art criticism:

> Monsieur Degas, who in his admirable dance pictures had depicted the moral decay of the venal female rendered stupid by mechanical gambols and monotonous jumps, manifested this time, in his studies of nudes, an attentive cruelty, a patient hatred. . . . But in addition to the note of scorn and

loathing one should notice the unforgettable veracity of the figures, captured with an ample, biting draftsmanship, with a lucid and controlled passion, with an icy feverishness; one should notice the warm, resonant color, the mysterious and opulent tone of these scenes, the superbly lovely patches of flesh turned blue or pink by the bath water . . .[37]

After noting that the paintings had been pronounced obscene, he remarked, "Ah, works have never been less so, have never been so free of fussy reticence and trickery, and so fully, decisively chaste. They even glorify the disdain of the flesh, to a degree that no artist since the Middle Ages has dared to attempt."[38]

While the exhibition had been getting under way, Durand-Ruel, at the invitation of the American Art Association, had been organizing in New York the largest of his attempts to redress his financial situation in France with the help of foreign sales; by June he had reason to feel encouraged. The show, billed as "Works in Oil and Pastel by the Impressionists

Jockeys in the Rain, c. 1886

of Paris" (although it included many non-Impressionists and even a few *pompiers*), opened on April 10 in the American Art Galleries, on Madison Square, with three hundred and ten pictures by thirty-two artists, among them Cassatt, Caillebotte, Degas (represented by twenty-three items, most of them now unidentifiable), Desboutin, Fantin-Latour, Forain, Guillaumin, Manet, Monet, Morisot, Pissarro, Renoir, Seurat, Signac, and Sisley. It aroused enough curiosity to warrant being prolonged for a month in the exhibition rooms of the National Academy of Design. Some of the local critics equaled Wolff in their pompous unperceptiveness; a writer in *Art Age,* for instance, described the new French school as "communism incarnate,"[39] and one in the *Sun* dismissed Degas as merely a fellow who "draws badly."[40] But in general the press was favorable; about a fifth of the works on view were sold, Mary Cassatt was an effective proselyter; and there was significant evidence of alarm among Manhattan dealers who had invested heavily in Bougereau, Cabanel, Meissonier, and Gérôme. Durand-Ruel now believed — rightly, as things turned out — that in the long run he would be saved by the Americans.

In Europe, too, things were looking up for the Impressionists and their colleagues, although there were still hard times ahead for Pissarro, Sisley, and Gauguin. At the beginning of 1886, Renoir, Redon, and Zandomeneghi had been asked to show their work in Brussels at the annual exhibition staged by the avant-garde Cercle des XX (so called because originally composed of twenty artists); Pissarro, Morisot, Lebourg, Raffaëlli, and Seurat were to be among the participants the following spring. In the spectacular Expositions Internationales organized by Petit in his new gallery in the Rue de Sèze during 1886 and 1887, Monet, Renoir, Sisley, Morisot, and Raffaëlli were among the invited. By May 1887 Monet was able to inform Durand-Ruel, a bit maliciously, that, under the direction of Theo van Gogh, the Boussod and Valadon Gallery — still Goupil's to the older generation of artists — was buying up works by Renoir, Sisley, Degas, and Monet himself from other dealers and from collectors and reselling them almost immediately. In short, the final victory over the academic Establishment was at hand. And so, depressingly if quite naturally, was the final collapse of the alliance formed nearly twenty years earlier in the Café Guerbois and the studios of the Batignolles and the Ninth Arrondissement. After the eighth group exhibition of secessionists from the Salon, no one even thought of proposing to continue the series.

The year 1886 was also marked by the publication in April, after a successful run as a serial in the daily newspaper *Gil Blas,* of Zola's *L'Oeuvre.* The novel, in recounting the failure and suicide of a modern painter, relied closely enough on the history of Impressionism to be read as a condemnation of the whole modern movement. There was, of course, nothing very specific about the connection: the tragic hero, Claude Lantier, could be identified as readily with Gervex as with Manet, Cézanne, or Monet. But the book was loaded with evidence that Zola had never quite understood the aims of his artist-friends in the Batignolles group, that he had confused Impressionism with literary Naturalism, and that now, a famous writer installed in a fine villa on the Seine, he pitied the old comrades who had not turned out as well as he had. Moreover, he added to the irritation of the old comrades by defending the story in terms that exempted no one, not even Manet and Degas, from his complacent condescension. Moore describes a dinner party, organized to celebrate the appearance of *L'Oeuvre,* at which Madame Charpentier argued, partly as a provocation, that the protagonist, after all, was not a man of talent:

> Seeing that all were siding with Madame Charpentier, Zola plunged like a bull into the thick of the fray, and did not hesitate to affirm that he had gifted Claude Lantier with infinitely larger qualities than those which nature had bestowed upon Edouard Manet. This statement was received in mute anger by those present, all of whom had been personal friends and warm admirers of Manet's genius. . . . It must be observed that M. Zola intended no disparagement of M. Manet, but he was concerned to defend the theory of his book — namely, that no painter working in the modern movement had achieved a result equivalent to that which had been achieved by at least three or four writers. . . . And, in reply to one who was anxiously urging Degas' claim to the highest consideration, he said, "I cannot accept a man who shuts himself up all his life to draw a ballet-girl as ranking co-equal in dignity and power with Flaubert, Daudet, and Goncourt."[41]

He seems to have been obsessed by this idea of a rivalry between modern painters and modern novelists (himself included, of course), for in 1883 he had written to Huysmans concerning the latter's praise of Degas in the recently published *Art moderne:*

> I am afraid we are not always in agreement. I am not ready to demolish Courbet and proclaim Degas the greatest modern artist. The more I advance and the more I cut loose from merely curious corners of observation, the more I love the great, abundant creators who present us with an entire world. I know Degas very well, and have known him for a long while. He is nothing but a constipated fellow with a very pretty talent.[42]

After 1886 Cézanne, Pissarro, Monet, and Renoir avoided Zola. Degas confessed that the novelist's detailed card-index kind of Naturalism "has on me the effect of a giant putting together a postal directory,"[43] and maintained that *L'Oeuvre* had been written "simply to prove the great superiority of the man of letters over the painter."[44]

19. Celebrity

Z OLA'S PHRASE "shuts himself up" had some truth in it, for strangers were notoriously unwelcome at 19 bis Rue Fontaine-Saint-Georges, and even old friends, after ringing the downstairs bell, were apt to be subjected to a long wait while a concealed, suspicious Degas peered down from a sort of medieval turret flanking the studio and decided whether he wanted to interrupt his work. He reacted violently to the intrusion of critics into what he called his "fortified enceinte,"[1] and on one occasion, after the publication of an unauthorized, though favorable, article in *La Revue de Paris,* he exploded into what was almost a denial of his vocation:

> Is painting done to be looked at? Do you understand me? One works for two or three friends who are alive and for others who are dead or unknown. Is it any business of journalists if I make pictures, boots, or cloth slippers? Painting concerns one's private life.[2]

One day in the late 1880s he said to George Moore, who was secretly preparing a critical essay:

> I think that literature has only done harm to art. You puff out the artist with vanity, you inculcate the taste for notoriety, and that is all. . . . You do not even help us to sell our pictures. A man buys a picture not because he read an article in a newspaper, but because a friend, who he thinks knows something about pictures, told him it would be worth twice as much ten years hence as it is worth today. . . . *Dites?*[3]

This insistence on being left alone ceased completely, however, when the daylight in the atelier faded and he returned to his apartment in the Rue Pigalle. Then he dressed for the evening — with a touch of démodé dandyism during his middle years — and, if he did not have guests coming, prepared to leave for the Opéra, the Cirque Fernando, the Théâtre des Variétés, Les Ambassadeurs, the Café La Rochefoucauld or, very often, a dinner engagement. The steady flow of invitations he received can be attributed partly to the loyalty of friends, to the fact that a bachelor is a useful fill-in for a hostess, and to sympathy for a man without local relatives. (In 1878 his sister Marguerite, the last member of the family to remain with him in Paris, had emigrated to Buenos Aires with her architect-husband, Henri Fevre, and their children.) But from accounts of him at table it is clear that a principal reason for his social success was his talent for keeping a conversation going. "I can't play piquet or billiards," he once lamented to Bartholomé, "or curry favor with people, or paint in front of a landscape, or simply be agreeable in society."[4] He was right on every count except the last, although "agreeable" was not exactly the word for some of his more virtuosic, more reckless dinner-table performances.

Throughout the 1880s and 1890s, when the principals were not out of the city, Friday evening meant dinner in Henri Rouart's big town house at 34 Rue de Lisbonne. The quarter, a tree-lined network of short streets mostly carved out of the nearby Parc Monceau by Second Empire real estate promoters, echoed with the nineteenth-century use of art to legitimate capitalist enterprise; between the Rue de Lisbonne and what was left of the eighteenth-century park where the brand new Rue Rembrandt, Rue Murillo, Avenue Ruysdaël, Avenue Van-Dyck, Rue de Vézelay (Mérimée and Viollet-le-Duc had given Romanesque a certain cachet), and Avenue Velasquez. And the legitimating assumed a concrete, thoroughly defensible form when one entered number 34, which had been designed — by Fevre shortly after the collapse of the Commune — to accommodate, in the jammed-together manner of the period, one of the largest painting and sculpture collections in Paris, put together patiently and personally by Rouart by keeping an eye on the auctions in the Hôtel Drouot and on the offerings of unconventional dealers like Martin, Tanguy, and Theo van Gogh. Among the pictures, which tapestried the walls from the floors to the high ceilings and proliferated onto easels, were eventually fifty-three Corots, fifteen Millets, fifteen Delacroix, fifteen Degas (if one counts the copy of Poussin's *Rape of the Sabines*), fourteen Daumiers, ten Boudins, eight Courbets, seven Jongkinds, and works by El Greco, Goya, Fragonard, Chardin, Prud'hon, Isabey, Théodore Rousseau, Lépine, Diaz, Harpignies, Bonvin, Bouguereau (inexplicably), Puvis de Chavannes, Fantin-Latour, Cassatt, Cézanne,

Forain, Manet, Monet, Morisot, and Pissarro. The sculpture included
Egyptian wood funerary statues, Greek Classical fragments, marble busts
of the French seventeenth and eighteenth centuries, Romantic bronzes, and
anticipations of the twentieth century in some pieces by Medardo Rosso.
In such a house Degas was back, emotionally if not stylistically, in the
world of passionate connoisseurship he had glimpsed as a boy in the homes
of La Caze, Marcille, and the elder Valpinçon; and he was also, after the
years of exhibiting and arguing with his secessionist allies, back in the
reassuring climate of the *grande bourgeoisie* and of something like the extended families he had known in Naples and New Orleans. Among the
other regular dinner guests were a mathematics professor and, most prominently, a group of industrialists, engineers, and artillery officers, nearly all
of them members, with Rouart, of the influential caste of Ecole Polytechnique old boys. "These gentlemen," Jacques-Emile Blanche once pointed
out, "were accustomed to precision; they were specialists whose technical
language, scientific knowledge, and sense of order and discipline pleased
Monsieur Degas greatly."[5] Hovering in the background and providing a
fund of affection for the childless bachelor were Rouart's grown-up daughter, Hélène, and his four sons, who ranged from Louis, born in 1869, down
at two-year intervals through Alexis, Eugène, and Ernest. Degas was especially fond of Ernest, who became a painter, and of Louis, even though the
boy became an art critic. The single perceptible flaw in the pattern of moral
and intellectual comfort supplied by Friday night was Madame Rouart, a
sharp-featured, pursed-lipped woman who seems never to have understood
why her husband was so attached to that talkative, often irascible artist.

Tuesday evening meant dinner with Henri Rouart's younger brother,
Alexis, for a while out on the eastern edge of Paris in the Boulevard Voltaire
and then, by the second half of the 1880s, in a house at 36 Rue de Lisbonne
that had also been designed by Fevre. Here, although many of the guests
were the same as those who appeared next door on Friday, the talk and
atmosphere were usually quite different, for Alexis had an eclectic mind
that was not at all the heavyweight Ecole Polytechnique sort, and he had
an art collection that was the result more of happy rummaging than of
consistent objectives. Japanese prints were mixed in with watercolors by
Eugène Lami, and Indian sculpture with Tanagra figurines. There were,
however, five pastels by Degas, a nearly complete set of Degas prints (kept
up to date by the artist himself, who knew that the lot was to go eventually
to the Cabinet des Estampes), and lithographs by Daumier, Devéria, Gavarni, Géricault, Lami, and Raffet that Alexis had been accumulating since
his adolescence.

Thursday evenings and two or three lunch hours during the week were apt to be spent with the Halévys at 22 Rue de Douai, within sight of 19 bis Rue Fontaine-Saint-Georges and behind a Second Empire façade of volutes, angels, bracketed balconies, and Composite columns that was the creation, according to Daniel Halévy, "of a delirious stonemason who had passed through Rome."[6] Here the atmosphere was an agreeable blend of affluence, social assurance, irreverent intelligence, and familial intimacy. Ludovic Halévy was the son of the dramatist and historian Léon Halévy, the nephew of the composer Fromental Halévy, and the grandson of the architect Hippolyte Lebas, who had designed Notre-Dame-de-Lorette and part of the Paris Bourse. After leaving Louis-le-Grand the young man had become a civil servant in the new Bonapartist regime and later the private secretary of the Duc de Morny, who was Napoleon III's bastard half brother, a promoter of fashionable Deauville, and a hustling businessman with a Corsican parvenu's disrespect for very important persons. (One day James Rothschild, cofounder of his dynasty's Europe-wide consortium, appeared in the office. "Take a chair," Morny said, without bothering to get up. "I am Rothschild," the ruffled banker replied. "Oh," said Morny, "then take two chairs.")

Beginning in 1861, Halévy had moved from this apprenticeship in impudence to the theatrical partnership with Henri Meilhac. He had to his credit a long list of skits, plays, and librettos, the last mostly for Offenbach's operettas but also for Bizet's *Carmen* and, somewhat indirectly, Johann Strauss's *Die Fledermaus*. At one point in the 1870s he had had a dozen pieces running or rehearsing in Paris at the same time. He had added two best-selling novels and in 1884 membership in the Académie Française, after which, though he was just past fifty, he became mostly a retired writer managing a still profitable literary estate. Presumably he had decided that a logical corollary to *il faut être de son temps* was that one should stop when one's consonant time, which for him had been the carefree years of the Second Empire, was over. ("The customers," he had remarked to Offenbach in the 1870s, "aren't what they were twenty years ago, and we aren't either.") This uninterruptedly successful career, which was doubly remarkable in view of the slender talent behind it, had been rounded out by a happy marriage with the well-connected Louise Bréguet, a member of the powerful Bréguet family of instrument-makers and physicists and the niece of the celebrated chemist and statesman Marcellin Berthelot; and by the birth of two sons, Elie in 1870 and Daniel two years later, who in the mid-1880s were brilliant students on their way to becoming professional historians and political essayists. Degas was on old-schoolmate terms with Ludovic and on almost a brother-and-sister basis with Louise, who as a girl had known his parents and all the Degas children and had been one of Marguerite's close friends.

Halévy's cousin Geneviève, the daughter of his uncle Fromental, was occasionally one of the attractions of Thursday evening. She was a striking, witty, ambitious, mildly neurasthenic woman who had gone through several years of relative penury as the wife of Georges Bizet and who, after the composer's untimely death in 1875, had set about using the royalties from the worldwide success of *Carmen* to launch herself socially. A dramatic portrait of her in her widow's costume, painted by Degas's Villa Medici comrade Elie Delaunay, had been one of the hits of the Salon of 1878, and she had soon become known for her clothes, receptions, and repartee. (Asked by an advanced bluestocking for an opinion on incest, she said, "Madame, all I'm up on is adultery.")[7] In 1886 she married Emile Straus, a lawyer for the Rothschild interests and a rumored Rothschild illegitimate son, and established herself in a town house in the Boulevard Haussmann, decorated with a collection of paintings that ranged from eighteenth-century portraits of the mythological Nattier sort to nineteenth-century *pompiérisme* and Impressionism. Here she maintained a salon at which one might encounter politicians, financiers, Réjane, Maupassant, Goncourt, the young Proust, Degas, Forain, Puvis de Chavannes, generals, musicians, and a group of aristocrats that included the beautiful, fabulously rich Comtesse Greffulhe, who would become a model for the Duchesse de Guermantes of *A la recherche du temps perdu*. Degas wavered in his attitude toward Geneviève between fascination and an impulse to deflate. He obtained permission to watch her having her hair combed, he often accompanied her to the shops of the important couturiers, he canceled engagements in order to be with her when she had an open day on her social calendar, and in one of his letters he reproached himself for having temporarily neglected her. But he dismissed the Delaunay picture as a piece of "studio mourning,"[8] he referred to her as a "person devoured by society,"[9] and when she wondered why he liked going with her to the dressmaker's for a fitting he said, "It's the red hands of the little girl who holds the pins."[10]

Another of his Rue de Douai favorites was Madame Hortense Howland, an elegant, lettered Parisienne whose wealthy American husband had returned to the United States after providing her with a comfortable annual income and a house in the Rue de La Rochefoucauld, where her neighbor across a shared garden was Gustave Moreau. As a teen-age intellectual during the Second Empire she had been influenced by the popular Ecole Normale professor Victor Cousin, a mixer of philosophical systems who was also the author of studies of seventeenth-century *précieuses* and female Jansenists. In the mid-1870s she had been intimate with Fromentin, who addressed to her some of the letters on Dutch and Flemish painting that became the basis for his book *Les Maîtres d'autrefois*. By the mid-1880s she had established herself as a hostess whose guest list included Nadar, Degas, Cassatt, Moreau, Sickert, Jockey Club members, Symbolist poets, art critics, and the extravagant aesthete Robert de Montesquiou. Degas called her *belle amie,*[11] threatened to weep when she left the Ninth Arrondissement for a voyage to America, and at the same time dismissed much of the conversation in her salon as "tittle-tattle."[12]

Among the men in the Halévy circle the most important were Ernest Reyer, Albert Boulanger-Cavé, and Charles Haas. Reyer, who had grown up during the maturity of Rossini and Donizetti and had succeeded Berlioz as the critic for *Le Journal des Débats,* was a link with the great musical past (he had covered the Cairo première of *Aida* for his paper), a gifted composer, and a peculiarly placid talker with a knack for provoking explosions from more opinionated people. Boulanger-Cavé had moved as a young man in the entourages of both Delacroix and Ingres, served briefly as a theater censor during the early Second Empire, and then decided, with the help of some inherited money, to become a permanent loafer, a sort of bourgeois aristocrat; Daniel Halévy called him "a do-nothing Ariel"[13] but admired his taste and wit. Haas was also a man of leisure, although he was nominally employed now and then as a roving administrator in businesses controlled by the Rothschilds. In his time (he was a year older than Degas), aided by green eyes, blond curls, a faun's beard, and the best tailor in Paris, he had been a famous Lothario, with several social lionesses and the twenty-year-old Sarah Bernhardt on his list of conquests. Then he had become an inspector of historical monuments under Mérimée, an adviser on objets d'art for both Bonapartist and Legitimist aristocrats, an insider at the court of Napoleon III, and the second Jewish member of the Jockey Club (the first was a Rothschild). On the verge of sixty, still slim, seductive, and carefully urbane, he was a romantically representative survival, a Monsieur Second Empire, to nostalgic young snobs like Blanche and Proust. Twenty years later something of his way of life and some of his traits — for example, the habit, acquired from the Goncourts, of comparing his friends to figures in old master paintings — would reappear in the Swann of *A la recherche.* Degas, perhaps a bit enviously, derided him as "a ladies' man,"[14] found his conversational effects too "managed,"[15] and evidently preferred the low-pressure talk of Boulanger-Cavé, whom he described as "an alliance of sloth with finesse."[16] Less categorically, Halévy remarked, "For going to [suburban] Asnières I would take Haas, but for going to Constantinople I would rather have Cavé."[17]

The other survivors of the Batignolles group did not appear in the Rue de Lisbonne and the Rue de Douai. A remnant of the relationships of the Guerbois era was preserved, however, by Berthe Morisot and Eugène

Manet, who in 1883 had acquired a large ground-floor apartment with an adjoining garden at 40 Rue de Villejust (today the Rue Paul-Valéry), two blocks from the Arc de Triomphe. Here, in a combination of atelier and living room hung with paintings by her brother-in-law Edouard and filled with First Empire furniture, Berthe organized monthly dinners attended regularly by Degas and Renoir and fairly often by Monet, Sisley, Fantin-Latour, Puvis de Chavannes, Astruc, and Mallarmé. She was now an intimidating, white-haired matron who struck one of her visitors, the poet and novelist Henri de Régnier, as being "haughty and enigmatic . . . in her infinitely distinguished frigidity,"[18] but who in fact kept warm in her heart and mind her memories. At the beginning of 1884, much as if nothing had happened since Alfred Stevens's prewar Wednesday night parties, she reported again to Edma, "Degas is still the same, witty and paradoxical."[19] Later that year she and Eugène surprised him by sending him as a present Edouard's *Departure of the Steamboat,* one of the larger oils they had bought back during the mostly disappointing post-decease auction at the Hôtel Drouot; and they received an affectionate letter of acknowledgment:

> You wanted to please me greatly, and you have succeeded. Behind your gift there are several special intentions of a delicately thoughtful sort that have deeply affected me. I'll be over shortly to see you and thank you.[20]

Some of the "special intentions" probably involved the circumstance that the picture, which is a preliminary version of the better-known *Departure of the Folkestone Boat,* had been painted during the summer holiday of 1869 when Degas and Manet were together at Boulogne-sur-Mer.

The long series of notebooks begun by the student Edgar came to an end in 1886, probably because he no longer had a strong need to record picture ideas and worry about ego identity. The gap in biographical material thus created is not, however, as serious as it could have been, for the Degas of the late 1880s and early 1890s was a confessional letter-writer and a man who interested his literate contemporaries, both as an artist and as a celebrity who was beginning to acquire the mythical dimensions of a *monstre sacré.* His little paintings of danseuses, racehorses, café-concert divas, and faceless women in tubs were being bought at rising prices by wealthy collectors as various as Mrs. Havemeyer, the banker Isaac de Camondo, the composer Ernest Chausson, the impresario Paul Gallimard (at one point the owner of the Théâtre des Variétés), the perfumer Alfred Chéramy, the porcelain manufacturer Charles Haviland, the Tokyo and Paris art dealer Tadamara Hayashi, and the society dentist Georges Viau. His appearance, walk, and idiosyncrasies were being recorded, and his remarks collected. In short, the lifelong observer was now very much the observed.

He had never been what might be described as a fine figure of a man, and some of the defects in his physical make-up — the concave face, a certain lack of luster in the eyes, skin, and hair, and a tendency toward a round-shouldered stoop — had been accentuated by middle age, to the point of giving a general first impression of mediocrity. In 1888 van Gogh, linking looks to a supposed outlook, categorized him as a "notary," a word that in the bohemia of nineteenth-century Paris connoted a middle-class conformist. Around the same date, Moore insisted that "for those who know him the suit of pepper-and-salt and the blue necktie tied around a loose collar are full of *him,*" but granted that "the casual visitor of the Café de la Rochefoucauld would have to be more than usually endowed with the critical sense to discern that Degas was not an ordinary man."[21] Apparently the one visually striking thing about this "ordinary man" was his gait, which Moore described as "rolling" and Thadée Natanson recalled as having become by the 1890s a peculiarly complex and surprisingly rapid strut:

> At the racetrack or in the street he advanced leaning on his cane, with his belly somewhat out in front and his legs following in the indolent manner of a duck, but this way of walking was nevertheless rapid enough to make the flaps of his caped cloak fly around his shoulders.[22]

It was the kind of locomotion Freud would interpret as "a symbolic substitute for stamping on the body of Mother Earth"[23] and that non-Freudians can see as a less specific form of compensation, applicable to more than one feeling of inadequacy. It was also, in spite of its strange capacity for speed, the walk of a Parisian stroller, a born *flâneur,* who was ready at any moment to stop, settle back on his heels and cane, and then, as remembered by the critic Arsène Alexandre, "examine things and people with a sort of recoil of the bust and a bridling up of the head."[24]

His small manias were of the same obsessional stuff as his devotion to art, his need for independence, and his hatred of phoniness and *arrivisme.* Having developed a temporary passion for lace-trimmed handkerchiefs from Normandy, he mobilized the idle Boulanger-Cavé for a search, sent off a special order to Dieppe, and bought enough in Rouen, according to one of his letters, to provoke roughly a tripling of the local price. He then turned to canes and began to haunt the special workshops of the Rue du Faubourg-Saint-Denis and the Gare du Nord quarter in the hope of adding to his collection of antique knobs. He detested central heating, huge lampshades, people who did not arrive on time, trucklers who addressed him as *maître,* and omnibus passengers who wore large bonnets secured by protruding hatpins; and he became particularly vehement on the subject of overweight dowagers in strapless evening gowns:

What's it to us that they have shoulders, when their faces are old and their necks are worn? These women would be ready to appear completely naked and turn in every direction just to demonstrate that they still have scapulae. How the Orientals must laugh at us![25]

His anachronistic education had included an attentive reading of one of the masterpieces of Romantic Classical gastronomic literature, Jean-Anthelme Brillat-Savarin's *Physiology of Taste,* and he had firm notions about the proper way to dine: cats, dogs, and young children, he felt, should be kept out of the room, and there should be neither flowers as a centerpiece nor perfumed guests at the table to compete with the smell of the food. He loved the odor of burning toast, to the extent that he sometimes thrust a piece of bread into a fireplace for the pleasure of inhaling the pungent result.

The making of *mots* was much in vogue during the last third of the century, and the better-known makers were in the habit of delivering their sallies with a ramming emphasis and an air of self-satisfaction that to a modern sensibility suggests the delivery of vaudeville gags. Whistler, for instance, was famous for his triumphant cackle, a shrill "eh what," and a tendency to let his monocle drop from his eye as final punctuation. The playwright Henry Becque concluded a bright retort with a grating, whinnying *woin* (pronounced roughly "vwahng"), Zola with a patronizing *hein, mon bon* (huh, my dear fellow), the caricaturist Caran d'Ache with *c'est drôle ça, tu sais* (that's funny, you know), and Stevens, as described by Goncourt, with "an interrogative *hein,* a thoroughly disagreeable *hein* that was like a belch in your face." Degas contributed to this period style by frequently winding up a *mot* with a loud *dites, quoi?* (what do you say to that?), and sometimes he added an ironical, oddly professional nuance to the performance by immediately extending his hand as if to be congratulated.[26] But he was also addicted to throwaway lines uttered in a low voice, and Blanche was struck by a combination of the peremptory with the fearful:

> At certain times Monsieur Degas's attitude is that of a cavalry major on a drill ground: if he makes a gesture, the gesture is imperious, expressive, like his drawing. But he soon adopts a defensive position, like a woman hiding her nakedness. It is the habit of a recluse veiling or protecting his personality.[27]

The opera singer Jeanne Raunay thought that "he was above all timid" and that "he found it convenient to mask this timidity by assuming a forceful, blustering manner."[28]

His *mots,* like his pictures and sculpture, often mixed acute observation with economy of means and a touch of the passing maliciousness that

Henri Bergson called "a momentary anaesthesia of the heart," and they usually juxtaposed apparently incompatible frames of reference, much as his art might combine realism with artificiality or use a timeless classicizing idiom to depict lowbrow ephemerality. He praised Renoir as "a cat playing with a multicolored ball of wool,"[29] described an academic colorist as "a *pompier* who has caught fire,"[30] and dismissed the retiring but ambitious Moreau as "a hermit who knows the train schedules."[31]

He was not, of course, always intent on turning out phrases for circulation in Paris studios and salons, and Redon, after spending an hour with him in Vollard's gallery, was agreeably impressed by a different style:

> The chatting of Degas is not solid, substantial. It is entirely made up of abridgments, needlepoints, delicate facets. He has read nothing, except some book or other of 1830, some studio gossip in which Ingres or Delacroix is mentioned. He knows pictures extremely well. He has seen all the pictures there are, he knows them from top to bottom, and he sees what is in them. The main interest in his talk is in the rage he exhales against the false and the absurd. I told him how pleasantly surprised I was, in view of his reputation for being a tiger, by his communicative sociability. He said he maintained that legend of ferocity to get people to let him alone. When I left him my mind was awake and alert. Afterward, I don't know why, I thought of Stendhal. He must have talked the way Degas does. Or so I imagine.[32]

On other occasions the charm seems to have come from a rapid and peculiarly inconsequent flow of fantasy and persiflage intended for immediate consumption. The diary Daniel Halévy kept for a number of years in the Rue de Douai provides some hints of what the flow may have been like:

> *December 26, 1890.* Dinner. After dinner Elie and I corner Degas. It was delightful.
> "I should like," he began by saying, "to have in Paris a sober place where serious music would be performed and where one could smoke and drink. In England there is a café, a tavern, where choruses sing Handel."
> "But that's unreasonable," I objected. "You won't find in Paris two hundred smokers and drinkers who love good music."
> "You don't know what you're talking about," he said. "There are even some Buddhists in Paris."[33]

> *January 22, 1891.* He talked about someone who had gone off to become a settler in Canada.
> "I was very happy," he said, "to see him escape from journalism."
> "He was in journalism?"
> "He could have been."[34]

Another friend, the curator Paul-André Lemoisne, wrote, "The talk of Degas was extremely hard to describe, partly because of its attractive un-expectedness and variety and also because it was quite different in an intimate exchange between friends from what it was when addressed to strangers or to people he disliked."[35] Other acquaintances noticed that it was again different when aimed at fellow artists, for then it was apt to be seasoned with affectionate abuse and with words that would not become acceptable in French drawing rooms until after World War II. "Bonnat," he once said to the now very successful comrade from Louis-le-Grand and the Villa Medici, "in life you are a good fellow, but in painting you are just *un con*."[36] (Literally "a cunt," figuratively "a damned fool" or "a mean bastard.")

By the late 1880s his aesthetic theories and opinions were fixed, and Berthe Morisot was impressed enough to write some of them down after the dinners in the Rue de Villejust and pass them on to her young daughter, Julie Manet:

> Degas said that the study of nature was worthless, since painting is an art of conventions, and that it was infinitely better to learn to draw from Holbein. He said that Edouard [Manet], although priding himself on slavishly copying nature, was in fact the most mannered painter in the world, never made a brush stroke without first thinking of the old masters, and did not, for example, draw fingernails, because Frans Hals had not drawn them.
>
> At dinner with Mallarmé he said, "Art is falseness." And he went on to explain that, since objects look the same to everyone, you are an artist only at certain times, by an effort of the will. . . .
>
> He recalled a joke of Edouard's on introducing [the Naturalist novelist] Paul Alexis: "He does cafés after nature."[37]

This emphasis on the mode of representation was linked to a continuing interest in such conventional arts as ballet, opera, and music in general, and also to a profound, if sometimes ironically exaggerated, disapproval of Monet's retinalism and of the crowds of open-air amateurs who were beginning to invade the countryside around Paris on Sunday afternoons. During one of his many conversations with Vollard, he said:

> If I were in the government I would have a brigade of gendarmes for keeping an eye on people who paint landscapes after nature. Oh, I wouldn't want anyone killed. I would be satisfied with a bit of birdshot to begin with.[38]

He admired Mantegna, the Pollaiuolo brothers, Ghirlandaio, and Botticelli, and shocked Gérôme one day at the Café La Rochefoucauld by maintaining that "there have been three great draftsmen in the nineteenth century: Ingres, Delacroix, and Daumier."[39]

Although convinced that drawing was more important than coloring, he insisted, in a talk with Jeanniot, on the need for free handling and on the danger of being too explicit:

> At the moment there is a fashion for pictures in which you can see the time of day, as on a sundial. I don't like that at all. A painting calls for a certain mystery, some vagueness, some fantasy. If you dot all the *i*'s you wind up being a bore.[40]

His term for a slickly finished picture was *bouguereauté*.[41] He regretted the academic erosion of traditional themes; after looking at a Nativity he remarked to Daniel Halévy, "How many lovely subjects there were! It's really unfortunate that we have allowed them to be taken from us by imbeciles."[42] At the same time he was contemptuous of the Salon artists who, after years of insults, were beginning to imitate the motifs and techniques of the Impressionists and their secessionist allies and to agree that *il faut être de son temps*. "They shoot us down," he said, "and then go through our pockets."[43]

His opposition to painting landscapes after nature did not keep him from spending a good deal of time in rural or semirural settings. Nearly every summer, usually in August, he went to the château at Ménil-Hubert for an intended visit of a few days and then stayed on and on, sometimes for several weeks, yielding to the urging of the Valpinçons and working frequently in a park pavilion they let him use as a studio. At other periods of the year he might be found week-ending in the vicinity of Louveciennes, where Pissarro, Sisley, and Henri Rouart often painted, or in La Queue-en-Brie, a village on the Marne side of Paris in which the Rouart family had a country house. In 1893 Halévy added another piece to the pattern by buying a large place at Sucy-en-Brie, a locality within walking distance of La Queue-en-Brie. Clearly, the exile from the "fortified enceinte" and the overheated stove in the Ninth Arrondissement did not find a spell of green space and fresh air very disagreeable.

But there was no question of Romantic personification, empathy, and communion: in a letter of 1887 to Henry Lerolle he complained that "when we are in love with nature, we can never know whether she loves us in return."[44] Nor was there any feeling of being nourished physically and spiritually by Mother Earth; on the contrary, he was capable of being darkly, pseudoscientifically imaginative on the subject of the animosity nature might have toward innocent Parisians. During the wet August of 1884 he wrote to Rouart from Ménil-Hubert:

> In France one should no longer believe in anything except rain. Here we are in a hollow. A large park, extremely tall trees close together, and water that emerges under your feet. There are meadows where you seem to be walking

on sponges. Why shouldn't the cattle grazing and maturing on this humid grass contract rheumatism? And transmit it to us when we eat them?[45]

He felt better in places transformed by human activity, and in an undated note from Paris he scolded Rouart for having chosen Argelès-Gazost, a picturesque hamlet in the high Pyrenees, as a vacation spot:

> Stop looking for wild scenery. Every year you have the same regret. . . . Long live the suburbs. I keep coming back to that subject because I feel that in it I have grasped a great truth. . . . Come back to the place at Louveciennes and write me a letter. Louis XIV's aqueduct is there, Monsieur Rouart, and it's impressive, and so are the Marly reservoirs. And one thinks of Madame du Barry, who would not have had her head chopped off if she had loved her pavilion a little less.[46]

In still another exchange with Rouart he argued that nature "consoles" us chiefly by budging: "If the leaves of the trees did not move, how sad the trees would be — and so would we."[47]

The generally perceptive Jeanne Raunay felt that he was "a bit of a snob,"[48] especially when he was pretending not to be one. What she had in mind can be seen in an entry in Daniel Halévy's diary concerning the Marais, a Paris quarter which was inhabited mostly by Jewish artisans from Eastern Europe and with which Degas had become acquainted during his manic search for rare canes:

> "I should like," he said in this connection, "to get to know these Marais working-class families. You go into buildings that look filthy — with very narrow entrances. And you find bright, well-lighted, extremely clean apartments. The doors are open on the stairway landings; everyone is cheerful, everyone is working. Moreover, these people do not have the servility of merchants in shops. It's a delightful society."[49]

At lunch one day in 1888 in the Rue de Douai he fulminated against the democratization of education that had been initiated by the reforms of Jules Ferry as minister of public instruction and had rapidly become a feature of the new republican order:

> "It consists," he said, "in making people unfit for a lot of métiers that would enable them to earn a living. In the old days the daughters of concièrges became danseuses; now they have diplomas from the town hall."[50]

Pushing the matter of class farther into the past, and adding a jab at the new bathrooms of the Third Republic, he said of the subjects of Louis XIV, "They were dirty perhaps, but distinguished; we are clean, but common."[51]

As his celebrity grew, his opposition to Establishment honors and to other signs of his having arrived became more pronounced — and more irrational, in the opinion even of his admirers. He taunted Halévy constantly, and not always very amiably, about having topped a career in show business by becoming a member of the stuffy Académie Française. "There are successes," he observed to Jean-Louis Forain, "that take the form of a panic."[52] In 1888 he rejected a warmly flattering invitation from the Belgian critic Octav Maus to participate in a festival of modernism organized by the Cercle des XX in Brussels; in 1889 he insisted on the withdrawal of his work from the Exposition Universelle that marked the centenary of the fall of the Bastille (and of which the Eiffel Tower was the main attraction); in 1890 he went into a quivering rage because one of his lithographs appeared in a Paris exhibition without his permission, which he made clear he would have refused.

And shortly after that he reacted with particular fury to a threat of governmental favor, which materialized because Charles de Freycinet, a former lieutenant of Gambetta's, became prime minister and appointed the writer Henry Roujon, one of Mallarmé's best friends, to the post of director of fine arts. Mallarmé immediately went to work and soon managed, with some influential help, to persuade the state to buy Whistler's *Portrait of the Artist's Mother* and Renoir's *Girls at the Piano;* he then put on the pressure for Degas, with such success that one day, innocently pleased with himself, he appeared with an offer to acquire a picture for the Musée du Luxembourg (for the Louvre, that is, eventually). "Fortunately," Degas said later, "there was a table between us."[53] Mallarmé remembered "easels flapping under his fingers"[54] during the stormy interview. To Halévy, who saw nothing criminal in Roujon's action, the reply was another tirade:

> These people want to make me believe I have arrived. . . . To arrive is to be on a wall next to a portrait of a woman by Bougereau. . . . They have the chessboard of the fine arts on their table, and we artists are the pieces. They push this pawn and then that pawn. I'm not a pawn. I don't want to be pushed.[55]

Although self-esteem was involved, there was also a rather rollicking enjoyment of himself being crustily independent. He told Halévy, "I don't want you to defend me the way you do, by saying I'm an old lunatic. You must say I'm a philosopher. Not a lunatic. A philosopher, an old philosopher."[56] He tried to say "philosopher" once more and broke down in puffs of laughter.

His relations with many of his mature contemporaries were a mixture of mutual respect and only occasional acidity. "Renoir," he told Vollard, "can do anything."[57] And Renoir returned the admiration. Pissarro, in a letter to his son Lucien, said, "Degas is without any doubt at all the greatest artist of our time."[58] With Whistler things were not quite so smooth, for though Degas thought highly of the nocturnes, *The Artist's Mother,* and the etchings, he found the "Ten O'Clock" lecture much too precious and its author too dandified. "The butterfly role," he remarked to Sickert, "must be very tiring. I prefer being the old ox."[59] During the late 1880s the friendship with Cassatt was interrupted by his criticism of one of her pictures, but she recovered her equanimity, and in 1892, when she was struggling with a large mural for the Columbian Exhibition that was to open in Chicago, she wrote from Paris to Mrs. Potter-Palmer, who was in charge of the Women's Art Building at the fair:

> I have been half a dozen times on the point of asking Degas to come and see my work, but if he happens to be in the mood he would demolish me so completely that I could not pick myself up in time to finish for the exhibition. Still, he is the only man I know whose judgement would be a help to me.[60]

After looking at some of Redon's lithographs of nightmarish monsters, he said, "As for what he means, often I don't understand very much, but as for his blacks, oh his blacks, it's impossible to print anything more handsome,"[61] and Redon reciprocated in 1889 by writing in his diary:

> Degas's admiration for Ingres is a mental love affair; his heart is not in it. . . . But Degas is an artist, and one who is free and very exciting. . . . His name, more than his work, is synonymous with character. . . . Around him will always turn any discussion of the principle of independence. . . . So he is an occasion for respect. Absolute respect.[62]

Bonnat confessed, "I don't like to talk with Degas very long, because after I have left him, I feel tempted to change my way of painting."[63] One day in 1889, however, the two men found themselves together on the top deck of an omnibus in Biarritz, and as a result of their conversation Bonnat received as a gift the portrait of himself painted in the Rue de Mondovi more than a quarter of a century before. "Each of us," Degas said gently, "has followed his road. Life is funny."[64]

His relations with younger artists were unpredictable. The obviously talented Henri de Toulouse-Lautrec, for instance, seems to have had everything in his favor for Degas's approval. His subject matter included the music hall, the café-concert, the theater, the circus, and the brothel; he preferred the city to the country; and he loved drawing, prints, movement, time notations, and unexpected mise-en-scènes. In other words, he was the only major nineteenth-century painter who could be called a Degas disciple.

Moreover, he had the right geographical and social connections, for he was a tenant in the 1880s of the building where Degas's studio was located, and he was on good terms with the Dihaus, the family of musicians, to whom he was distantly related. Yet all this was not enough. Degas, after an introduction by Marie Dihau in 1889, quickly shifted from fatherly encouragement to criticism and finally to disavowal. Lautrec, he decided, was merely "a period painter" who would be remembered as "the Gavarni of his time."[65] Told that the disciple was appearing "a bit in your vestments," he replied with one of the most brutal and least witty of his wisecracks: "Yes, by cutting them down to his size."[66] Possibly he was irritated by an excess of worship: early one morning after a night in Montmartre bars, Lautrec burst into Marie Dihau's apartment with a band of drunken companions and ordered everyone to kneel in front of the portrait of her at the piano which Degas had painted in the 1860s (and which remained on her wall until her death in 1935). Possibly too there was an element of moral fastidiousness, for such Moulin Rouge danseuses as La Goulue (The Glutton), Grille-d'Egout (Sewer Grill), La Môme Fromage (The Cheese Kid), and Nini-Patte-en-l'Air (Leg-in-the-Air Nini) were vulgarly wanton in ways far beyond the behavior of a ballerina or a café-concert diva. In any event, the lack of rapport was plain. And it was all the more surprising when compared with the indulgence shown toward Vincent van Gogh and Paul Gauguin, neither of whom was very respectable and both of whom developed aesthetics radically different from that of Degas.

Vincent, as he preferred to be known, arrived in Paris from Antwerp at the beginning of March 1886 and installed himself with his brother Theo, at first in the Rue de Laval and then farther up the Montmartre slope at 54 Rue Lepic, a few minutes from the Café de la Nouvelle-Athènes. He was thirty-three, an absinthe addict, depressingly dirty, violently erotic, and given to choleric paroxysms that soon led Theo's friends and clients to refuse invitations to the Rue Lepic. But he was already displaying, on canvas and in café conversations, the passion for painting that during the next four years, in Paris, Arles, Saint Rémy, and Auvers-sur-Oise, would produce masterpieces, insanity, and suicide. He met Seurat, Pissarro, Degas, Gauguin, Toulouse-Lautrec, and the young Emile Bernard, who became the inventor of the variety of Symbolism referred to sometimes as Synthetism or Cloisonnism.

Degas, temporarily back in La Nouvelle-Athènes, talked about southern France and recommended that Vincent go to see Delacroix's portrait of Alfred Bruyas, Courbet's patron, in the museum at Montpellier. When the topic shifted to sex, Degas said, "I am saving myself for the women of Arles."[67] And although Gauguin seems to have thought otherwise, there is plenty of evidence that Vincent liked and appreciated his middle-aged interlocutor. Writing to Bernard from Arles in 1888, he said that the "calm and modeled" nudes of Degas were a kind of perfection that, "like coitus," can for a moment "make the infinite tangible for us."[68] In another letter of the same year to Bernard he presented a generous personal version of Balzac's theory that sexual intercourse may weaken an artist's creative drive:

> Why do you say that Degas has trouble having an erection? Degas lives like a little notary and does not love women because he knows that if he loved them and spent a lot of time kissing them he would become mentally ill and inept in his art. Degas's painting is vigorously masculine and impersonal precisely because he has accepted the idea of being personally nothing but a little notary with a horror of sexual sprees. He looks at the human animals who are stronger than he is and are kissing each other and having erections, and he paints them well, precisely because he himself is not at all pretentious about having erections.[69]

Vincent's visit to Montpellier, in line with Degas's recommendation, resulted in his discovery, immediately reported to Theo, that "Delacroix's portrait of Bruyas resembles me and you like a new brother."[70] The commitment to the asylum in Saint Rémy was marked by one of the most poignantly ironical letters in the whole correspondence: "I dream of accepting straightforwardly my profession of lunatic, much as Degas has taken the form of a notary. But I don't feel myself quite strong enough for such a role."[71] There is no documentation on what Degas thought about Vincent the man. That he admired the artist is proved, however, by his purchase, some time after the final act of the tragedy in Auvers, of two of the violently lyrical pictures painted in Paris in 1887.

Gauguin also began an important series of journeys in 1886. From June to November of that year he was at Pont-Aven, a village on the southern coast of Brittany, still working in an Impressionist manner but savoring what he called the archaic customs of the province and enjoying himself as the picturesque leader of the local colony of American, English, Swedish, and French landscapists. In 1887, from April until the end of the year, he was in Panama and Martinique, hoping in vain to be able to "live like a savage"[72] and deepening his feeling for arbitrary colors. In the summer of 1888 he was back at Pont-Aven, where his *Vision after the Sermon,* with its arabesques, emphatic contours, and flat patches of unrealistic hues, marked his repudiation of everything he had learned from Pissarro. He spent an unhappy autumn with van Gogh in Arles, and two more seasons in Brittany, and then, in April 1891, left for Tahiti.

During these years of stylistic evolution there were some spells of disagreement with Degas, but on the whole the feelings of the two men for each other were warm — and they continued to be so until Gauguin's death, in 1903. In 1888 Degas bought one of the Pont-Aven pictures, and Gauguin wrote to Bernard, "I am extremely flattered. As you know, I have great confidence in his judgment."[73] There seems to have been an argument about the departure for Tahiti; Degas thought that one could paint just as well in the Batignolles, and later he said to Vollard:

> Poor Gauguin. Out there on his island he must be thinking all the time of the Rue Laffitte. I advised him to go to New Orleans, but he thought the place was too civilized. He has to have people with flowers on their heads and rings in their noses.[74]

However, one evening in 1891 at the Halévys a question about Gauguin evoked a prompt defense: "He is a fellow who is dying of hunger and whom I esteem profoundly as an artist."[75] And when the pictures began to arrive from Tahiti their principal promoter was Degas. In 1893 he persuaded an unenthusiastic Durand-Ruel to present them in a one-man show, and during the exhibition, before a bemused Louis Rouart, he explained Gauguin's motivation by reciting La Fontaine's fable of the lean wolf who prefers an empty belly to well-fed domestication and having to wear a collar.[76]

The friendship with Georges Jeanniot and Albert Bartholomé was on a different plane. Jeanniot, born in 1848, was a former captain of the regular army and the son of the director of the Ecole des Beaux-Arts at Dijon; his reputation as an artist was based largely on his illustrations for *La Vie moderne, Le Journal amusant* (of which he became the editor), and special editions of the novels of Alphonse Daudet, Hugo, and the Goncourts. Degas appears to have liked him because of his military background, his kindheartedness, and his reporter's outlook — and also perhaps because of sympathy, for Jeanniot was deaf and hence a rather isolated, lonely man. Bartholomé, of the same age as Jeanniot and also an army veteran, came to Degas's attention in the early 1880s by exhibiting in the Salon a series of pastels executed in the academically Realistic style of the popular Jules Bastien-Lepage. In 1884 he won a Salon decoration, and by that time the friendship between the two men was advanced enough for Degas to write, "Your medal ought to make me indignant, but I applaud as if it were of gold."[77] In December of that year Bartholomé's young wife was gravely ill, and Degas sent them an apology for having temporarily neglected them:

> You two have always been, and were from the very beginning, full of goodness and comfort for me. Now you are both afflicted, the one by malady and the other by worry and uncertainty, and I choose this moment not to pay back what you have given me. That is the behavior of a man who wants to finish and die all alone, with no happiness at all.[78]

Some months later the couple sent him a pumpkin from the country and received a literary flourish in reply: "It's there. I looked at it again this morning — at its red loins and creased buttocks, as Goncourt would think and write about it. . . ."[79]

Madame Bartholomé died, apparently of cancer, in 1887, and Degas urged her husband to model a Christ for her grave, partly as a distraction and partly as a way of mourning. Bartholomé did so, and then, abandoning pastel, went on to become one of the best-known academic sculptors in France, in a style that updated Canova's Neoclassicism with some vaguely Egyptian and Primitive touches. In 1891, universalizing his mourning for his wife, he began work on his masterpiece, the huge *Monument aux Morts* that now dominates the central avenue of the Père Lachaise Cemetery in Paris. Degas remained steadfast in his friendship during this brilliant success, though he could not resist saying, "Bartholomé, you'll be like Guillaume, making a clean sweep of honors and decorations while your tear-filled eyes are fixed on heaven."[80] Eugène Guillaume was a cousin of Madame Henri Rouart's who was a widowed sculptor and who eventually became the director of both the Villa Medici and the Ecole des Beaux-Arts and a member of the Académie Française.

In one of his letters to Lucien, Pissarro wrote, "The long and short of it is that Degas . . . is very good-hearted and sensitive when other people are unhappy."[81] This was easily verifiable. When Madame Bartholomé was dying, Degas wrote to her sister-in-law, the Marquise de Fleury, "My hard heart is breaking."[82] When the collector Alphonse Cherfils fell ill in the Pyrenees, Degas immediately took the train from Paris to Pau. Through a process-server in Carpentras he tactfully made arrangements to provide the partly paralyzed Valernes with a small pension. "When you have worries," he said, "you think of your friends."[83] He was scrupulous about attending funerals, so much so that Cassatt found him a bit odd and tiresome in this respect.

Such behavior did not, however, counteract his reputation for what Caillebotte had called sourness. In 1886 he was a model, in Octave Mirbeau's novel *Le Calvaire,* for the artist Joseph Lirat, a misanthrope given to making cleverly malicious remarks. Two years later he appeared, slightly disguised as Georges Decroix, the protagonist of Félicien Champsaur's *L'Amant des danseuses.* In it, he is presented sympathetically as a painter of ballerinas and prostitutes, but is nevertheless said to have a melancholy philosophy. Goncourt, in an entry in his *Journal* in 1889, denounced "this constipated painter Degas, this fellow with his spiteful words swotted up and worked over during nights made sleepless by his failure as an artist."[84] The young Paul Valéry, who, as a friend of Ernest Rouart's, began to frequent the Rue de Lisbonne around 1893, thought that Alceste, the roughly outspoken hero of Molière's *Misanthrope,* looked "weak and easy"[85] when compared with Degas. One of the few writers to resist such judgments was Maupassant, who in 1888 sent the supposed Alceste a copy of the novel *Pierre et Jean* inscribed: "To Edgar Degas, who paints life as I would have liked to paint it."[86]

Jeanne Raunay felt that the sourness could be explained in part as an affectation acquired during the reign of Louis-Philippe:

> Degas . . . loved to imagine that he was redoubtable. We should not forget that he was born in the Romantic era and that Satanism was à la mode among littérateurs and painters when, very young, he began to develop his likes.[87]

Jeanniot also got the impression of something put on: "He valued his reputation for spitefulness and rudeness; in his eyes it had the advantage of keeping bores at a distance and providing him with an aura that amused him."[88] Vollard saw it as a means for keeping visitors away from the studio, and Degas himself said as much to Redon. To one of his hostesses, he also tacitly indicated that often his unsociable behavior was simply a performance — Degas playing the part of the misanthropic Monsieur Degas: "What's this I hear? What's this I hear? You are going about saying I'm not wicked, that people have made a mistake concerning me. If you take that away from me, what will I have left?"[89]

This is a reminder of the earlier evidence of the notion of the self as a role. We are back with the Baudelairean spleen suggested by the twenty-one-year-old Edgar's self-portrait, with the imp on the moonlit road from Rome, with the hateful "me" in Florence, with the ironical persona visible in the hat-doffing mirror image of 1865, and with Manet's remark to Morisot in 1869: "He lacks naturalness." The pattern also fitted well with the emphasis in Degas's art on theater, urban spectacle, processed reality, artificiality, voyeurism, and the presence of a concealed observer. It was perhaps inevitable that the Jaques who regarded the world as a stage should have wound up becoming, very consciously, one of the players.

Even so, it is plain that behind the performance there was genuine irascibility, morosity, and misanthropy. Caillebotte had perhaps been right in suspecting that one cause for all this was Degas's resentment at not having "the high rank his talent entitled him to," for in the long run being a modestly rewarded major artist in a philistine society that bestowed honors and town houses on the likes of a Cabanel or a Bouguereau must have been galling, whatever one might say about wanting to be "illustrious and unknown."

But there are other explanations. Degas was now a solitary, sensitive, aging bachelor, afraid of going blind and afflicted with some kind of physical or psychic sexual inadequacy. Like Alceste, he was impatiently intelligent and full of stiff-necked pride, and he could have joined Molière's personage in confessing: *Je n'ai point sur ma langue un assez grand empire*[90] (I do not have enough sovereignty over my tongue). Jeanne Raunay wrote, "He had been mistaken so many times, he found it difficult to believe in sincerity; he treated words with suspicion."[91] He seems to have been permanently affected by the failure of his father's bank and by the subsequent behavior of René; in 1891 he broke all relations with Moore because the latter had mentioned the affair in print. Daniel Halévy wrote, in this connection:

> He could not endure the thought that the honor of the family name had been stained. It is impossible to measure the extent to which his inner being was shaken. His vision of the world was darkened, and I think that at that moment the rather unsociable Degas whose image has persisted came into existence.[92]

More generally, his whole approach to life and art — the dialectical play between appearance and reality, between the refined and the vulgar, and between an idealizing idiom and a reductionist content — left him exposed to disenchantment, and so did his observer's stance. With Shakespearean logic, he moved from the detachment of Jaques toward the misanthropy of Timon of Athens.

He had moments of remorse. Asked during a dinner at the Halévys to repeat some apparently spiteful *mot* about Bonnard, he said, "No, I was being stupid. I was making fun of an old comrade who is very nice and of whom I am extremely fond."[93] And in 1890, thinking back over the years, he sent Valernes an apology that was really addressed to everyone he had offended:

> You have always been the same man, my old friend. . . . Now I want to ask your pardon for something that comes up often in your conversation and more often in your thoughts. It's that in the course of our long relations concerning art I have been, or have seemed to be, *hard* with you.
>
> I was particularly hard with myself. You must remember that, for you reproached me for it and expressed surprise that I should have so little confidence in myself.
>
> I was, or I seemed to be, hard with everyone, because of a sort of drive toward brutality that arose in me out of my doubts and my bad humor. I felt myself so badly made, so badly equipped, so flabby, whereas it seemed to me that my *calculations* about art were so right. I was sulky with everyone and with myself. I sincerely beg your pardon if, with this damned art as a pretext, I have wounded you in your fine and noble mind, perhaps even in your heart. [Emphases in original.][94]

20. Poetry, Travel, and Color

O N FEBRUARY 17, 1889, Mallarmé wrote from Paris to Berthe Morisot, who was spending the cold months on the Côte d'Azur, to inform her that, among other things, there had been a delay in the publication of a volume of his poetry for which Degas and the horse painter John-Lewis Brown (French despite the name) had promised some engravings as illustrations:

> The good Lewis Brown, very affected by the death of a step-grandchild, pulls a proof from time to time . . . but Degas, to whom I'm going to send a quatrain on stamped paper, is giving the publishers some time off. His own poetry is distracting him, for — and this will be the notable event of the winter — he is now into his fourth sonnet. In fact, he is no longer of this world, or is perturbed by the constraints of a new art, in which, upon my word, he conducts himself very prettily. All this does not keep him from exhibiting in the Boulevard Montmartre [in Theo van Gogh's gallery], alongside a set of incomparable landscapes by Monet, some wonderful danseuses, jockeys, and women in tubs.[1]

The quatrain, one of the many *loisirs de la poste* (postal leisures) in which Mallarmé ingeniously incorporated a friend's street address, was duly dispatched, and it reveals a change from the Rue Pigalle to a shrub-surrounded place in a byway near the Place de Clichy:

Rue, au 23, Ballu
J'exprime
Sitôt Juin à Monsieur Degas

> *La satisfaction qu'il rime
> Avec la fleur des syringas.*[2]

(Street, at number 23, Ballu I'll express as soon as June comes to Monsieur Degas my satisfaction that he rhymes with the flower of the syringas.) Degas replied:

> I have taken two days to write you in prose, and you two days in verse. If I felt like spending a peaceful winter, I would attempt my sonnet about the dog — the little dog that plays the trumpet with its tail. I would certainly take the winter on it, and the revisions would drag on into spring. I admire you: you can play with such weighty things and then run to the post office with them. Many thanks, but I must say that you humiliate me ad lib.[3]

In spite of the mock humility, he continued to work on his poetry, with the same zeal that he displayed when he was temporarily obsessed with making prints or with collecting Norman handkerchiefs and antique canes. He studied Théodore de Banville's *Petit Traité de versification française*, one of the best résumés of the Parnassian school's arguments in favor of verse that is crisply wrought in detail and definite in outline. He bought a volume of Ronsard's sonnets and a dictionary of rhymes, and consulted Henri Rouart's son Alexis, who was also an amateur poet, on Friday nights before dinner.

Eventually, perhaps over a period of three years, he produced twenty sonnets, a quantity of less formal pieces, and probably a large number of items now lost, for a surviving notebook full of crossed-out lines suggests a good deal of what was, in the end, destructive revising. Some of his admirers regretted the time taken from painting and did not think much of the results, and one day he received an anonymous remonstrance in verse:

> *Sous tes lauriers, Degas, si nombreux et si beaux,
> Tu peux, sans hésiter, te livrer au repos;
> Cesse de tourmenter une Muse rebelle.*[4]

(Under your laurels, Degas, so numerous and so fine, you can without hesitation give yourself up to rest. Stop tormenting a rebellious Muse.) Valéry, however, disagreed with such carping. "I do not doubt," he wrote, "that this amateur who knew how to take pains over a work . . . could have become, if he had concentrated all his energy on the task, a most remarkable poet, of the 1860–1890 type."[5] Today a sympathetic reader of the best of the poems may feel that Valéry's opinion, with its qualifiers included, was amply justified.

The sonnets follow, with variations, the Petrarchan rhyme pattern and stress the logical development of an idea in the sestet after its expression in the opening octet. Although there are echoes of Baudelaire and even of

Boileau, the most evident stylistic influence is that of the finest of the Parnassians, Hérédia, whom Degas knew personally and frequently consulted and whose sonorous, beautifully concise sonnets were published in a collected edition in 1893 under the title *Les Trophées*. As Valéry's phrase "of the 1860–1890 type" indicates, there is no question of Symbolist ambiguity or fin-de-siècle twilights. The subject matter is largely what might be expected from Degas. He mourns and moralizes ironically with Cassatt after the loss of her parrot Coco. A tribute to Rose Caron begins by evoking her long arms and ends:

> *Si mes yeux se perdaient, que me durât l'ouïe,*
> *Au son je pourrais voir le geste qu'elle fait.*[6]

(If I lose my eyes, may my hearing last; at the sound I will be able to see her gesture.) A sonnet titled *Thoroughbred* is a Longchamp playlet in which a colt appears in a dew-drenched dawn under the conduct of a stable boy, goes through its paces, receives its reward of oats, and then, freed of bridle, saddle, and blanket, gallops off across the meadow: *Tout nerveusement nu, dans sa robe de soie* (Quite nervously naked, in its robe of silk). One piece on the ballet tells the little darlings with their Montmartre mugs to dance with effrontery, for *les reines se font de distance et de fard* (queens are made of distance and cosmetics); another returns to the theme of appearance and reality by presenting a danseuse who weaves marvelous patterns with her feet of satin and then abruptly reveals that her *élévation* leaves something to be desired:

> *D'un rien, comme toujours, cesse le beau mystère.*
> *Elle retire trop les jambes en sautant,*
> *C'est un saut de grenouille aux mares de Cythère.*

(A mere nothing, as always, dissipates the lovely mystery. She pulls up her legs too much in a jump and becomes a frog jumping into the ponds of Cythera.) These theatrical sonnets give way at one point in 1890 to a rondeau that celebrates the union of Eros and Thanatos by telling a sardonic tale of a funeral at which the mourners lose their carriages to a wedding party:

> *Les six landaus n'arrivaient pas;*
> *Mais tout était prêt pour le mort.*
> *On eut voulu passer d'abord*
> *Et les landaus n'arrivaient pas!*[7]

(The six landaus did not arrive; but everything was ready for the dead man. One would have liked to have been first. And the landaus did not arrive!)

Degas sent the poem to Bartholomé with the comment "What a subject. Inexhaustible."[8]

One evening at Berthe Morisot's dinner table the new poet complained to Mallarmé, "I have lost my entire day over a cursed sonnet, without advancing a step. And yet it's not ideas that I lack. I'm full of them. I have too many."[9] Mallarmé replied, "But, Degas, it's not with ideas that you make verses. It's with words." The incident is not, as sometimes alleged, proof of the artist's naïveté about the writer's craft. He did, however, assume that clarity was a literary virtue, and he failed utterly to see the justification for the obscurity that resulted from Mallarmé's poetic attempt to "give a purer sense to the words of the tribe."[10] Valéry wrote:

> I think Mallarmé was rather afraid of this character so different from his own. As for Degas, he spoke very amiably of Mallarmé, but mostly of the man. The work seemed to him the fruit of a mild insanity that had taken over the mind of a marvelously gifted poet.[11]

The impatience increased when something of the style of the verse appeared in prose, as it tended to do as Mallarmé grew older. On February 27, 1890, in Morisot's studio in the Rue de Villejust, he repeated his moving but frequently hermetic lecture (which he had delivered originally in Belgium) on Villiers de l'Isle-Adam, and Régnier remembered being in the specially invited audience of some forty persons:

> During this reading I sat next to Degas, who showed his ill humor by shaking his head and shrugging his shoulders, for although he liked Mallarmé as a person, he did not appreciate the writer and poet — which is not at all surprising, since his favorite author was Brillat-Savarin. He used to have *The Physiology of Taste* read to him, if he did not ask for *The Thousand and One Nights*.[12]

Reportedly the exasperated painter stalked out before the end of the lecture, but Morisot's daughter, Julie, in an interview published long afterward, says that he did not and that he "would have been incapable of such a discourtesy."[13]

The implication of Régnier's account — that Degas did not have much of a literary background — is supported by Redon's assertion that "he has read nothing" and by other sources. Daniel Halévy, in a diary entry for 1890, remarked, "He has read very few things, and knows those things by heart. His mind was formed by itself."[14] Another entry recorded a conversation in the Rue de Douai in 1891:

> Degas attacked my uncle [Jules Taschereau], who reads two volumes a day. "Don't read," he said. "It's because of laziness that you read, mental laziness.

One should be able to sit for hours looking into the fire and rethinking cherished thoughts. One ought to have personal thoughts." [15]

Such evidence is contradicted, however, by dozens of references to reading in his letters and notebooks, by the several paintings that reveal extensive documentation, and by the contents of his library, which included the works of Corneille, Racine, La Fontaine, Voltaire, Musset, Vigny, Hugo, Flaubert, Stendhal, Sainte-Beuve, Maupassant, Mérimée, Gautier, and Renan. And an evident explanation for the contradiction is that he had once read a good deal but had stopped doing so by the time of his celebrity in his fifties.

One reason for his stopping was his deteriorating eyesight. Whatever the cause — organic or neurotic — it was also a convenience: it aroused dramatic sympathy, went well with his role of Alceste, and helped to shield him from intruders. André Mycho, Desboutin's son, referred to it by quoting a French proverb: "No one is as blind as the man who does not wish to see." [16] Vollard, who seems to have known Degas at least by 1893 and perhaps a little earlier, remembered seeing him consult a watch just after failing, or refusing, to recognize an acquaintance of thirty years. Jeanne Fevre, the painter's niece, insisted that even in his last years he never became completely blind. Nevertheless, there does appear to have been something organically wrong, particularly in his right eye, and of course a neurotic ailment can be just as real and provoke as much anguish as any other kind. The words *la vue, la vue* (the eyesight) are a constant refrain in his letters. In 1893, planning a trip to Carpentras, he informed Valernes:

> You will see a rather lugubrious apparatus on my eyes. The ophthalmologist is attempting to improve my sight by masking the right eye and letting the left one see only through a slit. All is going well, at least well enough for me to get about, but I can't adapt myself enough to work. [17]

In another experiment he spent a week in Brussels living mostly in the dark. But none of the treatments brought a permanent improvement.

Even if his eyes had been better, he probably would not have read much during these years, for he was very busy doing other things. In the spring of 1890 he took a lease on three floors of a small building at 37 Rue Victor-Massé (the former Rue de Laval, renamed in 1887 to honor the recently deceased composer of *Les Noces de Jeannette*), and here — without immediately giving up the place at 23 Rue Ballu — he began an elaborate installation that eventually became a private museum on the floor above the ground floor, living quarters on the next, and a studio on the top. He persuaded the art dealer Portier to help him find furnishings, started to haunt the department stores, and at the end of April wrote to Bartholomé:

> I still have furniture on my mind. Portier has looked at the wine-colored carpet and in particular at the first-rate carpet, the collector's item, the expensive one. . . . You know, that carpet attracts me. I pull on that carpet like a cat. I think of what one might have come up with at the time of the Crusades, secondhand or in the form of booty.[18]

In June Madame Halévy inspected the arrangements and, as reported in Daniel's diary, found them "charming" in general but thought that "a comical effect" was produced by having the bathtub and water closet in almost the same room as an iron bed and a collection of pictures. Degas firmly and ironically disagreed: "No, Louise, they are handy where they are, and you know I'm not a fop. I take my morning bath, put on my flowered nine-franc-fifty dressing robe, lie back contentedly on the bed, and tell myself that all this is what a lifetime of work leads to."[19]

Sabine Neyt had died shortly before the move from the Rue Pigalle, and he had engaged a housekeeper named Zoé Closier as her successor. Zoé was a round woman in her forties with a round face, round eyes, large round glasses, and the serious, authoritative air of a schoolmistress, which reportedly she had once been. Unlike Sabine and the talented young Clotilde of the 1870s, she was an execrable cook: Valéry never forgot the "rigorous insipidity" of her overdone veal, watery macaroni, and stringy orange marmalade, which was supposedly based on a recipe from Dundee. She complained because her employer spent money on drawings by Ingres instead of buying her a new blue apron, and she remained unimpressed when he tried to terrorize her by suggesting that he might get married. But she talked well, read to him, ran errands to Durand-Ruel's, kept the place clean, and resolutely blocked unwanted visitors; and in time she became the equivalent for him of the famous, devoted, rather Cerberean Jenny Le Guillou who had nourished and protected Delacroix for thirty years.

"It is impossible," he told Halévy, "for me to live far from my studio."[20] That was true in the long term but not in the short, for among the more striking of the many contradictions in his make-up was the fact that he was a confirmed Parisian, a Ninth Arrondissement villager, and at the same time one of the most traveled artists of the nineteenth century. The contradiction was conspicuous during the late 1880s and early 1890s, which were marked by trips to Cauterets, Lourdes, the Basque coast, Madrid, Andalusia, Cádiz, Tangier, Toulouse, Carcassonne, Geneva, Carpentras, Burgundy, and Interlaken, along with the usual stays in Normandy.

Although there were health, family, and friendship reasons for most of these journeys, he obviously went on them also because he found the going itself good.

The village of Cauterets offered romantic associations, a stirring site in the Pyrenees, and fourteen hot sulfurous springs whose nasty-tasting water was said to cure many common ailments, in particular those of the respiratory system. Marguerite d'Angoulême, queen of Navarre and the sister of Francis I, had written some of the amorous tales in her *Heptaméron* in a local abbey. Other noteworthy, and frequently amorous, visitors had included Rabelais, Chateaubriand, Taine, Hugo, Thiers, Heine, and George Sand; and during the last decades of the nineteenth century the resort ranked only slightly below Baden-Baden and Vichy as a gathering place for aristocrats, boulevardiers, and generals with microbes from the colonies. Degas was there during August and September in 1888, 1889, and 1890, ostensibly for treatment of bronchitis and very clearly in search of relaxation, fresh air, and glimpses of the beau monde. He took a room in the Hôtel d'Angleterre, a first-class establishment that provided a good restaurant and a view of the surrounding mountains. One letter announced that he had met the Comtesse de Mailly-Nesle, a reigning Paris beauty who later became the wife of the tenor Jean de Reszke; another said that the Baron Henri d'Ernemon was his neighbor for dinner and a buttonholer at the *buvettes,* the basins at which one lined up for the morning gargling; in another he gossiped about the arrival of two of Charles Haas's old mistresses. Thinking perhaps of Manet's color print *Polichinelle,* a proof of which he owned, he enjoyed the afternoon Punch and Judy show — especially its audience of rowdy children — in the town square. He received a visit from his friend and patron Paul Lafond, the curator of the municipal museum at nearby Pau and the purchaser of the New Orleans *Portraits in an Office.* (Lafond appears, on the left, with Alphonse Cherfils in the Daumier-like *Amateurs.*) He amused himself by hiring a Paris Opéra musician to astonish the evening strollers by playing, hidden among the trees and shrubs, the section of the Elysian Fields scene of Gluck's *Orfeo* in which the good spirits dance to the accompaniment of a flute solo. But finally he tired of the sudden changes in mountain weather from stifling summer heat to thunderstorms or autumnal fogs.

During the 1890 season he spent a morning with Lafond at Lourdes, thirty kilometers from Cauterets. By this date Bernadette Soubirous, the nearly illiterate girl who in 1858 had had a vision of the Virgin Mary in a local cave, was dead, the spring she had supposedly caused to gush forth was flowing commercially, a marble church in the Romanesque Byzantine style had just been completed, and the town was booming as a kind of sacred spa. Degas was at first horrified by the dying invalids, by the miracle-mongering, and in general by what, in a letter to his sister Marguerite, he called "a crusade at reduced prices in which there are . . . believers and thieves."[21] But later, in the Rue de Douai, he reacted sharply to Elie Halévy's rationalist denunciation of the place:

> Elie said, "It's ignoble." Degas said, "Ignoble? Well, I saw a bit of everything. There were women singing with an admirable exaltation; there were those who were as calm as if they were at a store counter. Others were putting on an act. . . . I saw porters who were convinced by the miracles. . . . You are going to talk about reason. What does that mean? Nothing causes people to say as many stupid things as reason does. One should not resort to it, or at most only as an instrument for climbing into an omnibus."[22]

He overstated his case, as he often did when challenged. But the exchange illustrates his ambivalence toward religion. Although far from being an ardent believer, he was moved, at Lourdes as at Assisi more than thirty years earlier, by the faith of others. Moreover, as an artist, a traditionalist, and a man preoccupied with the theatrical dimension of reality, he was willing to suspend his disbelief when confronted by a woman singing with exaltation in a small Pyrenees town, by the vox humana stop of an Umbrian organ, by a Giotto fresco, or simply by an affecting ritual. After attending a requiem Mass with Daniel Halévy, presumably at Notre-Dame-de-Lorette, he looked up at the high vault and said, "That Catholic liturgy, that great, turning wheel . . ."[23] On another occasion he remarked, "The Mass is much more beautiful than *Parsifal,* which is a poor copy."[24] His niece wrote that he regarded the Roman Catholic Church as "the only fragment of antiquity still alive in our world."[25] In short, he was what might be called culturally religious.

The journey through Spain, in the company of Giovanni Boldini, was an extension of the 1889 season at Cauterets. Giuseppe de Nittis had died in 1884, and Boldini was now the most fashionable Italian painter in Paris, admired both for his flattering portraits of women and for the brio of the long brush strokes with which he slashed and scarred a canvas, and celebrated, in spite of his having a dwarfish silhouette, as a new Casanova. He had become well acquainted with Degas in a Paris Italian dining and talking club called Le Cercle de la Polenta, at the Café La Rochefoucauld, and at Dieppe, where he was often the guest of the Duchesse Caracciolo, mother of the little Olga who visited the Halévys; and the Spanish holiday may have been his idea, for he had spent some time in Andalusia in 1877. Degas had hesitated at the prospect of two weeks of Boldini's *opera buffa* exuberance, and in a letter to Bartholomé he refers to *ce rastaquouère*[26] — a term usually reserved for flashy South American adventurers. But neither Bartholomé nor Lafond, each of whom had had experience as a tourist in Spain, was available as a companion. Boldini took the night train down from Paris, Degas proceeded by way of Lourdes and Pau, and they got together at Bayonne, Bonnat's home town, on September 6. They crossed the border at Hendaye, with Degas consulting his watch as usual; they reached the Hôtel de Paris in Madrid at six-thirty on the morning of Sunday, September 8, and at nine o'clock they were in the cool, Neoclassical halls of the Prado. After lunch Degas reported to Bartholomé:

> We have been eating extremely well since our arrival in Spain, although people are always talking about being poisoned. The heat announces something really formidable in Andalusia. The bullfight for which we are preparing ourselves will not take place until four-thirty. Even the bulls are waiting to avoid sunstroke. Nothing, nothing can give one an idea of Velázquez.[27]

At Tangier, on September 18, mounted on a mule, he was part of a cavalcade that a guide in a robe of violet silk led over a sandy beach, through dusty country lanes, and into the town at last, chattering all the while in an incomprehensible French. Recalling that Delacroix had been there in 1832, Degas wrote to Bartholomé, "In nature one loves the people who have not been unworthy of touching it."[28] He dreamed of rereading *The Thousand and One Nights* after visiting Granada and the Alhambra on the way back up from Cádiz. But it is clear that disagreements with Boldini were spoiling his pleasure, for his concluding comment on the trip is a weary allusion to "these centuries I am traversing in bad company."[29]

In 1890 during the first part of September he extended his descent from Paris into a circular tour of France by moving eastward across the Midi and then up through Provence and Savoy into Switzerland. He began by going again to Lourdes, this time with Haas, "the ladies' man," and another Cauterets regular, the Vicomte de Borelli. At Toulouse he halted for a dinner in the restaurant of the Hôtel Tivollier ("fine southern cooking"), a walk through the warm autumn night around the Romanesque basilica of Saint Sernin, and some sitting in a café.[30] At ten-thirty the next morning, on the twentieth anniversary of the fall of the Second Empire, he was composing a note to Bartholomé from a café on the Place aux Herbes (now the Place Carnot) in the recently, and excessively, restored medieval townscape of Carcassonne:

> I feel like writing to you from this spot and in front of the market shaded by handsome plane trees. *Ministransque potantibus umbram platanus* [*sic*]. And I am drinking anisette and water. I have just come down from the fortified

old city (Viollet-le-Duc) and I'm waiting until eleven o'clock for lunch. . . . It's a long way from Pau to Geneva.[31]

In Geneva he spent two days with his brother Achille, who was ill; at Carpentras he called on Valernes. Bartholomé came down from Paris, and before returning north the two men went to Diénay, a village twenty kilometers north of Dijon in which Jeanniot had a summer home.

The good weather was not yet over, so plans were soon under way in the Ninth Arrondissement for what promised to become the most amusing journey of the year. The idea, which may have arisen out of memories of the 1858 light-carriage trip from Rome to Tuscany, was to go from Paris to Diénay and back — a total distance of six hundred kilometers — by road instead of rail, and thus have time to savor the architecture, landscapes, and food of Burgundy. Bartholomé joined the project, and by the end of the month he and Degas had borrowed a gig of the tilbury type and hired a lumbering white horse who made up in clownish charm for what he lacked in Thoroughbred elegance.

On September 30, 1890, they set out from Montgeron, a southern suburb of Paris where the Halévys were staying that year. Bartholomé took the reins, and Degas promised to keep their friends informed. The white horse eyed the two artists suspiciously at first, and showed signs of vexation and impetuosity until he reached the long, straight stretch of road in the Forest of Sénart. At six-thirty, in Melun, forty-five kilometers from Paris, a bulletin was issued: "He is tired, and our thoughts are for him. Oats are all, say the Scriptures. Better than kind words."[32] The next report was less laconic:

> Montereau, Hôtel du Grand Monarque (the real one), lunch, sheep's foot, fried gudgeon, sausage and apple sauce (admirable), steak with cress, cheese, fruit, biscuits (admirable). The horse made a very fine descent on Montereau. Departure at three-thirty for Villeneuve-la-Guyard. There you must always stop at the Hôtel de la Poste. Dinner: panada with milk, brains with browned butter sauce, jugged hare, leg of mutton with mixed beans (first rate), salad, choice of desserts, a light, natural wine.[33]

The weather stayed brisk and bright, the horse got used to his new masters, and the flow of bulletins continued:

> *Saint-Florentin, October 3, one-thirty.* Bartholomé is the man for the job. Under that Trappist's beard beats the heart of a coachman. All aboard for Flogny.
>
> *Tanlay, October 4, Saturday morning.* Are eighteen liters of oats a day enough?
> *Aignay-le-Duc, October 5, Sunday noon.* At Copain's, where we are having lunch, we have just found some unimaginable pickles. A garden in vinegar.

The Seine is here, and our horse has taken a leg bath. There is only one country, Monsieur, and it's ours.

Moloy, October 6, twelve-thirty. Almost there, since this place is eleven kilometers from Diénay. We say to you that the true traveler, the man of feeling, should never arrive.[34]

Jeanniot had an etcher's press, and Degas devoted most of the five days he spent at Diénay to turning out, from memory, colored monotypes of the landscapes he had just passed through. On October 12 the travelers hitched the white horse to the tilbury again and started back to Paris, Degas with indigestion and Bartholomé with a hand swollen from an insect bite. By way of Montbard, Tonnerre, and Sens they reached Melun on October 18, and there they were welcomed back to the Ile-de-France by Forain. "He arrived," Degas reported in a final bulletin from a local restaurant, "on his tricycle, in a Garibaldian costume. Standing up and with his mouth full of food, he is discoursing on the future of cycling."[35]

During the summer of 1891 another stay at Cauterets was abandoned in favor of a call on Valernes at Carpentras. A letter of 1892 to the Fevres, in Argentina, describes part of the traveling of that year's August and September:

Three weeks in Normandy with that old animal Valpinçon, who has asthma and a bit of swelling of the legs and no courage at all. From there a race across France by way of Tours, Bourges, Clermont-Ferrand, and Valence to Carpentras.[36]

From Carpentras he went on to Geneva, where Achille's illness was becoming more and more disquieting. At the end of the following August, in stickily hot weather, he was at Interlaken to see Edmondo Morbilli, now suddenly old and infirm and being nursed heroically by Thérèse. But the occasions for such charitable visits to Switzerland were soon over, for Edmondo left Interlaken to spend his few remaining months of life in Naples, Achille and his New Orleans wife moved from Geneva to an apartment on the Paris Left Bank, and at the end of October 1893 Edgar wrote to Désiré Dihau:

You had not forgotten my poor Achille. Well, it's finished. He came back to die where he was born. His wife wanted him buried by the family alone. I am announcing his end to a few friends.[37]

He was much affected by the loss of his brother, and perhaps even more by the close spectacle of a physical dissolution and the vivid reminder of his own insubstantiality. He noticed, he told his Buenos Aires relatives, that death made Achille look young, like a retouched photograph. On December 4, 1893, with a hint of hypochondria, he wrote:

> I am doctoring my bladder a great deal with turpentine and Contrexéville mineral water and by cutting down on coffee, liqueurs, etc. I am still, however, having pains in the back. My eyesight is growing dimmer.[38]

A few weeks later he had the body of a cousin removed from the Degas family vault in the Montmartre Cemetery in order to make room for himself. (In fact, he still had twenty-three years to live.) Evidently he also felt a need to close ranks with survivors, for at some point around this date there was a complete reconciliation with René, who had become the managing editor of a new mass-circulation daily, *Le Petit Parisien,* and was living in the Rue Lepic with his second wife and their three children.

By adding up all the time he spent on traveling, dining out, making *mots,* and worrying about going blind, one can see that the Degas of these years was not working as hard as usual. And in portraiture the quantitative decline was accompanied by a qualitative one, so much so that one has to search for evidence of the old acuteness. Exceptionally, an ingratiating Lepic, holding one of his rumpled, short-faced griffons, looks out from a pastel done in 1888, a year before his death. The engineer, engraver, collector, and art dealer Michel Manzi is depicted, in a pastel of 1889, watching an incised copper plate he has just immersed in a bath of acid. The setting, in line with the theories developed by Degas and Duranty twenty years earlier, is the subject's laboratory and atelier in the Rue Forest, a back street near the Place de Clichy. Manzi was a Neapolitan who had fought for the unification of Italy and then emigrated to Paris, where he joined the Italian colony led by de Nittis, Zandomeneghi, and Boldini and finally became technical director of Goupil's print workshop. Around 1892 he brought out a much praised album of reproductions of some of Degas's drawings and pastels.

More interesting than these two painted portraits, however, are two pieces of sculpture modeled in 1892 and later cast in bronze by the founder Hébrard. The first, catalogued as *Head Resting on One Hand, Bust,* and long thought to represent Madame Bartholomé, has now been convincingly identified as an effigy of Rose Caron. It is the one that, Degas wrote in a letter of 1892 from Ménil-Hubert, he was going to "pounce" on after the end of his summer travels.[39] Presumably the poetic floating hand was the happy result of a desire to allude to Caron's gestures and a fear of repeating the disastrous attempt to model Hortense Valpinçon with arms. The second piece, catalogued *Head, Study for the Portrait of Mme. S.* and the larger of two items with that title, represents the danseuse and mime Mathilde Salle,

Nude Woman Standing at Her Toilette, 1890–1892

whom he had portrayed in pastel in 1886, and affords an occasion for some extended art-historical and psychological speculation. The neckless head, the rough surface (of clay in this instance instead of wax or plasteline), and the blurred eye strongly suggest the influence of Rosso's *Large Laughing Woman,* which was executed in Paris in 1891; and the suggestion is reinforced by the fact that the Italian sculptor often appeared at Rouart's house in the Rue de Lisbonne. But by this time Degas had become more free, more expressive, and in a sense more subjective in his handling of all his various media. Moreover, he may have been projecting into the strange motif of the blurred eye an awareness of his own infirmity. He may even, since the artistic imagination works on several levels, have had simultaneously in the back of his mind the tale of the three one-eyed dervishes in *The Thousand and One Nights.*

In 1891 he planned a series of lithographs of nude dancers and women in bathrooms. Only one print on the nude-dancers theme was done, and it was an etching reworked in pastel. Seven lithographs on the bathroom theme were executed, and of these the *Nude Woman Standing at Her Toilette* is generally regarded as the best. While he was doing the series the *bricoleur* in him emerged once more: sometimes he drew on celluloid and transferred the result to the stone, sometimes he painted directly on the stone with a brush and lithographic ink, and often he resorted to the scraper for highlights. His compulsion to revise also returned, with the result that in the last state of one of the pictures the subject is scarcely recognizable. In a letter written at the end of 1892 to the Fevres, he complained of "operations that are too complicated," of the need to hire "a rascally workman" to prepare the stones, and of a feeling that "it's getting late in my brain and my eyes."[40] He thereupon abandoned etching and lithography for the rest of his career.

He was more at ease in the less complicated medium of monotype, and he was happy with what he had done at Diénay. After his return to Paris he continued to produce landscapes, occasionally in pastel alone but more often in pastel over a monotype base; and during the winter of 1892–1893 he exhibited twenty-one of them at Durand-Ruel's. He was delighted with the paradox that his first — and only, as things turned out — one-man show was devoted to natural scenery instead of to the danseuses, horses, and bathroom nudes that had made his reputation. Asked by Halévy whether the pictures were Romantic "states of the soul," he said, "States of the eyes. We painters don't use such pretentious language."[41] Pissarro reported to Lucien, "They resemble color printing. Very curious. A bit slovenly and askew, but with a breathtaking delicacy of tone."[42] Boldini wrote to Signorini, who was still living in Florence:

News of the *novellissima* and most *incredibilissima* sort. Degas has exhibited twenty-four [*sic*] landscapes in Durand-Ruel's gallery. . . . Impressions of the Spanish countryside gathered during the trip we made together four years ago. All done from memory, for his is of iron. As you can imagine, the interest is great. All are pastels on paper. No sign at all of Impressionist brushwork, which has become a banality. [43]

Bartholomé thought he recognized parts of the Burgundy countryside as viewed from the tilbury; Daniel Halévy believed that some of the pictures had been inspired by loose paving blocks of granite in the Rue de Douai; other viewers asserted that a coal scuttle had been emptied on the table at 37 Rue Victor-Massé. The titles of the works referred to places in Provence, Picardy, and the Pyrenees, in addition to Burgundy and Normandy. Talking later to Vollard, Degas explained, "In the railway carriage I put my nose out the door from time to time." [44]

In all the speculation, the specific titles, and the jokes there was a measure of truth, some anti-Impressionist maliciousness, and a great deal that was beside the point, for these landscapes are almost as synthetic as the Babylon of Semiramis. They are at once a rejection and a conceptual manipulation of nature. Many of them illustrate admirably a passage in a letter of 1890 to Valernes in which Degas promised to come down to Carpentras "to talk about Delacroix and about everything that can cast a spell over Truth and give it the appearance of Madness (which is the art we have the duty to exercise)." [45] The light seems to come from nowhere, or from the earth itself. No one is around, not even the usual implied observer. When, as in *Autumn Landscape,* a promontory is used as a *repoussoir,* it looks far away and as if seen through out-of-focus field glasses. The sometimes nearly abstract forms produced by the controlled-accident monotype technique jostle each other and then disappear, like some of Turner's forms, into what Constable called tinted steam. And often an illusion-destroying scribble of pastel over the original monotype coating of oil pigments is allowed to set up some color counterpoint and at the same time remind the viewer of the picture's other mode of existence as a processed batch of tangible matter — as cuisine, to use the term favored by French painters in talking about the craft in their art.

The tendency toward arbitrary hues that is apparent in the monotype-pastel landscapes is also evident in the pastel danseuses and bathroom nudes executed during these years. In *Before the Curtain,* from around 1890, a diagonal slashes the composition into a quiet color section and a noisy one, the artificial light of the opera house turns human skin into a chalky inorganic substance, and the two women are brutally foreshortened from above into a cascade of green and a puddle of brown on an abstract red, green, white, and brown rug. In *After the Bath,* variously dated by Degas specialists but probably painted in the early 1890s, everything except the monumental henna-headed bather is reduced to a sweeping curve and some creases in a flattened yellow, white, blue, and red space. A parallel color development in oil can be seen in the bright *Dancers, Pink and Green,* which is usually assigned to 1890. Thus, if one accepts the assumption, derived remotely from idealist philosophy and common in the nineteenth century, that color is a function of the carnal senses whereas form and drawing are functions of the intellect and the moral judgment, one can say that as he grew older Degas became more sensual and more inclined to indulge in what, in the ethically loaded language of this kind of art appreciation, are commonly referred to as orgies of color.

The change becomes all the more odd when one notices that he continued to stress, as he had throughout his career, his high opinion of draftsmanship. Talking about his funeral (a subject apparently much on his mind at this time), he said that all he wanted in the way of obsequies was for Forain to get up and say, "He was very fond of drawing."[46] Line, he told Sickert, offered more opportunities for interesting innovation than did color.[47] He frequently repeated the story of how Ingres had said to him, "Draw lines, young man, lots of lines." In 1892 he planned a trip to Nantes simply to look at Ingres's portrait of Madame de Senonnes, which was in the local museum; and by that date he was well into the acquisition of the drawings by his idol that would become a key part of the collection at 37 Rue Victor-Massé. Tacitly accepting the idealist sense-intellect assumption, he described them as "marvels of the human mind."[48]

Several reasons for his apparently inconsistent behavior can be advanced. His failing eyesight may have caused him, to a degree of which he was not completely aware, to want stronger color stimuli, much as a person who is increasingly hard of hearing may unconsciously want more decibels. The shift in his drawing style toward simplified details, thickened lines, and bold, abrupt abbreviations of form that accompanied the use of arbitrary hues supports this possibility. Another factor, difficult to assess, may have been the historical context, for by the 1890s Seurat, van Gogh, Gauguin, and Cézanne had all used intensified color in ways that had little to do with the representation of visual reality, Whistler had flung his pot of paint in the public's face, and Fauvism was less than ten years in the future. Also, it should not be forgotten that Degas had long admired Delacroix almost as much as Ingres. He was not at his first essay in inconsistency.

All these reasons, however, are modified by the observation that in the present instance the inconsistency was, to a considerable extent, merely apparent. Degas remained Degas in spite of his stylistic evolution, and the new sensuality was under the control of the old intellect. Often the color orgy was visibly a kind of chromatic draftsmanship, a variety of *bricolage* that involved utilizing the pastel stick as a drawing instrument instead of just a vehicle for laying down hues to be blended with a finger or a stump, in the traditional eighteenth-century way. Typically, the first stage in the creation of a work was to cover the paper, or perhaps merely a section of it, with a network of flecks, whorls, scrawls, cross-hatching, and long parallel lines in scruffed half-tones and glowing reds, turquoises, yellows, and greens. The powdery pigments were protected from the danger of smudging and made to adhere to the support by means of a special, supposedly secret fixative (perhaps merely white shellac dissolved in pure methyl alcohol) that Degas obtained from his friend Luigi Chialiva, a Roman painter, chemist, and expert picture-restorer who had joined the Italian colony in Paris. A second network of linear hues was added in such a fashion as to let the lower one partly show through, the secret fixative was applied again, and so on with successive layers. (Degas would certainly have liked the brightness, transparency, and fast-drying quality of twentieth-century acrylic.) The technique was in varying degrees an equivalent of the juxtaposed commas of Impressionist brushwork, an imitation in opaque media of Venetian underpainting and glazing, and a pastel version of the irregular sort of overpainting that is called scumbling by oil practitioners. When everything went right, it could produce a textured, stratified, line-and-color structure that, though not lacking in sensuous appeal, was as much an incarnation of intellect in matter as any other kind of drawing could be.

The maker of such structures was plainly not misanthropic and hypochondriacal every day. In an undated note he informed Alexis Rouart, "I am doing a lot of work. Durand-Ruel is selling my articles and asking for more. I feel good."[49] (The dealer was now completely out of debt.) One of his early dance pictures, the exact title of which is uncertain, was sold for eight thousand francs in 1890 at the auction of the May collection in Georges Petit's gallery; in 1893 his *Absinthe,* shortly after provoking a useful scandal at an exhibition in London, was acquired in Paris by Isaac de Camondo for twenty-one thousand francs. He was now, in spite of Zoé's deplorable cooking, regularly inviting his friends to dinners in his new apartment-atelier-museum at 37 Rue Victor-Massé. In 1892 he felt prosperous enough to contemplate, if only half-seriously, spending nine hundred francs of the profits from his Durand-Ruel one-man show on Sir Richard Burton's recently published fifteen-volume English translation of *The Thousand and One Nights.* Since neither his eyesight nor his English was adequate for Burton's tortured, pseudo-archaic prose style, he planned to recruit the Halévy boys for reading sessions in the Rue de Douai.

Music was one of his most constant pleasures. In 1892, in a letter to Daniel Halévy, he described himself as intoxicated with the operas of Weber while working in his pavilion among the tall trees in the park of the château at Ménil-Hubert:

> If you want an idea of the nature of my thoughts, take the chorus of *Euryanthe* and hear me singing falsetto, the whole day long: "When we seek the king himself . . . hunter lost in the forest, hunter lost in the forest." With an interrupted, falling strain for "in the forest." Lovely, disquieting, airy, firm, steady.[50]

Later that summer, during his trip through central France, he had another of his combined musical and religious shocks, and reported it to Valernes:

> At Bourges in a deluge of rain I took shelter in the cathedral. Thunder claps echoed under the vault of the nave with a fearsome din. Lightning flashes blazed through the stained glass windows. And at that moment a mysterious musician decided to awaken the organ and play the *Dies Irae.*[51]

In 1890 he was at the Théâtre Royal de La Monnaie in Brussels for the production of Reyer's opera *Salammbô,* which was based on the Flaubert novel and graced with the singing of Caron in the title role and of the great baritone Maurice Renaud as Hamilcar.

Back in Paris the musical evenings were as numerous as they had been before the Franco-Prussian War. Stevens organized violin recitals in his new and luxurious apartment near the Boulevard de Clichy. Over on the Left Bank, Henry Lerolle's soirées featured the music of Chausson, who was Lerolle's brother-in-law, and of the young Claude Debussy, who often played the piano; and the guests, in addition to Degas, included Renoir, Henri Rouart, Forain, Régnier, and Mallarmé. In the Rue de Douai, the Dieppe girl Marie Lemoinne — nicknamed Yoyo, presumably because of the quality of her voice — sometimes started things off with a solo, and Degas, Louise Halévy, and Daniel joined in for some ensemble numbers, often from one of Gluck's operas.

Degas had not evolved at all in his musical tastes: on one occasion he asked for some airs from a now largely forgotten eighteenth-century pastoral, Pierre Monsigny's *Rose et Colas.* Once when a woman guest began to play a piano sonata he stopped her by saying, "When I hear a development by Beethoven I feel as if I were walking alone in a forest full of all my troubles. Give us something else."[52] His opposition to Wagner's innovations increased proportionately as the number of French Wagnerian cultists swelled under the blended influences of literary Symbolism and fin-de-siècle aestheticism; and it reached a peak of raillery when, in the spring of 1893, the Paris Opéra scheduled its first production of *Die Walküre* (at a time when the work had long since entered the repertoire of German, American, and British houses). One day a couple of weeks before the opening night he had lunch at a place on the Champ de Mars with Zandomeneghi (whom he had nicknamed "the Prince"), Manzi, Mathilde Salle, Bartholomé, and Camondo; and that evening the Halévys asked him whether the party had talked about the rehearsals at the Palais Garnier. "Oh," he said, "the others wanted to. But there was Zandomeneghi the Prince, who had just heard [Cimarosa's] *Il Matrimonio Segreto* at Bologna, there was Manzi, and we said that was enough and began to sing. The others insulted us and we kept going: la la la — la la la — lalalalala."[53]

Meanwhile, the weekly social rituals of the *grande bourgeoisie* continued. Valéry, remembering the Rue de Lisbonne, wrote, forty years later:

Every Friday Degas, faithful, sparkling, unbearable, animated the dinner at Monsieur Rouart's. He spread wit, terror, gaiety. He pierced, he mimicked, he lavished sallies, fables, maxims, jokes, all the features of the most intelligent unfairness, the most infallible taste, the narrowest and at the same time the most lucid passions. He abused littérateurs, the Institut [de France], bogus hermits, artists who arrive; he quoted Saint-Simon, Proudhon, Racine, and the bizarre pronouncements of Monsieur Ingres. I can still hear him.[54]

21. The Affair

D URING THE LAST TWO DECADES of the nineteenth century a large
number of rational, decent Frenchmen behaved in a stubbornly
irrational, thoroughly indecent fashion. They were also, like
some of the Tory squires of England and the unreconstructed
Southerners of the United States, the die-hard losers in an ideological
conflict involving a defense of values that are apt to be dismissed today as
either dissimulation or lost-cause sentimentality. Hence the period simultaneously inhibits and demands careful reporting, and it is no use pretending that there is a good way out of the difficulty. For if we observe the
usual rules for such reporting — if we practice empathy, evoke context,
avoid anachronistic moralizing, and remember that history should not be
seen exclusively from the viewpoint of the winners — we are bound to
wind up, in some degree, with an appearance of having condoned iniquity.
And if we ignore the rules we are certain to fail to understand what
happened.

Renoir's flare-up in 1882 against "the Jew Pissarro" was a sign of far
worse to come. In 1883 the daily newspaper *La Croix,* an organ of the
relatively new and rashly demagogic order of the Augustinians of the Assumption, was founded, and soon it was spreading the ancient Roman
Catholic varieties of anti-Semitism that depicted the Jews as rapacious
usurers and the murderers of Jesus. Here and there in the French provinces
the grisly ritual-homicide legend, which had inspired Chaucer's "Prioress's
Tale," was revived and updated. At about the same time, Socialist politi-

cians began to flirt seriously with the notion that a dose of anti-Semitism might help to motivate the French working class in an anticapitalist direction. Xenophobia, half-baked social Darwinism, and pseudoscientific anthropology contributed to the trend; and in 1886 Edouard Drumont, an unscrupulous pamphleteer with a talent for verbal savagery, pulled all the elements together in a violent twelve-hundred-page tract titled *La France juive* (Jewish France). He began with some standard mythologizing about Aryans and Semites, moved on to a catalogue of alleged Jewish crimes, made an impassioned plea for the liberation of the country from the asserted financial control of aliens, and included a generalized portrait to help possibly naïve Gentiles to identify members of what he called "the tribe crawling over France":[1]

> The principal signs by which you can recognize a Jew are the well-known hooked nose, the blinking eyes, clenched teeth, projecting ears, fingernails that are square instead of round and almond-shaped, an excessively long torso, flat feet, round knees, extraordinarily turned-out toes, and the soft, velvety hand of a hypocrite and a traitor.[2]

The book became a best seller. In 1890 Drumont took an active part in the organization of La Ligue Antisémite Nationale Française (one of several "leagues" that would shortly be formed); two years later he created a newspaper he called *La Libre Parole* (roughly, *Speaking Freely*); and in a matter of months he had half a million daily readers for his ideas. In detail none of this whole phenomenon was unfamiliar: Fourierists and other leftists, for instance, had denounced Jewish bankers during the reign of Louis-Philippe, and the Goncourts had published their anti-Semitic *Manette Salomon* during the Second Empire. There were no precedents in nineteenth-century France, however, for the scale and ferocity of what had been building up since the early 1880s.

The majority of French Jews tended at first to ignore the danger, partly perhaps because they wished to avoid any hint of provocation and largely because they felt sure that the thing would soon go away. Anti-Semitism, they argued, was a German and Russian malady. It could be imported temporarily into France, but it could not take root in the emotional life of a nation that during the preceding hundred years had issued the Declaration of the Rights of Man, freed its Jewish citizens of all their medieval legal disabilities, rid itself of a series of kings and emperors, and finally, with the advent of the Third Republic, emerged with a secular democracy administered mostly by civilians and opposed to all forms of obscurantism. Moreover, the accusations of the anti-Semitic agitators were absurd. There were only about eighty thousand Jews in all of France (against five million in Russia, two million in Austria-Hungary, and six hundred thousand in Germany), and, with the exception of the recent immigrants in the Marais quarter of Paris, they were all deeply committed to assimilation, so much so that many no longer observed any of the rules of Judaism and therefore could hardly be considered Jews. They were political moderates, staunch republicans, and superpatriots: in 1890 they paid for the erection of two statues of Joan of Arc, one in Nancy and the other in Paris. In short, they were neither numerous nor alien.

So the argument went, and it was a reasonable one. But of course Drumont, the Assumptionists, and their followers were not interested in reason; they were after the odd theory or fact that might feed their fanaticism. And such food, unfortunately, could be found. For instance, assimilation should have been rendered easier, and more plausible as a defense against prejudice, by the circumstance that French Jews were simply an ethnic group, since they differed from other French citizens only in cultural (including religious) terms and not as a race — not, that is, in terms of physical characteristics. They themselves, however, misled by the deplorable science of the period and to some extent by collective vanity, rejected the saving ethnic concept and insisted on talking about their supposed racial features, often in ways as ridiculous as the caricature in *La France juive*. (An official report of the philanthropic Alliance Israélite Universelle went so far as to assert that in "the Jewish race" the cranial dimensions were "without exception . . . superior to the corresponding dimensions of the Christian cranium.")[3] At the linguistic level, the French-like-other-Frenchmen claim was marred by the strong German accent of the many former Alsatians among the fifty thousand Jews in Paris. And at all levels the defense case was weakened by the presence in the French capital of a larger number of powerful, extremely visible representatives of international Jewish finance — Bamberger, Camondo, Reinach, Stern, Deutsch, Heine, Ephrussi, Goudchaux, Lippmann, Bischoffsheim, Koenigswarter, Cahen, Hirsch, Günzbourg, Léonine, May, Straus, and of course the Rothschilds. They were ex-residents of Berlin, Saint Petersburg, Munich, Constantinople, Genoa, Madrid, and London. Their town houses loomed among the trees along the avenues around the Parc Monceau. The titles of nobility many of them bore were of foreign origin: the "baron" of the Rothschilds, for example, came from Austria; the "comte" of the Camondos from Italy, although the family was from Turkey; and the "baron" of Jacques de Reinach also from Italy, although he himself was from Germany.

To be sure, there was a cap-wearing Jewish proletariat in Paris, and bankers were not invariably Jewish (though those who were not were likely to be Protestants and as such bracketed with the Jews by Catholic anti-

Semites). Even so, during the long economic depression of these years it was understandably not very difficult to convince jobless workers and ruined shopkeepers that their troubles were due to Jewish avarice and that, to take a specific example of anti-Semitic propaganda, the terrible collapse in 1882 of the Union Générale, one of the few Catholic-owned banks, was brought about by the Rothschilds instead of (as is probable) by overexpansion. Nor, with all those Germanic names to harp on, was it hard to arouse suspicions of treachery among Frenchmen who were still shaken by their defeat in the Franco-Prussian War.

During the latter part of the 1880s the humiliation of 1870 and the related xenophobic jingoism were also elements in what was known, with excessive precision, as the Boulangist movement. General Georges Boulanger had a blond beard, a black horse, foolishly anti-Bismarck sentiments, a tendency to lie to everyone, and a vague plan to replace the parliamentary Third Republic with a presidential regime based on plebiscite. As minister of war in 1886 he improved the food and lodging of the troops, made more use of brass bands, and had sentry boxes painted in the national blue, white, and red. On Bastille Day of that year, during the big military review at Longchamp, the frenzied crowd cheered him as no one had been cheered since the return of Napoleon III from Solferino in 1859; at the Alcazar the song "On Returning from the Review" gave his popularity another boost. In 1888, taking advantage of an electoral law that allowed a candidate to stand in more than one district, he won election to the chamber of deputies in three different departments; and on January 27, 1889, backed by an unnatural coalition of leftists, monarchists, Bonapartists, and anti-Semites, he swept all but one of the twenty Paris arrondissements. But then he failed to lead the waiting crowd in a march to seize power, and during the next two months the government changed the electoral law and frightened him with threats of arrest. On April Fools' Day, 1889, he fled to Brussels. His coalition collapsed, and a year later, completely discredited, he shot himself on his mistress's grave. He had never had what was needed to become a dictator. His tragicomic adventure had revealed, however, the fragility of French parliamentary democracy and, on the part of many, an ominous distrust of civilian politicians and a remarkable willingness to believe almost anything that was said by a man in uniform. Even Mallarmé had voted for him, and one can guess — on the basis of later behavior — that Degas had, too.

The general's remaining followers had a kind of revenge on their republican enemies. In February 1889 the French company that was cutting a canal through the Isthmus of Panama went bankrupt, mostly because of graft and mismanagement, and thousands of small investors lost everything. After a long hesitation a judicial inquiry was ordered. In the autumn of 1892 Drumont's *Libre Parole* and the leading Boulangist paper, *La Cocarde,* accused the government of complicity with the company's directors, a Royalist deputy charged that more than a hundred and fifty members of the chamber were involved, and soon the whole odoriferous story came out, without much need of an official investigation. The company, crippled by a lack of funds from the start, had felt obliged to encourage investment by bribing Paris journalists to keep silent about the way things were going, and had eventually found itself spending a sizable amount of what money it had on what was essentially a vast blackmail operation. In 1888 a lottery loan had been floated as a last, desperate effort to attract new shareholders; this required legislative approval and therefore more buying of good will. The bribery had been managed by the financier Jacques de Reinach, who died mysteriously at the beginning of the inquiry, and by two other Jews, the bogus medical doctor Cornélius Herz and a German adventurer named Léopold Arton. Herz had also, on some unknown basis, been blackmailing Reinach, and he had been allowed to buy a large share in *La Justice,* a newspaper linked to Clemenceau. Naturally, nearly everyone flatly denied everything, and among the veteran professional politicians of what would be referred to as "the Republic of Pals" there was a disposition to accept a pal's story. So finally the only briber who went to prison was Arton, and the only receiver of bribes was Charles Baïhaut, a former minister of public works, who had made the mistake of confessing. But the stench lingered for a long while around the chamber of deputies, and in the next elections Clemenceau lost his seat.

Thus by the mid-1890s the French public had been rendered hypersensitive to a number of themes — racism, nationalism, militarism, and corruption — that would reverberate through the furious, fascinating drama, half civil war and half detective thriller, that was about to divide the nation. Besides, and this was perhaps even more important, the men and instruments were on hand to orchestrate the themes and build up the crescendos. In 1881 a new law had freed the press from nearly every constraint, including the traditional ones concerning incitement to violence against political or religious groups, and the result had been a proliferation of some of the liveliest, funniest, most vicious, and most quarrelsome newspapers in the world. Most of them agreed with the subtitle of *La Libre Parole:* "France for the French." Many of the editors, however, were far from having a predictable political line, and of these the witty, polemical Marquis de Rochefort-Luçay, who wrote under the name of Henri Rochefort and belonged to the same family as the duke who had married Célestine Musson's older sister, was an example. Rochefort had been an anti-Bonapartist during the Second Empire and a supporter of the Commune in 1871, and as a result had been sent to the penal colony in New Caledonia. After the amnesty of former Communards in 1880 and the voting of the new press law, he had founded *L'Intransigeant,* which had lived up to its name by campaigning for the Radicals, switching to General Boulanger in 1889, veering back to the Socialists, and finally settling down on the extreme right.

What became "the Affair" began as simply a case on the evening of September 26, 1894, when a Parisian cleaning woman turned over to an officer of the French counterespionage service two bags of scraps from the wastepaper basket of the military attaché at the German embassy, where she worked. She was paid by the French service to do this regularly, and usually the results were extremely meager. But that evening the scraps included an unsigned, undated letter that turned out to be a list, a *borde-reau,* of documents the author was handing over to the German attaché: the principal items were a description of the new French 120-millimeter gun, a note on the covering troops along the Alsatian frontier, and a copy of the provisional firing manual of the French field artillery. This information was not in itself vitally important, yet it was of a nature to suggest that the writer of the *bordereau* was an officer in the war office.

After a hasty investigation, suspicion settled on Captain Alfred Drey-fus. Although no motive could be found, he was an artilleryman, an Alsa-tian, a Jew, and a rather unpopular member of the general staff; and to minds that were already made up, his handwriting seemed to match that of the *bordereau.* On October 15 he was hustled off in secret to a prison on the Left Bank. The news of his detention leaked out, and on November 1 *La Libre Parole* ran a front-page banner headline: HIGH TREASON — ARREST OF THE JEWISH OFFICER A. DREYFUS.[4] Almost the entire press, taking the captain's guilt for granted, began to howl for action by the minister of war, General Auguste Mercier. According to *Le Matin* and *Le Temps,* Dreyfus had been seduced into treason by a female Italian agent, *une magicienne d'amour,* who had given him a secret philter. In *L'Intransigeant,* Rochefort accused Mercier of "carelessness, stupidity, and bad faith,"[5] and *La Libre Parole* announced, "The affair will be hushed up because the officer is a Jew."[6] The harassed Mercier told *Le Figaro* that the proof of Dreyfus's treachery was overwhelming. In such a context the court-martial, which took place *in camera,* became simply a ritual; on December 22 the seven military judges, convinced by doctored evidence, unanimously pronounced the accused guilty and sentenced him to life imprisonment. A special law was passed to make it possible to send him to Devil's Island, a hot, desolate rock off the coast of Guiana.

The country applauded. The French army, people felt, was not like the corrupt civilians who had let the culprits in the Panama scandal go unpunished. On the right and the left the traitor was denounced. A Royalist wrote in *Le Figaro,* "I believe that if you opened Dreyfus's brain you would find nothing in it that was human."[7] In the chamber of deputies the Socialist leader Jean Jaurès expressed his regret that, because of a clause in the law concerning political crimes, the criminal could not be shot. The unanimous verdict at the court-martial had swept away the doubts of almost everyone except the Dreyfus family and, oddly, the anti-Semitic Goncourt, who in his *Journal* qualified the condemned captain as "this scoundrel, of whose treason I am nevertheless not convinced."[8]

Degas appears to have been slow to react and then to have made up in intensity for the time lost. An entry in Daniel Halévy's diary for November 5, 1895, says, "Degas is very sad. . . . He has become a passionate believer in anti-Semitism."[9] At about this time he began to have Zoé read *La Libre Parole* to him at the breakfast table. Apparently she also read *L'Intransigeant* occasionally, for Valéry remarked, "He thought that Rochefort was full of a miraculous sort of good sense."[10] By March 1896 his reputation as an anti-Semite was such that André Gide, on a vacation in North Africa, wrote in his *Journal* concerning a slightly eccentric Tunisian friend:

> He has sent Degas a cane in the form of a palm stem, along with a letter saying, "What pleases me about you is that you do not like Jews, that you read *La Libre Parole,* and that you think, as I do, that Poussin was a great French painter."[11]

The new — or perhaps merely reinforced — prejudice had no immediate effect, however, on the regular lunches and dinners in the Rue de Douai, for the Jews to be encountered there were not Jews like other Jews. Haas, for instance, had long since been converted to Roman Catholicism by one of his mistresses. Reyer appears to have been closer to Nordic mythology than to the Old Testament. Geneviève Straus remained a Jew, but very nominally; once when a Catholic priest suggested conversion she replied, "Monsieur l'abbé, I don't have enough religion for us to bother changing it."[12] Ludovic Halévy and his two sons were products of the assimilation process that had got under way after the emancipation of French Jews in 1791 and by the 1890s had affected four generations. Ludovic's patriarchal grandfather, Elie Halévy, had been an immigrant from the Würzburg ghetto at the close of the eighteenth century; he had become a Parisian professor, cantor, and poet and had celebrated Bonaparte's achievements in Hebrew verse. His son Léon, Ludovic's father, had drifted away from Judaism and adhered enthusiastically to French classical culture, to the ideals of the Revolution of 1789, and to the industrial socialism of Saint-Simon. He had written a history of the modern Jewry of the Enlightenment and had married a Christian. Ludovic was raised as a Catholic; his wife, Louise, came from a Swiss Protestant background; and they had raised their two sons as Catholics. Daniel, now in his mid-twenties, was so culturally confused as to indulge in a bit of Jewish self-hatred and refer in an essay to "the corrupt idiosyncrasies" of his "race,"[13] and he appears to have been undisturbed by the intolerance of his hero Degas.

The latter's warm friendship with the Halévys — half a century old — was deepened during these years by an extraordinary succession of losses of acquaintances and relatives that left him feeling mortal, isolated, and in need of affection. Eugène Manet died in 1892; Yves Morisot-Gobillard in 1893, at about the same time as Achille; Paul Valpinçon, Caillebotte, and Edmondo Morbilli in 1894; Ellen Andrée, Berthe Morisot, and Marguerite de Gas Fevre in 1895; and Valernes in 1896. The death of Marguerite was the worst blow, for she had always seemed a special, delightful person to her oldest brother, and her dying so far from France added to the horror for him. He immediately set about making arrangements to have her brought back to Paris and buried next to Achille and Célestine in the family vault in the Montmartre Cemetery. He also began to organize, at Durand-Ruel's, a retrospective exhibition of the work of Berthe Morisot. Their long relationship had had its tense moments, mostly because of what she had called his bad disposition, but it had never been broken; and in a farewell note to her daughter, Julie, written the day before she died, Berthe revealed that she had been thinking of him toward the end — still as the "Monsieur" Degas of the 1860s.

Although his bronchitis was getting worse, he had decided that the hot sulfurous springs at Cauterets were not good for his bladder, and so in 1895, 1896, and 1897 he spent his August periods of rest, medication, and name-dropping at Mont-Dore, a watering place situated on the banks of the Dordogne high up among the forest-covered extinct volcanoes of Auvergne — one of the few provinces of central France with which he was not yet familiar. The Gauls, the Romans, the Vandals, and George Sand had been there; and since the end of the First Empire the warm mineral water from the eight local springs had been piped conveniently into a single Etablissement Thermal, a huge building conceived in the Romantic Classical style and recently modernized in the Beaux-Arts manner. He did not like the local inhabitants, but he enjoyed the scenery, the altitude, and the daily ceremony of putting on an amusing sweat suit and marching from the first-class Hôtel de la Poste, where he stayed, across the street to the Etablissement for his prescribed treatment. In 1895 he reported to his correspondents in Argentina:

The stay here seems to be improving my health a great deal. . . . Lovely Auvergne, terrible Auvergnats. Good food, good bed. A flannel outfit, with trousers that enclose the feet, and galoshes. An hour every morning of perspiring and breathing in a temperature of between twenty-eight and thirty degrees.[14]

He had breakfast with an agent from Goupil's gallery in New York, lunch with an anti-Semitic journalist from *Le Figaro,* and a dinner with Madame Howland, "a poor snob in exile with her dog."[15] He was disappointed because the Comtesse de Mailly-Nesle, now Madame de Reszke, failed to appear at a banquet arranged by his doctor.

By this time his printmaking spells and his collecting of canes and Norman handkerchiefs had been replaced by a mania that was even more uncontrollable. In an undated letter to Martelli, who was now back in Tuscany, Zandomeneghi wrote:

Degas is abandoning everything in favor of his new lust for photography. . . . After getting off this note, I'll send you, between two pieces of cardboard, my portrait enlarged from a small negative produced . . . in his studio. You will be able to admire not only my likeness but also a beautiful photograph that is quite different from the usual commercial work. You will think you are looking at a Velázquez.[16]

The letter was probably written in 1895, for although Degas had almost certainly used a camera before, perhaps at Dieppe in the 1880s, "his new lust" had become particularly noticeable during his first stay at Mont-Dore. In a note from there to Henri Rouart, dated August 12, he wrote, "In the evening I digest my dinner and practice photography by twilight."[17] In several letters to his Parisian furnishers, the firm of Tasset and Lhote at 31 Rue Fontaine, he ordered plates by the dozen, six enlargements, and finally a new camera, and on one occasion he was so excited that he sent Tasset a telegram. Back in Paris in September, he wrote to Ludovic Halévy, "I'll drop in on you one fine morning with my apparatus. Greetings to Louise *la réveleuse*" ("the developer," with a punning reference to the anarchist and alleged incendiary Louise Michel, who was called Louise la Pétroleuse).[18] On December 22 Daniel went with him to the furnishers in the Rue Fontaine, where Tasset's pretty daughter Delphine took care of the more delicate development assignments:

[Degas] showed me his latest proofs — one of Renoir and Mallarmé, one of the Manet family, one of Madame Howland. "It's beautiful," he said of the last, "but she will not see it. She would have it licked by her dog. She is a brute. The other day I showed her my fine portrait of Haas, and she said, 'It's mottled and will have to be retouched.' A brute."[19]

The "proofs" were evidently enlargements, for Renoir and Mallarmé seem to have posed during November, at 40 Rue de Villejust, and the picture of Madame Howland, along with the one of Haas, can be dated to 1887. The mention of "the Manet family" is puzzling, since a print has not survived, and by 1895 Berthe Morisot and the three Manet brothers were dead. Perhaps the reference was actually to "the Mante family." Degas had already done pastels of Madame Mante and her daughters, and he may have been interested in the girls' father, Louis-Amédée Mante, who was a bassoonist at the Opéra and a well-known pioneer with the camera.

In fact, this whole photographic episode is somewhat puzzling. For instance, one might have expected Degas to exploit the peculiarities of the medium and produce a collection of looming *repoussoirs,* accelerated perspectives, and figures cut by frames. But in his preserved camera work we see that he did almost nothing of the sort; in terms of such effects his paintings are far more "photographic" than his photographs. Also, one might have expected Degas the observer, the *flâneur,* and the voyeur to come up with a batch of candid shots of people unaware of being looked at. But again he did almost nothing of the sort; on the contrary, his figures often look like coerced models who were thoroughly, even painfully conscious of the apparatus being pointed at them. And how coercive, painful, and uncandid that operation could become is revealed by Daniel Halévy's account of an evening in the Rue de Douai, in December 1895, with his cousins Henriette Taschereau and Mathilde Niaudet and his uncle Jules Taschereau:

> After dinner Degas went to his studio with Uncle Jules to get his camera. . . . They returned together, and then the evening of pleasure was finished. Degas raised his voice, became dictatorial. . . . He had placed Uncle Jules, Mathilde, and Henriette on the little sofa in front of the piano. He went back and forth in front of them; he ran from one corner of the salon to the other with an expression of infinite happiness; he moved lamps, changed reflectors, tried to light the legs by putting a lamp on the floor. . . . He said, "Taschereau! Grab that leg with your right arm and pull it over. There, there. And then look at that young person next to you. More affectionately, more — come on! You smile very well when you want to. And you, Mademoiselle Henriette, lean your head — more! more! let it go! Rest on your neighbor's shoulder." When she didn't do as he wished he took her by the nape and forced her into position; he seized Mathilde and turned her face toward my uncle. Then he stepped back and exclaimed happily, "We're ready to go!" The pose was held for two minutes, then again for two minutes, and so on. . . . At eleven-thirty everybody left, Degas carrying his camera, as proud as a child carrying a rifle.[20]

This was probably the way he had directed Duranty and Emma Dobigny twenty-five years earlier in *Sulking,* at a time when he still had faith in his theory of wordless expression; and the theory tended to produce in photography the same ambiguous staginess that it had in painting. Even the picture of Renoir and Mallarmé, which Valéry considered "by way of being a masterpiece" and one of the best portraits of the poet he had seen, suggests two actors in an unknown play. And it involved "nine gasoline lamps and a terrible quarter of an hour of immobility for the subjects."[21]

The photographs do not, of course, all show the signs of theatrical production. There are delightfully straightforward pictures of little girls, a nobly simple portrait of the Belgian poet Emile Verhaeren, and some studies of interiors manifesting the same interest in lamplight Degas had shown in such paintings as *Interior* and the portraits of Madame Camus. Quite often he also exhibited what Charles Ephrussi, commenting on the fifth secessionist show, had called "tone values of an astonishing exactitude that puts each thing in its place," and in doing so he revealed an acute awareness, surprising in a Louis-le-Grand Latinist, of recent advances in photographic technology. His orders to Tasset from Mont-Dore, for instance, specify panchromatic plates from the Lumière brothers' plant in Lyons — plates with a relatively new emulsion sensitive to the gray tones corresponding to the brightness of all the colors of the spectrum, including the difficult reds.

To mention these virtues, however, is to be reminded of some serious faults. Degas went on being fascinated by his new art for several years, and on the basis of his enthusiasm in 1895 we can assume that he took a large number, perhaps hundreds, of photographs. But only a packet of them — somewhere between forty and sixty, according to the rigor of the attributor[22] — has survived. We have nothing at all, for example, from those dozens of plates sent to Mont-Dore. And, although some prints simply may have been lost, the scarcity can be blamed mostly on his heedless amateurishness combined with the same delight in experimentation, problem-solving, and *bricolage* that ruined a lot of paintings, engravings, and pieces of wax sculpture. Madame Howland was partly right in calling the portrait of Haas mottled. The picture of Renoir and Mallarmé is marred by a mirror that reflects a glaring light, Madame Mallarmé and her daughter, and Degas himself, hunched over his camera. That evening of bullying Mathilde, Henriette, and Uncle Jules finally yielded nothing except a horizontal-vertical double exposure and then, with Jeanne Niaudet and Ludovic, Daniel, and Elie Halévy added to the list of suffering models, still another double exposure. In one of his letters to Tasset from Mont-Dore in 1895, Degas revealed that he had bought a red lantern at Avignon with the intention of doing some developing on his own. In another he said, "But nothing appears, my dear Monsieur Tasset, on these cursed panchromatics. . . . An instant in the bath and all is black." [23] At last he confessed, "What I proposed to you yesterday seems to me absurd. I am trying to photograph almost in darkness. Do you have any tips for such a case?" Daylight, he told his audience in the Rue de Douai, was too easy for a photographer.

One reason, in Paris at least, for his using the camera in the evening was that he wanted to reserve the daytime for painting. In 1895 he executed his last important, successful portrait, a study of Henri Rouart and his son Alexis, in which the real subject appears to be the wisdom of age and the fatuity of youth, for Henri, seated (he had arthritis), dignified, and benevolent, makes Alexis, in ill-fitting clothes topped by a ridiculous derby, look like a complete nincompoop. To 1894 can be assigned *Woman with a Towel,* in which the colored draftsmanship of *After the Bath* has evolved into an intense vibration that has been aptly described as "colored rain." [24] Both the color and the draftsmanship continued to evolve during the rest of the decade, and they reached another high point in a series of Russian dancers — some fourteen pastels and five sketches — probably inspired by a folk-dance number in a Paris theater and drawn in a slashing, thick-contoured manner that admirably matches the linked forms and dynamism of the dance. A few scholars have suggested, partly because of the apparent lateness of the drawing style, that the series was based on the Gopak dance performed in Paris in 1909 by the visiting Diaghilev company; other researchers have opted for a folk spectacle presented at the Folies-Bergère in 1895. The first possibility is ruled out, however, and the second seriously weakened by an entry in Julie Manet's diary for July 1, 1899, concerning an evening at 37 Rue Victor-Massé:

> Monsieur Degas was so nice, he was really a sweetheart. He talked about painting, and then suddenly he said to us, "I'm going to show you some orgies of color I am working on at the moment." He took us upstairs to his studio, which greatly affected us, for he almost never reveals what he has in hand. He brought out three pastels representing women in Russian costume wearing flowers in their hair, pearl necklaces, white blouses, brightly colored skirts, and red boots, and dancing in an imaginary landscape that was more real than the real. The movements were depicted in an astonishing drawing style, and the costumes in very beautiful hues. In one picture the women were lit by a pink sun, in another their dresses were more boldly rendered, and in the third the sun had just vanished behind a hill, leaving a clear sky against which the women stood out in half tints. The tone value of the whites against the sky was marvelous and completely real. This third picture

was perhaps the finest, the most taking. It was extraordinary, it carried you away. Monsieur Degas asked us which we thought the most effective, and then he showed us some torsos and some ballerinas, all of which must pay for the paintings he is buying for his collection.[25]

His phrase "working on at the moment" plainly implies a project begun earlier in that summer of 1899, and such a date fits the evidence of a drawing style that is rougher than what he was doing in 1895. But of course, given his habit of transforming and assembling old memories, notes, and sketches, what Julie saw in 1899 may have stemmed remotely from an earlier evening at the Folies-Bergère.

As the passage suggests, the private museum at 37 Rue Victor-Massé was growing rapidly. In 1894 a Delacroix had been acquired. In a series of

Three Russian Dancers, 1899

letters to Henri Rouart's brother, Degas enthusiastically describes the purchase, probably in 1895, of ninety-three rare and "magnificent" lithographs by Gavarni.[26] During the following year he bought two portraits by Ingres. In April 1897 he made a special trip to Montauban, the small town north of Toulouse where Ingres was born, to negotiate an exchange of photographic reproductions with the local museum. The intense emotional commitment that accompanied his collecting appears in an express letter of 1898 to Durand-Ruel concerning what may have been a version of *Oedipus and the Sphinx:*

> Don't deprive me of the little copy by Ingres; don't affront and afflict me over it. I really *need* it. I'll go look at it again by daylight. It is a little lacking in vigor, but it pleases me. I have been thinking about it all night.[27]

By this time he had also invested in a number of his contemporaries, including a rather unexpected one — the Montmartre model Suzanne Valadon. "I'll die in the poorhouse," he told the Halévys, "but it's wonderful."[28]

The poorhouse was not, of course, much of a menace. His own work was selling at constantly rising prices, and in 1896 his reputation was increased by the official acceptance of seven of his pastels by the Musée du Luxembourg. They had been part of the collection bequeathed by Caillebotte to the nation and had been spared during the uproar, fomented to some extent by Gérôme, that led to the rejection of twenty-nine of the sixty Impressionist pictures in the bequest. In short, Degas the anti-arriviste had arrived after all. His growing fame, however, brought with it some problems he did not know how to handle. In 1893, for instance, he sold *The Collector of Prints* to the Havemeyers through Mary Cassatt for a thousand dollars and then, as was his habit, asked to keep the picture for a while to add a few touches. He kept it for two years, after which he announced that, because of the rapidity with which the prices of his work had been rising, he wanted three thousand dollars. Henry Osborne Havemeyer, as he usually did in such circumstances, paid without a murmur, but Louisine Havemeyer said that the incident "cost Degas Miss Cassatt's friendship for a long time."[29] He was also upset by the way several of his old friends began to cash in on his success. Tissot, Duret, Michel-Lévy, and Renoir were among those who sold at high prices works they had bought for small sums or had received as gifts; and each got a scorching denunciation from Degas. "It is sad," he said, "to live surrounded by scoundrels."[30]

In the meantime the Dreyfus case was evolving. During the spring and summer of 1896 the new head of the French counterespionage service, Lieutenant Colonel Marie-Georges Picquart, gradually became convinced, on the basis of more scraps from the German attaché's basket and another handwriting comparison, that the real traitor, the real author of the *bordereau,* was Major Marie-Charles-Ferdinand Walsin-Esterhazy, a handsome, debauched descendant of an illegitimate branch of the Hungarian Esterhazys, who was known around Paris as a chronic borrower of francs and the lover of a prostitute in the Rue de Douai called Four-Fingered Margaret. Picquart's superiors ordered him to keep quiet, and he reluctantly obeyed. But fresh light continued to be shed, sometimes inadvertently. On September 15, 1896, the daily newspaper *L'Eclair,* in an attempt to answer all doubts about Dreyfus's guilt, overshot the mark and revealed that at the court-martial, in clear violation of both civil and military law, documents not shown to the defense had been produced to influence the judges. On November 6 Bernard Lazare, a young Jewish intellectual close to the condemned captain's family, summarized a number of contradictions and irregularities in a pamphlet entitled *Une Erreur judiciaire: La Vérité sur l'affaire Dreyfus.* At about this time Major Hubert-Joseph Henry, a member of the counterespionage service who knew how weak the supposed proofs of treason were, began secretly to forge evidence so as to be ready in the event of another trial. On November 10 *Le Matin* published a reproduction of the *bordereau.* On December 3 Madame Dreyfus's appeal to the chamber of deputies, based on the revelations in the *L'Eclair* article, was rejected on the grounds of *res judicata,* and at the end of the year Picquart, who was becoming a nuisance, was sent off to a post in Tunisia. General Mercier and the other officers involved in the railroading in 1894 could breathe again, and so could the politicians who, knowingly or not, had been covering up for the officers.

During the summer of 1897, however, Picquart returned to Paris on leave and, torn between his conscience and his military code of obedience, talked with a lawyer-friend, who in turn talked with the vice-president of the senate. As a result, a number of influential people, among them Clemenceau, joined those agitating for a new trial. The minister of war declared publicly on three occasions that Dreyfus was a traitor, other politicians took refuge again in the doctrine of *res judicata,* and *La Libre Parole* began to talk about a powerful "Jewish syndicate" that was supposedly spending millions of francs on a campaign of dupery.

On January 10, 1898, to the accompaniment of shouts of "Long live France!" and "Down with the syndicate!" from an assembled crowd, a court-martial cleared Esterhazy of all the charges against him. Picquart was arrested for divulging military secrets. But the agitation in favor of "revision" continued, and on the morning of January 13, in Clemenceau's new paper, *L'Aurore,* Zola published a long open letter to the president of the Republic, entitled "J'accuse." Among other things he accused General Mercier of having violated the rights of the defense at the court-martial of 1894; he accused the war office of having ordered the acquittal of Esterhazy; and he accused the new war minister of knowing that Dreyfus was innocent and suppressing the proof "for political reasons and in order to save the compromised general staff." He added, "And these people can sleep!" During the following week anti-Semitic demonstrations broke out in twenty French provincial towns. In Algiers an inflamed mob looted shops in the center of the city, overwhelmed the police, and finally sacked the Jewish quarter.

The Dreyfus Affair was now fully under way, and the country was divided into two camps: the Dreyfusards, who favored revision, and the anti-Dreyfusards, who opposed it. Old friendships were shattered, families were broken, and inviting people to dinner became a dangerous operation for a hostess. Among the Dreyfusards were Monet, Pissarro, Clemenceau, Jaurès (who had changed his mind), Proust, Zola, Gide, Jacques-Emile Blanche, Thadée Natanson, Octave Mirbeau, Anatole France, Aristide Briand, Léon Blum, Ludovic Halévy, Elie Halévy, Daniel Halévy, Geneviève Straus, Louise Michel, Jacques Bizet (Geneviève's son), the young poet Charles Péguy, the novelist Jules Renard, the veteran historian Ernest Lavisse, the humorist Alphonse Allais, and a sizable contingent from the élitist, literary Ecole Normale Supérieure. On the whole the Dreyfusards justified Clemenceau's frequent references to them as "the intellectuals" (a neologism he is said to have coined), and they thus constituted the first massive appearance of a class that would henceforth have a considerable influence on French political life. But the anti-Dreyfusards were by no means composed exclusively of rabid journalists, gouty generals, and noisy priests from the sticks, for they included Cézanne, Degas, Forain, Gérôme, Renoir, Rodin, Valéry, Jules Verne, Léon Daudet, Charles Maurras, Maurice Barrès, Alexis Rouart, Henri Rouart and his four sons, Frédéric Mistral, Paul Bourget, José-Maria de Hérédia, François Coppée, Pierre Louÿs, the literary critics Jules Lemaître and Ferdinand Brunetière, the Communard leader Gustave Cluseret (who balanced the presence of Louise Michel in the other camp), most of the Latin Quarter, and nearly all of the Académie Française.

The position of the Dreyfusards was relatively simple: they represented the France of Voltaire and the Declaration of the Rights of Man; they felt sure that an innocent man had been sent to prison; and they thought that the country was in danger of being taken over by the reactionary forces of militarism and clericalism. The position of the anti-Dreyfusards was more complicated, for it was more a matter of sensibility than a product of rational analysis. To them the French nation was not an abstract idea invented by eighteenth-century *philosophes;* it was a people welded together by the sacrifices of its soldiers, by the Roman Catholic religion, by a long succession of monarchs, and by hundreds of years of living on the same rich, lovely soil. Barrès thought of France as something given, something beyond argument:

> A nationalist is a Frenchman who has become aware of his formation. Nationalism is the acceptance of a determinism. There can be no question of free thinking. I can live only in relation to my dead. They and my land give me my orders.[31]

From such premises it seemed to follow that Jews, Protestants, Freemasons, and the new "intellectuals" could not be true Frenchmen; they were what Barrès dismissed as "the rootless" and what the less lenient Maurras called *métèques,* a word that combined the pejorative, ethnocentric connotations of such terms as "wop" and "sheeny" with a classical allusion, for in ancient Athens the Metics were resident foreigners without full political rights. It seemed to follow also that to weaken the prestige of the army by discrediting the general staff was to imperil not only the physical defense but also the continuity, the very essence, of the nation. Thus the more sophisticated anti-Dreyfusards tended, as the controversy deepened, to shift their ground from the facts about the court-martial of 1894 toward, in the largest sense of the phrase, reasons of state. France, they were willing to argue, was more important than an isolated instance of justice or injustice, and Dreyfus was less important than the reckless Dreyfusards who were sapping military morale. "Even if their client were to be proved innocent," Barrès wrote, "they would remain criminals."[32]

    Degas loved his country in much the way recommended by Barrès and Maurras. To him also France was first of all an unarguable datum, a physical thing that had nothing to do with Voltaire and the Declaration of the Rights of Man; it was the spongy green earth of Normandy, a glass of anisette in front of the plane trees at Carcassonne, a white horse standing in the Seine under an October sky, a pickle in Burgundy. At the same time it was a continuity whose mysterious reality seemed to him to call for the nondiscursive and ultimately untranslatable language of painting. He much admired Delacroix's huge *Saint Louis Winning the Battle of Taillebourg,* which was the glory of the Galerie des Batailles at Versailles, and he liked in particular the figure of the canonized French king pounding the skulls of the English knights with a mace in the middle of the melee. "The blue of

Saint Louis's mantle," he said to Valéry, "is France."[33] Apparently, however, he was capable of putting at least some of this combination of sensuousness and mysticism into words, for on December 22, 1895, Daniel Halévy was present at 37 Rue Victor-Massé for a sort of levee that moved from the usual Drumont and *La Libre Parole* into a nonstop patriotic oration:

> Degas was still in bed, at a quarter past nine, and he said good morning with that air he has only in bed, when he looks like a child. . . . Then he installed himself for breakfast. Zoé read the paper, and he interrupted her with grand, extraordinarily eloquent discourses on the French nation. We went out together. He talked about France, about photography, about photography, about France, the whole confounded in the same exaltation.[34]

Many of the ideas that went with his nationalism resembled those of Joseph de Maistre, who was one of his favorite authors, according to Blanche, and who in the years after Waterloo had denounced the liberal beliefs and empirical methods of the *philosophes* with the same fury that the anti-Dreyfusards were now displaying toward the views of the Dreyfusards. De Maistre considered philosophy "the worst plague in the universe."[35] Degas, Valéry said, "scoffed at the people he called thinkers,"[36] and once mockingly asked the philosopher Léon Brunschvicg to explain Spinoza "in five minutes."[37] De Maistre disliked scientific and technological progress; so did Degas. De Maistre wrote:

> The cradle of a man should be surrounded by dogmas, and when his reason awakes he must find all his opinions already in place, at least all those concerning his conduct. Nothing is as important for him as prejudices.[38]

"Monsieur," Degas once said to Forain, "prejudices are the strength of a society. *Dites?*"[39]

Another of his favorite writers at this time, still according to Blanche, was Emmanuel Las Cases, whose *Mémorial de Sainte-Hélène,* based on conversations with the exiled former emperor, did more than anything else to establish the Napoleonic legend. That Degas was a believer in the legend is doubtful. But he was fascinated by soldiers. He sat spellbound when General Philippe Duhesme, the officer who had supplied the stirring first-person account of the cavalry charge at Gravelotte for Halévy's book *L'Invasion,* appeared in the flesh in the Rue de Douai and talked about the maneuvers in which he had just participated. On January 2, 1896, Daniel noted a "big explosion from Degas": "We must hope that we'll soon be finished with art and aestheticism. . . . What interests me personally is work, business, and the army."[40] On February 7, 1897, he became expansive about the distinguished soldier and statesman Laurent Gouvion-Saint-Cyr, who had served nearly everywhere during the Napoleonic Wars:

> "He didn't even have a uniform. He was always in a frock coat, a frock coat, on horseback on the battlefield. He was the one who saved the day at Eylau. . . . In the evening he installed himself in a convent and played the violin, which was his passion. . . . But even so the soldiers worshiped him. They said, 'That bugger will get us out of a fix.' "[41]

After a moment, referring to the growing vogue of Art Nouveau, he said, "Ah, in the old days they beat the drum at the barracks door. Today they play the lyre."

One wonders, nearly a century later, why he and many other honest anti-Dreyfusards did not see how their patriotic mystique, their *douce* France, and their idealized military caste were flawed by the brutality and the intellectual vulgarity of anti-Semitism, by the plain probability that Dreyfus was innocent, and by the growing evidence that the so-called great chiefs of the French army were a shabby gang of political generals. But a number of factors, some of them nearly universal and the others specific, should be kept in mind. Racism and nationalism are normally resistant to factual argument, and they are apt to become impervious during a period of collective fear, spy fever, group phantasms, and reawakened atavisms. With imperial Germany substituted for the Soviet Union, the atmosphere in France during the 1890s can be compared with that of the United States during the McCarthy phase of the Cold War. Moreover, ordinary Frenchmen could not be at all sure of what had actually happened at the court-martial in 1894. Ninety per cent of the daily press (including René's paper, *Le Petit Parisien*) was anti-Dreyfusard, and among the literary and artistic magazines the Dreyfusard *Revue blanche* of the avant-garde intellectuals was more than matched by the venerable, academic, anti-Dreyfusard *Revue des Deux Mondes*. Solemn liars on the general staff constantly hinted at the existence of proofs of Dreyfus's treason that could not be disclosed without a risk of provoking a war with the Triple Alliance. Much of the controversy was at the *ad hominem* level, and many people made the mistake of finding the affirmations of General Mercier more impressive than the sudden righteousness of a Panama-tainted politician like Clemenceau. Finally, of course, much depended on one's personal traits and the company one kept, and in this context Degas seems to have been predestined to become an anti-Dreyfusard and remain one. Valéry recalled:

> Degas had political ideas. They were simple, peremptory, essentially Parisian. At the slightest indication he inferred, he exploded, he broke off. "Adieu, Monsieur," and he turned his back on the adversary forever. . . .

Politics in the Degas style were inevitably like himself — noble, violent, impossible.[42]

He and Henri Rouart fanned each other's nationalist ardor. The four Rouart sons were wild anti-Dreyfusards, and so, of course, were the Ecole Polytechnique old boys and the army officers — sometimes including General Mercier himself — who appeared at Rouart's for the dinner on Friday night. Blanche (from a Dreyfusard viewpoint, naturally) would write:

> In the town house in the Rue de Lisbonne Monsieur Degas was completely himself. . . . With people of whose friendship he was sure, he unbridled his frenzy as a dispenser of condemnations, as a fanatic, as a flag-waver from a past era. The others humored him in his manias and shared his prejudices.[43]

He also felt at ease with Jean-Louis Forain, who in the satirical weekly *Psst!* caricatured the Dreyfusards with a venom rare even in the Paris of the 1890s.

In the Rue de Douai the situation was an evolving one. Although Geneviève Straus had reacted to the announcement of the verdict against Dreyfus by putting on a black dress, the Halévys had behaved for two years much in the manner of the majority of French Jews, whose circumspection would be remembered by Léon Blum with disapproval:

> The dominant feeling was "It's something in which the Jews should not get mixed up." All the elements in this complex feeling were not of the same quality. There was certainly some patriotism and even a touchy patriotism. There was respect for the army, confidence in its leaders, and a reluctance to think they were biased and fallible. But there was also a sort of selfish and timorous prudence.[44]

The selfish prudence had become less and less defensible under the double impact of the mounting wave of anti-Semitism and the accumulating proof that Dreyfus was innocent, and by the summer of 1897 Ludovic Halévy and his two sons had discovered, as millions of assimilated European Jews would discover a generation later, that there was, after all, some substance in the *Libre Parole* refrain "Once a Jew, always a Jew" — though it was not the substance Drumont intended. In spite of their Christianity and their Frenchness, they were Jews because they felt themselves to be members of a community formed by centuries of suffering and isolation, and in a sense they were Jews simply because the anti-Semites said they were. Their eagerness to assimilate had led them to overlook the fact that assimilation requires acceptance.

Their home now became a center for the young Dreyfusards who were

Elie's and Daniel's friends. During several months, however, the family's relations with Degas continued much as before. There were evenings when Yoyo sang Gluck. On November 14, 1897, Louise Halévy brought off the tour de force of having to dinner the anti-Dreyfusards Degas and Jules Lemaître at the same time as the Dreyfusards Ernest Reyer and Anatole France, and somehow everyone remained civilized. Degas, one day at lunch, tactlessly and jubilantly recounted that he had just thrown a naked model out of his studio because she had said something vaguely pro-Dreyfus and that, though she was not a Jew, she was a Protestant and therefore almost as bad. The staunchly Protestant Louise eased the tension around the table by remarking, "A model? A Protestant? Odd métier for a Protestant."[45] Although Daniel noted on November 25 that "Papa was very much with his nerves on edge, Degas very anti-Semitic,"[46] one of the latter's letters indicates that he dined in the Rue de Douai as late as December 23, 1897.

The inevitable explosion seems to have occurred during the first weeks of January 1898, so it may have been provoked, directly or indirectly, by the events leading up to the court-martial of Esterhazy and the publication, on January 13, of Zola's "J'accuse." But both the immediate cause and the chronology remain a bit vague, for Daniel interrupted his diary at this point with a page of undated memoirs:

> Our friendship was about to end suddenly, and in silence except for some degrading words. For the last time, we had Degas at our table. Who were the other guests? I don't remember. Probably some young people who did not control what they were saying. Degas was silent. Conscious of the danger hanging over us, I watched his face. His lips were closed, his eyes almost constantly turned toward the ceiling, as if he were separating himself from the company around him. . . . At the end of the dinner he disappeared. The next morning my mother read in silence a letter addressed to her and then, refusing to understand, silently handed it to Elie. He said, "It's the language of exasperation."[47]

Degas never again saw Ludovic Halévy alive. He also broke with Haas, Reyer, Geneviève Straus, Camondo, and Pissarro. On March 21, however, after a preliminary "Ha! You?" he seemed pleased to see Daniel Halévy, who had decided to risk a visit to 37 Rue Victor-Massé. They talked about Daniel's forthcoming marriage, and Degas said, "It is a good thing to get married. Ah, loneliness."[48] From about this time forward he adopted the attitude that the Halévys were nice people taken in by Dreyfusard propaganda. They were *jobards,* easy marks. In his conversations with Forain he frequently referred to "my poor Halévys."[49]

The routine of his life continued as before, with a few variations and without the lunches and dinners in the Rue de Douai. During August and September 1898 he gave up his watering places in favor of a stay at Saint-Valéry-sur-Somme, the little fishing port in Picardy to which, back in the reign of Louis-Philippe, Auguste had taken the Degas children on an occasional holiday. René de Gas now had a summer home in the town, and so did the landscapist Louis Braquaval, a disciple of Boudin's who for the moment was specializing in English Channel skies and maritime shimmer. Degas, who had been coming up from Paris now and then since 1895, called Braquaval "an open-air painter of intimate scenes,"[50] chaffed his grown-up daughter Louise as "the terrible Loulou,"[51] and enjoyed the family's primitive privy, a poetic, ivy-covered little shack that one came upon suddenly after a walk across a courtyard and through an adjoining garden. He later told some Parisian acquaintances, "It's charming, excellent, respectful. . . . And what a view! I left the door open in order to take in the sweep of the horizon, and I sang and hummed in order to warn anyone who might be approaching."[52]

Encouraged by Braquaval, he painted — probably on this trip, possibly on one of the earlier ones — some uncharacteristically close-up landscapes and village scenes, and even a little picture of the cows coming home in the evening. He took photographs of the surrounding countryside and used the enlargements as inspiration for studio-executed landscapes. Perhaps, though the results seem not to have survived, he also worked directly on the big prints with pastel, as he had frequently done with monotypes.

By this time his notoriety as an anti-Semite and an anti-Dreyfusard may have reached not only Gide's circle in Tunisia but also the French community on the island of Tahiti. In any event, on August 15 from Papeete Gauguin sent off a generous defense to a close Paris friend, the painter and engraver Georges-Daniel de Monfreid:

> I am pleased that you have made the acquaintance of Degas and that, while wishing to be useful to me, you have acquired some good relations for yourself. Yes, Degas has a reputation for being ill-natured and caustic . . . but all that is not directed at people whom he judges worthy of his attention and his esteem. He has the instincts that go with heart and intelligence. I am not surprised that he showed sympathy for you and your talent . . . and I am sure that you have had more pleasure from a genuine, specific compliment than you would have had from one of those that are addressed to everybody. In terms of gifts and conduct Degas is a rare example of what an artist should be. He has had as colleagues and admirers all those who are in power . . . and he has never asked for a favor. From him no one has ever heard or seen a nastiness, a piece of unscrupulousness, of scurviness. Just art and dignity.[53]

Pissarro, with even more generosity, also remained steadfast in his admiration, though it was directed more to the recent pastels than to character. "Degas," he told Lucien, "goes forward constantly and finds distinction in everything around us."[54]

While Gauguin was writing, the Dreyfus Affair was arousing interest again. On August 13 an officer going through the file on the case noticed that a letter that had been among the scraps from the German attaché's wastepaper basket, and had been pieced together by Major Henry in the counterespionage section, was on a sheet of paper with faint blue gray lines at the top and the bottom and faint gray claret lines in the middle. There could be no doubt that the document, which had been regarded as a key piece of evidence against Dreyfus, was a combination of two letters that had nothing to do with the Affair. On August 30 Henry admitted the forgery, and on August 31, with a razor he had been allowed to take with him to his prison cell, he committed suicide by cutting his throat. General Mercier, when he got the news, had a one-word comment: *Foutu* (Screwed). From Saint-Valéry-sur-Somme Degas wrote to Henri Rouart's brother, Alexis, "We cannot talk about *affairs* without weeping with anger."[55] On August 7, 1899, after a long and finally unsuccessful delaying action, the new court-martial that had become unavoidable opened in Rennes. Absurdly, the military judges again found Dreyfus guilty, although with extenuating circumstances, and sentenced him to ten years of detention. Then the government, aware that France was becoming both a pariah and a buffoon in world opinion, decided to pardon everyone concerned. This, to the consternation of the Dreyfusards, meant that the real traitor, Esterhazy, and all the criminal officers would go unpunished and that the innocent man, although out of prison, would have to go on fighting (until 1906, as things turned out) for his complete rehabilitation. But the decision had the advantage of saving what was left of French military prestige and rendering pointless a quarrel that had dangerously divided the nation. Although the bitterness lingered, the Dreyfus Affair was over.

Shortly after the end, the Dreyfusard Natanson and the anti-Dreyfusard Forain, who had not been on speaking terms for a couple of years, ran into each other in a Paris gallery. Forain smiled, raised a forefinger in a priestly gesture, intoned, *"Errare humanum est,"* and then murmured, *"Perseverare diabolicum."*[56] Degas took the defeat of his camp less philosophically and with much less good humor, as can be seen from a letter of around 1900 to Henri Rouart concerning the death of a Jewish acquaintance:

> So the poor wandering Jew has departed. He'll walk no more, and if one had been notified, one would have willingly walked a bit behind him. What did

he think since the dirty Affair? What did he think of the embarrassment we felt with him, in spite of ourselves? Did he ever talk to you about it? What went on in his old Jewish head? Did he ever have the idea of thinking back to the time when we were fairly ignorant about his terrible race? We'll talk about all this when I see you. Wednesday I was at your place in La Queue-en-Brie and I talked about an odd dream I had two days after learning of his death from Tasset. Imagine, in my dream I met him, with a little more hair on his head, and then, as if I had been awake, I had the presence of mind to stop myself just when I was about to say to him, "Well, well, I thought you were dead." Which proves that the memory functions in dreams. [57]

The possibility that the man in question was Pissarro is ruled out by — among several other things — the implication that he had frequented the house in the Rue de Lisbonne and had continued to do so after the start of the Dreyfus Affair. However, the superior, condescending, absolute tone, the tone of a mind loaded with unexamined premises, probably indicates, as does the phrase "my poor Halévys," the attitude Degas adopted toward Pissarro. There are no signs that he ever thought he had taken the wrong side in the great clash of the two Frances, nor that he realized how much more tragic the clash had been for him than for his Jewish friends, who were, after all, on the winning side. And there are only a few hints of his usual humanity, irony, and role-playing. Vollard wrote of meeting, one day at the entrance to 37 Rue Victor-Massé, a Jewish acquaintance who explained:

> "Degas and I had not been seeing each other since the Affair. But yesterday I received a note, asking me to come by the studio. He had learned of the death of my wife and wanted to tell me he would give me a portrait of her he had painted long ago." [58]

From echoes in others' accounts of his conversation, one learns that he excused the morning reading of *La Libre Parole* as a means for taking his mind off Zoé's cooking. Challengingly reminded that he had once much admired Pissarro's work, he replied, with straight-faced inconsequence, "Yes, but that was before the Affair." [59]

He had suffered heavy losses in affection and social intercourse because of deaths and his anti-Dreyfusard stance, and he compensated by moving closer to his remaining friends — and to their descendants, who were now grown up and about to continue, by a remarkable amount of intermarrying, the close-knit group that had been one of the emotional mainstays of his life. In May 1898 he was back at 40 Rue de Villejust, attending a musical evening organized by Berthe Morisot's daughter, Julie Manet, and by Jeannie and Paule Gobillard, the daughters of Berthe's sister Yves, whose portrait he had painted in the summer of 1869. The three young women, all recent orphans, were living together in the former Morisot-Manet apartment. In December 1898 Rouart's son Eugène married Henry Lerolle's daughter Yvonne, and at a reception in the Rue de Lisbonne Degas introduced Paul Valéry to Julie Manet and to Jeannie and Paule Gobillard. Julie and her cousins invited Valéry to the Rue de Villejust to see their collection of paintings by Berthe Morisot and Edouard Manet and the portrait of Yves by Degas. Shortly after this another Rouart son, Louis, married the other Lerolle daughter, Christine. (The two Lerolle girls appear in several paintings by Renoir, notably in his at-the-piano series, and in a photograph with Degas taken in the Lerolle apartment on the Left Bank.)

One afternoon toward the end of 1899 Degas invited Julie Manet and Ernest Rouart, now a painter, to the Rue Victor-Massé for tea. During the conversation, mimicking the mayor of the Ninth Arrondissement conducting a marriage ceremony, he said, "I declare you united."[60] Evidently his joke had an effect, for on March 16, 1900, he wrote to Louis Rouart, who was in Cairo with the Institut Français d'Archéologie Orientale (and had red hair):

> This is a very late reply to your affectionate letter, my dear carrot-head. I write so little, I have lost the habit. . . . By way of a brown-head we have Ernest, who, after having been timid and cold, is becoming nonchalant and hot. Wednesday around a quarter past seven he arrived on foot with Julie at his uncle Alexis's house, with such a married air that you would have been convulsed. "Already?" I said to him. And Julie, who opens her mouth only a bit more, seemed just as much at ease as he was. It's astonishing, as Monsieur Prudhomme (along with me) would say, how men and women are made for each other.[61]

A few weeks before this letter, during a soirée for which Pablo Casals supplied the music, Paul Valéry and Jeannie Gobillard had announced their engagement. In December 1900, in a double ceremony in the church of Saint-Honoré-d'Eylau, next to an *Adoration of the Shepherds* attributed to Tintoretto, Ernest married Julie and Paul married Jeannie. The Ernest Rouarts moved into 40 Rue de Villejust, and eighteen months later the Valérys rented a floor at the same address. Degas now had two more households, both charged with memories for him, to which he might be invited for dinner.

He was himself entertaining regularly in the Rue Victor-Massé. At a dinner around the beginning of May 1900, his guests were Forain, the journalist Maurice Talmeyr, and the Comtesse Emmanuela Potocka, a Frenchwoman in spite of her married name and one of the celebrated beauties of the period. For an evening in June, and for many lunches during these years, the principal guest was Paul Poujaud, a lawyer by profession and a connoisseur of music and painting by inclination; Degas saw him occasionally in Chausson's apartment near the Parc Monceau, enjoyed his talk, and relied to a surprising degree on his judgment. Some forty years later Poujaud would remember having seen, one afternoon in the Rue Victor-Massé, the picture of Auguste listening to Pagans singing in the Rue de Mondovi:

> I had had lunch alone with Degas. After the coffee he put his hand on my shoulder, smiling and confident, and motioned to me to follow him. He took me into his bedroom and showed me, hanging above the . . . iron bed, the precious painting. "You may have known Pagans," he said. "That's a portrait of him with my father." Then he left me alone. That was his way of presenting his pictures: with a sort of proud modesty. He did not remain for the examination. . . . A few minutes later he came back into the bedroom and, without saying anything, without a word from me, looked at my face. For him that was enough.[62]

On other occasions the same procedure of absence and silence was followed for the presentation of *Interior* and of favorite works in the growing Degas collection.

By the late 1890s the buying of Suzanne Valadon's drawings had developed into a personal relationship in which Degas manifested once again his generosity toward younger artists — and also his willingness to accept people, if he liked them, who were neither bourgeois nor very virtuous. Valadon was the daughter of a laundress and an unknown father. After working as a seamstress, a waitress, and a circus acrobat, she had become a model for Puvis de Chavannes, de Nittis, Zandomeneghi, Toulouse-Lautrec, Bartholomé, and especially Renoir. In 1883, at the age of eighteen, she had had an illegitimate son, who became known as Maurice Utrillo and who by his early adolescence was already a drunkard. She had long been sketching in secret, and one day around 1890 she showed some of her work to Bartholomé and Zandomeneghi, who sent her to Degas. He admired the naturalness and vigor of her talent and found her Montmartre urchin's face and effrontery exactly to his taste, and soon began to address her as Maria, her name as a model. She said later, "From that day I belonged to his group of familiars. He hung one of my sanguine drawings in his dining room. I dropped in at his studio every afternoon."[63]

For a while he climbed the hill regularly to her studio in the Rue Cortot, near the top of the Butte, and he missed her when she married a wealthy businessman and moved — temporarily, for she was soon divorced

— out of Paris. In a note written in January 1900, he said, "Every year I see arrive, terrible Maria, that handwriting of yours, jagged as a saw. But I never see the author arrive, with a portfolio of drawings under her arm. And I am getting very old. Happy New Year." [64] There were of course rumors, totally unsubstantiated, that they were having, or had had when he was younger, a love affair.

22. Into the Night

H<small>E DID SEEM</small> to be suddenly getting old. In a letter from this period to Hortense Valpinçon, now Madame Jacques Fourchy but still living in the château at Ménil-Hubert, he complained:

> I was going along not at all badly and felt young again, but things have taken a turn for the worse. For the past eight days I have been unable to see. It is hard on me not to be capable of dragging myself around a bit outdoors at the end of the day in the studio. And when I have not worked for a few hours, I feel guilty, stupid, unworthy.[1]

Two of his finest lamplit photographs — both taken in the apartment at 37 Rue Victor-Massé and both his in the sense that he made the arrangements, though René tripped the shutter — can serve as illustrations for this complaint. One of them, with himself in the foreground and a protective Zoé looming in the background, recalls Ingres's portrait of the weary, aging Luigi Cherubini with the muse Euterpe behind him. In the other, Degas is a tragic mask with wounded eyes gazing out from a pool of Rembrandt-like darkness. The gap was narrowing between the reality of his being a partly blind painter and his neurotic, defensive, piteous playing of the role.

Everything did not, of course, stop all at once. For a number of years to come, the sequences of gloomy days would be broken now and then by relatively bright, productive spells. His misanthropy, bad disposition, and growing sense of futility would be counteracted by flashes of ambition,

Zoé Closier and Degas, 1890s

curiosity, and something of his former inclination to distance himself. He kept, for a long while, his sardonic tongue, bristling independence, rapid strut, and the ability, when he felt like exercising it, to charm and amuse. But after roughly the turn of the century he was increasingly an artist surviving the failure of his powers, and eventually he became mostly a pair of remarkably solid old legs stomping into the Parisian night.

Although he now lacked the capacity, or perhaps the desire, to examine and record facial expressions, his *Dancers* of around 1899 is a spirited combination of witty angles and cut-offs, lyrical abstractionism, and strata of proto-Fauvist colored rain. He was continuing his series of pastels of faceless women washing their bodies and combing their thick masses of hair, with such preoccupation that in 1901 he remarked to Maurice Denis, "I can't get out of bathrooms, and yet I too would like . . . to paint like Raphael. Why can't I?"[2] When his eyes were not up to drawing and painting, he turned, a bit morosely, to sculpture, and the critic François

Thiébault-Sisson, writing for *Le Temps,* remembered watching him at work shortly after 1900 on what may have been the statuette *Woman Seated in an Armchair Wiping Her Neck,* or at least a version of that piece:

> In the dark, cluttered room in the Rue Victor-Massé which served him as a studio the melancholy old man was modeling a figurine. Curled up in a Louis-Philippe armchair, a young woman, her upper body nude, made the gesture of wiping her neck. Scrutinizing the model through his spectacles, Degas slowly, patiently, with little strokes of his sculptor's tool or his thumb, molded and remolded in red wax the projection of the shoulder.[3]

A note written in September 1903 to Henri Rouart's brother, Alexis, says, "I'm still here in the atelier, attacking my waxes. Without work, how sad old age would be!"[4]

Success had not silenced all the detractors. The critic Gustave Coquiot, for instance, finally summed up his opinion by writing, "He is, after all, a sort of combined scrivener, skulking martinet, and timorous bourgeois."[5] Other contemporaries, however, were ready by now to add nuances to their verdicts. In the novel *La Ville lumière* (The City of Light), published in 1903 by the Symbolist poet and art critic Camille Mauclair, Degas is easily recognizable in the figure of Hubert Feuillery, a brutal, eccentric, nervous, misanthropic painter of dancers who is basically a sensitive, honest fellow horrified by the lack of authenticity in the world. And some dialogue in the part of *A la recherche du temps perdu* entitled *Sodome et Gomorrhe* mentions Degas under his own name in a context that makes clear the authority he had acquired — and even the intellectual terror he inspired — in matters of aesthetic judgment. The moment is the end of a summer afternoon some time after 1902; the place is a terrace facing the sea at Balbec; and the principal speakers are the narrator Marcel and Madame de Cambremer, a provincial aristocrat eager to like the right things. Monet's water-lily series having been mentioned, Marcel risks an unexpected opinion:

> I said that I was familiar with it . . . and I added that it was unfortunate that she had not come the day before, since at that same hour she could have admired a light similar to that of Poussin. . . .
> "In the name of heaven," she said, "after a painter like Monet, who is simply a genius, don't name an old hack without talent like Poussin. Frankly, I find him the deadliest of bores. Whatever you say, I can't regard that sort of thing as painting. Monet, Degas, Manet, yes, there you have some painters. . . ."
> Suspecting that the only way to rehabilitate Poussin in the eyes of

Madame de Cambremer was to inform her that he was back in fashion, I said, "But Monsieur Degas assures us that he knows of nothing more beautiful than the Poussins at Chantilly."

"Really?" said Madame de Cambremer, who did not want to disagree with Degas. "I don't know those at Chantilly, but I can speak of those in the Louvre, which are horrors."

"He has an enormous admiration for those also."

"I must look at them again," she said after a moment of silence. "All that is a little far back in my mind."[6]

It is not unlikely that the young Proust, in the period before the Dreyfus Affair when he was often at Geneviève Straus's apartment in the Boulevard Haussmann, had heard Degas in person express his admiration for Poussin. But there is no need to assume a direct source, for the opinion of Gide's anti-Semitic Tunisian friend in 1896, the fame of the copy of *The Rape of the Sabines* in the Rue de Lisbonne, and Duranty's only half-fictional account of the painter Louis Martin's adventures in the 1860s show that Poussin had long been linked to the Degas stories circulating in Parisian studios and salons.

Valéry must also, of course, be counted among the contemporary writers who were fascinated by the work and personality of Degas, since one result, twenty-one years after the painter's death, was the publication of the book *Degas, danse, dessin* (Degas, Dance, Drawing). The prolific, serene member of the Académie Française who wrote the book was not, however, very much like the blocked poet and tortured amateur philosopher who was particularly close to Degas during the early 1900s, and so the work, though valuable as a biographical memoir and stimulating as a general essay on art, is without the sense of involvement it might have had. When Valéry, still in his early twenties, settled in Paris in 1894 he was a rising poet in the circle around Mallarmé. In 1895 he published *Introduction à la méthode de Léonard de Vinci*, and the following year *La Soirée avec Monsieur Teste*. In 1897 he wrote a few short magazine articles, and then for roughly twenty years he published nothing, devoting himself instead to mathematics, science, and getting up before dawn to fill notebooks with ethical and psychological aphorisms. He had a pattern of related, mutually reinforcing reasons for this long silence. He felt that publishing was a contamination of the private psyche; it obliged the writer to "be himself for other people."[7] He wanted to explore what he called "the Mysterious Me"[8] and to sacrifice to the God of the Intellect. Like one of his two heroes, Leonardo, he found that aiming at universality led to paralysis at the level of the particular; like his other hero, the totally detached, totally unproductive Monsieur Teste, he discovered that the perfecting of an idea precluded its realization. And in much of this he divined a vague affinity with the fierce painter of ballerinas:

> I had formed concerning Degas an idea of a character reduced to the rigor of a hard drawing, a Spartan, a Stoic, a Jansenist in art. . . . Shortly before meeting him I had written *La Soirée avec Monsieur Teste,* and this little essay . . . was more or less *influenced,* as people say, by *a certain Degas I had imagined.*[9]

Degas refused to have *Monsieur Teste* dedicated to him, on the grounds that he would not understand the book and that anyway he had had "enough of poets."[10] He called Valéry Monsieur l'Ange (Mister Angel),[11] in what may have been a reference to the young man's lofty intellectualism. But he obviously liked him, and he must have noticed that Valéry's distaste for publishing was not far from his own destructive perfectionism and his own paradoxical sentiment that painting was a private activity.

His low opinion of writers on art remained unchanged. The muses, he liked to argue, did not discuss their work when they got together at the end of the day; they simply danced. "Painting," he remarked, "is not at all difficult when you don't know anything about it. But when you know, oh, it's something quite different."[12] This opposition to what he considered verbiage based on ignorance did not, of course, keep him from expressing his personal aesthetic view, nor from attacking the views of other artists. He was willing to concede that painting needed to return to reality now and then in order to renew the challenge to itself, to keep its muscles in shape; and to convey this idea he had an unclassical version of the fable of Antaeus in which Hercules deliberately let the giant touch the earth from time to time. But that did not excuse others' attempts to paint sincere farms. When Delphine Tasset informed him that landscapists had invaded the spectacular, granitic scenery of the Creuse Valley in central France, his comment was beyond appeal: "They already had vipers."[13] Art, he continued to insist, was a matter of convention, artifice, and abstraction. "A drawing is not the form," he said to Valéry; "it's a way of seeing the form."[14] He thought that one of the great merits of Ingres was that he reacted against the kind of drawing based strictly on proportions and that he introduced arabesques of forms.

A snapshot taken sometime around 1903 shows him swinging down a path in the park at Ménil-Hubert, belly out front, hands in his trouser pockets, lapel flying; in spite of a beard that has turned white, he looks energetic, aggressive, and, to use one of Valéry's favorite words in referring to him, *impossible.* He was also taking long walks in Paris, riding on the outside top decks, the *impériales,* of street cars and omnibuses, and observing the behavior of Parisians, much as he had been doing for more than half a century. Sometimes he rode all the way out to the end of the line and back, just for the pleasure of looking. After one of these expeditions he put on, with Valéry as an audience, a performance as a mime playing the role of a woman who had sat near him on the *impériale.* She had passed her hands over her skirt, smoothed out the creases, settled into the curve of the street car banquette, pulled up tight her gloves and carefully buttoned them, licked her lips and bit them slightly, stirred in her underwear, given the end of her nose a tweak, flicked a curl back into place with one finger, checked the contents of her handbag, stretched her half-veil, and assumed the expression of a person who has completed a job. The street car had swayed and shook as it advanced. She had sat still for a few seconds. Then she had twisted her neck in her collar, narrowed her nostrils, pursed her lips, and begun to readjust everything — dress, gloves, veil, and so on. It was one of his good days. "He was delighted," Valéry commented, "and there was a bit of misogyny in his pleasure." [15]

Pissarro died in Paris on November 13, 1903, two weeks after the opening of the first Salon d'Automne, a resolutely post-Impressionist enterprise in which the stars were Pierre Bonnard, Albert Marquet, Henri Matisse, Georges Rouault, and Edouard Vuillard. The ranks were thinning again: Whistler and Gauguin also died in 1903; Zola and Desboutin had died in 1902, Toulouse-Lautrec in 1901, Sisley and Chausson in 1899, and Moreau and Mallarmé in 1898. On December 30, 1903, Degas sent off a mournful New Year's greeting to Bracquemond: "We really must try to see each other one day before the end." [16]

In May 1904, Daniel Halévy dropped in at 37 Rue Victor-Massé, having heard that Degas had been ill for two months with intestinal flu:

> He was at home, he called me into his studio, and I had a little shock at seeing before me, dressed like a tramp, an emaciated man — another man. He seemed touched and pleased to see me; he asked for news about everyone in my family. . . . He repeated, "Beauty is a mystery." At one point he said, "Since our misfortunes —" Which meant "since the victory of the Dreyfusards." I was neither embarrassed nor irritated. I listened to him with infinite respect, as if he had been recounting the history of another world. And he listened to me with affection. [17]

He still possessed, or hoped to possess, the key to what at the age of fifty he had called the cupboard in which he stored his plans. Shortly after his seventieth birthday he said to Ernest Rouart, "One must have a lofty notion, not of what one has done, but of what one will be able to do some day; without that, it's no use working." [18] His intestinal flu persisted, however, and so he set off for the Vosges and Jura highlands in search of pure air. On September 7, 1904, he wrote to Alexis Rouart from Pontarlier:

> It's raining. I'm in a café. I am thinking of my friends. . . . From Paris to Epinal, Gérardmer, Col de la Schlucht, over into Alsace, Munster, Turck-heim, Colmar, back into France, Belfort (full of Jews), Besançon, Ornans, and finally two weeks in Pontarlier, from which I radiate a bit. I'll return by way of Nancy.[19]

Several misspellings in the letter indicate that he could no longer see very clearly what he was writing.

During the next couple of years he attempted some portraits of members of the Rouart family, with results that vary from the sketchy to the grotesque. He dreamed of an impossible return to the making of monotypes, etchings, and lithographs. "If I had my life to live over again," he said, "I would work only in black and white."[20] In 1906 he made his last trip to Naples and spent several weeks in the city, settling family affairs. Back in Paris, he complained of the northern cold and decided that the weather had been better in the past. He also complained, much in the manner of later environmentalists, about the pollution caused by automobiles and, in general, about the dangerous effects of the modern passion for speed. "I pity our successors," he said to Georges Jeanniot. "They are heading toward monstrous hecatombs."[21] Less dramatically, he opposed technological progress because in it he smelled a threat to his cherished independence: he did not want to be the servant of a machine any more than he had wanted to be a pawn pushed by the fine arts administration — and in this he differed totally from the up-to-date Forain. The latter, equipped with a new telephone and eager to demonstrate it, arranged to have a friend call one evening when Degas was invited to dinner. The scene went off as planned: the phone rang, Forain rushed to answer it, exchanged a few words with the caller, and returned proudly to the dinner table. But all Degas said was "So that's the telephone. It rings and you run."[22]

On January 17, 1907, he wrote to Alexis Rouart's son Jean, who was enjoying the Pyrenees scenery at Foix, "You cannot believe how I am discouraged from writing by the state of my eyes, although I can still see a little. Writing means pain, disgust, anger. Can you read this letter? I can't."[23] The year was not, however, entirely bad. On August 6 he informed Alexis:

> I am still here at work, and have returned to drawing and pastel. I'd like to, and anyway I must, finish a few articles. Travel no longer tempts me. Around five in the afternoon I dash toward the suburbs. There is no lack of street cars to take you out to Charenton or somewhere else.[24]

Later in the summer he went as far as Laon, where Luigi Chialiva's son was doing architectural drawings in the great Early Gothic cathedral.

On the day after Christmas, 1907, the painter, collector, and art historian Etienne Moreau-Nélaton found him still at work:[25]

> It was four in the afternoon. . . . The door of the studio opened slightly and the master of the house, in a chestnut-colored hat, looked at me with an unseeing eye. I gave my name. "Ah, Moreau, come in then. But pay attention to that bathrobe, you scoundrel. Don't disturb the folds." A piece of salmon pink material was arranged on the corner of a chair, next to a bathtub that was the other prop for a pastel with which he had been fencing all day. Nearby was the pastel, pinned to cardboard; it had been done on tracing paper. It represented a young woman leaving her bath, with a servant in the background. In the foreground was the pink stuff that was not to be disturbed. The execution was a bit summary, as is everything done during this period by this man whose sight was weakening day by day. But what vigorous, magnificent drawing!

They talked about Delacroix, Corot, the auctions in the Hôtel Drouot, and the eccentric collectors Degas had met as a boy during his Sunday leaves from Louis-le-Grand. He repeated his Ingres stories, his denunciations of modern speed, his remark about the silent muses, and his joke about ordering the police to shoot open-air landscapists. From time to time he paused to sip from a little white faience cup:

> "Do you know what that is? Milk? No, it's an infusion of cherry stems. A diuretic drink. Alas, I am reduced to that. My bladder no longer has the necessary elasticity. I have to get up five or six times a night. What misery. And then whatever happens I have to make my aging legs function every day before dinner."

Although it was now the hour for his daily walk, he agreed to join Moreau-Nélaton in the latter's waiting fiacre, and the two men drove through the December evening down the Rue des Martyrs, past Notre-Dame-de-Lorette, into the Rue Laffitte, past the brilliantly lit Opéra, across the Pont Neuf, and into the Rue Guénégaud, where there was a specialist in the pasting of pastels and watercolors to firm supports. Then along the Quai Voltaire, past the building where Ingres had had his studio, across the brand new Pont Alexandre III, and into the Rue du Faubourg Saint-Honoré, where the fiacre halted in front of Moreau-Nélaton's house:

> Monsieur Degas, on the sidewalk, held out his hands toward me and then plunged them into the pockets of his inverness. Head high, nose in the

wind, his rolling gait made a bit heavier by age, he disappeared in the crowd of pedestrians.

In prospect he had more than an hour of walking, much of it uphill through the traffic of the dark Ninth Arrondissement, before turning in at 37 Rue Victor-Massé, very late for Zoé's dinner and his cup of cherry-stem tea.

The pastel he had been doing that day and the probably contemporaneous, savage *Woman Drying Her Hair* were among his last two-dimensional works of any importance. Henceforth he devoted himself to his wax statuettes and to arranging his collection, which, after some twenty years of household frugality and compulsive bidding at auctions, was nearing its final state. Its nostalgic core was Jean-Baptiste Perronneau's bonbon Rococo portrait of Madame Miron de Portioux, which had hung in the living room in the Rue de Mondovi, appears as a blur on the back wall in the 1869 portrait of Thérèse, and has since become part of a private collection in New York. He also owned a minor allegory by Giovanni Battista Tiepolo, a Dutch seventeenth-century landscape in the manner of Aelbert Cuyp, a miscellany of eighteenth-century Japanese woodcuts, and two El Grecos: the *Saint Ildefonso Writing at the Virgin's Dictation* that is now in the National Gallery in Washington and the *Saint Dominic Praying* now in the Boston Museum of Fine Arts. However, the bulk comprised, for reasons of both price and personal taste, nineteenth-century works; and these, like the acquisitions of any well-diversified museum, fell into the three principal categories of paintings, drawings (including watercolors), and prints. Sculpture was represented by a few Barye and Bartholomé bronzes, some Neapolitan puppets of the type called *pupazzi,* a plaster cast of Ingres's hand holding a pencil, and a bust of Degas himself by his friend Paul Paulin.

In the painting section Ingres was the major figure, with twenty canvases that included the portraits of Jacques-Louis Leblanc and Madame Leblanc (both now in the New York Metropolitan); an oil study (now in the Stockholm Nationalmuseum) for *The Envoys from Agamemnon,* the picture with which Ingres won the Prix de Rome; the portrait of the Comte Amédée-David de Pastoret (formerly in the Madame D. David-Weill collection, Paris); the strange little history painting depicting the Duke of Alba at the church of Saint Gudula in Brussels (Musée Ingres, Montauban); and *Roger Freeing Angelica* (London National Gallery), a replica of the work in the Louvre. (The term "replica" is used here in the restricted technical sense of a nearly exact copy made by the painter of the original or under his supervision.) Among the thirteen canvases by Delacroix were *The Comte de Mornay's Apartment* (Louvre); the portrait (London National Gallery) of Baron Schwiter, Tissot's friendly gondola-owner in the Venice of 1860; and a replica (Peter Nathan collection, Zurich) of the *Entombment* in the Boston Museum of Fine Arts. There were seven Corots, among them *The Roman Campagna, with the Claudian Aqueduct* (London National Gallery). The seven Manets included *Madame Manet on a Blue Sofa* (Musée d'Orsay), *The Departure of the Steamboat* (Oskar Reinhart collection, Winterthur, Switzerland), *The Ham* (Burrell Collection, Glasgow), and fragments of one of the large versions of *The Execution of the Emperor Maximilian* (London National Gallery). The eight Gauguins included *La Belle Angèle* (Musée d'Orsay), painted at Pont-Aven in 1869, and *Hina Tefatou* (New York Museum of Modern Art), painted in Tahiti in 1893. Van Gogh was represented by *Sunflowers* (Berne Kunstmuseum) and *Still Life with Fruit* (Chicago Art Institute). Among the seven Cézannes were a self-portrait of around 1880 (Oskar Reinhart collection) and a portrait of the collector Victor Chocquet (Mellon collection). There were also paintings of less, though not minor, importance by Bartholomé, Daumier, Cassatt, Jeanniot, Legros, Lepic, Morisot, Pissarro, Puvis de Chavannes, Renoir, Henri Rouart, Théodore Rousseau, and Sisley. Noticeably, Monet was not represented.

There were a hundred and ninety drawings by Delacroix, many of them finished in watercolor; among the latter were four sketches executed in Morocco in 1832 (all now in the Louvre) and three elaborated studies (Tate Gallery, London) for the frieze, symbolizing war, agriculture, and industry, of the Salon du Roi at the Palais Bourbon, the present seat of the French National Assembly. The ninety drawings by Ingres included some that had been intended as finished works and many that had been preparations for paintings: a good example (now in the Fogg Art Museum, Cambridge, Massachusetts) of the first sort was a version — actually a *calque,* or tracing, made by Ingres himself — of *The Forestier Family;* the second category was beautifully exemplified by a study (in a London private collection) for the *Large Odalisque* and by an early idea (Louvre) for the draped female figure embodying the *Odyssey* in the *Apotheosis of Homer.* This section of the collection was rounded out with fifteen drawings by Hokusai, twelve by Forain, ten by Manet, five by Daumier, and a scattering by Cassatt, Millet, and Valadon.

The print section was dominated by Daumier, with some eighteen hundred lithographs. Although many were taken from published albums or from the satirical journals *Caricature* and *Le Charivari,* an impressive number — including such masterpieces as *The Legislative Belly* and *The Rue Transnonain* — were connoisseurs' proofs, *belles épreuves,* pulled on rice paper. Gavarni, with more than two thousand lithographs, was of greater importance in terms of quantity but not, of course, in terms of quality. Manet was represented by a series of etchings that included *Lola de Valence,*

Olympia, Christ with Angels, The Gypsies, and *The Guitarist,* and by such lithographs as the colored *Polichinelle* of 1874 and the black *Barricade,* a glimpse of the Bloody Week of 1871. There were woodcuts and monotypes by Gauguin, drypoints by Morisot, lithographs by Géricault and Alfred De Dreux, etchings by Bracquemond, Desboutin, Legros, Millet, Pissarro, Whistler, and Valadon, a series of offprints of Charles Keene's caricatures in *Punch,* and unusual color prints by Cassatt that combined straight etching with drypoint, aquatint, and soft ground. The vogue of *japonisme* was recalled in diptych by Kiyonaga showing women in a bath house in Edo (which became Tokyo in 1868 after the fall of the shogunate), two albums of studies of feminine qualities by the same artist, two triptychs by Utamaro, forty-two landscapes by Hiroshige, fourteen Japanese albums with mixed contents, and one lot of forty-one separate prints by Eisho, Hokusai, Shunman, Shunsho, Toyokuni, Utamaro, and Yeizan.

Although put together by an alert, well-tutored critical mind whose choices would eventually be ratified by a large number of competent outsiders, the collection was thoroughly personal. It reflected the kind of education Degas had had, the friends he had made, and the sensibility with which he had been endowed; it threw light on his place in the history of art. Keeping it together in one building after his death was therefore desirable for reasons that went beyond the usual yearning of collectors to leave monuments to their names. Sometimes he thought of a donation to the Louvre, and in 1896 he had told the Halévys, "Yes, I want to give [the pictures in my collection] to my country, and then I'll go and sit in front of them, and I'll look at them and think of what a noble thing I've just done."[26] On other occasions he considered excluding the state and creating a museum of his own, with a privately appointed curator who would appoint the next curator and so on, thus ensuring a sort of apostolic succession. But he kept finding reasons for doing nothing about his projects. He complained that the paintings in a recent gift to the nation were badly hung (in the Paris Musée des Arts Décoratifs) and subjected to a direct, glaring light instead of to the indirect illumination he preferred. Some of the older oils in his collection needed backing with new canvas before they could be exposed to the unpredictable relative humidity, the temperature changes, and the generally dangerous environment of a public gallery; and the idea of letting profane, possibly inexpert hands touch his treasures filled him with a literally physical horror. Ambroise Vollard recalled:

> I recounted to Degas the manner in which, before my eyes, a picture re-mounter of my acquaintance had operated. . . . A fine-textured canvas having wrinkled during the gluing and produced air bubbles under the paint, the fellow lanced them with a razor. Degas stopped me. He was suffering visibly.[27]

A visit to the Musée Gustave-Moreau, recently opened in the town house in the Rue de La Rochefoucauld, effectively discouraged the notion of establishing something similar. "It's really sinister," Degas told Valéry. "You think you are in an underground burial chamber. All those canvases gathered together have on me the effect of a thesaurus, of a *gradus ad Parnassum.*" [28]

In any event, he might never have done anything about disposing of his collection, for such an action would have been in conflict with the personality traits that had led to its creation. Zola and Goncourt had been right, in ways they could scarcely have suspected, when they had referred to him as "constipated." He was almost a textbook example of the combination of obstinacy, parsimoniousness, independence, and possessiveness referred to by psychoanalysts as the anal character. He took pleasure in retention; he did not like to let go. To say this is not, of course, to indulge in a foolish reductionism that equates bowel movements with an admiration for Ingres and Delacroix; nor is it to rule out the contributions that several kinds of modern psychology and of historical and socioeconomic disciplines can make toward an understanding of this gifted, attractive, and often disagreeably complicated man. Even so, the Freudian categorization, or metaphor, remains strikingly apt in describing Degas the collector, and its aptness increases with his age — inevitably, for just as there is no one quite so poetically Irish as an elderly Irishman and no one quite so serenely Jewish as an elderly Jew, so there is no one (rebellious eighteen-month-old infants aside) quite so stubbornly anal as an elderly anal character. The thrifty sculptor and *bricoleur* who eked out his plasteline with pieces of cork was in his mid-seventies, as reported by one of his models, doling out only five francs a day for food for himself, Zoé, and the peasant girl who helped with the housework. The hoarder of canes and Norman handkerchiefs finally became so possessive, according to Vollard, as to refuse to let even close friends peek into the portfolios of prints in the Rue Victor-Massé

There were still some good days. A set of photographs taken at Ménil-Hubert shows him executing a sort of ballet charade with Hortense and her husband in front of the château. But there were more and more bad days. On August 21, 1908, he wrote to Alexis Rouart, "I'll soon be a blind man. Where there are no fish, one should not pretend to be a fisherman." [29] He talked about paying a visit to his nieces, Marguerite's daughters, who had returned from Argentina and installed themselves in a villa at La Colle-sur-Loup, a suburb of Nice, but he had lost his old enthusiasm for racing across France. He worried about his bladder trouble, his bronchitis, and possible intestinal obstructions and inflammation. The great era of the Friday dinners in the Rue de Lisbonne was over, for the Ecole Polytechnique old boys were for the most part dead or in provincial retirement, the four Rouart sons were married, and Henri Rouart was now an invalid. Most affecting of all — although it was not acknowledged as such — was the death, on May 7, 1908, in a Left Bank apartment a long way from the neo-Baroque façade at 22 Rue de Douai, of Ludovic Halévy. In a diary entry apparently written the next day, Daniel said:

> I was told that Degas was there. I recognized his attentiveness to death. . . . He said, "I want to see your father." My father was upstairs. We went up to the darkened room where his body was arranged. Degas, in a loud, authoritarian voice, ordered: "Light! All the light!" I called Francine, who pulled every curtain completely back. Degas bent over my father's body and examined the face close up. At last he turned toward me and said, "It is the Halévy we have always known, with, in addition, the grandeur that death gives. You must keep that image." He left.[30]

It is hard to know whether the staginess and grandiloquence in this post-script to the Dreyfus Affair were the result of Daniel's writing or of Degas's attempt to cover the feelings of guilt he must have had.

He had lived long enough to see, insofar as his dimming sight per-mitted, the beginnings of twentieth-century art and the end, or at least a radically new flowering, of the two great traditions initiated by the Italian Renaissance: the linear, as represented by Florence, Ingres, and himself; and the painterly, as represented by Venice, Delacroix, the Impressionists, and to some extent himself. In the autumn of 1908 Georges Braque had a one-man show at the Galerie Kahnweiler, and in the daily *Gil Blas* the critic Louis Vauxcelles (who in 1905 had coined the term Fauvism) spoke of a reduction of everything "to geometrical schemes, to cubes."[31] During 1909 Picasso had a show at the Galerie Vollard, and Cubists exhibited at both the Salon des Indépendants and the Salon d'Automne. Degas report-edly remarked that what these young artists were attempting was "more difficult than painting,"[32] which was open to more than one interpretation but was not exactly a rejection. Also during 1909, at Durand-Ruel's gal-lery, Monet exhibited examples of his water-lily series, in which the land-scape had disappeared in favor of an implicitly limitless expanse of unreal, precious colors and constantly changing aqueous light. "Your pictures," Degas said, "make me dizzy."[33]

At the time his retinas were absorbing a lot of brilliant hues and rapidly shifting shapes, for he was attending Diaghilev's first — and re-soundingly successful — Paris season, which had opened on May 19 at the Théâtre du Châtelet and featured Anna Pavlova, Tamara Karsavina, and Vaslav Nijinsky in, among other works, the ethereal perfection of *Les Sylphides* and the wild virility of the Polovtsian dances from Borodin's *Prince Igor*. Paul Lafond, who came up from Pau for the occasion, wrote that

Degas sketched some of the dancers, probably as usual from memory after the performances. If he did, the drawings have not survived in identifiable form. But in any event he had the satisfaction of being present for a halt in the decline of ballet in the West and for the triumph of the finest male dancer since Jules Perrot.

His own theatricality was by now infected by boring lapses into repetition of old numbers in his repertoire and by extravagant attempts to mimic himself, to out-Degas Degas. On July 4, 1909, at 40 Rue de Villejust, André Gide endured one of the lapses:[34]

> I dropped in at Valéry's place to inquire about the health of Jeannie Valéry, who may have to have an operation. Degas was with her, and had been fatiguing her for nearly an hour, for he is very hard of hearing and she has a weak voice. I found him aging but still himself: just a bit more obstinate, more dead set in his opinions, exaggerating his crustiness and always scratching the same spot on his head, where the itching is more and more concentrated. He said, "Ah, those who work from nature! What impudent humbug! Landscape painters! When I meet some of them out in the country, I always feel like shooting at them, popping away. Pow! Pow!" He raised his cane, squinted with one eye, and took aim at the pieces of furniture in the living room.

He also repeated his denunciations of art critics and his remark about the muses who danced instead of theorizing at the end of the day's work. He did, however, say one thing that Gide seems to have found interesting:

> "The day we began to write the word 'Intelligence' with a capital 'I,' we were screwed. There is no such entity as Intelligence. There is just intelligence concerning this or that. One should be intelligent only in relation to what one is doing."

This was perhaps directed at "the intellectuals," among them Gide, who ten years earlier had converted the Dreyfus Affair into a conflict over what Degas considered abstractions, hanky-panky, mere words. His rejection of *pompiériste* ideal beauty in his art was accompanied by a noticeable disposition toward nominalism in his everyday life.

His deafness, like his blindness, seems to have been partly a matter of mood, since several anecdotes concerning him make no mention of it. But it too was real, and it was getting worse. The aging process that for a while had been as imperceptible as rusting was becoming sadly obvious. Around the beginning of 1910 he stopped trimming his hair and beard. Obliged to urinate more and more frequently because of his bladder trouble, he often forgot to close the fly of his trousers. He wore down-at-heel shoes and shiny, greasy clothes around the studio; and if he had to change to go out, he was likely to strip naked in front of a visitor, without the slightest sign of embarrassment. He let his toothbrush dry out in a dirty glass; he left the toilet door open. Remembering a day at 37 Rue Victor-Massé, Valéry wrote:

> I reflected that this man had been elegant, that his manners, when he had wished, had had the most natural sort of distinction, that he had spent his evenings in the wings of the Opéra, that he had frequented the paddock at Longchamp, that he had been the most sensitive of observers of the human form. . . . Here he was, a nervous old man, nearly always gloomy, sometimes inattentive in a sinister, perfidious fashion, given to sudden spells of anger or wit, to childish impatience and impulsiveness, to caprice.[35]

That day, however, finally turned out to be one of the good ones, and Degas entertained his visitor by singing, in Italian, a Cimarosa cavatina.

In March 1910 he informed Alexis Rouart, "There is no end to my confounded sculpture."[36] In August he went out to the Halévys' house in suburban Sucy-en-Brie and had dinner with Louise Halévy, for the first time in twelve years. In December he engaged a model named Pauline for two sessions of posing for one of the several versions of the statuette *Dancer Looking at the Sole of Her Right Foot,* and nine years later she published a detailed account of her experience.[37] The first day was bad, for the one-legged, torso-twisted pose was impossible to hold after a few seconds, and Degas was in a vicious humor. He denounced Jews, the twentieth century, and modern egalitarianism; he complained about having had to abandon drawing and painting; he used "very free" language. At one point he suddenly asked her, "How many times a night do you have to get up to piss?" But the next day he was quite different. He explained that the evening before he had taken the street car from Place Pigalle out to the château of Vincennes, walked around the fortifications, taken another car back to Place Saint-Augustin, and then walked home. Reminiscing about his youth, he said, "Like all young men, I had a dose of the clap, but I never had much of a fling." After singing a few tunes from Italian opera, he amiably translated the words into French. At last he launched into a wordless singing of the minuet from *Don Giovanni* and, carried away by the insistent rhythm, invited Pauline down from the table on which she had been posing. Then the two of them began the best imitation they could manage of the stately dance, with the white-locked old man singing and bobbing in his long sculptor's smock while the naked, laughing girl balanced and bowed back and forth across the dusty studio floor.

In the spring of 1911 at the Galerie Georges Petit there was a large Ingres show that included *The Turkish Bath,* some history paintings, and many oil and pencil portraits. Degas went, and while there told a friend, "I can make out something in the pictures I know, but nothing in those I don't know."[38] In June, on a grassy stretch between the Halévy place at Sucy-en-Brie and the Rouart place at La Queue-en-Brie, he saw his first airplane, and after touching it here and there and moving around to a side in full sunlight, he remarked merely that it was "very small," which it was.[39] Meanwhile, he was continuing to arrive, for during the summer the national Museums Council, of which Bonnat was the chairman, accepted the Camondo legacy, which included nineteen pictures by Degas — notably *Racehorses in Front of the Stands, The Dance Lesson, The Rehearsal of the Ballet on the Stage, Absinthe, The Tub,* and *Women Ironing.* Moreover, this time there was no question of entering the Musée du Luxembourg first and waiting until ten years after death for the final consecration: the collection was accepted directly for the Louvre. (All these pictures now belong to the Musée d'Orsay, although they are temporarily housed in the Jeu de Paume gallery.)

The satisfaction he may have felt was spoiled, however, by a series of concentrated, irreparable losses. Alexis and Henri Rouart died within a few months of each other. Zoé, old and ill, had to stop working, and the niece she left in charge soon abandoned the responsibility to a girl who knew nothing about the long-established routine that governed the household. The final disaster was an announcement that the lease at 37 Rue Victor-Massé would not be renewed in 1912 as scheduled, since the building was to be demolished to make way for a more profitable utilization of the land. After more than twenty years of accumulation of associations, habits, small manias, and beloved objects, everything had to be wrenched apart and transferred; and the task of the friends — the Valérys, the Rouart sons, and in particular Suzanne Valadon — who took charge of the search for another apartment and studio was complicated by Degas's stubborn refusal to leave the Ninth Arrondissement. At last he agreed to go some twenty meters beyond the boundary and accept a place on the fifth floor at 6 Boulevard de Clichy, near the Rue des Martyrs, across the street from the Cirque Médrano (the former Fernando), and only two blocks from 37 Rue Victor-Massé. Durand-Ruel's sons, Joseph and Georges, sent some of their specialist workmen from the gallery to move the furniture and the paintings. The precious portfolios of drawings and prints were taken up the hill by a shuttling handcart, with Degas intently surveying each loading and unloading.

On July 17, 1912, he wrote from his new address to the Fevre girls at La Colle-sur-Loup, "My sister Thérèse has just died in Naples. I embrace you, my dear nieces. *I won't write again.* I'll be seventy-eight the day after tomorrow." [40] On December 10 of that year he went down to the Galerie Manzi-Joyant, near the Madeleine, for the sale of the Rouart collection, at which his *Dancers Practicing at the Bar* was bought by Mrs. Havemeyer for the record sum of 478,000 francs ($95,700). Asked how he felt about such a price, he replied, "I'm like a horse that wins the Grand Prix; I'm content with my bag of oats." [41] Congratulated by an Italian acquaintance, he said, *"Sono pazzi"* ("They're crazy"). [42] Madame Louis Ganderax, the wife of the editor of *La Revue de Paris,* rushed up with a qualified compliment: "Bravo! That's the Degas we love, the one who is not the Degas of the Affair." But he managed a polite answer: "Madame, it's all of Degas that I want you to love." [43] After the sale, walking back up the Rue Saint-Honoré with Daniel Halévy, he was in an excellent humor:

> "You see, my legs are good. I feel fine. Since my move to a new apartment I have stopped working. It's strange: I have arranged nothing. Everything is still there against the walls. I don't care. I leave everything. It's amazing how with age you become indifferent. . . . I sleep extremely well, eight or ten hours a night. Sleep and legs, that's what I have left." [44]

The demolition work in the Rue Victor-Massé proceeded rapidly. Vollard recalled, "When the last rubbish had been removed and a fence had been erected along the sidewalk, you might still occasionally see an old man peering through the cracks between the planks at the empty lot." [45]

For a while he had a habit, embarrassing to his friends, of sinking into a long silence and then suddenly saying, in a partly sardonic, partly affected way, "I am thinking of death." [46] At Nice, Cassatt found Jeanne Fevre, Marguerite's unmarried daughter, working in a hospital and persuaded her to go up to Paris to look after her uncle, and he accepted the arrangement with unexpected docility. Because he no longer did any serious work, his mental faculties deteriorated alarmingly, though not so much into ordinary senility as into an exaggeration, a perversion, of the detachment he had always tried to achieve. His acquaintances referred to him as being "far away" [47] and thought that even his voice had become "distant, musical." [48] The fatty tissue behind his eyeballs atrophied to such a degree that finally he seemed to be staring out of two dark holes in a tangle of white hair and white whiskers. His admirers compared him to Homer and to King Lear, and Natanson saw him as "an unemployable Montmartre model for God the Father." [49] Daniel Halévy went up to the fifth floor of 6 Boulevard de Clichy and discovered "a dirty, defeated Prospero in the dust, in the semidarkness . . . in an immense indifference." [50] He had lived to such an age that there was scarcely anyone left to remember the brown-eyed young man who had capered in a Perugia street at five o'clock in the morning.

Degas in the Boulevard de Clichy, 1914

The former Parisian patriot remained indifferent when it became possible to hear the distant thunder of enemy artillery massed along the Marne and when, at the end of August 1914, the Germans staged their first air raid on the capital. Although now past eighty, he continued his compulsive walking in both Paris and the suburbs, and on one occasion at least Arsène Alexandre found him just about as lucid and as short-tempered as always:

> During the war I happened to meet him on a train that was taking both of us back from autumnal excursions to Versailles. Even in the darkness after the arrival in Paris he refused all assistance and plunged with perfect surety into a street encumbered with automobiles. During the crossing, in reply to one of my deferential questions, he said, "At my age you don't believe in anyone, you no longer hold to anything, you are screwed."[51]

As late as the summer of 1915 he was going out to Auteuil to talk with Bartholomé, who had a villa and a garden in what was then an artists' colony in the Rue Raffet. Sometimes he could be seen in the Boulevard des Batignolles, sitting at a table in the Café Victor, not far from the location of one of Manet's studios. But by the end of 1916 he was being obliged to stay in bed more and more often, and after that the decline, in both mind and body, was steady.

He died from a cerebral congestion on Friday morning, September 27, 1917, at ten minutes past midnight, after receiving extreme unction from one of the canons of the Cathedral of Notre-Dame. He was eighty-three. A brief service was held in the church of Saint-Jean-l'Evangeliste, a short distance from the Degas family vault in the Montmartre Cemetery; among the hundred people present were Bartholomé, Bonnat, Cassatt, Joseph and Georges Durand-Ruel, Jeanne Fevre, Forain, Gervex, Daniel Halévy, Louise Halévy, Lerolle, Monet, Raffaëlli, Alexis and Louis Rouart, Vollard, and Zandomeneghi. There was no funeral oration, although the presence of a representative of President Raymond Poincaré gave the rites a slightly official flavor — and irritated Forain, who felt sure that Degas would not have liked this final annexation by the Establishment. Daniel Halévy noticed that the body was so light, it turned slightly when the undertakers shifted the coffin. Zandomeneghi wrote to the Italian critic Vittorio Pica, "That beautiful intelligence had faded away some time ago."[52] Cassatt reported to an American friend:

> We buried him on Saturday, a beautiful sunshine, a little crowd of friends and admirers, all very quiet and peaceful in the midst of this dreadful upheaval of which he was barely conscious.[53]

Illustrations
Notes
Bibliography
Index

Illustrations

All works are by Degas unless otherwise identified.

Picture Credits

Notes

References are mostly to publications listed in full in the bibliography. Where an author has several entries in the bibliography, a short form of the cited work's title is used. Numbers and pages of Degas's notebooks are those given in the Reff edition. All the translations are mine unless otherwise credited.

Preface

1. Canaday, p. 31.
2. Nicolson, p. 315.
3. Raynor, p. 23.

1. Class Profile

1. Raimondi, p. 17.
2. Valéry, p. 56.
3. Fevre, p. 20.
4. Rewald, "Degas and His Family," p. 105.
5. Ibid., p. 107.
6. Ibid., p. 105.
7. Lemoisne, I, p. 223.
8. Léon et al., p. 829.
9. Ibid., p. 840.
10. Ibid., p. 841.
11. Karl Marx, *Capital, the Communist Manifesto, and Other Writings* (New York: Modern Library, 1932), pp. 323–324.
12. Léon et al., p. 847.
13. Raimondi, p. 95.
14. Fevre, p. 20.
15. Léon et al., p. 919.
16. Honoré de Balzac, *Le Père Goriot,* p. 160 (Paris: Editions Garnier Frères, 1963).
17. Honoré de Balzac, *Un Homme d'affaires,* vol. 12 of *Oeuvres complètes* (Paris: Furne, Dubochet, and Hetzel, 1846), p. 127.
18. Raimondi, p. 81.

2. An Unsentimental Education

1. Fevre, p. 24.
2. Raimondi, p. 92.
3. Fevre, p. 29.

4. Valéry, p. 55.
5. Ibid., p. 156.
6. Boggs, "Degas and Naples," p. 274.
7. Ibid.
8. Ibid.
9. D. Halévy, *Degas parle*, p. 30.
10. Rivière, p. 8.
11. Prost, p. 49.
12. Dupont-Ferrier, p. 87.
13. Prost, pp. 52–55.
14. Lemoisne, I, p. 226.
15. Baudelaire, p. 924.
16. Lemoisne, I, p. 258.
17. Ibid., p. 258.
18. D. Halévy, *Degas parle*, p. 49.
19. Lemoisne, I, p. 258.
20. D. Halévy, *Degas parle*, p. 145.

3. Bonjour, Monsieur Ingres

1. Prost, p. 34.
2. Carlo M. Cipolla, *Literacy and Development in the West* (Harmondsworth: Penguin, 1969), pp. 94 and 115.
3. Fevre, pp. 25–27.
4. D. Halévy, *Degas parle*, p. 30.
5. Raunay, p. 269.
6. Valéry, p. 15.
7. Lemoisne, I, pp. 10–11.
8. See Valéry, p. 63, and *A Documentary History of Art*, edited by E. G. Holt, vol. III (Garden City, New York: Doubleday, 1966), pp. 34–35.
9. Jeanniot, p. 158.
10. There are several slightly differing versions of Degas's meetings with Ingres. See Lemoisne, I, pp. 260–261; Valéry, pp. 67–68; D. Halévy, *Degas parle*, pp. 57–59; Alexandre, "Nouveaux Aperçus," p. 147; and Fevre, p. 70.
11. Quoted by Pierre Francastel, *Peinture et société* (Paris: Gallimard, 1965), p. 115.
12. *Journal de Eugène Delacroix*, edited by André Joubin, vol. II [May 15, 1855] (Paris: Plon, 1932), p. 327.
13. Notebook 3, p. 96.
14. Notebook 6, pp. 14 and 9.

15. Stendhal, *Mémoires d'un touriste*. This and the preceding comment by him are quoted in James Pope-Hennessy, *Aspects of Provence* (London: Longmans, 1964), pp. 35 and 22.
16. Walter Friedlaender, *David to Delacroix* (New York: Schocken, 1968), p. 78.
17. Notebook 4, p. 93.
18. Notebook 5, p. 33.
19. Notebook 4, p. 4.
20. Notebook 6, p. 83.
21. Baudelaire, p. 70.
22. Notebook 6, p. 65.
23. Ibid., p. 23.
24. Ibid., p. 71.

4. From Naples to Tuscany

1. Plessis, p. 100.
2. Notebook 7, p. 12.
3. Reff, "The Landscape Painter," p. 42.
4. Notebook 7, p. 4.
5. Ibid., p. 19.
6. Boggs, "Degas and Naples," p. 274.
7. Letter of May 14, 1859. Reff, p. 95.
8. Letter of February 8, 1860. Boggs, *Portraits*, p. 12.
9. Boggs, *Portraits*, p. 10.
10. Notebook 8, p. 32.
11. Ibid., p. 35v.
12. Ibid., p. 34v.
13. Ibid., p. 37.
14. Raimondi, p. 127.
15. Bizet, p. 65, letter of May 16, 1858.
16. Lemoisne, I, pp. 227–228
17. Pool, "Degas and Moreau," p. 251.
18. Paladilhe, p. 17.
19. "More Unpublished Letters," p. 283.
20. Notebook 11, p. 104.
21. Notebook 10, p. 46.
22. Bizet, p. 38, letter of February 26, 1858.
23. Notebook 10, p. 37.
24. Notebook 11, pp. 50–53.
25. Ibid., pp. 56–57.
26. Ibid., p. 57.
27. Ibid., p. 58.
28. Ibid., p. 59.

29. Ibid., p. 60.
30. Ibid., p. 65.
31. Ibid., p. 66.
32. Ibid., pp. 68–72.
33. Ibid., pp. 74–75.
34. Ibid., pp. 78–79.
35. Ibid., p. 79.
36. Ibid., pp. 84–85.
37. Ibid., p. 86.
38. Ibid., pp. 87–88.
39. Ibid., pp. 92–93.
40. Ibid., p. 94.

5. *Florence*

1. Notebook 12, p. 21.
2. Ibid., p. 38.
3. "More Unpublished Letters," pp. 281–282.
4. Notebook 12, p. 44.
5. "More Unpublished Letters," p. 283, note 29.
6. Ibid., p. 283.
7. Notebook 12, p. 91.
8. Notebook 18, p. 96.
9. Lemoisne, I, p. 30; Cabanne, *Edgar Degas,* p. 103.
10. Lemoisne, I, p. 31; Cabanne, *Edgar Degas,* p. 103.
11. Lemoisne, I, p. 31.
12. "More Unpublished Letters," pp. 282–284.
13. Lemoisne, I, p. 229; Cabanne, *Edgar Degas,* p. 103.
14. Fevre, p. 38.
15. Cabanne, *Edgar Degas,* p. 103.
16. Lemoisne, I, p. 228.
17. Staley, p. 132.
18. Signorini, pp. 77 and 120–121.
19. "More Unpublished Letters," p. 283.
20. Ibid., pp. 284–285.
21. Notebook 13, p. 41.
22. Ibid., pp. 34–35.

6. *History, Horses, and Nudes*

1. Letter of January 21, 1857. *Correspondance générale d'Eugène Delacroix,* edited by André Joubin, vol. III (Paris: Plon, 1937), p. 369.
2. Letter to Albert Magimel, quoted in *Ingres,* exhibition catalogue (Paris: Petit Palais, 1967) p. xxx.
3. Fermigier, p. 30.
4. Duranty, "Notes sur l'art," *Le Réalisme,* July 10, 1856, quoted in Rewald, *Histoire,* I, p. 43.
5. Pool, "The History Pictures," p. 306.
6. Fermigier, pp. 65–66.
7. Baudelaire, pp. 1044–1045.
8. "More Unpublished Letters," p. 285.
9. Fermigier, p. 35.
10. Notebook 13, p. 50.
11. Notebook 14A, folio 599v.
12. Notebook 13, p. 113.
13. Baudelaire, p. 918.
14. Notebook 14, p. 1.
15. Notebook 15, p. 6, quoted in Reff.
16. Notebook 14, p. 1.
17. Boggs, *Portraits,* p. 86, note 26, citing Sterling, "Chassériau."
18. "Some Unpublished Letters," p. 91.
19. Notebook 19, p. 15.
20. *Lettres,* p. 256.
21. Lemoisne, I, pp. 230–231.
22. Allem, p. 73.
23. Broude, "Degas's 'Misogyny,'" p. 101.
24. Ibid., p. 101.
25. Moreau-Nélaton, *Manet,* I, p. 32.
26. Sérullaz, p. 16.
27. Moreau-Nélaton, *Manet,* I, p. 36.
28. Notebook 18, p. 161.
29. Ibid., p. 163.
30. Ibid., p. 206.
31. Ibid., p. 202.
32. Barthélémy, Chapter XLVII.
33. D. Halévy, *Degas parle,* p. 160.
34. Lemoisne, I, p. 41.

7. *Bonjour, Monsieur Degas*

1. Duranty, *Le Pays des arts,* p. 335, Paris, 1881, from *Le Siècle,* November 13–15, 1872.
2. Lemoisne, I, p. 73.
3. Ibid.

4. Ibid.
5. Ibid.
6. Ibid., p. 261. See also Valéry, p. 68.
7. Baudelaire, p. 1068.
8. Cabanne, *Edgar Degas,* p. 103.
9. Vollard, *Degas,* pp. 85–86.
10. Rivière, p. 108.
11. Pierre Cabanne, "L'Amitié de Degas et de Valernes," see Mercier (unpaged).
12. Fevre, p. 77.
13. Ibid., p. 80.

8. *Into the Present*

1. Jules Claretie, *L'Artiste,* June 1865. Cited in Lethéve, *Impressionnistes,* p. 33.
2. Baudelaire, p. 952.
3. Letter dated December 25, 1861, published in the *Courrier du dimanche.*
4. Rewald, *Histoire,* I, p. 45, citing Astruc, *Le Salon intime* (Paris, 1860), p. 108.
5. Zola, *Mon Salon,* p. 60.
6. Ibid., p. 80.
7. Ibid., p. 75.
8. Ibid., p. 77.
9. Ibid., p. 85.
10. Goncourt, *Manette Salomon,* p. 73.
11. Ibid., p. 249.
12. Ibid., pp. 314–316.
13. J. Elias, "Degas," in *Die Neue Rundschau,* 28, 1917, p. 1566. Quoted by Reff, *The Artist's Mind,* p. 175.
14. Notebook 21, p. 9.
15. Ibid.
16. Ibid., p. 17.
17. Ibid., p. 22v.
18. Ibid., p. 22.
19. Ibid., p. 36.
20. Ibid., p. 4.
21. Notebook 22, p. 5.
22. Pool, "Degas and Moreau," p. 256.
23. Notebook 22, p. 5.
24. Valéry, p. 197.
25. Translated and cited in Nochlin, *Realism and Tradition,* p. 50.
26. Fevre, p. 73.
27. Translated and cited by A. L. Lehmann, *Encyclopaedia Britannica,* vol. 16, p. 169, 1974. The comment was a reaction to a book by the philosopher Victor Cousin entitled *Du vrai, du beau et du bien.*
28. "L'oubli," from *Les Trophées.*
29. Baudelaire, p. 1266.
30. Pool, *Impressionism,* p. 124.
31. Silvestre, p. 179.
32. Lethève, *Impressionnistes,* p. 43.
33. Goncourt, *Manette Salomon,* pp. 175–177.
34. Guest, *The Ballet,* p. 200.
35. *La Presse,* November 18, 1866. Browse, p. 51.
36. Zola, *Mon Salon,* p. 165.
37. Cabanne, "L'amitié de Degas et de Valernes," in Mercier (unpaged).
38. Zola, *Mon Salon,* p. 165.
39. Notebook 22, pp. 3–4.
40. Ibid., p. 5.

9. *Talk and Music*

1. Lethève, *La Vie quotidienne,* pp. 52–53.
2. Easton, p. 163.
3. Crouzet, pp. 239–241.
4. Moreau-Nélaton, *Manet,* I, p. 103.
5. Silvestre, pp. 176–177.
6. Moreau-Nélaton, *Manet,* I, pp. 102–103.
7. Interview with Monet by François Thiébault-Sisson, *Le Temps,* November 27, 1900.
8. Cited in Rewald, *Histoire,* I, pp. 252–253.
9. Nochlin, *Realism and Tradition,* p. 69.
10. Horace, *Ars Poetica,* line 361.
11. Notebook 23, p. 44.
12. Ibid., pp. 45–46.
13. *Lettres,* p. 255.
14. Zola, *Thérèse Raquin,* pp. 187–188. This source was discovered by Reff, *The Artist's Mind,* p. 205.
15. Gimpel, p. 187, says the institution was the Boston Museum of Fine Arts; Reff, *The Artist's Mind,* pp. 206 and

328, note 35, suggests that it was the New York Metropolitan.

16. Monneret, II, p. 284.
17. Lemoisne, I, p. 63.
18. Goncourt, *Manette Salomon,* p. 402.
19. Boggs, *Portraits,* p. 23.
20. Morisot, pp. 23–32.
21. M. Cooper, pp. 9–10.
22. Goncourt, *Journal,* III, p. 960.
23. Lemoisne, I, p. 59.
24. Jeanniot, p. 158.
25. Morisot, p. 40.

10. Military Interlude

1. Brogan, p. 14.
2. Plessis, p. 222.
3. Brogan, p. 30.
4. L. Halévy, *Revue des Deux Mondes,* 2, 1934, p. 371.
5. Brogan, p. 74.
6. Moreau-Nélaton, *Manet,* I, p. 122.
7. Goncourt, *Journal,* II, p. 587.
8. D. Halévy, *Degas parle,* p. 157.
9. Morisot, p. 44.
10. Moreau-Nélaton, *Manet,* I, p. 125.
11. Ibid., p. 126.
12. E. Rouart, p. 13.
13. Morisot, p. 48.
14. Brogan, p. 63.
15. Morisot, p. 58.
16. Brogan, p. 74.
17. Morisot, p. 58.
18. Ibid., p. 62.
19. Ibid., pp. 65–66.
20. Brogan, p. 74.
21. Lambert, p. 336.
22. Dunlop, p. 58.
23. D. Halévy, *Degas parle,* pp. 63–64.
24. Notebook 24, pp. 105–107.
25. L. Halévy, *L'Invasion,* p. 64.
26. *Degas Letters,* no. 1. Not in French edition.

11. Economics and Ballet

1. Moreau-Nélaton, *Manet,* I, pp. 103–104.
2. Zola, *L'Oeuvre,* p. 66.
3. "Some Unpublished Letters," pp. 88–89.
4. William Gaunt, *The Pre-Raphaelite Dream* (New York: Schocken, 1966), p. 79.
5. Letter written in June, 1871, cited in Rewald, I, p. 314.
6. Pickvance, "Degas's Dancers," p. 257.
7. Guest, *The Ballet,* p. 14.
8. See the exhibition catalogue *L'Art en France sous le Second Empire* (Paris, 1979), pp. 429–430, for Gautier's poem and a drawing by Chassériau of Camara.
9. Baudelaire, p. 152.
10. Ibid., p. 76.
11. L. Halévy, *Revue des Deux Mondes,* 2, 1934, p. 557.
12. Christout, p. 57.
13. Goncourt, *Journal,* I, p. 1036.
14. Notebook 24, pp. 7 and 20–21.
15. Havemeyer, p. 256.
16. Broude, "Degas's 'Misogyny,' " p. 105.
17. Germaine Prudhommeau, "L'érotisme et la danse," in *Erotiques* (Paris: Union Générale d'Editions, 1978), p. 284. (No. 1–2 of *Revue d'Esthetique.*)
18. *The Echo,* April 22, 1876. Quoted in Pickvance, "Degas's Dancers," p. 259.
19. *The Graphic,* November 21, 1874. Quoted in Pickvance, "Degas's Dancers," p. 263.
20. *The Echo,* April 22, 1876. Quoted in Pickvance, "Degas's Dancers," p. 265.
21. *The Echo,* May 18, 1875. Quoted in Pickvance, "Degas's Dancers," p. 264.

12. New Orleans

1. Lemoisne, I, p. 70.
2. Ibid., p. 71.
3. Ibid., p. 71.
4. *Degas Letters,* pp. 17–19 and 32, dated November 19, 1872, and February 18, 1873. Not in French edition.
5. *Lettres,* p. 21.
6. Ibid., p. 16.
7. Ibid., p. 22.
8. Ibid., p. 27.

9. Valéry, p. 157.
10. *Lettres*, p. 28.
11. Jean-Jacques Rousseau, *Confessions*, II (Paris: Larousse, 1971), pp. 119–120.
12. *Degas Letters*, pp. 17–19. Not in French edition.
13. *Lettres*, p. 23.
14. Ibid., p. 26.
15. Ibid., p. 19.
16. *Degas Letters*, p. 32. Not in French edition.
17. Lemoisne, I, p. 18.
18. *Lettres*, p. 24.
19. L. Halévy, *Revue des Deux Mondes*, 37, 1937, pp. 547–548.
20. *Lettres*, p. 32.

13. *Organized Secession*

1. Goncourt, II, pp. 967–968.
2. M. Scolari and A. Barr, "Cézanne d'après les lettres de Marion à Morstatt," *Gazette des Beaux-Arts*, 17, 1937. Letter of April 12, 1866.
3. G. Poulain, *Bazille et ses amis* (Paris, 1932), pp. 78–79. Quoted by Rewald, *Histoire*, I, pp. 218–219.
4. *Degas Letters*, pp. 38–40. Not in French edition.
5. Zola, *L'Oeuvre*, pp. 165–166.
6. *L'Opinion nationale*, April 22, 1874. Quoted in Lethève, *Impressionnistes*, p. 63.
7. *La Presse*, April 29, 1874. Quoted in Lethève, *Impressionnistes*, pp. 61 and 69.
8. *Le Rappel*, April 20, 1874. Quoted in Lethève, *Impressionnistes*, pp. 61 and 63.
9. *L'Artiste*, May 1874, p. 309. Quoted in Pickvance, "Degas's Dancers," p. 257.
10. *La République française*, April 25, 1874. Quoted in Lethève, *Impressionnistes*, pp. 67–68.
11. *Le Charivari*, April 25, 1874. Quoted in Lethève, *Impressionnistes*, pp. 64–67.
12. Havemeyer, pp. 249–250. Mrs. Havemeyer mistakenly says she was "about sixteen" at the time of the purchase.
13. *Lettres*, p. 30. Here the letter is dated 1873, which is impossible in view of the mention of the burning of the Opéra.
14. Letter of August 31, 1876. Quoted in Rewald, "Degas and His Family," p. 122.
15. *Paris-Journal*, August 21 and September 25, 26, and 29, 1875; *Le Figaro*, August 20 and September 25.
16. "Some Unpublished Letters," pp. 89–90.
17. *Le Figaro*, April 1, 1876. Quoted in Lemoisne, I, p. 237.
18. *Le Figaro*, April 3, 1876. Quoted in Lethève, *Impressionnistes*, pp. 76–77.
19. L. Halévy, *Revue des Deux Mondes*, 42, 1937, p. 836.
20. *Le Moniteur universel*, April 11, 1876. Lethève, *Impressionnistes*, p. 79.
21. *L'Art*, April 1876. Quoted in Lethève, *Impressionnistes*, p. 80.
22. Lemoisne, I, p. 239.
23. *L'Opinion nationale*, April 2, 1876. Quoted in Lethève, *Impressionnistes*, pp. 77–78.
24. *Art Monthly Review*, September 30, 1876, p. 121. Quoted in Mallarmé, pp. 1623–1624.
25. *Viestnik Evropy*, June 1876. Zola, *Mon Salon*, p. 279.
26. Duranty, pp. 23–31.
27. Ibid., p. 43.
28. Ibid., p. 45.
29. Ibid., pp. 53–55.
30. *Le Siècle*, April 5, 1877. Quoted in Lethève, *Impressionnistes*, p. 83.
31. *Le Petit Parisien*, April 7, 1877. Quoted in Cabanne, *Edgar Degas*, p. 92.
32. *Le Temps*, April 22, 1877. Quoted in Lethève, *Impressionnistes*, p. 85.
33. *Le Sémaphore de Marseille*, April 19, 1877. Zola, *Mon Salon*, p. 283.
34. *L'Artiste*, May 1877, p. 332. Quoted in Lemoisne, I, p. 243.

35. *Le Figaro,* April 5, 1877. Quoted in Lemoisne, I, p. 241.
36. *Le Courrier de France,* April 6, 1877. Quoted in Lethève, *Impressionnistes,* p. 84.
37. *L'Impressionniste,* April 6, 1877. Quoted in Lemoisne, I, p. 240.
38. Letter of August 24, 1877, *Correspondance de Paul Cézanne,* edited by John Rewald (Paris: Grasset, 1937), p. 131.
39. Rewald, "Degas and His Family," p. 122.
40. Ibid., p. 123.
41. *Lettres,* p. 39.
42. Ibid.
43. Ibid., p. 40.

14. *The Celibate*

1. Juin, p. 10.
2. Notebook 11, p. 94.
3. *Lettres,* p. 27.
4. Ibid., p. 209.
5. Vollard, *Degas,* pp. 70–71.
6. Rivière, p. 18.
7. Cited in Jean Lacoste, *La Philosophie de l'art* (Paris: Presses Universitaires de France, 1981), p. 44.
8. Goncourt, *Manette Salomon,* p. 145–146.
9. Lethève, *La Vie quotidienne,* p. 203.
10. Ibid., p. 204.
11. Sevin, p. 41.
12. Vollard, *Degas,* p. 71.
13. Sickert, p. 185.
14. D. Halévy, *Degas parle,* p. 95.
15. Ibid.
16. Jules Michelet, *La Femme* (Paris: Flammarion, 1981), p. 43.
17. Baudelaire, p. 204.
18. Moreau-Nélaton, *Manet,* I, p. 103.
19. Bernard Dorival, *Cézanne* (Paris: Pierre Tisné, 1948), p. 110.
20. Sweet, p. 18.
21. Sickert, p. 186.
22. Cited in Bullard, *Mary Cassatt,* p. 1.
23. *Lettres,* pp. 270–271.
24. Jeanniot, p. 155.
25. D. Halévy, *Degas parle,* pp. 157–158.
26. Morisot, p. 169.
27. *Lettres,* p. 150.
28. Ibid., p. 55.
29. Ibid., pp. 196–197.
30. Ibid., pp. 269–270.
31. "Some Unpublished Letters," p. 91.
32. Vollard, *Degas,* p. 15.
33. Rivière, p. 18.
34. D. Halévy, *Degas parle,* p. 166.
35. Natanson, p. 51.
36. Goncourt, *Journal,* IV, p. 674.
37. Notebook 6, p. 21.
38. Notebook 26, p. 41.
39. Zeldin, I, p. 307.
40. Baudelaire, p. 1189.
41. Huysmans, *Marthe,* p. 35.
42. Catalogue of eighth exhibition of secessionist group, May 15, 1886.
43. Vollard, *Degas,* p. 42.
44. Baudelaire, p. 25.
45. Plessis, p. 74.
46. Mallarmé, p. 1453.
47. Goncourt, *Journal,* IV, p. 674.
48. Monneret, III, p. 193.
49. Moore, *Impressions,* p. 318.
50. Ibid.
51. Zeldin, I, p. 312.
52. Ibid.
53. Gautier, *Le Roi Candaule,* p. 85.
54. D. Halévy, *Degas parle,* pp. 159–160.
55. D. Rouart, *Degas à la recherche de sa technique,* p. 65.
56. Notebook 30, p. 208.

15. *Life and Art*

1. Rivière, p. 7.
2. Moore, *Confessions,* p. 102.
3. Ibid., p. 149.
4. Goncourt, *Journal,* II, p. 1037.
5. Adhémar and Cachin, p. x.
6. Rivière, p. 97.
7. Ibid., p. 91.
8. Moore, *Confessions,* p. 105.
9. Rivière, p. 76.
10. Ibid., p. 24.
11. D. Halévy, *Degas parle,* pp. 47–48.
12. Moore, *Impressions,* p. 302.

13. Ibid.
14. De Nittis, pp. 187–188.
15. Fénéon, p. 609.
16. Moore, *Impressions,* p. 304.
17. Lemoisne, I, p. 1.
18. Notebook 30, p. 20.
19. Goncourt, *Manette Salomon,* pp. 400–401.
20. Moore, *Impressions,* p. 304.
21. De Nittis, p. 188.
22. D. Halévy, *Degas parle,* pp. 166–167.
23. De Nittis, p. 188.
24. Joly, p. 374.
25. Monneret, I, p. 42.
26. Gimpel, p. 186.
27. Sweet, p. 31.
28. Segard, pp. 7–8.
29. Bullard, p. 12.
30. Moore, *Confessions,* p. 69.
31. *Lettres,* pp. 149–151.
32. Maria and Godfrey Blunden, *La Peinture de l'Impressionnisme* (Geneva: Skira, 1981), p. 173.
33. Forbes Watson, *Mary Cassatt* (New York: Whitney Museum of Art, 1932). Quoted by Dunlop, p. 168.
34. Dunlop, p. 168.
35. Bullard, p. 14.
36. Sweet, p. 182.
37. Boggs, *Portraits,* p. 51.
38. Rivière, p. 2.
39. *Lettres,* pp. 41–42.
40. L. Halévy, *Revue des Deux Mondes,* 42, 1937, p. 823.
41. Pickvance, *Degas 1879,* p. 57.
42. *Lettres,* p. 42.
43. Ibid., pp. 56–57.
44. Moore, *Impressions,* p. 119.
45. Ibid., p. 300.
46. Ibid., p. 313.
47. Lascault, p. 21.
48. Erismann, p. 113.
49. Adhémar and Cachin, p. xlv, no. 42.
50. Ibid., p. xlv, no. 44.
51. Joly, p. 373.
52. Brunschwig, p. 336.
53. Erismann, p. 118.
54. *Lettres,* p. 57.
55. Joly, p. 373.
56. *Entracte,* June 26, 1888. Cited by Shapiro, p. 161.
57. Moore, *Impressions,* p. 312.

16. Defections and Quarrels

1. Rewald, *Histoire,* II, p. 79.
2. Dorival, *Cézanne,* p. 106.
3. Monneret, II, pp. 266–267.
4. Rewald, *Histoire,* II, pp. 86–87.
5. Ibid., p. 92.
6. *Le Figaro,* April 11, 1879. Lemoisne, I, p. 245.
7. *Viestnik Evropy,* June 1879. Zola, *Mon Salon,* pp. 319–320.
8. Huysmans, *L'Art moderne,* p. 137.
9. Lemoisne, I, p. 246.
10. Monneret, II, p. 267.
11. *Revue bleue,* June 1879. Quoted in Lethève, *Impressionnistes,* p. 106.
12. Bazin, *L'Epoque impressionniste,* p. 26.
13. Hélène Adhémar, *Hommage à Claude Monet,* p. 187. Exhibition catalogue, Paris, 1980.
14. Ibid., p. 220.
15. *Lettres,* p. 51.
16. Huysmans, *L'Art moderne,* pp. 131–133.
17. *Gazette des Beaux-Arts,* May 1880, p. 485. Quoted in Lemoisne, I, p. 247.
18. *Le Voltaire,* June 18–22, 1880. Zola, *Mon Salon,* p. 333.
19. *Le Figaro,* April 9, 1880. Quoted in Lemoisne, I, pp. 246–247.
20. *La Vie moderne,* June 12, 1880. Quoted in Lethève, *Impressionnistes,* p. 110.
21. Rewald, *Histoire,* II, pp. 103–105.
22. Ibid., p. 105.
23. *Le Temps,* April 5, 1881. Quoted in Millard, p. 119.
24. *Le Figaro,* April 10, 1881. Cabanne, *Edgar Degas,* p. 93.
25. *Chronique des Arts,* 18, 1881, pp. 109–110. Reff, *The Artist's Mind,* p. 242.
26. Havemeyer, p. 254.
27. *Paris-Journal,* April 21, 1881. Quoted in Millard, p. 120.
28. Blanche, *Propos de peintre,* p. 54.

29. *Le Temps,* April 23, 1881. Quoted in Millard, p. 121.
30. *La Civilization,* April 21, 1881. Quoted in Millard, p. 120.
31. *Le Constitutionel,* April 24, 1881. Quoted in Millard, p. 123.
32. *Le Courrier du soir,* April 23, 1881. Quoted in Millard, p. 123.
33. Huysmans, *L'Art moderne,* pp. 248–250.
34. *La France nouvelle,* May 1–2, 1881. Quoted in Millard, p. 123.
35. Monneret, II, p. 83.
36. Rewald, *Histoire,* II, p. 126.
37. Ibid.
38. Ibid., p. 127.
39. Ibid., p. 130.
40. Monneret, II, p. 172.
41. Ibid., p. 267.

17. *Media*

1. Rewald, *Complete Sculptures,* p. 3.
2. Reff, *The Artist's Mind,* p. 262.
3. Monneret, III, p. 251.
4. Notebook 19, p. 8.
5. Jeanniot, p. 171.
6. Reff, *The Artist's Mind,* p. 249.
7. *Lettres,* p. 89.
8. Ibid., p. 90.
9. Ibid., p. 91.
10. Ibid., p. 93.
11. Vollard, *Degas,* pp. 112–113.
12. M. Pittalunga and E. Piceni, *De Nittis* (Milan: Bramante, 1963), p. 359.
13. L. Halévy, *Revue des Deux Mondes,* 43, 1938, p. 399.
14. Lemoisne, I, p. 239.
15. Adhémar and Cachin, p. xlvi, no. 49.
16. L. Halévy, *Revue des Deux Mondes,* 42, 1937, p. 826.
17. *Lettres,* pp. 45–46.
18. Ibid., p. 47.
19. Notebook 30, pp. 208–202. (Pagination is reversed.)
20. Ibid., p. 210.
21. Ibid., p. 196.
22. Pickvance, *Degas 1879,* p. 76.
23. *Lettres,* p. 55.
24. Sweet, pp. 52–53.
25. D. Rouart, *Degas à la recherche de sa technique,* p. 66.
26. *Lettres,* p. 60.
27. Blanche, "Portraits," p. 23.
28. Lemoisne, I, p. 260.
29. D. Halévy, *Degas parle,* p. 133.
30. Jeanniot, pp. 154–155.
31. Notebook 33, p. 3v. Reff, *The Artist's Mind,* p. 277.
32. Valéry, p. 223.
33. D. Halévy, *Degas parle,* p. 83.

18. *Victory and Disbandment*

1. Rewald, *Histoire,* II, p. 134.
2. *Lettres,* p. 71.
3. Monneret, III, p. 92.
4. Monneret, II, p. 23.
5. Théodore de Banville, *Nous tous* (Paris: G. Charpentier, 1884), p. 91.
6. Sérullaz, p. 77.
7. Pissarro, p. 30.
8. Cooper, *Courtauld Institute,* p. 26.
9. Ibid.
10. Ibid.
11. *Lettres,* p. 69.
12. Ibid., p. 79.
13. Ibid., p. 79–80.
14. Ibid., p. 83.
15. Ibid., p. 99.
16. Sickert, p. 185.
17. Ibid., p. 184.
18. *Lettres,* p. 95.
19. D. Halévy, *Degas parle,* p. 170.
20. *Lettres,* p. 110.
21. Ibid., p. 108.
22. Jeanniot, pp. 152–154.
23. *Lettres,* p. 70.
24. Ibid., p. 104.
25. Ibid., pp. 72–73.
26. Ibid., p. 73.
27. Ibid., p. 72.
28. Ibid., p. 48.
29. Ibid., p. 81.
30. Ibid., p. 113.
31. Ibid., p. 118.
32. Morisot, p. 126.
33. Pissarro, pp. 100–101.

34. Ibid., p. 100.
35. Rewald, *Histoire*, II, p. 168.
36. *La Vogue*, June 13–20, 1886. Quoted in Lethève, *Impressionnistes*, p. 126.
37. Huysmans, *Certains*, pp. 21–22 and 23–24.
38. Ibid., pp. 24–25.
39. *Art Age*, April 1886. Quoted in Rewald, *History*, p. 544.
40. *The Sun*, April 11, 1886. Quoted in Rewald, *History*, p. 531.
41. Moore, *Impressions*, p. 298.
42. Letter of May 10, 1883. Zola, *Oeuvres complètes* (Paris: Cercle du livre précieux, 1970), XIV, p. 1427.
43. Moore, *Impressions*, p. 319.
44. Valéry, p. 202.

19. *Celebrity*

1. *Lettres*, p. 158.
2. Lemoisne, I, p. 201.
3. Moore, *Impressions*, p. 302.
4. *Lettres*, p. 68.
5. Blanche, *Propos de peintre*, p. 258.
6. D. Halévy, *Pays parisiens*, p. 33.
7. J.-P. Crespelle, *Les Maîtres de la belle époque* (Paris: Hachette, 1966), p. 26.
8. D. Halévy, *Degas parle*, p. 40.
9. *Lettres*, p. 147.
10. Ibid.
11. Ibid., p. 104.
12. Ibid., p. 118.
13. D. Halévy, *Pays parisiens*, p. 95.
14. *Lettres*, p. 143.
15. D. Halévy, *Degas parle*, p. 136.
16. Sevin, p. 26.
17. D. Halévy, *Degas parle*, p. 136.
18. Régnier, *Proses datées*, p. 27.
19. Morisot, p. 118.
20. Ibid., p. 121.
21. Moore, *Impressions*, p. 306.
22. Natanson, p. 46.
23. Sigmund Freud, *The Problem of Anxiety*. Cited in N. Fodor and F. Gaynor (eds.), *Freud: Dictionary of Psychoanalysis* (Greenwich, Connecticut: Fawcett, 1963), p. 165.
24. Alexandre, "Monsieur Degas," p. 12.
25. D. Halévy, *Degas parle*, pp. 53–55.
26. Sevin, pp. 20–21.
27. Blanche, *Propos de peintre*, p. 239.
28. Raunay, p. 273.
29. Sevin, p. 33.
30. Ibid., p. 25.
31. Ibid., p. 32.
32. Letter of 1895 to Maurice Fabre. *Lettres d'Odilon Redon* (Brussels and Paris: G. van Oest, 1923), pp. 22–23.
33. D. Halévy, *Degas parle*, p. 45.
34. Ibid., p. 62.
35. Lemoisne, I, p. 142.
36. Sevin, p. 26.
37. Valéry, pp. 201–202. Hals did, of course, draw fingernails.
38. Vollard, *Degas*, pp. 58–59.
39. Jeanniot, p. 171.
40. Ibid., pp. 280–281.
41. *Lettres*, p. 27.
42. D. Halévy, *Degas parle*, p. 159.
43. Sevin, p. 23.
44. *Lettres*, p. 125.
45. Ibid., p. 83.
46. Ibid., p. 98.
47. Ibid., p. 119.
48. Raunay, p. 273.
49. *Lettres*, p. 267.
50. D. Halévy, *Degas parle*, p. 27.
51. E. Rouart, p. 12.
52. D. Halévy, *Degas parle*, p. 159.
53. Vollard, *Degas*, p. 104.
54. Valéry, p. 60.
55. *Lettres*, pp. 273–274.
56. Ibid., p. 275.
57. Sevin, p. 33.
58. *Lettres*, p. 52, note 2.
59. Sickert, p. 185.
60. Letter of December 1, 1892. Quoted by Dunlop, p. 168.
61. Natanson, p. 48.
62. Cabanne, *Edgar Degas*, p. 94.
63. D. Halévy, *Degas parle*, p. 64.
64. There are several versions of this incident. See Cabanne, *Edgar Degas*, p. 103; Valéry, pp. 237–239; Sevin, p. 26.
65. Sevin, p. 34.

66. Ibid., p. 35.
67. Letter from Vincent to Theo, January 9, 1889.
68. Letter to Bernard, summer 1888, p. 106 of Vollard edition.
69. Letter to Bernard, August 1888, p. 102 of Vollard edition.
70. Letter to Theo, November 1888.
71. Letter to Theo, March 24, 1889.
72. Gauguin, p. 101.
73. Ibid., p. 136.
74. Vollard, *Degas*, p. 45.
75. D. Halévy, *Degas parle*, p. 61.
76. Gauguin, p. 289.
77. *Lettres*, p. 77.
78. Ibid., p. 78.
79. Ibid., p. 107–108.
80. D. Halévy, *Degas parle*, p. 162.
81. Pissarro, p. 247.
82. *Lettres*, p. 125.
83. Ibid., p. 239.
84. Goncourt, III, p. 784.
85. Valéry, p. 10.
86. Fevre, p. 73, note 1.
87. Raunay, p. 281.
88. Jeanniot, p. 288.
89. *Lettres*, p. 10.
90. Molière, *Le Misanthrope* (Paris: Librairie Larousse, 1971), p. 103, line 1574.
91. Raunay, p. 281.
92. D. Halévy, *Degas parle*, p. 13.
93. Ibid., p. 64.
94. *Lettres*, pp. 178–179.

20. *Poetry, Travel, and Color*

1. Morisot, p. 145.
2. Mallarmé, p. 89.
3. *Lettres*, p. 87.
4. Fevre, p. 130.
5. Valéry, p. 141.
6. See *Huit sonnets de Degas* for this and the following quotations. The sonnets have also been published in Lemoisne, I, pp. 202–212.
7. Millard, p. 88.
8. Ibid.
9. Valéry, p. 140.
10. Mallarmé, p. 70.
11. Valéry, p. 58.
12. Régnier, p. 202.
13. Monneret, III, p. 183.
14. D. Halévy, *Degas parle*, p. 42.
15. Ibid., p. 55.
16. Millard, p. 19.
17. *Lettres*, p. 193.
18. Ibid., pp. 151–152.
19. D. Halévy, *Degas parle*, p. 40.
20. *Lettres*, p. 197.
21. Fevre, p. 101.
22. *Lettres*, pp. 275–276.
23. D. Halévy, *Degas parle*, p. 21.
24. Fevre, p. 75.
25. Ibid.
26. *Lettres*, p. 142.
27. Ibid., p. 144.
28. Ibid., p. 145.
29. Ibid.
30. Ibid., p. 181.
31. Ibid. The Latin he had in mind is line 146 of Virgil's fourth Georgic: *iamque ministrantem platanum potantibus umbras* (and the plane tree already ministering to wine drinkers with its shade).
32. Ibid., p. 161.
33. Ibid., p. 163.
34. Ibid., pp. 164–166.
35. Ibid., p. 173.
36. Fevre, p. 102.
37. *Lettres*, p. 208, where the letter is incorrectly dated 1895. Paris municipal records show that Achille died in 1893.
38. Fevre, p. 102.
39. *Lettres*, p. 196.
40. Fevre, p. 102.
41. *Lettres*, p. 278.
42. Letter of October 2, 1892. Minervino and Lassaigne, p. 129.
43. Monneret, III, p. 319.
44. Vollard, *Degas*, p. 57.
45. *Lettres*, p. 168.
46. Sevin, p. 45.
47. Sickert, pp. 183–184.
48. *Lettres*, p. 127.
49. Ibid., p. 202.
50. Ibid., p. 192.

51. Fevre, p. 56.
52. D. Halévy, *Degas parle*, p. 103.
53. *Lettres,* p. 279.
54. Valéry, p. 16.

21. *The Affair*

1. Brogan, p. 308.
2. Rebérioux, p. 33.
3. Marrus, p. 31.
4. Chérasse and Boussel, p. 46.
5. Ibid., p. 51.
6. Ibid., p. 62.
7. Ibid., p. 69.
8. Goncourt, IV, p. 711.
9. D. Halévy, *Degas parle,* p. 78.
10. Valéry, p. 111.
11. Gide, p. 77.
12. Marrus, p. 80.
13. Ibid., p. 34.
14. Fevre, p. 100.
15. *Lettres,* p. 214.
16. Vitali, p. 273.
17. *Lettres,* p. 225, in which the date is incorrectly given as 1896–1898. See Newhall, p. 63.
18. *Lettres,* p. 208.
19. D. Halévy, *Degas parle,* p. 88.
20. Ibid., pp. 91–93.
21. Valéry, p. 81.
22. Attribution is complicated by the many photographs in which Degas himself appears and which were obviously not "taken" by him, although he may have "composed" them.
23. Newhall, p. 64.
24. Peter Owen, *Painting* (Oxford: Oxford University Press, 1970), p. 177.
25. J. Manet, p. 238.
26. *Lettres,* pp. 202–204.
27. Ibid., p. 220.
28. D. Halévy, *Degas parle,* pp. 97–98.
29. Havemeyer, pp. 252–253.
30. D. Halévy, *Degas parle,* p. 116.
31. Miquel, p. 85.
32. Ibid., p. 86.
33. Valéry, p. 158.
34. D. Halévy, *Degas parle,* p. 87.
35. Daval, p. 76.

36. Valéry, p. 218.
37. Ibid., p. 160.
38. Daval, p. 76.
39. Sevin, p. 45.
40. D. Halévy, *Degas parle,* p. 94.
41. Ibid., pp. 105–106.
42. Valéry, p. 111.
43. Blanche, *Propos de peintre,* p. 289.
44. Marrus, pp. 254–255.
45. Raunay, pp. 474–475.
46. D. Halévy, *Degas parle,* p. 126.
47. Ibid., pp. 127–128.
48. Ibid., pp. 130–131.
49. Ibid., p. 155.
50. Vollard, *Degas,* p. 48.
51. Ibid., p. 47.
52. Raunay, pp. 280–281.
53. *Lettres de Gauguin à Daniel de Monfreid* (Paris: Georges Falaize, 1950), p. 129.
54. Letter of March 7, 1898. Pissarro, p. 451.
55. *Lettres,* p. 225.
56. Natanson, pp. 76–77.
57. *Lettres,* p. 232.
58. Vollard, *Degas,* pp. 1–2.
59. Sevin, p. 32.
60. Monneret, II, p. 92.
61. *Lettres,* p. 229.
62. Ibid., pp. 252–253.
63. Monneret, III, p. 12.
64. *Lettres,* p. 233.

22. *Into the Night*

1. *Lettres,* p. 228.
2. Adhémar and Cachin, p. x.
3. Thiébault-Sisson, p. 3.
4. *Lettres,* p. 234.
5. Crespelle, p. 16.
6. Marcel Proust, *A la recherche du temps perdu,* vol. 9 (Paris: Gallimard, 1942), pp. 285–288.
7. Jacques Charpier, *Essai sur Paul Valéry* (Paris: Seghers, 1956), p. 95.
8. See his poem *La Jeune Parque.*
9. Valéry, p. 17.
10. Reff, *The Artist's Mind,* p. 192.

11. Valéry, p. 151.
12. Ibid., p. 154.
13. *Lettres*, p. 231.
14. Valéry, p. 197.
15. Ibid., p. 126.
16. *Lettres*, p. 235.
17. D. Halévy, *Degas parle,* pp. 131–132.
18. Valéry, p. 146.
19. *Lettres*, p. 239.
20. Adhémar and Cachin, p. xx.
21. Jeanniot, p. 299.
22. Valéry, p. 165. There are several versions of this anecdote.
23. *Lettres,* pp. 240–241.
24. Ibid., 241.
25. Lemoisne, I, pp. 257–261.
26. D. Halévy, *Degas parle,* pp. 97–98.
27. Vollard, *Degas,* pp. 80–83.
28. Valéry, p. 64.
29. *Lettres,* p. 243.
30. D. Halévy, *Degas parle,* pp. 134–135.
31. E. F. Fry, *Cubism* (London: Thames & Hudson, 1966), p. 10.
32. Gimpel, p. 154.

33. Ibid., p. 435.
34. Gide, pp. 274–275.
35. Valéry, p. 47.
36. *Lettres,* p. 245.
37. Michel, pp. 623–638.
38. D. Halévy, *Degas parle,* pp. 138–139.
39. Ibid., pp. 139–141.
40. Fevre, p. 113.
41. D. Halévy, *Degas parle,* p. 150. There are several versions. See, for example, Jeanniot, pp. 173–174.
42. Sevin, p. 44.
43. D. Halévy, *Degas parle,* pp. 149–150.
44. Ibid., pp. 145–146.
45. Vollard, *Degas,* p. 118.
46. Lemoisne, I, p. 197.
47. D. Halévy, *Degas parle,* pp. 161–162.
48. Ibid., p. 143.
49. Natanson, p. 52.
50. D. Halévy, *Degas parle,* p. 183.
51. Alexandre, "Nouveaux aperçus," pp. 172–173.
52. Vitali, p. 273.
53. Hale, p. 263.

Bibliography

Principal Writings by Degas

The Notebooks of Edgar Degas. Edited by Theodore Reff. Oxford: Clarendon Press, 1976. 2 vols.

Huit sonnets de Degas. With an introduction by Jean Nepveu-Degas. Paris: La Jeune Parque, 1946.

Lettres de Degas. Edited by Marcel Guérin, with a preface by Daniel Halévy. Paris: Bernard Grasset, 1945.

Degas Letters. English translation by Marguerite Kay, with some letters not in the French version. Oxford: Bruno Cassirer, 1947.

"Some Unpublished Letters of Degas." Edited by Theodore Reff. *Art Bulletin,* 50, 1968, pp. 87–94.

"More Unpublished Letters of Degas." Edited by Theodore Reff. *Art Bulletin,* 51, 1969, pp. 281–286.

Scattered letters will be found in Duranty, *La Nouvelle peinture;* Fevre, *Mon oncle Degas;* Morisot, *Correspondance;* and Newhall, "Degas, photographe amateur." See the third section of this bibliography. There is no complete edition of Degas's correspondence.

Principal Sales Catalogues

Catalogues des tableaux, pastels et dessins par Edgar Degas et provenant de son atelier. Paris: Galerie Georges Petit. First sale, May 6–8, 1918; second, December 11–13, 1918; third, April 7–9, 1919; fourth, July 2–4, 1919.

Vente de l'atelier Degas: gravures, lithographies et monotypes. Paris: Galerie Manzi-Joyant. November 22–23, 1918.

Catalogue des tableaux modernes et anciens, collection Edgar Degas. Paris: Galerie Georges Petit. March 26–27, 1918.

Catalogue des estampes, collection Edgar Degas. Paris: Hôtel Drouot. November 6–7, 1918.

Studies and Related Material

Abbot, J. "La Fille de Jephté." *Bulletin of Smith College of Art,* No. 15, June 1934, pp. 2–12.

Adhémar, H. "Edgar Degas et la 'Scène de guerre au Moyen Age.' " *Gazette des Beaux-Arts,* 70, 1967, pp. 295–298.

Adhémar, H.; Sérullaz, M.; Beaulieu, M. *Degas, oeuvres du Musée du Louvre.* Exhibition catalogue. Paris, 1969.

Adhémar, J., and Cachin, F. *Edgar Degas, gravures et monotypes.* Paris: Arts et Métiers Graphiques, 1973.

Alexandre, A. "Degas, nouveaux aperçus." *L'Art et les artistes,* 29, no. 154, 1935, pp. 145–173.

———. "Monsieur Degas." *Les Arts,* special issue, no. 166, 1918.

Allem, M. *La Vie quotidienne sous le Second Empire.* Paris: Hachette, 1948.

Amayo, M. "The Art of the Ottocento." *Art News,* 72, no. 1, January 1973, pp. 58–60.

Bacci, B. M. *Diego Martelli, l'amico dei Macchiaioli.* Florence: Mazza, 1952.

Barazzetti, S. "Degas et ses amis Valpinçon." *Beaux-Arts,* nos. 190, 191, and 192, August 21, August 28, and September 4, 1936.

Barthélémy, Abbé J.-J. *Voyage du jeune Anacharsis en Grèce, dans le milieu du quatrième siècle avant l'ère vulgaire.* Paris: Bure *ainé,* 1788. 4 vols.

Baudelaire, C. *Oeuvres complètes.* Paris: Gallimard, Pléiade edition, 1968.

Bazin, G. *L'Epoque impressionniste.* Paris: Pierre Tisné, 1947.

———. *Impressionist Paintings in the Louvre.* London: Thames & Hudson, 1964.

Bazin, G.; Florisoone, M.; Leymarie, J. "L'Impressionnisme." Special issue of *L'Amour de l'Art,* nos. 3 and 4, 1947.

Beaulieu, M. "Les Sculptures de Degas, essai de chronologie." *La Revue du Louvre,* 19, 1969, pp. 369–380.

Bell, Q. *Degas, Le Viol.* Charlton Lectures on Art. Newcastle-upon-Tyne, 1965.

Bergerat, E. "Edgar Degas, souvenirs." *Le Figaro,* May 11, 1918.

Bizet, G. *Lettres: Impressions de Rome, la Commune.* Paris: Calmann-Lévy, 1908.

Blanche, J.-E. *Aymeris.* Paris: Editions de la Sirène, 1922.

———. "Portraits de Degas." *Formes,* 12, February 1931, p. 22.

———. *Propos de peintre, de David à Degas.* Paris: Emile-Paul Frères, 1919.

Boas, G. "Il faut être de son temps." *Journal of Aesthetics and Art Criticism,* vol. 1, no. 1, 1941, pp. 52–65.

Boggs, J. S. *Degas — Paintings, Drawings, Prints, Sculpture.* Exhibition catalogue. Los Angeles County Museum, 1958.

————. *Drawings by Degas.* Exhibition catalogue. Saint Louis: City Art Museum, 1967–1968.

————. "Edgar Degas and the Bellellis." *Art Bulletin,* 37, 1955, pp. 127–136.

————. "Edgar Degas and Naples." *Burlington Magazine,* 105, 1963, pp. 273–276.

————. *Portraits by Degas.* Berkeley and Los Angeles: University of California Press, 1962.

Boime, A. *The Academy and French Painting in the Nineteenth Century.* London: Phaidon, 1971.

Borie, J. *Le Célibataire français.* Paris: Le Sagittaire, 1976.

Boschot, A. *Portraits de peintres.* Paris: Editions d'Art et d'Histoire, 1954.

Bouret, J. *Degas.* Paris: A. Somogy, 1965.

Braive, M.-F. *L'Age de la photographie.* Brussels: Editions de la Connaissance, 1965.

Brogan, D. W. *The Development of Modern France: 1870–1939.* London: Hamish Hamilton, 1940.

Broude, N. "Degas's 'Misogyny.'" *Art Bulletin,* 59, 1977, pp. 95–107.

————. "Macchiaioli: Effect and Expression in Nineteenth-Century Florentine Painting." *Art Bulletin,* 52, 1970, pp. 11–21.

————. "Macchiaioli as Proto-Impressionists." *Art Bulletin,* 52, 1970, pp. 404–414.

Browse, L. *Degas Dancers.* London: Faber & Faber, 1949.

Brunschwig, C. *100 ans de chanson française.* Paris: Editions du Seuil, 1972.

Bullard, E. J. *Mary Cassatt: Oils and Pastels.* New York: Watson-Guptill, 1972.

Burrolet, T. "Bartholomé et Degas." *L'Information de l'Histoire de l'Art,* 12, 1967, pp. 119–126.

Burroughs, L. "Degas Paints a Portrait." *Metropolitan Museum of Art Bulletin,* January 1963.

Byrnes, J. B. "Edgar Degas, His Paintings of New Orleanians Here and Abroad." Catalogue of exhibition at the Isaac Delgardo Museum, May 1965.

Cabanne, P. "Degas chez Picasso." *Connaissance des Arts,* no. 262, December 1973, pp. 146–151.

————. *Edgar Degas.* Paris: Pierre Tisné, 1957.

————. "Degas et 'Les Malheurs de la ville d'Orléans.'" *Gazette des Beaux-Arts,* 59, 1962, pp. 363–366.

Canaday, J. "The Still Unknown Degas." *The New York Times,* March 28, 1975, p. 31.

Caradec, F., and Weill, A. *Le Café-concert.* Paris: Atelier Hachette/Massin, 1980.

Carson, J. M. H. *Mary Cassatt.* New York: David McKay, 1966.

Champsaur, F. *L'Amant des danseuses.* Paris: Dentu, 1888.

Chapman, G. *The Dreyfus Trials.* Saint Albans, England: Paladin, 1974.

Charles, F. "Les Mots de Degas." *La Renaissance,* April 1918.

Charlton, D. G. *Positivist Thought in France during the Second Empire.* Oxford: Oxford University Press, 1959.

Chérasse, J. A., and Boussell, P. *Dreyfus ou l'intolérable vérité.* Paris: Editions Pygmalion, 1975.

Chesneau, E. "Le Japon à Paris." *Gazette des Beaux-Arts,* 18, 1878, p. 387.

Chialiva, J. "Comment Degas a changé sa technique du dessin." *Bulletin de la Société de l'Histoire de l'Art Français,* 24, 1932, pp. 44–45.

Christout, M.-F. *Histoire du ballet.* Paris: Presses Universitaires de France, 1975.

Clément-Janin, N. *La Curieuse vie de Marcellin Desboutin.* Paris: H. Floury, 1922.

Coke, V. D. *The Painter and the Photograph.* Albuquerque: University of New Mexico Press, 1964.

Cooper, D. "Le Centenaire de l'Impressionnisme." *Revue de l'Art,* no. 28, 1975, pp. 78–85.

———. *The Courtauld Collection.* University of London: Athlone Press, 1954.

Cooper, M. *French Music. From the Death of Berlioz to the Death of Fauré.* London: Oxford University Press, 1961.

Coquiot, G. *Degas.* Paris: Ollendorf, 1924.

Crespelle, J.-P. *Degas et son monde.* Paris: Presses de la Cité, 1972.

Crouzet, M. *Un Méconnu du réalisme: Duranty.* Paris: Nizet, 1964.

Dabot, H. *Lettres d'un lycéen et d'un étudiant de 1847–1854.* Péronne: E. Quentin, 1900.

Daudet, L. *Paris vécu.* Paris: Gallimard, 1930.

———. *Salons et journaux.* Paris, Nouvelle Librairie Nationale, 1917.

Daumard, A. *Les Bourgeois de Paris au XIXe siècle.* Paris: Flammarion, 1970.

Daval, R. *Histoire des idées en France.* Paris: Presses Universitaires de France, 1977.

Davies, M. *National Gallery Catalogues. French School.* Second edition revised. London, 1957.

Dunlop, I. *Degas.* London: Thames & Hudson, 1979.

Dunstan, B. "Oil Painting Techniques of Degas." *American Artist,* November 1976, pp. 70–75 and 99–100.

———. "The Pastel Techniques of Edgar Degas." *American Artist,* September 1972, pp. 41–47.

Dupont-Ferrier, G. *La Vie quotidienne d'un collège parisien pendant plus de trois cent cinquante ans. Du collège de Clermont au lycée Louis-le-Grand.* Paris: E. de Boccard, 1921–1925. 3 vols.

Dupont-Ferrier, P. *Le Marché financier de Paris sous le Second Empire.* Paris: Presses Universitaires de France, 1926.

Duranty, L. E. *La Nouvelle peinture.* Edited by Marcel Guérin. Paris: H. Floury, 1946. First edition, 1876.

Easton, M. *Artists and Writers in Paris. The Bohemian Idea, 1803–1867.* London: Edward Arnold, 1964.

Erismann, G. *Histoire de la chanson.* Paris: Editions Hermès, 1967.

Feschotte, J. *Histoire du music-hall.* Paris: Presses Universitaires de France, 1965.

Fénéon, F. "Souvenirs sur Manet" (Interview with Henri Gervex). *Bulletin de la Vie Artistique,* October 15, 1920, pp. 606–611.

Fermigier, A. *Courbet.* Geneva: Skira, 1971.

Fevre, J. *Mon oncle Degas. Souvenirs et documents inédits recueillis et publiés par Pierre Borel.* Geneva: Pierre Cailler, 1949.

Fosca, F. *De Diderot à Valéry. Les écrivains et les arts visuels.* Paris: Albin Michel, 1960.

Fries, G. "Degas et les maîtres." *Art de France,* 4, 1964, pp. 353–359.

Galup, J. *Le Mont-Dore et ses fantômes.* Aurillac: Editions U.S.H.A., 1948.

Gauguin, P. *Lettres.* Edited by M. Malingue. Paris: Bernard Grasset, 1946.

Gautier, T. *Le Roi Candaule.* In *Nouvelles,* Paris and Geneva: Slatkine Reprints, 1979. *Le Roi Candaule* was first published in 1845.

―――. *Tableaux de siège, 1870–1871.* Paris: Charpentier, 1871.

Geffroy, G. "Degas." *L'Art dans les Deux Mondes,* December 20, 1890.

Gernsheim, H., and Gernsheim, A. *Creative Photography and Aesthetic Trends, 1839–1870.* London: Faber & Faber, 1962.

Gide, A. *Journal, 1889–1939.* Paris: Gallimard, Pléiade edition, 1949.

Gimpel, R. *Journal d'un collectionneur.* Paris: Calmann-Lévy, 1963.

Girard, L. *La Garde nationale, 1814–1871.* Paris: Plon, 1964.

Girardet, R. *Le Nationalisme français, 1871–1914.* Paris: Armand Colin, 1970.

Gogh, V. van. *Lettres à Emile Bernard.* Paris: Vollard, 1911.

―――. *Lettres à son frère Théo.* Paris: Bernard Grasset, 1937.

Goncourt, E., and J. de. *Journal, mémoires de la vie littéraire.* Paris: Fasquelle, Flammarion, 1956. 4 vols.

―――. *Manette Salomon.* Paris: Union Générale d'Edition, 1979. First published in 1866.

Grada, R. de. *I Macchiaioli e il loro tempo.* Milan: Silvano, 1963.

Guest, I. *The Ballet of the Second Empire.* London: Pitman; Middletown, Connecticut: Wesleyan University Press, 1974.

―――. *The Dancer's Heritage. A Short History of Ballet.* Harmondsworth: Penguin, 1962.

Hale, N. *Mary Cassatt.* Garden City, New York: Doubleday, 1975.

Halévy, D. *Degas parle.* Paris and Geneva: La Palatine, 1960.

―――. *Pays parisiens.* Paris: Bernard Grasset, 1932.

Halévy, L. "Carnets." *Revue des Deux Mondes,* 6, 1933; 2, 1934; 37, 1937; 42, 1937; 43, 1938. The period from 1870 to 1882 is covered.

―――. *L'Invasion.* Paris: Michel Lévy, 1872.

Havemeyer, L. W. *Sixteen to Sixty. Memoirs of a Collector.* New York: Metropolitan Museum of Art, 1961.

Hess, T. B. "Communicating Degas." *New York* magazine, March 28, 1977, pp. 74–77.

Hoctin, L. "Degas photographe." *L'Oeil,* no. 65, May 1960, pp. 36–43.

House, J. "New Material on Monet and Pissarro in London in 1870–71." *Burlington Magazine,* 120, 1978, pp. 636–642.

Huth, H. "Impressionism Comes to America." *Gazette des Beaux-Arts,* 19, 1946, pp. 225–252.

Huysmans, J.-K. *L'Art moderne.* Vol. VI of *Oeuvres complètes,* Paris: G. Crès, 1929. *L'Art moderne* was first published in 1883.

———. *Certains.* Vol. X of *Oeuvres complètes,* Paris: G. Crès, 1929. First published in 1889.

———. *Marthe.* Vol. II of *Oeuvres complètes,* Paris: G. Crès, 1928. First published in 1876.

Ives, C. F. *The Great Wave: The Influence of Japanese Woodcuts on French Prints.* New York: Metropolitan Museum of Art, 1974.

Jamot, P. *Degas.* Paris: Skira, 1939. First published in 1924.

Janis, E. P. *Degas Monotypes.* Cambridge, Massachusetts: Fogg Art Museum, 1968.

———. "The Role of the Monotype in the Working Method of Degas." *Burlington Magazine,* 109, 1967, pp. 20–27 and 71–81.

Jeanniot, G. "Souvenirs sur Degas." *La Revue universelle,* 55, 1933, pp. 152–174 and 280–304.

Johnson, D. *France and the Dreyfus Affair.* London: Blandford Press, 1966.

Joly, A. "Sur deux modèles de Degas." *Gazette des Beaux-Arts,* 69, 1967, pp. 373–374.

Juin, H. "Le Célibat est-il un crime?" *Le Monde,* April 22, 1976, pp. 1 and 10.

Jullian, P. "Charles Haas." *Gazette des Beaux-Arts,* 77, 1971, pp. 239–256.

Katan, M. "La Famille Halévy." *Evidences,* March 1955, pp. 7–13.

Koshkin-Youritzin, V. "Irony of Degas." *Gazette des Beaux-Arts,* 87, 1976, pp. 33–40.

Lafond, P. *Degas.* 2 vols. Paris: H. Floury, 1918–1919.

Lambert, A. *Le Siège de Paris.* Paris: Calmann-Lévy, 1965.

Lapauze, H. "Ingres chez Degas." *La Renaissance de l'Art Français,* March 1918, p. 9.

Larguier, L. *Fachés, solitaires et bourrus.* Paris: Albin Michel, 1949.

Lascault, G. "Eloge du caf'conç'." *La Quinzaine littéraire,* July 7, 1980, pp. 21–22.

Laver, J. *Vulgar Society: The Romantic Career of James Tissot, 1836–1902.* London: Constable, 1936.

Lemoisne, P.-A. *Degas et son oeuvre.* 4 vols. Paris: Arts et Métiers Graphiques, 1946–1949. The basic catalogue of paintings and pastels.

Léon, P.; Lévy-Leboyer, M.; Armengaud, A.; Broder, A.; Bruhat, J.; Daumard, A.; Labrousse, E.; Laurent, R.; Soboul, A. *Histoire économique et sociale de la France, III: L'Avènement de l'ère industrielle (1789–années 1880).* 2 vols. Paris: Presses Universitaires de France, 1976.

Lethève, J. *Impressionnistes et symbolistes devant la presse.* Paris: Armand Colin, 1959.

———. *La Vie quotidienne des artistes français au XIXe siècle.* Paris: Hachette, 1968.

Lévêque, J.-J. *Edgar Degas.* Paris: Editions Siloé, 1978.

Lhote, A. *Ecrits sur la peinture.* Paris and Brussels: Editions Lumière, 1946.

Liere, E. N. van. "Solutions and Dissolutions: the Bather in Nineteenth-Century French Painting." *Arts* magazine, 54, 1980, pp. 110–111.

Mallarmé, S. *Oeuvres complètes.* Paris: Gallimard, Pléiade edition, 1945.

Manet, J. *Journal: 1893–1899.* Paris: C. Klincksieck, 1979.

Manson, J. B. *The Life and Work of Edgar Degas.* London: G. Holme, 1927.

Marrus, M. R. *Les Juifs de France à l'époque de l'affaire Dreyfus.* Paris: Calmann-Lévy, 1972. A translation of *The Politics of Assimilation.* Oxford: Oxford University Press, 1971.

Martelli, D. *Gli Impressionisti,* Pisa: Tipografia Vannucchi, 1880. Reprinted in his *Scritti d'arte,* Florence, 1952.

Mauclair, C. *La Ville lumière.* Paris: P. Ollendorf, 1903.

Mayeur, J.-M. *Les Débuts de la IIIe République, 1871–1898.* Paris: Editions du Seuil, 1973.

Mayne, J. "Degas's Ballet Scene from 'Robert le Diable.' " *Victoria and Albert Museum Bulletin,* II, 1966, pp. 148–156.

Meier-Graefe, J. *Degas.* Munich, R. Piper, 1920.

Mercier, A. *De Valernes et Degas.* Exhibition catalogue, Musée de Carpentras, 1963.

Michel, A. "Degas et son modèle." *Mercure de France,* 131, 1919, pp. 457–478 and 623–639.

Millard, C. W. *The Sculpture of Edgar Degas.* Princeton: Princeton University Press, 1976.

Millet, J. "La Famille Mante, une trichromie, Degas, l'Opéra." *Gazette des Beaux-Arts,* 94, 1979, pp. 105–112.

Minervino, F., and Lassaigne, J. *Tout l'oeuvre peint de Degas.* Paris: Flammarion, 1974. A translation of the Italian edition, Milan: Rizzoli Editore, 1970.

Miquel, P. *L'Affaire Dreyfus.* Paris: Presses Universitaires de France, 1973.

Mirbeau, O. *Le Calvaire.* Paris: G. Crès, 1925. First published in 1887.

Mitchell, E. " 'La Fille de Jephté' par Degas." *Gazette des Beaux-Arts,* 18, 1937, pp. 175–189.

Monneret, S. *L'Impressionnisme et son époque.* With an introduction by René Huyghe. 4 vols. Paris: Denoel, 1978–1981.

Monnier, G. "Les Dessins de Degas du musée du Louvre." *La Revue du Louvre,* no. 6, 1969, pp. 359–368.

———. "La Genèse d'une oeuvre de Degas: 'Sémiramis construisant une ville.' " *La Revue du Louvre,* no. 5–6, 1978, pp. 407–426.

Moore, G. *Confessions of a Young Man.* Edited by Susan Dick. Montreal and London, McGill–Queen's University Press, 1972. First published in 1888.

———. *Impressions and Opinions.* New York: Benjamin Blom, 1972. First published in 1891.

Moreau-Nélaton, E. "Deux heurs avec Degas." *L'Amour de l'Art,* July 1931. Reprinted in Lemoisne, I, pp. 257–261.

———. *Manet raconté par lui-même.* Paris: Henri Laurens, 1926.

Morisot, B. *Correspondance.* Edited by Denis Rouart. Paris: Quatre Chemins-Editart, 1950.

Moses, P. *Etchings by Edgar Degas.* Exhibition catalogue. University of Chicago, May–June, 1964.

Natanson, T. *Peints à leur tour.* Paris: Albin Michel, 1948.

Newhall, B. "Degas, photographe amateur." *Gazette des Beaux-Arts,* 61, 1963, pp. 61–64.

Nicolson, B. "Degas as a Human Being." *Burlington Magazine,* 105, pp. 239–241.

———. "The Mind of a Realist." *Times Literary Supplement,* March 18, 1977, p. 315.

Nittis, J. de. *Notes et souvenirs.* Paris: Librairies Réunies, 1895.

Nochlin, L. *Impressionism and Post-Impressionism.* Englewood Cliffs, New Jersey: Prentice-Hall, 1966.

———. *Realism.* Harmondsworth: Penguin, 1971.

———. *Realism and Tradition in Art, 1848–1900. Sources and Documents.* Englewood Cliffs, New Jersey: Prentice-Hall, 1966.

Nora, F. "Degas et les maisons closes." *L'Oeil,* no. 219, 1973, pp. 26–31.

Paladilhe, J., and Pierre, J. *Gustave Moreau au regard changeant.* Paris: F. Hazan, 1971.

Peters, S. W. "Edgar Degas at the Boston Museum of Fine Art." *Art in America,* no. 6, November–December, 1974, pp. 124–125.

Pickvance, R. " 'L'Absinthe' in England." *Apollo,* 77, 1963, pp. 395–398.

———. "Degas's Dancers, 1872–1876." *Burlington Magazine,* 105, 1963, pp. 256–266.

———. *Degas 1879.* Exhibition catalogue. Edinburgh: National Gallery of Scotland, August–September, 1979.

———. "A Newly Discovered Drawing by Degas of George Moore." *Burlington Magazine,* 105, 1963, pp. 276–280.

Pionnier, E. *Essai sur l'histoire de la Révolution à Verdun.* Nancy: A. Crepin-Leblond, 1905.

Pissarro, C. *Lettres à son fils Lucien.* Edited by John Rewald. Paris: Albin Michel, 1950.

Plessis, A. *De la fête impériale au mur des fédérés, 1852–1871.* Paris: Editions du Seuil, 1976.

Pool, P. "Degas and Moreau." *Burlington Magazine,* 105, 1963, pp. 251–256.

———. "The History Pictures of Edgar Degas and Their Background." *Apollo,* 80, 1964, pp. 306–311.

———. *Impressionism.* London: Thames & Hudson, 1967.

Prost, A. *Histoire de l'enseignment en France, 1800–1967.* Paris: Armand Colin, 1968.

Raimondi, R. *Degas e la sua famiglia in Napoli: 1793–1917.* Naples: Sav, 1958.

Raunay, J. "Degas, souvenirs anecdotiques." *La Revue de France,* March 15, 1931, pp. 263–282, and April 1, 1931, pp. 619–632.

Raynal, M.; Leymarie, J.; Read, H. *Histoire de la peinture moderne de Baudelaire à Bonnard.* Geneva: Skira, 1949.

Raynor, V. "Degas in Black and White." *The New Leader,* September 15, 1975, pp. 22–23.

Rebérioux, M. *La République radicale: 1898–1914.* Paris: Editions du Seuil, 1975.

Reff, T. *Degas: The Artist's Mind.* New York: Metropolitan Museum of Art and Harper & Row, 1976.

———. "Degas's Copies of Older Art." *Burlington Magazine,* 105, 1963, pp. 241–251.

———. "Edgar Degas and the Dance." *Arts* magazine, 53, November 1978, pp. 145–149.

———. "Edgar Degas's 'Little Ballet Dancer of Fourteen Years.' " *Arts* magazine, September 1976, pp. 66–69.

———. "Further Thoughts on Degas's Copies." *Burlington Magazine,* 113, 1971, pp. 534–543.

———. "The Landscape Painter Degas Might Have Been." *Art News,* January 1976, pp. 41–43.

———. "New Light on Degas's Copies." *Burlington Magazine,* 106, 1964, pp. 250–259.

Régnier, H. de. *Nos rencontres.* Paris: Mercure de France, 1931.

———. *Proses datées.* Paris: Mercure de France, 1925.

Reitlinger, G. *The Economics of Taste.* 2 vols. London: Barrie & Rockliff, 1961–1963.

Rewald, J. *The Complete Sculptures of Degas.* Exhibition catalogue. London: Lefevre Gallery, November–December, 1976.

———. "Degas and His Family in New Orleans." *Gazette des Beaux-Arts,* 30, 1946, pp. 105–126.

———. *Degas Sculpture. The Complete Works.* New York: Harry N. Abrams, 1957.

———. *Histoire de l'Impressionnisme.* Translated from English by Nancy Goldet-Bouwens. 2 vols. Paris: Albin Michel, 1965.

———. *The History of Impressionism.* Fourth revised edition. New York: Museum of Modern Art, 1973; and London: Secker & Warburg, 1973.

———. "Le Portrait de la princess de Metternich par Degas." *L'Amour de l'Art,* March 1937, pp. 89–90.

Rewald, J., and Boggs, J. S. *Twenty-six Original Copperplates Engraved by Degas.* Exhibition catalogue. Beverly Hills: Frank Perls Gallery, 1959.

Rewald, J., and Nepveu-Degas, J. *Edgar Degas: Original Wax Sculptures.* Exhibition catalogue. New York: Knoedler Galleries, 1955.

Rich, D. C. *Degas.* New York: Harry N. Abrams, 1951.

Ristori, A. *Etudes et souvenirs.* Paris: P. Ollendorff, 1887.

Rivière, G. *Mr. Degas, bourgeois de Paris.* Paris: H. Floury, 1935.

Romanelli, P. "Comment j'ai connu Degas." *Le Figaro littéraire,* March 13, 1937.

Rosenberg, J. *Great Draughtsmen from Pisanello to Picasso.* Cambridge, Massachusetts: Harvard University Press, 1959.

Rosenblum, R. *J.-A.-D. Ingres.* London: Thames & Hudson, 1967.

Rouart, D. *Degas à la recherche de sa technique.* Paris: H. Floury, 1945.

Rouart, E. "Degas." *Le Point,* February 1937, pp. 5–22.

Rouault, G. *Souvenirs intimes.* Paris: E. Frapier, 1926.

Saarinen, A. *The Proud Possessors.* New York: Random House, 1958.

Sandberg, J. "The Discovery of Japanese Prints in the Nineteenth Century before 1867." *Gazette des Beaux-Arts,* 72, 1968, pp. 295–302.

Scharf, A. *Art and Photography.* Harmondsworth: Penguin, 1974.

Schreiber, H. *Le Plus Vieux Métier du monde.* Paris: Albin Michel, 1968.

Searight, S. *New Orleans.* New York: Stein & Day, 1973.

Segard, A. *Un Peintre des enfants et des mères, Mary Cassatt.* Paris: P. Ollendorff, 1914.

Sérullaz, M. *L'Impressionnisme.* Paris: Presses Universitaires de France, 1961.

Sevin, F. "Degas à travers ses mots." *Gazette des Beaux-Arts,* 86, 1975, pp. 18–46.

Shapiro, M. "Degas and the Siamese Twins of the Café-concert: The Ambassadeurs and the Alcazar d'Eté." *Gazette des Beaux-Arts,* 95, 1980, pp. 153–164.

Sickert, W. "Degas." *Burlington Magazine,* 31, 1917, pp. 183–191.

Silvestre, A. *Au pays des souvenirs.* Paris: Librairie Illustré, 1892.

Signorini, T. *Caricaturisti e caricaturati al Caffè Michelangiolo: 1848–1866.* Florence: G. Civelli, 1893.

Sloane, J. C. *French Painting Between the Past and the Present: Artists, Critics and Traditions from 1848 to 1870.* Princeton: Princeton University Press, 1951.

Staley, A., ed. *From Realism to Symbolism: Whistler and His World.* Exhibition catalogue. New York: Wildenstein; Philadelphia Museum of Art, 1971.

Sterling, C. "Chassériau et Degas." *Beaux-Arts,* no. 21, May 26, 1933.

Sterling, C., and Adhémar, H. *Ecole française, musée du Louvre.* Paris: Editions des Musées Nationaux, 1959.

Sterling, C., and Salinger, M. *French Paintings.* 3 vols. New York: Metropolitan Museum of Art, 1935–1936.

Sweet, F. A. *Miss Mary Cassatt, Impressionist from Pennsylvania.* Norman: University of Oklahoma Press, 1967.

Tannenbaum, L. " 'La Cigale,' by Henri Meilhac and Ludovic Halévy — and Edgar Degas." *Art News,* 65, no. 9, January 1967, pp. 55, 71.

Taylor, J. R., and Brooke, B. *The Art Dealers.* New York: Scribner's, 1969.

Terry, W. *Ballet.* New York: Dell Laurel Editions, 1959.

Thiébault-Sisson, F. "Degas." *Le Temps,* May 18, 1918, p. 3.

Trapp, F. A. "The Universal Exhibition of 1855." *Burlington Magazine,* 107, 1965, pp. 300–305.

Valéry, P. *Degas, danse, dessin.* Paris: Gallimard, 1965. First published in 1938.

Vanier, H. *La Mode et ses métiers. Frivolités et luttes des classes, 1830–1870.* Paris: Armand Colin, 1960.

Venturi, L. *Les Archives de l'Impressionnisme.* 2 vols. Paris and New York: Durand-Ruel, 1939. Contains memoirs of Durand-Ruel.

Vernillat, F., and Charpentreau, J. *La Chanson française.* Paris: Presses Universitaires de France, 1977.

Vitali, L. "Three Italian Friends of Degas." *Burlington Magazine,* 105, 1963, pp. 266–273.

Vollard, A. *Degas.* Paris: G. Crès, 1924.

————. *Souvenirs d'un marchand de tableaux.* Paris: Albin Michel, 1937.

Wagner, A. M. "Degas's Collection of Art: An Introductory Essay and Catalogue." Brown University, 1974. M.A. thesis.

Walker, J. "Degas et les maîtres anciens." *Gazette des Beaux-Arts,* 10, 1933, pp. 175–185.

Weisberg, G. P. *Japonisme: Japanese Influence on French Art, 1854–1910.* Exhibition catalogue with essays. Cleveland Museum of Art, 1975.

Wells, M. "Who Was Degas's Lyda?" *Apollo,* 95, February 1972, pp. 129–134.

Werner, A. *Degas Pastels.* New York: Watson-Guptill, 1969.

White, H. C., and White, C. A. *Canvases and Careers: Institutional Change in the French Painting World.* New York: John Wiley & Sons, 1965.

Wildenstein, D. *Degas.* Exhibition catalogue. New York: Wildenstein Galleries, 1949.

Zeldin, T. *France: 1848–1945.* vol. I, *Ambition, Love and Politics. The Oxford History of Modern Europe* series. Oxford: Clarendon Press, 1973.

Zola, E. *Mon Salon. Manet. Ecrits sur l'art.* Edited by Antoinette Ehrard. Paris: Garnier-Flammarion, 1970.

————. *L'Oeuvre.* Paris: Fasquelle, 1968. First published in 1886.

————. *Thérèse Raquin.* Paris: Fasquelle, 1968. First published in 1867.

Index